HUMAN
ASSOCIATIVE
MEMORY

THE EXPERIMENTAL PSYCHOLOGY SERIES

Arthur W. Melton · Consulting Editor

MELTON AND MARTIN · *Coding Processes in Human Memory, 1972*

MCGUIGAN AND LUMSDEN · *Contemporary Approaches to Conditioning and Learning, 1973*

ANDERSON AND BOWER · *Human Associative Memory, 1973*

HUMAN ASSOCIATIVE MEMORY

By JOHN R. ANDERSON
THE UNIVERSITY OF MICHIGAN
and
GORDON H. BOWER
STANFORD UNIVERSITY

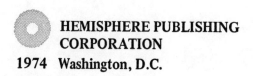

HEMISPHERE PUBLISHING
CORPORATION
1974   Washington, D.C.

A HALSTED PRESS BOOK
JOHN WILEY & SONS
New York   London   Sydney   Toronto

Second revised printing

Copyright © 1974, by Hemisphere Publishing Corporation

First printing

Copyright © 1973, by V. H. Winston & Sons, Inc.

Hemisphere Publishing Corporation
1025 Vermont Avenue, N.W., Washington, D.C. 20005

Distributed solely by Halsted Press Division, John Wiley & Sons, Inc., New York.

Library of Congress Cataloging in Publication Data:

Anderson, John Robert, 1947–
    Human associative memory.

    (The Experimental psychology series)
    1. Memory. 2. Association of ideas.
I. Bower, Gordon H., joint author. II. Title. III. Series.
BF371.A53   1973   153.1'2   73-5769
ISBN 0-470-02892-0

Printed in the United States of America

This book is dedicated to our wives

Sharon Anthony Bower

and

Lynne Marie Reder

CONTENTS

PREFACE

This book proposes and tests a theory about human memory, about how a person encodes, retains, and retrieves information from memory. The book is especially concerned with memory for sentential materials. We propose a theoretical framework which is adequate for describing comprehension of linguistic materials, for exhibiting the internal representation of propositional materials, for characterizing the "interpretative processes" which encode this information into memory and make use of it for remembering, for answering questions, recognizing instances of known categories, drawing inferences, and making deductions. This is all a very tall order, and we shall be gratified if a fraction of our specific hypotheses prove adequate for long. However, what is more significant is the overall framework and theoretical methodology within which specific hypotheses are cast: we sincerely hope that this framework would have a singular value that would outlive its specific details.

How have we arrived at the theoretical framework to be proposed? We will answer this question at two levels—first, in terms of a brief autobiography; second, in terms of a broader historical context. When the first author (JA) arrived at Stanford University as a graduate assistant to the second author (GB), there was an ongoing research program concerned with organizational and imaginal factors in various memory tasks. As we tried to become precise, even quantitative, in fitting organizational theory to free recall data, its difference from associationistic models of free recall seemed to evaporate, frankly because neither theory had been formulated with any real precision up to that time. Eventually, JA developed a semi-successful computer simulation model of free recall, FRAN; however, the data base of FRAN (or its memory representation) was fundamentally associationistic in character.

The problem with FRAN, as with other free recall models, is that it could not understand language: it treated a sentence as though it were a string of unrelated words. Consequently, it was decided to put FRAN aside and to search for a theory and model that would be able to represent the information in sentences and describe how they are learned and remembered. This required that both of us learn a fair amount of linguistics, psycholinguistics, and computational linguistics, a task in which we were aided by Herbert Clark and Roger Schank of the Stanford faculty. We had also begun some empirical investigations of sentence memory, expecting to find support for a Gestalt-like theory but instead finding associationist-like phenomena (these are reviewed here in Chapter 11).

The outcome of rather intensive ruminations and discussions was the theory, HAM (for Human Associative Memory) proposed herein. This was first worked out in detail in a long "dissertation proposal" by JA which had several goals: to present an associative theory of sentence memory, to report evidence relevant to it, to relate the theory to the historical tradition of associationism, and to indicate how a few standard "verbal learning" phenomena might be interpreted in terms of this approach. That document formed the basic outline for this book. The language parser and question-answerer of HAM were written as a LISP program by JA, and its operation is illustrated in Chapter 6 here. That proposal led us into a productive set of discussions and experiments, many of which are scattered throughout this book. Given the volume of results and the number of things we wanted to say about them, it became clear that a book rather than piecemeal publications was the appropriate way to communicate the theoretical framework and its supporting evidence.

In the Spring of 1972, we began collaborative writing of this volume; each day was filled with hours of fruitful discussions followed by our individual writing efforts. In these discussions we came to adopt characteristic roles—JA as the proposer, interpreter, and defender of HAM, and GB as the critic, provider of more problems, the demander of greater generality. However, like most fruitful interchanges, ours were free-wheeling, and we adopted various roles as the occasion demanded. Only a fraction of the analyses and problems solved appear in these pages. The discussions and writing turned out to be both personally and intellectually the most gratifying moments of our collaboration.

Now, let us briefly indicate the historical context of this work. First, our work falls within the tradition of philosophical associationism, which stretches from Aristotle through the British empirical philosophers to current psychology. We found so much of value in that rich intellectual tradition that we felt honor-bound to cite chapter and verse from it to show its contemporary relevance. This we do in Chapter 2, along with criticizing that tradition and anticipating how our theory of memory differs from it.

Second, this work owes a special debt to those scientists doing research on human memory, both researchers from the "verbal-learning" tradition and those using the "organizational" approach. Chapters 14 and 15 here explicitly deal with the verbal learning literature, whereas the influence of the organizational approach to memory should be apparent in chapters 3, 8, 11, 13, and 14.

The third intellectual tradition impinging on our research is the theoretical work in modern linguistics, especially that on transformational generative grammar of Noam Chomsky, his associates, and the whole movement he has promulgated. Although we deal with models of linguistic *performance* for only limited domains, we are nonetheless indebted to the formal analyses of the linguists for suggesting these models. Linguistic theories are reviewed in Chapter 5 and issues concerning the representation of propositional information occur repeatedly throughout our work (e.g., Chapters 7, 8, 9, 11, 13).

Our final intellectual debt is to the research workers in artificial intelligence, to those like Minsky, McCarthy, Newell, and Simon who have shaped the conceptual development of that entire area, but more specifically to those who have dealt with computer models for natural language understanding and for question-answering. A review of language understanding programs (those of Woods, Winograd, and Schank) is contained in Chapter 5, and a review of models for "long-term semantic memory" (specifically, Quillian's and that of Rumelhart, Lindsay, and Norman) is contained in Chapter 4. Our theoretical framework has a special likeness to that being developed by Rumelhart, Lindsay, and Norman at the University of California at San Diego, and that developed by Walter Kintsch at the University of Colorado. It is indicative of the *Zeitgeist* that our work was begun independently and in relative ignorance of theirs, and only later did we become acquainted with the details of their approach. Special visits to La Jolla and Boulder provided us with detailed information about their theoretical projects, and we are pleased to have this opportunity to thank these scientists and their research students for their intellectual help, encouragement, and hospitality.

These four distinct areas, then, provide the intellectual and historical backgrounds for our theory of human memory. As does every lengthy research project or book, ours has accumulated a number of specific debts to individuals who have helped bring this enterprise to fruition. First, we acknowledge the general support of the faculty and graduate students in cognitive psychology at Stanford University; the general climate of intellectual stimulation there clearly provided the reinforcing and educational contingencies needed to initiate, encourage, and maintain our theoretical enterprise. We appreciate those colleagues—Arnie Glass, Steven Kosslyn, Perry Thorndyke, and Keith Westcourt—who allowed us to report their previously unpublished experiments. Ed Feigenbaum was very helpful in our development of the simulation program and provided us with help when the simulation began to exceed the capabilities of the campus facility.

We solicited and received constructive comments from many colleagues, and the final version of the book is clearly better because of them. Bob Crowder, Jim Greeno, Reid Hastie, Marcel Just, Steve Kosslyn, Alan Lesgold, Elizabeth Loftus, Gary Olson, Lance Rips, Ed Smith, Dave Tieman, and Wayne Wickelgren all have commented on portions of the book. To them we give our thanks. A special note of thanks goes to Lynne Reder who read the book in its entirety and pointed out passages in need of better exposition.

The research reported here and preparation of the manuscript was supported through a research grant to GB, number MH-13950, from the National Institutes of Mental Health. We are pleased to acknowledge Drs. George Renaud and John Hammack of the NIMH staff for their helpful encouragement and support of this research and of its writing. Yale University also helped JA's writing by easing the burden on its new assistant professor and by making resources available for him to supervise the book through its final draft. During the final revisions, GB was supported by the Center for Advanced Study in the Behavioral Sciences and by research funds from NIMH.

We owe a special thanks to the several individuals who have been closely involved with the physical preparation of the manuscript. First among these is Joyce Lockwood, GB's secretary, who typed the first one and a half versions of the book, making sense out of our scrawls while exhibiting patient forebearance in the face of a frustrating barrage of corrections to corrections. The final one and a half versions of the manuscript were typed by JA's secretaries at Yale, Barbara Psotka and Glenna Ames. We appreciate the swift and reliable clerical help they have provided to us. A special thanks also goes to Larry Erlbaum, our publisher, for providing moral support as well as expediating those technical matters associated with shepherding a manuscript through to publication. Finally we are obliged to several authors and publishers who gave permission to quote or to reproduce figures from their publications, and we have acknowledged their contributions in the appropriate places of the text.

John R. Anderson and Gordon H. Bower

March, 1973

HUMAN
ASSOCIATIVE
MEMORY

1
INTRODUCTION

And I gave my heart to seek and search out by wisdom concerning all things that are done under heaven; this sore travail hath God given to the sons of men to be exercised therewith.

—Solomon

Two years ago, we set out to develop a theory of human memory, a theory which was to span a wide range of mnemonic phenomena. We are now humbled by the immensity of this task; human memory is a complex mental capacity, and our ability to comprehend man's mind appears at times quite limited. But Solomon calls us to the task of understanding, to be "exercised" by its sore travail. And so we tried. In countless hours of conversations, we discussed, proposed, role-played, argued, laughed, cajoled, reasoned, debunked, and just plain talked to one another about the problems of human memory. The time has come for us to commit to print a fraction of the things we have thought about human memory in the hope of helping others to think about this problem—which we consider to be the supreme intellectual puzzle of the century.

The theory of human memory which we will articulate will seem overly ambitious but still terribly programmatic; no one can realize this better than we ourselves. So why bother? What does Psychology need with another fragmentary theory of memory? After all, a long parade of memory theories since Plato's have been offered with great fanfare, hopeful enthusiasm, and persuasive arguments. Most of these were soon consigned to the loneliness of library tombs, accumulating dust to hide their insignificance. A very few of these writings become classics. But no one really believes the classics; they are read only to provide jousting partners for later opponents and voyagers on the seas of the unknown.

It is commonplace that the Zeitgeist in current psychology opposes global theories such as the one to be presented. It is said, instead, that one ought to work on limited hypotheses for small, manageable problems–categorization effects in free recall, verification latencies for negative sentences, search of items in short-term memory, and so on ad infinitum. Indeed, we have been told by many respected colleagues in psychology that we will surely fail because we "are trying to explain everything." Of course, we are not. Human memory is but a very small part of the psychological domain. To make a salient contrast, a criticism we are apt to receive from colleagues outside of psychology (e.g., artificial intelligence) is that we are far too narrow in our perspective and aims.

The reason for writing a theoretical book on human memory is the belief that we have something important to offer. In rejecting the earlier global theories, modern research on human memory has overreacted to the opposite extreme; it has become far too narrow, particulate, constricted, and limited. There is no overall conception of what the field is about or even what it should be about. There is no set of overarching theoretical beliefs generally agreed upon which provide a framework within which to fit new data and by which to measure progress. Were we describing an unhappy personality, we would say that the contemporary study of memory has lost its sense of direction, its sense of purpose, and it is drifting aimlessly with much talent but little focus. This point was stated forcibly by a recent, informed but highly critical review of the field (Tulving & Madigan, 1970).

CONCERN FOR SUFFICIENCY CONDITIONS

Laboratory studies of memory appear under the inexorable control of a distinct set of "experimental paradigms," a standard set of "tasks," which seem by their nature to spew out an unending string of methodological variations and empirical studies. But the phenomena studied are becoming further and further removed from the manifestations of memory in everyday life. There would be nothing necessarily wrong with this esoterica provided psychologists had some clear conception of how their research and theories would eventually fit together into a system adequate to explain the complexities of everyday human memory. But, on the contrary, it appears that we psychologists are totally unconcerned about having our psychological theories meet certain *sufficiency conditions*. It is not enough that a theory make adequate ordinal predictions for a particular situation and experiment; in addition, it should be shown that its principles are sufficient to play a part in the explanation of the total complexity of human behavior. For instance, one could require of a model of memory that it be sufficiently powerful to succeed in simulating question-answering behavior of the sort to be discussed in Chapters 12 and 13.

When we began to concern ourselves with sufficiency conditions, we were forced to fundamental reconceptualizations regarding the nature of memory. We found that memory could no longer be conceived as a haphazard jumble of associations that blindly record contiguities between elements of experience. Rather, memory now had to be viewed as a highly structured system designed to record facts about the world and to utilize that knowledge in guiding a variety of performances. We were forced to postulate entities existing in memory which have no one-to-one correspondence with external stimuli or responses. As discussed in Chapter 2, such structures violate the Terminal Meta-Postulate of classical associationism and stimulus-response psychology. It also became necessary to postulate the existence in the mind of highly complex parsing and inferential systems which function to interface the memory component with the external world. Furthermore, we were forced to postulate the existence of innately specified ideas in the form of semantic primitives and relations. We will therefore be proposing and arguing for a radical shift from the associationist conceptions that have heretofore dominated theorizing on human memory.

This shift is most apparent in the unit of analysis which we adopt. Unlike past associative theories, we will not focus on associations among single items such as letters, nonsense syllables, or words. Rather, we will introduce *propositions* about the world as the fundamental units. A proposition is a configuration of elements which (*a*) is structured according to *rules of formation*, and (*b*) has a *truth value*. Intuitively, a proposition conveys an assertion about the world. The exact structural properties of our propositional representation will be set forth in Chapter 7. We will suppose that all information enters memory in propositional packets. On this view, it is not even possible to have simple word-to-word associations. Words can become interassociated only as their corresponding concepts participate in propositions that are encoded into memory. However, propositions will not be treated here as unitary objects or Gestalt wholes in memory having novel, emergent properties. Rather, propositions will be conceived as structured bundles of associations between elementary ideas or concepts. However, our insistence that all input to memory be propositional imposes certain *well-formedness* conditions on the structure of the interidea associations. This notion of structural well-formedness is one that was completely lacking in past associative theories and was at the heart of many rationalist attacks on associationism.

NEO-ASSOCIATIONISM

We shall use the term "neo-associationism" to denote this new conception of human memory. While it introduces substantial deviations from past associationist doctrines, it still maintains a strong empiricist bias. We feel that the full significance of these theoretical assumptions can only be appreciated when one understands the associationist tradition out of which they came. Therefore, we have devoted Chapter 2 to an analysis of the associative tradition that extends from Aristotle through current American psychology. We will argue that a defining feature of associationism has been its *methodological empiricism*. That is, all associationists have accepted as their task the job of taking the immediate sense-data available to them and constructing their theory directly from these, always letting the data dictate the nature of the theory. This is contrasted in Chapter 3 with the *methodological rationalism* which attempts to first arrive at abstract, sufficient conditions, or constraints for the phenomena at hand, and then tries to relate these abstractions and conceptual constraints to the empirical world.

The contrast we are making between methodological empiricism and methodological rationalism corresponds (not surprisingly) to the more frequently made distinction between empiricism and rationalism. In the strong version of empiricism, the mind begins as tabula rasa, and all knowledge is a consequence of the passive encoding of experience. The strong version of rationalism claims that the mind begins highly structured and all significant knowledge derives from the mind's initial structure. According to the rationalists, the role of experience is simply to stimulate the mind to derive that knowledge. Methodological empiricism and rationalism are not concerned with the origins of human knowledge, but rather with procedures for developing a scientific theory. However, we can almost derive a definition of each by substituting "scientific theory" for "mind" in the above statements of empiricism and rationalism. That is, methodological empiricism claims a scientific theory can be built up from immediate data by the blind procedure of generalization; whereas, methodological rationalism insists the theory builder must bring the essential structure of the theory to the phenomena to be explained.

Neo-associationism represents a profane union of these two methodologies. There is no attempt at a "creative synthesis" of these two positions; we simply pursue both methods in parallel in constructing a theory. The result is a theory that irreverently intermixes connectionism with nativism, reductionism with wholism, sensationalism with intuitionism, and mechanism with vitalism. Depending on the theoretician's propensities, the mixture can be claimed to be either more rationalist than empiricist or vice versa. The mixture we will offer is still strongly empiricist, much more so than the other neo-associationist theories that we will examine.

The various neo-associationist theories of memory (e.g., Simon & Feigenbaum, 1964; Collins & Quillian, 1972; Rumelhart, Lindsay, & Norman, 1972), including our own, have been cast in the form of computer simulation models of memory. This is no accident. The task of computer simulation simultaneously forces one to consider both whether his theory is sufficient for the task domain to be simulated and also whether it can deal with the particular trends found in particular experiments. Chapter 4 is devoted to critically reviewing a selected few of the neo-associationist theories that have been advanced recently.

Chapter 5 is our final review chapter, and it examines the recent work in linguistics as well as in that specialized domain known as computational linguistics. Our theorizing and experimentation are specifically oriented towards memory for linguistically structured material. With such interests, one cannot help but make constant contact with the recent ideas in linguistics. The linguistic work, particularly of Chomsky, Fillmore, Lakoff, Katz, Ross, and their associates, is important for a second reason. These linguists have argued effectively for the importance of sufficiency conditions in linguistics. As a consequence, over the past decade rationalism and mentalism have become strongly entrenched in linguistics. The rationalist "revolution" has been imported from linguistics into psychology. Thus, the developments in linguistics are an important source behind the neo-associationist developments.

Thus, four substantial chapters are being devoted to an extensive historical and theoretical review of efforts related to our own. This is clearly out of character for a typical "research volume." The usual practice for American psychology is to restrict its focus to the last 5 or 10 years of experimentation centered around a narrowly circumscribed topic. This practice is lamentable since true scholarly endeavor would seem to require an appreciation of the historical and intellectual context within which that scholarship occurs. Without knowledge of that context, it is not possible to discriminate between significant theoretical advance as opposed to elaboration of an established paradigm. Chomsky (1968) has argued persuasively for a similar historical perspective in linguistics.

Our work began in the typical intellectual isolation of experimental psychology, but we constantly found ourselves being led into discussions of issues about which we know very little. Therefore, we have tried to trace the connections between our work and that which had occurred in past centuries or which was occurring in related fields. Our perception of what questions were important changed; similarly, the character of the theory and research to be presented is very different from what we had originally projected and from the typical fare that one finds in psychology. It can only be appreciated in the perspective of the historical context that we set in the first four chapters. One of the incidental advantages of a theory so constructed is that it provides the reader with an integrated viewpoint from which to perceive his own experimental research, related research in psychology and other fields, and the relation between this research and what has happened in past centuries.

Following these four review chapters, the remainder of the book serves as a forum for presenting our theory and research. We have 17 experiments to report that have not appeared before in print. We will also review and comment upon a large number of recent experiments that seem particularly interesting with respect to the issues that we are raising. Although there is no attempt to review extensively the literature in human memory, we do hope to establish theoretical connections among many different areas of experimentation in psychology.

To preview the contents of the later chapters, Chapter 6 provides a general overview of our model of long-term memory. We have christened the model HAM, an acronym for Human Associative Memory. The subsequent four chapters set forth most of the substantive theoretical assumptions of that model. The character of presentation varies considerably from one chapter to the next. In Chapter 7, entitled "The Structure of Knowledge," we propose a structure in which information will be encoded and stored in long-term memory. Following an informal presentation, we then develop the representation with some degree of formalism. Although it makes for difficult reading, the formalism does permit us to establish some important theoretical results. An informal discussion of the representation is included so that its salient features will be easily understood by those unfamiliar with set theory and formal grammars. In Chapters 8 and 9 we will discuss elements of our computer simulation of HAM. Chapter 8 will be concerned with how the external stimuli input to the system become transformed into the propositional representation developed in Chapter 7. This is what we call the "encoding problem." In Chapter 9 we will ask how the memory system recognizes that it has experienced something before. This issue, of how current stimuli contact old traces, is a point of notorious difficulty for other accounts of memory. Finally, in Chapter 10 we will present a stochastic model of how incoming information is encoded into long-term memory.

The remaining chapters will be concerned with relating our theory to various areas of research and experimentation. Chapter 11 will examine some of the salient research on sentence memory and indicate how HAM would explain it. In Chapter 12 we will examine the question of how long-term memory is searched for information, to decide whether or not some fact is known or some statement is true. This is the problem of *fact retrieval*. In Chapter 13 we will consider the more general inferential and problem-solving abilities that must be added to a fact-retrieval system before one approximates a question-answering system of the same competence as a typical human. In Chapter 14, we will discuss how our model would perform in the typical verbal learning paradigms such as paired-associate learning and free recall. Finally, in Chapter 15 we will discuss how different information inputs interfere with one another to produce forgetting. We will compare our model of this process with past theories of interference and forgetting.

THE FUNDAMENTAL QUESTIONS

There are well-known advantages to vagueness in constructing a theory; it protects the theory from disconfirmation. The typical strategy is to articulate the theory at those points where it makes contact with confirming evidence, but otherwise to shroud it in sufficient vagueness so that any other present or future data cannot unambiguously disconfirm the model. We have tried to avoid this tactic. Not only is our theory vulnerable to future disconfirmation; it also clearly fails to handle a number of the existing facts. The points of misfit will be openly acknowledged at the appropriate places. It is difficult to determine how serious these failures are. In a complex model like HAM it is always possible to introduce some special assumption that will handle any particular discrepancy. Also, the misfits may indicate a mistake in one particular assumption rather than a flaw in the grand theoretical design.

The fundamental issue at stake with respect to our theory is its neo-associationist character. This is not to be found in any particular assumption, but rather pervades diffusely throughout the whole enterprise. Our strong computer-simulation orientation has led to a class of controversial assumptions. Information processing in HAM tends to be in terms of discrete units called ideas and associations, and it proceeds in sequential steps, whereas parallel, interactive processes are assumed to be minimal. Can one really claim that a human processes information in this discrete, serial manner? But the physiology of the brain is very different from that of a serial, digital computer, and analogue, parallel processes would not seem out of character for that mysterious organ (cf. Von Neuman, 1958). Perhaps, then, our theory has been too strongly determined by what is easy to simulate on a computer rather than by considerations of psychological plausibility. That is one fundamental question.

Another source of difficulty with our theory may arise from our strong empiricist leanings. We have insisted that all knowledge in memory should be built up from input to the memory. We have denied that memory has any capacity to spontaneously restructure itself into more useful forms. Perhaps we have made memory too passive, too much of a tabula rasa. That is a second fundamental question.

On the other hand, we have granted the mind a great deal of self-structuring power in our assumptions regarding the perceptual parsers that transform external stimuli into memory input, or the various inferential and problem-solving abilities that enable the system to make intelligent use of the information recorded in memory. One is forced to postulate such powerful mechanisms in order to interface a memory with the world. The postulated mechanisms are enormously more complicated than any of the theoretical devices that have been previously postulated in associative theories. Perhaps, if we had complicated the proposed memory system, we could have simplified the interfacing apparatus. That is a third fundamental question.

Another possible flaw in the grand design has to do with our insistence on making the propositional representation fundamental. We will want to encode perceptual as well as linguistic input into this uniform propositional base. Perhaps we are choosing a representation that is too logical and abstract. Perhaps the primary representation of knowledge is of some diffuse, sensory sort; and our ability to encode information propositionally in this original base comes about only after much conceptual development and training in abstraction. This is a fourth fundamental question.

These are the sorts of questions that will hound us throughout this enterprise. We cannot claim that there is any great initial plausibility to our particular formulation. But we feel it is important that we develop that formulation as explicitly as possible and raise the questions we have about it. Our formulation provides a concrete realization of a certain theoretical position. It provides something definite for research workers to discuss, examine, criticize, and experiment upon. It is hoped that some resolution will be eventually achieved with respect to the fundamental theoretical questions. We hope that others will be encouraged to provide and motivate other explicit models of fundamentally different theoretical positions. If this happens, our goal will have been achieved, whatever is the final judgment with respect to HAM. We will have shifted the focus of experimental psychology from the articulation of narrow paradigms to an analysis of the significant questions concerning human memory. To attempt this may be a pretentious ambition, but it is a primary purpose and justification of this book.

REFERENCES

Chomsky, N. *Language and mind.* New York: Harcourt, Brace & World, 1968.

Collins, A. M., & Quillian, M. R. How to make a language user. In E. Tulving & W. Donaldson (Eds.), *Organization of Memory.* New York: Academic Press, 1972.

Rumelhart, D. E., Lindsay, P. H., & Norman, D. A. A process model for long-term memory. In E. Tulving & W. Donaldson (Eds.), *Organization of Memory.* New York: Academic Press, 1972.

Simon, H. A., & Feigenbaum, E. A. An information processing theory of some effects of similarity, familiarity, and meaningfulness in verbal learning. *Journal of Verbal Learning and Verbal Behavior,* 1964, **3**, 385–396.

Tulving, E., & Madigan, S. A. Memory and verbal learning. *Annual Review of Psychology,* 1970, **21**, 437–484.

Von Neuman, J. *The computer and the brain.* New Haven, Conn.: Yale University Press, 1958.

2
ASSOCIATIONISM: A HISTORICAL REVIEW

In our inquiry into the soul it is necessary for us, as we proceed, to raise such questions as demand answers; we must collect the opinions of those predecessors who have had anything to say touching the soul's nature, in order that we may accept their true statements and be on our guard against their errors.

—Aristotle

2.1. ASSOCIATIONISM: AN OVERVIEW

Associationism has a tradition that extends over 2,000 years, from the writings of Aristotle to the experiments of modern psychologists. Despite the existence of this clearly identifiable *theoretical tradition*, there is not a well-defined monolithic *theoretical position* which can be called associationism. Past associative theories differ one from another both in details and in basic assumptions. While all major associative theorists have agreed on a few fundamental points, there are more fundamentals on which there exist no such consensus. So, we are faced with an apparent paradox: How can we identify a coherent associative tradition but no coherent associative theory?

The unifying feature of associationism lies in its empiricist methodology, not in any substantive assumptions that it makes. That is, all associationists have taken as their task the job of using the immediate data available to them (e.g., introspections, stimulus-response contingencies, etc.) and constructing the human mind from these with minimal additional assumptions. Depending upon the data they considered important and upon personal idiosyncracies, different theorists achieved somewhat different mental reconstructions. However, because of the common methodology, their psychological systems tend to share certain metafeatures. Four such features seem to universally typify associationism:

1. Ideas, sense data, memory nodes, or similar mental elements are associated together in the mind through experience. Thus, associationism is *connectionistic.*

2. The ideas can ultimately be decomposed into a basic stock of "simple ideas." Thus, associationism is *reductionistic.*

3. The simple ideas are to be identified with elementary, unstructured sensations. (The meaning we want to assign to "sensation" is rather generous in that we intend to include internal experiences, such as involved in emotion.) Because it identifies the basic components of the mind with sensory experience, associationism is *sensationalistic.*

4. Simple, additive rules serve to predict the properties of complex associative configurations from the properties of the underlying simple ideas. Thus, associationism is *mechanistic.*

We claim that these four features of associative theories are defining features of associationism because they are the highly probable consequences of the empiricist methodology that constructs such theories.

It might seem that the empirical validity of these four metafeatures might then be crucial to evaluating associationism. If one of these assumptions were to be proven false, that would prove that associative theories are wrong. However, it is doubtful whether any of these assumptions is of the sort that it could be subject to empirical falsification. After all, they are metafeatures of the theory rather than definite predictions about observable behavior. These metafeatures become manifest in particular theories in the form of particular predictions that may be falsified or verified, but it seems that the metafeatures are not subject to empirical disconfirmation. But before pursuing this point further, we should examine the four meta-assumptions in more detail.

Connectionism. Regarding connectionism, one must distinguish whether the discussion concerns associationism as a theory of human memory or as a theory of all mental phenomena. Connectionism, with its implicit empiricism, is a controversial assumption within the general associative plan of trying to explain all mental processes with one basic principle. It is not at all obvious that all our mental processes have been connected together through experience. Indeed, in our own model we do not subscribe to the notion that the mind has been totally "wired up" by experience. Some of the important mental processes described in our model are much more naturally viewed as innate rather than acquired mechanisms.

In contrast to the doubtful character of connectionism as the universal principle of mental phenomena, it would seem entirely innocuous as a principle of memory. To say that memory consists of ideas connected by experience would seem to be almost tautological. In this respect, it is interesting to note the uncritical tendency among psychologists to apply the "associationistic" label to any theory of memory that refers to connections or associations. This practice is reducing associationism to an empty descriptive notion. Associationism as a theory of memory gets its cutting edge from the remaining three distinguishing features. They serve to impose some restrictions on the character of the "connections."

Reductionism. This is sometimes called "elementarism," and the doctrine is fairly clear: It is assumed that there are certain elements (the simple ideas) that are distinguished by the fact that all other ideas are built up from them. The phrase "built up from" is somewhat vague, but a formalization of that notion will be offered in Chapter 7, where the memory structure of HAM is discussed. Some readers might question whether reductionism has any empirical significance; wouldn't every theory of human memory subscribe to such a metaprinciple? The answer is "Definitely not." The classic counterexample (although there are others) is Gestalt theory, which argued many phenomena defied reductionistic analysis (see Chapter 3).

Sensationalism. Certainly no one would quarrel with the claim that representations of sensory data constitute part of the contents of the mind. However, from Plato to Chomsky, there have been radical rationalists who have denied the sensationalist's claim that all knowledge has a sensory base. Indeed, it will turn out that a few non-sensory elements are required in our model.

Mechanism. The mechanistic feature of associative theories is at once the most imprecise and the most controversial. Stated crudely, the claim is that man is a machine and his nature and behavior are to be understood in mechanical terms. Ever since Democritus gave his original mechanistic account of the human soul, the issue has been a controversy of some stature. Since La Mettrie attempted to refute Descartes' claim that man is not machine, the matter has been a violent debate (witness the recent book by Dreyfus, 1972). The problem, however, is that our concept of what it is to be a machine is exceedingly imprecise and is continually being revised as we construct more intelligent automata. However, we do have reliable intuitions about what it means to be mechanistic. Many principles in our model will be unanimously judged as mechanistic and, no doubt, distasteful for that reason to some readers. Mechanistic assumptions such as those in our model tend to display an affinity for simple, linear, and discrete processes and an aversion for mass, interactive, and continuously varying processes.

We have argued that these four features have significance with respect to theories of the mind, although connectionism without the other three is an empty claim with respect to human memory. Nonetheless, it seems unlikely that any single feature can be subject to direct empirical falsification. There is a certain vagueness inherent in each of these metafeatures. One can empirically falsify the manifestation of these features in a particular model (for instance, our own), but it seems that it will always be possible to come up with another set of similar assumptions to explain the offending data. Indeed, much of the history of experimental psychology is the continuing saga of antiassociationists demonstrating the weakness of a particular associative theory, only to find the theory quickly changed and no longer subject to the old attack. This elusiveness of the four metaprinciples should not be surprising since they reflect methodological biases that are not really subject to empirical disconfirmation.

To summarize our conclusions, we claim that associationism is a historical tradition distinguished by its attempts to reconstruct the human mind from sensory experience with minimal theoretical assumptions. This approach contrasts with rationalistic theories which have attempted to work from basic a priori principles. As a consequence of its empiricist methodology, all associative theories have been distinguished by the four metafeatures enumerated above. While these metafeatures can be manifested in empirical predictions that are subject to disconfirmation, the metafeatures themselves would seem fairly immune.

The Terminal Meta-Postulate

However, there is one feature which tends to haunt associative theories, which can be given precise statement, and which can be proven in error. This is the Terminal Meta-Postulate (TMP) which was so dubbed by Bever, Fodor, and Garrett (1968). This postulate should be viewed as a particularly likely manifestation of associationism's metafeatures. The postulate may be divided into three statements, one statement corresponding to each of three associative metafeatures.

1. *Sensationalist Statement.* The only elements required in a psychological explanation can be put into a one-to-one correspondence with potentially observable elements. These elements may themselves be observable stimuli or responses, or they may be derived from such observables. These derivatives have been variously known as intervening variables, mediating responses, sensations, perceptions, images, or ideas.

2. *Connectionistic Statement.* The elements in Statement 1 become connected or associated if and only if they occur contiguously.

3. *Mechanistic Statement.* All observable behavior can be explained by concatenating the associative links in Statement 2.

While many past associative theories have assented to the TMP, there are theories which are commonly agreed to be associative and which violate this principle. Many of the classical British associationists (see Section 2.3) admitted an irreducible principle of similarity and so would reject Statement 2, although all of the British associationists do seem to have accepted Statements 1 and 3. Aristotle (Section 2.2) rejected all three claims. We have followed his lead and have done likewise in our model. Therefore, to claim that the TMP is a defining feature of associationism, as some of our colleagues have, is just false.

Here we will illustrate a fundamental flaw in the TMP. In our demonstration we will be using the same example as employed by Bever et al. (1968). This is the mirror-image language which is typically employed as a structure that cannot be generated by *finite-state automata* or *regular grammars* (see Hopcroft & Ullman, 1969, for a formal exposition of such technical terms). Any mechanism satisfying the TMP cannot produce behaviors more complicated than can these formal automata or grammars. For instance, Suppes (1969) has established the equivalence between finite-state automata and S-R theory. Rather than becoming enmeshed in the formal theory of automata, however, we will try to make our points at a more conversational level.

In a mirror-image language, the sequence of elements in the first half of a string (or sequence) must be mirrored in the second half. For instance, if *a* and *b* were the only elements of the language, Table 2.1 gives examples of strings which are acceptable and strings which are not. Consider how a TMP system might try to deal with such a mirror-image language. Note that in grammatical strings, *a* can be followed by either *a* or *b*, and *b* can be followed by either *a* or *b*. Then, in accordance with Statements 1 and 2, we would have to postulate that the following

TABLE 2.1

A Mirror-Image Language

Grammatical	Ungrammatical
aa	ba
abba	aaab
bbbb	bbabaa
abaaba	bbabb

four associations are formed: $a \rightarrow a$, $a \rightarrow b$, $b \rightarrow a$, $b \rightarrow b$. These four associations do suffice to generate all the grammatical strings of our language. The first grammatical string in Table 2.1 could be generated simply with the association $a \rightarrow a$; the second could be generated by concatenating $a \rightarrow b$, $b \rightarrow b$, and $b \rightarrow a$, and so on for other strings. But the reader has probably already noted the difficulty. This TMP system generates too much. For instance, from the association $b \rightarrow a$ we can generate the ungrammatical string *ba*.

The basic problem with the TMP system is that it has no means of recording what it did early in the string so it can unwind the mirror image of that sequence in completing that string. To use a term popular in some psychological circles, a TMP system can have no "plan of action." It is easy enough to construct a system capable of generating all and just the strings of our mirror-image language. A context-free grammar to do this is given in Table 2.2. Also in Table 2.2 is a tree structure generated by the grammar. Bever et al. (1968) argue that it is the element X in the rewrite rule of the grammar which violates the TMP. However, this is to confuse a description of the formal grammar with the mechanism that implements the grammar. Nonetheless, when we examine such a mechanism we will find ample violations of the TMP.

However, before we turn to that mechanism, the reader should be clear about what is the problematical aspect of the mirror-image language in Table 2.1. The

TABLE 2.2

A Grammar for the Mirror-Image Language

Rewrite Rules

$X \rightarrow a\,X\,a$

$X \rightarrow b\,X\,b$

$X \rightarrow \phi$

difficulty is that this language permits an indefinite number of embeddings of strings within strings. This embedding introduces dependencies between elements at arbitrary distances in the final string. For instance, the first and last element of a mirror-image string must match. Such dependencies cannot be captured in a finite-state automaton.

In Table 2.3 is the flow chart of a minimal system that is adequate to generate mirror-image languages. This system requires a push-down stack (PDS), a device

TABLE 2.3

Flow Chart of Push-Down Stack Machine for
Mirror-Image Language

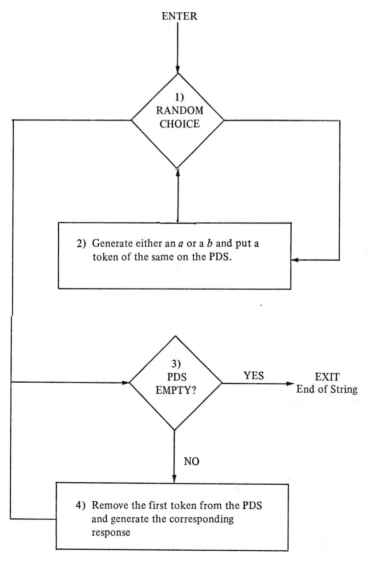

that stores objects and returns them according to the principle of last-in, first-out. This PDS clearly violates Statement 1 of the TMP. When we examine the flow chart, prescribing use of the PDS, we find further violations of the TMP. Consider how the string *abba* would be generated: The mechanism enters the random-choice box 1, and decides to move to box 2. Here it generates an *a* and puts an *a* token on the PDS. It cycles through the choice-box 1 and returns to box 2, this time to generate a *b*. Correspondingly, a *b* token is stored on the PDS. The contents of the PDS are now the tokens *b* and *a* in that order. The mechanism returns to choice-box 1 and then proceeds this time to decision-box 3. As the PDS is not empty, our mechanism proceeds to box 4, where it takes the first element from the PDS. This is a *b* token, and the system correspondingly generates a *b* response. It cycles through the choice-box 3 and back to box 4. Here it removes the last token from the PDS and generates an *a*. Upon returning to box 3, it finds the PDS empty and exits having successfully generated the string *abba.* The various operations we have been describing are clearly not encoded according to Statement 2 of the TMP or performed according to Statement 3. So we have violated all three conditions. Further violations of Statement 1 are the *a* and *b* tokens which were stored in the TMP. These *a* and *b* tokens are not responses nor response derivatives. Responses are not elements that reside for indefinite periods on push-down stacks. They rather occupy a brief moment in time and space.

Therefore, to generate the mirror-image language, we were forced to postulate a number of structures and processes only *abstractly* related to external observables. This is just what the TMP cannot abide. To end our discussion of the TMP on a technical note: In our "conversational" exposition we have been basically using the fact that a push-down automaton can and a finite-state automaton cannot accommodate the mirror-image languages. However, it is well known that any push-down automaton can be replaced by an equivalent finite-state automaton if we set a finite limit to the length of the push-down stack. A push-down automaton like that in Table 2.3 with a stack of length n can only generate (or recognize) mirror-image strings of length $2n$. But this is not objectionable, since there are certainly short-term memory limitations on the length of strings that we realistically can generate or recognize. Hence, it might be questioned whether we have shown the TMP to be in error, since there is a finite-state automaton that will handle mirror-image strings bounded by some upper length. However, this argument overlooks two important facts. First, the translation of a finite-stack push-down automaton into a finite-state automaton involves an enormous complication in terms of number of states. Essentially, each possible mirror-image string up to length $2n$ must be individually recorded by a distinct set of states. Secondly, by Statement 2 of the TMP, each transition in the state diagram must encode a contiguity in experience. But this is nonsense. We do not learn the mirror-image language by being exposed to all possible sequences of length up to $2n$; rather, a minute's study of the rules in Table 2.2 is sufficient. So this is one example of the importance of distinguishing questions of logical equivalence of two models from questions of their relative empirical plausibility. It is on the latter basis that we would reject any model based on the TMP.

To return to the main line of our historical exposition, in the following three sections of this chapter we will examine three types of associationism. The first is the associative analysis of human memory that Aristotle gave 2,300 years ago. His conception of memory was dominant until the time of the British associationists, beginning with Thomas Hobbes. The British empiricists extended the domain of associationism from Aristotle's original concern with human memory to encompass all mental phenomena; they also tried to make the associative doctrine a basis for their epistemology. The third type of associationism is the brand of associationism developed in America under the influence of functionalism and behaviorism.

Throughout this historical survey, we will try to distinguish the claims of associationism that are relevant to memory from those claims relevant to the more ambitious enterprise of reconstructing all of the human mind on a single principle. This distinction will be forced at times because, as we will see, some of the associationists denied that memory existed as a phenomena distinct from other aspects of consciousness.

2.2. ARISTOTLE'S ASSOCIATIONISM

Aristotle's associationism is found almost exclusively in his brief essay "On Memory and Reminiscence." However, it is best understood in the context of his general philosophy. In contrast to the extreme sensationalism of the sophists or the extreme rationalism of Plato, Aristotle provided a satisfying combination of empiricism and rationalism. In contrast to Plato, Aristotle supposed that all knowledge is derived through perception; there are no innate ideas. However, he supposed that the human mind does not contain a raw record of past sensory experience. Rather, Perception involves a creative action by Reason which imposes form on the incoming sensory data. The Reason makes use of various *analytical a priori propositions* in performing this task. Without the Reason to constantly structure and interpret incoming data, the mind would supposedly be a confusing mass of particulars. A role similar to the Reason in Aristotle's theory is exemplified in our model by such items as the perceptual and linguistic parsers and the inference-making processes. As with Aristotle's Reason, components of HAM's mechanisms are assumed to be innate rather than acquired from experience.

Aristotle's theory of memory is clearly sensationalistic. In fact, he believed that memory was part of the primary faculty of sense perception in that memory was the mechanism by which past sensory experience could be examined. A memory had the same relation to an original sense perception as a picture has to that of which it is a representation—i.e., memory provides a likeness of the original sensory experience. Even memory for "intellectual objects" such as numbers was alleged to involve the faculty of sense perception in that the intellect required its object to be presented to the mind by that faculty. Thus, as in all associationist theories, the structure of the input to and output from the memory component is identified with the structure of the percept. However, in contrast with many later theorists, Aristotle assumed that the mind imposed a great deal of structure upon the percept.

Aristotle's theory of perception, and hence his theory of memory, is also reductionistic in that he considered the perception of an object to be composed of the perception of its various sensible properties—color, smell, size, form, etc. Aristotle proposed the existence of a "common sense" which plays a central role in the construction of the object from its basic properties. It serves to unite the diverse sensations that come in by the various modalities and to cognize properties of the object which are not modality-specific (e.g., motion, number, shape, and magnitude). Aristotle took his theory about the encoding of the input with little modification from Plato's analogy of the wax-seal impression: "The process of movement involved in the act of perception stamps in, as it were, a sort of impression of the percept, just as persons do who make an impression with a seal [Beare, 1931, 450a30–450b1]." The important feature to note about this approach is that it identifies perception of an object as a necessary and sufficient condition for formation of a memory trace. This contrasts sharply with the emphasis commonly found in American associationism on the role of reinforcement in the formation of associations.

Aristotle's discussion of the retrieval process is commonly used to justify identifying him as the first associationist. He noticed something systematic in the chain of thoughts which resulted in the recollection of particular facts. He isolated three sorts of relationships that governed the succession of these thoughts: similarity, contrast, and contiguity of exemplars in past experience, which were to become the favored three principles of the British associationists. Aristotle also noted the importance of frequency, intensity, and good order in the construction of the associations. He thought that recollection involved a voluntary act of probing memory with some thought that was likely to bring about the desired memory by an associative train of thought: "Accordingly, therefore, when one wishes to recollect, this is what he will do: He will try to obtain a beginning of a movement whose sequel shall be the movement he desires to reawaken [Beare, 1931, 451b30]." Aristotle is making a distinction here between the selection of a probe, which is subject to strategic considerations, and the response of memory to this probe, which proceeds automatically. Aristotle called the automatic response of memory to a stimulus an "act of remembering," but if there was also strategic selection of the probe, he called the total act *recollection*. The former, the act of remembering, was allegedly a power possessed by all animals; but the latter, recollection, was possessed only by man, who alone had the faculty of deliberation and the capacity to make inferences. A similar distinction will appear in our model, separating the strategic selection of a probe from the automatic operation of a memory component in response to a probe.

At points in this examination of Aristotle's theory of memory, we have noted how closely it resembles our own in contrast to more recent formulations. Indeed, the British associationists, to be examined next, seem to have only introduced error into the Aristotelean conception. There are several reasons for this apparent advanced character of Aristotle's theory of memory. First, it is very sketchy. Many of the later errors occurred when the associationists took on the necessary task of filling in the details. Second, not content with Aristotle's original concern with human memory, later associationists extended the domain of associationism to all mental phenomena. Therefore, they could not provide the tailor-made analysis for human memory that Aristotle did. Finally, Aristotle's theory of memory was built upon the background of his careful and sophisticated epistemology. In contrast, the British associationists did not have such guidance to overview the construction of their associative theory. Rather, they tried to base their epistemology upon their analysis of the human mind.

2.3. BRITISH ASSOCIATIONISM

In the 200-year period from Thomas Hobbes ("Human Nature," 1650) to Alexander Bain (*The Senses and the Intellect*, 1859), associationism took on a very definite and ambitious form. Initially, with Hobbes and John Locke, associationism was just a minor part of free-wheeling empiricist expositions that boldly jumped from philosophy to psychology to sociology to political science. With Bishop Berkeley and David Hume, association psychology was called in to help buttress their epistemological views. With David Hartley, the connection between the psychological theory and the philosophical systems was cut. Hartley took the incomplete analyses of his predecessors and built a detailed psychological doctrine around them. Later associationists such as John and James Mill and Alexander Bain suggested variants on Hartley's system, but all basically conformed to the pattern Hartley had set forth.

One way to survey British associationism would be to provide a chronology of the 200-year period, noting what the principle figures said and how they differed one from another. However, excellent surveys of this kind already exist (e.g., Boring, 1950; Warren, 1921) and there is no need to reduplicate past efforts. Instead we shall try to extract and examine the global characteristics of British associationism. This is the way to isolate the weaknesses in their system that we must be careful to avoid in ours. In this analysis of British associationism it is necessary to focus on three aspects of their theory: first, their concept of an "idea," the unit out of which the mind was constructed; second, their concept of the association which connected the ideas together; and third, their concept of the associative process by which past experience determined current thought. There are serious weaknesses in each concept.

The Simple Idea—The Building Block of the Mind

As noted above, Aristotle identified the input and output of memory very closely with perception. This sensationalism is also present in the British associationism. Locke emphasized that all knowledge could be analyzed into discrete simple ideas like "roundness" and "redness," and that such simple ideas were all derived from experience—either directly through the senses or through reflection and self-observation. This conception of the simple idea was repeated by most of the later British writers.

Locke also outlined how complex ideas arose from associations of simple ideas. For instance, the complex idea of an apple would be composed, in part, from the simple ideas of roundness and redness. One of the immediate embarrassments to the associationists was that all the convincing introspective evidence for the association of ideas indicated that complex rather than simple ideas were linked by associations. It was never made entirely clear how complex ideas (which are interassociated bunches of simple ideas) could become directly connected by a single association in a way that could preserve the original mechanistic conception of an association as a link between two elements of the mind. It seems that a bunch of interconnected ideas could come to behave as a single idea.

In any case, according to the British associationists, the "terminal vocabulary" of the human mind is provided completely by elementary sensations and reflections. More complex ideas are just compounds of simple ideas. In more recent times, a similar notion dominated experimental psychology, namely, that behavior should be analyzable in a theoretical language that uses as its terms only stimuli and responses that are observable (at least in principle). This is the "Terminal Meta-Postulate" (TMP), which we discussed and criticized earlier. As shown there, a descriptive system satisfying the TMP cannot perform recursive mental operations, which are necessary to account for the creative aspects of language behavior and are probably necessary for other human behaviors as well. However, our concern with associationism is not with its adequacy as a model for human thought or language, but rather as a model for human memory, a subcomponent of our total mental hardware. Does the TMP lead to similar difficulties in the restricted domain of memory? There are some convincing demonstrations that it does.

The Need for a Type-Token Distinction

One of the problems with the TMP is that it would strain the storage capacity of any physical system. Consider James Mill's (1869) famous reconstruction of what is involved in the concept of a house:

> Brick is one complex idea, mortar is another complex idea; these ideas, with ideas of position and quantity, compose my idea of a wall. My idea of a plank is a complex idea, my idea of a rafter is a complex idea, my idea of a nail is a complex idea. These, united with the same ideas of position and quantity, compose my duplex idea of a floor. In the same manner my complex idea of glass, and wood, and others, compose my duplex idea of a window; and these duplex ideas, united together, compose my idea of a house, which is made up of various duplex ideas [pp. 115–116].

To paraphrase, a vast number of complex ideas and duplex ideas (associations of complex ideas) must be associated together to represent a house. Each of the complex and duplex ideas requires many associations between simple ideas. Thus, an enormous number (i.e., at least in the thousands) of simple ideas and associations would go into constructing the relatively simple concept of a house. The storage requirements to represent all our concepts and knowledge in such a format would be enormous. On this basis alone such a representation is untenable. However, such considerations of storage requirements did not weigh heavily on the British associationists. While some like Hartley occasionally lapsed into physiological speculations, the spirit of the age was such that pragmatic questions, like that of storage requirements in a physical system, were ignored. However, in this age of the computer, the problem immediately comes to mind.

In this age of the computer, the problem also has a well-known solution, the so-called type-token distinction (e.g., see Simon & Feigenbaum, 1964). However, the type-token distinction brings with it abandonment of the Terminal Meta-Postulate; i.e., elements are permitted which do not correspond to sensations or other externally observable referents like responses. The type-token distinction permits one to define each concept just once in memory. For instance, instead of embedding into the house concept the duplex idea of a window with all its complex ideas and associations, a single element is used to stand for the concept of a window in the definition of a house. This element is a "token" which "points" to the "type" for window. It is only the type node that collects together all the associations defining what a window is. This allows efficient structuring of information, since knowledge about windows needs to be stored just once in memory, even though the concept of a window can be used in constructing many other concepts. A significant feature of this analysis is that it introduces, as elementary unanalyzable units, some theoretical objects (namely, the tokens) which are not derived from elementary sensations. These tokens are not "copies" of sensations. If they were they would have to contain all the associative complexity of the type. Hence, the Terminal Meta-Postulate of British associationism is violated by the type-token distinction.

A similar difficulty stems from the fact that the same idea can enter into more than one association. For instance, suppose two sequences of colors were flashed at a subject—the first, red, blue, green, and the second, yellow, blue, orange. By the principle of contiguity, he could remember the first sequence by forming associations from the idea of red to the idea of blue and thence to the idea of green; by similar means he could represent and remember the second sequence. Letting arrows represent associations, these representations are illustrated in Figure 2.1a. Upon inspection, the difficulty with this representation should be immediately apparent. There is an association from red to blue and one from blue to orange. Given this structure, it is likely that the subject may recollect the sequence red-blue-orange, but this sequence in fact never occurred. This hypothetical example illustrates a very general point; if we have many associations leading to an idea and many associations leading from the idea, then the representation must have some way to determine which predecessors go with which successors.

One solution to this problem would be to have multiple copies of a particular idea and to use a new copy for each association. This would result in a representation like that shown in Figure 2.1b. One difficulty with this proposal is that it would require a great deal of storage to represent multiple copies of very complex ideas. A second problem arises when we ask how one would ever retrieve the old associations that an idea had entered into if every time we thought of the idea we found ourselves with a new, virgin copy of that idea. A better solution is again to introduce "tokens" of these ideas as in Figure 2.1c. These tokens are connected by further associations to the types which contain the prototypical representation of the ideas. Hence, it is possible to retrieve the old associations that an idea has entered into by following the associations from the prototypical type to its various tokens.

A further difficulty created by acceptance of the Terminal Meta-Postulate is that it committed the British associationists to a strong nominalist position. That is, all simple ideas were ideas of particular sensations, and all complex ideas were formed

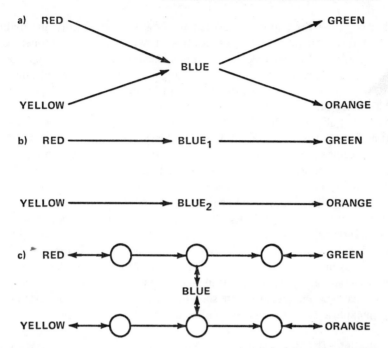

FIG. 2.1. Alternative associative structures: (*a*) the British conception; (*b*) with multiple copies of ideas; and (*c*) with the type-token distinction. See text for discussion.

from these particular ideas. Such an approach cannot tolerate any truly universal ideas—that is, elements that are completely abstracted away from particular elements of reality. How, then, were they to accommodate the fact that we appear to have ideas of universals, such as the generic idea of man? They argued that we have a word (e.g., "man") to denote the general idea, and that the word becomes associated to a complex idea composed of the collection of individuals to whom the generic title has been applied:

> The word, man, we shall say, is first applied to an individual; it is first associated with the idea of that individual, and acquires the power of calling up the idea of him; it is next applied to another individual, and acquires the power of calling up the idea of him; so of another, and another, till it has become associated with an indefinite number, and has acquired the power of calling up an indefinite number of those ideas indifferently. What happens? It does call up an indefinite number of the ideas of individuals, as often as it occurs; and calling them up in close connexion, it forms them into a species of complex idea [J. Mill, 1869, p. 264].

This analysis is unsatisfactory on multiple grounds. It is an enormous complication in the mental representation to insist that the general idea is an aggregate of all its individual instances. It is more economical to grant the mind the power to introduce a new element, the idea of the universal concept which is an abstraction from the instances. Moreover, without the distinction between particular and general ideas, it seems impossible to explain how we can identify the defining properties of a general concept as contrasted with accidental properties of particular instances. For example, all the knives one has seen may have had wooden handles, but having wooden handles is still not a defining property of knives. In contrast, serving the function of cutting is one of the defining properties of a knife.

The Terminal Meta-Postulate also denies the possibility of any innate knowledge and insists that all knowledge be a record of past experience—which, of course, is the extreme empiricist position. But, on this account, certain elements of our knowledge become inexplicable. For instance, as Hume demonstrated, there can be nothing in our experience to lead us to the notion of causality. So why do we perceive causality in the relation of events, and not just spatiotemporal contiguity? As Kant concluded, our understanding of causality (or at least our predisposition to perceive causality) must be a priori, or built in as part of our mental hardware.

So, the Terminal Meta-Postualte appears to have been the source of a host of related difficulties in the British associationist account of the mind. This questionable assumption was not part of Aristotle's original formulation. While it has been generally accepted in American associationism, particularly as a result of the behaviorist epistemology, we were soon forced to abandon it in our attempts to develop an explicit simulation model of human memory.

The Association—The Mind's Glue

In the previous section we examined and criticized the British conception of the idea. In this section we examine the associations which were alleged to hold the ideas together. We will begin by reviewing some of the agreed-upon properties of associations and will conclude by noting some difficulties with the British conception of an association. The problem with the British conception of the association is basically that it provides no useful way to represent the different relations that are expressed by different associations, nor for expressing the structural properties inherent in an associative configuration.

Contiguity and Similarity

Generally, the associationists distinguished between the *successive associations* which control the sequencing of thoughts in the stream of consciousness, and the *synchronous associations* which combine simultaneous ideas into more complex ideas. Contiguity in time was particularly important in the formation of a successive association, whereas contiguity in space was important for the formation of a synchronous association. Hartley attempted to reduce contiguity in space to a special case of contiguity in time, claiming that contiguity in space was effective only in that spatially contiguous objects or properties are likely to be perceived in temporal contiguity. However, all other major British associationists preserved the distinction between successive and synchronous associations. Much of what the British associationists included under the title of successive association is of little interest to our present concern with human memory, although such associations were supposed to play an important role in the British explanation of language and thought.

Similarity has frequently been mentioned as a principle governing the association of ideas. Both Hartley and James Mill, however, insisted that contiguity was the sole relation governing association and that similarity could be derived from it:

Resemblance only remains, as an alleged principle of association, and it is necessary to inquire whether it is included in the laws which have been above expounded. I believe it will be found that we are accustomed to see like things together. When we see a tree, we generally see more trees than one; when we see an ox, we generally see more oxen than one; a sheep, more sheep than one; a man, more men than one [J. Mill, 1869, p. 111].

This sort of associationistic argumentation has been attacked by numerous critics seeking an easy prey (e.g., Koffka, 1935; Köhler, 1947; Deese, 1965). These attacks are somewhat unjustified, since Locke, Berkeley, Hume, and Bain all accepted similarity as an irreducible law of associationism. Indeed, even John Stuart Mill rebelled against his father on this issue. On the same page as we find the preceding quote of the elder Mill, we can find this footnote added by J. S. Mill:

The reason assigned by the author for considering association by resemblance as a case of association by contiguity, is perhaps the least successful attempt at a generalisation and simplification of the laws of mental phenomena, to be found in the work. It ought to be remembered that the author, as the text shews, attached little importance to it. And perhaps, not thinking it important, he passed it over with a less amount of patient thought than he usually bestowed on his analyses [J. Mill, 1869, p. 111].

In the domain of human memory, contiguity does deserve a special status, since memories are generally of what has been spatially or temporally contiguous in our past experience. It is an interesting question, however, whether similarity among contiguous ideas or events facilitates our memory for them. One issue in the debate between Gestalt theory and modern associationism has been whether a concept of similarity is also needed for memory.

While most of the British philosophers admitted the possibility of association through similarity, they focused on the factor of contiguity. This is witnessed by the number of subprinciples enunciated within British associationism whose only purpose was to augment the principle of contiguity. Specifically, vividness of experience, frequency of experience, duration of experience, and recency of experience were all suggested as determining the strength of a particular association. This set of principles should sound very familiar to experimental psychologists, since they have generated a great many experiments on memory and verbal learning.

A point worth mentioning here is that the British associationists explicitly assumed that the mind could acquire new associations by "deliberate reflection," by thinking over a set of prior associations and noting new relations or inferences. For example, having learned how children keep dogs and cats for pleasure, a person may later be taught a new concept of a *pet*, as a domesticated animal kept for pleasure rather than utility; a later moment of critical reflection could then bring together the two associations relating "dog," "animal kept for pleasure," and "pet," thus setting up the internal contiguity necessary for the new association "dog-pet" to be formed. It is rather like the modern accounts of "mediated generalization," or how the associations A-B and B-C can strengthen the association A-C. What is wrong with the doctrine is not the unobservable character of its constructs (to which radical behaviorists would object), but rather that the mechanisms governing "reflection" are not given any satisfactory explanation and the theory becomes either totally descriptive or irredeemably vitalistic. To this day there is no well worked out theory of how the mind spontaneously interrogates its own knowledge to construct new knowledge.

The Mechanistic versus the Chemical Conception

One of the problems in interpreting British associationism is to determine what exactly an association was intended to be. Hume referred to it as "a gentle force which commonly prevails." In more recent times, psychologists have talked about the probability that one idea will elicit another. This notion is frequently referred to as "mental mechanics"; each association is simply a semideterministic link between independent ideas. Mental mechanics is to be contrasted with the "mental chemistry" view most clearly espoused by J. S. Mill (1889):

> When impressions have been so often experienced in conjunction that each of them calls up readily and instantaneously the ideas of the whole group, these ideas sometimes meld and coalesce into one another, and appear not several ideas but one. These, therefore, are cases of mental chemistry, in which it is proper to say that the simple ideas generate, rather than that they compose the complex ones [p. 558].

Warren (1921) argued that the chemical analogy is just as representative of British associationism as is the mechanical one. He quoted passages from Hobbes, Locke, Berkeley, Hume, and Hartley to show that they all admitted the possibility of the chemical analogy. It seems only James Mill rejected it. However, Warren failed to recognize that the writings of each of these authors was dominated by the mechanistic conception. None of the associationists, including J. S. Mill, developed the chemical analogy to any systematic conclusions.

Associations Express Relations

There is one problem with the conception of the association developed by the British school which cannot be rectified by either increasing the role of similarity or by introducing the possibility of the chemical analogy. The problem is that items that we know to be related in different ways are assumed to be connected in the mind by one and the same sort of association. For instance, in our mind a dining room is associated with eating, a glutton with eating, a fork with eating, and a steak with eating. How is it that we know that the relation expressed by the first association is one of location to act, the second is that of actor to act, the third of act to instrument, and the fourth of act to object? All are connected by the same one sort of associative link. No doubt James Mill would argue that these differences could be captured by considering each of the above examples as part of a larger network of associations, so that the relation in each case could somehow be "computed" from the position of the association in the network. However, no one has ever described exactly how this computation proceeds. All recent attempts to simulate human memory with an associative model have had to resort to labeling the associative links with the various relations they express (i.e., Anderson, 1972; Quillian, 1968; Schwarcz, Burger, & Simmons, 1970).

While most of the British associationists insisted that there was no need for relations, several notable exceptions are to be found at the periphery of the associationist's camp. Thomas Brown (1820) of the Scottish school had quite clearly seen the need to introduce the relation as distinct from the two interconnected ideas, and he made the relation an important part of his philosophy of the mind. Also in the last days of British associationism, Herbert Spencer (1890) proposed that associations expressed rudimentary relations which were distinct from the elements associated.

In addition to not admitting relations, the British theory also failed to have any conception of well-formedness in an associative structure. That is, they claimed that any idea could be associated with any other idea with which it is spatiotemporally contiguous. But on the contrary, as will be seen in the Gestalt analysis of perception, the elements tend to become organized into certain groupings which in turn tend to become organized into hierarchical structures. A similar need for hierarchical structures will arise when we deal with linguistic material. The point is, as Aristotle apparently understood, that the mind imposes a particular form on the incoming elements of experience. A system such as that proposed by the British associationists which denies such an organizing force would appear likely to produce a chaotic mass of uninterpretable associations.

The Associative Process

We have so far focused on what might be called the *structural* assumptions in British associationism. The two principle constructs considered were those of the idea and the association. We will now examine the *process* assumptions of British associationism.

As a general rule, the British associationists failed to discriminate among the process of encoding information, the memory structure that encoded that information, and the process of retrieving information from that memory structure. Let us consider in this light Hartley's classic statement of the law of association:

> If any sensation A, idea B, or muscular motion C, be associated for a sufficient number of times with any other sensation D, idea E, or muscular motion F, it will at last excite d, the simple idea belonging to the sensation D or, the very idea E, or the muscular motion F [Hartley, 1749, p. 102].

Note that there is no mention at all of a memory structure; rather, Hartley is stating a functional principle that relates a history of past experiences to a current psychological event. Hartley argued that remembering was a mental activity basically no different from thinking or imagining. Remembering just like these other activities was determined by the sequencing of associations in the mind. The only difference was "the readiness and strength of the associations by which they (the memories) are cemented together." If we do not assume that each step (association) in the thinking through of a problem had to be embodied in a memory trace, why assume this about memory. In our opinion, the fatal flaw in Hartley's argument is the assumption that a pure associative analysis is applicable to thinking or imagining. Aristotle was correct in restricting the associative analysis to memory.

This refusal of the British associationists to recognize the existence of memory traces is another instance of the extremities to which one can be led by an untempered empiricist approach. We will shortly return to this question of whether it is necessary to postulate memories. This was a point of debate between John Watson and Bertrand Russell. Watson, taking a similar position to Hartley's, argued that memory was just a matter of "verbal habits." It is to American associationism, in which Watson played such an important role, that we now turn.

2.4. ASSOCIATIONISM IN AMERICA

The bridge between British associationism and American associationism is the experimental psychology that developed in Europe under the influence of such figures as Wundt, Müller, and Külpe. The focus of the German research was on the introspective analysis of consciousness. The Germans introduced some novel theoretical ideas into the British conception—for instance, apperception, imageless thought, and the determining tendencies. However, the main effect of the German work was to articulate and develop the structural assumptions of the associative doctrine developed in Britain. There are excellent analyses of this early period in German psychology (e.g., Boring, 1950; Mandler & Mandler, 1964) that clearly describe the important issues and concepts. We have nothing to add to these sources. However, if the significance of our theory of memory is to be appreciated, it is important that we provide a separate analysis of certain developments that occurred in America.

Since most of the first generation of American psychologists received their training in the German laboratories, one might have expected to find in America a similar concern for articulating the structural assumptions of associationism. However, this was not the case. Over the first half of this century, associationism in America has almost completely disintegrated as a coherent theoretical position. In America associationism very nearly died due to its wide acceptance in academic psychology. Just as a scientific theory can be killed by scientists' widely ignoring it, so can a theory almost die from neglect because everyone accepts its basic premises and proceeds to work on technical details within the framework of those premises, details which may not be critically relevant to the truth of that framework. Remember that associationism began as a set of "structural" ideas regarding how our mind is constructed—regarding the content of our memories, how our memories are acquired, and especially how our memories are organized. What happened to associationism in America was that it was accepted and adopted by functionalism and then behaviorism, but it lay fallow while these schools and their exponents pursued other aims.

Functionalism

The psychology practiced by the Germans is known as structuralism—that is, the concern is with the observation, analysis, and description of the elements and contents of the mind—our sensations, feelings, thoughts, decision-making considerations, emotional conflicts. A deliberate attempt was made to reconstruct the patch quilt that is our conscious experience from these mental elements. The favored technique for gathering data was introspection, direct "observation" of one's own mental states and mental acts.

In America the cards were heavily stacked against this Teutonic brand of structuralism, despite Titchner's valiant efforts to make it palatable to his American colleagues. At the turn of the century, pragmatism and functionalism were the philosophical doctrines capturing the imaginations of American psychologists, and William James and John Dewey were the dominant intellectual figures. Pragmatism and functionalism were both very "action-oriented" programs, on the one hand analyzing philosophical ideas in terms of their consequences for practical actions, and on the other hand using the effective actions carried out by a particular "function of the mind" to characterize and elucidate that part of the mind (e.g., volition, imagination, memory). One appeal of such approaches is their potential for action research in real-life settings, with consequences for policy changes in educational or social practices. It was this seductive appeal to "relevance" that attracted American psychologists; it was also the forerunner of the present-day concern of behaviorists with the "control of behavior." Many of the early American psychologists were educational psychologists, employed in settings demanding effective, practical educational proposals. How very different all this was from the world of the withdrawn German introspectionist sitting in a quiet dark laboratory muttering to himself, straining to describe the essence of an afterimage!

Associationism was adopted by Functionalism because it was the most serviceable "learning theory" at hand to meet the needs of the educators. But associationism would have to change its previous emphasis and goals to make it more useful and relevant. A leading figure in American psychology, Edgar Robinson (1932), tells us why:

Now it would be foolish to deny that the theory of associationism under British care put an unwarranted emphasis upon the intellectual functions, and the contentions of the theory became strongly colored by philosophical doctrines of mind to which we, today, feel superior [p. 5].

British thought, until well into the nineteenth century, was strongly associational, but the associationism of our times is not to be understood as simply a continuation of the British tradition. The emphasis that our writers have put upon association requires for its explanation reasons why the conception has had a peculiar fitness for the American environment. Perhaps because the American public has had an eager faith in the practical advantages of learning, the American scholar has felt a great call to be useful. Our philosophy has tried several doctrines, but pragmatism has been its one wholehearted theory. Our physics has been a little mathematical, but very experimental. Our psychology has had its doctrines of sensation and of instinct, but these have been minor matters as compared with association, which opens up the school room. We can see why, then, among the numerous conceptions that might have dominated psychological thought, association should have a genuine appeal. The texture of experience is something about which nothing can be done. Innate capacities are merely the limits within which an energetic improver of humanity can work. But association strikes at the heart of education. It holds a promise that changes can be worked in human nature, because it is, in fact, a theory of such changes [pp. 4–5].

In such hands, association becomes the instrument of behavior change, of "behavior modification," a means for altering human nature. Because of this emphasis on behavior change, "memory" became the study of behavior modifications resulting from experience; the theory of memory was transmuted into "learning theory." Association was virtually ignored as a principle for reconstructing the structural organization of a person's world knowledge; association simply became the name for the hypothetical substrate of the brain acted upon by a set of procedural rules for controlling and modifying behavior. The theory of dynamics crowded out the deeper view of static organization. The quotation from Robinson summarizes the spirit of the times and helps us understand why associationism took the turn it did. That is, American pragmatism favored a strongly functional analysis of mental life and behavior change, which orientation was simply incompatible with the theoretical elaboration of associationism, which is primarily a structural theory.

Behaviorism

The radical behaviorism of John Watson was an ideological explosion on the American scene that immediately preempted the schools of functionalism and pragmatism. It was a philosophical as well as a psychological theory regarding mind and behavior; even today, some 60 years later, the ideas of John Watson are very much with experimental psychologists; some of his preachings are our very staff of life.

We will not attempt here a careful exposition of the views of behaviorism. To briefly mention but a few main tenets: Watson emphasized that psychology should be an objective science, with its subject matter describable in physicalistic terms (i.e., stimulus histories and observable behaviors of an organism), that introspections were unreliable observation bases, and that substantive psychological theories must predict objective behaviors. Watson argued in particular against the postulation of any psychological event, action, or state which did not have immediately observable indicants or consequents. These indicants were invariably alleged to take the form of muscular or glandular responses at some bodily location. Thus, specific emotional feelings might be identified with particular patterns of response by the viscera, glands, and smooth muscle system; thinking was identified with subvocally talking to oneself; the imagining of lifting a weight was nothing but slight tensions in appropriate muscles of the forearm, and so on. Watson emphasized observable, peripheral activities (responses, behaviors) as the only objective meaning assignable to statements regarding mental states or processes. He also adopted wholesale two further ideas current at the time: first, from Pavlov and Bechterev, the notion of the conditioned reflex was adopted as the basic unit of skilled performance, and as a paradigm (and vocabulary) for describing all learning; second, from early associationism, Watson adopted the idea that complex movements, performances, or skills are analyzable into a number of separate, simple units (reflexes), put together in novel patterns or sequences to form new complex behaviors. This is very like Locke's idea of how new concepts are formed by new combinations of elementary sensory ideas.

Behaviorism became wedded to functionalism in the years 1920 to 1960 in American "learning theories," in the systematic positions of Thorndike, Guthrie, Hull, Miller, Spence, and Skinner. Association was adopted as a primitive notion by all; but the operation of various secondary laws became of issue to many of the systematists. The development and enrichment of the associative organization of memory held no importance at all for these theorists. A list of the "hot controversial" issues of the 1930–1970 period serves in part to illustrate how far from center stage were developments in associationism:

1. What is the effective stimulus for transposition (relational) responding (e.g., Spence versus Köhler)?

2. Do animals learn by selecting entire hypotheses to solve a problematic situation or by gradually strengthening correct responses? Does the animal learn about all the components of a complex stimulus to which he responds or only about a selected cue on each trial (e.g., Lashley versus Spence)?

3. Can learning occur without reward or punishment (e.g., by contiguous experience alone)?

4. What is the common property of all reinforcing events? Of all punishing events (e.g., drive or need reduction hypothesis)?

5. Does reward influence what is learned or only what is performed (e.g., latent learning, latent extinction)?

6. Can stimulus-stimulus associations be learned without responses or reinforcements (sensory-sensory preconditioning experiments)?

7. Can learning occur without the overt response actually occurring (curare studies)?

8. Is the learned response best characterized as a muscular movement or as an approach by any means to a significant external stimulus ("place versus response" issue)?

9. Do responses of the autonomic nervous system ("involuntary") and skeletal ("voluntary") musculature differ in their fundamental laws of learning? Can involuntary responses be conditioned in the operant manner through the actions of rewards and punishments?

10. Do rewards act automatically to strengthen preceding responses or is the effect mediated by awareness of the S-R reinforcement contingencies? Do rewards act by their satisfying effects or by providing directive information?

This sample is representative of the class of controversial issues occupying the energies of American learning theorists during the past 50 years. They are questions posed largely within the stimulus-response framework, and they concern interpretations of the controlling effect on behavior of reinforcing and discriminative stimuli. Few of these controversies center around the structure of knowledge, the correct representation of the myriad bits of learnings that a person (or animal) acquires over its lifetime. If stimulus-response (or S-R) psychologists were pressed on this question of the structure of knowledge, they would probably reply that "knowledge" is coordinate with a set of S-R pairs: in situation S_i, make response R_j. The S's and the R's might be rather complex situations and performances (e.g., swerving a car to avoid a pedestrian; answering "Washington" when asked to name the capital of the U.S.A.), but these are themselves analyzable in terms of sequences of stimuli, responses, and response-produced (proprioceptive) stimuli. (This latter notion, used in many S-R discussions of thinking, is that a response has stimulus consequences which feed back as possible cues for later responses. For example, coordinated walking depends upon stretch-receptors in the leg and hip muscles feeding back signals to the spinal cord regarding the relative locations of the limbs in the stepping cycle.)

The S-R listing above could be augmented in theory by permitting "implicit mediating responses" and their implicit stimuli. A good example of an implicit response is "silently saying" a word to oneself; the implicit proprioceptive stimulus from such silent speech is a bit difficult to imagine, but might possibly be identified with particular time-varying patterns of tension in the articulatory muscles of the larynx, tongue, and lips. The presumed distinction between such implicit S-R events and the nebulous "ideas" of earlier associationism was based on the following restrictions:

1. The postulated implicit R's were restricted to those which are fractional copies of large-scale responses; essentially, if the experimenter could just "turn up the gain on the amplifier," these implicit responses would look and sound just like overt responses, and have all of their properties (e.g., be learned according to the same laws).

2. The only implicit stimuli are those corresponding to feedback from implicit responses.

With these sorts of restrictions on the implicit S's and R's, the addition of such pairs to the S-R listing of knowledge does not, in our opinion, appreciably expand the power of S-R theory to deal with the structure of memory (Fodor, 1965, has argued for a similar opinion). The criticisms associated with the Terminal Meta-Postulate apply full force to this variety of S-R theorizing. There are, furthermore, in our opinion rampant confusions and misconceptions regarding what can and what cannot be represented and reasonably explained in terms of mediating S-R chains (e.g., Osgood, 1968; Staats, 1969). The apparent power of mediating events comes about because S-R theorists literally abandon Strictures 1 and 2 above, and allow their "mediating" S-R events to take on precisely the surplus meanings of such notions as *idea, concept, meaning, image,* and *referent* which had been current in the mentalist vocabulary of British associationism.

Behaviorism and Neo-Associationism

In later chapters we will be proposing a neo-associationist theory which goes counter to many of the philosophical commitments of behaviorism since it uses notions like *idea, concept, feature,* and *image* as basic elements and uses relational associations as the "glue" for connecting these terms together into significant patterns. In this section, we critically analyze the memory representations implied by behaviorism; we also bring up and answer some standard criticisms we can anticipate from some S-R quarters against our neo-associationism.

There will be essentially two main criticisms that the strict S-R theorists could level against the general viewpoint of HAM. Like most present-day cognitive theories, HAM requires the postulation of a complex memory structure (data base plus interpretive procedures) which cannot be directly observed (or "operationally defined") but which we presume to intervene between a person's initial contact with some information and his later use of his memory of that information to guide a variety of performances. B. F. Skinner, an eloquent behaviorist, has criticized the postulation of *any* intervening variables, states, or structures that are not directly observable. He states his objection to any sort of postulated inner states as follows (also, see Figure 2.2):

> In each case we have a causal chain consisting of three links: (1) an operation performed on the organism from without—for example, water deprivation; (2) an inner condition—for example, physiological or psychic thirst; and (3) a kind of behavior—for example, drinking. . . . The objection to inner states is not that they do not exist, but that they are not relevant to a functional analysis. We cannot account for the behavior of any system while staying wholly inside it; eventually we must turn to forces operating on the organism from without. Unless there is a weak spot in our causal chain so that the second link is not lawfully determined by the first, or the third by the second, then the first and third links must be lawfully related. If we must always go back beyond the second link for prediction and control, we may avoid many tiresome and exhausting digressions by examining the third link as a function of the first. Valid information about the second link may throw light upon this relationship but can in no way alter it [Skinner, 1953, pp. 34–35].

The situation to which Skinner refers may be seen in Figure 2.2, where arrows depict functional relationships between variables. With one independent variable and one dependent variable, it is clearly uneconomical to introduce the intervening variable ("thirst"), since it is eliminable by functional arrow 3 relating just the observable variables. On this point there is no argument. The counterargument— stated effectively by Bergman (1953) and N. E. Miller (1959)—is that intervening

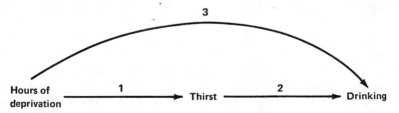

FIG. 2.2. An illustration of Skinner's argument for the elimination of intervening variables.

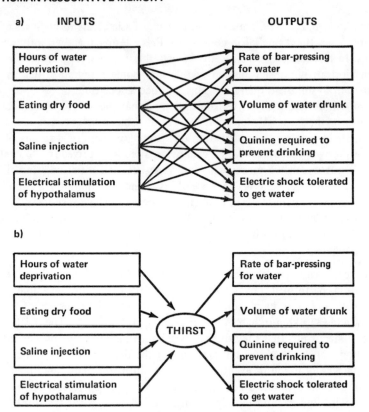

FIG. 2.3. An illustration of Miller's argument for the utility of intervening variables.

variables become economical in situations where there are multiple input and multiple output variables. The situation is properly depicted in the top and bottom panels of Figure 2.3 (adapted from N. E. Miller, 1959). In the top panel, with 4 independent determinants of "thirst" and 4 dependent indicators, there are 16 different functions to be discovered ($m \times n$ in general). The bottom panel, which introduces an intervening variable, also illustrates the economy of the postulation; here, only 8 ($m + n$ in general) relations must be determined, 4 relating the input variable to degree of thirst, and 4 relating thirst to the output variables. If this were a "unitary" intervening variable, then the former 16 S-R functions would be decomposable into 4 S-T and 4 T-R functions as shown in the bottom panel of Figure 2.3.

Most "neo-behaviorists" accepted the logic of this argument, saw the value of intervening variables, and so proceeded to postulate them with abandon. Clark Hull's theory, for example, was based on the postulation of one after another intervening variable (see Koch, 1954, for a critical review). Most of these concerned performance variables like stimulus intensity, drive intensity, incentive motivation, response fatigue, and the like. The basic associative intervening variable was simply "habit strength," conceptualized as an S-R bond. Thus, regarding the structure of knowledge, the main intervening variable in Hull's system was still just an S-R connection. This basic assumption exemplifies the so-called Terminal Meta-Postulate mentioned earlier which supposes that the only admissible elements (terms) in a description of behavior are those that map one-to-one onto observable stimuli or responses. Just as the failure of the TMP was a fundamental weakness of the empiricism of British associationism, so does it also point to a similar weakness in stimulus-response psychologies. Our theory, in rejecting the TMP, therefore is rejecting not only Skinner's radical behaviorism but all S-R associative conceptions. They are just not powerful enough to capture the complexity of human memory or language.

Behaviorism and the Reconstruction of Memories

Lest these criticisms of behaviorism appear too arid and abstracted away from the context of human memory, which is the focus of this book, let us examine the early behavioristic account of memory due to Watson, since it puts the issues in bold relief.

Watson did not think that "memory" was a useful term; he thought it had no place in an objective psychology. Insofar as the term has meaning, it refers, says Watson, to retention of a habit. He especially emphasized our memories of psychomotor skills such as golfing, swimming, and, for animals, running mazes and escaping from puzzle boxes. Here, memory considered as activation of a sequence of habitual reflexes does not seem too terribly implausible (except to ethologists, cyberneticists, and other connoisseurs of animal behavior or human skilled performance). But for describing man's ability to recollect past events, Watson relied heavily on the formation, retention, and reactivation of verbal and visceral habits to carry the burden of explanation. He explains as follows:

> What the man on the street ordinarily means by an exhibition of memory is what occurs in some such situation as this: An old friend comes to see him, after many years' absence. The moment he sees this friend, he says: "Upon my life! Addison Sims of Seattle! I haven't seen you since the World's Fair in Chicago. Do you remember the gay parties we used to have in the old Windmere Hotel? Do you remember the Midway? Do you remember _____," ad infinitum. The psychology of this process is so simple that it seems almost an insult to your intelligence to discuss it, and yet a good many of the behaviorists' kindly critics have said that behaviorism cannot adequately explain memory. Let us see if this is a fact.
>
> When the man on the street originally made the acquaintance of Mr. Sims, he saw him and was told his name at the same time. Possibly he did not see him again until a week or two later. He had to be re-introduced. Again, when he saw Mr. Sims he heard his name. Then, shortly afterwards, the two men became friends and saw one another every day and became really acquainted—that is, formed verbal and manual habits towards one another and towards the same or similar situations. In other words, the man on the street became completely organized to react in many habit ways to Mr. Addison Sims. Finally, just the sight of the man, even after months of

absence, would call out not only the old verbal habits, but many other types of bodily and visceral responses [Watson, 1930, pp. 235-236].

He sums up by saying:

By "memory," then, we mean nothing except the fact that when we meet a stimulus again after an absence, we do the old habitual thing (say the old words and show the old visceral—emotional—behavior) that we learned to do when we were in the presence of that stimulus in the first place [p. 237].

The basic difficulties of this viewpoint are easily brought out. Most of them hinge upon an inadequate conception of linguistic competence. Indeed these criticisms of Watson's views appeared clearly in writings by Bertrand Russell in 1927, in reply to Watson's 1924 book. It is with some embarrassment that we note that Russell's critique was not noted and appreciated by psychologists until about 30 to 40 years after it was written. The criticisms can be listed quickly. First, people need not respond overtly and verbally to an event at the time of witnessing that event in order later to show retention of knowledge about that event. Common examples are remembering scenes, episodes, or pictures in mental imagery that has no linguistic counterpart. An artificial laboratory example is to have a subject later report verbally the names of pictures of famous people shown to him while his vocal apparatus is occupied, say, with rapidly subtracting threes successively from a starting two-digit number.

A second, and more critical, point is that recollection of Mr. Addison Sims can be stimulated and retrieved by a multitude of different stimuli (queries or "probes"). One whole class of retrieval cues refers to visual appearances of Mr. Sims himself, although seen perhaps in radically changed settings. Another whole class of cues is linguistic queries, such as: "Do you know a Mr. Sims?" "Do you know anyone from Seattle?" "Who did you meet at the World's Fair?" etc. Finally is a whole class of ill-defined "retrievals" wherein our knowledge of some earlier event is used for later effective actions, such as reserving a room at the Windmere Hotel when next in Chicago because of its past association with happy times. In short, knowledge about the events surrounding meetings with Mr. Sims is a complex set of conceptual relations, and a very diverse variety of inputs (perceptual and linguistic) can tap into that knowledge structure. It is senseless to argue for retrieval here on any basis of "similarity" between the retrieval cue and a knowledge structure; one's answer to "Who did you meet in Chicago?" might possibly be explained in terms of the similarity of that probe to an earlier implicit statement like "Here I am in Chicago meeting Mr. Sims"; but it would not explain why a trivial surface variation on the probe such as "*Why* did you meet in Chicago?" elicits an entirely different answer.

A third difficulty with Watson's "verbal habit" account of memory is that it ignores our ability to paraphrase and recast linguistically the basic conceptual facts about events. One can say "I met Mr. Sims on the commuter train to Chicago" just as well as "While riding into the Windy City on the 8:35, I bumped into Joe"; for an appropriate audience and context, these two sentences assert the same propositions or conceptual relations despite their having almost no content words in common. Also, one may use either sentence indiscriminately to recall the same fact. Moreover, one may translate a learned set of conceptual relations into entirely different domains to make the recollections palpable; for example, if one were bilingual, his experiences with Mr. Sims might be described in a foreign language; if an artist, he might draw sketches of Mr. Sims, and so on. In such cases there is no possibility that one is reproducing overt responses which occurred upon the earlier occasion of meeting Mr. Sims. Russell (1927) expresses the case regarding Watson's view of memory as follows:

> It is not our actual language that can be regarded as habitual, but only what our words express. In repeating a poem we have learned by heart, the language is habitual, but not so when we recount a past incident in words we never used before. In this case, it is not the actual words that we repeat, but only their meaning. The habitual element, therefore, if it really accounts for the recollection, must not be sought in words. This is something of a difficulty for the Watsonian theory of language. . . . [Two different sentences may] have nothing verbally in common, yet they may relate the same fact, and I may use either indifferently when I recall the fact. Thus my recollection is certainly not a definite verbal habit. Yet words are the only bodily movements by which I make known my recollections to other people. If the behaviorist tells me that my recollection is bodily habit, and begins by telling me that it is a *verbal* habit, he can be driven by such instances to the admission that it must be some other kind of habit. If he says this, he is abandoning the region of observable fact, and taking refuge in hypothetical bodily movements invoked to save a theory. But these are hardly any better than "thoughts."
>
> This question is more general than the problem of memory. Many different forms of words may be used to express the same "meaning," and there seems no reason in mere habit to account for the fact that we sometimes use one form of words and sometimes another when we "think" of that which all the various forms of words express. The association seems to go, not direct from stimulus to words, but from stimulus to "meaning" and thence to words expressing the "meaning.". . . It is such facts, among others, that make it difficult to explain the mechanism of association, whether in memory or in "thought" in general, if we assume that words, or even sentences, are the terms associated [Russell, 1927, pp. 73-75].

The words of Russell have surprising cogency in our post-Chomskian world of linguistic deep-structure. In current-day terms, Russell was arguing that habits defined over surface strings of verbal units (words) will not suffice to account for paraphrastic descriptions of witnessed events.

Although the criticisms above have centered upon how our linguistic competence confounds a simplistic S-R view of event memory, we hasten to point out that the logical point is the same as that made earlier regarding the theoretical economy made possible by introducing thirst as an intervening variable. Just as we should not identify "thirst" with hours of deprivation nor with drinking, so should we avoid identifying our memory of the Sims episodes with a particular verbal descriptive sequence. Multiple "responses" sensitive in varying ways to multiple "stimuli" are made possible by the memory structure representing those episodes. The memory structure in HAM is here conceived to be a network of associative relations among abstract semantic concepts—an interrelated set of "meaningful propositions"—and for sufficiently rich structures there are almost limitless stimulus probes by which we can tap a limitless supply of answers ("responses") from such an abstract structure. In this sense, the prior "$(m + n)$ versus $(m \times n)$" argument for theoretical economy applies as well to this postulation of a meaningful conceptual structure as our encoding of and memory of the Sims episodes.

Although our point (or Russell's, really) regarding multiple inputs and outputs of a memory structure has been argued with respect to verbal memories, we strongly suspect that a similar argument could be made for the memories established by simple Pavlovian or operant conditioning procedures with either man or animal. A man can easily detect and frame for himself propositions expressing such contingencies as "When this blue light comes on, if I press this lever, I will get a nickel; otherwise, I get nothing for pressing." That simple knowledge structure will "mediate" effective responding in a variety of altered circumstances. For example, the experimenter may alter details of the response (e.g., "use your left hand instead of your right"), or pay off in convertible tokens rather than nickels, or verbally alter the contingencies (i.e., "there will be no more nickels"), and the subject will quickly adjust his response appropriately. Also, the person exposed to these contingencies can use what he has learned to describe the contingency verbally, either to himself or to a friend in need of nickels.

These examples are still using the verbal subject. What of animals in such simple learning tasks? What complex "abstract structure" is, say, a dog learning when a tone is consistently followed by a painful, noxious stimulus? There is no reason to deny *a priori* that dogs and other nonverbal organisms can form the equivalents of elementary propositions encoding the temporal sequence of significant events. To be absurdly concrete, suppose the dog acquires an associative structure expressible as the proposition: "In experimental situation S, a high-pitched tone is followed within a few seconds by a painful stimulus to my left front paw." If this proposition is combined with other general propositions, such as "If a limb is about to be injured, move it away to avoid injury," the dog could "derive" the command to flex its left paw when the tone sounds.

The claim is that such conceptual propositions capture the flavor of the dog's behavior, especially in new situations. (This was Edward Tolman's main position.) Thus, it is known that the overt paw-flexion response need not occur during learning. Blockage of the neuromuscular junctures with a curare-like drug prevents all overt responses, yet the tone-shock association may be established under curare, and then later tested with positive results (i.e., conditioned paw withdrawals to the tone) after the drug has worn off. Also the tone-pain association institutes a totally different "repertoire of responses" in the dog from the tone in other situations. Thus, in a later appetitive instrumental conditioning situation, the tone will serve as a "conditioned emotional stimulus" suppressing appetitive behavior. The tone can also be used as a "punishing" event, supporting passive avoidance learning; also, its onset can initiate various kinds of previously learned escape behavior, and its termination can "reinforce" escape behavior. There is, thus, a diverse class of different behaviors affected by the tone-shock experience. Beyond this, there are probably other means to induce a similar memory structure in the dog. For example, the tone could be paired with other painful stimuli like burns, loud noises, nausea, or pinpricks delivered to the left paw.

The tenor of these comments is that for even a nonverbal organism and for a singularly simple connection such as "tone-shock," we still require for its representation an intervening propositional structure which can account for multiple determinants, multiple contexts of retrieval of that information, and multiple varied "behavioral indices" related to that learning. Thus, our arguments against the behavioristic conception of memory can also be advanced with some plausibility for elementary conditioning with animals, although admittedly the arguments lack the force of those available on the issue when dealing with language-rich human adults. Part of the battle fought by E. C. Tolman, arguing for a "cognitive theory" to explain animal behavior, was concerned with just such points.

Interference Theory

We have argued in the foregoing that the successes and excesses of functionalism and behaviorism led to the intellectual stagnation of associationism as a theory of memory. The primary exception to this stagnation has been the appearance of the associative interference theory of forgetting. Although suggested by a number of earlier researchers (e.g., Müller & Pilzecker, 1900), modern interference theory dates its beginnings from McGeoch's (1932) formulation, and it has been developed and researched by several generations of intellectual offspring of McGeoch. The British associationists had concentrated almost exclusively on the conditions favorable for acquisition of new information; the interference theorists turned the tables and concentrated instead on the conditions that promoted forgetting of already-learned materials. This yielded some new perspectives on the problems of memory.

A rich set of concepts and interlocking facts has been developed under the auspices of modern interference theory. The learning of laboratory materials tends to interfere with memory for other laboratory material that was learned before and after it. The basic variables in these experiments and multiple variations thereof have by now been quite systematically explored and catalogued. The facts of interference are very important to associationism because they appear to be so easily explained within an associationist framework. We consider these facts sufficiently important that we will devote a later chapter (Chapter 15) to reviewing the well-established facts about interference and illustrating how our model, HAM, can accommodate these facts.

The work of the interference theorists is, in our opinion, the major substantive accomplishment of associationism in America. Postman's assessment of the scene over a decade ago is still right on target:

Interference theory occupies an unchallenged position as the major significant analysis of the process of forgetting. The only serious opposition has come from the trace theory of the Gestalt psychologists, but that point of view has thus far proved experimentally sterile and resistant to rigorous test. As a result, the recent years have seen little debate about the basic assumptions of interference theory. Developments in the study of forgetting have consisted largely of extensions and refinements of interference theory and of methodological advances in the measurement of retention [Postman, 1961, p. 152].

Of the criticisms that might be leveled against interference theory, one of the most serious from our point of view is that interference theorists have not devoted much effort to systematically developing the associative theory of memory in which their theory of forgetting is embedded (see Melton, 1961, for a similar opinion). There has been little concern for demonstrating that their conception of memory meets the necessary "sufficiency conditions" for a theory adequate to the full range of mnemonic phenomena. They have adopted the restrictions of behaviorism, so that the "S-R habit" is the only conceptual tool interference theorists have for explicating or representing the knowledge that a person possesses. They have a weak view of the retrieval process and provide no account of interference, deduction, and reconstruction in acts of remembering. Interference theory is also conspicuously remiss in characterizing the associative organization of long-term memory in a realistic way, and it fails to clarify exactly how that associative organization is brought into play when we add new facts, new strategies, and new procedures to our knowledge. Interference theory, like other branches of psychology, has not provided a realistic model of language use, nor of learning and forgetting of propositional materials. Its exponents have said relatively little about interference with thematically meaningful materials, and some researchers have even doubted that interference has any bearing on memory for meaningful materials. What interference theory lacks is approximately what our theory, HAM, supplies; namely, a systematic theory about how the person brings his cognitive equipment to bear upon comprehending, storing, retrieving, and using propositional information for inference, question answering, and action.

For these tasks, for theories about the structure of memory and the nature of language comprehension, the clear theoretical leaders in the past decade have been a small number of computer scientists who work on models of mental organization. In our opinion, it is these computer simulation models of semantic memory that begin to actualize the full potential of associationism as a theory of mental organization. We call them the "neo-associationists"; we shall review their critically important work in Chapter 4.

REFERENCES

Anderson, J. R. FRAN: A simulation model of free recall. In G. H. Bower (Ed.), *The psychology of learning and motivation.* Vol. 5. New York: Academic Press, 1972.

Bain, A. *The senses and the intellect.* London: Edwin S. Parker, 1859.

Beare, J. I. De memoria et reminiscentia. In W. D. Ross (Ed.), *The works of Aristotle.* Vol. 3. Oxford: Clarendon Press, 1931.

Bergman, G. Theoretical psychology. *Annual Review of Psychology*, 1953, 4, 435–458.

Bever, T. G., Fodor, J. A., & Garrett, M. A formal limitation of associationism. In T. R. Dixon & D. L. Horton (Eds.), *Verbal behavior and general behavior theory*. Englewood Cliffs, N. J.: Prentice-Hall, 1968.

Boring, E. G. *History of experimental psychology*. New York: Appleton-Century-Crofts, 1950.

Brown, T. *Lectures on the philosophy of the human mind*. Edinburgh: Tait, Longman, 1820.

Deese, J. *The structure of associations in language and thought*. Baltimore: Johns Hopkins Press, 1965.

Dreyfus, H. L. *What computers can't do*. New York: Harper & Row, 1972.

Fodor, J. A. Could meaning be an r_m? *Journal of Verbal Learning and Verbal Behavior*, 1965, **4**, 73–81.

Hartley, D. *Observations on man, his frame, his duty and his expectations*. London, 1749.

Hobbes, T. Human nature. In W. Molesworth (Ed.), *The English works of Thomas Hobbes*. Vol. 4. London: Bohn, 1840. (Originally published: 1650.)

Hopcroft, J. E., & Ullman, J. D. *Formal languages and their relation to automata*. Reading, Mass.: Addison-Wesley, 1969.

Koch, S. Clark L. Hull. In W. Estes, S. Koch, K. MacCorquodule, P. Meehl, C. Mueller, W. Schoenfield, & W. Verplanck (Eds.), *Modern learning theory*. New York: Appleton-Century-Crofts, 1954.

Koffka, K. *Principles of Gestalt psychology*. New York: Harcourt, Brace & World, 1935.

Köhler, W. *Gestalt psychology: An introduction to new concepts in modern psychology*. New York: Liveright, 1947.

Mandler, J., & Mandler, G. *Thinking from association to Gestalt*. New York: Wiley, 1964.

McGeoch, J. A. Forgetting and the law of disuse. *Psychological Review*, 1932, **39**, 352–370.

Melton, A. W. Comments on Professor Postman's paper. In C. N. Cofer (Ed.), *Verbal learning and verbal behavior*. New York: McGraw-Hill, 1961.

Mill, J. *Analysis of the phenomena of the human mind*. London: Longmans, Green, Reader & Dyer, 1869.

Mill, J. S. *A system of logic, ratiocinative and inductive*. London: Longmans, Green, 1889.

Miller, N. E. Liberalization of basic S-R concepts: Extensions to conflict behavior, motivation and social learning. In S. Koch (Ed.), *Psychology: A study of a science*. Vol. 2. New York: McGraw-Hill, 1959.

Müller, G. E., & Pilzecker, A. Experimentelle Beiträge zur Lehre vom Gedächtnis. *Zeitschrift Psychologig Ergänzungaband*, 1900, #1.

Osgood, C. E. Towards a wedding of insufficiencies. In T. R. Dixon & D. L. Horton (Eds.), *Verbal behavior and general behavior theory*. Englewood Cliffs, N. J.: Prentice-Hall, 1968.

Postman, L. The present status of interference theory. In C. N. Cofer (Ed.), *Verbal learning and verbal behavior*. New York: McGraw-Hill, 1961.

Quillian, M. R. Semantic memory. In M. Minsky (Ed.), *Semantic information processing*. Cambridge, Mass.: M.I.T. Press, 1968.

Robinson, E. G. *Association theory today*. New York: Century, 1932.

Russell, B. *Philosophy*. New York: Norton, 1927.

Schwarcz, R. M., Burger, J. F., & Simmons, R. F. A deductive question-answerer for natural language inference. *Communications of the Association for Computing Machinery*, 1970, **13**, 167–183.

Simon, H. A., & Feigenbaum, E. A. An information processing theory of some effects of similarity, familiarity, and meaningfulness in verbal learning. *Journal of Verbal Learning and Verbal Behavior*, 1964, **3**, 385–396.

Skinner, B. F. *Science and human behavior*. New York: Macmillan, 1953.

Spencer, H. *The principles of psychology*. New York: Appleton, 1890.

Staats, A. W. *Learning, language and cognition*. New York: Holt, Rinehart & Winston, 1969.

Suppes, P. Stimulus-response theory of finite automata. *Journal of Mathematical Psychology*, 1969, **6**, 327–355.

Warren, H. C. *A history of the association psychology*. New York: Scribner's 1921.

Watson, J. B. *Behaviorism*. New York: Norton, 1930.

3
RATIONALIST COUNTERTRADITIONS

Reminiscence is the faculty of the soul by which it receives the forms it had known before being associated with the body.

—Plato

3.1. THE RATIONALIST APPROACH

Experimental psychology in America is pervaded by the firm conviction that any theory of memory will have to be basically associative in character. This claim, we are convinced, is fundamentally wrong. This chapter reviews two counterexamples to this mistaken generalization, namely, Gestalt theory and the reconstruction hypothesis, both exemplifying the rationalist methodology. Unfortunately, both of these approaches will turn out to be rather sketchy when considered as memory theories. This is not surprising because, in the rationalist conception of matters, memory is a very complicated but essentially uninteresting topic for study.

As a consequence of their sketchiness and vagueness, neither theory provides a strong alternative to our model, HAM, which is an unfortunate state of affairs. We will report as sympathetically as we can what these theorists have said in their writings about human memory. We leave to those with rationalist leanings the task of developing or extrapolating either of these theories to the point where they could become strong competitors to associative theories.

In contrast with the associationist's commitment to methodological empiricism, the rationalist approach attempts to begin with certain "truths" or "first principles" about the human mind. The primary methodology is use of intuition, insight, and reason. By these means the basic structure of a mental phenomenon is supposed to emerge, and one should eventually be able to formulate the abstract principles that are really at the heart of the phenomenon. Once these first principles have been formulated, the remaining task is to relate them to observations of particular real world phenomena. Lest anyone think that this is an absurd manner in which to proceed, he should realize that a similar rationalist methodology has been one of the principal means by which many of the major theoretical advances have occurred in the physical sciences.

We argued in Chapter 2 that the methodological empricism of associationism tended to leave it branded with certain higher-order properties or metafeatures. We think we can make a plausible case for the position that the methodological rationalism also tends to generate certain metafeatures in the theories it generates. Furthermore, in rough correspondence to each of the four features of associationism, it is heuristic to consider an opposing four features typically allied with rationalist theories. Corresponding to connectionism in associationism one typically finds *nativism* (innatism) in the rationalist theory; corresponding to reductionism one finds *holism*; corresponding to sensationalism one usually finds *intuitionism*; and corresponding to mechanism there may be *vitalism* (or antimechanism). We will give a brief discussion of each of these theses.

Nativism

The most extreme form of nativism was that stated by Plato: All knowledge of any importance was alleged to be innately recorded in the human mind. The point of experience was merely to bring out that knowledge in explicit form. Plato did not deny that sensory experience could be recorded in a more or less direct form in the human mind; but he argued that such knowledge was inconsequential and a source of error. The particular facts of the world were ephemeral, changing, and untrustworthy compared to the enduring truths of pure reason. Plato's nativism is very nearly the antithesis of connectionism, which asserts that all knowledge arises from linking together the elements of experience.

Subsequent rationalist theorists, however, have not taken nearly so extreme a position as that of Plato. Instead they have argued a more moderate position that a certain *class* of *principles* is innately given in the "apparatus of the mind" which constrains it to impose particular structures or to project hypotheses of a special type upon the multifarious flux of sensory experience. Some typical examples in the literature of rationalism are such distinctions as that between self versus others, or material versus spirit, and the alleged universality of such beliefs as the principle of causality, or the principle of inductive inference, or the belief that "laws of logic" dictate our "laws of thought." Other examples of pertinence to psychologists include the rationalists' belief that man's perceptual system is so preset that it "naturally" interprets a two-dimensional retinal mosaic as a projection of a three-dimensional visual space; or that it is so preset that it construes the physical world in accordance with the axioms of Euclidean geometry.

A recent and vigorous rationalist argument has been given by Chomsky (1968) and Katz (1966) for language acquisition. Chomsky assumes that the facts of language force us to conclude that the child, considered as a language-acquisition device, must begin life innately endowed with a small set of *linguistic universals* both as in regards to some basic concepts (e.g., syntactic or semantic distinctions) and in regards to grammatical principles (e.g., a bias for transformational grammars, a potential for distinguishing surface versus deep-structure propositions, a potential for cyclic recursion, etc.). According to this view, these various innate settings bias the child to construct a rather sophisticated "theory" of the grammar underlying his native language, and to do so despite the fact that the speech he hears around him is ungrammatical, chaotic, and prone to errors. It should be remarked in passing that our model HAM begins, as does Chomsky's language-acquisition device, with a rather rich set of syntactic primitives for analyzing sentences; these will be described in detail in Chapters 7 and 8.

The rationalism-empiricism controversy has revolved around the issue of innatism, not so much differing with regard to the existence of innate principles, but rather differing with regard to the nature of the types of mental *capabilities* which were assumed to be innate. For even John Locke, a strong critic of innate ideas in his *Essay Concerning Human Understanding*, assumed that the mind has an *innate* capacity to associate contiguous experiences, and to reflect upon experiences. The critical nature of these assumed innate mechanisms has been pointed out by Katz (1966) in regard to the rationalist-empiricist debate:

> The basis for the controversy is not, as it is often conceived in popular discussions, that empiricists fail to credit the mind with any innate principles, but rather that the principles which are accorded innate status by empiricists do not place any substantive restrictions on the ideas that can qualify as components of complex ideas or any formal restrictions on the structure of associations which bond component ideas together to form a complex idea. On the empiricist's hypothesis, the innate principles are purely combinatorial devices for putting together items from experience. So these principles provide only the machinery for instituting associative bonds. Experience plays the selective role in determining which ideas may be connected by association, and principles of association are, accordingly, unable to exclude any ideas as, in principle, beyond the range of possible intellectual acquisition [pp. 240-241].

Katz is arguing that associations that record contiguous experiences are not sufficient to constrain the nature of the mind nor of the child's interpretation of what his language is like. We hold a similar view, and so have endowed our model from the outset with a highly structured linguistic-perceptual "parser." Associations enter in HAM only in encoding ("learning") the structured output of a rather rich interpretative parser. Whereas associations represent and hold memories, the input to the memory component is structured logically in a manner resembling a Chomskian context-free phrase structure grammar. Therefore, HAM's memory for certain information is structured only insofar as its perceptual interfacing mechanisms impose a particular logical description onto its inputs; HAM's memory simply records rather passively the structural trees output by its parser. We have no detailed model for language acquisition; we know it is absurd to say that a baby should begin life with all the sophisticated interfacing and parsers with which we endow the "adult HAM." Exactly which parts and perceptual mechanisms of HAM should be degraded to get a viable model of the child is not obvious and is clearly not a simple scientific problem.

Nativism is not per se a theory of memory; in fact, the two notions are literally at opposite poles. Nativism becomes a meaningful position when it is used to characterize the properties of mental processes involved in perception (of space, of linguistic utterances) or in reasoning (inductive generalization, deductions). Of course, it is with respect to just these processes (perception, reasoning) that the rationalist attacks on associationism-empiricism have been most vigorous and successful.

Holism

Just as reductionism leads to theories that are cast in terms of the microproperties of experience, so holism leads to theories that are cast in terms of the global properties. This holist bias manifests itself at two levels in rationalist approaches to memory. First, there is the claim that the total memory structure has properties that cannot be predicted (or are very difficult to predict) from a knowledge of the underlying parts and their configuration. The whole is alleged to have novel properties that are quite unlike the properties of the parts comprising the whole. This is the doctrine of emergent properties to be examined in greater detail when we review Gestalt theory.

A second level revealing the holistic character of rationalist theories is in the insistence that it is in principle impossible to study the memory system by itself, that the functioning of the memory system is inextricably intertwined with the functioning of the total organism. Therefore, to understand memory, it is necessary to come to an understanding of the whole mind. For example, this attitude appears frequently in assertions that memory is not reproductive but rather reconstructive, or that remembering bears strong resemblances to "problem solving," or that all sorts of rules and inferential procedures are called in by "higher mental processes" in order for the person to reconstruct an event from memory. This viewpoint, that memory necessarily implicates diverse inference and problem-solving routines both at the time of input (e.g., comprehending a sentence) and at output (e.g., reconstructing an event), is at direct odds with our proposal that there exists a *strategy-free component* of memory (viz., that is modeled in HAM) that functions independently of the rest of the mental system; the strategies (e.g., use of mnemonic imagery in encoding, use of reconstructive searches in decoding, etc.) are assumed to operate in interfacing the memory system to the external world, but do not determine the operation of the memory once the input tree or probe (query) tree has been specified.

Intuitionism

In opposition to the empiricist tradition, the rationalist believes that intuitions about mental phenomena are much more important than any empirical data that he might obtain. His intuitions provide immediate access to the data central to the problem that he is studying, while empirical observations are always subject to contamination from unknown sources, to problems of replicability, multiple interpretations, questions of generalizability, and the whims of nature. So it is not surprising that the rationalist, when faced with an experiment that disconfirms his theory, will doubt the data and not the theory; the defense is frequently couched in teims of the alleged "artificiality" of the experimental situation in contrast to "real life" situations.

In most sciences, this is all that intuitionism amounts to, namely, a particular methodological bias about how to proceed in experimentation. However, in psychology intuitionism is something more because psychology is the study of the very animal that possesses these valuable intuitions. Hence, to the rationalist an important piece of data is the subject's introspections about the psychological processes under study. In contrast, the radical empiricist rejects intuitions as an acceptable form of data; and while milder mannered empiricists accept such data as indicators of internal processes, they refuse to regard intuitions as any more important than other data that can be brought to bear upon the matter. Clearly, the most successful form of this rationalist reliance on intuitive judgments is to be found in the modern linguistic tradition initiated by Chomsky which relies almost exclusively on intuitions of native speakers regarding the grammaticality of particular sentences (see Chapter 5 for an extended discussion). However, we shall also presently see that Gestalt theory and the reconstruction hypothesis place great emphasis on having their theories correspond to introspections about the memory processes.

Concerning human memory, intuitionism also manifests itself in judgments about what are the important matters that are worth explaining. While associationism focuses on the sensory contents of memory (i.e., the events that the subject reports remembering), the intuitionist is likely to focus on the subjective experiences of the "remembering act" itself. A good example would be the subjective experiences of a person caught mid-flight in a "tip of the tongue" state, in which a word or name hovers tantalizingly just outside the grasp of complete retrieval (see Brown & McNeill, 1966). As a second example, the rationalist is likely to emphasize how the mind abstracts an underlying schema or principle from a range of experiences with particular instances of a concept or rule, whereas the empiricist would emphasize storage of particular exemplars and only gradual and fragmentary abstraction of the schema or prototype (see Reitman & Bower, 1973). These points of divergence serve to contrast intuitionism with the "sensationalism" of the associative tradition. The intuitionist does not deny that sensory information is stored in some form in memory; rather he denies that this is the interesting feature of memory. He emphasizes instead processes such as abstraction, schematization, inference, and reconstruction.

Vitalism

Like mechanism, vitalism is a feature that is vague and hard to pin down, although we have reliable intuitions about what it implies. Originally, it was invoked by biologists who believed that the complexities of living organisms or the consciousness of human beings could not be explained in terms of reduction of these phenomena to the natural laws of physics and chemistry. Instead, it was proposed that new laws would have to be introduced to describe the vital forces behind such phenomena. Beyond this is the connotation of vitalism that relates it to the antithesis of mechanistic explanations. In psychology, for example, antimechanistic positions would include such things as the idea that "determining tendencies," "intentions," or "purposes" guide chains of associations (or responses) so as to achieve particular goals, and that they do so in a manner not reducible to mechanistic principles. With regard to vitalism, such examples now seem less antimechanical in the light of the developments in cybernetics, servomechanisms, equilibrium-seeking machines, executive programs, and algorithmic searches of problem graphs directed at achieving a hierarchy of goals (see Ernst & Newell, 1969). A plausible form of the antimechanistic position in psychology asserts that some psychological phenomena can never be captured or explained in any significant way by theories modeled on serial, digital computers. For instance, it might be asserted that one's immediate awareness and subjective experience of the world cannot be modeled in such a machine (see Hook, 1961). Or it might be argued that the mind is not remotely like a serial computer (but rather like a parallel, analog computer), that it exhibits holistic "field influences" in its actions in complex ways suggesting that present-day mechanistic accounts are misguided (see Dreyfus, 1972, for a recent critique from this viewpoint of research in artificial intelligence).

As was the case with the four metafeatures of associationism listed in Chapter 2, these opposing metafeatures of rationalism are not directly subject to empirical falsification. Rather, they insinuate themselves into particular predictions of particular models, and only the latter are subject to empirical falsification. Also, while these features are common properties of a rationalist model, they may also be accidental features of an associative model. For instance, our model HAM will be nativistic regarding the perceptual parsers, and perhaps vitalistic in that it assumes the existence of an executive program that directs the information processing. But other components of HAM are connectionistic and mechanistic in character.

3.2. GESTALT THEORY

Gestalt theorists were frequently criticized (see Buhler, 1926; Selz, 1926) for using other researchers' results as discoveries for Gestalt theory. The earlier researchers had already noted the significance of the results. So the Gestalters were asked what was so revolutionary about the theory they were proposing. To understand why Gestalters were able to shake the psychological world with shopworn demonstrations, let us consider just one example of how one class of demonstrations was incorporated into Gestalt theory. The illustration comes from research on *form qualities* or, as Christian von Ehrenfels (1937) called them, Gestaltqualitat.

The basic problem concerned the perception of form. In viewing a square, we experience more than four separate lines; we also perceive immediately the relationship of "squareness" that inheres in their particular configuration. Similarly, in hearing a musical tune, we perceive more than the individual notes; we perceive the melody, which is provided by the relationships among the notes. Before the time of the Gestalt theorists, the standard analysis of these phenomena, exemplified by Ehrenfels, was to assert that there were "non-sensory" elements in perception; in addition to perceiving the sensory elements (the Fundamente), it was said that we perceived their relationship (the Grundlage) as an additional element.

The important feature of this classical analysis is that it preserved the reductionism of associationism. It did not deny that all experience could be decomposed into a finite set of specifiable elements; it rather asserted only that higher-order, relational elements had also to be recognized in the analysis. The Grundlage was no more important than the Fundamente; indeed, according to Ehrenfels, the Grundlage was definitely subordinate, depending as it did on the Fundamente. Ehrenfels (1937) described his own results as follows:

> The decisive step in the founding of a theory of Gestalt-quality was my own assertion: When the memory-images of successive notes are present as a simultaneous complex in consciousness, then an idea (Vorstellung), belonging to a new category, can arise in consciousness, a unitary idea, which is connected in a manner peculiar to itself with the ideas (Vorstellungen) of the complex of notes involved [p. 521].

It was just this elementalism or atomism that the Gestalters objected to. They had made the same observations on form quality but they concluded something very different from them. They claimed that the elements in the perception of the whole were not preserved; rather, the perception of the relation transcended the elements and formed a new Gestalt. The new, emergent properties of the Gestalt could not be predicted by considering the elements themselves. In fact, perception of the elementary parts was transformed because of the whole. As Wertheimer (1944) described the matter:

> The whole cannot be deduced from the characteristics of the separate pieces, but conversely; what happens to a part of the whole is, in clear-cut cases, determined by the laws of the inner structure of its whole [p. 84].

This is a typical example of how the rationalist proceeds in a scientific endeavor. Nothing in the data about perception of squares or melodies directly indicated the need to overthrow elementalism. Within the established paradigm Ehrenfels had provided a fairly satisfactory elementalist analysis of the phenomena. Only a rationalist coming upon the phenomena with his preconceived model would have interpreted the phenomena in the way that the Gestalters did. With that theory the Gestalters were to reinterpret most of the mental world that the associationists had been so confident that they understood thoroughly. In this way, the elementary phenomena of Gestaltqualitat which were the source of satisfactory but not very inspiring analyses in the hands of associationists became ammunition for a revolution in the hands of the Gestalters.

After these brief historical remarks, we now examine the Gestalters' approach to human memory and how that view differs from associationism. However, first we will have to sketch in some of the details in the Gestalt theory of perception because, as had Aristotle and the British associationists before them, the Gestalters identified the input to the memory system with the perceptual data that the organism was registering. Indeed, as much as Aristotle, and more than the British associationists, the Gestalters refused to admit a truly separate faculty for memory. They supposed that mnemonic phenomena would be explained by the same principles that govern perception. "Association" was just a label for the coherence of elements resulting from the organization or assimilation of elements into a unitary perception or conception. Of course, people can remember their own thoughts and other data not immediately derived from perception, but the Gestalters claimed that the structure of this data was ultimately derived from perception. For this reason, Gestalt theory is sensationalistic; that is, it identifies the contents of memory with encodings of perceptual experience.

The Gestalt Theory of Perception

Since both Gestalt and associationist theories are sensationalistic, it is not surprising that the basic disagreements between them concern the nature of perception rather than the nature of memory. Gestalt theory and associationism confront each other on the topic of memory because both wanted to apply their analysis of perception to memory. The basic Gestalt objection was that the associative analysis was reductionistic and mechanistic, attempting to analyze experience into atomic sensations and then mechanistically build up all of human knowledge from these elements. Appropriately, Gestalt theory is usually dated as originating with the discovery of the phi phenomenon, the experience of apparent movement (e.g., the motion of flashed still pictures seen at the cinema) that could not be decomposed into a sequence of atomic sensations. It still stands today as a clear demonstration that the mind imposes organization on incoming sensory data, that the perception of the whole series takes on emergent properties above and beyond the properties of its parts (although modern neurophysiology [e.g., Barlow & Levick, 1965] suggests the Gestalters may have been wrong about the neutral mechanisms). However, the reductionist postulate of associationism is too elastic to be emphatically disconfirmed by such a demonstration. Only that specific brand of reductionism advocated by Titchner and his associates was upset by the phi phenomenon. They had conjectured (incorrectly) that the perception of motion would be made up from a continuous sequence of "still" perceptions of the object as it traveled through its course. Other associationists simply changed the specific brand of reductionism so as to permit the perception of motion as one of the atomic elements in their analysis.

The Gestalt-associationist controversy was not over what the atomic elements might be in a psychological analysis, but over whether such elements existed at any level. The Gestalters insisted that psychology would only succeed if it considered the whole phenomenon "from the top down." The "whole" was alleged to have emergent properties that could not have easily been predicted by examining the parts. These wholistic properties determined how the parts would be perceived, and not vice versa. According to the Gestalt account, there was nothing mysterious or magical about the emergence of new properties in a whole. Emergent properties are found in many *dynamic* processes that have turned out to be quite amenable to scientific analysis. Köhler, the physicist among the Gestalt group, frequently invoked the concept of "dynamic self-distribution," as in the following quotation:

> Dynamic distributions are functional wholes. Take, for example, a simple electric circuit. The differences of potential and the densities of the current distribute themselves among the conductors in such a way that a steady or

stationary state is established and maintained. No part of this distribution is self-sufficient; the characteristics of local flow depend throughout upon the fact that the process as a whole has assumed the steady distribution [Köhler, 1947, p. 136].

The Gestalt literature is replete with such references to physical processes, all done to demonstrate that the postulation of "dynamic principles of organization" was respectable and scientific. However, one can concede the respectability of such concepts but still criticize the Gestalters for failing to provide an explicit or systematic process interpretation of relevant psychological phenomena. Instead, their work was largely a matter of argument and demonstration that the prevailing mechanistic interpretation of psychological phenomena was not adequate.

Koffka and Wertheimer used the phrase "law of Prägnanz" to reference essentially the same concept as Köhler's "principle of dynamic self-distribution." As Koffka (1935) described the law of Prägnanz"

It can briefly be formulated like this: psychological organization will always be as "good" as the prevailing conditions allow. In this definition the term "good" is undefined. It embraces such properties as regularity, symmetry, simplicity and others which we shall meet in the course of our discussion [p. 110].

The well-known Gestalt laws of similarity, proximity, closure, and good continuation in determination of perceptual groupings and perceptual organization can be seen as special instances of the law of Prägnanz"

The dynamic organization of experience not only creates wholes, but also segregates whole units from one another. These are not independent processes; the fusion of parts into unit-wholes necessarily implies that those parts not members of the same unit-whole will be segregated, separated, and assigned to other units. Köhler conceived of a hierarchy of successive segregation of parts followed by unification. An illustration is provided in Figure 3.1. At one level of analysis, each dot is segregated from every other. However, at another level they merge into a black "figure 8" against its background of white dots. At a still higher level, the "8" and its background merge into a single unit which is segregated as a picture from the surrounding frame. As Köhler (1947) described the matter:

Groups which consist of separate members have a special interest for theory inasmuch as they prove that a given unit may be segregated and yet at the same time belong to a larger unit. In our last example one dot represents a continuous detached entity. None the less it is a member of a larger whole, the number, which is detached from a wider area. There is nothing peculiar about such a subordination of units. In physics, a molecule constitutes a larger functional whole which contains several atoms as subordinate wholes. Functionally, the atoms belong to the molecule-unit; but in this unit they do not altogether lose their individuality [p. 144].

This description corresponds in part to the associationist conception of how ever more complex ideas are compounded out of simple ones. However, it is important

FIG. 3.1. An example that demonstrates a hierarchy of perceptual unification and segregation.

to emphasize the difference in the two conceptions. In the Gestalt account, at each level with the formation of a whole-unit there would be new emergent properties arising which would not be derivable by any simple summation of the properties of its parts. Furthermore, the Gestalters would reject the possibility of a fixed set of ultimately simple ideas, which belief was fundamental to the associationist's viewpoint.

The Gestalt Theory of Memory

As noted earlier, the Gestalt theorists identified the input to memory with perception. Gestalters would propose that the outputs from memory would also have a structure isomorphic to the original perception. To bridge the temporal gap between the input and the output, the Gestalters postulated the existence of an enduring *memory trace*, which conception is central to their theory of memory. They assume that the current input creates an active process which will remain in a "subdued" form as a trace. This information is stored in substantially the same form as the original perception. As Köhler (1938) described the matter:

> Neural events tend to modify slightly the state of the tissue in which they occur. Such changes will resemble those processes by which they have been produced both in their pattern and with respect to other properties [p. 236].

Recall simply involves a reactivation of the trace; effectively, it is a renewal of the same perceptual process as that corresponding to the original input. So, one idea was that the trace is an active process continuing in the nervous system.

A second, unrelated Gestalt principle was that of *isomorphism*, which supposed that the structure of phenomenal experience would be isomorphic to the structure of the underlying neural processes (whatever that means). The combination of these two ideas led to an apparent paradox; why is it that we are not simultaneously conscious of all past experiences that have been recorded as memory traces? To solve this problem, Koffka proposed that a trace would be represented in consciousness only if the dynamic processes underlying it were of sufficient intensity. Most memory traces, of course, would be too weak to reach consciousness. Recall, then, involves amplifying the intensity of a particular trace. This notion, coincidentally, is approximately the same as that of Freud (1933), who assumed that certain ideas and memories lay dormant in the unconscious until activated ("cathected") with an appropriate charge of libidinal energy to raise them over the threshold of consciousness.

Just as the associationists, the Gestalters proposed that the individual elements were connected together in memory and that recall involved going from one element (the cue) to another (the response). However, they rejected the associationist's claim that the memory trace consisted simply of the two independent elements plus a connecting bond. The elements were thought to be *fused* together or organized into a unitary trace. Köhler (1947) stated the alternatives thusly:

> We do not know what happens in recall. The only thing which we seem compelled to assume is some connection between the traces of two processes, A and B, so that reactivation of A leads to recall of B rather than of any facts with which A has not been associated. Now, in this respect two hypotheses are possible. If we believe that, in becoming associated, A and B remain two mutually neutral facts which merely happen to occur together, then some special bond, such as a particularly well conducting group of fibers, may be regarded as an adequate basis of the association. In full contrast to this view, we may, however, reason as follows: When an A and a B become associated, they are experienced not as two independent things but as members of an organized group-unit. This may perhaps now be taken for granted. But with this premise the neural situation cannot consist of two separate parts of which one corresponds to A and the other to B. Rather, the unitary experience indicates that a functional unit is formed in the nervous system, in which the processes A and B have only relative independence. If this is the case, we cannot expect two separate traces to be left when A and B are no longer experienced. Traces, we said, tend to preserve the organization of the original process. Thus only one trace will be established, which represents the functional unit by which it was formed. And in this trace, A and B will exist only as relatively segregated sub-units. Consequently, by virtue of their inclusion within one trace, A and B will be just as well "connected" as they could ever be by means of a special bond [pp. 269-270].

Since the traces formed in memory were permanent recordings of the units formed in perception, the Gestalters could easily explain the classical laws of association. The factors of contiguity, similarity, cause and effect, and so on, underly the "laws of association" because these factors corresponded to Gestalt laws governing the formation of organized units—namely, the laws of proximity, similarity, and good-continuation. Moreover, unlike the associationists, the Gestalters could handle the mnemonic advantage of meaningful material, since meaningful material was alleged to be easily organized into conceptual units.

The Asch Demonstrations

Particularly compelling illustrations of this Gestalt viewpoint in memory have been provided in demonstrations by Asch and his co-workers (see Asch, 1969; Asch, Ceraso, & Heimer, 1960; Prentice & Asch, 1958). Asch investigated the perceptual arrangements which lead to what he calls "coherence" or "unitary" patterns of two otherwise distinguishable visual forms. These are more easily illustrated (see Figure 3.2) than described; Asch's papers should be consulted for other examples. Asch is typically asking one question with these examples: "If I want to have two forms or properties naturally cohere in memory, how should I best arrange for them to be related perceptually at the time I present them for memorization?" In the top two lines of Figure 3.2, a constitutive relation is illustrated; for example, the shape of a rhombus is exemplified in outline by small pluses (the mode, or second form). Presentation of a list of such unitary figure-mode combinations results in far better "associative recall" (of the two forms appropriately paired) than does presentation of outlined figures paired with a row of mode forms alongside (the nonunitary displays on the right of Figure 3.2). Asch would say that the figure on the left is seen as a single unit, as "a rhombus composed of pluses," so that the two forms are inextricably bonded (organized) together. In contrast, the nonunitary display on the right is seen as two isolated units (an outline rhombus and a row of pluses), related only by their spatial contiguity (as are all other pairs in Asch's nonunitary list); consequently, the isolated figures are difficult to organize into a single unit. Therefore, after studying a list of such nonunitary pairs, the subject will be poorer at recalling "plus" when cued with an outlined rhombus than will

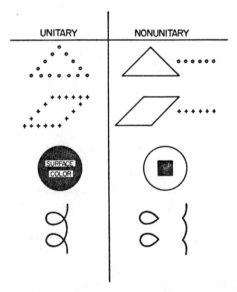

FIG. 3.2. Examples of unitary relations among components of a figure. (Reproduced from Bower, 1970a.)

be the subject exposed to the unitary figure. The third line of Figure 3.2 illustrates a similar coherence between a form and its surface color; one can more easily associate a "circular shape" with a "red color" if it is seen as a "red circle" rather than a "red patch" inside a "circular-shaped form" (see Asch, 1969; Arnold & Bower, 1972).

A similar mnemonic benefit arises from unitary pronunciation of the two elements of a verbal paired-associate item. Asch (1969) used pairs of nonsense syllables (like DAT-NIC) with subjects instructed to pronounce them cyclically either as a fused unit ("DATNIC") or as separate syllables ("DAT"-"NIC"). Arnold and Bower (1972) extended the finding with (consonant vowel)-(consonant) pairs, with some subjects instructed to pronounce each unit of the pair separately (e.g., LO-M as "low-emm"), whereas others were instructed to fuse the elements into a single syllable (e.g., "LOM"). Subjects learned under either incidental or intentional learning instructions, and retention was tested by cued recall of each pair with the left-hand member (e.g., present LO as a cue for recall of M; or DAT as a cue for recall of NIC). In all cases, recall was about twice as good for subjects given "unitary pronunciation" instructions as for subjects told to use "separate-unit pronunciation" rather than fused pronunciation. It may be noted that in all these cases the recall test cue is the separate unit itself (e.g., LO or DAT), which, being more similar to its code during acquisition of the pair, would seem to involve less generalization decrement than when input required fused elements. Nonetheless, the powerful effect of perceptual unitization in memory was sufficient to offset this differential generalization decrement for the two cases.

Such demonstrations illustrate the importance of perceptual relationships in determining how easily two properties or forms become associated in memory. They are not the sort of result that classical associationism was prepared to deal with, since the basic relations of "contiguity" of the two forms are more or less equated in the unitary versus the nonunitary pairs. In terms of our theory, HAM, such results as Asch's are obviously relevant to the type and complexity of the description issuing from the "perceptual parser," which serves in turn as the input to memory. It is plausible to assume that Gestalt laws of grouping would be built into the perceptual parser, and that it would contain as part of its descriptive vocabulary such primitive relations as "form x is composed of y's," or "x is the surface of y," or "x fits into y as part to whole," etc. Given these relational primitives, then the description delivered to HAM's memory by the perceptual parser will be very much simpler and compact (and require fewer "associations" to be learned) for unitary displays than for nonunitary displays. To illustrate, "a rhombus composed of small pluses" is a shorter perceptual description than is "an outline rhombus to the left of a row of small pluses." Recall differences would accordingly be expected to follow these differences in complexity of the perceptual descriptions input to HAM's memory.

To summarize: Asch's demonstrations illustrate nicely the sort of criticisms Gestalt psychologists have been making with regard to classical associationist theory, but it is unclear how seriously they upset more modern associative notions like our own.

The Gestalt Theory of Forgetting

The Gestalters also tried to use a few of their insights regarding perception to explain forgetting. If the trick could be done successfully, they would have interference theory (modern associationism) at a distinct disadvantage in regard to parsimony. By invoking their dynamic laws of perception, the Gestalters would not need to introduce any new postulates for memory. The same "dynamic laws of organization" that are alleged to impose structure upon a perceptual field would also tend to transform incoherent and poorly organized memory traces over time into traces that displayed better organization. If the transformation were too drastic, the trace would lose its original identity and would thus effectively disappear. But if the transformation were not too extreme, recall of the trace would display some systematic distortion in the direction of a better organization. A long history of research has been aimed at testing this prediction of systematic distortion of memories, particularly regarding a person's memory for geometric forms. The literature was reviewed by Riley (1962). His conclusion was that the mass of empirical evidence on the issue is largely negative with respect to the Gestalt position. There are assuredly distortions in memory for forms, but they seem to be predictable not so much by Gestalt "good figure" biases as by (a) assimilation of the memory of the input figure to a common cultural stereotype (proactive interference ?), and/or by (b) assimilation of the input form to a common verbal code or label used at the time of input, which coding distorts the reproduction of the form in a relatively constant manner over varying retention intervals.

In addition to the alleged autonomous effects of organizing principles within the trace, Gestalt theorists also assumed that a trace could be transformed through interactions with other traces and processes. We have already noted that Gestalters held that unification and segregation of a perception took place at several levels. Correspondingly, memory traces were alleged to form a hierarchical structure of groupings. This idea has recurred in a slightly changed form in the writings of the modern "organizational" theorists (see Miller, 1956; Mandler, 1967; Bower, 1970b). According to the Gestalters, because of this hierarchical structure, what might be considered an individual trace at one level participated in a larger trace system at a higher level and was thus connected to other traces. So, via the dynamic laws of organization, traces would mutually affect one another within hierarchies. It was by this means that the Gestalters tried to explain the facts of interference uncovered by modern associationism (see Chapter 15). For example, to handle effects of similarity on retroactive interference, it was supposed that similar traces would tend to disappear into larger trace systems by virtue of the law of similarity.

The Gestalt Theory of Retrieval

Koffka (1935) stated that a current stimulus would serve to recall a fact with which it had been associated by setting up an active neural process that would communicate with the original trace. He introduced a particularly opaque concept to try to illustrate how the current process would make contact with the memory trace. The underlying principle is that a dynamic system such as memory would tend to move in the direction of equilibrium. With this in mind, the reader may evaluate for himself the following quote from Koffka (1935) which gives the Gestalt notion of retrieval:

> It is therefore no new hypothesis if we apply this general principle to the problem of the selection of a trace by a process: This selection must have something to do with the nature of the process, it must further one kind of development of this process rather than others. Let us call the kind of development which is thus being furthered the stability of the process, just to have a convenient name. The actual choice will then depend upon this stability. Those traces will communicate with the process which will give it the particular stability it needs. When we say that in this way our problem has become a problem of organization we say nothing new, but with this formulation we connect our problem with others, the solution of which has been previously indicated. Again, in this aspect also, memory appears not as an entirely new function with completely new laws, but as a special case of a very general function [p. 598].

This conception of retrieval allegedly permits the Gestalters to explain why the active process corresponding to a probe tends to evoke traces of similar mnemonic processes, because one principle of good organization in perception is the law of similarity. By this means, they believed they could give a decent account of how the famous *Höffding step* was accomplished. The Höffding step refers to the problem of how the perception of a particular object (e.g., a particular cameo of Abe Lincoln) can selectively retrieve past memories of the generic representation of the object in memory. Höffding (1891) had used this required contact between the "percept" and "idea" to demonstrate the need for a law of similarity in any psychological reconstruction of recall. (Indeed, we use something like it in HAM.) The Gestalt theorists argued that it was their version of the law of similarity that was needed to explain the communication between the probe and the trace. For example, Köhler (1947) noted that the single vertical line in Figure 3.3B was a much better probe for recall of Figure 3.3A than were the series of bars in Figure 3.3C. This was the case despite the fact that the series of bars represented a much larger part of the original pattern than did the single bar. However, the series of bars was presumed to set up a perceptual process very dissimilar to that of Figure 3.3A, and so could not communicate with the trace of this original pattern.

A basic problem of this "similarity" approach to retrieval is that it is vague and unrevealing. Between any three multidimensional objects or events A, B, C, there are a multitude of possible comparisons; on some dimensions, event A may be closer to B; on other dimensions, A may be closer to event C. The question is how to weight the various components of "similarity" so as to come out with unambiguous predictions; different weightings of this or that similarity lead to different predicted outcomes. Without independent assessment of "psychological distances," explanations of phenomena in terms of the "similarity" of the probe and the retrieved trace will tend always to have high post hoc credibility but low predictive validity.

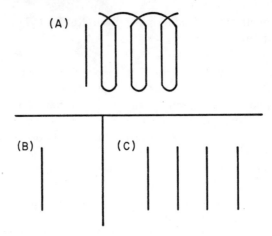

FIG. 3.3. Gestalt demonstration: The probe in (*B*) is a much better cue for recall of (*A*) than the probe in (*C*).

A Difficulty with Gestalt Theory

The most serious difficulty with the Gestalt theory of memory is that it has not been given an extended, explicit formulation by any of its proponents. The Gestalters, particularly Köhler, always wrote as if the only explicit or satisfactory formulation of their principles would be a neurophysiological one. Given our incomplete knowledge of the nervous system, they excused themselves from the task of concretizing their theory. In sympathy, one must consider that they may have been correct in their claim that an adequate expression of Gestalt theory awaited a more detailed neurophysiological theory. The great stumbling block to a formalization of their theory is the claim that the whole has emergent properties. One needs a basis for lawfully predicting what the emergent properties will be when a set of elements are united. A neurophysiological theory appears to provide the only possible basis. (The particular neurological speculations of Köhler have not fared at all well in the empiricist's marketplace; see Lashley, Chow, & Semmes, 1951; Sperry & Milner, 1955.)

It should be clear that the Gestalt theorists were not saying that there can be no adequate theory of the interactions arising when elements are merged into a whole. An analogy to chemistry should make the Gestalt position clearer. When oxygen and hydrogen are combined, the resultant is water. For a long while in chemistry, there were no means by which to explain what the properties of water would be (e.g., its wetness) from the properties of the elements oxygen and hydrogen (which are gases). In a very real sense, water was a "whole" whose emergent properties could not be explained from the properties of its parts. About all that the chemists could do was to give a descriptive statement, describing the properties of the emergent substance produced when oxygen and hydrogen were combined. Psychology, the Gestalters claimed, is at this stage of explanation. The Gestalt "law of Pragnanz" corresponds to the chemist's descriptive statements about the results of putting elements together in certain ways. Today chemistry has satisfactory theories regarding the emergent properties of chemical compounds. In the case of water, the emergent properties came to be understood in terms of the angle at which the two hydrogen atoms attach themselves to the oxygen atom. This level of analysis and its attendant properties were not available to the earlier chemists. Similarly, the Gestalters would argue, we do not yet have a satisfactory neurophysiological level of analysis, but the time will come when such an analysis will verify the Gestalter's claims.

We will close our discussion of Gestalt theory by emphasizing its importance to the topic of human memory. Because it is imprecise, its value is not so much that it provides another way of understanding memory, but rather that it makes us constantly think critically about and defend the reductionistic and mechanistic assumptions in a theory like HAM. Corresponding to the Gestalt demonstrations of the dangers in reductionism and mechanism in perception, there are demonstrations in memory, such as those of Asch mentioned earlier, which show that good, unitary figures are better remembered than nonunitary patterns.

There is a second class of memory phenomena that makes the same point regarding the benefit of "good organization" of the material to be learned, and this is the matter of "mnemonic devices." It has been known since ancient times that the best way to remember arbitrary sets of material is to introduce meaningful relations between the to-be-remembered items. The essential character of all such mnemonic devices (see Bower, 1970a; Norman, 1969) is that, in Gestalt terms, they attempt to merge the disjoint elements to-be-associated into a unitary perceptual or conceptual whole. For instance, if a subject is asked to remember the paired-associate pair *cow-boot*, a most effective device would be for him to image a cow wearing large rubber boots. Or, if he finds imaging difficult, he might produce a linguistic proposition of the form "The cow is wearing boots." An important characteristic of such mnemonic devices is that they make the information to be remembered more memorable by adding further information. But this addition of further information should mean more elements to associate together, so, on most associationist accounts, such mnemonics should make the task harder rather than easier. It was evidence of just this sort that forced the staunch associationist Müeller, as quoted by Katona (1940), to concede that we can learn "by uniting members of a series into solid groups through collective apperception [p. 23]."

It should be understood that we are not claiming that such demonstrations constitute incontrovertible evidence against associationist theories. Such claims would make this book rather pointless. Besides, we have argued in Chapter 2 that associationism is a metatheoretical position that is not directly subject to empirical falsification. The fact that the best remembered material appears to go against the spirit of associationism is an embarrassment to every existing associationist theory. However, being embarrassed is not the same as being proven false. In fact, it will turn out that we can handle many such phenomena in our theory HAM when we fully develop its assumptions in later chapters—about how information is encoded, about how processing time is distributed in the creation of associations, about the interaction between associative structure and new associations, and so on.

3.3. THE RECONSTRUCTION HYPOTHESIS

A standing debate in psychology concerns whether the mind should be analyzed into just static *elements* or qualities of consciousness, into just mental *processes*, or into both such aspects (see Boring's [1950] discussion of the schools of act and content in Germany). The Gestalters' analysis of memory tended to be a static one. That is, they spoke of each experience being recorded in memory as a separate trace, although they assumed that these traces could change spontaneously over time or through interaction with other traces. Recall was to be construed as a reactivation of that trace, as the reappearance of the original perception before "the footlights of consciousness" (to use William James' expression). It is just this sort of "reappearing trace" theory that Bartlett (1932) and Neisser (1967) have objected to most vehemently. Their alternative is what we have called the *reconstruction hypothesis.* They have argued that in perception or thought we *construct* mental objects out of the elementary sensory or cognitive data at hand rather than passively register and classify the events. This is the "analysis by synthesis" model of perception. Neisser, following Bartlett, has also argued that the same sort of approach can be applied to memory, that in remembering we bring to bear our total conceptual repertoire in reconstructing the original experience that we are trying to remember. In one of the more cogent descriptions of this position, Neisser (1967) writes as follows:

> This is not to say that the stimuli themselves are copied and stored; far from it. The analogy being offered asserts only that the role which stored information plays in recall is like the role which stimulus information plays in perception. In neither case does it enter awareness directly, and in neither case can it be literally reproduced in behavior except after rather special training. The model of the paleontologist, which was applied to perception and focal attention in Chapter 4, applies also to memory: out of a few stored bone chips, we remember a dinosaur. To assert otherwise, to defend the Reappearance Hypothesis, would be to adopt an attitude reminiscent of naive realism in perception. It represents a fallacy in both contexts. One does not see objects simply "because they are there," but after an elaborate process of construction (which usually is designed to make use of relevant stimulus information). Similarly, one does not recall objects or responses simply because traces of them exist in the mind, but after an elaborate process of reconstruction (which usually makes use of relevant stored information) [p. 285].

The fundamental difficulty with this approach is its vagueness and incompleteness of statement. By analogy, memory is likened to "constructive processes in perception"; but these are themselves in dispute, not explicitly formulated, and not very well understood. For instance, there is no commonly agreed upon formulation of analysis-by-synthesis models of pattern recognition nor any consensus concerning what stored information they require. Nor is there any clear demarcation between such models as contrasted with "passive classifiers" which (by using stored information) feed forward expectations or hypotheses regarding what is the most plausible next stimulus (see Morton, 1969). Also, no matter how much construction and "fleshing out" of a memory may go on, it surely must begin with and be guided by some coherent bits of information, some "bone chips." And what are these but memory traces? How does the system decide which groups of "bone chips" go together? How does a cue retrieve one rather than another set of "bone chips" to begin the task of reconstruction? What are the reconstructive activities? Are they just "problem-solving" or "story-telling" routines that make use of formerly learned material to fill in, in a thematically plausible manner, a fragmentary, degraded memory trace? The paleontologist's "construction" of a dinosaur from a few bone chips is a striking metaphor, but why should we believe that it is not misleading?

Bartlett's Schema

These and numerous other such queries can be raised regarding the reconstruction hypothesis. We may look into Bartlett's (1932) book, *Remembering*, to try to find answers. For Bartlett, the important organizing factor behind such reconstructive recall was what he called the "*schema*." As he defined it, the schema was "an active organization of past reactions, or of past experiences, which must always be supposed to be operating in any well-adapted organic response [p. 201]." Bartlett is borrowing this notion of a schema from Head (1920), who had used it to refer to something like a person's moment-by-moment "knowledge" of where his various limbs (arms, legs) are located in space around his trunk. This "model" or schema is updated moment by moment by information that comes in as the person moves a limb or adjusts his posture; the "model" is also responsible for sending out commands to other bodily parts to make compensatory adjustments so as to maintain the body in upright balance. However, Bartlett wanted to use this notion to explain the vastly more varied and complicated behavior that we call remembering. The schema concept had been designed to handle the moment-to-moment adjustment of limbs in postural movements, and it is not obvious how it applies to the behavioral flexibility characteristic of human memory.

Bartlett (1932) clearly realized this difficulty with Head's notion of a schema. For example, he stated the problem of retrieval from memory in the following terms:

> A new incoming impulse must become not merely a cue setting up a series of reactions all carried out in a fixed temporal order, but a stimulus which enables us to go direct to that portion of the organized setting of past responses which is most relevant to the needs of the moment [p. 206].

To solve the retrieval problem, Bartlett proposed a particularly opaque process:

> An organism has somehow to acquire the capacity to turn around upon its own "schemata" and to construct them afresh. This is a crucial step in organic development. It is where and why consciousness comes in; it is what gives consciousness its most prominent function [p. 206].

Of great importance in this constructive activity is the subject's general attitude about the material he is trying to recall. It is this which determines the reconstruction of a schema in recall:

> It may be that what then emerges is an *attitude* towards the massive effects of a series of past reactions. Remembering is a constructive justification of this attitude; and, because all that goes to the building of a "schema" has a chronological, as well as a quantitative significance, what is remembered has its temporal mark; while the fact that it is operating with a diverse organized mass, and not with single undiversified events or units, gives to remembering its inevitable associative character [p. 208].

We find such crucial passages a little hard to follow.

Neisser (1967) interprets Bartlett's schema concept as a cognitive structure, which he defines as a "nonspecific but organized representation of prior experience [p. 287]." The schemata, according to Neisser, are produced by the constructive act of recall. We do not store the schemata in memory, however; rather what is stored in memory are traces of the processes by which the original experience was constructed. So, for instance, the mnemonic representation underlying a perceptual memory would be traces of the perceptual processes that occurred during the original perception. Thus, we do not remember what happened but rather how we cognized what happened.

Neisser's Executive

Bartlett's idea of the person "turning around" upon his schemata and reconstructing them has been interpreted by Neisser (1967) in terms of problem-solving routines carried out by an *executive*, a concept borrowed from computer science. The executive component of a computer program is characterized as follows:

> Most computer programs consist of largely independent parts, or "subroutines." In complex sequential programs, the order in which the subroutines are applied will vary from one occasion to the next. In simple cases, a conditional decision can lead from one subroutine to the next appropriate one: "transfer control to register A if the computed number in register X is positive, but to register B if it is negative or zero." In other situations, however, the choice between register A and register B may depend on a more complicated set of conditions, which must be evaluated by a separate subroutine called "the executive." Common practice is to make all subroutines end by transferring control to the executive, which then decides what to do next in each case [pp. 295-296].

Readers with philosophical acuity will see the executive as a vitalistic vestige within the mechanical model, a vestige to which all varieties of irreducible "faculties" are assigned. The decisions it makes, the goals it sets, the priority-rankings of subgoals it will work on, its cutoff time for stopping work on fruitless subproblems, etc., are not explained by the program itself; rather they are an assumed set of capabilities and "values" assigned to the program by its designer.

The designer, in some respects, is mimicking the effects of an evolutionary history in installing these components in the "innate wiring" of the machine. In the informal discussions of cognitive psychologists, the executive is assigned diverse and wondrous abilities; it has free will, purposes, intentions, goal priorities, etc. For example, the executive "decides," in the light of motivational and situational constraints, whether or not to begin reconstructing a memory to satisfy a given retrieval cue, or whether to switch attention from one train of thought to a newly arriving stimulus of some significance. In these respects, the executive plays somewhat the same explanatory role as the old "inner homunculus" of prescientific theories.

This concept of an executive is certainly alien to the spirit of stimulus-response associationism, which would want to inquire into why the executive behaves as it does. The counterargument is that something like an executive is almost a logical necessity for running complex, hierarchically organized programs, and the informal abuses of the concept in loose discussions should not be counted against the basically mechanical nature of the concept. At any level of behavioristic (or mentalistic) analysis, certain capabilities and operations have been accepted temporarily as primitives (e.g., the ability to "decide" whether two symbols match). The fundamental difference between the executive and the homunculus is that the executive is a mechanistically specified computational algorithm: its designer knows exactly the "rules" by which it operates. On the other hand, the homunculus is just another unanalyzed man, whose behavior can be predicted no better than that of the person within which the homunculus resides.

Winograd's Program

In searching for a concrete realization of what Bartlett and Neisser must be saying, we have found a recent dissertation by Terry Winograd (1971) to be a useful theoretical paradigm. Winograd's aims were in the direction of artificial intelligence, not psychology, and he certainly is not consciously in the tradition of Bartlett and Neisser. Nonetheless, his dissertation offers an interesting illustration of what it might mean to store procedures for reconstructing a memory rather than to store the memory itself. In Winograd's system, knowledge is expressed in terms of programs that will operate on the world or on other programs. For instance, linguistic assertions are stored in the data base as procedures that may be evoked when the system is faced with some task to perform such as answering a question or constructing a particular block scene in its small toy environment. By representing knowledge as procedures, Winograd (1971) claims to have gained "greater flexibility than a program with a fixed control structure, in which the specific knowledge can only indirectly control the process of understanding [p. 13]." It is not clear how to evaluate Winograd's claim that representing knowledge as procedures is superior to systems that represent knowledge as data separate from program. There is no denying that Winograd's system is one of the most impressive natural language understanding systems in computer science. We will examine its virtues in more detail at later points in the book. However, it appears to us that the credit for the success of the system really goes to its abstract, logical structure and not to its use of procedures for representing knowledge. It would seem possible to translate from Winograd's program representation of knowledge into a network representation which is logically equivalent. In fact, at points in his dissertation Winograd seems to concede this point or similar ones. For instance he writes: "Is there anything in common between grammars which are networks and grammars which are programs? The reader may have already seen the 'joke' in this question. In fact, these are just two different ways of talking about doing exactly the same thing! [p. 201]"

Evidence for the Reconstruction Hypothesis

Bearing in mind the Winograd type of explication, it would seem that the Bartlett-Neisser reconstructive hypothesis is a workable idea. But why should anyone favor it over the reappearing-trace hypothesis? Several lines of evidence are traditionally marshaled for this viewpoint. They mostly concern the fact that some memories are strongly biased by the particular mood, motives, interests, beliefs, and personality of the person who is remembering. One of Bartlett's famous demonstrations illustrated how recall of an Indian folktale ("The War of the Ghosts") became progressively transformed over time to fit into the cultural assumptions of his English subjects. Further, Neisser notes how adaptive memory is, that our memories are seldom repeated exactly but rather appear in new combinations appropriately suited to the tasks at hand. If the trace hypothesis were correct, Neisser (1967) argues, then we would expect that "repetition of earlier acts or thoughts should be the natural thing, and variation the exception [p. 280]." He also notes the importance of motivation or interest to memory, that we tend to remember what we want to.

Important to the reconstructive hypothesis is the analysis that Bartlett and Neisser give to perception. Both argue against the simple imprinting of impressions on a relatively passive wax tablet, which has been the underlying metaphor in associationist conceptions of perception, and to a lesser extent in the Gestalt conception. They argue rather that perception must involve an active process of using the elements of experience to construct a meaningful perception out of them. Gregory (1970) has offered a similar view of perception. If this analysis of perception is correct, then Bartlett and Neisser would have parsimony on their side in their analysis of memory. If the original perception is constructed, why not just assume that the memory of the perception also results from the same sort of constructive procedures.

As mentioned earlier, we find these remarks or arguments rather unconvincing. We readily admit that a trace theory which has only the potential to revive old experiences verbatim is inadequate for the complexities of human memory. Indeed, we have argued this same point at several places in the last chapter. But that is no reason to dispense entirely with a trace system; rather we feel that the trace system should be properly viewed as only one component of a total mental system that has the capacity for such things as deduction, strategic probing, inference, strategic guessing, selective attention, and so forth.

There is no doubt, however, that both Bartlett and Neisser would insist that a theoretical separation of memory from the rest of the mental system is inherently misguided. Indeed, in a sense, they would deny that "uncontaminated" experimentation on human memory could be a realistic or desirable goal. Neisser (1967) states his position as follows:

> The simplifications introduced by confining the subject to a single motive and a forced set of alternative responses can be justified only if motivation and cognition are genuinely distinct. If—as I suppose—they are inseparable where remembering and thinking are concerned, the common experimental paradigms may pay too high a price for simplicity [p. 305].

Concluding Observations

In conclusion, it is interesting to note that the Gestalt memory theory and the reconstruction hypothesis agree on the four metafeatures of a rationalist approach, but yet they are really quite different. As theories of memory, the issue of *nativism* is not really applicable to them. But both theories are clearly *holistic* in the two senses outlined in Section 3.1. Firstly, they emphasize the interactions among the contents of the total memory system; and secondly, the memory system is seen in unity with the rest of the faculties of the mind. But the principles which govern the interactions within whole memories and which unify the memory system with other systems are the dynamic laws of organization in Gestalt theory, whereas in reconstruction theory they are the procedures for generating plausible constructions, given certain traces as clues. A similar sharp contrast of the two theories is seen in the kind of *intuitions* which have guided the development of the theories and which the theories try to explain. The Gestalters concentrated on intuitions about how innate organizing forces structure whole units, whereas Bartlett and Neisser emphasize intuitions about how a person's attitudes and interests actively determine the character of his memories. The fourth rationalist feature, *vitalism*, was manifest in the dynamic laws of Gestalt theory but in the form of a purposeful "executive" within the reconstruction hypothesis.

In these two chapters we have examined two contrasting methodologies for constructing a theory of human memory. Methodological empiricism attempts to work from raw data to more and more general statements about memory. In contrast, methodological rationalism begins with lofty first principles and then attempts to relate these to empirical phenomena. In terms of a spatial metaphor we may say methodological empiricism works from the bottom (raw data) up but that methodological rationalism works from the top (lofty principles) down. Having now completed our review of both the rationalist and empiricist attempts at theories of memory, we must conclude that both methodologies appear subject to serious difficulties. The regrettable feature that seems characteristic of rationalist enterprises is that of stagnation. After the initial insights and intuitions have given shape to the theory, there is an absence of any further development or articulation of the hypotheses regarding memory. It is rarely made explicit with detail and rigor how a memory system so conceived will explain the empirical phenomena at hand. Subsequent experimentation seems to be little more than repeated demonstrations that there *really* are processes like the theory postulates. In terms of the top-down metaphor we used to describe rationalist theory construction, it seems that the theory never obtains a broad, elaborated, and firm empirical foundation. The theory remains suspended in mid-air, as it were.

Of course, it is just as easy for the rationalist to retaliate with criticisms of the empiricist enterprise. By focusing on the need to build a theory around particular data, the empiricist may frequently miss the fundamental characteristics of the phenomena at hand. We see evidence for this in the preceding chapter—for instance, with respect to associationism's blindness of the flaws in the Terminal Meta-Postulate. The empiricist methodology has a myoptic view of the world. In terms of our bottom-up metaphor, the empiricist methodology seldom gets beyond unconnected low-level theories, a complaint which runs rampant among surveyors of the contemporary scene of confusion (e.g., Tulving & Madigan, 1970). The connecting theoretical superstructure is never successfully imposed on these low-level theories. Moreover, the rationalist would argue that by the very nature of the enterprise, it is unlikely that the low-level theories could ever produce an adequate foundation for the necessary superstructure.

As indicated before, the neo-associationist methodology tries to proceed simultaneously from an abstract characterization of the problem downwards and from the empirical data upwards. It is too early to tell whether this methodology avoids the problems of the pure rationalist and the pure empiricist. Perhaps we will just be compounding the difficulties of both approaches. It is unclear whether it is any easier to get a meeting in the middle than it was for the rationalists to touch empirical ground or for the empiricist to reach the lofty goal of a sufficient and unified theory. The next chapter reviews some of the recent computer simulations of human memory which tend to be neo-associational in character and which use this combined approach.

REFERENCES

Arnold, P. G., & Bower, G. H. Perceptual conditions affecting ease of association. *Journal of Experimental Psychology*, 1972, **93**, 176–180.

Asch, G. E. A reformulation of the problem of associations. *American Psychologist*, 1969, **24**, 92–102.

Asch, G. E., Ceraso, J., & Heimer, W. Perceptual conditions of association. *Psychological Monographs*, 1960, 74 (3, Whole No. 490).

Barlow, H. B., & Levick, W. R. The mechanism of directionally selective units in rabbit's retina. *Journal of Physiology*, 1965, **178**, 477–504.

Bartlett, F. C. *Remembering: A study in experimental and social psychology*. Cambridge: The University Press, 1932.

Boring, E. G. *A history of experimental psychology*. New York: Appleton-Century-Crofts, 1950.

Bower, G. H. Analysis of a mnemonic device. *American Scientist*, 1970, **58**, 496–510. (a)

Bower, G. H. Organizational factors in memory. *Cognitive Psychology*, 1970, **1**, 18–46. (b)

Brown, R., & McNeill, D. The "tip of the tongue" phenomenon. *Journal of Verbal Learning and Verbal Behavior*, 1966, **5**, 325–337.

Buhler, K. Die "Neue Psychologie" Koffkas. *Zeitschrift für Psychologie*, 1926, **99**, 145–159.

Chomsky, N. *Language and mind*. New York: Harcourt, Brace & World, 1968.

Dreyfus, H. L. *What computers can't do*. New York: Harper & Row, 1972.

Ehrenfels, C. von. On Gestalt qualities. *Psychological Review*, 1937, **44**, 521–524.

Ernst, G. W., & Newell, A. *GPS: A case study in generality and problem-solving*. New York: Academic Press, 1969.

Freud, S. *New introductory lectures on psychoanalysis.* Trans. by J. H. Sprott. New York: Norton, 1933.

Gregory, R. L. *The intelligent eye.* New York: McGraw-Hill, 1970.

Head, H. *Studies in neurology.* Oxford: Oxford University Press, 1920.

Höffding, H. *Outlines of psychology.* London: Macmillan, 1891.

Hook, S. *Dimensions of mind: A symposium.* New York: Collier Books, 1961.

Katona, G. *Organizing and memorizing.* New York: Columbia University Press, 1940.

Katz, J. J. *The philosophy of language.* New York: Harper & Row, 1966.

Koffka, K. *Principles of Gestalt psychology.* New York: Harcourt, Brace & World, 1935.

Köhler, W. *The place of value in a world of facts.* New York: Liveright, 1938.

Köhler, W. *Gestalt psychology: An introduction to new concepts in modern psychology.* New York: Liveright, 1947.

Lashley, K. S., Chow, K. L., & Semmes, J. An examination of the electrical field theory of cerebral integration. *Psychological Review,* 1951, 58, 123–136.

Mandler, G. Organization and memory. In K. W. Spence & J. A. Spence (Eds.), *The psychology of learning and motivation.* Vol. 1. New York: Academic Press, 1967. Pp. 328–372.

Miller, G. A. The magical number seven, plus or minus two: Some limits on our capacity for processing information. *Psychological Review,* 1956, 63, 81–97.

Morton, J. The interaction of information in word recognition. *Psychological Review,* 1969, 76, 165–178.

Neisser, U. *Cognitive psychology.* New York: Appleton-Century-Crofts, 1967.

Norman, D. A. *Memory and attention: An introduction to human information processing.* New York: Wiley, 1969.

Prentice, W. C. H., & Asch, G. E. Paired-associations with related and unrelated pairs of nonsense figures. *American Journal of Psychology,* 1958, 71, 247–254.

Reitman, J., & Bower, G. H. Structure and later recognition of exemplars of concepts. *Cognitive Psychology,* in press.

Riley, D. A. Memory for form. In L. Postman (Ed.), *Psychology in the making.* New York: Knopf, 1962.

Selz, O. Zur Psychologie der Gegenwart: Eine Anmerkung zu Koffkas Darstellung. *Zeitschrift für Psychologie,* 1926, 99, 169–196.

Sperry, R. W., & Milner, N. Pattern perception following insertion of mica plates into visual cortex. *Journal of Comparative and Physiological Psychology,* 1955, 48, 463–469.

Tulving, E., & Madigan, S. A. Memory and verbal learning. *Annual Review of Psychology,* 1970, 21, 437–484.

Wertheimer, W. Gestalt theory. *Social Research,* 1944, 11, 78–99.

Winograd, T. Procedures as a representation for data in a computer program for understanding natural language. *M.I.T. Artificial Intelligence Laboratory Project* MAC TR-84, 1971.

4
COMPUTER SIMULATION
MODELS OF MEMORY

In terms of the continuum of intelligence, the computer programs we have been able to construct are still at a low end. What is important is that we continue to strike out in the direction of the milestone that represents the capabilities of human intelligence. Is there any reason to suppose that we shall never get there? None whatever. Not a single piece of evidence, no logical argument, no proof or theorem has ever been advanced which demonstrates an insurmountable hurdle along the continuum.

—Feigenbaum and Feldman

4.1. COMPUTER SIMULATION AND NEO-ASSOCIATIONISM

In this chapter three neo-associationist models of human memory will be reviewed. Given our definition of neo-associationist theories—i.e., the results of the parallel application of empiricist and rationalist methodologies—there is no necessary reason why neo-associationist models should so often take the form of simulation programs. That they have probably reflects the peculiar demands of computer simulation. That is, one must not only adopt the rationalist approach and develop a program sufficient to simulate a particular class of human behaviors, but he must at the same time adopt the empiricist approach and build the program around individual psychological experiments.

Starting in the mid-1950s with the truly seminal work of Newell, Shaw, and Simon (e.g., 1958), a new approach to computer programming and computer usage developed. In particular, the computer came to be viewed as a general symbol-manipulating machine rather than just a rapid arithmetic calculator. Newell, Shaw, and Simon had the perspicacity to see that it might be used to characterize human thinking and problem solving. To this end, they began developing "list-processing" languages for computer programming (such as IPL) which were heuristic in helping to describe and operate upon hierarchically organized information structures. Probably the most important language today in artificial intelligence and computer simulation is LISP. It originally was developed at M.I.T. by John McCarthy while he was working on the theory of computation (see McCarthy, Abrahams, Edwards, Hart, & Levin, 1962). Its popularity and widespread usage is mainly a consequence of its orientation towards symbolic data structures and its facilities for programming of recursive operations. Originally LISP was definitely not a user-oriented language and many programmers cursed its very existence. Under practical demands, however, it has become oriented with amazing sensitivity to the research needs of artificial intelligence and computer simulation (cf. Teitlebaum, Bobrow, Hartley, & Murphy, 1971). Many of the new generation of computer languages (e.g., PLANNER—see Hewitt, 1970) are really extensions of LISP. Our simulation work has been programmed exclusively in LISP.

For present purposes the significant aspect of LISP is its data structure. The atomic building block in the data structure is the *ordered pair* by which two symbolic elements (memory locations) may be conjoined. One standard feature in LISP is the *property list* by which one element may be related to others by means of particular *relations*. So at the very base of LISP, the data primitives are objects that bear striking correspondences to the unlabeled associations (ordered pairs) and the labeled associations (property lists) that concerned us in Chapter 2. With these primitives it is easy and natural to construct arbitrarily complicated memory networks. Other symbolic programming languages have also been designed to facilitate the construction of such associative networks. It is small wonder then that modern computer simulation should be so strongly tainted by an associative flavor. This is clearly a case of the medium determining the message.

One could say equivalently that computer simulation models of memory are *connectionistic*. As argued in Chapter 2, any model of memory must in some sense be connectionistic. However, it is the stark mechanical nature of these connections that gives simulation models a considerable associationistic character. But it is important to understand that, when a cognitive simulator decides to use a network of associations as his data base, the considerations that are motivating him may be very different from the traditional psychological concerns. That is, cognitive simulators often are not trying to capture the associative trains of thought, the contiguities of stimuli and responses, or other more or less immediate data. Rather, they are using an associative network because such representations are considered in computer science to be desirable for constructing large general-purpose data bases. Moreover, the "accepted" computer languages of artificial intelligence, such as LISP, make it difficult to use any radically different data representation.

While the computer simulation models display strongly the mechanistic and connectionistic character of traditional associationism, they do not seem much committed to reductionism and sensationalism. These features are not well developed in any simulation model. Concerning the rationalist metafeatures, there is some pattern in the commitments of the simulation models. With respect to nativism, the models do assume some wonderful and powerful mechanisms that preprocess and analyze stimulus input, that store and search memory, and that compute answers to questions from the data base. But little is said about how these mechanisms ever came to exist in the mind. The *intuitionistic* feature is very strong in all these models insofar as the programmer's intuitions and requirements of computational elegance have played a strong role in determining the initial form of the theory. In no case can the theories be thought of as just generalizations from the data, whereas this was the case for many past associative constructions. The *vitalistic* feature in terms of a powerful and sophisticated executive program appears very strongly in a system like ELINOR (see Section 4.4) but is almost totally lacking in EPAM or SAL (see Section 4.2). Finally, the *holistic* feature which emphasizes mass interactive effects is almost totally lacking in current research. The nearest approximation is the assumption in Quillian's model of spreading activation throughout the memory system (see Section 4.3). Effects depending on the interaction of a number of simultaneous processes tend to be shunned because they are difficult to simulate on a serial, digital computer. Once again we have an example of the medium determining the message.

These remarks attempt to place computer simulation in a historical perspective within psychology. That is, we have described the posture of simulation work on the various "metafeatures" that have characterized and divided past psychological research. We feel that it is an enlightening exercise to examine the theories from this perspective. It is important for the reader to realize how often technological capabilities and constraints have determined theoretical decisions in this field. We now turn to examination of three simulation programs which we feel are particularly important psychologically. These models are also interesting because they contain many similarities to HAM but also many contrasts. By examining these alternatives the reader will have a better framework within which to evaluate HAM.

4.2. EPAM AND SAL

The original aim of the designers of EPAM (Feigenbaum, 1963; Simon & Feigenbaum, 1964) was to create a program which could learn to discriminate among a number of stimulus patterns, and could learn to associate a "response" to each stimulus pattern so identified. The name of the program captures these aims: EPAM is an acronym for Elementary Perceiver and Memorizer. Towards this end EPAM embodies many assumptions regarding the memory structure, mechanisms regarding the way in which stimulus information is recognized, and acquisition rules concerning how new information is to be added into the memory structure. Hintzman (1968) developed a simpler model, SAL (an acronym for Stimulus and Association Learner), which was based on ideas similar to EPAM and which he used to interpret a number of learning experiments. Unlike the later models to be reviewed, EPAM and SAL are the only ones explicitly concerned with learning and forgetting, particularly with how the learning of new information causes old information in memory to become inaccessible.

The Discrimination Net

The basic memory structure in both EPAM and SAL is the *discrimination net*. The purpose of a discrimination net is to sort a complex stimulus to its corresponding representation in memory. The stimulus is first analyzed by the perceptual system into a set of attribute-value pairs or features. The perceptual system which extracts these features has never in fact been modeled for EPAM, although it has been for a few other pattern recognizers (e.g., for some review, see Kolers & Eden, 1968, and Dodwell, 1970).

The discrimination net is a sequential network (tree) of tests on these stimulus features; an example is illustrated in Figure 4.1. In that figure, a circular node refers to a test question, whereas branches radiating out below a test node represent different "answers" to the query at the test node. In Figure 4.1, TEST A examines some high-priority feature of the stimulus. If the outcome of this test is r_1, the program moves down to the TEST 1 node where a test will be made of a second feature; if the outcome of TEST A is r_2, the program moves to TEST 2 and asks a different question, and so on. By branching through a sequence of such tests, the original stimulus description "falls out the bottom" of the sorting tree into a particular "terminal node" representing its unique storage location in the memory. This terminal node may have pointers (or cues) to other associated information with which the current stimulus is to be connected.

Such a sorting tree is one kind of a content-addressable store; the description list of a stimulus directly informs an executive program how to traverse the pathways of the discrimination net in order to find the terminal node in memory corresponding to that stimulus. The tests are presumably laid out serially in such fashion as to minimize the average amount of stimulus analysis and feature identification required in order to identify the high-frequency stimulus patterns. In principle there are no restrictions on the complexity of the tests contained at test nodes. In practice, the early versions of EPAM and all versions of SAL tested for the presence or absence of a particular feature or attribute-value pair on the description list of a stimulus. Thus, the output of the test was either *yes* or *no*. A later version of EPAM used tests for the value of a specified attribute, so multiple output branches were possible. This increases the breadth of the tree and reduces the depth of the tree needed to distinguish among a fixed set of patterns.

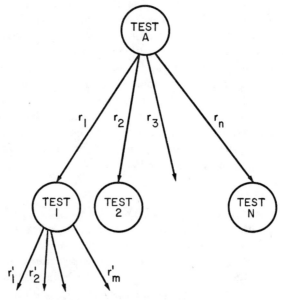

FIG. 4.1. A schematic illustration of a discrimination net used in EPAM and SAL.

Acquisition in a Discrimination Net

The research of Feigenbaum and Simon on EPAM and of Hintzman on SAL was focused primarily on the learning of novel stimulus patterns by adults; in particular, they have examined the learning of nonsense syllables in the paired-associate and serial learning paradigms. One advantage of nonsense syllables is that they form unfamiliar patterns that are easily composed and that can be made of varying degrees of difficulty; yet, they are patterns for which we can be reasonably sure about the elementary units entering into the subject's analysis (i.e., as letters in particular positions in a string). Since such nonsense syllables are unknown patterns, the experimental subject cannot sort them through his discrimination net at the outset of the learning task. Therefore a major component of his learning task is to grow new test nodes in the discrimination net so as to identify the nonsense syllables of the set being learned.

As mentioned earlier, EPAM and SAL grow a discrimination net by adding nodes which test for presence versus absence of a particular feature, thus producing binary sorting trees. For nonsense syllables, the features were identified as the alphabetic letters in the three serial positions (left, middle, right). Thus, the syllable *XIH* would be characterized by the three features of having an *X* in Position 1, *I* in Position 2, and *H* in Position 3. A typical test node would be identified as *-I-*, which asks whether the letter *I* is in the second position of the stimulus pattern being sorted.

In what order are tests of the several features of a pattern added to the expanding network as learning proceeds? The answer is that the three positions are assigned an empirically based priority order or "noticing order," namely, first-letter first, last-letter next, and middle-letter last. Features of the pattern currently being studied are added as test nodes according to the following rule: If the highest priority feature (first-letter) of the pattern has not already been positively identified in sorting it, then add this to the network as a test node; if the highest priority feature has already been positively identified, then use the next feature in priority in order to construct a test node; if the second-priority feature of the pattern has already been used for sorting it, then add its third-priority feature as a test node. Use of the third feature will, of course, exhaust the complete description of such patterns.

The hope is that the system, much like the person it is simulating, can learn to discriminate reliably among the set of training patterns without having to learn the complete description of every pattern. To this end, EPAM and the initial version of SAL (called SAL-I) adopted a sort of "minimal effort" principle. If a net were sufficiently elaborated to correctly identify a particular stimulus, then presentation of that pattern would be assumed to cause no alteration in the network. If the net misidentified a particular pattern and made an error, the net would be "patched up" only locally to handle this particular perturbing pattern; a test node would be added, tailor-made to handle the immediate local problem of distinguishing the currently perturbing stimulus. This "local laziness" built into EPAM and SAL-I was the source of some of its interesting predictions regarding learning. In particular, this feature causes forgetting due to interference of new "local" learning with prior retrieval routes.

(a)

(b)

(c)

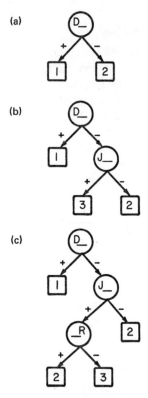

FIG. 4.2. An illustration of how retroactive inference occurs in EPAM's discrimination network. See text for discussion.

An example would be helpful in explicating the behavior of such a model. For convenience of exposition, we shall use the task modeled by SAL-I, viz., the learning of "CVC-digit" paired associates. Suppose the first two pairs studied were *DAX*-1 and *JIR*-2. Then SAL would only develop a net like that shown in Figure 4.2a. Test nodes are indicated by circles; terminal nodes containing digit responses are indicated by squares. Referring to Figure 4.2a, if the first letter is *D*, the pattern is sorted down the "+" branch where it finds and gives a 1 as its response; if *D* is absent, the pattern is sorted along the "–" branch to a terminal which yields response 2. This net suffices for the pairs *DAX*-1, *JIR*-2. The minimal effort principle dictates that if there are no further nonsense syllables to be differentiated, then the net in Figure 4.2a will not undergo further elaboration since it never makes an error in classifying members of the training set.

But this is a trivially small set of patterns to discriminate. Suppose a third pair, *JUB*-3, is added. It will initially be sorted to terminal 2, and the program will respond erroneously, indicating that a new test should be added to the right-hand branch of the tree. Because of EPAM's fixed noticing order, this test will refer to the first letter (note, terminal 2 had been identified before only as "not *D*--").

Adding this first-letter test following the error on *JUB*-3, the new net will look like that in Figure 4.2*b*. A high-priority feature of the perturbing pattern, namely *J*--, has been established as a test node, with the positive branch leading to response 3, the response of the currently perturbing pair, whereas the old response 2, from the former node (of Figure 4.2*a*), has been placed at the terminal of the negative branch.

The net has now learned locally how to deal with the pair *JUB*-3. Unfortunately, this local learning with *JUB* now creates difficulties with *JIR*, which formerly was sorted correctly to the response 2 terminal. Now *JIR* will be sorted to terminal 3, because it shares the test feature *J*-- with *JUB* which gave rise to this node. In order to deal with this confusion, a new test node must be added onto the old terminal 3 of Figure 4.2*b*. The program uses the next feature in the noticing order of *JIR*-2, namely, the last letter *R*. The net as elaborated in Figure 4.2*c* results, and it suffices to sort the three nonsense syllables *DAX*, *JIR*, and *JUB*. Of course, larger and more complex sets of syllables will require correspondingly more complex discrimination nets.

This example illustrates the phenomenon of retroactive interference, the way in which new learning can produce "forgetting" of old associations in the network. Because of the "local patching-up" principle, EPAM, while dealing with the immediately offending pattern, does so by losing its access route to a prior association. This sort of confusion and mutual interference between patterns depends crucially on the similarity of the two stimuli or the common elements in their description lists, e.g., that *JIR* and *JUB* both begin with *J*. In experimental studies of memory, of course, retroactive interference does depend directly on stimulus similarity.

In a later version of his model, dubbed SAL-II, Hintzman relaxed this principle of minimal effort, assuming that new test nodes could be added with experience even though the net was currently successful in differentiating the training set of stimulus patterns. SAL-II added new test nodes and gradually built up more complete internal descriptions of each pattern, even long after the system had stopped making errors on the training set. This result corresponds to providing "overlearning" beyond the point of mastery on the set of training patterns. A consequence of this overlearning on the initial set of patterns by SAL-II is that interpolated learning of a second, similar set of patterns causes less retroactive interference than in the control case where the initial set is not overlearned. This outcome corresponds to a well-validated experimental conclusion, that overlearning reduces the amount of retroactive interference. SAL-II implies this outcome because during overlearning it acquires fairly complete internal representations of the patterns of the original list, with most patterns being sorted by positive identification of their three features. Therefore, unlike the case in Figure 4.2, SAL-II can protect itself from interference that is due to partial feature overlap between new and old stimuli.

The Associative Process

The foregoing discussion describes the development of the discrimination net for recognizing stimuli. For most applications of the model, an additional associative process is required by which information sufficient to generate a response is stored at the terminal to which a stimulus pattern is sorted. This associative process is necessary for generation of the response term in a paired-associate task or the next-successor term in a serial-list learning situation. This response generation is achieved by storing at (or associating to) each terminal node a cue or partial list of cues which in turn is to be sorted through a discrimination network for responses. The terminal arrived at in this second sort contains parameters for generating the desired physical response. In case the responses in a paired-associate task are already familiar, well integrated, and differentiated from one another before S-R pair learning begins, then the response-cue retrieved by sorting the stimulus suffices to retrieve the correct response without further ado. This is the situation simulated by Hintzman's SAL model where single digit responses were employed. However, in EPAM, Feigenbaum and Simon explicitly tackled this response-learning component, since they wanted their model to be able to generate nonsense syllable responses. Their solution was to store at the terminal node to which the stimulus was sorted a "partial description-list" just sufficient to locate the correct response in a response-discrimination net.

The Push-down Stack

One of the basic empirical weaknesses of EPAM and the initial versions of SAL was their failure to show proactive interference, which is the deleterious effect on retention of a list by having the subject learn earlier lists. A second difficulty of the models was that they could not permit a given stimulus to remain associated to several different responses in several different lists. Provided the stimulus (call it A) is sorted to the same terminal node in different lists, then EPAM can give at most only one response to it, namely, that generated by the response-cue stored at the terminal node. Thus, if stimulus A becomes associated to response C in List 2, the system has no way to maintain and recall its association to response B from List 1.

These are serious deficiencies for a model which purports to simulate human memory. To deal with these problems, Hintzman introduced in his SAL-III version the idea that multiple responses could coexist at a terminal node in the stimulus-sorting network. In order to rank-order the several responses at a terminal node in terms of their priority to the stimulus, Hintzman used the notion of a temporally ordered list or "push-down stack" (abbreviated PDS). The most recent correct response to a stimulus occupies the topmost position in the push-down stack; the next-most-recent response is in the second location in the stack, etc. It is assumed that when the model is asked to respond to a stimulus, it gives that response on the top of the PDS, i.e., the most recent correct one. This assumption produces strong retroactive interference in the A-B, A-C paradigm since later-learned responses will be favored. This priority for recently reinforced responses corresponds to the *response competition* factor in modern interference theory, whereas disruption of prior retrieval routes by growth of the discrimination net corresponds to the *unlearning* factor in contemporary accounts. As Keppel (1968) indicates in his extensive review, there is evidence for both factors in retroactive interference.

Hintzman showed how this PDS mechanism could explain several phenomena in paired-associate learning. These included facts regarding recall latencies before versus after list mastery, the relation of S-R pair recognition to cued response recall, and the continued joint availability of *A-C* and some *A-B* associations following interpolated learning when the subject is asked to recall the responses learned from both lists (the so-called MMFR test).

The PDS postulate does not itself explain proactive interference in retention. In order to handle proactive effects, therefore, Hintzman introduced the further assumption that over time, responses residing in a given PDS will "spontaneously rise" to the top, pushing out responses located at higher levels of the PDS. Consequently, with the passage of time, responses learned in earlier lists would tend to extrude responses learned in later lists, causing them to be lost from the system; that is, of course, a mechanism that implies proactive interference, that old learning can displace new learning.

The unattractive part of Hintzman's theory is the "spontaneous rising" of lower responses in the PDS, causing the list to "pop its top off." That assumption seems unpalatably ad hoc, as Hintzman himself recognized. An alternative assumption, close in spirit to the theory we will present, is that the person maintains the several responses at the stimulus terminal node, but there are perturbations over time in their ordering on the list. Thus, although the system might know at the end of training that the PDS at the terminal for the stimulus contains the responses from Lists 3, 2, 1 in that order, with the passage of time the order of the responses is reshuffled to obtain, say, the order 2, 3, 1. We suggest that the reshuffling may be a consequence of conscious ruminations by the subject about the material he has learned. We will discuss these details in Chapter 15.

The Type-Token Distinction

For our purposes, two further ideas are to be noted in the EPAM (or SAL) model. One of these is the type-token distinction introduced by Simon and Feigenbaum (1964); similar notions have been adopted by all later neo-associationist models. EPAM represents any complex idea in all its complexity only once, at what is called its "type-image." Once the complex pattern or idea is familiarized (by forming a type-image of it), EPAM can use it as a unit in the construction of new images. But in these later, constructive efforts, EPAM only requires a token image which points to the location in the network of the original type-image.

The necessity for having this distinction arose in EPAM-II, which stores a representation of the stimulus (a partial copy or "image") at that terminal node to which the stimulus is sorted. This image is said to be "the internal informational representation of an external stimulus configuration that the learner has stored in memory [Simon & Feigenbaum, 1964, p. 386]." In language very reminiscent of John Locke, they say, "An image may be elementary or compound. A compound image has, as components, one or more elementary or compound images which may themselves be familiar and which possess their own terminal nodes in the discrimination net [p. 386]." Thus, Simon and Feigenbaum have reintroduced the elementary and complex ideas of classical associationism, but with the type-token distinction added. In this way, EPAM deals directly with what we earlier called the Paradox of Mill's House, which illustrates the need for higher-order elements or nodes.

Critical Comments on EPAM

Critical remarks could be lodged against EPAM concerning its deficiencies as a general model for perceptual pattern recognition and as a general model of an associative information store. As a model of perceptual recognition we can find at least four deficiencies. First, it is clear that serial discrimination nets place far too much reliance on veridical identification of single stimulus features in a strong order of priority. Thus, if one or more of the high-priority features are not identified or are misidentified by the stimulus analyzers which supply a description list to EPAM, then there is little hope that the pattern will be correctly identified by a serial sorting tree. But we know that human pattern recognition typically operates with much redundant information, so that character perception may be accurate with an exceedingly blurred or degraded stimulus input (e.g., as from a brief visual flash of a word or from a fragmentary visual pattern). This suggests that we typically rely on multiple redundant cues rather than a few critical ones for stimulus recognition. This is the decision strategy implemented in the Pandemonium model of pattern recognition (Selfridge, 1959). Second, as a model for pattern perception, EPAM appears to be lacking a recognition mechanism which enables it to "know" whether or not it has previously seen the current stimulus. Every stimulus, no matter whether novel or old, gets sifted in a definite path through the sorting tree, with some subobjects but not others being positively identified, finally ending at a terminal node already filled in by a previous response. In this sense, the system always has a ready classification and response for any and all stimuli; but it is unable to decide that a particular stimulus pattern has never been seen before. Third, the model is not now formulated with sufficient complexity to permit the operation of a prevailing semantic context to bias its perceptions of words in context. Fourth, the model performs static recognition of single objects or characters, but is inadequate for dealing with realistic scenes containing multiple objects arranged in depth in a variety of relations.

More serious objections may be lodged against EPAM as a theory of our memory store. Whether or not it is a plausible model for the content-addressability needed for the units of a human memory, it fails many of the desiderata for an extendable theory of human memory. Although it is clear how EPAM learns nonsense syllables, it is not clear how EPAM learns word pairs, or serial lists of words, or propositions expressed in sentences. No analysis of semantics or word meanings or reference is suggested. The only relationship that apparently is recordable in EPAM is the fact that particular subobjects cooccur; that is, it can record that a pattern "is composed of" subobjects *a, b, c,* etc. Since there is no word-meaning store, it is unable to record new predications and is unable to deal with questions relevant to that factual base; it can say only which elements cooccurred with or followed which other elements. Of course, EPAM was not designed to deal with language processing and question answering; therefore we are not being entirely fair in pointing out its deficiencies in this respect. Conceivably, one could develop a semantically based EPAM, where the meaning of a word is the series of semantic feature tests it can pass in being sorted, and where a proposition is recognized as already known by being sorted through a network of concepts linked by relational predicates. That kind of approach to semantic memory has not been followed so far as we know. Insofar as it appears tractable, it would seem rather like the semantic network models of Quillian (1968, 1969). We turn now to reviewing Quillian's work because of its truely seminal role in the development of recent simulation models of semantic memory.

4.3. THE TEACHABLE LANGUAGE COMPREHENDER

Quillian's theoretical ideas have been given two major statements (Quillian, 1968, 1969); we shall concentrate here on the model, described in his 1969 paper, called the Teachable Language Comprehender (or TLC). First, let us try to determine in what sense TLC is a model of memory. In addressing this question, Figure 4.3 will serve as a useful aid. The figure is solely concerned with the processing of linguistic material since this has been Quillian's primary concern. To simplify matters, it is supposed that the linguistic data which a person must process may either be an *input* to be coded and stored into memory, or a *probe* requesting information from memory. In either case, the raw linguistic data must be subjected to some analysis to transform it into a format which can be interpreted and used by the memory. If the received linguistic form is an input, it is to be encoded as a new addition to the existing memory structure; if it is a probe, the memory component is to produce a suitable answer as output. The memory's *output* is transformed by the language generation routine into a form suitable for speaking or writing.

Language Analysis

In his published work, Quillian has mainly focused on the role that memory is to play in language analysis. It is important, therefore, to understand the theoretical biases that have determined his approach to language analysis. The linguistic input is structured sequentially or linearly in time. Quillian realized that, while this structure is suitable for production by our oral apparatus, it tends to hide all sorts of meaning relationships that may obtain between nonadjacent words, concepts, or phrases in the sentence. In terms of a distinction usually attributed to Chomsky (1957), the *surface structure* of a sentence is the raw linguistic material, but it must be analyzed into a *deep structure* that more clearly reflects the important semantic distinctions and logical relationships among the concepts that are being asserted in the surface string. Accepting the metatheoretical commitments of transformational grammar (e.g., Katz & Postal, 1964), some computational linguists (e.g., Matthews, 1962; MITRE, 1964; Petrick, 1965), have thought that this analysis should be syntax-based. That is, the input should be parsed according to an ordered set of syntactic rules, the output of this parsing would be a labeled tree of the logicogrammatical relations implicit in the surface form, and then this deep-structure tree would be subjected to a semantic interpretation (see our discussion in Chapter 5). Quillian represents part of the growing disenchantment with this assumption (see also Schank, 1972; Winograd, 1971). Quillian argued

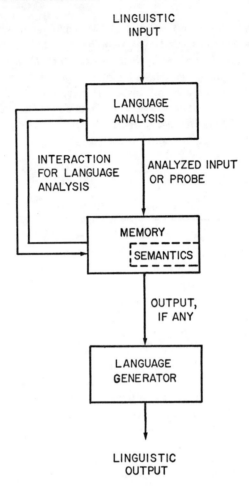

FIG. 4.3. A schematic outline of the flow of information in TLC during the processing of linguistic information.

instead that the analysis should be semantics-based, with the parsing being guided by semantic considerations.

The Nature of a Semantic Theory

Quillian also rejected the conception of semantics which was at that time dominant in the viewpoint of transformational grammar articulated by Katz and Fodor (1963). They had claimed that the semantic information required to properly analyze any language (English in particular) is a very restricted part of the listener's total world knowledge. They felt that the meaning of a word could be expressed as a list of its values on a small set of "universal" semantic features or meaning components such as [± Concrete], [± Animate], and [± Male]. The meaning of a "surface sentence" was supposed to be calculatable from (a) the meanings of the lexical items, (b) their logical interrelationships stipulated by the syntactic deep-structure corresponding to the surface sentence, and (c) a set of "semantic projection rules" whereby the meaning of a phrase is amalgamated from the meanings of its parts, and the meaning of a clause or sentence is amalgamated from the meanings of its constituent phrases. Such semantic approaches are mainly concerned with what might be called the meaning relationships between the words or the "sense" of a sentence as contrasted to the reference of the sentence. Katz and Fodor (1963) rather explicitly bypass the notion of reference in their account of semantics; they notice, correctly, that the reference of an expression depends on the prior knowledge the speaker has about the world (e.g., the referent of "the author of *Hamlet*"), as well as the context of the utterance. Since these components are subject to so much situational variation and idiosyncratic experience of the person processing the utterance, Katz and Fodor argued that the world knowledge shared by speakers could not be systematized, certainly not with sufficient compactness and economy to serve as a reliable basis for a theory of semantics. In brief, they felt that allowing "world knowledge" and reference to enter into one's formal characterization of the semantics of a sentence was a last-resort effort, leading to a hopeless, unanalyzable, and indefinitely circumscribed field for linguistic analysis.

In sharp contrast to this standard transformational position, Quillian supposes that the person, in understanding text, brings to bear nearly all of his "world knowledge," including referents of definite descriptions, the context in which the expression occurs, facts about physics, and myriads of pieces of information related to the concepts in the text. Thus, to harken back to Figure 4.3, Quillian assumes the linguistic analysis routine is drawing information from all of memory, not just a circumscribed semantic subpart. Quillian argues that such information is needed in order for the listener to "fully comprehend" a piece of text. Quillian is not alone in these biases. The Katz and Fodor conception of semantics has been subjected to attack from all sides. From computer science, there have been frequent assertions (e.g., Lindsay, 1963; Winograd, 1971) that the listener must have a "model of the world" if he is to properly understand language. Philosophers of language such as Searle (1969) and Suppes (1971) have argued that the semantic projection rules provide no usable account of the meaning and truth conditions for even the simplest predications. Bolinger (1965) argued that no criteria existed for constraining the set of markers to be finite in number, and that it was misguided to try to circumscribe the meaning of a word by a few of its general features. The generative semanticists (see our discussion in Section 5.3) have challenged both the assumption about the primacy of syntax over semantics and the failure to consider reference. Olson (1970), from a more psychological point of view, argued that semantic judgments about ambiguity, anomaly, and paraphrase could not be properly analyzed without notions of reference, of the speaker's world knowledge, and of the situational context of the utterance.

So, the consensus today seems to be in favor of Quillian's plan to use general world knowledge in language analysis. Thus, language understanding requires a powerful and sophisticated memory system. However, we doubt that the task of language analysis provides a good empirical testing ground for a theory of memory. We suspect that language analysis is a far too diffuse, indeterminate, and unbounded domain within which to try to empirically validate competing hypotheses regarding the structure of human memory. There are simply too many degrees of freedom in the relation between a memory structure and linguistic processing in order for successful language analysis to constrain the memory representation to any significant degree. Testament to this belief is supplied by the swarm of "reasonably successful" (by usual criteria) language-analysis programs that have appeared in the past 5 or so years in computational linguistics. We have in mind the programs of Green and Raphael (1968), Schank (1972), Schwarcz, Burger, and Simmons (1970), Slagle (1965), Winograd (1971), and Woods (1968, 1970), among others. Most of these programs successfully analyze (i.e., semantically interpret) a subset of grammatical English sentences, using some special-purpose "world knowledge" along with simpler semantic information. Most of these programs adopt somewhat different memory representations of important world knowledge, and they clearly have different heuristics, tricks, rules, and procedures for parsing an input sentence. Because successful language analysis depends so heavily on a good set of heuristics or procedures for using knowledge, the structure of the memory representation (which is our concern) tends to occupy a lesser role in these programs.

Quillian's Representation of Memory

Despite our belief that language analysis is an inappropriate testing ground for theoretical claims about the structure of memory, we nonetheless feel that Quillian's proposed structure is a reasonable one that has had an important influence on our thinking and that of other psychologists. The basic building block in Quillian's TLC is the *labeled association* or, as he prefers to call it, "property information" predicated of some unit. The following quotation tells the story:

> First, *all* factual information is encoded as either a "unit" or as a "property." A unit represents the memory's concept of some object, event, idea, assertion, etc. Thus a unit is used to represent anything which can be represented in English by a single word, a noun phrase, a sentence, or some longer body of text. A property, on the other hand, encodes any sort of predication, such as might be stated in English by a verb phrase, a relative clause, or by any sort of adjectival or adverbial modifier [Quillian, 1969, p. 462].

Inspection of Figure 4.4, from Quillian's paper, will help us understand these ideas. In this diagram, words are used to represent "type nodes" for a concept, whereas asterisks denote tokens which point to the type nodes. In this fragment of the mental dictionary, the word *client* points to a unit (the top bracket in the figure) the first element of which points to the immediate superordinate category (or "superset") to which the concept belongs. Thus, the link from *client* through the first element of its defining unit is essentially encoding the fact that a client is a person. The second element in the "client unit" points to a predicate or property that distinguishes clients from other persons, namely, that they employ professionals. In this particular case, the property is equivalent syntactically to a relative clause. A concept could be defined by listing any number of properties

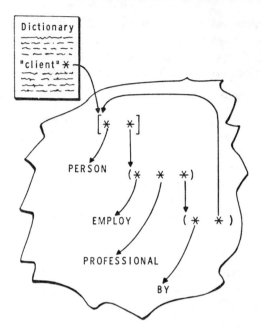

FIG. 4.4. A piece of information in TLC's memory. (From Quillian, 1969.)

after its immediate superset, indicating jointly how the general concept is to be modified or refined to compose the specific concept being defined. Quillian includes as properties not only standard "adjectival" qualities like color, height, weight, sex, etc., but also any verb and its object, or any preposition and its object.

Furthermore, new concepts can be composed by new combinations of old concepts, using a single node to point to an entire conceptual list. Thus, the concept of *John's house* would be composed by a pointer to superset *house*, and properties such as *belongs to John, in Palo Alto, color brown, style rancho*, and so on, with further distinguishing information. The pointer to the superset *house* enables access to all general properties the system may already know about houses, e.g., that they are man-made structures, composed of wood or brick or stucco; having-as-parts walls, floors, roof; are lived in by people, etc. Since there is no limit to the number and nesting of properties that can be associated to a given unit, it is clear that concepts and predicates of practically unbounded complexity could be built up and represented in this memory format.

To return momentarily to our defining criteria of associationism, it is clear that Quillian's memory format adopts some but not all of the metafeatures of associationism. His theory is mechanistic and connectionistic since the memory structure is formed from simple connections between units, and these memory structures exhibit no emergent properties. However, it is consciously not *reductionistic* in that there is no commitment to build up the memory structure from a base set of elementary ideas. He offers instead what might be called the *configurational theory of meaning*; that is, every unit in the network is defined only in terms of other units in the network. Such systems, like a dictionary in a foreign language for the nonspeaker, are forever cut off from reference to the sensory world. Clearly such a memory has to be interfaced eventually to a perceptual component, but Quillian willingly postpones that issue. For that reason his theory would not be classified as *sensationalistic* in its present form.

Language Analysis in TLC

The thrust of Quillian's work was to try to do as much linguistic analysis as possible by semantic means alone, before any kind of syntactic information is brought to bear in interpreting the sentence. Also, Quillian wants the output of the language-analysis routine to have the same structure or format as the information found in memory, since this will facilitate recording the new information in memory.

Quillian (1969) writes that there are three principal obstacles to the task of language comprehension:

1. Since words usually have multiple meanings, how is one (or some set) of these to be selected to serve as superset of the word's new unit? (In other words, precisely which old concepts are referred to in this piece of text?)

2. How is TLC to compose properties adequate to express what the text asserts about these concepts?

3. Because, in continuous text, a great many words refer to things discussed earlier in the same text, how is TLC to know when this occurs so that it can somehow amalgamate all the statements made about some given thing throughout a text [p. 464]?

His one mechanism for solving all these problems is the *intersection search*. Collins and Quillian (1972) describe the intersection search as follows:

The locating of paths between concepts, then, is basic to both comprehension and retrieval. Quillian's (1968, 1969) program searches for paths between concepts using what is called an *intersection technique*. This systematically proceeds outward along all the pointers or paths leading from each concept which is referred to by the words in the sentence. Where a word can refer to several different concepts, the search proceeds outward from all these possible concepts (though a less likely meaning of a word starts off more slowly). At each concept encountered as the search proceeds outward, a tag is left indicating where the search originated. Because many different branches are taken at each concept encountered, the search continually widens like a harmless spreading plague. When the search originating from one word encounters a tag originating from another word, a path linking the two concepts has been found. The later in the search a path is found, the longer the path will be. Because the length of paths reflects semantic distance in memory, such a search produces semantically probable paths first. The use of tags in the model is a way to implement in a computer the idea of activation, either in terms of priming concepts or in terms of spreading to related concepts. These are very old ideas in psychology [pp. 326-327].

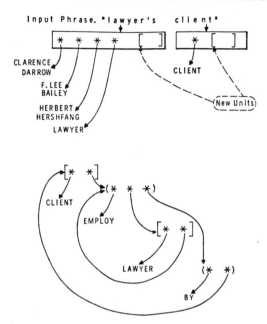

FIG. 4.5. This structure represents TLC's understanding of the phrase "lawyer's client." (From Quillian, 1969.)

TLC supposes that the text that it is reading is essentially directing it to form new concepts. These are formed by placing old concepts into some relation. It does this by creating new units or nodes which point to the appropriate supersets and relations among the appropriate concepts. Figure 4.5, taken from Quillian (1969), illustrates the graph structure built when the system hears the phrase "---lawyer's client---" as a part of a linguistic input. These words access their corresponding units in memory (represented by the boxes in Figure 4.5), and in each of these a new "empty" unit is momentarily created which is to be filled by pointers to the relevant concepts and relations that presumably will be found by the intersection-search routine. In its search it examines properties of each concept. For example, from the *client* graph shown in Figure 4.4, it looks at the attribute EMPLOY and checks for an immediate connection to LAWYER. Since it will find no immediate connection here, the program turns from the attribute EMPLOY to consideration of its value, PROFESSIONAL, and checks this candidate for any word in the input text it can identify with PROFESSIONAL. It discovers that it can identify LAWYER with PROFESSIONAL since it knows, as another fact in memory, that lawyers are professionals. So TLC tentatively identifies LAWYER with CLIENT in the graph structure diagrammed in Figure 4.5 to get the "client employs lawyer" relation.

Identification of this relationship found in the input is only tentative until certain syntactic information or inflections of these words and their environments of other words are checked out. These features will determine whether the relation of the two words is really to be formed, or whether they are just two words that chance to fall close to one another in a surface utterance but which bear no significant relation to one another in the intended meaning. These features are checked out in various ways. For example, there are so-called "form tests," such as whether *client* comes before *lawyer* (e.g., compare *lawyer's wife* with *wife's lawyer*), whether they are separated by a particular function word like *of*, whether one or another of the text words has a particular ending, etc. A form test can be stored with a property; for instance, a test form associated with the verb EMPLOY checks that the text word identified with the property's value (EMPLOY-LAWYER) have an *'s* as its ending and be followed immediately by the source word (*client*). If a battery of such tests are passed by the input text, then the tentative relation found earlier is considered acceptable, and the text is "understood" according to the structural relationships in Figure 4.5. Any further anaphoric references to and predications about this "lawyer's client" in the text will be attached to the concept thus created.

The advantage of Quillian's semantics-based approach is that it will understand in appropriately different ways phrases that are identical in syntactic construction but different in their underlying meaning. Although the system understands *lawyer's client* as a client who employs a lawyer, it does not misunderstand *young client* as a client who employs a youth, but rather interprets it as *a client whose age is young*. It also correctly understands by its form tests the difference between *doctor's lawyer* and *lawyer's doctor*. The intersection search finds and accepts quite different connection pathways for such expressions. Quillian (1969) shows 14 such examples of the system's correct understanding, mainly of two-word phrases, but also a few full sentences. But it is difficult to tell from such selected examples how really effective Quillian's intersection-search model is. His reported examples are surely nonrandom, and, in any case, their success must rest heavily upon the peculiarities of the subset of English he had loaded into TLC when it worked on these examples.

In searching for weaknesses of a "parsing" model, one usually looks for counterexample sentences for which a given "parsing" theory will fail. In the case of Quillian's intersection model, the counterexamples would be those in which two otherwise highly associated concepts that are close together in the text are nonetheless implicitly dissociated by the surrounding text. Winograd (1971) offers a class of counterexamples, using sentences of the type "He hated the landlord so much that he decided to move into the house on Harvard St." It would be difficult to restrain TLC's intersection search from locking onto the close association between *landlord* and *house*, concluding incorrectly that the fellow in question was moving into rather than out of the landlord's house.

The Superset Relation

Quillian was very much concerned with the efficient structuring of information in memory. For instance, he introduced the type-token distinction into TLC to avoid reduplicating concepts throughout the network. He also used instance-to-superset associations to streamline the efficiency of the model's representation of knowledge. The subordinate concepts of a particular superset usually share a great many features. For example, all birds have wings, feathers, beaks, and lay eggs. Therefore, great efficiency would be gained if these properties were stored once with the superordinate concept rather than duplicated repeatedly with each of the many subordinate concepts. The superset relation may be used to infer that the subordinate concept (e.g., canary) has the property (e.g., feathers) stored with the superordinate concept (i.e., bird).

These superset relations are extremely important for Quillian's model of comprehension. Recall, for instance, that the *lawyer's client* phrase was understood because the system identified a relation between the two concepts at the intersection *professional*, which is a superset of *lawyer*. As Quillian (1969) says:

> The first condition which two units must meet to be identifiable [for comprehension] is that they have what we call a "superset intersection in memory." This is said to occur:
>
> 1) If the two units are the same unit.
>
> 2) If one unit is superset of the other, or superset of the superset of the other, or superset of that, etc. In this case, we will say that one unit lies directly on the "superset chain" of the other.
>
> 3) If the two units' superset chains merge at some point [p. 467].

The TLC breadth-first search strategy is designed to find superset intersections between the units under current consideration. This strategy uses the general rule that set inclusion is a transitive relation and any property ascribed to a general class is true of every subset, instance, or individual of that class.

There is no doubt that the superset relation is a very important means for storing and retrieving information in memory efficiently. A single property which applies to a class need not be attached redundantly to every single instance of that class. However, it is doubtful that information is stored in human memory as efficiently as Quillian was advocating, i.e., that general properties are associated only to the general class of instances. On the contrary, it seems that we frequently do store with subordinate concepts the information that is also stored with the superordinate concepts. For instance, it is highly implausible when we report that humans have color vision, that we are inferring this from the fact that humans are primates and that all primates have color vision. Our point is that if information has been stored at an instance-node, and has frequently been asserted or predicated of that instance in the person's linguistic community, then there is little reason to suppose that the "instance-to-predicate" link will be *detached* just because the person has learned a more general predication that implies this link. The difference between Quillian's and our presuppositions also concerns the relative costs of storage versus inference; we feel that in the human brain, storage is cheap and inference (of any great degree) is bothersome and costly, whereas in a computer, inference or deduction is relatively cheap whereas storage space is scarce and dear.

A difficulty with the superset relation, as Quillian uses it, is that it is a hybrid that blurs important conceptual distinctions. Quillian sometimes uses "superset" as it is normally used in mathematics, to refer to a set that properly contains another set, e.g., *mammal* is a superset of *dog*. At other times, he uses the superset relation to convey the mathematical relation of set membership. For instance, he claims that *lawyer* is a superset of *Clarence Darrow*. Finally, Quillian (1969) uses the same relation to express a phase in the life span of a single individual:

> Thus suppose one wished to construct a new unit to represent Joe Smith as a boy, or one to represent Joe Smith from the point of view of his wife, or one to represent Joe Smith when angry. Each of these could be constructed as a new unit having as superset a pointer the previous Joe-Smith Unit...[p. 463].

It is clear why Quillian wants to express all these diverse relations by the single superset relation. Each relation appears to have the same inference potential; that is, if a property is true of an item's superset, it should be true of the item itself. Nonetheless, it is not overly technical or picayune to complain about Quillian's use of the superset relation to express these three different conceptual relations. Quillian's model is designed to be able to express the knowledge that we have about the world. Part of our world knowledge is the ability to systematically identify and distinguish situations or propositions which express proper superset relations, set-membership relations, and different phases of a single individual's life. Such information would not selectively be retrievable if all these relations were to be expressed in memory by "superset."

Moreover, it turns out that the true superset relation and the set-membership relation do not have identical inferential properties. For instance, the proper superset relation is transitive, whereas the set-membership relation is not. For example, a dog is a mammal and a mammal is a living thing, so therefore a dog is a living thing. However, it does not follow from *Spot is a dog*, and *dog is a species* that *Spot is a species*. This confusion of set inclusion and set membership is found in a number of memory models including that of Rumelhart, Lindsay, and Norman (1972) which will be reviewed next. The distinction between the two relations will be carefully made in our memory model.

Quillian's Contributions

Although we have been rather critical of Quillian, we should conclude our review by emphasizing again the importance of his work as a source of many good ideas for later models. Among these seminal ideas one might list the following:

1. Quillian emphasized the notion of memory as a propositional network structure that contains our total world knowledge. This contrasted sharply with the prevailing conception in experimental psychology where memory is viewed as a haphazard collection of habits or traces. Quillian further argued for the importance of that world knowledge to the task of language analysis.

2. He reintroduced the concept of labeled associations or properties. While a similar notion is to be found in earlier language-analysis programs, Quillian was the first to make the identification between property information and the associations that have dominated in psychology.

3. He developed the notion of the "deep-structure" of the sentence as the structure of its conceptual representation in memory. Function words are to be represented in memory by labels on the associative links and/or by differences in graph configuration.

4. He emphasized that the output of the linguistic analysis routine should be in the same representational formalism as the structure of memory. This was to facilitate the encoding of the sentence into memory.

5. He successfully argued for efficiency as an important motivating principle in determining the structural characteristics of memory. He identified the importance of "superset" and similar relations in the efficient structuring of memory. He argued for "inference" as a means for reducing memory storage, as a way to answer questions, and as implicitly involved in language comprehension.

Related Psychological Models

Quillian's model was proposed as a program for natural language analysis. It helped overthrow the "syntactic parsing" viewpoint that had prevailed in computational linguistics up till that time, and it pointed the way for the introduction of more semantics into language-analysis programs. Since Quillian's initial paper, several other language-analysis programs have appeared which use, with more or less success, interactions between the syntactic and semantic components to effect analysis of linguistic input. As mentioned earlier, these include programs written by Woods (1968), Schwarcz, Burger, and Simmons (1970), Slagle (1965), Schank (1972), Winograd (1971), and Green and Raphael (1968). Simmons (1970) provides a review of most of the programs developed before 1969. The programs due to Woods, Winograd, and Schank are reviewed in Chapter 5. These programs are within the tradition of computational linguistics, with the efficiency and power of the heuristics for syntax parsing being of central concern. But there is relatively little concern in these programs for how human memory might be organized or how one might test experimentally a few of the many assumptions embedded in these programs. There have appeared a few programs in the past decade which are explicitly concerned with simulation of human memory: ones by Reitman, Grove, and Shoup (1964) and by Frijda and Meertens (1969) which were more concerned with thinking and verbal analogies than with learning; a proposed program by Kintsch (1972b) which adopts a case-grammar propositional base as a lexical deep-structure, but which is addressed more to semantic organization and production rules than to learning; and finally, a program by Rumelhart, Lindsay, and Norman (1972) which represents memory as a network of caselike relationships among concepts.

These several theories have been written largely independently of one another. Since we are working on a similar model, it is clear that such network models for simulating human memory are a current "Zeitgeist" in theoretical psychology. Frijda's (1972) excellent review of this class of models serves to gel, to concentrate, and to focus the aims of the various theoretical programs on memory models. Except for the latter program by Rumelhart et al., these theories are less fully formulated than Quillian's, and each is notably lacking in supporting data (however, see Kintsch, 1972a). Rather than reviewing all these theories, we shall focus on the Rumelhart et al. (1972) theory, because it is in some ways the most ambitious and it is also the most closely related to our own theoretical orientation. Rumelhart, Lindsay, and Norman have dubbed their program ELINOR, and we will so call it in our review.

4.4. ELINOR

The basic building block of ELINOR is the *n-ary relation*, written formally as R(*a, b, ..., n*), which is intended to encode elementary linguistic propositions. For instance, "The rock crushed the hut" would be encoded as a ternary relation, CRUSH (rock, past, hut). Figure 4.6 illustrates how these *n*-ary relations are represented in memory. The relation R is connected to its *n* arguments by *n* labeled associations. Each association is labeled with a name that indicates the semantic role of the argument in the relation. For Figure 4.6, the relation R is the main verb, and the links to the nouns are labeled by the case role they play with respect to the verb of the proposition. Inspection of Figure 4.6 will show that any *n*-ary relation can be decomposed into *n* labeled pairs of the form <*a* r *b*>, meaning "element *a* has relation r to element *b*." For the proposition in Figure 4.6, the labeled associations are <crush, instrument, rock>, <crush, time, past>, and <crush, object, hut>. In making this identification between their representation and the labeled association, Rumelhart et al. have made explicit the close connection between their model and traditional associative conceptions. However, they introduce a major revision to past associative theories by the imposition of a propositional structure on these associative links. This assumption of "propositional well-formedness" has been made by a number of recent models including our own.

Figure 4.6 uses what Rumelhart et al. call their *longhand* notation for memory structures. However, for some structures illustrated in their paper they use a *shorthand* notation which can be adopted when the relations are binary. To contrast the two, the longhand representation of a binary relation is given in Panel *a* of Figure 4.7 where relation R connects to its two arguments *A* and *B* by associations labeled L_1 and L_2. The shorthand representation is shown in Panel *b* where a single link between the two arguments is labeled with the relation R.

Unlabeled Graphs?

A brief digression on notation may be illuminating here. In private discussions with us, Norman and Rumelhart have suggested that labeled associations can always be rewritten as unlabeled graphs, by defining the label itself as a node. For example, Panel *a* of Figure 4.7 could be decomposed into the graph structure in Panel *c*. In Panel *c*, instead of associating a relation R to its argument *A* by L_1, R is first associated to L_1 by an unlabeled association. It has been proposed that in this

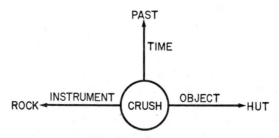

FIG. 4.6. The encoding given by ELINOR from "The rock crushed the hut."

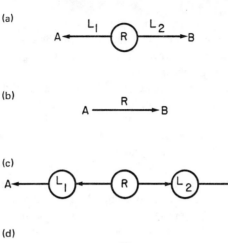

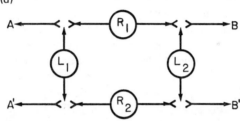

FIG. 4.7. Various ways to encode binary relations in ELINOR: (*a*) longhand; (*b*) shorthand; (*c*) An extension of longhand which eliminates labels; and (*d*) a logically adequate version of (*c*).

manner labeled associations can be entirely eliminated from the network. If this were a viable position, why then have we been so careful to distinguish the labeled association as a quantum departure from the theoretical machinery of classical associationism?

The issue hinges on the difference between logical equivalence as contrasted to computational efficiency for the two classes of networks. A labeled associative network can be searched much more efficiently than the unlabeled network, particularly for retrieving the answers to questions of the form "Retrieve the L_1 of relation R." For the input "The rock crushed the hut," such questions would be "What object was crushed?" or "What instrument did the crushing?" In the labeled graph of Panel *a* in Figure 4.7, the argument A can be directly retrieved by evoking the L_1 function (link) starting at node R. In our model HAM, for example, there is a primitive function called "GET (R of a)" which outputs a list of *b*'s that are stored as $<a \ R \ b>$ relational triples in memory. Consider, however, the unlabeled associative structure in Panel *c* of Figure 4.7. When the command is GET (L_1 of R), it will "fire off" or search down all links out of node R, looking for the node L_1, all of which can be a very time-consuming operation if R occurs in many propositions. Second, consider the dilemma of the system once L_1 is reached from node R in Panel *c*. If L_1 refers to a case-grammatical relation like instrument or location, there will be multiple paths leading from L_1, one path corresponding to each time the case-grammatical relation was used in a different proposition. The system will have no basis for selecting the correct path out of L_1. So the system diagramed in Panel c of Figure 4.7 does not really provide a viable structure for memory retrieval.

A simple method to patch up the Panel c structure to avoid this difficulty (of not knowing where to search from node L_1) is to introduce the familiar type-token distinction. We have a separate token node for each instance of the relation. These tokens are all connected to a single type node. This is illustrated in Figure 4.7d, where circles around letters denote type nodes, while angular brackets denote token nodes that point to their corresponding type nodes. The diagram shows two relational triplets: A is the L_1 of R, and B is the L_2 of R. The type-token distinction is shown for each unit.

Let us see now how the system in Figure 4.7d would respond to the command to "Get the L_1 of R_1." Suppose that the command sends signals in parallel out along all connections out of the type nodes of L_1 and R_1. A monitor watches in parallel for an intersection node somewhere in the system, indicated as that node which receives two signals at once. The top angular node that is encoding "the L_1 of R_1" will thus be selected; then, following the arrows out of that intersection node will lead the machine eventually to the type node called A.

Such a system, incorporating the structure of Figure 4.7d and a Quillian-like intersection search routine, is at least a workable memory-search model. However, the unlabeled associations are purchased at the cost of requiring many more links, requiring parallel activation of all paths from the retrieval cues, and monitoring of a vast network of nodes in parallel to detect an intersection node. We consider those costs too much to pay for unlabeled associations.

Relations versus Concepts

While ELINOR can be cast in an associative framework, it contains many distinctions that are not found in past associative representations. One is the distinction between *concepts* and the *relations* that take these concepts as arguments. (Kintsch, 1972b, also uses a similar distinction in a central way.) Rumelhart et al. (1972) describe the difference as follows:

> A concept is a node in the memory system which corresponds to an object or idea that can be named or described. Whereas relations have free variables (ranges which must be filled), concepts have none. They are complete by themselves. Concepts act as the constants which replace the ranges of relations to generate descriptions of particular events. A relation with a particular set of instances as its ranges is itself a concept (of the type called a *proposition*) which can enter as a constituent in still more complex events [p. 216].

Examples of relations are verbs and comparative adjectives. One motivation for the concept versus relation distinction is an observation that is often attributed to Fillmore (1968). He noted that within a simple proposition there is usually one item, namely, the relation or the verb, that has the power to determine what other elements should appear in the proposition. For instance, "go" requires a direction, "hit" an object, "give" a recipient, etc. The other items, the concepts which are constrained by the relation, do not have the power to similarly determine what other elements may appear in the proposition with them. In this sense, as the graph structure in ELINOR indicates, the relation is the "central" element of the proposition.

The Meaningstore

In contrast to other associative models, there is a distinction in ELINOR between general world knowledge and dictionary information about what a word means. The latter is stored in an area of memory called the *meaningstore*. The definition of a relation is essentially a listing of the type of arguments (noun cases) it can take plus a statement of a superordinate relation that contains it as an instance. Later unpublished work by Rumelhart, Norman, and their students has concentrated quite intensively on the representation of particular verb meanings. Consider, as an example, the definition of "fall" that is given in Figure 4.8. The gist of the notation is that "fall" is defined as a movement that requires an object, takes gravity as an instrument, and requires a downward path. Other verbs are similarly defined, by listing a superordinate verb, distinguishing adverbs, plus the noun cases the verb may take. In contrast, the definition of a concept consists basically of a series of properties attributed to it. For example, consider the definition of "mountain" in Figure 4.9. To paraphrase the definition, a mountain is a natural formation found on the surface of the earth, and it rises abruptly to a high summit.

There are two important features to note about these definitions. First, they are encoded in the same associative formalism that is used to encode linguistic propositions. Second, they can be distinguished from the general mass of known facts by virtue of a DEF arrow pointing from the word's type node to its defining structure. Therefore, unlike the Quillian model, there is a separation between the

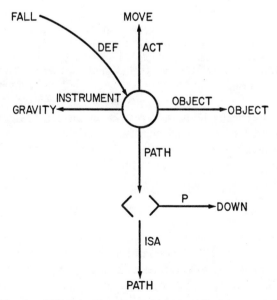

FIG. 4.8. Definition of "fall" in ELINOR.

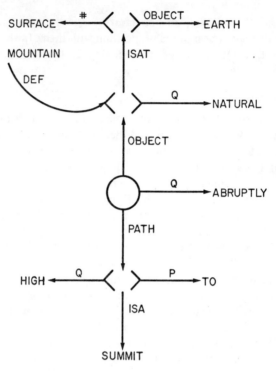

FIG. 4.9. Definition of "mountain" in ELINOR.

semantic component versus general world knowledge, or between analytic versus synthetic information.

Concepts, Events, and Episodes

Rumelhart et al. (1972) also make a distinction between what they call *concepts, events,* and *episodes* as follows:

> When examining the kinds of things that must be represented in a model of human LTM [Long Term Memory], it is convenient to distinguish among three classes of information: *concepts, events,* and *episodes. Concepts* refer primarily to particular ideas. An *event* is action-based, denoting a scenario with its associated actors and objects. An *episode* is a series of events or actions. Although these different classes of information can be logically distinguished, they are all represented in the same memory format [p. 203].

It would appear that in this passage Rumelhart et al. are using concepts to refer to *both* what they call concepts and what they call relations in other parts of their paper. It would appear that an "event" simply denotes a relation plus associations to the concepts that serve as its arguments. For instance, Figure 4.6 would encode the event described by "The rock crushed the hut." In other words, an event corresponds to what they call at other times a proposition. But in an earlier quote (Rumelhart et al., 1972, p. 18) they noted that a proposition is just another type of concept. Their terminology is somewhat confused between the four terms *concept, relation, proposition,* and *event.* The episode, however, introduces new complexities into their model that have yet to be considered. By means of the episode, they are attempting to make systematic the conceptual macrostructure in which events are embedded. They introduce propositional connectives like WHILE and THEN to make explicit the causal and temporal relations between the various events. Thus, an episode might be of the form "Event E_1 WHILE Event E_2 THEN Event E_3 THEN Event E_4." Basically, the connectives THEN and WHILE are just labels on associations that connect propositions. An illustration of an encoded episode is shown in Figure 4.10 from the Rumelhart et al. paper. The episode consists of five base events or propositions strung together by WHILE and THEN connectives: (John sees Mary) WHILE (Mary is eating Saturday noon at Luigi's) THEN (John pulls a knife) THEN (John stabs Mary) THEN (Mary dies).

The episode structure permits ELINOR to encode *procedures* that it can evoke later to operate on the world or on its own memory structure. For instance, a cooking recipe could be stored in memory as strings of commands: "Add 1 cup of flour, THEN add an egg WHILE gently stirring, THEN ...." With the necessary interpretive routines defined, ELINOR could use this memory representation to bake a cake. This potential of ELINOR is particularly intriguing because it seems to open up for associative models a broader domain of applicability than just memory. In particular, this provides a means to store and initiate skilled action sequences. Also, insofar as cognitive problem-solving techniques are "internal action" routines (see Bartlett, 1958), like a "recipe" on how to solve particular classes of problems, the learning of procedures can be used to represent the acquisition of problem-solving skills, learning (study) skills, and so on.

Generalization and Discrimination

Following strong in Quillian's footsteps, Rumelhart et al. plan to outfit their model with procedures for inductive generalization. The occasion for evoking the

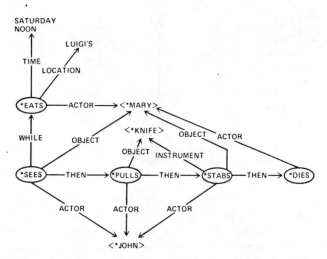

FIG. 4.10. Encoding of an episode. (From Rumelhart, Lindsay, & Norman, 1972.)

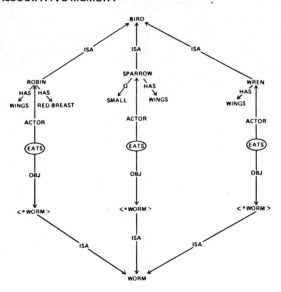

FIG. 4.11. *Above:* A memory structure in ELINOR that is "ripe" for spontaneous inductive generalization. *Below:* the memory structure after the generalization and after further facts are acquired. (From Rumelhart, Lindsay, & Norman, 1972.)

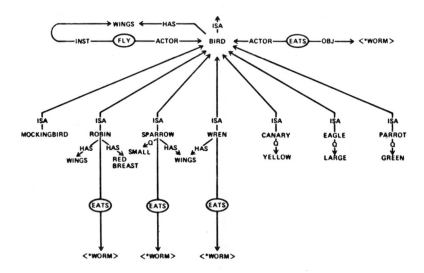

procedures is that the system has learned a number of separate facts about instances of a more general concept. Figure 4.11 from the Rumelhart et al. paper illustrates the procedure. Suppose that the system has learned separate facts about robins, sparrows, and wrens; e.g., that a sparrow is a bird, is small, has wings, and eats worms. This is the situation depicted in the upper part of Figure 4.11. It is supposed that a "generalization routine" is initiated which searches for inductive generalizations regarding what the system knows. It first retrieves all known instances of a general concept (following the inverse ISA paths) and checks these for common predicates. If a predicate is discovered which is shared by a sufficient number of instances and is not contradicted by any, then a generalization is formed and that predicate is promoted up to the next higher level and attached to the general class node.

The bottom half of Figure 4.11 shows that this generalization has been made for the properties "eats worms" and "has wings," based on the information known explicitly about robins, sparrows, and wrens. It should be noted that in promoting the shared predicate to the superset, it is not "erased" from the instance nodes to which it was formerly attached.

The influence of generalizations can be seen if we now give the system a new piece of subset information, e.g., that a canary is a bird. The system then can infer that canaries probably have wings and eat worms; similarly, the same predicates are inferable for any other objects we introduce to the system as birds. It is this inferential capability that gives generalizations their "generative" power; the system now "knows" many propositions that are true. But it knows these by inference rather than by having stored them directly.

Suppose, on the other hand, that in attempting to generalize over a class of instances, the system comes across conflicting information. For instance, a particular predicate is true for a substantial number of instances but implicitly or explicitly is false for other instances. In this case, the system will *subdivide* the general concept into the two subclasses of instances, by creating two new subclass nodes representing the two sets of instances. The distinguishing property that triggered the subdivision is then attached to that subclass node representing the instances for which that predicate is true, whereas the conflicting instances are linked to the other subclass. What is not clear in the Rumelhart et al. paper is what new linkages are made for instances which have no information associated to them regarding the candidate predicate, so the system does not know whether the proposed generalization is true or false of such instances. Perhaps these unknown instances are not linked to either subclass, but rather maintain only their link to the general class node.

Now, in the usual situation, our familiarity with examples of a given class grows slowly over time. Therefore, it will frequently be the case that the ELINOR system would form a generalization on the basis of early evidence which is contradicted by later instances. After inducing from evidence on robins, wrens, and sparrows that all birds can fly, the system overgeneralizes by supposing that penguins and ostriches (which are birds) can also fly. Rumelhart et al. suppose that the system handles such contradictory evidence not by erasing the generalization, nor by subdividing the class of birds—as they say, "it is too late for sub-division"—but by attaching the contradictory evidence directly to the offending instances. Thus, if we later asked the system whether a penguin could fly, it would answer *no* from a direct link to the *penguin* node and block the answer *yes* obtainable by a two-step inference through the *bird* superset.

Our opinion is that these procedures for generalization and discrimination in ELINOR are rather poorly worked out; they amount to little more than an inexact restatement of the supposed canons of induction discussed by philosophers for centuries. Moreover, the events which will trigger off the making of a generalization are not well identified. Our personal opinion is that high-powered generalizations are not frequent occurrences in human thought (otherwise science would be easy); when generalizations do occur, they are triggered by specifically motivating problems or queries. Most of the generalizations that the average child or layman knows are ones he has been told directly. In our model, HAM, we were not therefore so concerned with simulating the inductive capabilities of the human mind.

The Production Rules

From the description so far, it is clear that ELINOR is *connectionistic* in the associative tradition. It is also *mechanistic*. In fact, Rumelhart et al. addressed themselves in earnest to the traditional mechanistic task of associationism, viz., how to construct complex ideas from simpler ones. They formalize no less than 14 rules for the construction of new concepts and relations from old ones. Some of these are rules for modifying old concepts to form new concepts, some are for modifying old relations to form new relations, and some are rules for forming new modifiers ("operators") themselves out of combinations of more primitive elements, e.g., *tiny → very/small* and *partly → not/completely*. To give one illustration, the following rule generates a new relation from an old one:

$$R(V_1, ..., V_n) \rightarrow O/R(V_1, ..., V_n),$$

where O is an operator, R is a relation, and the V_i are argument variables. This says that one relation, R, can be rewritten in terms of a modification of a second relation. Thus, for example, the relation stroll(actor, path, time) is derived from slowly/walk(actor, path, time). Operators of this type are typically what we otherwise call "adverbs."

It is important to try to get clear on just what these formation rules do for the ELINOR system. Rumelhart et al. (1972) state that the rules "explicitly describe the *procedures for generating* new concepts and relations from old ones [p. 212, our italics]." But quite clearly they do not achieve this; they are not generative procedures, but rather descriptions of the type of structures they wish to admit into memory. The rules do not describe the processes governing the construction of new structures, nor do they characterize the causal events that trigger the use of particular rules. To see this, consider the rule illustrated above, relating *stroll* to *slowly/walk*. When would that particular rule be used in the memory? So far as we can tell, it would be used only when ELINOR was expanding its "meaningstore" by listening to definitions, so that it would hear and assimilate propositions such as "to *stroll* is defined as to *walk slowly*" or the like.

These "formation rules" of Rumelhart et al. therefore appear to be only a classification system which abstractly characterizes the kinds of complex relational structures admissible in ELINOR's memory. It is almost as though they had proceeded as follows: Select a concept which one would like to have in the internal lexicon of ELINOR, say, *lamb*; figure out how to define that concept in terms of other concepts, e.g., *young sheep*; generalize the form of the definition-type, e.g., the new concept is a qualifier Q operating on an old concept C; finally, declare the form of the definition-type to be a "formation-rule" for forming new concepts from old ones, e.g., $C \rightarrow Q(C)$. However rules are not operative procedures. They have about the same status as production rules in a phrase-structure grammar, i.e., they state what are "acceptable" structures (for the meaningstore, in this case). Later in their paper, Rumelhart et al. seem to agree with this interpretation of their formation rules: "What we have done for this model is to place certain restrictions on the general format that the meaningstore entries must take, and to specify to some extent the kinds of information that must be stored at primary nodes [p. 226]."

Comments on the ELINOR System

Our sketch of the ELINOR system has been necessarily brief and incomplete, and the original paper should be consulted for further details regarding how the type-token distinction is used, how concepts are defined, how memory structures are built up, and how they are interrelated. The authors introduce a rich variety of concepts and hypotheses regarding the structuring of memory.

The ELINOR system as described in the Rumelhart et al. paper would seem to have several deficiencies. Its procedures for inductive generalization and discrimination appear destined to create a rather "messy" memory network in the long run. Second, the "acquisition mechanisms" by which the system learns new information are not specified for propositional information, nor is their linguistic parser specified in the Rumelhart et al. paper. Third, memory search and retrieval schemes are not specified in their paper. Routines are clearly needed to try to match the current linguistic input to information already stored, to determine whether the input is already known, or is true, or is comprehensible and possible. If the input is a question, then a barrage of "memory match-up" and inference routines needs to be specified to get an answer from ELINOR. From personal communications, we understand that these investigators do have programmatic ideas regarding these lacunae of their earlier papers, so we may expect progress reports on all these problems.

A fourth problem with ELINOR is that its authors use the subset-superset relation (which they call the ISA relation) to refer variously to a proper subset relation between classes and to membership of an individual in a set. In our earlier discussion of Quillian, we criticized a similar amalgamation of logical functions carried by this one relation, and the same criticisms apply to the ELINOR system. Basically, the criticism is that since people are aware of and can utilize these differing relations, it is senseless to write a model which does not recognize this distinction at the outset.

To editorialize, perhaps the most disturbing aspect of the ELINOR project is that a group of competent experimental psychologists have produced a model that seems to lack any supporting experimental data. As they confess: "We have been developing a semantic memory system whose support comes from intuitive considerations [Rumelhart et al., 1972, p. 233]." Moreover, the character of these intuitions or their role in model building is not explicated as it frequently is in linguistic investigations. Although they do refer to an experiment by Collins and Quillian (1969) as evidence for their postulate about generalization, that experiment was sensitive only to the existence of a hierarchy of concept subordination which is a characteristic of most semantic-memory models. Besides, subsequent experiments (e.g., Conrad, 1972; Schaeffer & Wallace, 1970—see our discussion in Chapter 12) have placed in doubt the reliability and interpretation of the original result by Collins and Quillian. The Rumelhart et al. paper does not cite any experimental evidence to support the concept versus relation distinction, the structure of "episodes," the encoding of procedures ("recipes") in the data base, or other features distinctive of their model. Rather the paper seems mainly devoted to defining and illustrating a rich variety of concepts and distinctions. Still it is an important "position paper" in cognitive psychology, setting forth the basic goals and approach of what will doubtless be a significant contingent of future researchers.

REFERENCES

Bartlett, F. *Thinking: An experimental and social study.* London: Allen & Unwin, 1958.

Bolinger, D. The atomization of meaning. *Language*, 1965, **41**, 555–573.

Chomsky, N. *Syntactic structures.* The Hague: Mouton, 1957.

Collins, A. M., & Quillian, M. R. Retrieval time from semantic memory. *Journal of Verbal Learning and Verbal Behavior*, 1969, 8, 240–247.

Collins, A. M., & Quillian, M. R. How to make a language user. In E. Tulving & W. Donaldson (Eds.), *Organization of Memory.* New York: Academic Press, 1972.

Conrad, C. Cognitive economy in semantic memory. *Journal of Experimental Psychology*, 1972, **92**, 149–154.

Dodwell, P. C. *Visual pattern recognition.* New York: Holt, Rinehart & Winston, 1970.

Feigenbaum, E. A. Simulation of verbal learning behavior. In E. A. Feigenbaum & J. Feldman (Eds.), *Computers and thought.* New York: McGraw-Hill, 1963.

Fillmore, C. J. The case for case. In E. Bach & R. T. Harms (Eds.), *Universals in linguistic theory.* New York: Holt, Rinehart & Winston, 1968.

Frijda, N. H. Simulation of human long-term memory. *Psychological Bulletin*, 1972, 77, 1–31.

Frijda, N. H., & Meertens, L. A. A simulation model of human information retrieval. In *The simulation of human behavior: Proceedings of a NATO Symposium, Paris, 1967.* Paris: Dunod, 1969.

Green, C., & Raphael, B. Research on intelligent question answering systems. In *Proceedings of the ACM.* Princeton, N. J.: Brandon Systems Press, 1968. Pp. 169–181.

Hewitt, C. *PLANNER.* MAC-M-386, Project MAC, M.I.T. October 1968. Revised August 1970.

Hintzman, D. L. Explorations with a discrimination net model for paired-associate learning. *Journal of Mathematical Psychology*, 1968, 5, 123–162.

Katz, J. J., & Fodor, J. A. The structure of a semantic theory. *Language*, 1963, **39**, 170–210.

Katz, J. J., & Postal, P. N. *An integrated theory of linguistic descriptions.* Cambridge, Mass.: M.I.T. Press, 1964.

Keppel, G. Retroactive and proactive inhibition. In T. R. Dixon & D. L. Horton (Eds.), *Verbal behavior and general behavior theory.* Englewood Cliffs, N. J.: Prentice-Hall, 1968.

Kintsch, W. Abstract nouns: Imagery vs. lexical complexity. *Journal of Verbal Learning and Verbal Behavior*, 1972, **11**, 59–65. (a)

Kintsch, W. Notes on the semantic structure of memory. In E. Tulving & W. Donaldson (Eds.), *Organization of Memory.* New York: Academic Press, 1972. (b)

Kolers, P. A., & Eden, M. *Recognizing patterns.* Cambridge, Mass.: M.I.T. Press, 1968.

Lindsay, R. K. Inferential memory as the basis of machines which understand natural language. In E. Feigenbaum & J. Feldman (Eds.), *Computers and thought*. New York: McGraw-Hill, 1963.

Matthews, G. H. Analysis by synthesis of natural languages. *Proceedings of the 1961 International Conference on Machine Translation and Applied Language Analysis*. London: Her Majesty's Stationary Office, 1962.

McCarthy, J., Abrahams, P. W., Edwards, D. J., Hart, T. P., & Levin, M. I. *Lisp 1.5 programmers manual*. Cambridge, Mass.: M.I.T. Press, 1962.

MITRE. English preprocessor manual. Rep. SR-132, The Mitre Corp., Bedford, Mass., 1964.

Newell, A., Shaw, J. C., & Simon, H. A. Elements of a theory of human problem solving. *Psychological Review*, 1958, 65, 151-166.

Olson, D. R. Language and thought: Aspects of a cognitive theory of semantics. *Psychological Review*, 1970, 77, 257-273.

Petrick, S. R. A recognition procedure for transformational grammars. Unpublished doctoral dissertation, M.I.T., 1965.

Quillian, M. R. Semantic memory. In M. Minsky (Ed.), *Semantic information processing*, Cambridge, Mass.: M.I.T. Press, 1968.

Quillian, M. R. The teachable language comprehender. *Communications of the Association for Computing Machinery*, 1969, 12, 459-476.

Reitman, W., Grove, R. B., & Shoup, R. G. Argus: An information processing model of thinking. *Behavioral Science*, 1964, 9, 270-281.

Rumelhart, D. E., Lindsay, P. H., & Norman, D. A. A process model for long-term memory. In E. Tulving & W. Donaldson (Eds.), *Organization of Memory*. New York: Academic Press, 1972.

Schaeffer, B., & Wallace, R. The comparison of word meanings. *Journal of Experimental Psychology*, 1970, 86, 144-152.

Schank, R. C. Conceptual dependency: A theory of natural-language understanding. *Cognitive Psychology*, 1972, 3, 552-631.

Schwarcz, R. M., Burger, J. F., & Simmons, J. R. A deductive question-answerer for natural language inference. *Communications of the Association for Computing Machinery*, 1970, 13, 167-183.

Searle, J. R. *Speech acts: An essay on the philosophy of language*. Cambridge: Cambridge University Press, 1969.

Selfridge, O. G. Pandemonium: A paradigm for learning. In D. V. Blake & A. M. Vittey (Eds.), *Proceedings of the Symposium on Mechanization of Thought*. London: Her Majesty's Stationary Office, 1959.

Simmons, R. F. Natural language question-answering systems: 1969. *Communications of the Association for Computing Machinery*, 1970, 13, 15-30.

Simon, H. A., & Feigenbaum, E. A. An information processing theory of some effects of similarity, familiarity, and meaningfulness in verbal learning. *Journal of Verbal Learning and Verbal Behavior*, 1964, 3, 385-396.

Slagle, J. R. Experiments with a deductive question-answering program. *Communications of the Association for Computing Machinery*, 1965, 8, 792-798.

Suppes, P. *Semantics of context-free fragments of natural languages*. (Tech. Rep. No. 171, Psychology Series, Institute for Mathematical Studies in the Social Sciences) Stanford, Calif.: Stanford University, March 1971.

Teitlebaum, W., Bobrow, D. G., Hartley, A. K., & Murphy, D. L. BBN-LISP Tenex Reference Manual, July 1971. Bolt, Beranck and Newman Inc.

Winograd, T. Procedures as a representation for data in a computer program for understanding natural language. *M.I.T. Artificial Intelligence Laboratory Project MAC-TR-84*, 1971.

Woods, W. A. Procedural semantics for a question-answering machine. *Proceedings of the 1968 Fall Joint Computer Conference,* 33, 457-471.

Woods, W. A. Transition network grammars for natural language analysis. *Communications of the Association for Computing Machinery*, 1970, 13, 591-606.

5

CURRENT DEVELOPMENTS IN LINGUISTICS

One would expect that human language should directly reflect the characteristics of human intellectual capacities, that language should be a direct "mirror of mind" in ways which other systems of knowledge and belief cannot.

—Noam Chomsky

5.1. PSYCHOLOGY AND LINGUISTICS

It is wise to begin by pointing out that neither our theory nor our research is intended to, or does, say anything definitive about linguistics. In the same vein, it appears that little of the work occurring in linguistics has anything definitive to say about the problems of human memory to which we address ourselves. Nonetheless, it is important that we access the state of affairs, as we see it, in linguistics today. We do this because the major emphasis in our research concerns the way that a memory system deals with linguistic material. Although we occasionally discuss how perceptual materials would be handled in our theory, even these analyses are really determined by the way our model treats linguistic input.

Competence versus Performance Models

There is a famous distinction between competence and performance in linguistics that has been emphasized by Chomsky (1965):

Linguistic theory is concerned primarily with an ideal speaker-listener, in a completely homogeneous speech-community, who knows its language perfectly and is unaffected by such grammatically irrelevant conditions as memory limitations, distractions, shifts of attention and interest, and errors (random or characteristic) in applying his knowledge of the language in actual performance. This seems to me to have been the position of the founders of modern general linguistics, and no cogent reason for modifying it has been offered. To study actual linguistic performance, we must consider the interaction of a variety of factors, of which the underlying competence of the speaker-hearer is only one. In this respect, study of language is no different from empirical investigation of other complex phenomena.

We thus make a fundamental distinction between *competence* (the speaker-hearer's knowledge of his language) and *performance* (the actual use of language in concrete situations). Only under the idealization set forth in the preceding paragraph is performance a direct reflection of competence. In actual fact, it obviously could not directly reflect competence. A record of natural speech will show numerous false starts, deviations from rules, changes of plan in mid-course, and so on. The problem for the linguist, as well as for the child learning the language, is to determine from the data of performance the underlying system of rules that has been mastered by the speaker-hearer and that he puts to use in actual performance [pp. 3-4].

In contrast to the competence models of the linguist, what we will propose in the forthcoming chapters will involve certain aspects of a theory of language performance. Specifically, detailed proposals will be made regarding the way incoming speech is analyzed and represented in memory. This performance model contains specific assumptions about the speaker's linguistic capacities, assumptions that are similar to some controversial ones in linguistics. Therefore, it behooves us to examine how these assumptions are treated in linguistics.

Since our theory is a performance model, the considerations that motivate our theoretical decisions are not identical to the considerations that determine the linguist's competence model. For judging a competence model, the linguist takes as his criteria formal simplicity and ability to account for the intuitions of the language user. An oft-mentioned goal for a linguistic theory is that it be able to explain our judgments of grammaticality or predict which strings of words will be (should be) judged to be grammatical sentences. We do not reject these criteria as uninteresting; rather we feel a greater need to account for memory data, and that has been the determining factor in our research.

In Chapter 8 we will present a model of how HAM would *parse* an incoming sentence. In parsing a sentence, HAM sets up a representation of its information that is appropriate for storage in and retrieval from long-term memory. Thus, we will be primarily concerned with the problems of language analysis and comprehension rather than language generation. This contrasts with much of the formal work in linguistics, which tends to produce models appropriate for language generation (the "speaker") rather than for language comprehension (the "listener"). As Chomsky (1971) points out, current linguistic theories are abstract specifications of language competence and are not really concerned with analysis or generation in the performative sense. However, these linguistic theories are more easily translated into performative models of generation than performative models of analysis. Sections 5.2 and 5.3 review the formal linguistic work of this sort. Section 5.2 reviews the work of Noam Chomsky, which largely set the groundwork for the transformational grammar approach in linguistics. Section 5.3 considers some challenges to Chomsky's conceptions that have arisen within the transformational approach. Finally, Section 5.4 reviews three language-analysis programs from computational linguistics—those of Woods, Winograd, and Schank. Only in such computational linguistic work does one find models suggestive of how language analysis might proceed in the human head. Section 5.4 is very important preparation for Chapter 8, since the parser programmed in HAM is only a psychologically plausible synthesis of work in computational linguistics. The remainder of this initial section will be devoted to considering the classical psychological accounts of language and to discussing a few of their inadequacies.

Traditional Psychological Theories of Language

The most influential psychological accounts of language have all been cast within the general rubric of S-R learning theory. Thus they all make the fatal error of accepting the Terminal Meta-Postulate of associationism (see Chapter 2 for a history of this postulate in associationism and a critique). The Terminal Meta-Postulate, it will be recalled, assumes that associations can exist only between stimuli and responses which are overt or isomorphic derivatives of overt, observable elements. The critique we gave illustrated that linguistic phenomena such as recursive embedding require positing abstract elements that are neither overt nor covert stimuli or responses. For instance, a construction with embedded relative clauses is "The man who seduced the woman who is married to the banker robs banks." The problem created by recursive embeddings is the syntactic dependencies between elements before and after the embedding. In this example, there is a dependency in number between the main subject "man" and the main verb "robs." Because these embeddings are recursive, an indefinite number of terminal elements (i.e., words) may intervene between the dependent elements. The only formal means available to capture dependency between elements separated by arbitrarily many embeddings is by the introduction of nonterminal elements which serve to "keep track of" the dependency commitments and which are only *abstractly* related to the observed output of elements.

For this reason alone, we can know that S-R theories of language are inadequate for representing the complexities of natural language. Still it is worthwhile to consider the basic learning mechanisms that have been postulated to account for language acquisition to see what can be done with them. Although incomplete, these theories reflect attempts to deal with issues that have been largely ignored by linguists and computer scientists. The difficult problem in the psychology of language is to combine the linguist's concern that a theory be sufficient to the complexity of language with the traditional psychological concern that theory meet the necessary conditions of psychological plausibility and experimental validation.

Psychological Theories of Syntax

In linguistics it is common practice to make a distinction between what is called syntax (the rules which determine which linguistic structures are well formed or grammatical) and semantics (the rules which determine what a well-formed linguistic utterance will mean). It is useful to make a similar distinction in our analysis of the traditional theories of S-R psychology. From the behaviorist point of view, an undeniably salient "syntactic" feature of language is that certain types of word sequences are much more likely than others, that the rare sequences are likely to be judged as strange, ungrammatical, or nonsense. It is clearly the task of the behaviorists to explain why this should be so. Their basic explanation is to hypothesize that past instrumental conditioning sequences have set up language habits (e.g., Watson, 1930; Skinner, 1957; Staats, 1968). We say "Please pass the butter" and not "Butter please the pass" because we have been reinforced for saying one and not the other. However, this mechanism, by itself, clearly will not do. Man is notorious for saying sentences that he has never encountered before and therefore never could have been reinforced for uttering.

However, the mere fact of human creativity poses no difficulty for the learning theorist. He need only view the generation of a sentence as the product of a sequence of individual word-to-word associations. That is, each word in the sentence serves as the stimulus for the production of the next word in the sentence. Which words are produced in response to which other words is seen as a reflection of the person's past associative history. For instance, we have been reinforced in the past for saying plural nouns rather than singular nouns after the adjective "two," and so in our speech "cats" and not "cat" will follow "two." The novelty of speech is a consequence of the chaining of such word-to-word associations. The nth word in a sentence may elicit many possibilities as the $(n+1)$st word since the nth word has been associated to many other words. Similarly, there is a large number of $(n+2)$nd words that can be elicited by the $(n+1)$st. While all the first-order sequence (i.e., nth to $[n+1]$st, and $[n+1]$st to $[n+2]$nd) must be based on experience, higher-order sequences (i.e., nth to $[n+1]$st to $[n+2]$nd) can be novel. Staats (1971) draws the habit structure of Figure 5.1 as a conceivable network of word-to-word associations. This would generate such potentially novel sentences as "Give her a red car."

In fact, Staats argues, it is not even necessary that we explicitly learn all the individual word-to-word associations in such a habit structure. For instance, a child might learn to associate "him," "her," and "me" to "give." Then, whenever he heard "give" he would covertly produce all three of these words. As a consequence of occurring overtly together in response to "give," the three words "him," "her," and "me" would become interassociated and form what Staats calls a *response hierarchy*. Then, suppose the child learned to associate "him" to "throw." Now when he heard "throw" he would covertly produce not only "him" but also "her" and "me" which previously were associated to "him." Consequently, "her" and "me" would become associated to "throw" without any overt training trials.

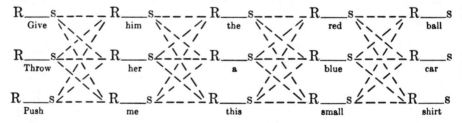

FIG. 5.1. A sequence of response hierarchies that will generate novel sentences. (From Staats, 1971.)

Accepting this conception of how language is acquired, one is soon led into an interest in research on verbal learning using such classic paradigms as the paired-associate task. In this way, it is claimed, we can directly study the basic principles which determine how one word can become a stimulus controlling the emission of another word as a response. One of the prime claims of this book is that this viewpoint completely misses the true significance of verbal learning. In later chapters we will try to provide a better perspective on verbal learning. Here we would merely emphasize that verbal learning cannot derive its legitimacy from such extrapolations because this S-R explanation of language acquisition is quite wrong.

First, the argument against the Terminal Meta-Postulate showed that certain linguistic phenomena could not be captured in the language of stimuli and responses. Moreover, it would seem obvious that word-to-word associations have little to do with acquisition of a grammar. It is hard to imagine how a person could so consistently find his way through a fantastic morass of associations such as Figure 5.1 in order to generate even the simplest remarks in a coherent, directed discourse. Let us consider some implications of Figure 5.1. As Staats argues, "her" would become associated with "him" as well as with "the," "a," and "this." How is it, then, that we never generate "Give *her him* a red car," in which the implicit her-him association becomes overt? Again, why is it that responses are always appropriate? That is, we say "Give her a red car" typically when she wants a red car. It is vitalism of the worst form to assume that the mind always manages to wander through such associative mazes in such a foresightful manner.

Theoreticians like Skinner or Staats are certainly expert at producing reconstructions of habit structures that could have produced the observed behavior, but this is all lamentably post hoc. What is lacking is any demonstration that habit structures could ever develop and behave in such predictable ways. Consider a computer simulation program that developed associations between any pairs of words that it was reinforced for producing together, that formed associations between covert responses like Staats proposes, etc. Ignoring the question of whether its output would ever be semantically appropriate, would it even be grammatical? It seems too much to believe. It is well known (Miller & Selfridge, 1950) that constructions generated by conforming to English word-to-word patterns (first-order approximations to English) are seldom grammatical. A sentence is generated with "a plan" that extends beyond what the next word is going to be.

Furthermore, it is not entirely clear that "grammatical behavior" is acquired through the usual principles of operant reinforcement and shaping. Although more studies of language acquisition are needed, a not untypical observation is that parents seldom correct their child's grammar either by punishing bad constructions or rewarding good constructions. Rather parents seem more concerned with shaping the truth of the child utterances, correcting misconceptions the child utters, punishing dishonesty, and rewarding truth and insightfulness. Given this reinforcement history and a belief in the omnipotence of reinforcement in language acquisition, it is strange indeed that we tend to grow up to become grammatical liars rather than ungrammatical tellers of truth. Our linguistic competence must be more abstract than a set of S-R bonds between words and must depend for its development on something more profound than the principle of reinforcement.

This is not to say that we find much value in pronouncements about a language-acquisition device (e.g., McNeill, 1968) that come from certain antibehaviorist circles. Viable models of language acquisition and performance will come about only when psychologists set themselves seriously to the task of specifying in detail such models, simulating them, and experimentally testing their predictions.

Psychological Theories of Semantics

The work of the S-R behaviorists in the domain of semantics, while incomplete, will probably have some lasting value. There are really two problems of semantics or meaning—the *first-person problem* and the *third-person problem*. When I utter something or hear something, my introspective experience is seldom one of just a string of noises. The utterance has significance for me. Explicating this personal significance is the "first-person problem" of semantics. On the other hand, what a person says or hears has a clear (though usually indeterminate) relation to his environment and to his behavior. A good example of this is the mesh between what is said by each person during a conversation. The problem of explicating this contextual coherence in a person's verbal behavior is the "third-person problem" of semantics. As behaviorists, the S-R theorists only consider the third-person problem a legitimate scientific question. However, they are often led to speculate about first-person meaning as part of the solution to the third-person problem. That is, to explain the correlation between language, behavior, and environment, the learning theorists are naturally led to speculate about what the utterances mean to the speaker-hearer.

In a S-R analysis, some of the third-person problem can be handled without any reference to the first-person problem. Classic examples of these successes are the explanations (e.g., Skinner, 1957; Staats, 1968) of how internal and environmental stimuli come to control naming behavior or what Skinner calls "tacting" (e.g., "That's red," "That's a dog," "I have a stomach ache"). The basic paradigm is once again that of instrumental conditioning in which the naming response becomes reinforced to the appropriate class of stimuli. Frequently, the response is produced only by deliberate imitation or matching to an adult's pronunciation of a new word, and it is clearly arguable whether imitation is analyzable in strictly S-R terms or whether it requires internal "cognitive representations" of the stimulus being modeled (see Bandura, 1971). Frequently, also, the only conceivable reinforcement is social approval and it often seems rather farfetched to claim even that as a reinforcer. However, the basic learning mechanisms of stimulus discrimination and generalization seem to describe the way in which the naming response becomes settled onto the appropriate range of stimuli. Another aspect of a word's third-person meaning is the control that various phrases and commands (e.g., "Please pass the salt") have over our behavior and that of other people. Skinner (1957) has called these "mands," and thinks of them as learned by the operant conditioning paradigm. One highly operational approach to meaning is Noble's (1952) which measures words' meaningfulness (m) by the mean number of word associations it elicits in 60 seconds of free association. Meaningfulness, so defined, is generally correlated with better performance in most verbal learning tasks. But it is now well known that the m measure correlates with a large number of other dimensions of verbal units. For instance, with words, m correlates highly with a word's concreteness (or imagery value), and Paivio (1971) has shown that m is a relatively weak variable of word learning when concreteness is controlled.

Traditionally, learning theory has supposed that much of the first-person meaning of a word is acquired through classical conditioning. For instance, words are assumed to acquire emotional connotations by this means. Thus, the word "bad" acquires its negative evaluation by being paired with various negative experiences. After a number of such pairings, the word "bad" begins to elicit such negative reactions on its own (see Maltzman, 1968, for a review of research into semantic conditioning). Also, Bandura (1969), Mowrer (1960), and Staats (1968) have suggested that words can act as stimuli to elicit sensory responses. For instance, after having heard the word "cat" so many times while seeing a cat, the word comes to evoke such perceptual experiences even when a cat is not physically present. In this way, words can come to evoke various types of imagery. Paivio (1971) presents extensive documentation of the importance of the imagery-evoking value of a word in various tasks such as verbal learning. As we noted above, it appears that the importance of the more traditional variable meaningfulness, m, is due to a confounding with imagery value.

From a different approach, Osgood (see Osgood, Suci, & Tannenbaum, 1957) developed the *semantic differential* for comparing and judging the connotative meaning of words. The basic procedure has the subject rate a set of concepts (e.g., "my mother," "Chinese," "modern art") on a series of seven-point scales defined by antonymic pairs (e.g., good-bad, hot-cold). By factor-analyzing a large set of such ratings, three underlying factors have been uncovered: an Evaluative Factor, a Potency Factor, and an Activity Factor. Osgood (1968) thinks of these affective features as three independent elements that have become classically conditioned to the concepts. For example, "my mother" receives a high evaluative rating because she has been associated with pleasant experiences. Further, Staats (1968) describes how language can be used to transfer the meaning from one word to another. Consider, for instance, the sentence "Motorcycles are dangerous." The predicate "dangerous" has already acquired negative meaning, and this sentence now associates that connotation to "motorcycles." Staats identifies this process as higher-order classical conditioning in which the unconditioned stimulus "dangerous" is paired temporally with the conditioned stimulus "motorcycle." Further analysis reveals, however, that this cannot be all there is to the matter. For instance, from Staats' account one would expect "Motorcycles are not dangerous" to have the same effect, whereas it surely does not. While association principles may operate in transferring meaning from one word to another, such principles are not sufficient in themselves. Certainly syntactic considerations intervene to determine when the temporal contiguity principle of conditioning should apply and when it should not.

In more general terms, this last criticism goes to the heart of the weaknesses in learning-theory analyses of meaning. It is not that significant variables and factors have not been uncovered, or that the learning processes hypothesized are not relevant. Rather the problem is that there has been no attempt to embed these ideas in a theoretical framework sufficiently powerful for the total complexity of language. The reason for this is very simple; until the past decade there has been little recognition of how complex language really is. The linguistic developments that occurred under the leadership of Noam Chomsky are principally responsible for this recognition. On several points, he and his followers have demonstrated the inadequacy of the traditional S-R analysis of language (e.g., Chomsky, 1959, 1968; Fodor, 1965; Bever, Fodor, & Garrett, 1968).

On the other side of the coin, we may note that the semantic notions developed within linguistics have proven largely sterile. That is, modern linguistic theories have been designed to account for a few rather abstract sets of intuitions—judgments of paraphrase, ambiguity, anomaly, perhaps grammaticality, but not much else. The behaviorists, on the other hand, saw that an adequate psychological theory of meaning would have to be woven into the total fabric of the person's interactions with his social community and his physical world. That is, language is the vehicle by which we communicate ideas, describe the world, plan actions, persuade and influence others, express emotions, etc. An adequate theory of what the utterances mean must indicate how arbitrary sequences of sound can have such profound influences over our lives. Language is not just a structured system of rules; rather, it is a very important instrument by which we get things done. Any psychological account of meaning that fails to make contact with this fact is at least as much in error as the traditional S-R theories.

Clearly, as Osgood (1968) has urged, what is required is "a wedding of insufficiencies" of the two approaches. In later chapters we indicate the beginnings of a possible marriage. We will propose a model that seems adequate for many aspects of natural language question answering. While the total use of language is much greater than the question answering with which we will be concerned, our work is hopefully a step in the right direction. But more of this anon. For now, we examine the revolution brought about in linguistics and psychology by Noam Chomsky.

5.2. CHOMSKIAN TRANSFORMATIONAL LINGUISTICS

The practice of linguistics in Europe and America before the nineteenth century was very different from the twentieth century linguistics practiced in America when Chomsky came upon the scene. The earlier linguistics had been highly subjective, speculative, and unsystematic. The favored technique was to use the classical grammars of Greek and Latin as frames within which other languages were described. All this was changed by the Bloomfieldian school of linguistics which developed in America during the twentieth century. American linguists were seized by a sense of practical urgency as they were faced with the prospect that hundreds of native Indian languages were soon to die out. They needed a methodology that would permit them to successfully record for posterity these soon-to-be-extinct languages. The traditional Latin and Greek grammars were rather artificial structures that distorted the basic data that was to be recorded. Therefore, American linguists were very receptive to the arguments offered by Leonard Bloomfield for a more empiricist, less mentalistic linguistics, for a methodology that was less determined by preconception and more receptive to the structure inherent in the language under study.

Bloomfield, himself, was more concerned with the need to make linguistics scientific than with any practical mission. In many ways, the position of Bloomfield in linguistics was identical to that of Watson in psychology. Like Watson, Bloomfield held a particular interpretation of scientific rigor and objectivity which eschewed all reference to unobservable mental events. As a consequence of this behavioristic bias, the Bloomfieldians had little to do with the study of cognitive meaning. Since the Bloomfieldian was not permitted to define the meaning of a word in terms of mental events, he was forced to refer to external situations to express the meaning of a phrase. While it was possible to give precise definitions of certain scientific terms in this way (e.g., "salt" is sodium chloride), most of the words (e.g., love or hate) of our language defy such definitions. Therefore, Bloomfield (1933) concluded: "The statement of meanings is therefore the weak point in language-study, and will remain so until human knowledge advances very far beyond its present stage [p. 140]."

Then, it is not surprising that in American linguistics, semantics has been neglected in favor of syntax and phonology. In their approach to these aspects of language the Bloomfieldians were structuralists in that they assumed that each language had its own unique syntactic and phonological structure that had to be discovered. Great emphasis was laid upon "discovery techniques" which would permit the linguist to discover the structure without using preconceived biases. Perhaps, the culminating work in this tradition is Zellig Harris' (1951) book *Methods in Structural Linguistics*, in which a rigorous attempt was made to define these discovery procedures.

Structural linguistics was the initial intellectual environment of Noam Chomsky. He was one of Harris' students and in his early work showed little sign of challenging the Bloomfieldian conception of linguistics. More than anything else, the early Chomsky seemed concerned with the lack of rigor found in much of the linguistic work. However, his first monumental work, *Syntactic Structures* (1957), contains the beginning of his disenchantment with Bloomfieldian linguistics. He rejected the goal of a formal discovery procedure for linguistics as too ambitious and unrealistic. Rather, Chomsky argued, we should set our sights on the lesser goal of an evaluation procedure by which one might determine which of a number of grammars best describes a given language. As Chomsky defined a grammar, it was a formal system of rules which would generate all the grammatical sentences in a language and none of the ungrammatical ones. To produce such grammars for natural languages was a goal clearly consistent with Bloomfieldian goals. However, Chomsky also put some secondary emphasis on the need to capture the speaker's intuitions about a language, such as his judgments of ambiguity and synonymy of sentences. This mentalistic emphasis on the speaker's intuition would increase in importance in later works of Chomsky.

Finite-State Grammar

Chomsky's most important contribution in *Syntactic Structures* was the examination of the generative power of various classes of formal linguistic models which were then compared with the complexities of natural language. He examined three types of grammars, the weakest of which is the *finite-state grammar*. In such a grammar, the generative mechanism transits from one state to another, generating a new word with each transition. Chomsky uses Figure 5.2 to illustrate a fragment of such a grammar. It would generate such sentences as "The old man comes" or "The men come." Such a finite-state grammar is basically what Staats was proposing in Figure 5.1. As we have noted before, such a finite-state grammar suffers the fatal weakness associated with any model that accepts the Terminal Meta-Postulate. That is, in such a grammar, it is very difficult or impossible to state contingencies between elements that are an arbitrary distance apart. But, as noted before in our earlier discussion of center embedding, there are such dependencies in natural language (e.g., between subject and verb). Chomsky only considered the finite-state grammar because of its popularity as a model in psychology and communication theory. He gave a formal proof of its inadequacy.

Phrase-Structure Grammar

The second class of linguistic models considered by Chomsky are the *phrase-structure grammars* which make explicit the hierarchical structure of a sentence and which permit dependencies to be expressed between elements at arbitrary distances. A phrase-structure grammar can be conceived of as a sequence of rewrite rules in which *nonterminal elements* are rewritten as other nonterminal elements or terminal elements. Figure 5.3 gives a fragment of a hypothetical phrase structure grammar for English. In this grammar, the symbols (S, NP_s, VP_s, REL_s, NP_p, VP_p, REL_p, R, T, N_s, V_s, N_p, V_p) are the nonterminal elements, and the terminal elements are all the various words of English. By applying these rules, various types of sentences of English may be generated. Figure 5.3 illustrates how the sentence "The man who hits the ball kisses the girls" would be generated. Note that although the singular subject, "man," is separated from the verb "kisses," the grammar was still able to capture the number-dependency between the two. This is because the initial rule in the generation of the sentence ($S \rightarrow NP_s + VP_s$) rewrote the start symbol as a singular noun phrase and a singular verb phrase. All subsequent rewritings of the noun phrase and verb phrase then preserve this information about number. Capturing such dependencies had been a problem with finite-state grammars.

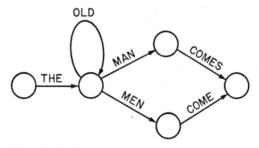

FIG. 5.2. A finite-state grammar: a set of state transitions.

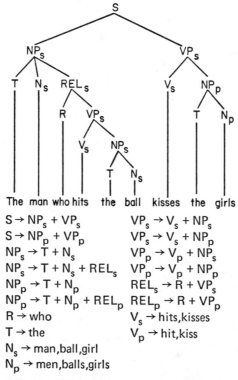

$$S \rightarrow NP_s + VP_s \qquad VP_s \rightarrow V_s + NP_s$$
$$S \rightarrow NP_p + VP_p \qquad VP_s \rightarrow V_s + NP_p$$
$$NP_s \rightarrow T + N_s \qquad VP_p \rightarrow V_p + NP_s$$
$$NP_s \rightarrow T + N_s + REL_s \qquad VP_p \rightarrow V_p + NP_p$$
$$NP_p \rightarrow T + N_p \qquad REL_s \rightarrow R + VP_s$$
$$NP_p \rightarrow T + N_p + REL_p \qquad REL_p \rightarrow R + VP_p$$
$$R \rightarrow who \qquad V_s \rightarrow hits, kisses$$
$$T \rightarrow the \qquad V_p \rightarrow hit, kiss$$
$$N_s \rightarrow man, ball, girl$$
$$N_p \rightarrow men, balls, girls$$

FIG. 5.3. A phrase-structure grammar: a set of
rewrite rules.

Phrase-structure grammars of the context-free sort described by Chomsky cannot generate all conceivable languages. No one has been able to find constructions in English that are beyond the generative power of a phrase-structure grammar, but there apparently are certain constructions in other languages which are. Furthermore, there are reasons for rejecting a context-free phrase-structure description of English. Basically, this is because it fails to capture certain intuitions that we have about the relatedness of sentences of the language. For instance, active and passive pairs (e.g., "The boy hit the girl" and "The girl was hit by the boy") are generally judged synonymous but have very different phrase-structure generations. It was for this kind of reason that Chomsky proposed supplanting the phrase-structure grammar with a *transformational grammar*.

Transformational Grammar

Chomsky's basic idea was to have a phrase-structure grammar that would first generate underlying phrase structures like that given in Figure 5.4a. Then transformations could be applied to the initial phrase structure to produce different phrase structures. For instance, the passive transformation could be applied to the active phrase structure of Figure 5.4a and thus create the passive phrase structure of Figure 5.4b. This particular transformation involves such things as reordering the subject and object noun phrases, introducing the verb auxiliary "was," and creating

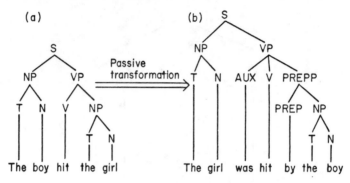

FIG. 5.4. The passive transformation maps phrase structure (*a*) into phrase structure (*b*).

a prepositional construction with "by." Other transformations involve similar formal operations as well as deletion of nonessential elements. Our description of the passive transformation is somewhat simplified over Chomsky's, but it serves to illustrate how the transformation operates on the total phrase structure to produce another phrase structure. In contrast, the rewrite rules in a phrase-structure grammar only operate on a single nonterminal element of a phrase-structure tree.

Transformational grammar constitutes a considerable increase in generative power over the phrase-structure grammar. It is able to capture our intuitions about the similarity between active and passive sentences, since they are presumed to both derive from the same underlying phrase structure. The difference is that a passive transformation has been applied in the derivation of the passive sentence. However, one of the problems that has plagued transformational grammar is that it is too powerful a generative mechanism. It is possible to formulate in transformational grammar all sorts of linguistic operations that do not correspond to anything found in any natural language. For instance, to define a passive transformation is no different formally than to define a transformation that reverses word order (e.g., "The boy hit the girl" becomes "Girl the hit boy the"). Yet such a reversal transformation is not found in any language. So one of the projects that has occupied Chomsky and others is specifying what types of transformations are found in natural language. Transformations like the reversal transformation which are structure-independent (i.e., apply to any phrase structure) seem not to be found in natural language. These limitations on the types of permissible transformations has been taken by Chomsky in more recent years (e.g., 1968) to reflect universal properties of the human mind.

Semantics

The reader may have noted a complete absence of any mention of semantics in the discussion above. This reflects the Bloomfieldian influence on the early Chomsky. However, by the time he published *Aspects of the Theory of Syntax* (1965), Chomsky had begun to speculate in earnest about the semantic component of language. Using a trichotomy suggested by Katz and Postal (1964), Chomsky proposed that language was to be analyzed into three components, a syntactic component, a phonological component, and a semantic component. The syntactic component in *Aspects* was not greatly changed over Chomsky's earlier formulation in *Syntactic Structures*. That is, phrase-structure rules were presumed to form the "base component" of the grammar. The phrase structures generated by the base component were now referred to as "deep structures." A transformational component was proposed that mapped the deep structures onto surface phrase-structures. The phonological component operated on the surface structures generated by the transformational component to convert them into phonetic patterns (e.g., spoken utterances). The semantic component operated upon the deep structure to produce a semantic interpretation. Following the suggestion of Katz and Fodor (1963), Chomsky proposed that semantic interpretation involved combining the semantic features of the individual words to produce a description of the entire sentence. Special filtering rules were defined to reject any combination of semantic features that was anomalous. (See Section 4.3 for further discussion of the semantic feature analysis of Katz and Fodor.)

This conception of semantics is purely *interpretative*. The base component generates a deep structure on the basis of the formal rewrite rules of its phrase-structure grammar. The semantic component has no role in the generation of the deep structure or in the selection of transformations applied to generate a surface structure. The semantic component only serves to interpret what the syntactic component generates. As a psychological model of the causal sequence by which a sentence is generated, this scenario is utterly ridiculous. It would claim that we first decide what utterance we are going to say and then decide what meaning we want to convey, which is surely just the wrong way around. But of course, this is not a proposal for a performance model, but rather a formal competence model that attempts to interrelate the syntactic, semantic, and phonological structures of a sentence. Whether it can successfully do that is an empirical question, but not a psychological question. We will soon discuss the work of some linguists, calling themselves "generative semanticists," who deny that Chomsky's approach can achieve this goal of interrelating the three components of natural language so long as it uses a purely interpretative semantics.

One significant difference between the *Aspects* model and the model in *Syntactic Structures* is that transformations are assumed to be meaning-preserving; that is, a transformation was viewed as something which would not affect the meaning of the ultimate sentence. This is because the deep structure is the element that receives semantic interpretation, not the surface structure. Therefore, all semantically significant elements of the sentence must be represented in the deep structure before the transformations are applied. The transformations only reorder and smooth out the elements of the sentence. In *Syntactic Structures*, transformations were considered that changed a phrase structure like Figure 5.4*a* (The boy hit the girl) into its negative (The boy did not hit the girl), or which embedded a new clause (The boy hit the girl who kissed him), and so forth. Such *meaning-changing* transformations are no more to be found in the transformational component of *Aspects*. Rather, their work was presumed to be done by phrase-structure rules of the base component.

This, then, is the basic formal framework that Chomsky established in his work on transformational grammar. Within that framework many insightful analyses of the structural properties of particular languages have occurred. The hope is that study of particular languages from this viewpoint will not only increase our appreciation of their individual properties, but also help uncover some so-called *"language universals."* Particularly important are the *formal universals* that reflect general constraints on the possible types of grammatical rules. However, such attempts to extend Chomsky's transformational grammar have sometimes led to critiques and defections rather than refinements or further specification of the theoretical framework. If the framework seems restrictive and prevents expression of significant generalizations by others, there comes a questioning of the framework, just as Chomsky challenged the Bloomfieldian framework. Such challenges have appeared in linguistics during the past few years.

5.3. NEO-CHOMSKIAN LINGUISTICS

The most fundamental challenge to Chomsky's transformational grammar has come from *generative semantics*, which we will soon discuss. However, certain linguists like Charles Fillmore (1968, 1971) and John Anderson (1971) (not one of the authors!) have accepted the general framework of transformational grammar, but have proposed substantial modifications to the deep structure. Their modified transformational grammar, which is called *case grammar*, is of interest to us because the deep structure has many properties in common with the memory structures with which we and similarly oriented psychologists (e.g., Rumelhart, Lindsay, & Norman, 1972; Kintsch, 1972) have been working.

Case Grammar

One strong challenge opposes the assumption of standard transformational theory that the deep structure should be developed in terms of the grammatical relations that can be expressed by immediate domination in a phrase structure. For instance, in Chomsky's grammar, the deep-structure relation, "subject of sentence," is defined as the noun phrase that is dominated by the *S* node in the phrase structure. Similarly, relations like "main verb of" or "object of" a construction are defined in terms of various deep-structure configurations. The difficulty arises because items serving a particular deep-structure role can serve rather different semantic roles. For instance, Fillmore would argue that the subjects of the following sentences each serve a different semantic role:

John runs.	(1)
John is afraid.	(2)
The window broke.	(3)
The medicine cures.	(4)
Chicago is hot.	(5)

The subject in Sentence (1) serves the logical role of the *agent* of an action, in

Sentence (2) the role of an *experiencer*, in Sentence (3) that of a *passive object*, in Sentence (4) that of an *instrument*, and in Sentence (5) that of *location*.

In case grammar the deep structure of a sentence is developed in terms of such *semantically-relevant syntactic relations*. That is, instead of using configurational concepts like "subject of sentence" and "object of sentence," the deep structure of a case grammar uses semantic concepts like "agent doing the action" or "instrument with which the action was performed." Each of these concepts is represented by a different case in the deep structure. According to Fillmore (1968):

> The case notions comprise a set of universal, presumably innate, concepts which identify certain judgments human beings are capable of making about the events that are going on around them, judgments about such matters as who did it, who it happened to, and what got changed [p. 24].

The exact cases chosen seem to vary considerably from author to author and from one article to the next. Fillmore (1971) states that he is currently "comfortable" with the case relations of agent, experiencer, instrument, object, source, goal, place, and time.

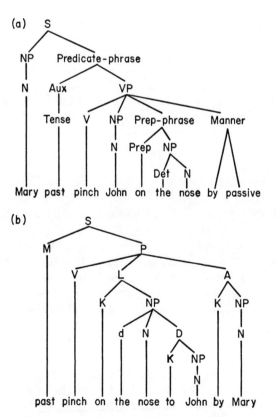

FIG. 5.5. A comparison of Chomsky's deep-structure representation (*a*) with Fillmore's case structure (*b*).

Figure 5.5 illustrates how the deep structure of the sentence "John was pinched on the nose by Mary" would be represented in Chomsky's grammar (panel *a*) and in Fillmore's grammar (panel *b*). In Fillmore's representation, the sentence (S) is rewritten as a modal element (M) and a proposition (P). Nearly all of his proposals deal with how the proposition is to be analyzed, and he has not developed the modal component which includes such things as tense, negation, mood, and aspect. The proposition is rewritten into a verb (V), plus a sequence of case elements (in Figure 5.5 the case elements are L for locative and A for agentive). Each case element is rewritten as a general case tag (K, the "Kasus") plus a noun phrase (NP). In Figure 5.5, "John" would be identified by Fillmore as *D*, a *dative* element (or experiencer), which is dominated by the *locative* element, "nose." Clearly, the case representation makes more salient the semantic roles of the elements in the deep structure. Consequently, it is argued, the task of producing a semantic interpretation of the deep structure has been made this much easier. It also happens that such deep structures help explicate paraphrase relationships between sentences. For instance, the sentence "John was pinched on the nose by Mary" can be paraphrased as "Mary pinched John's nose." Both sentences would derive from the same deep structure in Fillmore's case grammar, but would have quite different deep structures in the standard transformational grammar of Chomsky.

The deep structure generated by case grammar has certain properties which make it attractive as a model for human memory, since memory seems to be organized semantically. In Chapter 8 we will discuss how subjects show considerable recognition-memory confusions between sentences like the above-paraphrased pair in which semantic relations are maintained but syntactic relations are greatly changed. To accommodate such facts at the outset, one might prefer a memory structure in which connections were determined by semantic relationships as in case grammar rather than by purely syntactic relations.

In memory systems such as Rumelhart, Lindsay, and Norman's (1972) or our own, propositions are always encoded in terms of deep-structure constructions. The individual branches of the deep-structure trees are recorded as associations which connect nodes or "ideas." Case relations or other semantic functors are used to label the associative links. These semantic labels help to organize long-term memory and to direct searches for particular information in that memory. In his 1968 formulation (see Figure 5.5*b*), Fillmore preferred to use case labels as nodes that dominated the noun phrases. However, more recently (1971), Fillmore has produced linguistic reasons for preferring a deep-structure representation in which case relations label links in the phrase structure. Thus, there is some convergence in the representation advocated by linguists and by memory theorists.

Generative Semantics

Fillmore's original 1968 position would be described in the linguist's jargon as that of a *deep-structure interpretivist*. That is, while he questioned Chomsky's choice of a deep-structure representation, he did accept Chomsky's claim that semantic rules would operate on the deep-phrase structure generated by the base component to derive a semantic interpretation. In contrast, the generative semanticists (e.g., George Lakoff, James McCawley, John Ross) have argued that language is best viewed as starting with a semantic interpretation from which an utterance is generated by application of transformations. Certainly, if this were a performative model of sentence generation, the generative semantics approach would be more intuitive than that of the interpretivists. However, since the issue concerns abstract competence models, it is a matter of considerable controversy in linguistics whether the generative semantics position is superior to the interpretivist position. Some have argued in fact that the two positions are not different in a formal sense.

The work of the generative semanticists tends to be highly particulate. They provide careful, in-depth analyses of a certain linguistic phenomenon (e.g., pronominalization) and discover that certain generalizations seem impossible to capture in the interpretivist framework. The general model that they propose instead goes roughly as follows: There is a phrase-structure component that generates, not deep structures in the standard transformational sense, but rather phrase structures that represent the semantic content of the sentences. Unlike the earlier deep structures, the terminal elements of these semantic phrase structures would not be words (e.g., of English), although exactly what they are remains unspecified. Lakoff (1970) speaks of "a small finite number of atomic predicates" that "do not vary from language to language [p. 223]." All meaning then is built up in terms of these primitive but unspecified elements. (These primitives sound suspiciously like the "simple ideas" of British associationism.) Then, to these "abyssal structures," a series of transformations are applied that serve to introduce lexical items and to accomplish all the reordering, addition, and deletion of elements that is necessary in any transformational grammar.

This would seem a rather different conception of language, but Chomsky (1971) has questioned whether it really is anything but a "notational variant" of his standard transformational grammar. He notes that his transformational grammar generates a set of formal objects, quadruples $\langle S, d, s, p \rangle$, where S is a semantic interpretation, d is the deep structure, s the surface structure, and p the phonological representation. Chomsky argues that generative semantics generates identical quadruples. Moreover, in both theories d is related to s by the transformational component, and s to p by the phonological component. The only difference would appear that in generative semantics the deep structure d is generated from S by application of transformations, whereas in the standard theory the deep structure d is interpreted to arrive at a semantic representation, S. But this is just a matter of notation, Chomsky argues, since the transformations that map S to d are just converses of the rules of semantic interpretation of the standard theory. Since we are speaking of a formal competence model, Chomsky argues, it is meaningless whether the rules map the deep structure into the semantic interpretation or the reverse. In either case, the formal relationship between the two is specified with equal adequacy.

Lakoff (1971) protested against Chomsky's attempt to pass off generative semantics as a notational variant of the standard theory. First, he argued that the character of the semantic representation in generative semantics is very different from that in the standard theory of *Aspects*:

> The *Aspects* theory assumes that semantic readings are formal objects of a very different sort than syntactic phrase markers, and that projection rules are formal operations of a very different sort than grammatical transformations. One of the most important innovations of generative semantics, perhaps the most fundamental one since all the others rest on it, has been the claim that semantic representations and syntactic phrase markers are formal objects of the same kind, and that there exist no projection rules, but only grammatical transformations. In his discussion of his new "standard theory," Chomsky has therefore adopted without fanfare one of the most fundamental innovations made by the basic theory [p. 269].

Secondly, Lakoff argues that there is no place in generative semantics for anything like the deep structures originally envisaged by Chomsky. In generative semantics there is a sequence of phrase structures $P_1, ..., P_1, ..., P_n$ beginning with the abyssal semantic representation (P_1) and finally resulting in the surface structure (P_n). Transformations are used to carry out each step, P_j to P_{j+1} in the sequence. The abyssal structure in either Chomsky's theory or in generative semantics has no lexical items. It is Chomsky's claim that there is a block of transformations that introduce all the lexical items into the phrase structure. We can call P_i the phrase structure created by this block of transformations. Subsequent to P_i all transformations are "upward-to-the-surface cyclic" rules which reorder elements, delete elements, etc. Thus, the phrase structure P_i has a distinguished status in the derivational history of the sentence. The phrase structure P_i is the point in the derivational history at which lexicalization (word insertions) is complete so that a different class of transformations begins to operate. This phrase structure P_i is Chomsky's deep structure. Lakoff's claim is that in general a phrase structure so defined does not exist because it is impossible to always keep all the lexical insertion transformations prior to the upward-to-the-surface cyclic transformations.

Lakoff's arguments regarding the need to mix the order of the two types of transformations can only be fully appreciated with more linguistic background than can be provided here. However, a particularly simple example from Lakoff and Ross (1968) will serve to show the character of the arguments. Their example concerns the peculiarity of idioms such as "bury the hatchet" or "kicked the bucket." Consider Sentences (6) to (11):

They buried the hatchet.	(6)
The hatchet was buried.	(7)
The gladiator kicked the bucket.	(8)
*The bucket was kicked by the gladiator.	(9)
I've been had.	(10)
*Someone has had me.	(11)

Sentences (6) and (7) illustrate that some idioms can be passivized. Thus, as Chomsky would want, with these sentences lexicalization could precede the passive transformation. However, other examples show the passive transformation sometimes must precede the lexicalization. For example, the "kicked the bucket" idiom does not permit such passivization and Sentence (9) is consequently ungrammatical. Similarly, the "been had" idiom can only exist in the passive, and the active Sentence (11) is ungrammatical. Thus, Lakoff and Ross argue, lexical insertion only occurs with these idioms after the passive transformation has or has not been applied. If it had preceded the passive transformation, there would be no way to prevent the optional passive transformation in Sentence (8) or to force it in Sentence (10). Consequently the ungrammatical Sentences (9) and (11) could result. Rather the idiom "kicked the bucket" must be inserted in derivation after it is too late for the passive transformation to reorder the phrase. Hence, this is one example of an upward-to-the-surface cyclic rule (i.e., the passive transformation) preceding a rule of lexicalization.

Since the process of lexicalization is so important to the arguments of generative semantics, it would be worthwhile to examine one example in some detail. This example, adapted from Lakoff (1970), involves the verb "persuade" in a sentence of the order "*X* persuaded *y* to hit *z*." At some point in the derivation of this sentence (presumably near to the abyssal structure), the representation of the sentence is that given in Figure 5.6*a*. This can be paraphrased as "*X* caused that it should

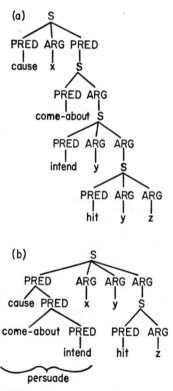

FIG. 5.6. An example of lexicalization after reordering transformation: Structure (*a*) is transformed into Structure (*b*); then the lexical item *persuade* is introduced.

come about that y should intend that he (y) should hit z." After a sequence of transformations that delete elements, raise elements, and rearrange phrases, the phrase structure in Figure 5.6b results. It is only then that the lexical item "persuade" is inserted, replacing the entire subtree that means "cause to come about to intend." Further transformations would then have to apply before obtaining the sentence "X persuaded y to hit z."

In this example, there are some transformations that rearrange phrase structure, then a lexicalizing transformation, then some further rearranging transformations. Intuitively, this is not an unreasonable psychological model of how "persuaded" might be introduced in the generation of the sentence. That is, a person would begin with some very abstract nonverbalizable conception, then rearrange elements in that conception until he could give a fairly simple lexical realization of his conception, and then introduce the appropriate words. Therefore, from a psychological point of view, generative semantics is much more appealing than the original transformational model. However, even generative semantics suffers one fatal flaw as a model for human performance. While it is suggestive of a plausible model of sentence generation, it is completely useless with respect to achieving a model of sentence analysis. That is, it is very difficult technically and often impossible to turn the transformations around and derive an abyssal structure from the surface sentence.

It is difficult to judge what the final outcome will be in this debate between the generativists and the interpretivists. It would appear that as more of the language falls under the transformational analysis, the more it is becoming apparent that some fundamental reconceptualizations are required in Chomsky's (1965) position. For instance, Fillmore (1971) has changed his original (1968) lexicalist case analysis and turned to a position more similar to that of the generative semanticists.

5.4. COMPUTATIONAL LINGUISTICS

The scientists who have seriously approached the problem of natural language analysis are the computational linguists who have attempted to implement language-understanding programs on computers. There were a few early attempts to use the transformational model of Chomsky directly as a model of language analysis. For instance, one might attempt "analysis by synthesis" (e.g., Matthews, 1962), in which one simply generates all the sentences of English, looking for the to-be-analyzed sentence. A somewhat more practical algorithm for language analysis (Petrick, 1965; MITRE, 1964) attempted to analyze the sentences by applying the transformations in reverse order. Woods (1970) discusses the difficulties inherent in these attempts to reverse the transformational sequence. First of all, it is difficult to determine exactly what surface structure to assign to the to-be-analyzed sentence. Without such a surface structure it is impossible to begin to apply the reverse transformations to it to derive a deep structure. But even with the surface-structure problem solved, fatal difficulties still remain. While it is usually unambiguous which forward transformations to apply to a phrase structure in generating a sentence, the ambiguity quickly gets out of bounds with respect to backward transformations. At each point in unwinding the transformations there are often several possible reverse transformations that could be applied to the current phrase structure. Thus, there is an exponential explosion of the number of possible reverse transformational sequences that could be applied. That is, if n transformations must be reversed and there are r possible reverse transformations at each point, there are r^n possible reverse sequences.

Because of such difficulties, it therefore became clear that some new attack on language analysis was required. Despite long-standing biases, it does not seem that language analysis and language generation involve the same mechanism that is "put in forward gear" for one and "put in reverse" for the other. We will examine three recent proposals for how language analysis may proceed efficiently. The first proposal, that of *augmented transition networks*, stays fairly close to the transformational tradition that was just examined. Second, we will consider a parser developed by Terry Winograd which is much more *procedure-oriented*. Finally, we will examine some of the radical notions of Roger Schank about "conceptual analysis." His work is clearly the most deviant from the mainstream transformational tradition in linguistics, and perhaps the most promising.

Woods' Augmented Transition Network Grammars

Earlier versions of augmented transition networks for grammatical analysis of sentences have been developed by Thorne, Bratley, and Dewar (1968), and by Bobrow and Fraser (1969), but the most powerful and sophisticated to date is that reported by Woods (1970). The basic notion behind such systems is to begin with a finite-state grammar (see Figure 5.2) and strengthen it to the point where it is capable of handling English. The advantage of finite-state grammars is that they are as usable for language analysis as for language generation. In language generation, as the finite-state grammar moves (transits) from one state to another, it generates one word associated with each transition. Thus, each transition determines the output of a word. In contrast, in language analysis each incoming word determines a state transition. That is, the finite-state mechanism transits from a particular state along the arc labeled with the next word in the sentence. The analysis given to the sentence is determined by the path taken through the finite-state network. Thus, with finite-state grammars, language analysis is in fact just language generation put in reverse.

The problem with such finite-state grammars is that they are incapable of handling the recursive embedding of linguistic constructions. Chomsky's solution to this problem was to move to context-free phrase-structure grammars. However, this option adopted by Chomsky was the beginning of the difficulties for language analysis. Instead Woods (1970) suggests a rather different move to take care of such complexities in language:

Suppose, however, that one added the mechanism of recursion directly to the transition graph model by fiat. That is, suppose one took a collection of transition graphs each with a name, and permitted as labels on the arcs not only terminal symbols but also nonterminal symbols naming complex constructions which must be present in order for the transition to be followed. The determination of whether such a construction was in fact present in a sentence would be done by a "subroutine call" to another transition graph (or the same one). The resulting model of grammar, which we will call a *recursive transition network*, is equivalent in generative power to that of a context-free grammar or pushdown store automaton, but as we will show, allows for greater efficiency of expression, more efficient parsing algorithms, and natural extension by "augmentation" to more powerful models which allow various degrees of context dependence and more flexible structure-building during parsing. We argue in fact that an "augmented" recursive transition network is capable of performing the equivalent of transformational recognition without the necessity of a separate inverse transformational component, and that this parsing can be done in an amount of time which is comparable to that of predictive context-free recognition [p. 591].

Figure 5.7 provides a simple transition network to illustrate what Woods is discussing. The first network in Figure 5.7 provides the "mainline" network for analyzing simple sentences. From this mainline network it is possible to call recursively the second network for analysis of noun phrases or the third network for the analysis of prepositional phrases. Woods (1970) describes how the network would recognize an illustrative sentence:

> To recognize the sentence "Did the red barn collapse?" the network is started in state S. The first transition is the aux transition to state q_2 permitted by the auxiliary "did." From state q_2 we see that we can get to state q_3 if the next "thing" in the input string is an NP. To ascertain if this is the case, we call the state NP. From state NP we can follow the arc labeled det to state q_6 because of the determiner "the." From here, the adjective "red" causes a loop which returns to state q_6, and the subsequent noun "barn" causes a

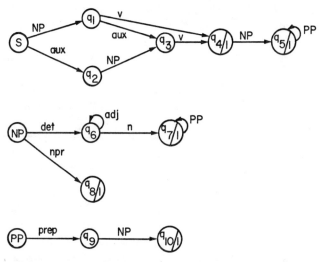

FIG. 5.7. A sample transition network. S is the start state. q_4, q_5, q_6, q_7, q_8, and q_{10} are the final states. (From Woods, 1970.)

transition to state q_7. Since state q_7 is a final state, it is possible to "pop up" from the NP computation and continue the computation of the top level S beginning in state q_3 which is at the end of the NP arc. From q_3 the verb "collapse" permits a transition to the state q_4, and since this state is final and "collapse" is the last word in the string, the string is accepted as a sentence [pp. 591–592].

We have illustrated in Figure 5.7 what is known as a *recursive transition network* which is equivalent to a context-free phrase-structure grammar. In our discussion of Chomsky's work, it was pointed out that a phrase structure grammar was inadequate for certain complexities of natural language. What is needed in addition are mechanisms that will permit fragments of the sentence to be permuted, copied, and/or deleted. Chomsky's solution, to introduce transformations into the grammar, was a disastrous move from the point of view of language analysis. On the other hand, Woods' solution is to increase the computational power of his recursive transition networks. As one moves through these "high-powered" networks, called *augmented transition networks*, structure-building operations are called upon which no longer construct only the surface structure of the sentence, but rather something like a deep structure:

> The augmented transition network builds up a partial structural description of the sentence as it proceeds from state to state through the network. The pieces of this partial description are held in *registers* which can contain any rooted tree or list of rooted trees and which are automatically pushed down when a recursive application of the transition network is called for and restored when the lower level (recursive) computation is completed. The structure-building actions on the arcs specify changes in the contents of these registers in terms of their previous contents, the contents of other registers, the current input symbol, and/or the result of lower level computations. In addition to holding pieces of substructure that will eventually be incorporated into a larger structure, the registers may also be used to hold flags or other indicators to be interrogated by conditions on the arcs [Woods, 1970, p. 593].

At each transition in the network, it is possible to define arbitrarily complicated tests to see if the transition should be taken, and to perform arbitrarily complicated structure modifications if the transition is taken. Thus, like a transformational grammar, an augmented transition network has the full computational power of a Turing machine and is therefore presumed to be adequate in principle to any of the complexities of natural language. Moreover, unlike transformational grammar, it has maintained some of the efficiencies with respect to language analyses that are inherent in a finite-state grammar.

One of the attractive features of Woods's parser, which is one found in all successful parsers, is that difficulties due to *multiple parsing* and *backtracking* are minimized. Such problems occur because, as a parser begins reading a sentence, there are ambiguities about what to make out of the initial phrases. For instance, depending on whether the sentence is active or passive, the first noun phrase encountered is either the logical subject or the logical object in the deep structure. Whether a sentence is active or passive is not determined until the verb construction is encountered following the noun phrase. So for a short time it is unclear what role to assign to the initial noun phrase in the deep structure. Less efficient parsers pursue multiple parses in serial or in parallel, attempting to parse the noun phrase both as logical subject and as logical object. Woods' parser avoids this difficulty of multiple parsing by storing the first noun phrase in a register and waiting until the verb construction is analyzed before committing itself. Woods also indicates that even when the network has made a mistake and committed itself to the wrong parse, it is not necessary to "backtrack" (as do some parsers) to the point of the mistake and begin the parse all over again from that point. Woods (1970) gives an example of how the need for backtracking is sidestepped:

> For example, when one is at the point in parsing a sentence where he is expecting a verb and he encounters the verb "be," he can tentatively assign it as the main verb by putting it in the main verb register. If he then encounters a second verb indicating that the "be" was not the main verb but an auxiliary helping verb, then the verb "be" can be moved from the main verb register into an auxiliary verb register and the new main verb put in its place [p. 602].

While Woods' parser is clearly designed as an artificial intelligence program (that is, as a program that would get the job done as efficiently as possible), it is in some respects a plausible psychological model of language analysis. Kaplan (1971) has set forth some of its psychological virtues. It processes sentences in the same left-to-right linear order as we do—a feature not true of many of the previous parsers. Also unlike previous parsers, the amount of computation time needed to analyze a sentence does not grow exponentially with the length of the sentence. In addition to these gross features, Kaplan argues that it is also possible to explain within this framework some of the more detailed features of sentence comprehension in man. For instance, by ordering the arcs leading out of a particular state, it is possible to bias the interpretation of an ambiguous sentence so that the network will choose the same interpretation as a human does. By similar means it is also possible to make sentences which subjects find hard to analyze, similarly hard (in terms of amount of computation) for the network. For instance, passive sentences are more difficult than active sentences for Woods' network because more state transitions must be followed in analyzing the passive sentence.

The purpose of Woods' parser is to try to uncover the sentence's syntactic deep structure, and this aim would seem to be its fatal flaw. We noted earlier in discussing generative semantics that attempting to find a deep structure may only obfuscate the analysis of a sentence. Moreover, from the point of view of a psychologically plausible model, a deep-structure syntactic analysis is clearly uninteresting. What we really want is a representation of the semantic content of the sentence, and Woods' parser only gets us part of the way. The other two parsers to be considered have as their goal the derivation of a semantically satisfactory representation of the sentence.

The Winograd Procedural System

There are two major sources available for Terry Winograd's work. The first is his dissertation (1971), and the second an article (1972) that occupied a total issue of *Cognitive Psychology*. We will principally rely on the former document because it contains technical details omitted from the latter. Winograd's parser is not very different from that of Woods, although it appears to be at first glance. Winograd's parser is written as a sequence of programs which can recursively call one another during the parsing of a sentence. There is a program associated with each major grammatical group in the sentence. For instance, there is a program associated with the total sentence. That program will call a noun phrase program to parse the subject of the sentence, and then a verb phrase program to parse the predicate. These programs can call other programs within recursive loops, so that it can go on indefinitely. The potential isomorphism between Woods' and Winograd's parsers becomes apparent when one realizes that where Woods recursively transits from network to network, Winograd transits from program to program. (Compare the networks in Figure 5.7 from Woods with the flow charts in Figure 5.8 from Winograd.) It is true that Winograd's grammar is based on Halliday's (1967, 1970) systemic grammar, while Woods' linguistic theory remains much more closely tied to Chomsky's standard transformational grammar. However, either grammar could be programmed in either computational formalism, so it would appear that no theoretical advantages arise from the decision to implement the parser as a set of programs or as an augmented recursive transition network—a point which Winograd partially concedes in his dissertation.

The advance of Winograd's program over Woods' lies in the area of semantics. Winograd did not conceive of semantics as a narrowly defined domain whose sole function is to account for judgments of paraphrase, ambiguity, and anomaly. Winograd realized that an adequate theory of meaning must be woven into the total conceptual fabric of his program. The purpose of language is to talk about things, and language only becomes interesting when we have a real world to talk about. Therefore, Winograd's language-comprehension program operates as an individual who has its own little world to talk about to its interrogator. Winograd simulates a robot that lives in a world composed of a tabletop, a box, and a number of blocks and pyramids of different sizes and colors. The robot can see its world and has one hand by which it may manipulate the objects in its world.

Winograd's system consists of three interrelated parts—*syntax, inference,* and *semantics.* The syntax we have already discussed. By "inference" Winograd refers to his knowledge representation and his procedures for reasoning with that knowledge. Such an inference system is necessary if a program is to intelligently respond to commands and answer questions. Very simple assertions about the world such as property statements about individuals, like "Boise is a city," are stored directly in Winograd's data-base. However, more complicated assertions that involve logical connectives and quantifiers like "All canaries are yellow" or "A thesis is acceptable if it is long or it contains a persuasive argument" are stored as theorems which can be evoked whenever deductions are required to answer a question or to fulfill a request. These theorems are contained in memory as procedures. So for instance,

DEFINE program SENTENCE

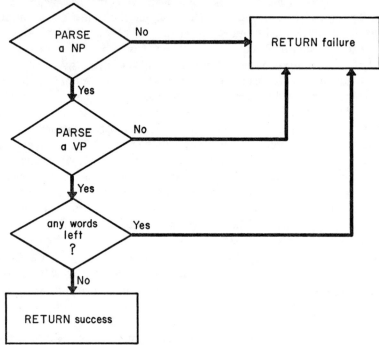

DEFINE program NP

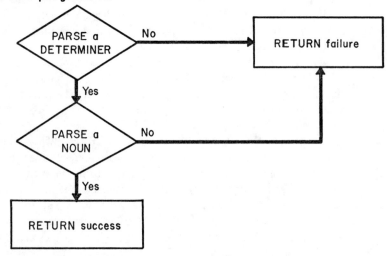

(Continued)

DEFINE program VP

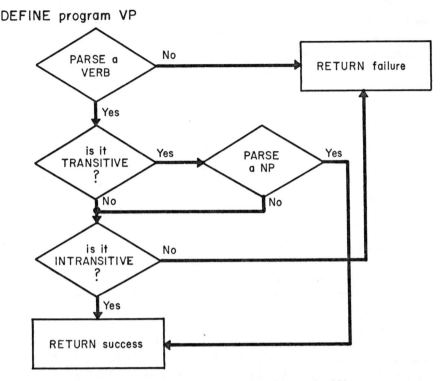

FIG. 5.8. A simple parsing program. (From Winograd, 1972.)

the statement "A thesis is acceptable if it is long or it contains a persuasive argument" is translated into the following procedure to prove that a thesis is acceptable: First, check if it is long by counting its pages, and if the number of pages passes a criterion, conclude it is acceptable. Secondly, if it fails this test, read the thesis to see if it contains any persuasive argument. If it does, it is also acceptable. Winograd uses the programming language PLANNER, developed by Hewitt (1970), for encoding these procedural theorems and for executing the procedures whenever they are needed. Much of the success of Winograd's efforts must be credited to the advances built into the PLANNER language. The language PLANNER has numerous facilities for incorporating heuristics to guide deduction, and so avoids some of the inefficiencies associated with other theorem-proving systems.

In Winograd's system, the function of semantics is to provide the bridge between syntax and inference. Traffic on this bridge travels both ways. Winograd defined a number of programs, called "semantic specialists," whose function is to take the output of the parser and translate it into statements, theorems, or programs acceptable for integration with the inference system. For instance, there is a "noun-group specialist" that would give as the meaning of "a red cube" a procedure that could be activated to identify such an object. However, the semantic specialists can also be evoked to use the inference capacities of the system to censor the behavior of the parser. For instance, the noun group specialist can be evoked after a noun group has been tentatively identified by the parser. If it is impossible to interpret the noun phrase meaningfully, the parser is redirected to attempt other syntactic constructions. For instance, in the sentence "John rode down the street in a car," the parser may initially identify "in a car" as modifying "the street." However, when the noun-group specialist sent the construction "A street which is in the car" to the inference system, the parse would be rejected because it is known that streets contain cars and not vice versa.

Such a system can easily take into account the context in which a statement is made while it is trying to understand the statement. For instance, pronouns like "it" or definite descriptions like "the big block" simply evoke programs that will search to see if the referent of the phrase is contained in a record of past discourse or a list of objects in the current scene. The system keeps track of the order in which items have been mentioned in past discourse. Therefore, upon hearing the noun phrase "the block," it will determine which block has been most recently mentioned and assume that this is the intended referent of the phrase.

If one were to find fault with Winograd's system, it would be that language comprehension is still syntax-based. That is, while semantics interprets and censors the output of the syntactic parser, it cannot suggest to the parser how the sentence should be analyzed. This leads to a number of difficulties for Winograd's system. For instance, it could never understand ungrammatical sentences, although humans are forever uttering and comprehending such malformed constructions. Even a Tarzan-like muttering such as "eat boy food" is perfectly comprehensible to most people. However, since Winograd's semantic system waits patiently for the parser to make tentative syntactic sense out of such a string of words, the conceptual knowledge of his program can never be brought to bear as it so clearly does in the human case.

This failing also leads to certain inefficiencies in the program's way of dealing with the problem of lexical ambiguity in otherwise well-formed sentences. Many words in a sentence have multiple interpretations (e.g., "bank" can mean a river bank or a monetary institution). If n words in the sentence each have r meanings, there are r^n possible interpretations of the sentence. This rapidly gets out of hand as the sentence becomes long and n gets large. Winograd's system will reject some of these interpretations as semantically impossible. For instance, "ball" in the phrase "striped ball" cannot mean a society dance. However, most of the interpretations cannot be rejected on logical grounds. For instance, there are four semantically possible interpretations of the sentence "The man hits the colorful ball," although only one is at all obvious (see Katz & Fodor, 1963). The way Winograd handles such multiple ambiguities is to examine all possible interpretations, assign each a plausibility, and select the most plausible. But this is quite inefficient when the number of possible interpretations becomes large. What is needed is a means by which the semantic component can use its conceptual expectations to determine the proper interpretation of each word in the sentence and to ignore all others.

Schank's Conceptual Dependency Analysis

Roger Schank (Schank, Tesler, & Weber, 1970; Schank, 1971) had directed his research at the problem of how conceptual expectations could be used to direct the parse of an incoming sentence. His system is an example of a *verb-based* parser. That is, the parser's prime task is first to discover the main verb or act in the sentence. Having discovered that, it then consults a *verb dictionary* to determine what kind of syntactic constructions to expect and how to interpret these conceptually. The parser builds around the verb a conceptual representation of the sentence that involves case-like noun categories such as actor, object, instrument, recipient, and a directive case. Knowledge of the verb helps the system determine what type of case roles to expect, so that even when there is no noun filling a particular case role in the sentence, the parser will try to provide an appropriate though implicit one. Hence, given the sentence "I am in love," the parser will determine "love" is the underlying act and supply a dummy "someone" as the conceptual object of that act.

In Schank's view, sentential syntax should be used to parse a sentence only when all conceptual means have failed. Syntax is important in sentence generation but not in sentence comprehension:

> For example, we are familiar with the fact that it is much easier to understand a foreign language than it is to speak it. Whereas, we need the "grammar" rules of a language to generate from our conceptual base, it seems plausible that the process of understanding can work sufficiently well with a knowledge of the words of this foreign language and a very few of the major realization patterns. This is because the conceptual base into which we are mapping during the process of understanding this foreign language is the same one as we ordinarily utilize. It has the same rules of organization of its parts (namely concepts). If we are aware of the word-concept couplings of this foreign language, we now only need to arrange these concepts according to our usual (i.e. language-free) manner. Thus, it would seem that humans can fare rather well without realization rules during parsing. If this is the case, we must require of any simulation that it do likewise [Schank, Tesler, & Weber, 1970, p. 4].

The output from Schank's parser are conceptual dependency diagrams which are structures that differ somewhat from the traditional phrase structures considered until now. As Schank describes a conceptual dependency diagram, it is "a bundle of interconnected concepts (not words), where each concept is dependent on some other concept for explication of its meaning and where pieces of the conceptual network thus formed have their various sentential realizates [Schank, 1971, p. 8]." As an example, consider Figure 5.9, which gives the conceptual dependency diagram for "The big man took the book." The main conceptual link is the double-headed arrow which connects the actor "man" and the act "trans." The relationship between the act and actor of a conceptualization is one of mutual dependency as indicated by the bidirectional arrow. The adjective "big" points to "man", indicating that it is an attribute conceptually dependent upon the noun it modifies. The verb "take" has been replaced by the conceptual act "trans" which underlies all verbs of transition. A symbol p modifies the double-headed arrow indicating the action took place in the past. The object "book" is connected by a labeled dependency link to the act.

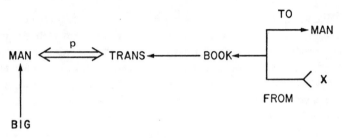

FIG. 5.9. An example of a conceptual dependency diagram generated by Schank's parser.

Finally, the dependency diagram has been enriched with a recipient case (indicated by the bent arrow connected to "book") which indicates that the book transited from some person or place, X, to the man. This fact of the book's transition was not directly expressed in the sentence, but is something the parser can infer from its knowledge of the verb "take" and the concept "trans."

It is difficult to determine whether any significant facts really rest on the choice of a conceptual dependency diagram over the more traditional phrase-structure representation. Schank has not yet made a convincing case for the peculiar graphical properties of his representation. However, we have personally observed that his parser is relatively successful with such a representation. This at least indicates that the traditional phrase structure is also in need of some motivation. The problem of adequately motivating the representation generated by a parser is a very serious one and is an issue to which we will devote some effort in later chapters with respect to our own model.

Schank in recent work (1971) has indicated that the syntactic and conceptual expectancies that direct his parser are not sufficient. He argues that a successful language-understanding program will have to bring higher-level contextual and general world information to bear on the comprehension process. He provides the following example to make his point:

Fred: Hi.
John: What are you doing with that knife?
Fred: Thought I'd teach the kids to play mumblypeg.
John: I could use a knife right now. (agitated tone)
Fred: What's the matter?
John: Damn Mary, always on my back. She'll be sorry.
Fred: I don't think a knife will help you.
John: You're just on her side. I think I ought to . . . . . [Schank, 1971, p. 4].

Clearly, at this point in the conversation our expectations about what John is about to say take into account more than what is contained in the incompleted sentence. These expectations are based on such things as the previous conversation, our knowledge of what knives can be used for, how quarrels can end, etc. Schank argues that if a human can bring these sorts of considerations to bear to form complex expectations, so should a computer, and the computer should use these expectations to guide the parse.

Roger Schank, unlike the past linguists or computer scientists we have considered, is firmly committed to the psychological task of modeling the human as he understands a sentence. Because of Schank's psychological commitments, his parser is subject to experimental test, whereas the other theories have protected themselves from potential embarrassments from this quarter. However, Schank's level of theorizing is such that it is difficult to make contact with the data that psychologists typically gather. We will present data (Chapter 10) to indicate that the graph-structural properties of his conceptual dependency diagrams are different from the properties of the associative representation of the sentences in memory. However, it is doubtful whether this constitutes much of an embarrassment to Schank's overall efforts to provide a model of the language-comprehension process. His real contribution would seem to be in his efforts to guide the parser in an intelligent manner. Unfortunately, much of that work is scattered throughout the insides of his program in the form of particular heuristics, decisions to represent particular verbs in particular ways, etc. One might bring evidence to bear on one or more of these special decisions, but that would have little consequence for the grand scheme.

Concluding Remarks

One serious criticism that can be leveled at the parsers reviewed is that they do not learn how to parse; rather they are programmed to parse. Practically, this means that these efforts will never handle more than a small subset of any real language like English. In a powerful program like Schank's, as each word is introduced into the lexicon, it is necessary to enter information about the type of conceptualizations in which it can appear, any of its syntactic peculiarities, and other information relevant to intelligently parsing constructions in which that word appears. Clearly, it would be an inordinately burdensome task to program a parser that could handle an appreciable portion of the lexicon of the English language. What is necessary is a system with basic acquisition devices so that it could program its own parser, given some experience with a language. Also such a model would provide a much more elegant and satisfactory theory of parsing. It is not very enlightening to have a huge listing of special patterns and idiosyncracies that are relevant to untangling a particular natural language. This is what a theory of natural language comprehension like Roger Schank's rapidly becomes as it is extended to larger subsets of English.

Unfortunately, no one has a detailed and programmable theory of language acquisition. In our language-analysis program, we will also fail to deal with this problem. That is, HAM's parser will be preprogrammed with many of the tricks and heuristics necessary for analyzing English. While these tricks and heuristics are part of an adult's linguistic knowledge, they clearly are not part of a child's initial linguistic competence. We think we can be excused for our failure to provide a theory of language acquisition because our principle concern is with memory and not with language understanding. With respect to memory, we will be careful to identify what are the original structures and processes and how this initial memory system develops through experience into the adult system. So without further ado we will turn to describing our model of memory, HAM. As we do, the reader should be careful to be comparing it with the ideas we have presented in these first chapters.

REFERENCES

Anderson, J. M. *The grammar of case.* Cambridge: The University Press, 1971.

Bandura, A. Social-learning theory of identificatory processes. In D. A. Goslin (Ed.), *Handbook of socialization theory and research.* Chicago: Rand McNally, 1969.

Bandura, A. *Psychological modeling; Conflicting theories.* Chicago: Aldine-Atherton, 1971.

Bever, T. G., Fodor, J. A., & Garrett, M. A formal limitation of associationism. In T. R. Dixon & D. L. Horton (Eds.), *Verbal behavior and general behavior theory.* Englewood Cliffs, N. J.: Prentice-Hall, 1968.

Bloomfield, L. *Language.* New York: Holt, 1933.

Bobrow, D. G., & Fraser, J. B. An augmented state transition network analysis procedure. *Proceedings of the International Joint Conference on Artificial Intelligence*, Washington, D. C., 1969, 557–567.

Chomsky, N. *Syntactic structures.* The Hague: Mouton, 1957.

Chomsky, N. Verbal behavior (a review of Skinner's book). *Language*, 1959, **35**, 26–58.

Chomsky, N. *Aspects of the theory of syntax.* Cambridge, Mass.: M.I.T. Press, 1965.

Chomsky, N. *Language and mind.* New York: Harcourt, Brace & World, 1968.

Chomsky, N. Deep structure, surface structure, and semantic interpretation. In D. Steinberg & L. Jakobovits (Eds.), *Semantics: An interdisciplinary reader in philosophy, linguistics, anthropology and psychology.* London: Cambridge University Press, 1971.

Fillmore, C. J. The case for case. In E. Bach & R. T. Harms (Eds.), *Universals in linguistic theory.* New York: Holt, Rinehart & Winston, 1968.

Fillmore, C. J. Some problems for case grammar. Unpublished manuscript, 1971.

Fodor, J. A. Could meaning be in r_m? *Journal of Verbal Learning and Verbal Behavior*, 1965, **4**, 73–81.

Halliday, M. A. K. Notes on transitivity and theme in English. *Journal of Linguistics*, 1967, **3**, 37–81.

Halliday, M. A. K. Functional diversity in language as seen from a consideration of modality and mood in English. *Foundations of Language*, 1970, **6**, 322–361.

Harris, Z. S. *Methods in structural linguistics.* Chicago: University of Chicago Press, 1951.

Hewitt, C. PLANNER: A language for manipulating models and proving theorems in a robot, artificial intelligence. Memo No. 168 (Rev.), Project MAC, Massachusetts Institute of Technology, Cambridge, Massachusetts, August 1970.

Kaplan, R. M. Augmented transition networks as psychological models of sentence comprehension. Unpublished manuscript, 1971.

Katz, J. J., & Fodor, J. A. The structure of a semantic theory. *Language*, 1963, **39**, 170–210.

Katz, J. J., & Postal, P. N. *An integrated theory of linguistic descriptions.* Cambridge: M.I.T. Press, 1964.

Kintsch, W. Notes on the semantic structure of memory. In E. Tulving & W. Donaldson (Eds.), *Organization of Memory.* New York: Academic Press, 1972.

Lakoff, G. Linguistics and natural logic. *Synthese*, 1970, **22**, 151–271.

Lakoff, G. On generative semantics. In D. Steinberg & L. Jakobovits (Eds.), *Semantics: An interdisciplinary reader in philosophy, linguistics, anthropology and psychology.* London: Cambridge University Press, 1971.

Lakoff, G., & Ross, J. R. Is deep structure necessary? Unpublished manuscript, 1968.

Maltzman, I. Theoretical conceptions of semantic conditioning and generalization. In T. R. Dixon & D. L. Horton (Eds.), *Verbal behavior and general behavior theory.* Englewood Cliffs, N. J.: Prentice-Hall, 1968.

Matthews, G. H. Analysis by Synthesis of Natural Languages. *Proceedings of the 1961 International Conference on Machine Translation and Applied Language Analysis.* London: Her Majesty's Stationary Office, 1962.

McNeill, D. On theories of language acquisition. In T. R. Dixon & D. L. Horton (Eds.), *Verbal behavior and general behavior theory*. Englewood Cliffs, N. J.: Prentice-Hall, 1968.

Miller, G., & Selfridge, J. Verbal context and the recall of meaningful material. *American Journal of Psychology*, 1950, **63**, 176–185.

MITRE. English preprocessor manual, Rep. No. SR-132, The Mitre Corp., Bedford, Mass., 1964.

Mowrer, O. H. *Learning theory and the symbolic processes*. New York: Wiley, 1960.

Noble, C. E. An analysis of meaning. *Psychological Review*, 1952, **59**, 421–430.

Osgood, C. E. Towards a wedding of insufficiencies. In T. R. Dixon & D. L. Horton (Eds.), *Verbal behavior and general behavior theory*. Englewood Cliffs, N. J.: Prentice-Hall, 1968.

Osgood, C. E., Suci, G. J., & Tannenbaum, P. H. *The measurement of meaning*. Urbana: University of Illinois Press, 1957.

Paivio, A. *Imagery and verbal processes*. New York: Holt, Rinehart & Winston, 1971.

Petrick, S. R. *A recognition procedure for transformational grammars*. Unpublished doctoral dissertation, M.I.T., 1965.

Rumelhart, D. E., Lindsay, P. H., & Norman, D. A. A process model for long-term memory. In E. Tulving & W. Donaldson (Eds.), *Organization of Memory*. New York: Academic Press, 1972.

Schank, R. C. *Intention, memory and computer understanding*. Stanford Artificial Intelligence Project Memo. No. AIM-140, Stanford University, 1971.

Schank, R. C., Tesler, L., & Weber, S. *Spinoza II: Conceptual case-based natural language analysis*. Stanford Artificial Intelligence Project Memo No. AIM-109, Stanford University, 1970.

Skinner, B. F. *Verbal behavior*. New York: Appleton-Century-Crofts, 1957.

Staats, A. W. *Learning, language and cognition*. New York: Holt, Rinehart & Winston, 1968.

Staats, A. W. Linguistic-mentalistic theory versus an explanatory S-R learning theory of language development. In D. Slobin (Ed.), *The ontogenesis of grammar*. New York: Academic Press, 1971.

Thorne, J., Bratley, P., & Dewar, H. The syntactic analysis of English by machine. In D. Michie (Ed.), *Machine intelligence 3*. New York: American Elsevier, 1968.

Watson, J. B. *Behaviorism*. New York: Norton, 1930.

Winograd, T. Procedures as a representation for data in a computer program for understanding natural language. *MIT Artificial Intelligence Laboratory Project MAC-TR-84*, 1971.

Winograd, T. Understanding natural language. *Cognitive Psychology*, 1972, **3**, 1–191.

Woods, W. A. Transition network grammars for natural language analysis. *Communications of the ACM*, 1970, **13**, 591–606.

6

AN OVERVIEW OF HAM

I see no reason to believe that intelligence can exist apart from a highly organized body of knowledge, models, and processes. The habit of our culture has always been to suppose that intelligence resides in some separated crystalline element, call it consciousness, apprehension, insight, gestalt, or what you will, but this is merely to confound naming the problem with solving it.

—Marvin Minsky

6.1. THE INFORMATION-PROCESSING APPROACH

A disappointing outcome of our review of memory theories is that there appears to have been relatively little progress, at least until fairly recently. Indeed, one could argue that Aristotle's sketchy outline was the most advanced conception. Although it is too early to decide whether the neo-associational models reviewed in Chapter 4 will constitute a significant theoretical advance, they certainly provide that prospect.

The progress now being made in theories of memory has to do, we think, with the advent of the information-processing approach in psychology. Until the last two decades there were only three principal ways to study the mind. First, there was introspection where one observed the operation of his own mental processes insofar as they were accessible to observation and description. The unreliability of introspection, as a source of data, has been greatly exaggerated. In the imageless thought controversy, for instance, the real issue did not seem to be what the basic introspections were, but rather how to interpret them. The original assumption of the introspectionists was that the data of introspection would simply and unambiguously determine a satisfactory psychological explanation. But this simply asks more of introspection than it can provide. Introspections are valid psychological data, but they cannot be expected to ever constitute or easily generate a theory. There is just too much "low-level processing" going on below the level of consciousness, not open to introspection which must be inferred from behavior. Skinner's (1953) analysis of how we learn to introspect about private mental events—to discriminate them, label them, describe them, and generally to be aware of them—suggests very severe limitations on the sorts of revelations that can be expected to come from "self-observation."

The behaviorist-functionalist approach was another attempt to arrive at a psychological theory via a particular experimental methodology. In this approach, man is viewed as a "black box" into which various stimuli go and out of which various responses come. For the radical behaviorist, the task of psychology is, *experimentally*, to record what responses are elicited by what stimulus conditions and, *theoretically*, to make generalizations about these stimulus-response contingencies. The nature of the processes going on inside the black box is of little interest to this account because the behaviorist does not believe that knowledge will advance one's ability to predict and control the behavior of the black box; as Skinner says, "The Outside Story has to be told first." On this account, the task of psychology is that of specifying the input-output functions that will serve to predict specified behaviors under specified conditions. The layman has always thought that this approach is unduly restrictive, and he is right. As we argued in Chapter 2, the task of specifying that grand input-output function is conceptually intractable unless one is permitted to speculate about the mental structures and processes underlying the behavior.

The problem remains of how to specify these structures and processes. In this age of scientific materialism, the layman has a ready solution: Let's talk about brain structures, neurons, electrical potentials, biochemical transmitters, and the concrete, physical happenings that we all know ultimately underlie man's behavior. The physiological psychologist pursues this solution in earnest. It is another attempt to arrive at a theory by an experimental methodology and it has similar fatal flaws. The neural activity involved in the typical question answering of a human is undoubtedly a matter of enormous complexity. We could never grasp it in terms of which neuron is exciting which others in what ordered patterns; at that level, the matter is simply too complex. The problem is analogous to trying to understand question answering in a computer program at the level of the electrical circuitry of the computer. And, almost certainly, the computer is much simpler physically than the human brain. The level of analysis is just too microscopic to be of any psychological utility. In the computer, we must talk of and characterize abstract objects called programs and data structures. So, also in understanding man, we must resort to postulation of abstract mental structures and processes.

The information-processing approach, then, is not a methodology for experimenting; it is rather a methodology for theorizing. An attempt is made to characterize abstractly the commodity, information, which is to be handled by the mental processes. One of the early characterizations of "information" measured its uncertainty in terms of *bits* (see Shannon, 1948). The uncertainty approach led to some interesting research (see Garner, 1962), but it was relatively useless as a theoretical tool. The problem was that the bit gave a very poorly articulated characterization of the information. More recent information-processing theories have attempted to characterize the information in terms of such things as chunks, features, associations, semantic markers, phrase structures, lists, discrimination nets, and propositions. As the descriptions of the information have become more articulated, the theories composed out of them have become more successful. The basic units in our theory will be semantic primitives (simple ideas), complex ideas constructed from these, and associations that connect the ideas. From these, propositional structures will be composed to provide a higher-order level of analysis.

6.2. HAM'S STRUCTURES AND PROCESSES

Having a viable characterization of the information, it then becomes possible to characterize the processes that transform or make use of the information as it proceeds through the system. Such characterizations are frequently given in terms of flow charts, and we follow this convention in introducing HAM. Figure 6.1 is an outline of the information flow occurring between the reception of stimuli and the emission of various responses. We will have very little to say about many of the system components in Figure 6.1. Our major theoretical contributions will all concern the component labeled "memory." Nonetheless, we have added the many arrows and components to illustrate how the memory component fits into the total mental picture.

First, we assume that the external information is registered by sensory receptors, transformed and recoded into higher-order features, and then held in

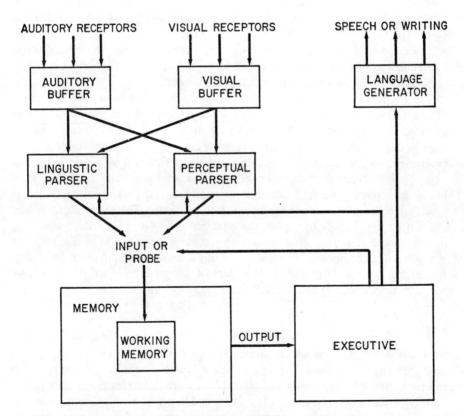

FIG. 6.1. The architecture of HAM's mental system.

limited-capacity auditory and visual buffers. We have absolutely nothing to say about these sensory processes except that they happen. In the next stage, the task of the parsers is to analyze what is in these buffers and to produce a meaningful description of it, suitable for transmission to and storage in long-term memory. The linguistic parser is designed to operate on symbolic information. It does not produce a description of the signals residing in the buffers, but rather a description of the conceptualization referenced by the symbols in the buffer. Its primary function is obviously to translate natural language statements into conceptual descriptions, but it presumably can be evoked to handle other symbolic systems such as formal logic. We will examine in Chapter 8 how the linguistic parser functions and how it is to be interfaced with long-term memory.

In contrast to the linguistic parser, the perceptual parser simply tries to build up a description of the sensory contents contained in the buffers. Given current evidence about lateralization of function (e.g., Gazzaniga, 1967; Gazzaniga & Sperry, 1967; Kimura, 1963; Milner, 1968), it is intriguing to speculate that in most adults the linguistic parser may be localized in the left cerebral hemisphere and the perceptual parser may be in the right hemisphere. Obviously, the same stimulus can be analyzed and given very different descriptions by the two parsers. The linguistic parser would take a visual stimulus like the words "Nixon cried" and send off to memory a conceptualization equivalent to "The president of the U.S.A. shed tears," whereas the perceptual parser would build up a conceptualization equivalent to "The pattern, *Nixon*, occurred to the left of the pattern *cried*." We will develop in the next chapter the representation in which these conceptualizations are expressed. It will be argued there that the output of either parser is expressed in the same representational format.

The outputs of these parsers are sent as inputs or probes to be matched to the contents of long-term memory. This is the process generally known in psychology as stimulus recognition. It will be discussed in detail in Chapter 9. These probes and their matching structures in long-term memory are sent from the long-term memory component to the executive (the arrow labeled "Output" in Figure 6.1). The executive has very general control over all information processing in the system. It has at its disposal powerful problem-solving and inferential capacities which can be used in deciding how to direct the information processing. These capabilities will be called upon periodically to explain the intelligence displayed by HAM in allocating its mnemonic resources. The final component in Figure 6.1 is the language generator. This component is evoked to output answers to questions, to request further information to disambiguate a piece of discourse, and so forth. Again, we will have almost nothing to say about the language-generation process.

An Example

With this outline of the system architecture, it will be informative to trace a particular piece of information through encoding, storage, and retrieval. When a novel sentence is received like "In a park a hippie touched a debutante," it is analyzed into a binary graph structure like Figure 6.2. This graph structure is initially held in working memory. The parser and its use of working memory are examined in Chapter 8. A separate tree structure is composed for each proposition in

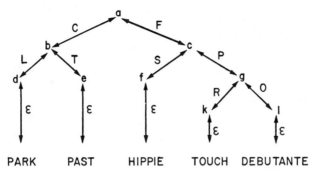

FIG. 6.2. A prototypical output from the parser.

the sentence. Because our example sentence involves only one proposition, the graph structure in Figure 6.2 is a simple tree. The graph in Figure 6.2 is composed of nodes interconnected by labeled arrows. The nodes are represented by lower case letters and the labels on the arrows by upper case letters. The letters representing nodes are arbitrarily chosen and simply facilitate reference to a particular node. In contrast, the labels indicate specific semantic relations holding among the nodes. There is just a finite set of possible semantic relations or labels. Note also that function words like *a* are not maintained in HAM's representation. Any semantic information conveyed by choice of function words is expressed in graph-structure configuration and by the choice of labels.

Each propositional tree is divided into two subtrees—a *context* subtree and a *fact* subtree. The arrow labeled with a *C* points to the context subtree and the arrow with an *F* to the fact subtree. Intuitively, the nodes in the tree represent *ideas* and the links *relations* or *associations* between the ideas. Therefore, in Figure 6.2, node *a* represents the idea of the total proposition, node *b* the idea of the context, and node *c* the idea of the fact. Effectively, the proposition is asserting that fact *c* is true in context *b*. The context node *b* is further subdivided into a *location* node *d* and a time node *e*. The arrows leading to these nodes are labeled *L* and *T*, respectively. Similarly, the fact node *c* leads by an *S* arrow to a subject node *f* and by a *P* arrow to a *predicate* node *g*. That is, the fact is composed of a predication *g* being asserted about a subject *f*. Finally in this example, the predicate node *g* leads by a *R* arrow to a *relation* node *k* and by an *O* arrow to an *object* node *l*. So, what is being predicated of *f* is that it has relation *k* to *l*.

This completes the binary divisions in the proposition. The node *d* represents a particular park, *e* a particular past time, *f* a particular hippie, *k* a particular touching, and *l* a particular debutante. These are connected by the *membership* relation, ϵ, to the general concepts of *park, past, hippie, touch,* and *debutante*. These general nodes already exist in memory and represent our ideas of each concept. Connected to each is an associative structure giving the meaning of the general idea. A much more complete analysis of HAM's representation is provided in Chapter 7. There we also attempt to motivate the structural assumptions that underlie these representations.

The concept nodes, in which the tree structure is anchored, are assumed to be preexisting in memory before receipt of the sentence. However, all the structure above the concept nodes is new and records the novel information in the sentence. To encode this sentence, each of the 13 working-memory links above the concept nodes must be transformed into long-term memory associations. A stochastic model describing this encoding process is developed and tested in Chapter 10.

When the parser receives a question (e.g., "Who touched the debutante?"), it constructs a probe tree to represent the query. This probe tree is held in working memory while HAM attempts to match it to a corresponding structure in long-term memory. The best-matching long-term memory structure is generated as the output. The executive uses the information in the output in its attempt to generate an answer to the question. If the information is insufficient, the executive may construct a new probe and send it to memory requesting further output. Three of our later chapters—9, 12, and 13—will be devoted to examining various aspects of this retrieval process.

The executive can also be a source of information input to memory. That is, the executive can reflect upon its own opinions and form spontaneous propositions of its own—e.g., "I guess I don't really agree with Nixon's policy" or "I've just discovered that the fourth power of 3 is 81." These also can be sent to long-term memory as inputs and encoded.

From this description it should be clear that the executive has very general powers and plays a central role in the information processing schematized in Figure 6.1. It directly receives outputs from memory, can send probes and inputs to memory, and determines the generation of speech. Finally, it can communicate with the parsers and send useful information to them (e.g., that a particular parse does not make sense).

The Strategy-Free Component of Memory

A particular mnemonic performance in the laboratory is behavior whose characteristics are determined by all the components mentioned in Figure 6.1. However, our concern is really only with the long-term memory component. We have to consider the other components only out of the need to make contact with experimental data. The executive is a particularly annoying source of complication in the analysis of the memory experiments, for it determines the mnemonic strategies, heuristics, and tricks that a subject may evoke to make his learning task easier. Research aimed at delimiting the information-processing characteristics of human memory often finds itself bogged down in a tangle of idiosyncratic tricks employed by subjects (see Anderson, 1972; Prytulak, 1971; Reitman, 1970; Tieman, 1971).

We shall assume that long-term memory, itself, is strategy-invariant, that probes are always matched to memory in the same way, that identical outputs will be generated to identical probes, and that a given input always is represented and encoded in the same manner. Mnemonic strategies enter the picture in terms of the strategic selection of probes and inputs which are to be sent to memory and in terms of interpretations given to the output. That is, we claim that all these troubles are to be localized in the "executive component" of Figure 6.1. We will argue in Chapter 14 that verbal learning paradigms such as paired associates or free recall are particularly likely to elicit such strategic complications. That is, subjects restructure and edit what they encode in memory in order to make it more meaningful. Most of our research is concerned with sentences or larger linguistic units. It was our hope that, with such material, subject-imposed structure would be less frequent, and the transformations between stimuli and memory representations would be more direct and predictable. However, we are sometimes forced to consider the complications of unexpected mnemonic strategies even with such sentential materials.

It is a claim of considerable empirical import to state that there is a core strategy-free memory component common to all memory performances. The claim is equivalent to asserting that memory performance can be analyzed into a large set of mnemonic strategies plus this common strategy-free component. If so, the task of analyzing a particular memory performance can be divided into two smaller and hence more tractable subproblems—that of specifying the memory component and that of specifying the prevailing strategy of the subject. Moreover, if we succeed in characterizing the core memory component common to all behaviors, we have only one of these subproblems left in analyzing any further memory performances, viz., specifying the strategy adopted in the particular situation. The reader should appreciate that this decomposition may in fact be impossible for human memory. As noted in Chapter 3, both the Gestalters and the reconstruction theorists asserted that it was impossible to extricate memory from such matters as problem solving and inference. If they are right, this whole theoretical enterprise will come crashing down on our heads.

A Formalization of the Strategy-free Component

Formalization is an appropriate goal for any scientific theory. However, there are dangers in forcing a theory prematurely into a formal cast. This tends to stunt the theory, fix it in its misconceptions, and prevent needed insight and revision. For whatever reason, certain types of reconceptualizations are easier if the theory is in a "rough and ready" form. This rough and ready form need not lack in clarity or precision, but it often lacks succinctness and elegance. Many of the ideas we will present are still in this state of informal development.

However, there does come a point when formalization becomes a stimulus rather than a hindrance to further theoretical development. It serves to separate the central assumptions from the tangential and to identify the points where further thought is required. Some of our theoretical ideas are achieving this needed formalization—particularly our ideas about the strategy-free component of memory. We will now provide a formal definition of this strategy-free component. This definition provides the superstructure for the formal developments in the next chapter. We will characterize the strategy-free component $\mathfrak{M}$ as an ordered six-tuple:

$$\mathfrak{M} = \; < \mathfrak{I}, \mathfrak{P}, \mathfrak{O}, \mathfrak{S}, \mathfrak{E}, \mathfrak{D} >$$

where $\mathfrak{I}$ is the set of possible inputs
$\mathfrak{P}$ is the set of possible probes
$\mathfrak{O}$ is the set of possible outputs

$\mathcal{S}$ is the set of possible memory structures

$\mathcal{E}$ is an encoding (or "learning") function such that $\mathcal{E} : \mathcal{I} \times \mathcal{S} \times t \rightarrow P(\mathcal{S})$, where t is the time for which the input is studied, and $P(\mathcal{S})$ is the power set of $\mathcal{S}$ (i.e., the set of all possible subsets of $\mathcal{S}$). The encoding process $\mathcal{E}$, is the mechanism by which the structure of memory is modified to record new information. $\mathcal{E}$ maps into more than one possible memory structure because the encoding process is probabilistic rather than deterministic. (See Chapter 10.)

$\mathcal{D}$ is a decoding function such that $\mathcal{D} : \mathcal{P} \times \mathcal{S} \rightarrow P(\mathcal{O})$. This is the mechanism by which memory, $\mathcal{S}$, is probed, $\mathcal{P}$, to determine what is recorded there. The function maps onto the powerset of the outputs, $P(\mathcal{O})$, to accommodate the probabilistic character of the decoding process.

The elements $\mathcal{P}, \mathcal{I}, \mathcal{O}$, and $\mathcal{S}$ will be discussed in Chapter 7. They constitute the *structural components* of the theory. The decoding function $\mathcal{D}$ is discussed in Chapter 9 on stimulus recognition, and the encoding function $\mathcal{E}$ in Chapter 10 on learning. They constitute the *process assumptions* of our theory.

A word of warning is appropriate here about our use of the word *encoding*. In the psychological literature it is most often used to refer to the transformation of a stimulus into an internal representation. We will use the term in this way sometimes—for instance, in our discussion of parsing in Chapter 8. However, "encoding" has acquired a second meaning in our research—that exemplified in the above definition of the strategy-free component of memory. Here it refers to the transformation of the temporary representation of information in the input tree into a permanent representation in long-term memory.

6.3. THE SIMULATION OF HAM BY COMPUTER

One advantage of the abstract character of an information-processing theory is that one need not be concerned with the details of the physical realization of the theory in the brain. However, the characterization is sufficiently explicit that it should be capable of implementation in a number of physical systems. In particular, we should be able to implement HAM as a simulation program in a serial, digital computer. We have accomplished a partial simulation of the system outlined in Figure 6.1. The core strategy-free memory component is fully specified as a series of programs and data structures in the programming language, LISP.

It is important to be clear about the relationship between the theory and this simulation program. We make no claim that there is any careful correspondence between the step-by-step information processing in the simulation program and in the psychological theory. Rather, there is a *functional* correspondence to be made between various *mental processes* we postulate and various *programs* (LISP functions) that we have implemented. A particular program is equivalent to a mental process in terms of its *effect* on the abstract informational structures, but not necessarily in other respects. So, for instance, there will be no necessary correspondence between the time for a program to run and the time for the process to occur in the head.

Thus, the computer simulation of our theory is to be construed in the same sense that one construes computer simulations of theories in physics or in other sciences. We are simulating at a gross level some effects the theory predicts, but no ontological significance should be attributed to the operations (LISP functions or electrical componentry) that are evoked to produce the simulation. The computer is only a *computational tool* for explicitly checking the predictions of the theory, for determining whether all the specified mental processes are in fact fully specified, and whether they can work together as claimed.

This stance is not always taken with regard to computer simulations advanced as psychological theories. The claim is sometimes made (e.g., Newell & Simon, 1961) that the program is the theory. That is not the case for HAM, and we wish to make this denial explicit. HAM represents a very complicated set of speculations about human memory. Only some of these are represented in the simulation program. Moreover, the simulation program does not serve as an embodiment of this subset of the theory; rather, it is but one test of the adequacy of that subset.

Despite these disavowals, the reader is sure to suspect that the task of computer simulation has been a strong influence on the character of our theory. It has, and we worry about it. That is, one factor that has determined our theory is that it should be easy to simulate on a digital computer. Algorithmic computability is likely to be confused with psychological simplicity or plausibility of a process. Furthermore, programming a computer is a great stimulus for theoretical creativity. A solution to a programming problem often suggests a corresponding psychological mechanism. We would hardly want to criticize the machine for stimulating our creativity, but we do realize it stimulates us in the direction of computer-like mechanisms, and the brain is not a serial, digital computer. However, the tactic of developing a theory so that it is simulatable does not differ in principle from developing a theory so that it is mathematically tractable. The practice of simplifying theories to make them tractable is quite acceptable in science because of the necessity of testing scientific claims. However, it is a practice that is dangerous because computational tractability is not always compatible with scientific accuracy. Whether our theory is seriously flawed by this influence remains to be determined.

Our simulation program functions in a question-answering task domain. That is to say, we have programmed an interactive system to which we may assert facts and of which we may ask questions. The program accepts English sentences from a teletype, the sentences representing either assertions or questions. If it receives an assertion, it will type back a description of the memory structure it has formed in the course of encoding that assertion. If it receives a question, it will search its memory for an appropriate answer. This simulation program may be regarded as a test of the sufficiency of our theory. That is, it demonstrates that the theory is sufficient to generate behavior approaching the complexity of that found in the world outside the laboratory.

The Interface Problem

However, much more than HAM's strategy-free memory component must be simulated in order to have an operative system. This strategy-free component by itself comprises what is called a *fact-retrieval system* in the literature of artificial intelligence. That is, it is a memory system which, given a description of the desired information (a probe), will search memory for some piece of information that is similar to it, and then return this information as output. However, much more program must be written if one is to interface such a fact-retrieval system with the outer world, in order to produce a well-behaving *natural language question-answering system.* A linguistic parser must be written to transform natural language sentences into appropriate input for the memory. A number of executive routines must be written to guide the parser, to selectively search the vast memory network for useful answers to questions, and to make appropriate inferences about the information retrieved from long-term memory. This task of writing the parsing, inference, problem-solving, and decision programs is what will be referred to as the *interface problem* in question answering.

If one could efficiently handle both fact retrieval and interfacing, he would have a very powerful program indeed. Given the large memories that computers are coming to possess, we could simply feed into our computer the Encyclopaedia Britannica, and overnight HAM would become the most knowledgeable creature on this planet. The barrier to this goal is, of course, the interface problem. The adult who can comprehend the Encyclopaedia Britannica is a very competent speaker or reader of the language, has an enormous store of world knowledge, and is very adept at inference and problem solving. He has gained this sophistication from many long years of interaction with his world. It is that vast sophistication which must be programmed into our question-answering simulator in the form of the interface. But, of course, this is a job of unending proportions.

It is our opinion, therefore, that we should forget this Utopian goal of an all-purpose question-answer. However, we think it would be worthwhile to program a subset of the adult's sophistication into our program. Although it is infeasible to program the question-answerer with all our knowledge of the language, we could nonetheless give it sufficient knowledge to understand at least a subset of English. Although it could not solve all the problems or answer all the questions, it is of interest to see whether it handles a significant subset in a principled manner. This has been our goal in simulating HAM. Only a partial solution to the interface problem has been programmed, but enough so that we can have limited interaction with our fact-retrieval program.

A question we are sometimes asked is, Why not build up from this initial base? Why not write some more programs to increase HAM's ability to parse and comprehend sentences? Why not add some more inferential routines to increase the intelligence with which it answers questions? We started down this enticing, seductive path; but we slowly came to the realization that this was no way for experimental psychologists to proceed. Whatever is the value of such an approach for workers in artificial intelligence, from a psychological point of view it rapidly becomes fruitless and unenlightening. The end product of such an enterprise would appear to be thousands of lines of program that described the countless heuristics, procedures, tricks, and rules that the human has learned in his lifetime. We would have translated one incomprehensible mass of particulars, the human mind, into another incomprehensible mass, a computer program. But the task of a science is surely to reduce particulars to general laws rather than to translate particulars from one idiom into another.

Is there any way to study problem solving, language comprehension, or other elements of the interface problem? The answer would seem to be to look for the general principles underlying particular procedures. A good example of this strategy is the research done with the General Problem Solver, GPS (Ernst & Newell, 1969), in which an attempt was made to give a general model in which all problem solving of a well-defined sort could be understood. In particular, problem solving was viewed as searching for operators that would reduce the difference between a current state of the system and the desired goal state. However, for each problem to which GPS is applied, one must program in a characterization of the state space, the "rules of the game," and the set of permissible operators. Thus, while such research helps us understand problem solving, it does not avoid the need to separately encode each of the myriad of problem-solving heuristics into the program. We still need a seemingly endless list of characterizations of individual problem-solving tactics.

Perhaps a developmental approach would provide the needed theory of complexity. That is, one would like to characterize the initial processes and structures that permit acquisition of particular problem-solving abilities, or which permit acquisition of a language. This could be one way to obtain an efficient characterization of the adult competence. Also such a developmental theory holds out interesting prospects for research in artificial intelligence. If we could implement those structures and processes on some physical machine, we may get a self-evolving program which could eventually consume the Encyclopaedia Britannica. Our approach to describing the memory component in HAM is developmental in just this way. That is, we believe that it is simply hopeless, if not ridiculous, to try to specify all the information and procedures residing in the typical human memory. Rather we have characterized how that information and those procedures would be generated in HAM, if HAM were given the appropriate learning history.

A Sample Dialogue

To concretize our general description of the simulation program, we offer a sample dialogue we have had with it. Even though the conversation is not particularly inspiring, it does serve to illustrate some of the complexities in question answering. In the following, the symbol I references the informant who asserts facts to HAM and asks questions; likewise, H refers to HAM. To begin the discourse, the informant asserts a particular fact:

I: In a park a hippie touched a debutante.
H:

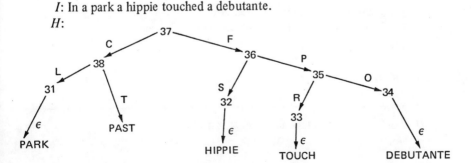

HAM's programmed response to this assertion is to parse it and then print out the above tree diagram for our inspection. Actually, a list encoding of the tree is printed out since the program has no graphic-display capabilities. This tree is the memory structure that is to represent and encode the assertion.

> *I*: Who was touched by the tall hippie?
> *H*: The tall hippie—which one?

HAM protests that it does not know of any *tall* hippies. So, we inform it that the current hippie under discussion is tall:

> *I*: The hippie was tall.
> *H*:

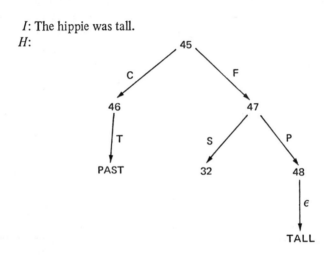

> *I*: Who was touched by the tall hippie?
> *H*: The debutante.

HAM can now generate the correct answer to this question. It should be noted that in the tree structure for "The hippie was tall," the same node (denoted here as 32) is used for hippie as was used in the previous conceptualization. This is because HAM interprets us to be talking about the same particular hippie (and we are). The next sequence illustrates HAM's procedures when it encounters a word not in its current lexicon.

> *I*: The sailor was kissed by the debutante.
> *H*: Sailor—I do not know this word—do you really mean it?
> *I*: Yes.
> *H*: What is its root form?
> *I*: Sailor.
> *H*: What type is it?
> *I*: A person.
> *H*: Would you like to talk about what it means?
> *I*: No.

The first possibility HAM considers is that "sailor" may be a typing error and that the informant really meant some word that it knows. Therefore, HAM asks, "Do you really mean it?" All lexical items are stored only once in the lexicon in their root form. Therefore, HAM must determine that "sailor" is the root form (e.g., instead of the plural form). Next, the parser needs to have some crude characterization of the word—whether it is a location, a person, a verb, etc. Finally, HAM asks whether the informant would like to tell it more about the meaning of this word. There are two ways for HAM to learn more about the meaning of *sailor*. First, the informant can explicitly provide such defining information. This is what HAM is requesting the informant to do in this example. Second, HAM can build up knowledge about the concept from a set of semantic contexts in which the word occurs. This is what the informant insists that HAM do in this case. The informant so insists because he knows all the programs for the former possibility have not been written and debugged.

The work by HAM to make sense of the word "sailor" turns out to be wasted in this instance because the sentence uses the definite article "the" preceding sailor. This definite article signals reference to some particular sailor, but HAM does not yet know of any particular sailor. Therefore, the sentence has to be recast using the indefinite article "a" which does not refer to a particular sailor. However, since a particular debutante has already been introduced, the definite article may be used with it.

H: The sailor—which one?
I: A sailor was kissed by the debutante.
H:

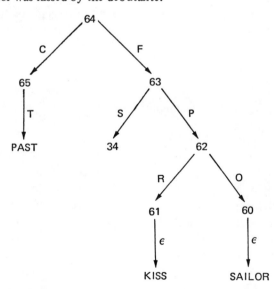

I: Who kissed the sailor?
H: The debutante.
I: Who touched the sailor?
H: I do not know the answer.

I: A prostitute who kissed the sailor was touched by the hippie.
H:

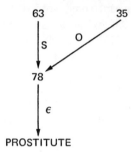

This last structure set up by HAM deserves some comment. HAM previously set up a structure to encode "A sailor was kissed by the debutante." It now uses part of that structure to encode the new proposition "The prostitute kissed the sailor." HAM adds a new subject-branch to the original structure; consequently, it now has encoded in memory "A prostitute and the debutante kissed the sailor." Similarly, HAM builds on the old structure for "In a park a hippie kissed a debutante" in order to encode the new proposition "The hippie touched a prostitute." It would then have encoded in memory a structure equivalent to "In the park the hippie touched the prostitute and the debutante." It may be noted in this regard that it was never asserted that the prostitute was touched *in the park*; but HAM's memory-matching routines conjecture that this was the location of the second act.

In essentials, the episodes described to date have the hippie touching two people and the sailor being kissed by two people. HAM maintains its memory-structure associations updated according to their recency of experience, and hence will respond with the most recent individual. This is illustrated by the following answers.

I: Who kissed the sailor?
H: The prostitute.
I: Who was touched by the hippie in the park?
H: The prostitute.
I: Who kissed the sailor in the park?
H: I do not know the answer.

The last question introduces one of the fuzzy problems in question answering. HAM has stored the fact that the sailor was kissed by the prostitute, but no mention has been made that this act occurred in any particular place. Since the query mentions a specific park, should HAM reply with "prostitute" or not? The current program balks and refuses to give an answer. Presumably an intelligent program would reply, "The sailor kissed the prostitute, but nothing was said about where that act occurred."

There is little to be gained from extending this sample dialogue because there is not much more that HAM can do that is of general interest. HAM's conversations are not so clever as those produced by some question-answering programs in artificial intelligence (e.g., Winograd, 1972) and we have not labored overmuch on developing a "smart" simulation. We shunned the many tricks known in the trade which would have made the proceeding simulation more lifelike, but which were empty of psychological significance. There are two reasons for our lack of concern about a clever-appearing simulation. First, as indicated previously, the time came when it seemed that further development of the program was only a way to exercise our skills in programming. However, the point was also quickly reached at which the simulation program became of such a size that it was beyond our limited financial resources to continue it in earnest. That is, not only was theorizing and experimentation more satisfying for us than was programming, it was also very much cheaper.

To the extent that the simulation is operative and successful, it serves to indicate that the memory system to be described in subsequent chapters meets certain sufficiency conditions for theories of human memory. To the extent that the simulation falls short of being adequately impressive, it remains uncertain whether we are just poor programmers (that has two senses!), or whether HAM is fundamentally wrong. In any event, the simulation per se has played little role in predictions and experimentation that we will be reporting. To be sure, the simulation would produce the results we predict from HAM's theoretical mechanisms, but the predictions have always been so obvious that no simulation was required to establish them. The logical status of this simulation contrasts with an earlier, less ambitious program of ours, FRAN (see Section 14.4 for a review), where the simulation really did play an essential role in generating experimental predictions. In this regard, then, HAM is rather much a "verbal theory" spelled out in the idiom of information processing which is currently popular among cognitive psychologists and comprehensible to them. Although not all aspects of our hypotheses have been programmed, the desire that we should be able to do so has kept a firm check on our flights of theoretical fancy. We offer these remarks to advise the psychologist that what he will find in the following pages is just the familiar language of current cognitive psychology, and to forewarn the computer scientist not to expect pages of code describing a snappy AI program. We now proceed to do our own thing.

REFERENCES

Anderson, J. R. FRAN: A simulation model of free recall. In G. H. Bower (Ed.), *The psychology of learning and motivation.* Vol. 5. New York: Academic Press, 1972.

Ernst, G. W., & Newell, A. *GPS: A case study in generality and problem solving.* New York: Academic Press, 1969.

Garner, W. R. *Uncertainty and structure as psychological concepts.* New York: Wiley, 1962.

Gazzaniga, M. A. The split brain in man. *Scientific American*, 1967, **217**, 24–29.

Gazzaniga, M. A., & Sperry, R. W. Language after section of cerebral commisures. *Brain*, 1967, **90**, 131–148.

Kimura, D. Right temporal damage. *Archives of neurology*, 1963, 8, 264–271.

Milner, B. Visual recognition and recall after right temporal-lobe excision in man. *Neuropsychogia*, 1968, **6**, 191–209.

Newell, A., & Simon, H. A. GPS, a program that simulates human thought. In H. Billing (Ed.), *Lernende Automaten.* Munich: R. Oldenbourg KG, 1961. pp. 109–124.

Prytulak, L. S. Natural language mediation. *Cognitive Psychology*, 1971, **2**, 1–56.

Reitman, W. What does it take to remember? In D. A. Norman (Ed.), *Models of human memory.* New York: Academic Press, 1970.

Shannon, C. E. A mathematical theory of communication. *Bell System Technical Journal,* 1948, **27,** 379–423, 623–656.

Skinner, B. F. *Science and human behavior.* New York: Macmillan, 1953.

Tieman, D. G. Recognition memory for comparative sentences. Unpublished doctoral dissertation, Stanford University, 1971.

Winograd, T. Understanding natural language. *Cognitive Psychology*, 1972, **3,** 1–191.

7
THE STRUCTURE OF KNOWLEDGE

> *Let us remind ourselves that the task on which we are engaged is not merely one of English grammar; we are not school children analyzing sentences into subject, extension of subject, complement and so on, but are interested not so much in the sentences themselves, as in what they mean, from which we hope to discover the logical nature of reality.*
>
> *—F. P. Ramsey*

7.1. THE REPRESENTATION PROBLEM

The most fundamental problem confronting cognitive psychology today is how to represent theoretically the knowledge that a person has: what are the primitive symbols or concepts, how are they related, how are they to be concatenated and constructed into larger knowledge-structures, and how is this "information file" to be accessed, searched, and utilized in solving the mundane problems of daily living. The choice of a representation is central, since how one handles this issue causes widespread effects throughout the remainder of his theoretical efforts. As computer scientists working on problem solving have known for years, a good structural representation of the problem already constitutes half of its solution (see Amarel, 1968).

There are several possible ways to represent the knowledge derived from linguistic or perceptual inputs—as description-lists, analog pictures, two-dimensional arrays, attribute-value strings, trees, etc. The basic unit of knowledge in HAM will be the *proposition*, which corresponds in essentials to a complete conceptualization (i.e., an assertion or statement). The structure of these propositions will be described later in this chapter. However, before turning to that, we shall briefly indicate some of the criteria for a psychologically plausible representation of knowledge.

We wanted a standard format in which to represent incoming information, in order to store it in a retrievable form. We have searched for considerations that could motivate a particular choice for this representation and will list five that we have thought of.

1. The representation should be capable of expressing any conception which a human can formulate or understand.

2. The representation should allow for relatively efficient search for and retrieval of known information. That is, specific information should remain relatively accessible even when the data-files grow to encyclopedic proportions.

3. The representation should saliently exhibit the substantive information extracted from a given input. It should not be influenced by the peculiarities of the particular natural language in which that information was communicated. This hope for language-invariance amounts to a wish for a universal *interlingua* in which any conception in any language could be expressed, but for which the format would not be specific to a particular language. Furthermore, we would hope that sensory or perceptual information provided by "scene descriptions" would be expressible in the same formalisms. In such a manner, the system would provide a common currency in terms of which linguistic and perceptual information could be brought together to be compared, modified, combined, and coordinated in usage.

4. For reasons of parsimony, the representation should involve a minimum of formal categories. That is, it should make a minimum of *formal* (structural or syntactic) distinctions at the outset; more complex distinctions would be built up by the construction rules for concatenating primitive ideas. One motivation for minimizing the formal categories is for the sake of simplicity and elegance in the theory. Another motivation is that the fewer and simpler are the innate distinctions the mind must make, the more likely it is that the neural apparatus of a child can implement at least that much analysis of the input.

5. The representation must allow for easy expression of concatenation operations, by which "duplex ideas" can be constructed out of "simple ideas." This means, for example, that the representation should allow easy expression of conceptual hierarchies, or multiply embedded predications, or allow one to predicate new information of any old information-structure.

We believe that these five systematic considerations help delimit what is a plausible representation; they clearly are not sufficient to determine the representation uniquely. There is a considerable gap between these general specifications and a finished representational format, a gap that presently can be filled only by one's intuitions, best guesses, and biases. Because we are aware of this gap, we would therefore welcome further criteria to motivate our representation or alternative ones more satisfactory than our own.

As noted above, the proposition is the principle unit in the representation of knowledge in HAM's long-term memory. HAM's long-term memory passively records the propositional trees that it receives as input, preserving identically their structure. Therefore, our discussion here will refer indiscriminately to the structure of propositions either in long-term memory or in the input, since these exhibit identical properties.

The linguistic parser accepts a sentence and is presumed to deliver as output a set of atomic propositions related in specified ways. These atomic propositions will be represented as binary labeled trees of a particular sort to be specified. The trees will consist of a set of memory nodes linked by labeled arcs. The full set of atomic propositions and their relations within a given sentence are then represented as one large graph structure, which the memory system automatically tries to "learn" or "store." If the tree is successfully stored, the nodes and the links of the input tree will become permanent elements of long-term memory. The nodes correspond intuitively to the *ideas* of British associationism, and the links to the *associations.* Long-term memory in HAM consists of a huge network of such intersecting trees. In a later section we shall be concerned with how the total long-term memory is organized. For the moment, however, we will focus on the character of an individual tree as it is input to and stored in long-term memory.

Perhaps a word is in order regarding alternative representations for HAM's memory. We seriously considered adopting one of the linguistic representations discussed in Chapter 5, such as Chomsky's deep-structure in *Aspects*, Fillmore's deep case structure, the generative semanticist's abyssal structure, or Schank's conceptual structure. However, with each of these representations there were some difficulties that caused us to balk. Each of these linguistic representations is concerned with explicating the structure of a single sentence, and, except for Schank's, each is aimed primarily at capturing relevant linguistic intuitions and generalities. Moreover, some of the information contained in the linguistic representations is undoubtedly specific to the peculiarities of language. For instance, some of Fillmore's case concepts, such as "instrument," appear to be motivated primarily by the fact that many languages have particular syntactic constructions for expressing instrumentality. However, we have seen no compelling argument for such a separate case distinction in a memory representation. We would argue that a memory formalism such as our own should not be designed specifically to fit the peculiarities of a given natural language, since it must also be capable of encoding *nonlinguistic* information that arises from perceptual sources like a visual scene. In contrast to the linguistic approaches, our concern has been instead with an *effective* memory representation of the information asserted by sentences. An "effective representation" would be one that is realistic and economical in terms of the memory storage requirements, that permits efficient search of its contents in carrying out various memory tasks, that facilitates the various deductions required in question answering, and so on. We felt that these linguistic formulations were rarely designed for efficiency in such enterprises. In currently popular jargon, regardless of their appeal as models of linguistic *competence*, they were not necessarily ideal as models for *performance*. Furthermore, we were not acquainted with any particular psychological data which strongly suggested that the memory structure of a proposition should take one or another linguistic form.

We will therefore propose a particular "deep-structure" of our own, one which bears a certain resemblance to Chomsky's *Aspects* grammar and also to predicate calculus. Although we will try to motivate each distinction in this deep-grammar, we confess that we are somewhat tentative about the exact details of the representation. We know that HAM's formalisms can represent any assertion or question. What is in doubt is the aptness or correctness of the representation. Although memory data will be presented to favor HAM's representation over salient alternatives, the reader should not forget the tentative nature of these proposals.

The Sensationalistic Bias

As mentioned earlier, perceptual scene-descriptions should be represented in the same sort of information structures as linguistic descriptions. In this regard, we share the sensationalist bias of past associative theories in believing that the mind has been shaped through evolution to encode perceptual information, and that all inputs to memory are basically perceptual descriptions (albeit descriptions which may sometimes be rather abstract). That is, when the memory component encounters a proposition such as "In the park the hippie touched the debutante," what it in fact encodes is a description of the perception of a scene corresponding to that sentence. Both in the evolution of man and in the development of the child, the ability to represent perceptual data in memory emerges long before the ability to represent linguistic information. We believe that language attaches itself parasitically to this underlying conceptual system designed for perception (Bever, 1970, has proposed a similar view). Indeed, it could be argued that natural languages can be learned initially only because their organization corresponds (at least in the simple cases) to the perceptual organization of the referential field.

Such speculations are made plausible by recent results reported by Moeser and Bregman (1972; in press) on the learning of miniature "languages" by adults. The languages involved three to five phrase-structure rules involving four grammatical categories, and the terminal vocabulary was nonsense syllables. Subjects in one experiment (Moeser & Bregman, 1972) received a large amount of training (3,200 trials), being exposed to many grammatical strings exemplifying all rules, with periodic tests for recognition of novel grammatical versus ungrammatical strings. In one condition, the subjects merely saw the syllable strings alone, with no referential field. These subjects showed practically no learning of any of the syntactic rules, even after 3,200 trials. In an alternate condition, a systematic referential field (a string of geometric shapes) was presented along with the grammatical string, and the syllables in each syntactic category had a particular referential function in terms of that perceptual field (e.g., altering color, orientation, or borders of a central figure). The presence of the semantic referents alongside the grammatical string of nonsense caused a dramatic turnaround in results; all subjects now readily learned the grammatical rules, and showed productivity in distinguishing novel grammatical from ungrammatical strings even without the pictures. In commenting upon the strategy employed by subjects in this latter condition, Moeser and Bregman (in press) report:

> ... when semantic referents are present the learning strategy consists of
> (a) learning to associate each word with its referent, and (b) learning the
> specific rules of the reference field (the ways in which these referents can be
> organized), and then (c) learning to map words referring to relevant aspects of
> the visual field onto the sentence positions [p. 23].

Such studies, then, show that the organization of the perceptual field plays a significant role in the acquisition of grammatical relations. They also make plausible the view that, in the beginning, simple syntactic organization reflects aspects of the perceptual organization of the referential field.

The interfacing of language with the memory system, even if parasitical, has important consequences. For example, it permits men to exchange their experiences verbally, to inform one another, to reinforce or punish or question one another, and generally to enjoy the many fruits of a technology for communicating with one another. Moreover, language eventually facilitates the development of abstract conceptual structures that appear far removed from a description of immediate perceptual experience. By this and other similar means, language plays a central role in our capacity for abstract thought. Abstraction of a sophisticated type would seem unlikely without some kind of language. However, the structures that develop in memory never free themselves of their origin. Even the most abstract structures seem capable of being reduced to perceptual data, and Section 7.4 suggests a way by which this reduction might be accomplished. The language of the mathematical grammarians seems at times to be little more than uninterpreted symbols, mere tiles shuffled about according to string-formation rules. But real languages always remain close to their perceptual base in their interpretation. The perceptual derivation of even abstract concepts is almost so obvious as to be missed. Many of these abstract concepts arise from metaphors that use perceptual terms (Asch, 1961), such as the "depth" of thought, a "piercing wit," a "heated debate," a "raging passion," a "well-tuned" car, a "stormy meeting," etc. Theoretical discourse is replete with figurative metaphors, as the quotation marks in the following passage (from Whorf, 1956) illustrate:

> I "grasp" the "thread" of another's arguments, but if its "level" is "over my head," my attention may "wander" and "lose touch" with the "drift" of it, so that when he "comes" to the "point" we differ "widely," our "views" being indeed so "far apart" that the "things" he says "appear" "much" too arbitrary or even "a lot" of nonsense [p. 146].

Of course, these sensationalist claims for our memory structure currently have the status of pure dogma—or, less pejoratively, a promissory note to be cashed in the future. We have little to say in the way of specific experimental predictions about memory for perceptual material or its relation to memory for linguistic material. We have worked exclusively with sentence analysis, and have only hinted at the nature of the interface between perceptual material and the memory component. As difficult as it is to produce a theory of the interface between language and memory, it appears far easier than constructing the necessary perceptual system. Therefore, our predictions will concern memory for linguistic material. Nonetheless, we have tried to develop a representation that would be relatively indifferent to whether it is encoding perceptual or linguistic material. In this way fundamental modifications would not be required should the theory be extended someday to perceptual material.

7.2. THE PROPOSITIONAL REPRESENTATION

In choosing a representation for propositional information we have tried to be as frugal as possible and not assume more than the bare minimum necessary. The attitude has been not to permit a further complication to the representation unless it is absolutely required. The primary concepts will be presented as a set of semantic distinctions HAM makes in its propositional trees. Each distinction will be commented upon as it is introduced. Later, in Section 7.3, these rules will be presented more formally.

The Subject-Predicate Distinction

To put it plainly, the purpose of long-term memory is to record facts about various things, events, and states of the world. We have chosen the subject-predicate construction as the principal structure for recording such facts in HAM. In HAM we predicate of some subject S that it has a certain property P. Consider the four example sentences in Figure 7.1 and their representations in HAM. In each case, a particular node (called the *fact* node) sprouts two links or arcs, one arc, labeled S, pointing to the subject node, and a second arc, labeled P, pointing to the predicate node. The fact node represents the idea of the fact being asserted. James Mill would have called it a *duplex* idea, formed from the complex ideas of the subject and of the predicate. It is an idea that has some of the same functional properties as the subordinate ideas to which it points. For instance, we can predicate properties of such ideas (fact nodes) just as we can predicate of simple ideas like "a balloon." To illustrate, a fact can be said to be false, or probable, or amusing, or fortunate, etc. Figure 7.2 illustrates how one may predicate a property of a fact, asserting in this case that "It is fortunate that Caesar is dead." This approach permits representation of a number of such predications embedded inside one another to arbitrary depths. For instance, one can encode and represent "It is false that it is believed that it is fortunate that Caesar is dead."

The subject-predicate distinction is an ancient and honorable one which can be traced at least as far back as Aristotle. Roughly speaking, it permits one to introduce a topic (the subject) and then to make some comment about it (the

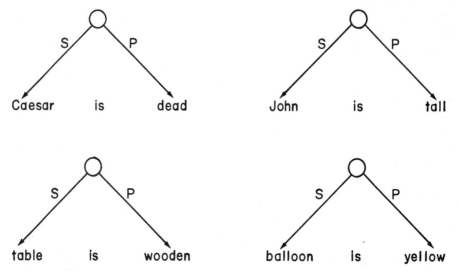

FIG. 7.1. Examples of how the subject-predicate construction may be used to express simple propositions.

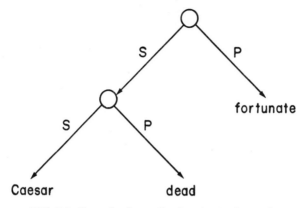

FIG. 7.2. Example of a predication about a fact node.

predicate). It is often observed that predication is the principle function of language. For instance, the "logical" subject-predicate distinction plays a very central role in Chomsky's transformational grammar (Chomsky, 1965). Furthermore, it is frequently the practice in computer science (e.g., Quillian, 1969) to represent all sorts of information in terms of a listing of object-property pairs or attribute-value pairs. But such pairs are basically just subject-predicate constructions. Philosophers have often argued that the subject-predicate distinction is more than an accident of language, that it basically reflects the way we understand reality. For instance, it has played a central role in philosophical debates regarding the distinction between universals and particulars (see Loux, 1970; Ramsey, 1931; Russell, 1911-12). Behavioristic psychologists (e.g., Mowrer, 1960; Staats, 1968; see our discussion in Chapter 5) have remarked upon the similarity between stimulus-response conditioning and predication. In conditioning as in predication, one item (the response or the predicate) becomes attached to another item (the stimulus or the subject) due (in part) to temporal contiguity. So, in adopting a subject-predicate distinction, we have many prestigious precedents. However, the role of predication in HAM's representation is somewhat different from these other uses, as will become apparent.

The Relation-Object Distinction

Predication frequently involves more than ascribing a simple predicate like "wooden" or "dead" to the subject. Rather, the predication often says that the subject bears a certain relation, r, to an object, o. Examples of how such relation-object predications would be encoded in HAM are illustrated in Figure 7.3. Our representation is now even closer to the deep-structures proposed by Chomsky (1965). It may be recalled that Chomsky's grammar rewrites the sentence as a noun phrase plus a verb phrase, and rewrites the verb phrase as a verb plus a noun phrase (object). For instance, Figure 7.3b involves a verbial construction for which HAM's representation is isomorphic to the deep-structure assigned to it by Chomsky's grammar.

Earlier, in Figure 7.2, we illustrated how something can be predicated of a fact node, e.g., "It is fortunate that Caesar is dead." In a similar vein, one can predicate

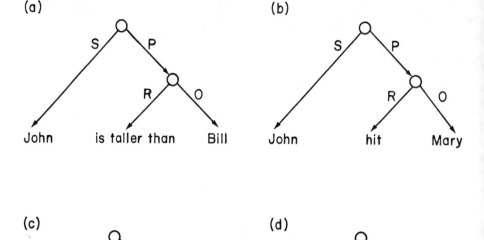

FIG. 7.3. Examples of the use of the relation-object construction.

something about a predicate node. Figure 7.4 illustrates the representation for the sentence "John cruelly hit Mary" and, for contrast, the representation of "John vigorously hit Mary." In Figure 7.4a, the predicate "cruel" modifies the predicate "the hitting of Mary," since "cruel" is a comment on the act. In contrast, in Figure 7.4b, "vigorous" just modifies the verb "hit," since "vigorously" is a so-called adverb of manner. Thus, some adverbs will modify the total predicate (the "action-object" combination), whereas others will modify just the relation (the

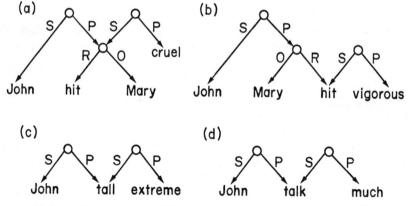

FIG. 7.4. Examples of predications about predicate and relation nodes.

"act"). For some sentences it is ambiguous whether the adverb is modifying the predicate or the relation. For instance, the sentence "John amusingly hit Mary" is ambiguous between "John hit Mary in an amusing manner" and "It was amusing of John to hit Mary."

One can, of course, predicate things of surface adjectives or properties, or of intransitive verbs, all of which will be written as S-P constructions in HAM's deep-structure. Intensifiers like *very, extremely, mildly, moderately*, etc., are typical examples. The structure assigned to "John is extremely tall" in HAM is shown in Figure 7.4c, whereas Figure 7.4d shows the structure for "John talks a lot," where an intransitive verb is modified.

The rules introduced so far represent unary relations with the subject-predicate rule, p(s), and binary relations with the subject-relation-object rule, r(s, o). It might seem that our formalism should be extended to allow for expression of general n-ary relations—i.e., $r(x_1, x_2, ..., x_n)$ as in the ELINOR system of Rumelhart, Lindsay, and Norman discussed in Section 4.4. For instance, ELINOR would represent "John gave the book to Mary" in functional notation as "give (John, book, Mary)," and "John opened the door with a key" would be represented as "open (John, door, key)," where the successive noun-arguments of the verb-relation occupy distinguished case roles. In Fillmore's case grammar, many verbs typically take more than just two cases (nouns), suggesting a possible need for n-ary relations in a long-term memory representation. However, we believe that this use of n-ary relations fails to capture a certain feature of such verbs that is very important in a memory representation. Often when a verb appears with more than two cases, it turns out that the underlying proposition is really asserting a causal relation between a predicate and another atomic proposition. Roger Schank (1972), in particular, has pointed out these implicit causatives in multiple case verbs.

Figure 7.5 shows the representation that these sentences should have in HAM. In Figure 7.5a, "John gave the book to Mary" becomes "John transferred the book, causing Mary to possess it"; in Figure 7.5b, "John opened the door with a key" becomes "John turned the key, causing the door to be open." By such means, then, one would be able to express n-ary relations $(n > 2)$ in our binary formalisms. Moreover, unlike the formalism of Rumelhart et al., our formalism would make salient the causal connections inherent in such higher-order relations. Our representation also makes salient the so-called *presuppositional* information as contrasted to the *implicational* information in sentences such as "John gave Mary the book." The presupposition is that John previously possessed the book, whereas the implication is that Mary has it now. This expanded representation would then permit direct answers to questions such as "Who has the book now?" without requiring further inferences.

The Context-Fact Distinction

The prior distinctions provide no means for representing where and when a fact occurred. Some facts like "John is the father of Bill" or "Giraffes have long necks" are true in any context, and no stipulation of a context is needed. However, it is usually necessary to specify the context in which a fact is true. Figure 7.6 illustrates how contextual information about time and location will be represented in HAM;

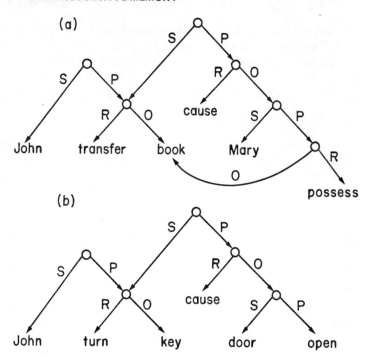

FIG. 7.5. How multicase sentences might be represented in the subject-relation-object formalism of HAM. Note that implicit causatives are often embedded in such sentences.

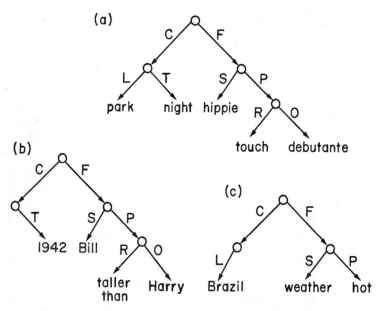

FIG. 7.6. Use of the context-fact distinction in encoding the following example propositions: (*a*) During the night in the park the hippie touched the debutante. (*b*) Bill was taller than Harry in 1942. (*c*) In Brazil the weather is hot.

two further duplex ideas are introduced into the representation to accomplish this purpose. First, we introduce the duplex idea of a context, which is composed in turn from the complex ideas of a place ("park") and a time ("night"). Second, the duplex fact-idea is combined with the duplex context-idea to construct a duplex idea of the total proposition being asserted. As mentioned above, the context modification of a fact node is optional. Also, the context node does not require expansion into both a time and a place specification. Figure 7.6b and c illustrates context ideas which are rewritten with only a time or only a location specified. Thus, Figure 7.6b may be read "John would be taller than Harry anywhere in 1942," and Figure 7.6c may be read "In Brazil the weather is hot at any time."

The context element specifies the spatiotemporal portion of reality for which a particular fact is true. This information can be very important in reasoning about the world. For instance, if we are asked whether John is now taller than Harry, it is important that our memories have recorded that it was the year 1942 when he was taller. If John was a man and Harry a child in 1942, we should hesitate to say that John is still taller. If both were grown men in 1942, we would be likely to suppose John is still taller. Thus, specification of context is important to a realistic memory because of the ephemeral nature of the particular facts about the world. Often knowledge of such facts is worthless unless we can further specify where and when they were true.

Furthermore, context information can often be called into service to resolve inconsistencies of "factual" inputs. To take a trivial example, the statement "The weather today is hot and freezing" is contradictory, whereas "The weather today is hot in Mexico and freezing in Antarctica" is perfectly acceptable. Besides time and location information, there is another contextual-like information that plays an important role in resolving inconsistencies. This is information about the source of a particular proposition. For instance, HAM may have stored "John thinks the weather is hot" and "Mary thinks the weather is freezing." Here, the contradicting assertions about the weather occur embedded as objects of propositions stating the source of the assertions (i.e., "John thinks X" and "Mary thinks Y"). The apparent contradiction can now be ascribed to the sources. Note that in this example, the source would not be given under the context branch of a proposition but rather as an embedding proposition.

A particular context node can become associated with a large number of facts. It is also possible to predicate features directly of a context. For example, Figure 7.7 illustrates how HAM would encode "San Francisco was cold, wet, and windy on Christmas." In this way, HAM could represent a lengthy description of a complex situation. Such situational descriptions prove to be very important in problem-solving applications within artificial intelligence (see McCarthy & Hayes, 1969; Raphael, 1971). Problem solving is often formulated as the task of finding a set of *operators* or *actions* that will transform one state of the world (a situational description) into a desired goal state (another situational description). Thus, our memory formalism would be well suited for use in representing "situational spaces" for problem solving.

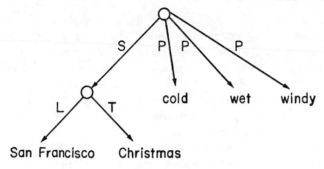

FIG. 7.7. Example of predications about a context.

Terminal Quantification

So far we have introduced four binary distinctions used in HAM's representation. In each case, a duplex idea is composed from simple ideas. Such binary trees will form the input to HAM. The trees always terminate in nodes which already exist in memory. (In this way the input trees are "anchored" or "hooked into" the existing memory structure.) For expository purposes, these nodes have been represented in Figure 7.1 through 7.7 by the corresponding English words. However, it is now time to reveal this oversimplification and to indicate the actual manner in which the trees will be linked into memory nodes.

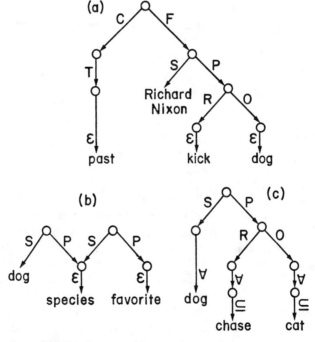

FIG. 7.8. Examples of terminal quantification.

A careful distinction is made within HAM between *concept* nodes and *individual* nodes. A concept node represents the general idea of some class concept like *dog* or *table*. It represents a set which may have individual members. In contrast, individual nodes reference the particular objects, properties, and events that fill our lives; examples are "Germany," "my dog Spot," "Richard Nixon," or "the hippie's touching of the debutante." When an input proposition is about a particular individual there are two ways of terminating the input tree, as illustrated by Figure 7.8. In one case, the node corresponding to that individual already exists in memory, as is the case with "Richard Nixon" in the proposition "Richard Nixon kicked a dog." In this case the tree (Figure 7.8a) can terminate directly with that node. However, in the case of an indefinite description like "a dog," there is no prior representation in memory of the particular individual being kicked; instead, we have only a representation of the class (e.g., dog) to which this newly designated individual belongs. In this case, then, HAM must create a new node to represent the individual in question, and connect this node by a link to the concept node. The link is labeled with the symbol ϵ for set membership. Note that in Figure 7.8a, the time "past" and the relation "kick" are similarly represented in terms of set memberships, since the proposition refers to a particular past time and a particular instance of the set of actions known as kickings.

We wish to allow for the possibility of predicating something of the concept itself. For example, Figure 7.8b shows for the concept of "dog" the predication "Dog is my favorite species." This is the one circumstance in which it is possible to use a concept node directly as the terminal node of a tree. This circumstance, in which something is predicated of the concept per se, should not be confused with the circumstance in which something is predicated of all *individuals* in the set referenced by the concept. A different representation is required, as is illustrated for "dogs" in Figure 7.8c. Here the proposition "Dogs chase cats" is rendered in HAM as "all dogs chase some cats." A node corresponding to a prototypical or generic dog is created which is connected to the dog concept by a generic link, which is labeled with the symbol for universal quantification $\forall$ (meaning "for all"). Such generic links provide HAM with the expressive power of universal quantification in a predicate calculus. Thus, if a node n_1 is related to a node n_2 by a generic link, this is to be interpreted as meaning "For every member of the set n_2, the proposition involving n_1 is true."

Figure 7.8c also illustrates how existential quantification is represented, specifically with respect to the concepts "chase" and "cat." The subset relationship is introduced here, with the label on the links in Figure 7.8c being $\subseteq$ denoting set inclusion. A subset of the total set is created (representing "some cats"), and then the generic relation branches out of that selected subset whenever something specific is to be asserted about all individuals in that subset. That is to say, while the proposition is not true of every member in the total set of cats, it is true of every member in some subset of cats. Thus, Figure 7.8c could be read "For every dog there is a subset of all cats which he chases." In predicate calculus notation, Figure 7.8c would be written as: $\forall(x)[\text{dog}(x) \rightarrow (\exists y)[\text{cat}(y) \text{ \& chase}(x, y)]]$. (Later we shall take up the issue of the ambiguity in "scope" of existential and universal quantifiers.)

The Deep Grammar

We have now set forth the few structural rules of the trees that will serve as input to HAM and as "memories" in HAM. These rules are summarized by the *deep grammar* of Table 7.1, which stipulates what qualifies as well-formed input trees that will be "accepted" by HAM. The interpretation of each rule in Table 7.1 is that the label on the left of the rule can be rewritten as a node and zero, one, or two labels as specified on the right. The table indicates the constraints that a relation leading into a particular node places on the relations that lead out of that node. For instance, Rule 7.1c indicates that TIME and LOCATION links may lead from a node *n* to which a CONTEXT relation leads. Rule 7.1c may be also read as an instruction to be followed in constructing the tree: "At the bottom of a CONTEXT link, place a node *n*, and from node *n* put out a TIME link and a LOCATION link." The TIME and LOCATION links are in parentheses in rule 7.1c to indicate that they are optional; that is to say, it is possible to have just a TIME or just a LOCATION specified.

Rules 7.1a and 7.1b are special in that they start the construction of the tree. Rule 7.1a with PROPOSITION is used if the FACT is to be qualified with a context, whereas Rule 7.1b is adopted if qualification is unnecessary. In either case,

TABLE 7.1

The Deep Grammar

PROPOSITION	n CONTEXT	FACT	7.1a
FACT	n SUBJECT	PREDICATE	7.1b
CONTEXT	n (TIME)	(LOCATION)	7.1c
PREDICATE	n RELATION	OBJECT	7.1d
OBJECT	n CONTEXT	FACT	7.1e
SUBJECT	n SUBJECT	PREDICATE	7.1f
CONTEXT FACT TIME	n (ϵ $\hbar_s(t)$)		7.1g
LOCATION SUBJECT	n MEMBER		7.1h
PREDICATE RELATION	n SUBSET		7.1i
OBJECT MEMBER SUBSET GENERIC	n GENERIC		7.1j

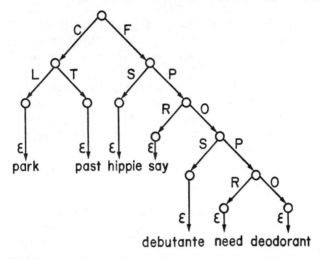

FIG. 7.9. Example of a tree structure generated by rewriting OBJECT: "In the park the hippie said the debutante needed a deodorant."

nothing is left of the start element in the resulting tree. Rules 7.1*e* and 7.1*f* deserve special notice insofar as they allow HAM to decompose OBJECT or SUBJECT as either a PROPOSITION or a FACT. Figure 7.9 provides an example of a tree structure generated by rewriting the OBJECT.

Rules 7.1*a* through 7.1*f* stipulate the branching in acceptable input trees. No more than two relations ever lead from a node. However, it is possible to have an arbitrary number of links leaving a node, each labeled with the same relation. This is the manner in which *conjunction* is expressed in HAM's memory. For instance, as in Figure 7.10, we may predicate more than one thing about a particular subject: "John hates cats but loves dogs." We have encoded this in Figure 7.10 by creating two separate predicate links leading from the fact node. However, this possibility

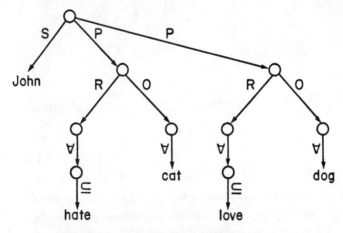

FIG. 7.10. Example of conjunction of predicates.

for conjunction should not obscure the basic *binary structure* of HAM's representation. In Chapter 9 we will provide a discussion of how this binary structure leads to certain efficiencies in the memory representation over other possible structures.

So far we have confined our discussion to Rules 7.1*a* through 7.1*f*, which specify the binary structure of the input trees. Rule 7.1*g* specifies that any branch in the tree may end directly in a node from memory (the set $\bar{\Pi}_s(t)$ is the set of memory nodes at time *t*–see Sections 7.3 and 7.4). Finally the Rules 7.1*h* through 7.1*j* specify how we may apply the quantifiers–i.e., member (ϵ), subset ($\subseteq$), or generic ($\forall$)–to any of the terminal branches.

Intersection of Trees

The deep grammar only generates simple tree structures. But often a total proposition needs to be analyzed into an intersecting set of such trees. An intersecting tree is illustrated in Figure 7.11*a*, which encodes the proposition "In a dark alley a baby cried." Such intersecting subtrees could either be input all at once or input separately to HAM. In the separated case, first HAM would encode the subtree for "An alley was dark," as shown in Figure 7.11*b*. As a consequence of encoding this tree, node 1 of Figure 7.11*b*, which represents the particular context, would have been set up in memory. Suppose the second tree of Figure 7.11*c* is then input to the memory. Since node 1 had already been established as a memory node, it serves as a terminal node in the input tree of Figure 7.11*c*, which encodes the proposition "In context 1, a baby cried."

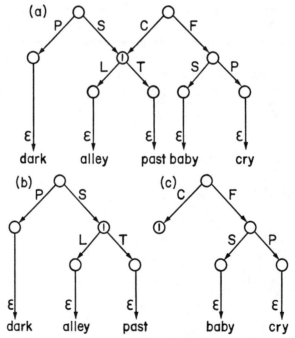

FIG. 7.11. Example of intersecting subtrees which can be separately input to HAM.

All such intersecting trees have the character that one tree is *predicating* something of a particular node in another tree. For instance, in Figure 7.11*a* the subject of the predication is the context node 1, and the predicate is *dark*. The input order of the two intersecting trees is immaterial to HAM's final representation of the information. That is, the same structure would develop in memory if HAM first input the proposition "In an alley a baby cried" and then input "The alley was dark." It is possible formally to make such predications about any node in the input tree. Of course, each duplex node in the tree represents a certain combination of ideas. A significant outcome of our representation is that predications are possible about only certain of the possible combinations of ideas, namely, context (time plus location), predicate (relation plus object), fact (subject plus predicate), and proposition (context plus fact). A moment's reflection will show, however, that there are many other possible combinations of ideas about which it is not possible to make direct predications, e.g., (time plus relation), (subject plus relation), (location plus object), (time plus subject plus object), and so on. In fact, there are some 26 possible combinations of two, three, four, and five elements in a five-element proposition. But our representation allows us to predicate about only four of these combinations; these are the allowable duplex ideas about which we can speak. The interesting point is that it is impossible to conceive of wanting to predicate anything of the other 22 combinations. We regard that fact as very compelling evidence for the representation that we have adopted. Our initial reasoning was that every node in memory should have a character corresponding intuitively to that of an "idea" in past associationist theories. One intuitive characteristic of an idea is that it has properties or predicates that could be true of it. Given our deep grammar, then, HAM simply will not accept any of the 22 nonpredicatable combinations as legitimate ideas. People don't seem to do so either.

Equivalence to Second-Order Predicate Calculus

Our formalism appears to have all the expressive power of the second-order predicate calculus. The predicate calculus requires several syntactic devices such as the notions of implication, falsity, the ability to compose *n*-place relations (where *n* is arbitrary), and the ability to quantify both over relations and over individuals (see Robbin, 1969). All these features are now available in HAM's deep grammar. We earlier illustrated the composition (or decomposition) of *n*-place predicates (e.g., the verb *give*), and have just discussed quantification over relations and individuals. Implication in our system is a relation holding between two propositions, whereas falsity is a predicate that applies to an embedded proposition. These devices are illustrated in the sentence "If John doesn't hit Mary, Bob will" (see Figure 7.12). A rephrasing of the tree structure in Figure 7.12 would be "(John hit Mary is false) implies (Bill hit Mary)."

One feature of the predicate calculus that is problematical for associative networks concerns the *scope* of existential and universal quantifiers. To illustrate the problems here, let us consider the ambiguous sentence "All dogs chase some cats." One interpretation of this sentence, which was represented previously in

Figure 7.8c, is "Each dog has a particular set of cats which he chases." This would be represented in the predicate calculus as $(\forall x)[\text{dog}(x) \rightarrow (\exists y)[\text{cat}(y)\ \&\ \text{chase}(x,y)]]$. The problem is how to represent the second, less likely, interpretation of this sentence, viz., "There is one particular set of cats which are distinguished by the fact that all dogs chase them." This is rendered in predicate calculus notation as $(\exists x)[\text{cat}(x)\ \&\ (\forall y)[\text{dog}(y) \rightarrow \text{chase}(y,x)]]$. In the first interpretation the scope of the universal quantifier $(\forall)$ is outside the expression and thus includes the scope of the existential quantifier $(\exists)$. In the second interpretation, this order of quantifier scopes is reversed.

In our representation, the scope of the subject quantifier is always interpreted as containing the scope of any quantifiers in the predicate. This subject-determination of scope appears also in people's interpretations of ambiguous sentences; in one investigation of this phenomenon, Johnson-Laird (1969) found that doubly quantified sentences were predominantly interpreted with the greater scope belonging to the quantifier on the surface subject. Thus, his judges tended to interpret "all philosophers have read some books" as meaning "some books or other" (i.e., different books for different philosophers); on the other hand, the passive transform "Some books have been read by all philosophers" tends to be interpreted as "Some books in particular." Presumably these interpretive biases for scope can be trained in or trained out according to cultural usage.

The question arises, however, whether HAM has a representation of our "dogs and cats" sentence for which the scope of the existential quantifier on the object, "cat," contains the scope of the universal quantifier on the subject, "dog." Figure 7.13 presents a possible solution within HAM's formalisms. Here, "some cats" has been made the subject of a fact, which is then related to the proposition "All dogs chase them" by the relation "are distinguished by." In this way, the scope of "cat," as subject of the main clause, contains the scope of "dog," which is the subject of the embedded object clause. Obviously, by this circumlocution it should be possible to represent arbitrarily complicated relationships of scopes. The fact that

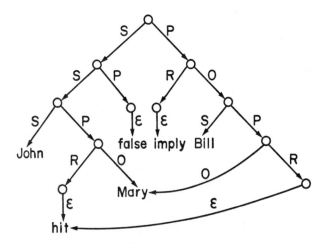

FIG. 7.12. An example of implication in HAM.

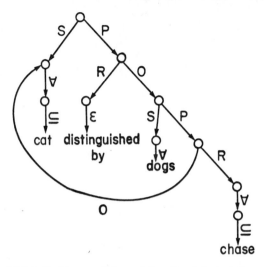

FIG. 7.13. Representation of the other interpretation of "All dogs chase some cats." Compare with Figure 7.8c.

circumlocution is required is not necessarily an embarrassment. The full expressive power of predicate calculus cannot be captured in natural language without much circumlocution. It seems reasonable to suppose that neither human language nor human memory evolved in a way that enables them to deal easily with the expressive powers of the formal languages that have been developed only in the past century of man's history.

The Structure of Probe Trees

The discussion so far has focused on the structure of the trees that are input to the memory. HAM will attempt to store these trees in long-term memory by forming associations corresponding to each of the links in the tree. This storage process will be examined at length in Chapter 10. We will now consider the structure of the probe trees which are sent into memory during information-retrieval tasks. These trees correspond to questions; their function is to specify what information is to be retrieved from memory to satisfy a particular need or purpose. Since the structure of the input trees largely determines the structure of the memory representation, the retrieval process will be most efficient if the structure of the probe is as similar as possible to the structure of the input. In deciding how the memory probes should be structured, it is important to recognize that there are basically two ways of probing memory for information. Either we can present a proposition and ask whether it is true (e.g., "Did the boy hit the girl?"), or we can ask for some information that will serve to complete a proposition ("Who hit the girl?"). The former are called *yes-no questions* and the latter *wh-questions* (*wh* for who, what, which, when, etc.). For a

(a)

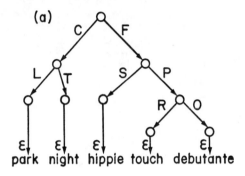

ε↓   ε↓   ε↓   ε↓   ε↓
park night hippie touch debutante

(b)

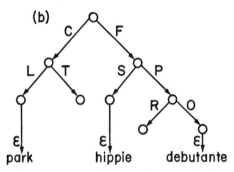

ε↓   ε↓   ε↓
park   hippie   debutante

FIG. 7.14. Examples of probe trees: (*a*) for
yes-no questions, and (*b*) for wh-questions.

yes-no question, the structure of the probe tree is identical to that of the input tree
for the proposition whose truth is being queried. Thus, Figure 7.14*a* could equally
represent the input tree for "In the park during the night a hippie touched a debutante," or the probe tree for "Did a hippie touch a debutante during the night in a
park?" The difference between the question and the assertion lies in what the
processor does with the propositional trees—whether it stores it or attempts to
verify it as true or false.

In contrast, the structure of a probe tree for a wh-question differs somewhat
from the structure of the corresponding input tree. Corresponding to each queried
element of the proposition, there will be a "dummy" terminal node in the probe
tree. Unlike the terminal nodes of an input tree, these "queried terminals" of the
probe tree are not preexisting nodes in memory. For instance, Figure 7.14*b*
presents the probe tree for "When did the hippie do what to the debutante in the
park?" The time and relation nodes in this tree are just "dangling," not anchored to
any particular nodes in memory. When the decoding process matches the probe tree
to trees existing in memory, it will fill in these queried terminals with the memory
nodes of the matched trees. The matched memory nodes should correspond to the
right answers to the question.

This concludes the discussion of how HAM is to represent incoming inputs
(facts) and probes (questions). We have tried to indicate the various considerations
that motivated our particular choice of representation. To review, these
considerations were:

1. The representation should be capable of expressing any conception of which a human is capable. HAM's representation was shown to be at least equal to the second-order predicate calculus with respect to its expressive potential.

2. Binary-branching and labeling of links turns out to be useful in the memory matching routines to be described in succeeding chapters.

3. The representation should be designed to make salient the substantive information that is being input. It should not be influenced by the peculiarities of any natural language in which that information might have been communicated.

4. For reasons of parsimony, the representation should involve a minimum of conceptual categories.

5. It should be possible to predicate properties of any of the duplex ideas introduced by the representation, but not possible to predicate properties of any combination of ideas not represented by a node.

These five considerations go a long way in the direction of specifying what the representation should be. However, we must admit that these alone are not sufficient constraints, so that unsystematic biases and intuitions have also played a role in determining the choice of a representation. We wish it were otherwise.

7.3. FORMALIZATION OF THE PROPOSITIONAL TREES

The assumptions of HAM's representation were stated informally and diagrammatically in the previous section. However, there are certain advantages to presenting the representation in as formal a manner as possible, and that is the purpose of this section. A formal presentation brings out precisely just what is being assumed; it also eases the way for carrying out derivations of theorems. Later, in Section 7.4, several important consequences of our assumptions about memory will be proven.

Our goal in this section is to specify exactly what propositional trees are acceptable inputs to HAM. As the memory structure is just a passive encoding of these input trees, a specification of the acceptable inputs will take us a long way to the goal of specifying the character of the memory structure. HAM's deep grammar will be presented as a set of formal *productions* or *rewrite* rules for trees. The reader should keep in the back of his mind that we are really just describing more precisely the labeled tree-structures of the last section. Those readers who find the formalization unrevealing can skip to Section 7.4 without much loss of comprehensibility. For easy reference, Table 7.2 exhibits the notation symbols to be used in the following text. In that table we are using script capitals to denote sets and ordered *n*-tuples of sets, capital letters for associative relations, and lower-case letters for nodes.

To begin with the set notation, then, a finite labeled graph is an ordered triple $\mathcal{G}$ = $\langle \mathcal{R}, \mathcal{N}, \mathcal{A} \rangle$, where:

$\mathcal{R}$ is a finite set of relations
$\mathcal{N}$ is a finite set of nodes
$\mathcal{R} \cap \mathcal{N} = \emptyset$ (i.e., the empty set)

TABLE 7.2

Notation

$\mathfrak{M} = <\mathfrak{I}, \mathcal{P}, \mathcal{O}, \mathcal{S}, \mathcal{E}, \mathcal{D}>$

$\mathfrak{I}$ = set of input trees

$\mathcal{P}$ = set of probe trees

$\mathcal{O}$ = set of output trees

$\mathcal{S}$ = the memory structure

$\mathcal{E}$ = encoding function

$\mathcal{D}$ = decoding function

$\mathfrak{I}(t) = <\mathcal{R}, \mathfrak{N}_I(t), \mathcal{Q}_I(t)>$ = input tree at time t

$\mathcal{O}(t) = <\mathcal{R}, \mathfrak{N}_O(t), \mathcal{Q}_O(t)>$ = output tree at time t

$\mathcal{P}(t) = <\mathcal{R}, \mathfrak{N}_P(t), \mathcal{Q}_P(t)>$ = probe tree at time t

$\mathcal{S}(t) = <\mathcal{R}*, \mathfrak{N}_S(t), \mathcal{Q}_S(t)>$ = memory structure at time t

$\mathcal{R}$ = set of relations in a finite labeled graph

$\mathcal{R}*$ = the set of relations in $\mathcal{R}$ plus their inverses

$\mathfrak{N}$ = set of nodes

a, b, c, etc. = particular nodes

X, Y, Z, etc. = particular relation

X^{-1} = inverse-X relation

$\mathcal{Q}$ = set of links

$<a \; X \; b>$ = an individual link; node a has relation X to node b

$\lambda = <\mathcal{R}, \emptyset, \emptyset>$ = the null graph

$\mathfrak{N}_f$ = future nodes

$\mathfrak{N}_S$ = memory nodes

$\mathfrak{N}_P$ = set of nodes in memory corresponding to individuals

$\mathfrak{N}_C$ = set of nodes in memory corresponding to concepts

$\mathfrak{N}_B$ = base set of nodes

Iff = If and only if

$(\forall X)$ = for all X

$(\exists X)$ = there exist X

$a \in A$ = a is a member of the set A

$a \notin A$ = a is not a member of set A

$A \subseteq B$ = the set A is contained in the set B

$\emptyset$ = the empty set

$A \cup B$ = the union of the sets A and B

$A \cap B$ = the intersection of the sets A and B

C = context

F = fact

S = subject

P = predicate

R = relation

O = object

T = time

L = location

ϵ = is-member-of

$\forall$ = generic (for all)

$\subseteq$ = is-subset-of

$\mathcal{C}$ is a finite set of triples such that if $<a\ X\ b> \in \mathcal{C}$, then $a, b \in \mathcal{N}$ and $X \in \mathcal{R}$. Essentially, each member of $\mathcal{C}$ is a particular link of the graph. In the pictorial representation we have been using, if $<a\ X\ b> \in \mathcal{C}$, then a is the origin of the link, b the terminus, and X the label of the link. As a simple example, consider the graph of Figure 7.15, which encodes the sentence "It is false that it was a boy who hit Harry." That graph would be represented formally by the following triple: $<$ [C, F, P, S, R, O, L, T, $\forall$, $\subseteq$, ϵ], [$a, b, c, d, e, f, g, h, j, k, l$, past, hit, Harry, person, boy, false] [$<a\ C\ b>$, $<b\ T\ c>$, $<c\ \epsilon$ past$>$, $<a\ F\ d>$, $<d\ P\ e>$, $<e\ R\ f>$, $<f\ \epsilon$ hit$>$, $<e\ O$ Harry$>$, $<d\ S\ g>$, $<g\ \epsilon$ person$>$, $<l\ S\ h>$, $<h\ S\ g>$, $<h\ P\ k>$, $<k\ \epsilon$ boy$>$, $<l\ P\ j>$, $<j\ \epsilon$ false$>$] $>$. First, we list here the types of labels that we use on links in this tree; then we list a set of nodes, some of which are nonterminals (a through l) which have been especially created in memory to encode this tree, and some of which are preexisting terminal nodes (past, hit, etc.); finally, we list all the triples in the tree, giving the relation existing between the two nodes in the triple. This long listing is the information in a labeled tree. It also brings home the point that a picture is worth a thousand words.

Having given the formal definition of a finite labeled graph, we now use it to characterize four of the six objects in the formal specification of the strategy-free component of memory, $\mathcal{M} = <\mathcal{J}, \mathcal{P}, \mathcal{O}, \mathcal{S}, \mathcal{E}, \mathcal{D}>$ (see Section 6.2). We will define in this formalism the set $\mathcal{J}$ (the inputs), the set $\mathcal{O}$ (the outputs), the set $\mathcal{P}$ (the probes), and the set $\mathcal{S}$ (the memory structures). It will prove necessary in the following to introduce a variable t that gives the time from the point of HAM's birth. The notation $\mathcal{J}(t)$ will be used to reference the input at time t, and similarly for the notations $\mathcal{O}(t)$, $\mathcal{P}(t)$, and $\mathcal{S}(t)$. Now we introduce the following definitions:

$$\mathcal{J}(t) = <\mathcal{R}, \mathcal{N}_I(t), \mathcal{C}_I(t)>$$
$$\mathcal{O}(t) = <\mathcal{R}, \mathcal{N}_O(t), \mathcal{C}_O(t)>$$
$$\mathcal{P}(t) = <\mathcal{R}, \mathcal{N}_P(t), \mathcal{C}_P(t)>$$
$$\mathcal{S}(t) = <\mathcal{R}^*, \mathcal{N}_S(t), \mathcal{C}_S(t)>$$

where $\mathcal{R} = $ [F, S, P, R, O, C, T, L, ϵ, $\forall$, $\subseteq$]. This is the full set of link labels that we

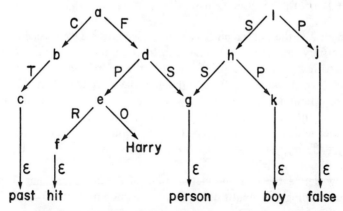

FIG. 7.15. Input tree for "It wasn't a boy who hit Harry."

introduced earlier. The set $\mathcal{R}^*$ which appears in the definition of $\mathcal{S}(t)$ will be defined in the next section of this chapter. These definitions are not particularly revealing; they say simply that the object on the left is a kind of labeled graph, connecting some nodes by a set of links.

This section will provide a precise characterization of the set of inputs, $\mathcal{I}$. The next section will provide a definition of the set of memory structures, $\mathcal{S}$. Chapter 10 will attempt to explicitly define $\mathcal{E}$, the encoding function. So this aspect of $\mathcal{M}$, concerned with input and its storage, will achieve formal definition. Implicit with our definition of the input trees is a definition of the probe trees, $\mathcal{P}$. A probe is just an input tree without the restriction that its terminal nodes must be memory nodes. However, the other two elements of our memory component, the decoding process $\mathcal{D}$ and the outputs $\mathcal{O}$, will not receive formal definition. The decoding process is implemented as a LISP function in our simulation, and it does generate output trees. However, the program is complicated, and in chapters dealing with the decoding process we have focused only on psychologically significant aspects. When the reader is introduced to the vagaries of the decoding process in Chapter 9, he will appreciate why we have been remiss in providing a complete formalization.

The Set of Acceptable Inputs, $\mathcal{I}$

To specify $\mathcal{I}$, we will introduce a grammar that will generate all the finite labeled graphs acceptable for input to memory. The grammar specified here will just be a formal restatement of the deep grammar given in Table 8.1. Our specification of this *Input Grammar*, $\mathcal{G}_I$, is similar to the formalisms of Pfaltz and Rosenfeld (1969) in their definition of *web grammars*. As Pfaltz and Rosenfeld point out, the specification of grammars that generate graphs is somewhat more complicated than specification of sentence grammars, because graphs lack the simple linear ordering that sentences have. To begin with the set notation, the Input Grammar is an ordered 5-tuple, $\mathcal{G}_I = \langle \mathcal{N}_f, \mathcal{N}_s, \mathcal{R}, \lambda, \mathcal{P}_I \rangle$, where

$\mathcal{N}_f$ is a set of potential or future nodes
$\mathcal{N}_s$ is the current set of memory nodes
$\mathcal{N}_f \cap \mathcal{N}_s = \emptyset$
$\mathcal{R} = [C, F, L, T, S, P, R, O, \epsilon, \subseteq, \forall]$.

The element λ is the null graph from which all graphs are to be generated. It serves as an arbitrary start symbol in the construction of the graph. $\mathcal{P}_I$ (not to be confused with $\mathcal{P}$, the set of probe trees) is the set of nine production rules, P_0 through P_8, which we will define. In defining these production rules, we need the concept of a terminal node. Intuitively, a terminal node is a bottom node which is pointed to by other nonterminal nodes in the input tree, but which does not point to any other nodes in the input. To state this formally, a is a terminal node in the graph $\mathcal{I}_J = (\mathcal{R}, \mathcal{N}_J, \mathcal{C}_J)$ if and only if $a \in \mathcal{N}_j$ and $(\forall X, y) \langle a\,X\,y \rangle \notin \mathcal{C}_j$ (that is, a is not the origin of any link).

We now define the nine production rules of the input grammar. These can be viewed as mapping one input tree, $\mathcal{I}_1$, into a second input tree, $\mathcal{I}_2$, which contains some modification.

Rule P_0: This first rule serves to introduce three new nodes in the tree, connected by subject and predicate links. The nodes a, b, c are selected from the set $\mathcal{N}_F$ of future nodes; node c is the root of the new subject-predicate construction. Graphically, this rule says that we can create or add the structure

Formally, we have

$$P_0: \mathcal{I}_1 \to \mathcal{I}_2$$

where $\mathcal{N}_2 = \mathcal{N}_1 \cup [a, b, c]$
    $a, b, c \in \mathcal{N}_F$
    $\mathcal{C}_2 = \mathcal{C}_1 \cup [<c \, S \, a>, <c \, P \, b>]$.

The formal lines may be read as follows: rule P_0 takes tree $\mathcal{I}_1$ into $\mathcal{I}_2$, where the nodes of $\mathcal{I}_2$ are those of $\mathcal{I}_1$ plus a, b, c (which are selected from the set of future nodes), and where the links in $\mathcal{C}_2$ are those in $\mathcal{C}_1$ plus the subject-link connecting c to a, and the predicate-link connecting c to b. This rule is used whenever we want to start constructing a propositional tree from scratch. In a computer simulation, we may think of the elements a, b, c from the set $\mathcal{N}_F$ as cells from a free-cell storage array which is available for recording incoming information.

Rule P_1: Consider any arbitrary node a in a tree; we then make up a subject-predicate construction around this node. This rule may be represented graphically as

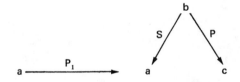

Formally, the rule is stated as follows:

$$P_1: \mathcal{I}_1 \to \mathcal{I}_2$$

where $a \in \mathcal{N}_1$
    $\mathcal{N}_2 = \mathcal{N}_1 \cup [b, c]$
    $b, c \in \mathcal{N}_F$
    $\mathcal{C}_2 = \mathcal{C}_1 \cup [<b \, S \, a>, <b \, P \, c>]$.

Rule P_2 allows us to combine the root node of a proposition, e, with a preexisting subject-predicate construction, making the root node the object of the subject-predicate construction.

Graphically, the diagram for this rule is

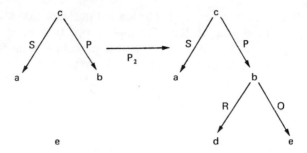

In this rule, node d is selected from $\mathcal{N}_F$ and made to stand for the relation between a and e. Formally, we have

$$P_2: \mathcal{I}_1 \rightarrow \mathcal{I}_2$$

where $a, b, c, e \in \mathcal{N}_1$
$\qquad \mathcal{N}_2 = \mathcal{N}_1 \cup [d]$
$\qquad d \in \mathcal{N}_F$, and e a root node
$\qquad \mathcal{C}_2 = \mathcal{C}_1 \cup [<b \; R \; d>, <b \; O \; e>]$.

This rule is very important in making prior propositions the objects of new predications, e.g., "John hates the fact that George smokes."

Rule P_3, which is similar to P_2, allows the division of a predicate node b into a relation node plus an object node. The diagram for the rule is:

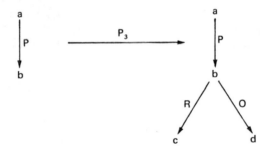

Formally, the rule is as follows:

$$P_3: \mathcal{I}_1 \rightarrow \mathcal{I}_2$$

where $a, b \in \mathcal{N}_1$
$\qquad \mathcal{N}_2 = \mathcal{N}_1 \cup [c, d]$
$\qquad c, d \in \mathcal{N}_F$
$\qquad <a \; P \; b> \in \mathcal{C}_1$
$\qquad \mathcal{C}_2 = \mathcal{C}_1 \cup [<b \; R \; c>, <b \; O \; d>]$.

That is, the initial tree $\mathcal{I}_1$ has nodes a and b related by a predicate link; rule P_3 maps this into a tree which adds R and O links from b to new nodes c and d, respectively. The rule is obviously used in expanding predicates into relation-object pairs.

Rule P_4 permits us to embed a fact node (or root node) a inside a context-plus-fact construction. The diagram is

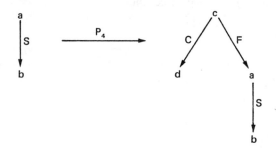

The formal definition is:

$$P_4 : \mathfrak{I}_1 \rightarrow \mathfrak{I}_2$$

where $a, b \in \mathfrak{N}_1$
$\mathfrak{N}_2 = \mathfrak{N}_1 \cup [c, d]$
$c, d \in \mathfrak{N}_F$
$<a \; S \; b> \in \mathfrak{A}_1$
$\mathfrak{A}_2 = \mathfrak{A}_1 \cup [<c \; C \; d>, <c \; F \; a>]$.

This rule, P_4, is used for attaching any sort of context to a fact. The next rule, P_5, states that a context node can be rewritten as either a Time link (T) or a Location link (L) or both. Pictorially, the rule is:

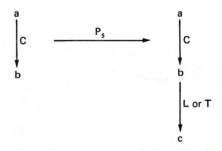

Stated formally, the rule is:

$$P_5 : \mathfrak{I}_1 \rightarrow \mathfrak{I}_2$$

where $a, b \in \mathfrak{N}_1$
$\mathfrak{N}_2 = \mathfrak{N}_1 \cup [c]$
$c \in \mathfrak{N}_F$
$<a \; C \; b> \in \mathfrak{A}_1$
$\mathfrak{A}_2 = \mathfrak{A}_1 \cup [<b \; X \; c>]$, where X = T or L.

This rule is straightforward. To generate a Time *and* a Location link out of the context node, b, one would simply call rule P_5 twice, choosing T or L accordingly.

These initial rules have only involved nonmemory nodes (i.e., nodes from the set, $\mathcal{N}_F$, of future nodes). However, rules must also be stated that will anchor the input trees into terminal nodes that are memory nodes. The following rule allows the *conversion* of any terminal node a in the input tree into a corresponding memory node b. There is no appropriate diagram to show, since one is merely replacing a terminal node a of the input tree with a node b preexisting in memory. Formally, the replacement rule is as follows:

$$P_6: \mathcal{I}_1 \rightarrow \mathcal{I}_2'$$

where $b \in \mathcal{N}_s$
$\quad a \in \mathcal{N}_1 \cap \mathcal{N}_F$
$\quad a$ is a terminal node in $\mathcal{I}_1$
$\quad \mathcal{N}_2 = [\mathcal{N}_1 - a] \cup [b]$
$\quad \mathcal{Q}_2 = (\mathcal{Q}_1 - \mathcal{Q}^*) \cup [<c \times b> | <c \times a> \in \mathcal{Q}_1]$
$\quad \mathcal{Q}^* = [<c \times a> \in \mathcal{Q}_1]$.

This says that all X-relational links from c to the node a (the set $\mathcal{Q}^*$) are now replaced by X-relational connections to the memory node b. This rule is what directly "plants" the input tree (the a terminal nodes) into the ground of known concepts (the b-nodes).

The next rule, P_7, introduces various quantifiers on the links into terminal nodes. The quantifier can be either the generic relation ($\forall$), which is to be interpreted as "For all (every, each, any) members of the set b"; the set-membership relation (ϵ), which is interpreted as "This instance a is a member of the set b"; or the subset relation ($\subseteq$), which is interpreted as "a is some arbitrary subset of the set b." The pictorial representation is

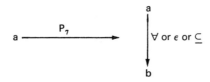

The rule is stated formally as follows:

$$P_7: \mathcal{I}_1 \rightarrow \mathcal{I}_2$$

where $a \in \mathcal{N}_1$
$\quad a$ is a terminal node
$\quad \mathcal{N}_2 = \mathcal{N}_1 \cup [b]$
$\quad b \in \mathcal{N}_F$
$\quad \mathcal{Q}_2 = \mathcal{Q}_1 \cup [<a \times b>]$, where $X = \forall, \epsilon,$ or $\subseteq$.

Once terminal b is replaced by a concept node preexisting in memory (e.g., *dog*), then the interpretation of $\forall$, ϵ, and $\subseteq$ are "all dogs," "a particular dog," and "some dogs," respectively.

The final rule, P_8, permits conjunction (*and*) in the input graph. That is, more than one link may leave the node a so long as they are labeled with the same relation X. Graphically, P_8 appears as the expansion:

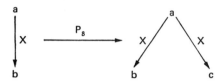

The formal statement of the production rule is as follows:

$$P_8: \mathcal{I}_1 \rightarrow \mathcal{I}_2$$

where $a, b \in \mathcal{N}_1$

$\quad \mathcal{N}_2 = \mathcal{N}_1 \cup [c]$

$\quad c \in \mathcal{N}_F$

$\quad <a \, X \, b> \in \mathcal{A}_1$

$\quad \mathcal{A}_2 = \mathcal{A}_1 \cup [<a \, X \, c>]$.

This says that every relation X can be conjoined with itself. In the memory representation, the conjoined objects simply form a labeled push-down stack. Thus, "John likes girls" can be added onto the stack (conjunction) of things which John likes. Interestingly, rule P_8 provides for conjunctions at practically any link in an input structure. For example, one can express a conjunction of contexts in which a given fact is true, a conjunction of predicates that apply to some subject, a conjunction of facts true in a given context, a set of objects related by a given relation $\mathcal{R}$ to the subject, and so on. In HAM all of these conjunctions will be produced by rule P_8 and represented in terms of an appropriate push-down stack.

We observed earlier in Section 7.2 that of the 26 possible combinations of elements in a proposition, only four could have predications made directly about them—context (time plus location), predicate (relation plus object), fact (subject plus predicate), and proposition (context plus fact). We argued that strong evidence for HAM's representation was the observation that these were the only combinations that it seemed one would want to make predications of. The same observation can be made about conjunction. Again only these four combinations can be directly conjoined in the input structure, and it seems that these are the only combinations that one would want to conjoin.

At this point, an illustration of how these rules operate might prove useful. So let us consider how we would go about generating the intersecting tree structure "It wasn't a boy who hit Harry," which was given in Figure 7.15. The generation process is illustrated in Figure 7.16. First, we start with the null graph, λ, then by rule P_0 generate the predication $[<d \, S \, g>, <d \, P \, e>]$; then by rule P_3 we generate a relation-object construction with f as the relation and r as the object; then by applying P_4 we introduce a context-fact distinction; rule P_5 introduces a time

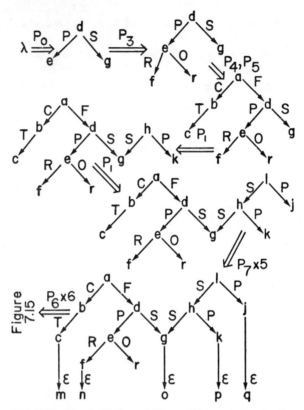

FIG. 7.16. The derivation of Figure 7.15 according to the input grammar.

element; rule P_1 is evoked to predicate a second fact, h, about the node g; rule P_1 is evoked again to predicate something about node h; then rule P_7 is evoked five times to provide for set-membership (ϵ) quantification on the nodes c, f, g, k and j. This quantifier is not required for node r, since it is going to be linked in the final tree to an individual node, namely, Harry. This pass through quantification yields the final graph structure shown in Figure 7.16. After this, the rule P_6 would be evoked six times to convert the terminal nodes m, n, r, o, p, and q into the memory nodes past, hit, Harry, person, boy, and false, respectively. This would then create the graph structure shown earlier in Figure 7.15.

The exact sequence in which these rules are applied is not crucial, provided that each rule is allowable when it is applied. For instance, the two applications of P_1 in Figure 7.16 could have preceded the applications of rules P_4 and P_5. The same structure would still have resulted in the end. Also, different sets of rules may be equivalent in their final effect.

Having specified the production rules of the grammar, we can now specify the set $\mathcal{I}$, which is the set of permissible inputs. This requires the logical notion of "derivable from." We say the graph structure $\mathcal{I}_n$ is derivable from the graph structure $\mathcal{I}_1$, (represented $\mathcal{I}_1 \xrightarrow{G} \mathcal{I}_n$), if there exists a sequence of graph structures

$\mathcal{I}_1$, $\mathcal{I}_2$, $\mathcal{I}_3$, ..., $\mathcal{I}_{n-1}$, $\mathcal{I}_n$ such that for each adjacent pair $\mathcal{I}_j$, $\mathcal{I}_{j+1}$ there exists $P_k \in \mathcal{P}_I$ such that $P_k: \mathcal{I}_j \to \mathcal{I}_{j+1}$. That is, $\mathcal{I}_n$ can be obtained from $\mathcal{I}_1$ by the application of a sequence of production rules. We can now define $\mathcal{I}$ as the set of all graphs which are anchored in memory nodes and which can be generated from the null graph, λ. Formally, $\mathcal{I} = [\mathcal{I}_j | \lambda \underset{G}{\to} \mathcal{I}_j$ and if a is a terminal of $\mathcal{I}_j, a \in \mathcal{N}_s]$. It is only trees from this input set $\mathcal{I}$ which HAM's parsers will construct and which will be sent to the memory component.

7.4. THE MEMORY STRUCTURE AND ITS PROPERTIES

Having explicitly characterized the inputs to memory, we now turn to examining the memory structure that is set up as a consequence of encoding these inputs. We begin by defining the memory structure.

Definition. At any time t, the memory structure $\mathcal{S}(t)$ is a finite labeled graph, $<\mathcal{R}^*$, $\mathcal{N}_S(t)$, $\mathcal{Q}_S(t)>$ where:

$\mathcal{R}^* = [F, F^{-1}, S, S^{-1}, P, P^{-1}, R, R^{-1}, O, O^{-1}, C, C^{-1}, T, T^{-1}, L, L^{-1}, \epsilon, \epsilon^{-1},$
$\forall, \forall^{-1}, \subseteq, \subseteq^{-1}]$

$\mathcal{N}_S(t)$ is a finite set of memory nodes

$\mathcal{Q}_S(t)$ is a finite set of ordered triples, $<a \times b>$, with a, $b \in \mathcal{N}_S(t)$ and $X \in \mathcal{R}^*$

A first comment on this definition is that the set of relations in memory $\mathcal{R}^*$ is exactly twice the size of the set of input relations, $\mathcal{R}$. For every member of $\mathcal{R}$ there is to be found in $\mathcal{R}^*$ both that relation, X, and its inverse, X^{-1}. Of course, X is also the inverse of X^{-1}; that is, $(X^{-1})^{-1} = X$. In psychological jargon, the inverse relation corresponds to a "backward association." The Symmetry Postulate introduced below makes critical use of such inverse relations. Each of the nodes in $\mathcal{N}_S(t)$ corresponds intuitively to an *idea* in past associationist theories. The ordered association corresponds to the traditional association in that it expresses a functional connection between the ideas, a and b (i.e., that a can lead to b), but with the added specification that a will lead to b only if the relation X is evoked. As noted in Chapter 2, labeled associations permit expression of the relations between associated ideas, something which was lacking in most traditional associative representations. We assume that the mind has a primitive retrieval process, which we shall call the *GET* process, which takes an idea a and a relation X, and returns as its values an *ordered list* of all nodes b, such that $<a \times b> \in \mathcal{Q}_S(t)$. The function GET is the basic process in terms of which all searches of memory will be defined. Functionally, the retrieval possibilities revealed by Get(a, X) are all that the graph structure of memory amounts to. The encoding of new information takes the form of adding new labeled associations; this is functionally equivalent to adding new retrieval possibilities.

Having specified what the memory structure is, we now impose a first restriction on the structure:

Symmetry Postulate

$(\forall t)$ if $<a \times b> \in \mathcal{Q}_S(t)$, then $<b \ X^{-1} \ a> \in \mathcal{Q}_S(t)$.

This postulate says that if an associative link exists in one direction between two nodes, then a symmetric inverse link must exist in the other direction. If a person knows the *simple* relation $<a \, X \, b>$, he should know the inverse relation $<b \, X^{-1} \, a>$. To critics with a bent for parsimony, symmetric associations may appear as superfluous redundancies, since one association could be inferred from another. However, consider the problem of how the information in the relation $<b \, X^{-1} \, a>$ could ever be retrieved if the memory system only had access to node b. Without the symmetric association $<b \, X^{-1} \, a>$, that information would not be accessible from b. So, symmetric associations are really needed to facilitate the directed search of memory for information of specified types.

At this point a picture might help convey the full graphical complexity of the structure that we envisage as existing in memory for a single proposition. Suppose the total input of Figure 7.15 had been successfully encoded into memory. Then residing in memory would be the structure illustrated by Figure 7.17. This is the only time we will show the full complexity of a proposition linked into memory, but this "longhand' may be permitted this time for expository purposes. Note that each association has a symmetrical inverse association. Also, the input of Figure 7.17 has not really been anchored to the words *past, hit, Harry, person, boy,* and *false*; rather, it is anchored in the idea nodes $m, n, r, o, p,$ and $q,$ and these idea nodes are connected to the words by the idea-to-word links labeled W. This distinction between words and ideas will be discussed in the next chapter. The word link, W, also has an inverse idea link, labeled I. The relations W and I have not been included in the set $\mathcal{R}*$ because they really do not serve to record facts about the world; rather, their function is to interface the memory structure with language.

The No-Forgetting Postulate

Our second restriction on the memory structure stipulates that no associations can disappear from memory once they have been encoded. Thus, this commits us to the claim that all forgetting at one level of analysis is a matter of losing *access*

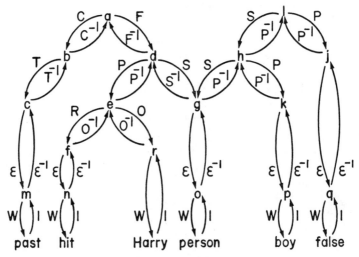

FIG. 7.17. Representation in memory of "It wasn't a boy who hit Harry."

to information in memory rather than losing the information itself from memory. This position (or its denial) appears almost impossible to establish experimentally. However, several arguments attract us to the position that all forgetting is a matter of lost availability. First, it can be demonstrated in many ways that a good deal of forgetting is of this variety—that information not retrievable under one circumstance is accessible under another. Interests of parsimony lead one to speculate that all forgetting is of this variety. Secondly, simulation of the loss of learnt information would pose a considerable additional programming burden in constructing our simulation of HAM. Finally, proofs of formal properties about a memory system like HAM can become very complicated if it is necessary to always consider the effects of forgetting. These various reasons incline us in favor of the No-forgetting Postulate. The postulate may be stated formally as follows:

$$(\forall t_1)(\forall t_2)[t_1 \leqslant t_2 \text{ implies } \mathcal{C}_S(t_1) \subseteq \mathcal{C}_S(t_2)]$$

In words, for all times t_1 and t_2 from HAM's birth, if t_1 is less than t_2, then the set of memory links at time t_1 is contained in the set at time t_2.

The First Empiricist Postulate

With respect to propositional memory, we are empiricists in that we believe there is no innate knowledge in the form of associations among memory nodes. All associations formed are records of past experience and are all derived from links in past input trees. The following postulate formalizes this assumption:

$(\forall t_1)$ if $<a \text{ X } b> \in \mathcal{C}_S(t_1)$, then both

(a) $(\exists t_2)$, $0 < t_2 \leqslant t_1$ *such that* t_2 *is the least t for which* $<a \text{ X } b> \in \mathcal{C}_S(t)$, *and either*

(b) *For any time* t_3 *in a finite interval up to and including* t_2, *either* $<a \text{ X } b>$ *or* $<b \text{ X}^{-1} a>$ *was a member of* $\mathcal{C}_I(t_3)$ *(i.e., a link in the input tree), or*

(c) $<a \text{ X } y>$, $<y \text{ X}^{-1} a>$, $<z \text{ X } b>$ *or* $<b \text{ X}^{-1} z>$ *was a member of* $\mathcal{C}_I(t_3)$, *where variables* y *and* z *denote nonmemory nodes* $\in \mathcal{N}_I(t_3)$ *that were matched and replaced by the memory nodes a or b, respectively.*

Let us explain this postulate step by step. Part (a) asserts that there was some time t_2 after birth ($t = 0$) when the association $<a \text{ X } b>$ first appeared in memory. Part (b) asserts that this association was encoded directly from an input tree given before t_2 or we have Part (c) to handle a special technical case. As we will discuss in Chapter 9, it is possible for part of an input tree to be matched to an existing piece of memory. If this occurs, HAM can use the existing piece of memory to encode the matched portion of the input tree. It is possible then, as Part (c) indicates, that one of the nodes, a or b, may have come from memory structure already established by a previous input, while the other node derives from encoding the unmatched portion of the input tree at time t_2. From Part (a) it follows that, with respect to associations in memory, the child is a tabula rasa; i.e., $\mathcal{C}_S(0) = \emptyset$. The claim that a child is a tabula rasa in this sense is part of every past associationist account. In fact, it is hard to find any respectable intellectual figure except Plato who actually claimed that we entered the world with a stock of facts ready made about our world.

The Second Empiricist Postulate

We will now strengthen the empiricist character of the theory by a second postulate. The first postulate restricted the *origin* of associations to be encodings of input trees; the second postulate will restrict the *acquisition* of new nodes (e.g., concepts, propositions) to be similar encodings of input trees. However, unlike the first empiricist postulate, this second postulate will not carry the implication that $\mathcal{N}_S(0) = \emptyset$. In fact, a contradiction would result if the second postulate were made as strong as the first in this respect. The formal statement of the postulate is as follows:

$(\forall t_1)$ *if* $a \in \mathcal{N}_S(t_1)$, *but* $a \notin \mathcal{N}_S(0)$, *then both*

(a) $(\exists t_2)$ $0 < t_2 \leqslant t_1$ *such that* t_2 *is the least* t *for which* $a \in \mathcal{N}_S(t)$. *Moreover, there is just one link* $<a \: X \: b> \in \mathcal{C}_S(t_2)$;

(b) *for any time* t_3 *in a finite interval up to and including* t_2, *either* $<a \: X \: b>$ *or* $<b \: X^{-1} \: a>$ *was a member of* $\mathcal{C}_I(t_3)$, *or*

(c) $<a \: X \: y>$ *or* $<y \: X^{-1} \: a>$ *was a member of* $\mathcal{C}_I(t_3)$, *where* y *denotes a nonmemory node* $\in \mathcal{N}_I(t_3)$ *that was matched and replaced by memory node* b.

The logical structure of this postulate is parallel to that of the First Empiricist Postulate. It begins by restricting discussion to those nodes in the set $\mathcal{N}_S(t)$ that were not in the original set, $\mathcal{N}_S(0)$. Part (a) asserts that at the time t_2 when the node a first appeared in memory, it was introduced as the consequence of encoding an associative link of the form $<a \: X \: b>$. Because of the Symmetry Postulate, the inverse association $<b \: X^{-1} \: a>$ must have also been encoded simultaneously. Parts (b) and (c) assert that $<a \: X \: b>$ was derived from the then-current input tree, $\mathcal{I}(t)$. Thus, all associations and nodes that appear in memory derive from direct encoding of input trees.

The Learning Postulate

We make one more transparently true postulate, viz., that some learning occurs. Formally, this says

$(\exists t)\mathcal{C}_S(t) \neq \emptyset$

This says that there comes a time t in every person's life when he learns something or, equivalently, when some associations are established in his memory. We hope this postulate is completely noncontroversial. Given this innocuous claim, the Second Empiricist Postulate, and the claim that the terminal nodes of input trees must be memory nodes, our first lemma follows:

Lemma 1: $\mathfrak{N}_S(0) \neq \emptyset$

That is, these three assumptions imply that the child must start with an initial set of memory nodes. We will refer to this set of innate ideas $\mathfrak{N}_S(0)$ as the base set, denoted as $\mathfrak{N}_B$.

Proof: To prove this lemma, we will assume $\mathfrak{N}_B = \emptyset$ and then show that it leads to a contradiction. Let t_1 be the least t such that $\mathfrak{A}_S(t) \neq \emptyset$. The Learning Postulate insures that such a t_1 exists. Consequently, the set of nodes at t_1, $\mathfrak{N}_S(t_1)$, is not empty. Since, by hypothesis, $\mathfrak{N}_B$ is empty, there is a least t_2, $0 < t_2 \leq t_1$, such that $\mathfrak{N}_S(t_2) \neq \emptyset$. Let a be a member of $\mathfrak{N}_S(t_2)$. The Second Empiricist Postulate insures that there is a $t_3 < t_2$ such that $a \in \mathfrak{N}_I(t_3)$. Consequently, $\mathfrak{I}(t_3) \neq \lambda$. But all non-null input trees must have terminals that are already memory nodes. Therefore, $\mathfrak{N}_S(t_3) \neq \emptyset$. This contradicts the assumption that t_2 is the least t such that $\mathfrak{N}_S(t) \neq \emptyset$. Hence, the assumption $\mathfrak{N}_B = \emptyset$ leads to a contradiction; so we must accept $\mathfrak{N}_B \neq \emptyset$.

The basic character of this proof is very simple. Since some nodes appear in memory, they must have been derived from an input tree. These first nodes came from a tree that was already anchored to memory nodes. Therefore, these first nodes could not have been the first memory nodes—that is the contradiction. This lemma introduces us to the base set, $\mathfrak{N}_B$, which is important because it is the initial set of atomic elements from which all further knowledge is alleged to be constructed. It corresponds to the set of simple ideas in past associationist accounts. The existence of this set of simple ideas follows inexorably from the other empiricist assumptions we have made. This illustrates our claim in Chapter 2. To the extent that one approaches theory construction with an empiricist bias, to that extent his theory will be forced into an associationist-like cast.

However, the simple ideas in our set $\mathfrak{N}_B$ are quite different from the simple ideas of past associative theories in one important respect; our base set consists of primitives that are innately specified. The standard view of the British associationists on this matter was that these simple ideas sprang up in the mind after appropriate sensory experience. They would suppose that our idea of red appeared in our mind as a consequence of sensory experiences of red objects. While many of the simple ideas in HAM's memory will also correspond to sensations, they exist in memory independent of experience. We are forced to this alternate formulation by our insistence that all input to memory takes the form of propositional trees anchored in preexisting memory nodes. Given this assumption, there is simply no way for us to allow the simple ideas to arise in memory in the way that the British associationists wanted. For experimental psychology, however, this is an inconsequential distinction. That is, it is difficult to conceive of any empirical test that would discriminate between HAM and the more traditional associative formulation of the origin of the simple ideas.

HAM: Empiricist or Rationalist?

Here is an appropriate point to emphasize the senses in which HAM is empiricist and the senses in which it is rationalist. The strategy-free component of memory, which we have been developing in this chapter, is clearly an empiricist construction. Despite that technicality about the ideas of the base set being innate, the strategy-free component does passively accept whatever is sent to it by the parsers and does indiscriminately proceed to encode links in that input. During decoding it generates output trees in response to probe trees in a similarly automatic manner. This corresponds rather closely to Aristotle's conception of memory (see Section 2.2).

However, Aristotle would not have permitted his memory to encode raw sensory experience. He insisted that Reason imposed *form* on incoming sensory data. Similarly HAM's linguistic and perceptual parsers intervene between the receipt of sensation and the sending of input or probe trees to memory. Just as Aristotle's Reason, these parsers impose form on experience. Similarly the trees output by HAM in the decoding process are not directly externalized in actions or words. As Chapter 13 discusses, deductive and inferential processes intervene to generate answers to questions. Aristotle had similar notions about the selective use of information in answering a question. So to conclude: With respect to the strategy-free component, HAM is empiricist, but there are rationalist elements in other parts of HAM's system. If HAM as a total system is to be described as associationist, it must be added that it is an Aristotelian associationism.

Connectivity in the Graph Structure

Since the base set of initial memory nodes $\mathcal{N}_S(0)$ is nonempty but the initial set of links $\mathcal{L}_S(0)$ is empty, it follows that the labeled graph representing the memory structure, $\mathcal{S}(t)$, cannot be connected for all t. By connected we mean that it would be possible to trace a path from any idea in $\mathcal{N}_S(t)$ through associative links in $\mathcal{L}_S(t)$ to any other idea in $\mathcal{N}_S(t)$. Since memory is not necessarily connected, there could be interassociated "clumps" of ideas that are segregated from the rest of the associative structure. The fact that our adult memories appear connected (i.e., that it appears that we can chain associatively from any idea to any other) is an interesting empirical fact; but it is in no way a necessary feature of memory.

Any memory node not in the base set must have some connections to other nodes. This fact is a simple consequence of the Second Empiricist Postulate. However, the simple ideas of the base set need not be involved in any associations. For instance, one might suppose that in a blind person there are visual primitives in his base set which have never been excited and associated to other nodes and which are consequently disconnected from the rest of the memory structure.

As argued in Chapter 2, the defining traits of an associative theory are connectionism, sensationalism, reductionism, and mechanism. Let us see how HAM lines up according to these features. The *connectionistic* character of HAM is transparent in its graph structure representation. The *mechanistic* character of the theory pervades diffusely through the entire theoretical enterprise. HAM's *sensationalistic* character is there in spirit, if not in detail. That is, all input to the memory component is basically encodings of perceptual events, and many of the ideas in the base set are to be identified with some neurological feature-detection routine or some other perceptual mechanism. However, we say our theory is sensationalist in spirit rather than detail, because these sensationalistic beliefs have not yet been realized by specific theoretical proposals.

Given the base set of simple ideas, we can start to make precise the sense in which HAM is reductionistic. Since these are the initial elements of memory, since all further memory structures derive from the encoding of input trees, and since these input trees must be anchored in memory, it is clear intuitively that all new ideas must in some sense be ultimately reducible into the terms of the base set. That is, all new ideas can be conceived of as *complex ideas* in the traditional associative sense. Their meaning is in some sense constructed from the meanings of the simple ideas. We will now attempt to make formal the sense in which this is true. First, we will describe the character of the memory structure in the ideal situation in which all input trees were perfectly encoded. In fact, this is not true, as will become clear when we formalize in Chapter 10 the process by which associations become encoded into memory. Nonetheless, it is enlightening to consider what the memory structure would be like if the following postulate held.

A Hypothetical Postulate of Perfect Encoding

$$(\forall t) \; [\text{if} <a \; X \; b> \; \epsilon \; \mathcal{C}_I(t), \text{then} <a \; X \; b>, <b \; X^{-1} \; a> \; \epsilon \; \mathcal{C}_S(t)] \, .$$

This postulate is cast in somewhat too simple terms because of the operation of the MATCH process (see Chapter 9) by which a link in the input $\mathcal{I}(t)$ can be matched to an association in memory and need not be encoded. However, given that the postulate is only hypothetical, we will not bother to represent such technicalities. The Perfect-Encoding Postulate implies:

Lemma 2: $(\forall a)$ *if* a ϵ $\mathcal{N}_S(t)$, *but* a $\notin$ $\mathcal{N}_B$, *then both*

(a) *there exists a sequence* $<a \; X_1 \; b>$, $<b \; X_2 \; c>$, ..., $<m \; X_m \; n> \; \epsilon \; \mathcal{C}_S(t)$, *such that* n ϵ $\mathcal{N}_B$ *and*

(b) $X_1, X_2, ..., X_m \; \epsilon \; \mathcal{R}$ *(rather than the augmented set $\mathcal{R}*$).*

Lemma 2 states that in the ideal world where Perfect-Encoding always occurs, every node a, not in the base set, would be connected by at least one string of associations to a node n that was in the base set. Part (b) asserts that none of the relations $X_1, X_2, ..., X_m$ are inverse relations (e.g., $\forall^{-1}, L^{-1}$); rather, all come from the set of relations $\mathcal{R}$ that are used in defining the set of acceptable inputs, $\mathcal{I}$. So, it is in this sense that the "meaning" of a complex idea is ultimately constructed from the meanings of simple ideas. Of course, the meaning of a complex node probably rests on more than this one chain of associations to a simple idea. It is probably embedded in a great network of associations and connected by multiple paths to a great many simple ideas. However, we want to prove here, given the Perfect-Encoding Postulate, that it is always possible to trace out at least one sequence of noninverse relations which lead to a simple idea.

Proof: We will outline a recursive procedure for constructing the sequence of associations which is claimed to exist. For any complex idea, a, there is a least time

t_1, such that $a \in \mathcal{N}_S(t_1)$. By the Second Empiricist Postulate, $a \in \mathcal{N}_I(t_1)$. Moreover, there exists a sequence $<a \ X_1 \ b>$, $<b \ X_2 \ c>$, ..., $<i \ X_i \ j> \in \mathcal{C}_I(t_1)$, such that j is a terminal node and $j \in \mathcal{N}_S(t)$ for some $t < t_1$. These links will all be encoded into memory according to the Perfect-Encoding Postulate. They form the first associations in the desired chain. If $j \in \mathcal{N}_B$, the complete chain is available in this one tree. If $j \notin \mathcal{N}_B$, find the least t_2 such that $j \in \mathcal{N}_S(t_2)$. Then we just reapply the procedure to the input in which j appears at t_2 in order thus to augment our chain of associations. Either we now have the complete chain desired, or we have a partial chain ending with a node k that first appeared in an earlier input $\mathcal{I}(t_3)$ where $t_3 < t_2$. This procedure can reapply as many times as needed to arrive at a node from the base set, $\mathcal{N}_B$. Provided that for each pair of times in the set $t_1, t_2, ..., t_r$, we have $t_{n+1} - t_n > \delta$, this procedure must converge, because eventually we would unwind back to $t = 0$ at which time all nodes of memory were contained in the base set.

What we envisage in this proof is illustrated by Figure 7.18. Node a first occurred in input tree 1 of Figure 7.18. In that tree, a was connected to the terminal c, among others. The node c first occurred in the input tree 2 and was connected to terminal d. We would follow this path through successively earlier input trees until we finally came to the base set node n in tree j. We would now have traced out one chain that links node a to n. Of couse, there are probably many

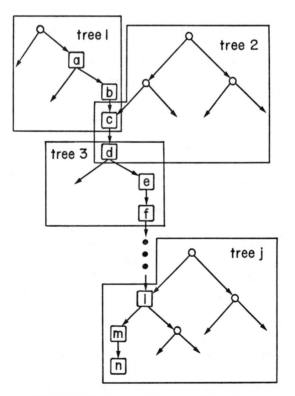

FIG. 7.18. Illustration of the proof of Lemma 2.

more chains to other nodes in the base set, and this multiplicity has not been illustrated in Figure 7.18.

This proof of Lemma 2 depended on the Perfect-Encoding Postulate. When we relinquish this postulate, the desired chain may not exist for every complex idea. Some of the links in the chain may have failed to be encoded. Without the Perfect-Encoding Postulate we can only prove something very much weaker about the character of simple ideas versus complex ideas. This weaker lemma says that the simple ideas can only have associations pointing to them which use relations from the set $\Re$, rather than from the total set $\Re^*$ which includes inverses.

Lemma 3: $(\forall t)$ if $a \in \tilde{\Re}_B$, then for all $<b \, X \, a> \, \in \, \mathcal{C}_S(t), X \in \Re$

Proof: Let a be an arbitrary member of the base set, and let $<b \, X \, a>$ be an arbitrary association to the node a, selected from $\mathcal{C}_S(t)$. By the First Empiricist Postulate, for some $t_1 < t$, either $<b \, X \, a>$ or $<a \, X^{-1} \, b> \, \in \, \mathcal{C}_I(t_1)$. Since $a \in \tilde{\Re}_B, a \in \tilde{\Re}_S(t_1)$, and hence a is a terminal node in the input tree $\mathcal{I}(t_1)$. Therefore, it must be $<b \, X \, a>$ that is the link in the input tree. Therefore, X cannot be an inverse relation, because input trees never use inverse relations.

Lemma 3 states that the nodes of the base set are unique insofar as they are only used in composing propositions about the world. By peculiar combinations of failure and success at encoding links in an input tree, it is possible for nonbase set nodes also to have the property that no noninverse relations lead to them. However, this is an *accidental* property of complex nodes, not a *necessary* property as it is for simple nodes.

From Lemma 3 the following lemma follows quite trivially:

Lemma 4: $(\forall t)$ if $a \in \tilde{\Re}_B$ and $<a \, r \, b> \, \in \, \mathcal{C}_S(t)$, then $b \notin \tilde{\Re}_B$

This is to say, contrary to the sentiments of British associationism, *the simple ideas are not directly associated together.* Rather they are only associated to elements not in the base set.

In the compounding of complex ideas, HAM is able to achieve the same power that is achieved through the type-token distinction in other neo-associationist models. Ideas in HAM can be made ever more complex by defining new ideas in terms of ideas already in memory. In HAM, this construction of complex ideas does not result in the so-called "Paradox of Mill's House" (see Section 2.3), because the complex idea, a, can be used in constructing a more complex idea, b, by incorporating into the definition of b a single association to a. Thus, it is not necessary to rewrite or rebuild into the definition b all the associative structure that is in the definition of a. The difference between the complex idea in HAM and the complex idea of British associationists is that in HAM the complex idea is not a conglomeration of primitive simple ideas; rather, it is itself a primitive element, a node, that can enter into associations just as readily as simple ideas do.

We have noted how complex ideas lead down through a network to a set of base nodes. However, we have been careful not to say that the meaning of a node is *just* this set of base nodes. It is not, and for this reason *HAM is not totally reductionistic*. Part of the meaning of an idea derives from the subject-predicate constructions into which it enters. For instance, the propositions "Dogs chase cats," "The hippie touched the debutante," and "Windows are made of glass" tell us something about, respectively, "dogs," "the hippie," and "windows." However, these subjects are not connected to their predicate constructions by downward links (i.e., links from the set, $\Re$). Nor should they be—the meaning that accrues to the subjects in these constructions is not *compositional*; rather, it is purely *implicational*. For instance, the meaning of "dog" is not composed out of the meanings of "chase" and "cat"; rather, the "chase cats" predicate permits us to infer something about an object which is a dog—namely, that it will chase cats.

7.5. THE CONCEPTUAL STRUCTURE OF MEMORY

At any time t, the set of memory nodes, $\mathcal{N}_S(t)$, can be subdivided into the set that correspond to *individuals*, $\mathcal{N}_P(t)$, and the set of memory nodes that correspond to *concepts*, $\mathcal{N}_C(t)$. Individuals are the objects and events that fill our everyday life. The philosophers often refer to them as *particulars*. In contrast, concepts are things that we never meet face-to-face. Concepts may be thought of as sets whose members are either individuals or other concepts. As an example of this distinction, "dog" is a concept, but my dog "Spot" is an individual. Philosophers like to refer to concepts as *universals*. The relevance to human memory of the metaphysical debates over the character of particulars and universals is not obvious. What is important for our purposes is simply that concepts correspond to sets that contain instances, whereas individuals do not. Thus, individual nodes will be connected to concept nodes by *member* (ϵ) and *generic* ($\forall$) relations.

The Metaphysical Postulate

We have dubbed the following postulate in honor of the 2,500-year running debate in metaphysics about the nature of universals and particulars,

(a) $(\forall t)\mathcal{N}_S(t) = \mathcal{N}_P(t) \cup \mathcal{N}_C(t)$
(b) $(\forall t)\mathcal{N}_P \cap \mathcal{N}_C(t) = \emptyset$
(c) $\mathcal{N}_B = \mathcal{N}_C(0)$

Part (a) of the above postulate guarantees that all memory nodes are either concept nodes or individual nodes. Part (b) guarantees that the two sets of nodes are disjoint. Finally, Part (c) guarantees that the base set should only contain concept nodes. This third restriction was made because it seemed preposterous to suppose that we are born with an innate stock of individual nodes representing such things as Spiro Agnew, Woodstock, my dog Spot, or the hippie's touching of the debutante in the park. As a very trivial consequence of Part (c), there is the following lemma:

Lemma 5: $\mathcal{N}_P(0) = \emptyset$

That is, the set of known individuals is initially empty.

Past associative theories have tended to be allied with a nominalist position in metaphysics. That is, they have denied the existence of universal ideas and insisted that all ideas were just representations of particulars. For reasons reviewed in Chapter 2, we find this position untenable and have opted for a conceptualist position which permits both particular and universal ideas. However, the empiricist bias of our theoretical enterprise has resulted in the fact that HAM seems much more suited as a model of how we acquire facts about particulars rather than facts about universals. Some of HAM's universal concepts are innately specified as part of the base set, but presumably HAM does not come by all its concepts in this manner. Surely, our concepts of a dog, of kicking, or of a powerset are not part of our innate genetic endowment; they are surely acquired. The problem is to specify how they are acquired and how their meaning is encoded in the memory structure.

Acquiring New Concepts

Most of the models of semantic memory (e.g., Collins & Quillian, 1972; Kintsch, 1972; Rumelhart, Lindsay, & Norman, 1972) are really systems of rules aimed at divining and setting forth the memory structures that underlie our universal concepts. However, these models typically give little attention to the issue of how this conceptual structure is to be acquired from interaction with the world. Rumelhart et al. (see Section 4.4) discuss how the memory component might spontaneously generalize from more particulate experience. However, we argued that this seemed an implausible mechanism for introducing new concepts into memory. Rather, it seems that whatever concepts we acquire are either told to us or develop after much conscious thought (implicit querying and tabulating) about some matter. In either case, it would seem that some source external to the memory component (the world or the executive) inputs a proposition to memory that serves to introduce a new concept.

If so, the interesting questions concern the structure of these concept-defining inputs and the functional characteristics of the processes and structures by which the inputs are encoded into memory. Tulving (1972) has recently postulated a distinction between *semantic* memory and *episodic* memory which seems similar to our distinction between memory for particular facts and memory for universal facts. Tulving speculated that the characteristics of these two memories were quite different. Since we want to argue that a single model, HAM, is adequate to both domains, our task is to outline how universal concepts may be acquired in a manner that is similar to particulars. While we do not claim to have an exhaustive analysis of this problem, the following is meant as a tentative beginning.

Our basic claim is that a universal concept is introduced into HAM as a consequence of encoding a propositional input that has one of its nonmemory nodes linked to a memory node by a subset ($\subseteq$) relation. When this proposition is encoded, this new memory node will represent a new universal concept. Such propositions we will refer to as *concept-defining propositions*. To make concrete this discussion, consider how the concept *canary* might be introduced into memory as a subset of the concept *bird*. For instance, the proposition "A canary is a yellow bird that sings" might be input to memory. Figure 7.19 illustrates the memory structure that would be established. A subset of birds is created (which is named

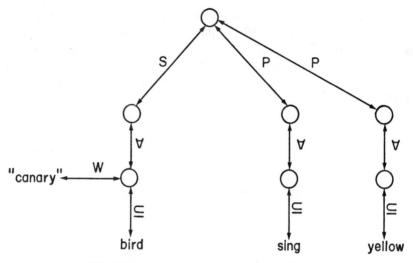

FIG. 7.19. Canary introduced as a subset of bird.

"canary" via the *word* (W) association). A generic instance of the concept is created which has the properties of being yellow and singing. Incidently, the subsets of "sing" and "yellow" introduced by the definition are the concepts of "canary singing" and "canary yellow." Thus, this one proposition has served to introduce three new concepts into memory.

As the above example illustrates, HAM can introduce some new concept, *a*, as a direct subset of an old concept, *b*. That is, it can directly enter the association <*a* ⊆ *b*> into memory. However, it is impossible for HAM to introduce this direct link if *a* is already a long-term memory node. As an example of a situation where HAM would want to introduce a direct subset link between two concepts already in memory, consider the following circumstance: We describe to HAM the species *platypus* and some of its features (e.g., has hair, has a bill, lays eggs). To encode this information, HAM would create a *platypus* node. Then suppose we assert to HAM: "A platypus is a mammal." It would be nice if HAM could input and encode the structure in Figure 7.20*a*. However, this input is not allowable because it contains

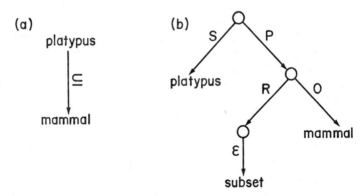

FIG. 7.20. Two representations of the fact that a platypus is a mammal.

as a nonterminal node, the memory node, *platypus*. (Remember nonterminals of inputs must be nonmemory nodes.) Therefore, because *platypus* was encoded into memory before HAM knew it was a mammal, HAM would have to resort to the subject-predicate construction of Figure 7.20*b* to encode the subset relation. In Figure 7.20*b* *platypus* has predicated of it that it has relation *subset* to mammal.

Of course, Figures 7.20*a* and 7.20*b* are equivalent in meaning. In fact, they serve to illustrate a very general equivalence between memory structures in HAM. That is, whenever there is in memory the link $<a \, X \, b>$, having the meaning "*a* has the relation X to *b*," it could have been expressed equivalently by the set of links $[<v \, S \, a>, <v \, P \, y>, <y \, R \, z>, <z \, \epsilon \, X>, <y \, O \, b>]$. However, single links as shown in Figure 7.20*a* are to be preferred because they are easier to search than are the subject-relation-object construction shown in Figure 7.20*b*. It is only on a few occasions like this that we must resort to the more complicated memory structure.

To return to our general discussion, it does seem possible to encode in HAM that various concepts are subsets or supersets of one another. As Figure 7.19 shows via the generic relation, it is also a simple matter to predicate properties of the generic member of a concept. It is also possible to predicate properties of the concept itself. For instance, Figure 7.21 illustrates how the proposition "Unicorns are mythical" would be represented. Here we predicate the property "mythical" not about any particular or generic unicorn, but rather about the concept itself. So, it should be obvious that HAM's formalisms can encode any information needed to define object concepts like "unicorn" or "canary."

Relational and Predicate Concepts

However, the task is less straightforward when one tries to define the concepts that will serve as predicates or relations. The problem is that in defining these concepts one must incorporate information about their *selectional restrictions* and about their *inferential potentials*. As one instructive illustration, let us consider the following definition of the predicate *to cry*: "*Crying* is when an animate creature sheds tears." This definition is stating a variety of facts about the concept *cry*.

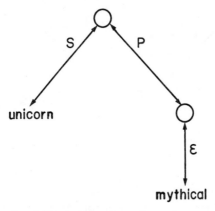

FIG. 7.21. A proposition about the concept "unicorn."

First, *cry* is said to be a subset of the concept *shed*. However, the concept is not distinguished by simple properties as was *canary*. Rather it has the selectional restriction that its subject must be *animate*. Thus, while plants can shed leaves, they cannot cry (except metaphorically). Second, we know that when a person has cried, it is *tears* that he has shed. This is part of the inference potential of the word *cry*.

Figure 7.22 shows the manner in which this information would be encoded into HAM's memory. First, a particular proposition about the world is entered into memory, namely, that "Some animals shed tears." This proposition introduces, as a subset of the concept *shed*, the concept we want to have for *cry*. The word "cry" becomes connected to this node through the word (W) association. The associative structure of the defining proposition in which *cry* appears serves to specify the desired selectional restrictions on its use as well as its inference potential. Figure 7.22 also serves to illustrate how the statement "John cried" would be encoded with reference to the new concept *cry*.

This example illustrates the uniform procedure that we would like to use in defining predicate or relation concepts. A true statement about the world is encoded into memory, and this serves to introduce the desired concept. This procedure is consonant with our general view that all new ideas enter memory as a consequence of encoding an input $\mathcal{J}(t)$ from the well-defined set, $\mathcal{J}$. Therefore, no new mechanisms are needed to handle predicate and relational concepts. In fact, the proposition that defined *cry* in Figure 7.22 is not very different from the proposition that defines *canary* in Figure 7.19.

As a final example let us consider how the relational concept *kick* would be defined in HAM. The true proposition "Some animals move their feet forcefully against some objects" would be encoded in memory (as illustrated in Figure 7.23). The proposition itself is rather uninteresting, but it does serve to introduce the concept *kick* as a subset of the *move* concept. That structure also serves to specify the selectional restrictions of *kick*. The subject of *kick* must come from the set of animals, which forms the subject of *move* in the defining proposition. The object of *kick* is specified differently in the underlying proposition. Part of the structure in Figure 7.23 encodes "The moving of the foot is against some *OBJECT*." The object

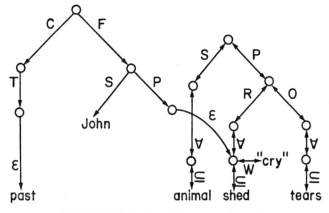

FIG. 7.22. Definition of the concept "cry."

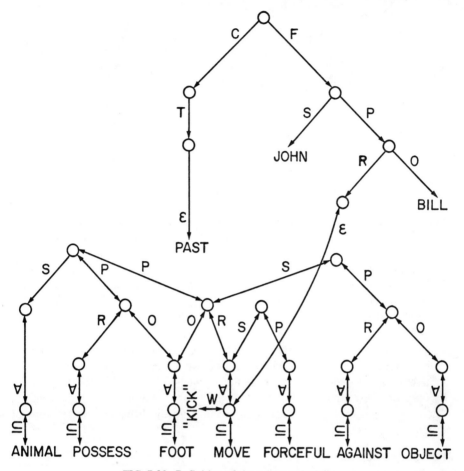

FIG. 7.23. Definition of the concept "kick."

of *kick* is not the object of move (i.e., foot), but rather the item *OBJECT* that occurs in the modifying subject-relation-object construction. This is not unlike having a free variable X appear in an equation. In general, the object of a relation is signaled by the appearance of the item OBJECT somewhere in the defining proposition.

We should notice the many inference potentials contained in the defining proposition for *kick*. If we have encoded "John kicked Bill," as is the case in Figure 7.23, we can know that John is a type of animal, that he possesses a foot, that he used his foot, that he moved it forcefully, and that the movement of the foot was against Bill. None of these facts is directly contained in the encoding of "John kicked Bill," but all are potentially derivable from the "meaning" of *kick*.

Figure 7.24 illustrates how HAM would encode into memory the proposition "John moved his foot forcefully against Bill." Compare this with the encoding of "John kicked Bill" in Figure 7.23. These two encodings are identical in meaning, and HAM would have to be able to recognize their synonymy. That is, if HAM has encoded the sentence in Figure 7.24, it should reply yes to the question "Did John

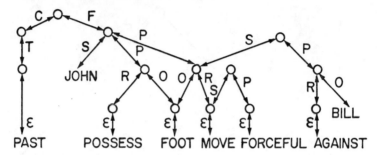

FIG. 7.24. Encoding in HAM of the proposition "John moved his foot forcefully against Bill."

kick Bill?" An important question for future research is how to define inference procedures that will automatically recognize such equivalences. They have not yet been implemented in our simulation program.

Our current method of representation of concepts in HAM would seem to have great potential for establishing such equivalences between memory structures, such as the equivalence of the structures in Figures 7.23 and 7.24. This approach contrasts with the stated purpose of an enterprise like Roger Schank's conceptional linguistics (e.g., Schank, 1972), in which there is just one structure for each equivalent set of propositions. In contrast to Schank, we are forced to have multiple representations as a consequence of two factors. First, we permit separate representation in memory of multiple overlapping concepts (e.g., *move* and *kick*). Second, we allow input trees to be anchored to any arbitrary concept in memory. Therefore, equivalent propositions can be built up by different combinations of different concepts.

Recognition Confusions

In regard to the question of how to represent synonymous sentences, a problem for all such approaches is to interpret data on confusions among different sentences in recognition memory. We will be considering such data in great detail in the third section of the next chapter. If we assume sentences in a synonymous set are equivalently represented, then on a later recognition test HAM would be unable to discriminate which member of the equivalent set of sentences was the one originally input. The logic of this inference has been the conventional wisdom in long use in psycholinguistics research, and indeed we use it extensively in Section 3 of the next chapter.

But there are worrisome features about this logic (see also Fillenbaum, 1970). A first problem is that a given sentence may have different internal representations depending upon the subject's "encoding strategy"—that is, depending upon what information the person wants or has need to extract from it. In particular, a sentence may be represented differently depending on whether it is encountered in everyday conversation or in a context in which the listener knows that verbatim reproduction will be required. A second problem is that subjects frequently forget to make the distinctions experimenters require of them in recognition memory tests. Instead of judging whether a test sentence is verbatim identical to an input sentence, they will occasionally lapse into judging whether a test sentence is *true*, given the information in the set of input sentences. This can be circumvented in part by multiple-choice recognition tests which pit different forms of synonymous and true sentences against one another. A third problem with recognition memory tests is that factors affecting forgetting, such as associative overlap and interference among different sentences of the study set, may interact with and alter the internal representation of a sentence between the time it is studied and the time it is tested.

A final problem with this inferential logic of confusions in recognition memory is that synonymity of meaning of two sentences tends to be discussed as an all-or-none distinction, whereas recognition confusions tend to be more-or-less. In the typical experiment, the subject does "false alarm" to (falsely recognize) conceptually synonymous sentences more than to totally unrelated (or false) sentences. However, he typically also discriminates at a high level between the verbatim input-sentence and conceptually synonymous test sentences. How is one to interpret such data? Theories like Schank's which suppose that synonymous sentences are represented identically have trouble explaining why there can be such a high level of verbatim discrimination. In contrast, theories which suppose that only surface strings are stored have trouble accounting for the higher "false alarm" rate for conceptually synonymous sentences.

HAM adopts a pallid compromise on this issue, opting for the rather weak assertion that the information that is extracted from a sentence and recorded into memory depends upon how the subject expects to use the material. In the absence of specific encoding instructions, subjects enter the experiment exhibiting particular encoding biases carried over from conversational usages; examples would be a bias for transforming passive to active sentences organized around the salient topic of the sentence, or a bias for converting comparative constructions to a common format using the simpler, unmarked adjective, so that a sentence like "Bill is shorter than John" is converted into "John is taller than Bill." There is also an encoding bias which replaces lengthy descriptions of concepts (e.g., "struck his foot forcefully against an object") by the names of those concepts ("kick"). These encoding strategies make use of interpretive mechanisms that make use of inference rules—e.g., shorter $(A,B) \leftrightarrow$ taller (B,A)—to derive and recognize equivalences among memory structures. In principle, some of these inference routines can be implemented in HAM, and we discuss several possibilities later, in Chapter 13. But until such "equivalence-seeking" mechanisms have been specified, the evidential status of recognition confusions is simply unclear regarding the internal representation of sentential information. Incidentally, this is a very general problem for all models of sentence memory; it is not a problem unique to HAM.

REFERENCES

Amarel, S. On representations of problems of reasoning about action. In D. Mitchie (Ed.), *Machine intelligence III*. New York: American Elsevier, 1968.

Asch, S. E. The metaphor: A psychological inquiry. In M. Henley (Ed.), *Documents of Gestalt psychology*. Berkeley: University of California Press, 1961.

Bever, T. G. The cognitive basis for linguistic structures. In J. R. Hayes (Ed.), *Cognition and the development of language*. New York: Wiley, 1970.

Chomsky, N. *Aspects of the theory of syntax*. Cambridge, Mass.: M.I.T. Press, 1965.

Collins, A. M., & Quillian, M. R. How to make a language user. In E. Tulving & W. Donaldson (Eds.), *Organization of Memory*. New York: Academic Press, 1972.

Fillenbaum, S. On the use of memorial techniques to assess syntactic structures. *Psychological Bulletin*, 1970, 73, 231–237.

Johnson-Laird, P. N. On understanding logically complex sentences. *Quarterly Journal of Experimental Psychology*, 1969, 21, 1–13.

Kintsch, W. Notes on the semantic structure of memory. In E. Tulving & W. Donaldson (Eds.), *Organization of Memory*. New York: Academic Press, 1972.

Loux, M. J. The problem of universals. In M. J. Loux (Ed.), *Universals and particulars*. New York: Doubleday, 1970.

McCarthy, J., & Hayes, P. Some philosophical problems from the standpoint of artificial intelligence. In B. Meltzer & D. Mitchie (Eds.), *Machine Intelligence 4*. Edenburgh: Edenburgh University Press, 1969. Pp. 463–502.

Moeser, S. D., & Bregman, A. S. Imagery and language acquisition. Preprinted paper. Simon Fraser University, Burnaby, B. C., 1972.

Moeser, S. D., & Bregman, A. S. The role of reference in the acquisition of a miniature artificial language. *Journal of Verbal Learning and Verbal Behavior*, in press.

Mowrer, O. H. *Learning theory and the symbolic processes*. New York: Wiley, 1960.

Pfaltz, J. L., & Rosenfeld, A. Web grammars. *Proceedings of the International Joint Conference on Artificial Intelligence*, Washington, D. C., 1969, 609–621.

Quillian, M. R. The teachable language comprehender. *Communications of the Association for Computing Machinery*, 1969, 12, 459–476.

Ramsey, F. P. Universals. *The foundations of mathematics*. New York: Harcourt Brace, 1931.

Raphael, B. The frame problem in problem-solving systems. In N. V. Findler & B. Meltzer (Eds.), *Artificial intelligence and heuristic programming*. New York: American Elsevier, Inc., 1971.

Robbin, J. W. *Mathematical logic: A first course*. New York: Benjamin, 1969.

Rumelhart, D. E., Lindsay, P. H., & Norman, D. A. A process model for long-term memory. In E. Tulving & W. Donaldson (Eds.), *Organization of Memory*. New York: Academic Press, 1972.

Russell, B. On the relations of universals and particulars. *Proceedings of the Aristotelian Society*, 1911–12, 1–24.

Schank, R. C. Conceptual dependency: A theory of natural-language understanding. *Cognitive Psychology*, 1972, 3, 552–631.

Staats, A. W. *Learning, language and cognition*. New York: Holt, Rinehart & Winston, 1968.

Tulving, E. Episodic and semantic memory. In E. Tulving & W. Donaldson (Eds.), *Organization of Memory*. New York: Academic Press, 1972.

Whorf, B. L. *Language, thought, and reality*. Cambridge, Mass.: M.I.T. Press, 1956.

8
THE ENCODING PROBLEM

Actual memories mostly are traces not of past sensations but of past conceptualization or verbalization.

—W. V. O. Quine

8.1. PARSING

The previous chapter characterized HAM's propositional trees and how they were used to represent information in long-term memory. However, memory must get connected to the outer world in some way. There are two aspects to this *interface problem*. The first is the *encoding problem* which is concerned with how events in the external world are to be translated into the internal memory representation. The second is the *retrieval problem* which is concerned with how that internal information becomes externalized—in speech or other memory performances. The retrieval problem will be of central concern in a number of later chapters—9, 12, and 13. The focus of this chapter is with how information, particularly linguistic input, is analyzed into a form suitable for use in long-term memory.

As outlined in Chapter 6 (see Figure 6.1), we assume that the external information is registered by sensory receptors, that it is then transformed and recoded into higher features, and that these higher-order features are held for awhile in limited-capacity auditory and visual buffers. It is at this point that the perceptual and linguistic parsers come to bear. Their function is to encode this buffered information into propositional trees that are in the same format as HAM's memory representation. The chief concern of this section will be with the linguistic parser whose prime function is to translate natural language statements into the propositional format. Later, at the end of this section, we briefly indicate how nonlinguistic stimuli such as visual scenes might be described with similar mechanisms and formalisms similar to those postulated for the linguistic case.

However, in neither of these cases will we be interested in the "raw" physical stimuli and their analysis. We will assume rather that considerable preprocessing has already occurred before the mechanisms that we will postulate come to bear. That is, we shall assume that, by whatever means, either the individual words or the basic visual objects of the scene have already been isolated and identified. These are the objects that reside as units in the buffers. Thus the linguistic parser is designed to operate on symbol strings, and to construct an internal representation of the conceptual information contained in such strings.

After discussing our parsing system and its successes and failures, we will turn in Section 8.2 to discussion of the precise interfacing between the parser, various short-term memory components, and HAM's long-term memory. This is a very important issue currently in the experimental contacts between psycholinguistics and research on short-term memory. Some psychological data on comprehension latencies will be discussed in connection with our interfacing proposal. Finally, in Section 8.3 we will examine various data (some new, some old) on recognition confusions in sentence memory. These data help serve to indicate the structural characteristics of the parser's output.

We have programmed a parser that translates English sentences into the binary labeled trees appropriate for input to HAM's memory. However, we want to emphasize that *by no means* have we solved the parsing problem for natural language. Our parser is not designed to be able to encode all English sentences. Rather all input to the system will be taken from a rather restricted subset of English that can express most conceptually distinct facts. Permitting a more syntactically varied class of input would increase the stylistic power of the subset, but with little or no increase of the conceptual content. We argued in Chapter 6 that psychologists should not be interested in a *complete* solution to the parsing problem, since it seems to involve a very large but mixed bag of language-specific and idiosyncratic tricks and procedures of probably little general significance.

The Surface Grammar

The subset of English we are currently working with is defined by the "surface grammar" in Table 8.1. The phrase structures for a range of sample sentences generated by the grammar are illustrated in Figure 8.1. The grammar contains no context-sensitive rules, and consequently it will generate an infinity of semantic anomalies. For instance, "That the cat flies very in the love is on top of the yellow heart" would be one such semantically anomalous sentence that the grammar would generate. However, it is anticipated that the user of the program can inhibit such sentences on the basis of his unformalized semantic intuitions. The purpose of the above grammar is to specify precisely which of the well-formed sentences in English will be accepted by our parser. These syntactic restrictions on input make the task of the parser much easier. The sole purpose for the simplification of the syntax of our input is to simplify the task of parsing.

Since the point of our research is not to promote a parser, but rather to promote HAM as a memory system adequate to meet the varied demands of natural-language question-answering, this simplification of the input sentences does not seem particularly damning from the point of view of our general theoretical enterprise.

TABLE 8.1

Surface Grammar for a Subset of English

1a	SENTENCE	ASSERT
1b		QUESTION
2a	ASSERT	CONTEXT NP PRED
3a		[Where, when] CONTEXTQUERY CONTEXT
3b		[Who, what, whom] PRED CONTEXT
3c	QUESTION	What [did, does, do] NP do (to NP) CONTEXT
3d		[Did, does, do] NP VP (NP) CONTEXT
3e		[Is, are, was, were] NP COMPLEMENT CONTEXT
3f		How [did, does, do] NP VP (NP) CONTEXT
4a	CONTEXT	(During NP) (in NP)
5a	NP	[Some, A, The] (ADJP) Noun (REL)
5b		CLAUSE
6a	PRED	[Is, are, was, were] COMPLEMENT
6b		VP (NP)
7a	CONTEXTQUERY	[did, does, do] NP VP (NP)
7b		[is, are, was, were] NP COMPLEMENT
8a	ADJP	(ADVP) Adj
8b		(ADJP) Adj
9	REL	Relative (NP) PRED CONTEXT
10	CLAUSE	that NP PRED CONTEXT
11a	COMPLEMENT	VP (by NP)
11b		ADJP
11c		NP
11d		PREPP
12	VP	Verb (ADVP) (PREPP)
13	PREPP	Preposition (NP)
14	ADVP	(ADVP) Adv
15	Noun	boy, cat, life, we, John, chair, etc.
16	Adj	big, funny, two, hard, etc.
17	Verb	run, jump, laugh, etc.
18	Adv	happily, very, vigorously, rather, etc.
19	Preposition	in, outside of, above, from, to, etc.
20	Relative	that, who, which, etc.

Note.—The elements completely in capitals are called *nonterminal* symbols. The nonterminal symbols are commonly used abbreviations of the form-class names: i.e., NP, noun phrase; VP, verb phrase; ADVP, adverbial phrase; PREPP, prepositional phrase; ADJP, adjective phrase; RELATIVE, relative clause; etc. CONTEXTQUERY is involved in questions about *where* or *when* something happened (see Rule 3a). It is possible to have conjunctions of these nonterminals. For instance, an NP conjunction is illustrated in Figure 8.1c.

The elements starting with capitals rewrite into words; their names correspond to those commonly given for the form-class of words they dominate. These are called *terminal symbols*. The elements totally in small letters are examples of *terminal words*.

Parentheses indicate that the element is optional and may not appear. Brackets indicate that one but only one of the bracketed elements must be chosen.

However, it would be clearly misguided for us to suggest that the mechanisms which we have developed for handling the subset will extend without substantial augmentation to the total of natural language. So, besides describing how our parser operates, we will append descriptions of the important theoretical additions that will be required to have a parser that successfully mimics how a human analyzes a sentence. While our parser is clearly not a complete model of sentence comprehension, we do believe that, as far as it goes, it is correct.

Operation of the Parser

The parser for HAM can basically be described in computer jargon as a "top-down, left-to-right, predictive parser." We will try to make clear what this

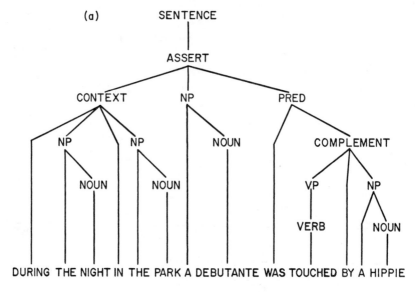

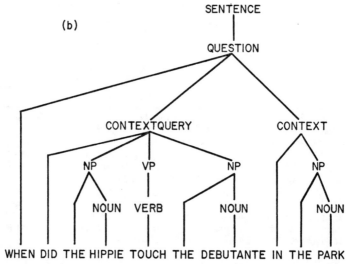

(*Continued*)

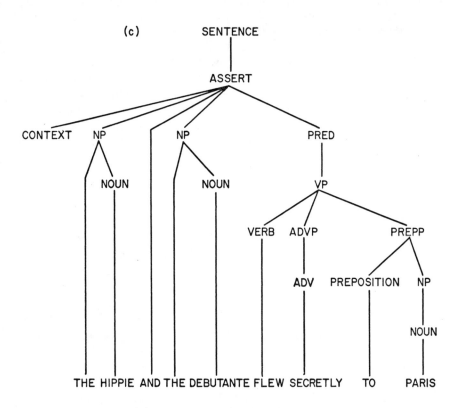

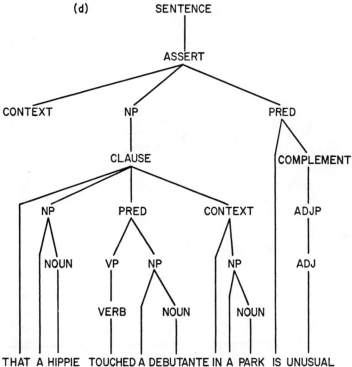

FIG. 8.1. Phrase structures generated by the surface grammar in Table 8.1.

description means. At the heart of the parser are 14 programs, one program associated with each of the first 14 rules in Table 8.1. The program names in the system are in each case the symbols on the left of the rewrite rules. The parser starts with the top-level program (the one called by SENTENCE) and recursively calls lower-order programs until it has properly analyzed each word in the sentence. When the rewrite rule associated with the program (e.g., Rule 2a: ASSERT → CONTEXT NP PRED) rewrites on the left into more than one symbol, the parser must completely analyze the first or leftmost symbol (i.e., CONTEXT) before proceeding to later symbols. These later symbols are stored on a temporary stack of to-be-analyzed units while the parser analyzes the first symbol. If the to-be-analyzed symbol is a nonterminal one (i.e., if it also occurs on the left of one of the first 14 rewrite rules), the parser will analyze that symbol by calling the program associated with it. On the other hand, if the symbol is a terminal element, there is no need to call any further programs, and the parser can select the next symbol from its stack of to-be-analyzed units.

The phrase structures associated by the surface grammar with a sentence define precisely the order in which programs are called in the parsing of the sentence. As an illustration, let us consider in detail the parsing of the sentence shown in Figure 8.1a, "During the night in the park a debutante was touched by a hippie." A depth-first, left-to-right traversal of that tree defines the order in which the programs are called. That is, first the program SENTENCE is called, which calls the program ASSERT, which calls the program CONTEXT. The program CONTEXT analyzes the symbol "during," then calls the program NP to analyze the phrase "the night," then analyzes "in," and finally calls the program NP again to analyze "the park." After this segment finishes, control is transferred from the CONTEXT program back to the ASSERT program. Having finished the context phrase, the next symbol on the ASSERT rewrite rule then calls the program NP to analyze "a debutante," and then finally calls the program PRED. PRED discovers the word "was," and this causes it to call COMPLEMENT to analyze the rest of the sentence. Finally, COMPLEMENT calls VP to analyze TOUCHED, analyzes "by," and then calls NP to analyze "the hippie." Control transfers back out from NP to COMPLEMENT to PRED to ASSERT to SENTENCE, ascending from the recursive depths back out to the top-level executive. Since there are no more words in the sentence, the analysis is both complete and successful. From this discussion, it should be clear why we call our program "top-down" and "left-to-right." The descriptor "top-down" refers to the hierarchical calling of programs and "left-to-right" to the manner in which the parser simultaneously proceeds through the elements of a rewrite rule and through the elements of the sentence.

Parsing Ambiguity

When the parser encounters a symbol associated with more than one rewrite rule (e.g., QUESTION, Rule 3, rewrites into six separate constructions), the parser can always determine the correct rule on the basis of the first one or two elements remaining in the sentence to be analyzed. For instance, Rule 3a is signaled by the appearance of the word "where" at the beginning of the sentence. This strict determination of the syntactic rules is an important characteristic of the subset of

English defined by our surface grammar. This feature saves our grammar from the need to back up or follow multiple parses as other parsers appear to do. Because it always selects the correct rewrite rule initially, we also categorize our system as a *predictive parser*. However, there are constructions in English for which such a parser could not always make the correct predictions. For instance, consider Sentences (1) and (2). In both of these sentences, it is ambiguous until the seventh word whether the fifth and sixth words ("the girl") are part of a conjunction—as in Sentence (2)—or part of a subordinate clause—as in Sentence (1).

I admired the boy the girl despised.   (1)
I admired the boy the girl and their parents.   (2)
I admired the boy that the girl despised.   (3)

This sort of ambiguity never arises for our parser simply because Sentence (1) is not a permissible construction according to the surface grammar. Rather that sentence would have to be constructed as (3) which avoids the ambiguity by the insertion of the relative conjunction "that" after the noun phrase "the boy."

There is evidence for the "psychological reality" of the notion that relative conjunction ("that . . .") materially aids sentence parsing. It has been shown in paraphrase tasks and phoneme-monitoring tasks (e.g., Fodor & Garrett, 1967; Hakes & Foss, 1970) that those sentences which have disambiguating relative pronouns like Sentence (3) are more easily comprehended than sentences like Sentence (1) which lack the relative pronouns. In general, whenever there is ambiguity (syntactic or semantic) at some point in a sentence about how it should be interpreted, we would predict at least momentary difficulty in comprehension, because of the need to consider multiple parses. For instance, Fodor, Garrett, and Bever (1968) have found that sentences with complex verbs were more difficult to comprehend than sentences with simple verbs. A complex verb was one which permitted more than one syntactic construction to follow it. As Sentences (4) and (5) illustrate, "believe" is complex because it may be followed by a sentential complement—as in Sentence (4)—or a simple object—as in Sentence (5). In contrast, the verb "discussed" in Sentence (6) is simple because it only permits object completion.

John believed that the minister was an idiot.   (4)
John believed the minister.   (5)
John discussed the book.   (6)

Also, MacKay (1966) and Foss (1970) report that pure sentential ambiguity will interfere with comprehension whether it is lexical ambiguity, as in Sentence (7), or underlying structure ambiguity, as in Sentence (8).

The tank was too hot to touch.   (7)
The elephant is ready to lift.   (8)

Construction of Propositional Trees

To return to the operation of HAM's parser, it could produce phrase structures like those in Figure 8.1, but HAM has no use for them. What HAM wants from its parser is something very different, namely, binary labeled trees of a form suitable for input into its memory. Thus, with each step in the parse HAM makes further additions to the tree it is building up in working memory. For instance, if it finds a construction "during NP" in analyzing CONTEXT (Rule 4a), the results of analysis of NP will be assigned to the TIME branch in a tree. Thus HAM's parser is much like Woods' (1970—see Section 5.4), in that there is little correspondence between the flow of control in the parser and the structures output.

Because the surface-phrase structure trees do not always correspond to the propositional trees, it is often the case that the results of the parse cannot be immediately integrated into the binary tree that is being constructed. For instance, in Rule 2a the NP element may either fill the role of logical subject or object in the proposition, depending on whether the sentence is active or passive. Whether the sentence is active or passive is not determined until the verb phrase of the sentence has begun to be analyzed. As another example, the adjective phrases uncovered in the NP parse (Rule 5a) must be put to one side until the noun is found to which they can be attached. Therefore, as Hunt (1971) forecast, we have had to set up a working memory to hold these partial results until the parse has proceeded far enough to indicate what should be done with the partial results. What to do with them is always uniquely determined by the end of the sentence because the grammar in Table 8.1 generates no syntactically ambiguous sentences (at least as far as the parser is concerned).

Syntactic Knowledge as Procedures

There is one important feature that this parser shares with Winograd's (see Chapter 5). That is, syntactic knowledge is expressed as procedures, programs, or processes for transforming a sentence into the desired underlying representation. This method of incorporating syntactic knowledge into procedures has an important and correct psychological implication—since the syntactic information is represented in the form of mental processes, it should not be explicitly retrievable upon demand. Thus, when queried, a naive informant should not be able to give systematic statements of his linguistic knowledge or list a set of syntactic rules. However, he will exhibit his possession of that knowledge whenever he receives an English sentence and proceeds to "understand" it (i.e., gives it a correct analysis and interpretation). This is presumably what Chomsky (1965) meant to reference when he spoke of our linguistic capacities as displaying a "tacit" knowledge of the grammar. The fact that grammatical knowledge is tacit in the naive speaker impresses us as a strong *psychological* argument for representing syntactic knowledge in the form of processes, rather than storing a set of rules which are uniformly applied by some general interpretive program. The *computational* arguments for the "procedure" approach cited by Winograd (1971) are not at all convincing. As Winograd (1971, p. 210) himself eventually admits, the two approaches are equivalent in their parsing power, since both have the power of a Turing machine.

The Word-Idea Distinction

Before proceeding further in discussing the parser, it is necessary to introduce one further complication to HAM's memory structure. Up until now we have employed the convenient fiction that the name of a node in memory can be the English word for the idea to which that node corresponds. In fact, this is false; the idea nodes are essentially nameless entities that acquire their meaning from the configuration of associations into which they enter with other ideas. Each English word, as a word, is also represented in memory, but by nodes different from the idea nodes that we have discussed so far. The orthographic and articulatory parameters corresponding to the word are accessible from the *word node*. These word nodes are connected by the member (ϵ) relation to the concept of "word."

For the purpose of simulating HAM with verbal material, it is necessary to make explicit the linkage between the word nodes and the idea nodes which they reference. We have found it useful to introduce two additional associative relations into memory, *WORD* and its inverse, *IDEA*. The WORD association connects an idea node to its corresponding word nodes. Because of the existence of synonymous words, any particular idea node can be connected to *more than one word node*. Similarly, because of the polysemy of English words, a particular word may be connected by the IDEA relation to *more than one idea node*. Figure 8.2 illustrates what we have in mind. In that figure we have used words to express the word nodes and pictures to express the idea nodes. "Ball" is connected to its two senses, "dance" to its one sense. These two relations, IDEA and WORD, may be thought of as two elements of our language-specific capacities, since they have no purpose other than providing a convenient interface between linguistic terms and the corresponding ideas.

Semantics

The semantic powers of our current parsing program fall far short of what we would like to see implemented someday. We will now describe what sorts of things the parser handles well, where its principal weaknesses lie, and how it might be improved. First, there is the matter of word synonymy which poses no problem at

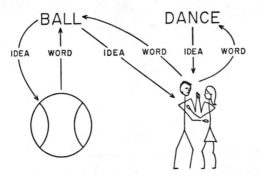

FIG. 8.2. The connection between words and ideas.

all for the parser. Since synonymous words are connected to the same idea node, synonymous words are represented by the same idea node in the tree that the parser sends to memory. For example, the input trees for the two sentences, "The boy hit the girl" and "The lad hit the girl," would be identical, since "boy" and "lad" reference the same idea node.

In contrast to the ease with which HAM handles word synonymy, its parser has no current mechanisms for handling polysemy—how to disambiguate a word on the basis of the sentence or larger context. For instance, how might "bank" be disambiguated in the sentence "I deposited my money in the bank"? There are two possible ways that this might happen. To give the more implausible first, the parser might, as Winograd advocates, consider explicitly all possible interpretations of "bank" and compute which is the most probable. Or somewhat similar to what Quillian did, we might have HAM send activation from words early in the sentence to associatively related concepts. In this way HAM can prime whichever interpretations of a polysemous like "bank" are associatively related to the initial words. Thus HAM, having previously stored propositions (associative structures) in which the ideas of "deposit" or "money" have co-occurred with the idea of a financial institution, would be able to prime the financial-institution interpretation of "bank" in this example sentence. The Quillian alternative seems well adapted to a parallel machine, which the brain may well be.

Disambiguating Reference

HAM does have primitive mechanisms for determining the referents of nouns or pronouns. Much as in Winograd's program, the appearance of a pronoun or of a noun preceded by "the" sets off a search for the referent of that term. In contrast, a noun preceded by "a" is interpreted differently as introducing a new member of the noun class rather than referring to an old member previously mentioned. Hence, no search is initiated in the latter case. Important to disambiguation of reference is the fact that HAM's long-term memory associations are ordered according to recency, so that the most recently used associations are the most available. (We will discuss the details of this ordering mechanism in the next chapter.) This ordering of the associations makes it very easy to determine the referent of a noun preceded by "the": HAM proceeds from the word node to the idea node for the noun. Then HAM retrieves the most available (most recent) ϵ^{-1} association leading from the idea node. This association leads to the appropriate referent node because when people use a phrase like "the man," they are usually referring to the last mentioned instance of a man, which will be the most available ϵ^{-1} association to the concept, man.

When the input noun has attached to it a definite description (e.g., the *big ugly* boy, the boy *who kicked the girl*, etc.), the determination of its reference is somewhat more complicated. The parser constructs a probe tree corresponding to the description (e.g., Was a boy big and ugly? Did a boy kick a girl?). These probes are sent to memory through the decoding function. In matching these probes to memory, HAM will instantiate the nouns. (The matching process is described in the next chapter.) HAM will then use these instantiations of the nouns as the desired referents—i.e., as the concept nodes to which new predications are to be attached.

Deciding the reference of third-person pronouns like "he" is different again. The parser can generally retrieve from its working memory (to be discussed in the next section of this chapter) the last few input trees that it has constructed. To find the referent of a third person pronoun, the parser first determines the appropriate semantic class of the referent, then searches back through these trees trying to find an item which is a member of the appropriate class. For instance, the class corresponding to "he" is "male person." So, the mechanism for deciding the referent of pronouns is quite different from that for nouns. The reference of definite nouns is determined by associations in long-term memory and by their relative availability. The reference of pronouns is determined by a search through a short-term store of input trees. Consequently, if one wants to refer to an individual that occurred some considerable distance back in the passage, he must use a noun construction rather than a pronoun. Pronouns and nouns seem to be used in this way in most texts.

Conceptual Knowledge

A significant weakness of our parser is that, with the exception of determining reference, it does not bring the knowledge in HAM's long-term memory to bear on the task of parsing. Thus, for instance, HAM cannot use conceptual expectations to help guide the parsing, as Roger Schank advocates (see Section 5.4). Such expectations are very important in properly analyzing pairs of sentences such as (9) and (10).

He hit the boy with long hair. (9)

He hit the boy with a wrench. (10)

In Sentence (9) the parser must recognize that the "with" prepositional phrase is probably a description of "the boy," whereas in Sentence (10) it probably gives the instrument of action. These decisions can be only based on our past knowledge about hitting, hair, boys, and wrenches. Actually, this pair of sentences would not be input to HAM's current parser, because both are prohibited by the surface grammar. Sentences (9) and (10) would have to be rendered as Sentences (11) and (12), in which the potential ambiguity is eliminated.

He hit the boy who had long hair. (11)

He hit with a wrench the boy. (12)

This example illustrates how the restrictions of our surface grammar save the parser from many a semantic embarrassment. It equivalently illustrates the kind of information our parser should be able to retrieve from long-term memory before it can begin to adequately parse a larger set of English sentences.

A general problem with our parser is that, just as Woods' or Winograd's, it is syntax-directed. That is, it will not consider a particular parse of the sentence unless there is syntactic evidence for that parse. However many ungrammatical utterances can be understood because of the semantic constraints among the words. The utterances of Tarzan to Jane, or of two-year olds to their parents, while not very grammatical, are comprehensible. Such informal facts suggest that our comprehension can be guided by semantic as well as by syntactic considerations. Presumably, what is required is a parser which tries to use both syntactic and semantic clues in parallel to analyze the sentence. When these two types of clues are redundant, the parser would follow whichever yielded the quicker solution. Perhaps, the syntactic analysis should be continued after the semantic analysis had yielded an interpretation to check the acceptability of the tentative parse. Similarly, semantic considerations could be evoked to check out any syntactically determined parse. In ungrammatical speech, a syntactic redundancy check would not be possible, and the parser would have to trust the semantics. Similarly, with anomalous sentences like "Colorless green ideas sleep furiously," the parser would have to be satisfied with a syntactic analysis.

The problem with this grand proposal is one of implementation. It is easy enough to see how to bring low-level sentential semantics into the parsing process. For instance, like Schank's (see Schank, Tesler, & Weber, 1970) SPINOZA, HAM could consult the conceptual representation in memory of the sentence verb (once it is located) to determine what sort of noun classes (cases) to expect and how to analyze them. But, as Roger Schank effectively argues (see our discussion in Section 5.4), the type of information that people bring to bear in comprehending a sentence may include information about the total linguistic and nonlinguistic context in which it occurs. Except for the simple matters of reference, which our parser already handles, no one has produced a language parser that extends beyond the boundaries of individual sentences. This clearly is the challenge for the future.

Scene Analysis

Our task in constructing a parser that would transform sentences typed to HAM into input trees of the desired form is an interesting and rather difficult task even for a restricted subset of English. It would have been considerably more difficult if we had demanded that the parser deal with all the complexities of English. However, even this seems a small task in contrast to the problem of getting the computer to derive similar input trees from visual scenes. This would be a truly Herculean task. In the first place, the input does not have the form of well-defined characters as does a typed sentence. A great deal of preprocessing effort must go into feature extraction—the lines, points of intersection, features, etc.—the units out of which the scene description will be built. But there have developed a few reasonably successful heuristic techniques for doing this (see Duda & Hart, 1972). The really unchartered ground concerns the problem of composing these elements into articulated descriptions of scenes. This problem domain has been called *scene analysis* in computer science.

In the first place, present scene-analysis programs are handicapped by the fact that they almost never have two "eyes." That is, visual information comes from just one television camera taking a static picture of the scene for the computer. Of course, people can get along fairly well with monocular vision, but we have motion parallax to help determine depth. In contrast, the computer typically works with a static, monocular view of the world. Now, it is a simple geometrical fact that an infinite number of three-dimensional arrays will project the same static, monocular, two-dimensional view. That we usually construct a particular 3-D scene from a static, monocular, 2-D array is testament to our past experience with the three-dimensional world. We are able to determine the 3-D scene by supplementing the 2-D information with constraints about what are the likely objects and configurations in the scene. That is, we know that certain places have certain objects in certain locations, that objects have certain shapes more often than others, that objects are not usually suspended in midair without support, etc. Much of this knowledge certainly comes from our history of moving through the environment using binocular vision and motion parallax to determine the statistics about real-world objects (see Gibson, 1950). The computer has no such learning history—all of its knowledge must be programmed in. So in many ways the computer scientists have saddled themselves with an inordinately difficult task. We wonder if a human would ever come to articulate his visual world if all he ever saw were successive stills.

Another difficulty with scene analysis has to do with the task itself rather than the technical constraints imposed by the mode of perception. How does one organize the description of a picture? A one-dimensional sentence has a natural linear ordering which makes much easier the task of specifying a syntax than does a 2-D picture. One solution has been to describe figures in terms of their boundaries which have natural orderings. But this approach has limited utility and breaks down when we come to scenes having multiple overlapping figures. The task of producing a satisfactory description for an arbitrary scene is without solution. Some of the more impressive work on the problem comes out of the M.I.T. Artificial Intelligence Lab and concerns the analysis of scenes composed of jumbles of blocks. This we will describe briefly to give an indication of how scene analysis might proceed.

Guzman's SEE Program

In some recent seminal work, Guzman (1968) has produced a program (named SEE) that would analyze a scene like Figure 8.3 and isolate out the objects and identify which surfaces belonged to which object. Guzman's program identifies various types of vertices between surfaces, each type providing some evidence about the linkage of the surfaces into a single object. Figure 8.4 shows four of the more common vertices along with their names. The Arrow provides evidence that the two regions bounded by the small angles are adjacent sides of an object. Similarly, the Fork provides evidence that the three pairs of sides are adjacent at each of the three edges. Figure 8.5 shows a cube with one Fork, three Arrows, and three Ells, with lines connecting the surfaces that are linked by the vertex heuristics of Guzman's program. Notice how the Fork and the Arrows provide the requisite information for segmenting the figure. The Tee vertex is also quite useful because a matching pair of Tee's (such as in Figure 8.6) suggests that one figure is occluding another. With these and a few other heuristics, Guzman was able to analyze figures as complicated as Figure 8.3.

A few criticisms might be lodged against Guzman's work. One criticism is that the program does not, in fact, produce a description of the scene it is analyzing; rather, its output is just a segmentation of the objects in the scene. Thus, given the

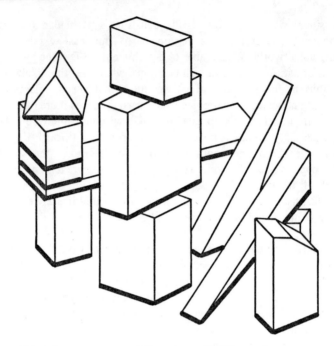

FIG. 8.3. A scene successfully segmented by Guzman's program.

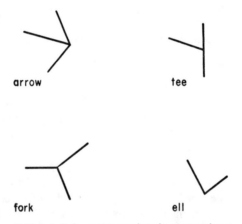

arrow   tee

fork   ell

FIG. 8.4. Informative vertices in segmenting a
scene.

scene of Figure 8.7a, it would not recognize that the objects were brick-shaped or that they formed an arch. Of course, given this scene, there is actually no necessary reason to do so. The 2-D representation in Figure 8.7a could have been projected by a great many 3-D objects besides blocks with parallel sides and right-angled corners. Secondly, there is no necessary reason to suppose that one block is supported by the other. The top block could in fact be somewhat above and in front of the arches we suppose support it. However, on the basis of past experience,

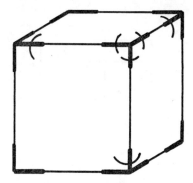

FIG. 8.5. Vertices on the cube indicate connections between surfaces.

we assume that such 2-D shapes correspond to bricklike blocks, and that blocks tend to be supported one on another rather than to be dangling in midair.

Starting with Guzman's system, Winston (1970) has programmed further procedures that will impose these relevant assumptions upon the scene and extract an appropriate description such as in Figure 8.7*b*. Winston has used such scene descriptions as starting points from which his program has been able to learn concepts of geometric structures such as an arch, a pedestal, a table, etc. The representation of this scene in Winston's system (shown in Figure 8.7*b*) is not a simple tree structure such as HAM's parser provides for sentences. However, it should not be surprising that complex graphs are necessary to encode the complex relations that exist in a visual scene. Figure 8.8 shows how Winston's graph structures can be converted into a *set* of tree structures suitable for input to HAM. This is to say that the descriptions output by Winston's scene analysis program could be considered the output of HAM's "perceptual parser" and as the input to HAM's long-term memory. The fact that we can translate Winston's graph structures into HAM is itself relatively uninteresting. The interesting question is whether there is any evidence for the "psychological reality" of either system of scene representation. On that question the reader will observe a profound silence from all quarters.

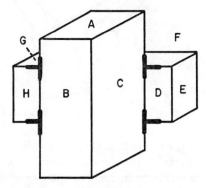

FIG. 8.6. T-vertex indicates an occluded
figure.

(a)

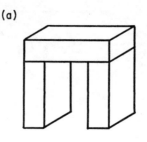

(b)

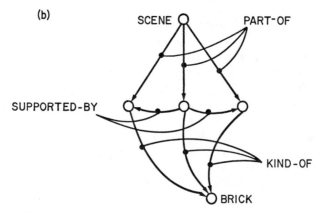

FIG. 8.7. An arch (a) and its description (b) by Winston's program.

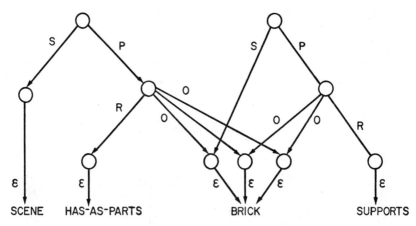

FIG. 8.8. Translation of Winston's description in Figure 8.7a into HAM's formalisms.

Much of the success in the research of Guzman and Winston depended on the particular task domain to which they applied their work. They were able to discover local cues in such block scenes enabling them to pick out the objects and identify various spatial relations among the objects. However, it is not obvious that such specialized techniques can be generalized to the description the nonrectilinear world, such as describing a human face, an outdoor scene, a football game, etc. Such problems seem rather far from quick solution.

8.2. MEMORY REQUIREMENTS OF THE PARSER

Our parser makes certain storage requirements on the system to hold information as it is parsed and input to memory. To meet these requirements we have postulated the existence of three types of mental storage mechanisms. These have marked similarities to those suggested by Hunt (1971). First, there are the visual and auditory buffers that retain acoustic or visual representations of the words in memory while they are being analyzed. These buffers would hold words for some time after they have been analyzed to permit backup should the first analysis attempted prove faulty. It is not clear exactly what the holding capacity of these stores is. Our immediate memory span for a string of words is about seven, but this measure probably involves a confounding of the buffer with the working store which we will discuss shortly. In any case, the size of the buffer implies clear limitations on how far back in the sentence we can retrieve the exact word representations in case they should be necessary for a reinterpretation of the meaning of the sentence. Various studies of loss from short-term memory (e.g., Reitman, 1971) suggest that interference by similar interpolated material may be a crucial factor in forgetting from the auditory buffer.

Secondly, the parser must be able to keep track of where it is in the parse of the sentence. In terms of our program-grammar (see Table 8.1), this bookkeeping involves keeping a constantly updated record on a push-down store (PDS) of the sequence of programs that resulted in reaching the current point in the analysis of the sentence. For instance, if the word "park" is being analyzed in the sentence "In the park the hippie touched the debutante," the system must know it is in the middle of executing an NP program, which was called by the CONTEXT program, which was called earlier by the ASSERT program, which was called by the main SENTENCE program. A record must be kept of the calling programs so that the system will know where to return control after it has finished executing the current program.

In actual fact, it is not always necessary to keep a complete record of the sequence of programs. For instance, in executing NP in the current example, one need not keep record of CONTEXT because control will be transferred from NP to CONTEXT, and then pass directly to ASSERT without the CONTEXT program performing any further computations. So a clever system would only store ASSERT and then omit record of the intermediary CONTEXT. The general strategy behind this economizing is that if one is analyzing the rightmost element in a rewrite rule, the program symbol associated with that rule need not be stored because the computation will not need to return to this program again. Because of this fact, with right-branching-sentences like Sentence (13) it is not necessary to store on the PDS a record of the nesting of programs that lead to the generation of the right-branching structure.

The boy hit the girl who kicked the dog who chased the cat who ate the mouse. (13)

An intelligent program would rather just store "ASSERT" knowing that at the end of the right-branching the program structure will directly unwind back to the ASSERT level. In contrast, when the program encounters center-embedded constructions such as Sentence (14), it is not possible to delete the records of the intervening programs that have been called.

The mouse who the cat who the dog who the girl who the boy hit kicked chased ate died. (14)

When the parser arrives at the element "boy" in Sentence (14), it would have to have already stored the backwards sequence NP REL NP REL NP REL NP REL NP ASSERT SENTENCE. The difficulty in holding such a long list of commitments may be one of the reasons why center-embedded sentences are so much more difficult to comprehend than right-branching sentences.

It is difficult to know what limit to place on the number of elements that may be saved on this PDS. However, it does seem reasonable to postulate that there is a limit and that this limit helps determine what sentences can be easily comprehended. Also, it seems reasonable that the PDS is "cleared out" at the end of each sentence. This seems consistent with results on running memory-span for sentences obtained by Jarvella (1971).

A third storage area is required in language analysis to hold partial tree structures as the sentence is parsed and total tree structures (called the "input trees") as they are matched to memory and then encoded. This storage area, which we call *working memory*, corresponds quite closely to the concept of a *short-term store* in models like those of Atkinson and Shiffrin (1968) or Anderson (1972a). That is, as information resides in this storage area it can become permanently recorded as part of long-term memory. In contrast to the Atkinson and Shiffrin short-term store, our working memory is not structurally separate from long-term memory, but rather it is a *currently active partition* of long-term memory. It is the area of long-term memory where structural modifications are presently occurring to associative linkages. This conception of a currently-active partition of long-term memory was introduced in Anderson (1972a) where the concern was with an associative model for free recall. Also in keeping with Anderson (1972a), we will assume that the size of this working memory is limited by the number of long-term memory nodes that can be held active in the working memory.

An Example

We have now postulated three separate memory restrictions that limit the parser as it tries to encode a sentence into memory. This position contrasts sharply with an assumption frequently made in the memory literature that there is but one short-term store for all information processing. A worked-out example will illustrate how these three storage mechanisms interact in the processing of a sentence. We will therefore consider how the two-sentence sequence of (15) and (16) would be analyzed. We will assume a limit of five on the number of words that may be stored in the acoustic (or visual) buffer. We will make no definite assumption about the size of the PDS holding the list of syntactic commitments nor about the size of working memory—only that processing these sentences does not exceed capacity in either store.

In a park a hippie touched a debutante. (15)

The debutante slapped the hippie. (16)

Beginning at the beginning of Sentence (15), the first word that is input is "In." Upon hearing this word, the parser would determine that an assertion was being made and call the program ASSERT. The original program SENTENCE would be stored on the push-down store (PDS). The program CONTEXT would then be called, and ASSERT would be stored on the PDS. The program CONTEXT would determine that there was no time expression of the form "during NP," since such an expression should initiate the sentence according to the restricted surface grammar. (A time link will be added later to the propositional structure when it discovers that the verb "touched" is in the past tense.) However, there is a locative expression in the surface string as indicated by the word "in." The next word heard is "a," which signals the beginning of an NP expression in the locative phrase "in NP." The NP program would then be called. The CONTEXT program would not be stored on the PDS, since NP was the rightmost branch in the CONTEXT rule (see Table 8.1). Rather, control would go directly back from NP to the ASSERT program which is already stored on the PDS.

After the third word, "park," had been heard, the memory configuration would be as set forth in Figure 8.9a. The acoustic buffer would contain a record of the words "In a park," and the contents of the syntactic PDS would be the current program NP, the ASSERT program to which control transfers after NP, and the SENTENCE program to which control will transfer after ASSERT is completed. In the square box of Figure 8.9a we show the working memory, and, as can be seen, with the introduction of "park," some structure has begun to appear. The concept node for park is connected by a word association (labeled with a W) to the word node for "park." That word node is not part of working memory. This is indicated in Figure 8.9a by the fact that the word is outside of the working-memory box. The concept node for "park," however, is contained in working memory. As the concept node is a node already encoded in long-term memory, it constitutes one of the terminal nodes in which the growing propositional tree will be anchored. A new node has been created to represent the particular park instance under discussion. It has been connected to the park concept node by a member link, labeled ϵ. It is also connected to the context node by a location link, labeled L, and the context node is connected to the proposition node by a context link labeled C. This is as far as the construction of the input tree can proceed on the basis of the words received so far. Note that the memory requirements on working memory (given by the variable S to the right of the box in Figure 8.10) is just one, since only the one park concept node is required from long-term memory.

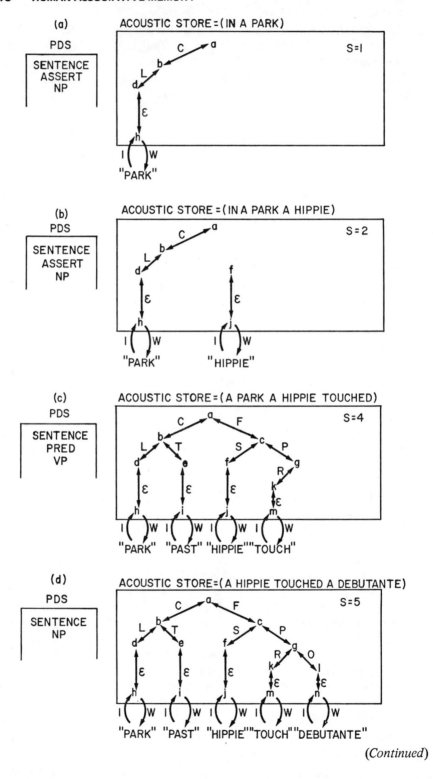

(Continued)

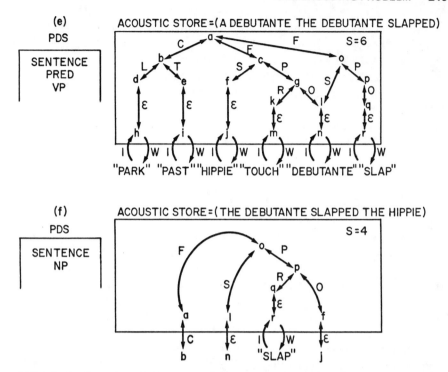

FIG. 8.9. Configuration of the various short-term memory stores during the analysis of Sentences (15) and (16).

We assume that the number of nonmemory nodes does not count as part of the capacity limitations. Rather, the critical variable will be the number of areas of memory (i.e., nodes) that can be simultaneously accessed and held actively excited in order to support the developing tree structures. Provided n memory nodes can be brought into the working memory, we suppose that arbitrarily complicated structures can be built upon them, involving arbitrarily many nonmemory nodes. Should the supporting memory nodes become inactive (fall out of memory) before the structure they support becomes part of long-term memory, then that structure would disintegrate, and encoding of it would cease. Hence, the measure of working memory capacity is the number of long-term memory nodes that are currently being recruited to support the structures being held.

To return to our parsing exercise, the next word in the sentence is "a," which signals the end of the current noun-phrase and the beginning of a new noun-phrase. Control returns to ASSERT and then passes to NP which is the second element in the rewrite rule associated with ASSERT (Rule 2 in Table 8.1). After the word "hippie" is heard, the memory configuration is as illustrated by Figure 8.9*b*. A member or instance of the "hippie" concept has been created to represent the referent of the current noun-phrase. The memory requirements for the working store are now two, since both the "park" and the "hippie" concept nodes have been recruited from long-term memory.

With the entry of the verb "touched," a flurry of activity takes place in the memory stores. The verb marks the end of the noun-phrase, and control returns from NP to ASSERT which now calls PRED. Since PRED is the rightmost element in the ASSERT rewrite rule, ASSERT is deleted from the PDS and, once the PRED subroutine finishes, control will transfer directly back from PRED to SENTENCE. PRED calls on the routine VP to analyze the verb. The verb is in the active voice, indicating that "hippie" should be the subject in the input tree. Also, "touched" is in the past tense, indicating that "past" is the correct time element (now added to the context node). Also, "touched" provides the relational element "touch" which is also incorporated into the deep-structure tree. Figure 8.9c shows the tree after all these additions have been made to it. The only element still missing is the object of the relational element "touch." Four long-term memory nodes are required to support this memory structure.

The next word to be heard is "a," which signals the end of the verb phrase and the beginning of a noun phrase. The symbols PRED and VP are removed from the PDS, and the NP program is introduced to analyze the incoming noun phrase. After the element "debutante" has been analyzed, the tree structure held in working memory is as illustrated in Figure 8.9d. The tree is now complete and ready to be stored in long-term memory. While it is being encoded it has to be held in the working memory. The details of the storage process will be described in Chapter 10.

At this point the entire sentence has been entered into working memory. Note from Figure 8.9d that only the last five words of the sentence are still in the acoustic buffer. The only way that the beginning phrase of the sentence, "In a park," could be retrieved is by generation from the input tree contained in working memory. In this sense, the working memory serves sort of like an intermediate memory store.

Analysis of the second sentence now begins. The first word, "The," signals that the CONTEXT element of the sentence is being omitted and that the sentence is starting with the surface subject. The next word, "debutante," is taken as referring to the debutante instance created in the previous sentence, so no new elements are added to the working memory of Figure 8.9d. Then, with the verb "slapped," a great flurry of activity takes place just as it had with the verb "touched" in the previous sentence. The parser infers that this is another fact about the same context and introduces "slap" as the relational element in the new input tree it is building. Thus, Figure 8.9e shows the total contents of working memory after the verb analysis. The number of long-term memory nodes now recruited by the working memory is six, which may well be approaching capacity.

Finally, the last two words "the hippie" are analyzed by the parser. The second input tree is now completed and ready for encoding in memory as indicated in Figure 8.9f. We assume in this example that the memory ceases to try to encode the previous tree and now focuses its efforts on the recent tree. Therefore, the first tree no longer occupies space in working memory since it is not being held for encoding. Note that many of the terminal branches of the new input tree are memory nodes created during the encoding of the previous tree. These new terminal nodes are the context node, the subject node ("the debutante"), and the object node ("the hippie").

In this example, there were never more than three elements on the syntactic PDS, and one element was always the highest-level program, SENTENCE. The sentences did not contain any embedded clauses and hence did not require long lists to be stored on the PDS. The reader might well wonder what the psychological equivalent is of the programs which HAM stores on the PDS. It is certain that people are not evoking LISP programs when they analyze a sentence. We will assume, however, that corresponding to our syntactic programs are recursive sets of mental processes that can be evoked to analyze various syntactic constructions. The PDS then is a means of recording where one set of mental processes was when a second set started up.

Center-embedding

We have already suggested that center-embedding sentences are more difficult than right-branching sentences because of the need to store a record of more commitments on the PDS. Another reason may have to do with the difficulty of keeping track of the information in the working store. Consider the predicament of the parser when it comes to the word "chased" in Sentence (17).

The lion that the dog that the monkey chased bit died.	(17)
The monkey chased the dog that bit the lion that died.	(18)
The dog that the monkey chased died.	(19)
The question that the girl that the lion bit answered was complex.	(20)

In the working store, the structure would be as diagrammed in Figure 8.10. That is, the parser has determined that "monkey chased" is the correct subject-verb combination and must now try to select the correct object from between "lion" and "dog" but has no basis for this decision. This dilemma of having to select between multiple candidates for a syntactic role never arises with right-branching constructions like Sentence (18). This analysis of the difficulty of center-embedding suggests that the difficulty should not be found with constructions like Sentence (19) which have only one embedding, since object ambiguity does not arise with these. In fact, constructions like Sentence (19) are judged to be fairly comprehensible by most college students. The real difficulty in comprehension begins with a *second* center-embedding. Also, center-embedded sentences like

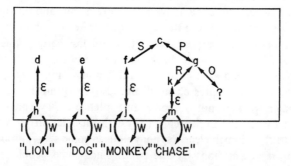

FIG. 8.10. Object ambiguity in parsing Sentence (17).

Sentence (20) should not be so difficult since semantic relations help constrain the possible complements of the verbs. In line with this, Schlesinger (1966) found that semantically constrained constructions like Sentence (20) were more easily comprehended than constructions like Sentence (17).

8.3. MEMORY FOR SYNTACTIC FORM
VERSUS SEMANTIC GIST

So far little consideration has been given to exactly which class of synonymous English sentences should be transformed into identical deep-structure trees. The vagaries of this problem may be illustrated by the five pairs of Sentences (21) to (30), each pair of which could be considered synonymous by one or another criterion of synonymity.

The boy phoned the girl up.	(21)
The boy phoned up the girl.	(22)
The boy hit the girl.	(23)
The girl was hit by the boy.	(24)
The car's exhaust pollutes the air.	(25)
The car pollutes the air with its exhaust.	(26)
The boy is taller than the girl.	(27)
The girl is shorter than the boy.	(28)
My favorite number is the fourth power of 3.	(29)
My favorite number is 81.	(30)

Clearly, the pair (21) and (22), exemplifying particle shift, should not result in different input trees. The active-passive pair (23) and (24) are mapped onto the same input tree by our present parser, but there is room for some dispute from our own data. That is, one might want to argue that the subject slot in the input tree should be filled by the surface subject (presuppositional focus) of the sentence rather than the logical subject. That is, Sentence (23) is really *about* the boy, whereas Sentence (24) is *about* the girl. The subject in the input tree, one might argue, should be the topic of the sentence. This would require having for every transitive verb two relations, the active relation (e.g., hit) and the passive (e.g., was hit by). Later we suggest evidence that either of these can be used depending on the utility of that mode of representation. It is still less certain whether a pair of sentences like (25) and (26) should have the same input trees assigned to them. The comparative pair (27) and (28) introduce still further complexities, since not only are surface syntactic structures changed, but also important lexical elements (the comparative adjectives) are not the same. In Sentence (27) we are dealing with the relation "taller than," and in Sentence (28) with the relation "shorter than." The pair (29) and (30), although clearly synonymous in some sense, probably should be given different representations by the parser since some people might not even know that the fourth power of 3 is 81.

The problem we will be discussing in this section is where one should draw the line between Sentences (21) and (30) in declaring for "synonymous" representations. At what point does the parser stop producing identical pairs of input trees for such synonymous pairs of sentences? On a priori grounds, it is very difficult to say. Deeper analysis and more computation will be required if the parser is to produce identical representations for sentences that have quite different surface structures, because the surface structure determines how the sentence parse will proceed. Therefore, if two very different parsing sequences are to result in identical input trees, the parser will have to perform more complicated tests, will have to store temporarily many partial tree structures, and will have to search memory to determine equivalences between pairs like "taller" and "shorter." On the other hand, this extra work in encoding equivalences tends to pay off later by making it easier to search the memory structure during question answering. For instance, HAM would not have to spend time discovering the memory structure for Sentence (27) and proving that it justifies an affirmative answer to a question such as "Is the girl shorter than the boy?" Rather the probe tree for the question would have a structure identical to the memory structure set up by the original Sentence (27) and so would directly contact it. So, on a priori grounds, there are both advantages and disadvantages to mapping synonymous sentences into identical input trees.

Therefore, we decided to consult some experimental evidence to see if any light could be shed on this issue from that corner. If we assume that two sentences A and B are mapped onto the same input tree, I, by the parser, we are led to a very powerful empirical prediction. Consider the situation where the subject has studied A or B and later must tell which it was he studied. One can predict that the subject will completely confuse the alternatives A and B because all he has in memory is an encoding of I, and he has no way of determining whether I came from A or B. So, the prediction is that if two sentences are parsed into the same input tree, they should be confused on a later recognition test. However, as with many other apparently clear-cut experimental predictions, this test turns out to be more complicated methodologically than what we have just set forth. We will examine these methodological issues in some detail for active-passive synonymous sentences and then turn to a more cursory examination of recognition confusions between other types of synonymous sentences.

Recognition Confusions with Active-Passive Pairs

The classic study of active-passive recognition confusions was performed by Sachs (1967). She had subjects listen to stories in which a critical active or passive sentence was embedded. At a delay of 0, 80, or 160 syllables from the original sentence, subjects were presented with a test comprised either of the original sentence, a sentence whose semantic content was changed, a sentence with the voice (i.e., active versus passive) changed, or a sentence with a very minor syntactic change (e.g., particle shift). The subjects were very likely (over 90%) to detect any change in the sentence at the 0-syllable–delay test. Of course, in that immediate test, they would still have a more or less exact acoustic representation of the sentence they had just heard. However, when tested at the 80- and 160-syllable delay, when they did not have benefit of immediate memory, subjects were only 60% accurate (chance is 50%) in detecting the voice change and hardly above chance at detecting other minor syntactic changes from the original sentence. In contrast, the subject maintained almost 80% accuracy in detecting semantic changes in the original sentence. This result suggests that active and passive sentences are identically represented in long-term memory; and as a consequence, voice information is lost but gist retained.

Although Sachs found relatively poor memory for voice, it was nonetheless above chance level. This small residual memory for voice has been confirmed in other experiments (e.g., Bregman & Strasberg, 1968; Anderson, 1972b). Wanner (1968) proposed that subjects in an *intentional* learning situation such as these might deliberately encode information about the form of the surface sentence. For instance, the subject might form to himself and remember a proposition like "The sentence about *Galileo* was in the active voice." Certainly, the introspections of subjects in such experiments do suggest this possibility. Wanner performed an experiment in which he showed that whether a subject would have long-term memory for a sentence's form depended on whether he had been warned that there would be a subsequent memory test. Recent experiments of ours suggest that the degree to which surface features of sentences are encoded depends also on whether the sentences are treated as part of a smoothly unfolding story ("natural discourse") or treated as independent, unrelated sentences presented without thematic context. These experiments used a measurement technique (verification latency) which appears extraordinarily sensitive to the form of internal representation of information.

Verification Latency Experiments

The subjects studied a series of active and passive sentences; in the first experiment, these sentences comprised a semi-interesting thematic story; in the second experiment, the same sentences were scrambled together to appear unrelated and were presented simply as isolated materials to be remembered. Except for this variation in materials, the two experiments were otherwise identical. The subject's memory for each of the critical sentences was tested either immediately after its presentation, or after a delay (averaging over 2 minutes) following presentation of the full set of sentences.

The memory test involved a "truth verification" task for which reaction times were measured. A probe or test sentence would be flashed on the screen before the subject, and his task was to decide whether that statement was true or false according to the set of sentences he had just read. Each "true" probe sentence was either a critical sentence of the study set or a voice transformation of the original sentence (i.e., active-to-passive voice, or vice versa). Each "false" probe sentence was constructed by reversing the logical subject and object of its corresponding original sentence. The voice and truth-falsity of the probe sentence were thus manipulated orthogonally to the voice of the input sentence.

We shall present first the data from the "story" experiment. These reaction-time results are shown in Figure 8.11, for the immediate probe tests at the top and for the delayed tests at the bottom of the figure. A first fact to note about the upper

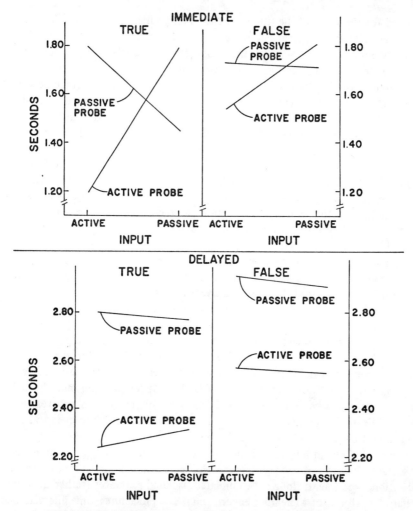

FIG. 8.11. Verification times from the "story" active-passive experiment.

data in the immediate condition is that there was a strong effect of *voice matching.* That is, active probes were more rapidly verified when the original sentence was active, whereas passive probes were more rapidly verified when the original was passive. This voice-matching effect was stronger for true sentences than for false sentences. Of course, when the voice matched for trues, there was physical identity between the immediately preceding study sentence and probe, whereas the subject and object were reversed for the false probes. Such a voice effect is to be expected for trues if the immediate representation of the sentence includes some more or less veridical representation of it, say in the acoustic buffer. Similar results as in this immediate condition have been reported by Olson and Filby (1972) and by Garrod and Trabasso (1972).

The data in the delayed condition (bottom of Figure 8.11) contrast sharply to those found in the immediate condition. In the delayed test, no significant effect remained for the voice of the study sentence, neither main effect nor in interaction with other effects. In particular, there was no interaction between the voice of the study sentence and voice of the probe sentence at the delayed test. Thus, according to this verification task, these materials produced no long-term representation of the voice of the original sentence studied. This outcome would occur if HAM encoded a sentence into a logical deep-structure independent of the voice of the surface sentence. A further interesting statistic is that in the delayed condition, subjects could still remember the voice of the original sentence with greater than chance accuracy (56%) when asked to remember the voice of the probe in contrast to its truth value. (Their truth judgments were 95% accurate.) Thus, it would seem that subjects *can* store auxiliary observations about the syntactic form of a sentence. However, when asked to make truth judgments, subjects access the representation of the sentence in memory and not the auxiliary information. Hence, the auxiliary information does not manifest itself in the reaction-time data obtained in the delayed tests.

It is also interesting to note that passive probes took 440 msec. longer in the delayed condition than did active probes. This can not simply be due to the fact that it takes longer to read the longer passive, since the active-passive difference was only 100 msec. in the immediate condition. The added time for the passive may represent the additional computation time required to transform a passive into a probe tree for input to memory. Because the surface structure of the passive is very different from the structure of the tree, it is not as simple for the parser to transform from the passive sentence to the probe tree as from the active sentence. In our parser, an additional program, the COMPLEMENT program, must be called in to analyze a passive sentence. So this evidence with actives and passives would seem to indicate that both are represented in an active-like format in memory.

But alas, things are not so simple. It appears that subjects can represent passive (or active) relations in long-term memory if the task emphasizes verbatim memory for surface features of the sentences. This conclusion arises from the second verification experiment, done with unrelated, isolated sentences (rather than with the narrative stories of the earlier experiment). The procedures, time intervals, and testing methods were identical to those of the earlier experiment. The results in this case are shown in Figure 8.12. It is informative to compare these data to those in Figure 8.11 from the story experiment. In the immediate testing conditions (top panel of Figure 8.12), the results are as before: A "voice matching" effect, with reaction times rather close to those observed earlier. The different result occurs at the delayed test, shown in the bottom panel of Figure 8.12. For the true data, an interaction now appears in the direction of a "voice matching" effect; in particular, active probes are answered quicker if they refer to an original active sentence than to an original passive sentence. There is also a slight suggestion that passive probes are responded to quicker for passive inputs than for active inputs. These two sloping lines (left bottom panel of Figure 8.12) suffice to produce a statistically significant interaction. This appears to mean that the information acquired from the input sentence is still represented in a voice-specific form for as much as 2 minutes after input of the sentences. In accord with this fact, subjects in this second experiment were correct 74% of the time when asked at the delay test to

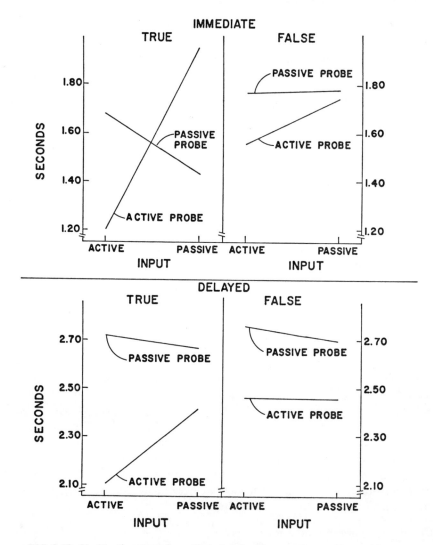

FIG. 8.12. Verification times from the isolated-sentence active-passive experiment.

remember the voice of the input sentence (compared to 56% in the "story" experiment and a 50% chance baseline).

This second set of results may be viewed in several ways. One way is to suppose that subjects give special treatment to surface features of the isolated sentences, and that this causes the voice features to be maintained in their working memory for a longer time than before. On this view, the "voice matching" effect found at the delayed test would eventually disappear, and the results would then look just like those in Figure 8.11 for the narrative material. This is perhaps the correct view, but we find it somewhat implausible because it assumes voice information can survive in working memory through a large number of intervening sentences all of which also must occupy working memory. An alternative and more intriguing view is to (*a*) represent and encode all inputs as "active" sentences in the logical deep-structure, thus converting passives to actives, or (*b*) represent and encode the input in accordance with the active or passive relation asserted in the sentence. The "natural" processing of sentences in the meaningful context of discourse, dialogue, and text is to adopt option (*a*) and convert sentences to the active deep-structures. However, when necessary or advantageous, the subject will adopt encoding strategy (*b*), which supposes that the parser takes a passive-complement construction directly into a passive-relation memory node rather than converting it into the active. For instance, this would suppose that just as we have conceptual nodes corresponding to the verbs "hit," "touch," and "drink," so would we also have unitary nodes corresponding to the relations "was-hit-by," "was-touched-by," and "was-drunk-by." This would permit us to predicate, say, of a "ball" that it "was-hit-by" John, and to write this in the deep-structure as an *S-R-O* proposition (with S = ball, R = was-hit-by, O = John). An auxiliary rule would then be needed to relate the active to the passive relation and to exhibit their inference potential, that is, $x \, R \, y$ iff $y \, R^1 \, x$, where R and R^1 denote "active" and "passive" relations, respectively. In this representation, then, the truth of a passive statement would be "derived" from a stored active relation or vice versa. This contrasts with our earlier view that all inputs are automatically converted to the "active" voice by the parser.

The overview we would urge is that it is not possible to say how the parser should treat active and passive sentences (i.e., how it will represent and encode them into long-term memory) without knowing the encoding strategies adopted under the influence of the input and/or expected testing conditions. We see no reason to decide by fiat or intuition that, in theory, our parser should always give identical representations for sentences differing in voice or some similar syntactic transformation; the better way is the cautious one of supposing that subjects have alternate parsing strategies, so that they can, when required, encode surface features of the input. This "weakens" the rules incorporated in the linguistic parser—now an extra parameter needs to be specified to indicate whether to convert or record passive relations directly—but yet the extra degree of freedom is clearly needed to capture the variability of the actual results.

Recognition Confusions in Sentence Memory

Despite these problems of interpreting slight differences in verification latencies, we may still search (as did Sachs, 1967) for indications of identical memory representations by use of a memory-confusions method. Most of the research using this methodology has employed presentation of lists of unrelated sentences. An early experiment using this procedure was one by Fillenbaum (1966), who found confusions in memory between an adjective (e.g., "open," "dead") and its negated opposite (e.g., "not closed," "not alive"). In the following, we will review research by Anderson (1972b) and Tieman (1971) that makes use of the technique. Sentences (31) to (34) from Anderson serve to illustrate the logic used in these experiments.

The boy was hit by the girl.   (31)

The girl hit the boy.   (32)

| The boy hit the girl. | (33) |
| The girl was hit by the boy. | (34) |

The subject was presented with Sentence (31) along with 59 other unrelated sentences to study, and then 10 minutes later was asked to choose the original sentence from among the four alternatives (31) to (34). The question of interest is not so much confusion between the synonymous pair (31) and (32) as it is the relative rates of false alarms to the synonymous alternative (32) as contrasted to the nonsynonymous alternatives (33) and (34). Both Sentences (33) and (34) are closer in surface structure to the original sentence than (32). Therefore, if the subject can remember the auxiliary encodings of the surface form, but cannot remember the actual sentence, he should false alarm to Sentences (33) and (34) in preference to Sentence (32). On the other hand, if Sentences (31) and (32) have a similar representation in memory because of their synonymy, the subject should false alarm to Sentence (32). A preponderance of false alarms to Sentence (32) would indicate that the subject has encoded the meaning of the sentence but often not enough information about surface form to discriminate between Sentences (31) and (32). So, this is a test of whether Sentences (31) and (32) are given similar representations in long-term memory. With respect to actives and passives, the outcome of this test was positive. In four alternative forced choice, such as a selection from Sentences (31) through (34), 50.7% of the choices were to the correct alternative, 25% to the synonymous alternative, 12.5% to one of the nonsynonymous alternatives, and 11.8% to the other. Thus, the synonymous alternative receives twice as many false alarms as either of the nonsynonymous alternatives.

Recognition Confusions with Other Types of Sentences

Anderson (1972b) employed a much wider variety of sentence pairs than just actives or passives. He attempted to delimit just what pairs of sentences would be confused. His conclusion was that any pair of sentences that were conceptually synonymous (i.e., synonymous because of the meaning of the words) was likely to be confused. As a sample of the types of confusions found, consider the four pairs (35) to (42), where sentences (35) to (36) express agent and instrument of action by different syntactic means; (37) to (38) and (41) to (42) involve an inference regarding the symmetry of "give-receive" and "newer-older", and the pair (39) to (40) and many others like it involve synonymity of lexical items.

| The car's exhaust will pollute the air. | (35) |
| The car will pollute the air with its exhaust. | (36) |

| The boy gave money to the girl. | (37) |
| The girl received money from the boy. | (38) |

| The blonde is the mother of that baby boy. | (39) |
| The blonde gave birth to that baby boy. | (40) |

| The garage is newer than the theatre. | (41) |
| The theatre is older than the garage. | (42) |

In each of these cases, the recognition-memory confusions within the pair far exceeded that of control sentences that were similar in only surface features. The fact that all such pairs are confused at levels far exceeding control baselines suggests that in many cases the linguistic parser is mapping such sentences into identical memory structures in response to their similar meanings. Needless to say, a sophisticated parser would be required to produce identical representations for such differing sentences.

The Imagery Hypothesis

However, there are other conceivable representations for such sentences besides our propositional system which would yield such confusions in memory. A currently popular suggestion (e.g., Paivio, 1971) assumes that subjects transform such sentences into visual images (whatever those are) and store the composite image in memory. Intuitively, the visual images for the pairs (35) through (42) would seem to be quite similar. So, from this viewpoint, it is not surprising that they are confused in recognition memory. One problem with this imagery explanation is that it is unclear exactly what is meant by an image. If we conceive of an image as a *perceptual description* of a scene and permit arbitrarily abstract concepts in the description (e.g., "It's a picture of a kind man helping a frightened dog"), then there is little or no difference between our representation and that of an image. We have already indicated how our formalism could describe visual scenes. If this is what is meant by an "image," then the imagery hypothesis does not really differ from our own.

However, Anderson (1972b) decided to test a version of the imagery hypothesis that is clearly an alternative to our own. As he described it:

> The remaining hypothesis about the memory structure, the naive imagery hypothesis, assumes that the subject stores a "picture" depicting the situation described by the sentence. . . . The reader should take care in how he parses the phrase "naive imagery hypothesis." I am not claiming all imagery theories of memory are naive. Rather, I am attempting to identify a particular subclass of the imagery theories which are distinguished by the fact that they conceive of images in *naive realist* terms. Therefore, if we reject this hypothesis because of a failure to find the predicted confusions, it does not mean that the memory structure underlying the sentence is not an image. All such a result would show is that, if it is an image, the image is sufficiently abstract in character that it can contain information that is not directly translatable into visual correlates. This type of "sophisticated image" is not the point-to-point representation of a visual scene which the naive imagery hypothesis proposes. It is difficult to conceive how such a "sophisticated imagery hypothesis" would differ from the conceptual structure hypothesis in its predictions about recognition confusions [pp. 11–12].

He went on to reason that such a hypothesis would predict confusion between certain pairs of sentences for which hypotheses such as our conceptual structure would not:

If we interpret a "picture" in naive realist terms, we find that some information retained in a conceptual representation is lost in the pictorial representation as is illustrated by sentences (43) through (46). Sentences (43) and (44) are conceptually distinct but would be represented by the identical picture of a lieutenant writing a name on a check. Sentences (45) and (46) are also conceptually distinct owing to different judgments about the agent responsible for the transaction of the money.

The lieutenant signed his signature on the check.	(43)
The lieutenant forged a signature on the check.	(44)
The baker gave the money to the barber.	(45)
The barber took the money from the baker.	(46)

However, the physical action depicted in a picture would be identical in both cases. Therefore, the naive imagery hypothesis would predict confusions between such pairs of sentences, while the other hypotheses would not. [pp. 11-12].

It is easy to generate several dimensions along which two propositions may differ *conceptually* but not in terms translatable naively into a pictorial difference. Example distinctions that seem conceptually but not pictorially distinct are things like *time* (tomorrow, yesterday), intention or emotion (dishonest, frightening), *causality* (because, due to), anchor point (a glass that is half empty versus half full), and so forth. In each case, the distinction is more or less clear conceptually, but yet a naive image is the same for the two sentences—hence, one would expect total confusions to such imaginally similar alternatives. However, in opposition to this prediction, Anderson (1972b) found that confusion to such imaginally similar (but conceptually different) distractors was hardly any greater than to imaginally different (by syntactically similar) alternatives. From such results, it was concluded that the naive imagery hypothesis was untenable.

However, a respected colleague, Stephen Kosslyn was uncertain about Anderson's conclusion. Rather, he argued that the image a subject would spontaneously generate for Sentence (43) would probably be quite different from the image generated for Sentence (44), and similarly for the others. For instance, in the image for Sentence (44), the lieutenant, a forger, is much more likely to be sporting a devilish moustache. Professional actors are trained to reveal their motives and intentions in overt cues; similarly, in imaging intentions or motives, we might make them manifest in overt signs. It was on the basis of cues like these, Kosslyn argues, that subjects might discriminate such pairs of "conceptually different" sentences. Therefore, he had his adult subjects prerate pairs of sentences according to how similar were the images they evoked; he then used for his memory experiment only those pairs of sentences that were rated as having very similar images. Conceptually distinct sentences that evoked similar images (according to the ratings) would be pairs such as Sentence (47) through (50).

George picked up the pen to write on the paper.	(47)
George picked up the pen to doodle on the paper.	(48)

> The lion killed the buffalo because he was hungry. (49)
> The lion killed the buffalo so he must have been hungry. (50)

However, with sentences like these rated to be nearly identical in images, Kosslyn still failed to find confusions between conceptually distinct sentences with similar images. It was as if adults could still preserve in memory a conceptual distinction which others had rated as being imaginally indistinguishable from a control sentence. A recent finding of Kosslyn's is that kindergarten children do *not* distinguish conceptually different sentences; sentences which are rated to be imaginally the same are totally confused by kindergarteners whether or not they are distinguished along some conceptual dimension. Although suggesting that young children rely more on perceptual reference than abstract concepts in interpreting propositions, this final result must await replication and elaboration before its significance is to be interpreted.

Tieman's Results

There is clear evidence from other sources that imagery is an important factor in determining recognition confusion in sentence memory for adults. David Tieman (1971) has examined the effect of learning instructions on later recognition confusions for pairs of comparative sentences such as (41) and (42). He studied the recognition confusions obtained when subjects were told to try to remember the "exact wording" of the study sentences, when they were told to remember the gist or meaning of the sentences, and when told to form an image of the referent of the sentences and remember that image. A four-alternative forced-choice test procedure was used, similar to Anderson's illustrated above. Tieman found that in the exact-wording condition, subjects made more errors to the syntactically similar distractors than to the semantically similar distractors. This result is not particularly surprising in light of the instructions. In the imagery condition, however, the semantically similar distractor received the most false alarms by far. The gist condition produced intermediate false alarms between these two extremes.

It is tempting to think that what Tieman was manipulating by his instructions was the *S*'s propensity to encode auxiliary information about the form of the sentence in contrast to the meaning of the sentence. However, the fact that there were more semantic errors in the imagery than in the gist condition suggests that whatever recorded the meaning of the sentence, it had imagery-like properties. Tieman also reported evidence to indicate that the image was not a naive realistic one. The amount of semantic confusion was the same for abstract, nonpicturable comparatives (e.g., more necessary, smarter) as it was for concrete, picturable ones (e.g., thicker, taller). The concreteness-abstractness of the adjectives also did not interact with the instruction variable in determining the overall level of performance or types of confusion errors.

This last result appears to contradict a result of Begg and Paivio (1969). They contrasted recognition memory for abstract sentences like (51) with concrete sentences like (52), using "Yes-No" tests rather than multiple-choice tests.

> The arbitrary regulation provoked a civil complaint. (51)

The spirited leader slapped a mournful hostage.   (52)

For concrete sentences, Begg and Paivio found the typical result: Subjects were very good at detecting semantic changes but relatively poor at detecting syntactic changes from the original sentence they had studied. However, with abstract sentences, they found just the reverse result: Semantic changes were more poorly detected than syntactic changes. Begg and Paivio argued that concrete sentences are represented in memory in terms of the imagery they evoke. Hence, with sentences like (52) there was considerable sensitivity to semantic changes (e.g., interchanging agent and recipient of the action) since semantic changes imply quite different images. In contrast, they argued that abstract sentences cannot easily evoke imagery and hence should be represented primarily in terms of surface, word-to-word associations. On this account, one would expect greater sensitivity to syntactic changes for abstract sentences, which is what they found.

It is not yet clear how to reconcile the Begg and Paivio data with Tieman's. One difference is the method of testing: Begg and Paivio used single-stimulus tests with the subject judging "old" or "new" to each test sentence singly; Tieman used multiple-choice tests with the four alternatives consisting of the original sentence plus the three distractors generated by interchanging the subject and object nouns and replacing the comparative adjective by its opposite (e.g., "shorter" for "taller"). Tieman's testing method would seem much the more sensitive insofar as the subject experiences a direct comparison between the original sentence and its several variants. It also minimizes differential response biases (to say "yes") to abstract versus concrete materials. A second difference was in the materials in the two experiments; Tieman used all comparative constructions which seemed quite comprehensible, whereas Begg and Paivio used subject-verb-object constructions some of which appear upon close examination to be ambiguous and somewhat difficult to understand. Recent work by Johnson, Bransford, Nyberg, and Cleary (1972) has confirmed that there was a marked difference in the comprehensibility of the abstract versus concrete sentences used by Begg and Paivio. It is not clear which of these several differences are responsible for the differing conclusions of the two studies, and systematic replications are clearly needed to resolve the differences.

Conclusions

The conclusions we can make after this review of recognition confusions are not particularly definitive. It seems clear that the behavior of the human parsing system can be quite variable. The same sentences can be mapped onto quite different representations. Variables that appear to influence the output of the parser include age of the subject, instructions, concreteness of the sentences, and context in which the material is presented. It seems that the attitude with which we originally had approached this research was quite naive. We had thought there was some standard behavior of the parsing system that could be easily uncovered by looking at recognition confusions. Rather, the parser's behavior is quite variable, and it often appears quite adaptive to task demands.

Some colleagues have urged on us that we should attempt to discover how the parsing system "normally" works by examining sentence memory in situations that are as naturalistic as possible. We think such advice is misconceived for two reasons. First, our purpose is not descriptive; our goal is not to uncover what the parser normally does. We rather want to uncover the basic mechanisms that underlie its behavior, the formal properties of the representations that it generates, and how various factors such as context and instructions control its behavior. Second, such advice is mistaken because it holds to the untenable position that there is some standard operation of the parser that may be characterized as "normal." Undoubtedly, in the "real world" the behavior of the parser is every bit as variable and subject to task demands as it is in the laboratory. To designate one mode of operation as normal would be to engage in an arbitrary legislation, lacking any psychological motivation.

So this existing research has done little more than map out the complexity of the parser's behavior. It should be clear that the parser which will generate the range of results we found in this section has a major computational task on its hands. In a way, these results further demean our own inadequate efforts at programming a parser. However, we hasten to add that there are no other simulation programs for parsing that are up to the task of adequately fitting all the data. Moreover, to keep an accurate perspective on the true dimensions of the interface problem, the reader is reminded of how advanced linguistic parsing is relative to perceptual parsing. We see these intellectual problems as being generations away from solution. We make no pretense that we have handled them in a very satisfactory manner.

REFERENCES

Anderson, J. R. FRAN: A simulation model of free recall. In G. H. Bower (Ed.), *The psychology of learning and motivation.* Vol. 5. New York: Academic Press, 1972. (a)

Anderson, J. R. Recognition confusions in sentence memory. Unpublished manuscript, 1972. (b)

Atkinson, R. C., & Shiffrin, R. Human memory: A proposed system and its control processes. In Spence, K., & Spence, J. (Eds.), *The psychology of learning and motivation.* Vol. 2. New York: Academic Press, 1968.

Begg, J., & Paivio, A. Concreteness and imagery in sentence memory. *Journal of Verbal Learning and Verbal Behavior,* 1969, 8, 821-827.

Bregman, A. S., & Strasberg, R. Memory for the syntactic form of sentences. *Journal of Verbal Learning and Verbal Behavior,* 1968, 7, 396-403.

Chomsky, N. *Aspects of the theory of syntax.* Cambridge, Mass.: M.I.T. Press, 1965.

Duda, R. O., & Hart, P. E. Pattern classification and scene analysis. Unpublished manuscript, 1972.

Fillenbaum, S. Memory for gist: Some relevant variables. *Language and Speech,* 1966, 9, 217-227.

Fodor, J. A., & Garrett, M. Some syntactic determinants of sentential complexity. *Perception and Psychophysics,* 1967, 2, 289-296.

Fodor, J. A., Garrett, M., & Bever, T. G. Some syntactic determinants of sentential complexity. II: Verb structure. *Perception and Psychophysics,* 1968, 3, 453-461.

Foss, D. J. Some effects of ambiguity upon sentence comprehension. *Journal of Verbal Learning and Verbal Behavior,* 1970, 9, 699-706.

Garrod, S., & Trabasso, T. A dual-memory information processing interpretation of sentence comprehension. Unpublished manuscript, 1972.

Gibson, J. J. *The perception of the visual world.* Boston: Houghton, 1950.

Guzman, A. Computer recognition of three-dimensional objects in a visual scene. M.I.T. Artificial Intelligence Laboratory Project MAC-TR-59, 1968.

Hakes, D. T., & Foss, D. J. Decision processes during sentence comprehension: Effects of surface structure reconsidered. *Perception and Psychophysics,* 1970, 8, 413–416.

Hunt, E. The memory we must have. Paper prepared for the C.O.B.R.E. Research Workshop on Coding Theory in Learning and Memory, August 2–5, 1971, Woods Hole, Mass.

Jarvella, R. J. Syntactic processing of connected speech. *Journal of Verbal Learning and Verbal Behavior,* 1971, 10, 409–416.

Johnson, M. K., Bransford, J. D., Nyberg, S. E., & Cleary, J. J. Comprehension factors in interpreting memory for abstract and concrete sentences. *Journal of Verbal Learning and Verbal Behavior,* 1972, 11, 451–454.

MacKay, D. G. To end ambiguous sentences. *Perception and Psychophysics,* 1966, 1, 426–436.

Olson, D. R., & Filby, N. On the comprehension of active and passive sentences. *Cognitive Psychology,* 1972, 3, 361–381.

Paivio, A. *Imagery and verbal processes.* New York: Holt, Rinehart & Winston, 1971.

Reitman, J. Mechanisms of forgetting in short-term memory. *Cognitive Psychology,* 1971, 2, 185–195.

Sachs, J. Recognition memory for syntactic and semantic aspects of connected discourse. *Perception and Psychophysics,* 1967, 2, 437–442.

Schank, R. C., Tesler, L., & Weber, S. Spinoza II: Conceptual case-based natural language analysis. Stanford Artificial Intelligence Project Memo AIM-109, Stanford University, 1970.

Schlesinger, L. The influence of sentence structure on the reading process. U.S. Office of Naval Research Technical Report, 24, 1966.

Tieman, D. G. Recognition memory for comparative sentences. Unpublished doctoral dissertation, Stanford University, 1971.

Wanner, H. E. On remembering, forgetting, and understanding sentences: A study of the deep-structure hypothesis. Unpublished doctoral dissertation, Harvard University, 1968.

Winograd, T. Procedures as a representation for data in a computer program for understanding natural language. M.I.T. Artificial Intelligence Laboratory Project MAC-TR-84, 1971.

Winston, P. H. Learning structural discriptions from examples. M.I.T. Artificial Intelligence Laboratory Project AI-TR-231, 1970.

Woods, W. A. Transition network grammars for natural language analysis. *Communications of the ACM,* 1970, 13, 591–606.

9
THE RECOGNITION PROCESS

Memory is the possession of an experience potentially revivable.
—Aristotle

9.1. THE MATCH AND IDENTIFY PROCESSES

The two preceding chapters were concerned with the processing and structuring of individual pieces of information as they are input into long-term memory. Chapter 7 displayed the structure of propositional trees acceptable to and recorded in HAM's memory, while Chapter 8 described the parsing system by which inputs are translated into our internal representations. In the present chapter we begin to examine the matter of accessing the information stored in memory. Here the concern is with how incoming information accesses and makes contact with those portions of long-term memory which are relevant to it. This is the central problem of "recognition." It is carried out in HAM by a process called MATCH which tries to find the best matching tree in memory corresponding to an input tree. The MATCH process is used not only during decoding (i.e., in answering questions), but also in encoding (i.e., comprehending and learning new statements). In particular, the MATCH process enables HAM to distinguish already known information in an input from novel information, and so enables HAM to restrict its efforts at encoding to the new information. In this way, HAM can make use of known information to reduce the task of encoding new information.

In reusing old information (subtrees of current predications), certain difficulties arise whereby the memory system could store unintended propositions (these will be illustrated later); consequently, following the MATCH process, a further process called IDENTIFY is evoked to check on how much of the matched information is in fact useable for encoding the current input. The purpose of this first section is to describe the operation of the MATCH and IDENTIFY processes. The subsequent Section 9.2 will report some experimental tests of these processes during encoding. Chapter 12 is devoted to an experimental examination of the MATCH processes during decoding. The final part of this chapter, Section 9.3, will illustrate how the MATCH process can be used to explain the many types of recognition that occur in the laboratory and in everyday life.

The MATCH Process

The function of the MATCH process is to make a correspondence between the current input or probe and some piece of the associative structure in memory. The exact details of the MATCH process are well defined and consistent. That is, there is a LISP function defined in our computer program which simulates how the MATCH process searches memory trying to bring the input or probe into contact with the appropriate memory structure. The exact details of the MATCH process will not be discussed here; a copy of the simulation program is available upon request. Here, we will emphasize those aspects of the MATCH process that are relevant to the experimental predictions to be examined.

As noted in Chapter 8, after a sentence has been parsed, a binary-branching input structure is held in working memory on which the MATCH process operates. The MATCH process always works on only one proposition in the input at a time. If there are multiple propositions in the current input (each proposition represented by a subtree of the input network), it will attempt to match *propositional subtrees* of the total input to trees in memory. The MATCH process always begins at those terminal nodes of the tree which are also memory nodes. In an input tree all terminal nodes are memory nodes, whereas in a probe tree only a subset of the nodes are (see our discussion in Section 7.2 on this point). MATCH tries to find paths in memory that (*a*) connect the terminal memory nodes, and (*b*) correspond to paths in the input tree it is trying to match. A memory path and an input path are judged equivalent if they possess the same number of links and the same sequence of relations labeling the links. The MATCH process attempts to find the graph pattern of paths through memory that gives the maximal match (measured in terms of the number of matched links) to the input.

The MATCH process is efficient in that it only examines those paths in memory between terminal nodes that could possibly match paths in the trees. It does so by use of labels on links. For instance, if a terminal node in the input tree is "dog" and it is linked in the input tree to a dominating node by a *member* relation ϵ, the MATCH process will not consider any links with $\subseteq^{-1}$ or $\forall^{-1}$ leading out of the "dog" node in memory; only ϵ^{-1} links giving "dog-instances" will be considered. This is one way that HAM uses the relational information on links to guide its search of memory. Of course, there could be a great many ϵ^{-1} associations to "dog." That is, the list returned by the function GET(dog, ϵ^{-1}) could be very long. (Recall from Chapter 7 that the function GET(dog, ϵ^{-1}) is a primitive that will retrieve a list of all elements b such that $<$dog ϵ^{-1} $b>$ is a long-term memory association.) This ordered list of nodes is referred to as the *GET-list*. The associates on this list are constantly updated according to their recency of mention. Since a recently mentioned instance of a dog is likely to be the instance HAM is searching for, HAM is likely to find the appropriate associate early in its search of the GET-list. Of course, none of the ϵ^{-1} associations on the GET-list may match the input. To prevent many long and fruitless searches of GET-lists, it is assumed that HAM will only search a GET-list to a probabilistically determined depth.

The fact that only a probabilistically determined portion is examined turns out to be very significant. This is the sole mechanism in HAM that produces forgetting. That is, old unused associations will tend to descend relatively far down in the GET-list and will hence become effectively inaccessible. We will expand upon this mechanism in Chapter 15, where we will discuss how the literature on interference and forgetting can be accommodated by this mechanism. It is important to realize that its motivation is not to produce forgetting but to make the MATCH function more efficient by preventing protracted but fruitless searches.

To explore the mechanics of how the MATCH process operates, it will be useful to trace through an example of how an input is matched to memory. A plausible search theory, we believe, involves a quasi-parallel simultaneous search from all terminal nodes of the input tree, possibly with the earlier elements in the left-to-right processing of the input getting started ahead of the later elements. From each node a search proceeds forth trying to find a match in memory to the input tree. This simultaneous search process is similar to one proposed earlier by Quillian (1968), but there are some notable differences. First, the searchers from different terminal nodes are independent of one another. Thus, an input proposition is not considered matched to memory until one of the MATCH processes, searching from a terminal node, achieves a complete match by itself. There can be no intersection or "meeting in the middle" of a number of search processes as there is in Quillian's model. Quillian seems to have only concerned himself with intersections of two searches in conceptual hierarchies (see Section 4.3 for a review of Quillian's model). Here it is relatively easy to define how an executive routine should respond to an intersection. However, when one has more than two MATCH processes searching propositional tree structures, as is the case with HAM, it is very complicated to define an executive routine that will appropriately respond to all possible patterns of intersection. It was so complicated that we decided it was implausible psychologically to have HAM attempt to use these intersections.

A second difference between HAM and Quillian's model is that in HAM each MATCH process searches memory in a serial fashion rather than parallel. In fact, MATCH time is linearly related (the precise model is developed in Chapter 12) to the number of associations searched during the attempted match. As a consequence, any associative fanning encountered at a particular node during the search (e.g., multiple ϵ^{-1} associations leading from a terminal node) will increase the mean MATCH time. This is because each of the fanning associative links will have to be considered sequentially to see if it leads to the best matching proposition. Thus, each fanning association can result in further associations to search and an increase in search time.

An Example

Despite our commitment in theory to this simultaneous search from all nodes, we will present an example where the MATCH process is only proceeding from one terminal node at a time. This is the actual routine programmed in the MATCH function. We will consider how the input tree in Figure 9.1a would be matched to the memory structure in Figure 9.1b. The input is an encoding of the sentence "In the park a hippie sang." The current MATCH program will select the leftmost terminal, *park*, at which to begin its search process. Since *park* is linked into the input tree by an ε relation, MATCH evokes the process GET(park, ϵ^{-1}) to obtain the list of all park instances that it knows. This list is ordered with instances to be called *a, b, c, ...* Suppose that instances *a* and *b* will not lead to substantial matches with the memory structure. Consequently, the MATCH process will search the memory structures accessible from these two nodes, and it will not recover any substantial matches. After attempting these two nodes, it then attempts the node *c*—provided three nodes does not exceed the probabilistically determined depth for searching the GET(park, ϵ^{-1})-list.

The MATCH process is a *recursive mental operation* in that, having matched the input node 1 to memory node *c*, linkages emanating from node *c* are similarly matched to the linkages in the input emanating from node 1. Node 1 in the input is connected by an L-link to node 2. Therefore, the MATCH routine evokes GET(*c*, L^{-1}) from node *c* in the memory tree, and returns to node *e*. Now the MATCH function attempts to match the associative structures from nodes 2 and *e*. There are two differently labeled links in the input tree leading from node 2. Suppose MATCH searches the *time* construction first. It will match the input link <2 T 3> to the memory association <*e* T *d*> and <3 ε past> to <*d* ε past>.

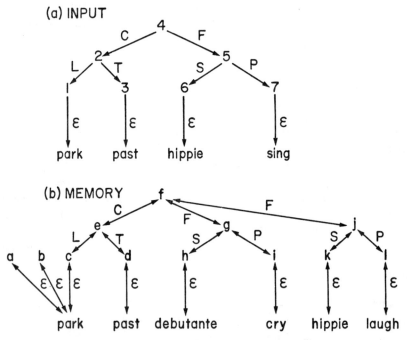

(a) INPUT

(b) MEMORY

FIG. 9.1. An input (*a*) is matched to a portion of memory (*b*).

At this point it has arrived at a terminal node in the input tree, *past*, and that terminal node matches the memory node. Therefore, it has found a tentative path through memory that matches a path between two of the elements in the input tree. MATCH files away on a temporary "matching candidates" list this particular match, between the memory structure $[<e \, L \, c>$, $<c \, \epsilon \, \text{park}>$, $<e \, T \, d>$, $<d \, \epsilon \, \text{past}>]$ and the input structure $[<2 \, L \, 1>, <1 \, \epsilon \, \text{park}>, <2 \, T \, 3>, <3 \, \epsilon \, \text{past}>]$.

There may be a great many ϵ^{-1} associations leading from *past*, but they do not affect search time in this example. On the other hand, search time was affected by the number of ϵ^{-1} associations leading from *park*, since HAM had to consider each one separately. With respect to *past*, however, the MATCH process had only to consider the possible ϵ associations leading from node d, and there was only one. If the MATCH process works as currently programmed, that is, selecting one terminal node of the input tree at a time and searching memory from it, then it becomes crucial which memory node is selected first. For instance, if there is little ϵ^{-1} fanning from *park* but much from *past*, it is clearly advantageous to begin at *park*. In contrast, if, as we really believe, search begins simultaneously from all terminal nodes, search time would be largely determined by the terminal node from which there was least fanning. There would be no need for HAM to concern itself with problems of selecting the best starter node.

The reader will note in this example that initially HAM wasted a lot of time searching for the appropriate ϵ^{-1} association, but now the search is proceeding much more expeditiously. In general, most of the wasted search time is due to fanning of associations at the bottom nodes in the input tree where many associations like ϵ are likely to be found. Once MATCH gets up into the duplex nodes, it is less likely to encounter many identically labeled associations, and hence the overall search will proceed faster through these higher portions of the tree.

To return to our example, we have matched the context subtree in the input to a corresponding piece of memory. The match process will now attempt to match the $<4 \, C \, 2>$ link of the input with a link from memory connected to node e. It will evoke GET(e, C), obtain the node f, and recursively apply the MATCH process to the memory node f and input node 4. In attempting to match the fact subtree from 4, it will first consider the *fact* subtree in memory, encoding "A debutante cried," which gives a complete mismatch to the input. It is informative to see how MATCH rejects this subtree of memory. It makes a tentative match between the input link $<4 \, F \, 5>$ and the memory link $<f \, F \, g>$. Subsequently, MATCH assigns $<5 \, S \, 6>$ to match the link $<g \, S \, h>$. Then it will attempt to match $<6 \, \epsilon \, \text{hippie}>$ to $<h \, \epsilon \, \text{debutante}>$. But it now has arrived at two terminal memory nodes, *hippie* and *debutante*, that fail to match. Therefore, it concludes that the *subject* branch it is currently examining is not an appropriate match, and it withdraws the tentative assignment of $<5 \, S \, 6>$ in the input to $<g \, S \, h>$ in memory. It then attempts to match the *predicate* branches from nodes 5 and g, but is similarly frustrated. Since the MATCH process can assign none of the memory structure from node g to the input tree from node 5, it also withdraws the tentative correspondence made earlier between $<4 \, F \, 5>$ and $<f \, F \, g>$. The MATCH process thus retreats back to the nodes 4 and f, which are its last still-matching nodes, and tries to find another fact subtree in memory.

The second node on the list returned when GET(f, F) was evoked is node j. MATCH tries to match j to node 5 in the input. It will succeed in matching the subject branch from node j to the corresponding input branch, since both branches terminate in the *hippie* memory node. MATCH has now found a second path in memory that corresponds to an input path and therefore adds to its stored match the correspondence between the input path [<4 C 2>, <4 F 5>, <5 S 6>, <6 ϵ hippie>] and the memory path [<f C e>, <f F j>, <j S k>, <k ϵ hippie>]. The MATCH process will then fail to find a match between the predicate branch from node 5 in the input and the predicate branch from node j in memory, because the first terminates in *sing* and the second in *laugh*. Since the match is not perfect, the MATCH process may continue to search to see if it can find a better match. The search will eventually be terminated by a "cutoff" time (see our discussion in Chapter 15). If MATCH cannot find a better match, it will accept this partial one. Remember that MATCH processes are also proceeding from the other terminal nodes in the tree. One of these other MATCH processes may have found a better partial match or a perfect match. HAM accepts the most complete match returned by any MATCH process.

Encoding upon Partial Matches

It should be noted that the MATCH process has made a strong and possibly incorrect claim in this illustration. It is claiming that the hippie who sang in the park is the same hippie recorded earlier in memory as laughing. Moreover, it is making this claim solely on the basis that they both were in a park at some time in the past. Given that hippies frequent parks, we should realize that the MATCH process is quite possibly wrong in this particular claim. The doubtful veracity of this match makes it problematical whether HAM should use the matched memory structure to reduce its encoding task. That is, HAM could encode the input in Figure 9.1*a* by simply adding another predicate branch to the memory structure in Figure 9.1*b*. This encoding of the input is illustrated by the memory structure in Figure 9.2. It should be noted that in this melding of the input tree of Figure 9.1*a* with the memory tree of Figure 9.1*b*, all the nodes 1 through 6 of the input tree have disappeared, being replaced by memory nodes *c* through *l*, and only node 7 of the input tree was encoded into memory. Thus node 7 is "new information" that has been added onto the preexisting information in memory.

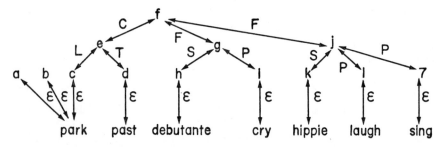

FIG. 9.2. The input in Figure 9.1*a* has been built onto the memory structure of Figure 9.1*b*.

However, it is unclear whether HAM should endorse all the implications of this modified memory structure in Figure 9.2. That is, it may not really be the same hippie, the same time, or the same park for the two acts of laughing and singing. An easy solution to this issue would be never to build an input upon a partially matched memory structure. However, there are good reasons not to go to this extreme either. After all, if it really were the same place, time, and hippie, then we do not want HAM to miss this fact. We do not want to have the same person, place, or time represented by two different instance nodes in memory. Moreover, there are clear advantages to HAM if it takes advantage of the redundancy (correspondences) between input and memory. That is, less time and fewer associations will be required to encode the input. As the information input to the typical human memory is probably highly redundant, it is important that the memory take pains not to reduplicate knowledge. No matter how efficiently HAM's memory is structured, to build up a normal adult memory will require nodes and associations numbering at least in the hundreds of thousands and probably in higher orders of magnitude. If maximum efficiency is not attempted in the representation, HAM will lose credibility simply because of the sheer vastness of the memory structure hypothesized.

So the question is, how is HAM to decide when it can "chance it" and attach partially matched input onto some corresponding memory structure? How would *we* react if someone informed us "A hippie sang in the park," and we remembered "A hippie laughed in the park"? Quite possibly we would set out to determine whether or not this partial correspondence was accidental. Suppose we knew that the hippie of our memory was Jerry Rubin and that the park was New York's Central Park. Then we might ask of our informant, "Was that Jerry Rubin who was in Central Park last Saturday?" If our informant assented, we would be fairly confident that the match obtained was not accidental. This is how we would like HAM to react to a partial match—by asking a question regarding its conjecture. That is, it should intelligently set out to determine whether or not to endorse the proposed identification.

In the simulation of HAM, where its interaction with the world takes the form of a teletype dialogue with its informant, one could have HAM, whenever it encounters a match, to announce that fact and request of the informant whether or not the match is spurious. Of course, this simply transfers the burden of decision from HAM to the informant. Nonetheless, we are seriously contemplating programming such a strategy because we make no pretense of having captured all of human intelligence. Rather, the goal is to simulate certain aspects of human memory. But all this is hypothetical; such informant-program interaction is not yet programmed. As the simulation currently operates, either it will accept any partial match between memory and input, or (if a parameter is changed) it will only accept perfect matches.

The IDENTIFY Process

When HAM does encode input trees using partially matched memory structures, there occur certain logical problems that have forced the postulation of a second mental process, IDENTIFY, which determines whether any unwarranted conceptualizations would occur if HAM built upon the partially matched memory structure. To establish that building on partial matches can have unwarranted and unwanted outcomes, consider the following example: Suppose HAM first hears the proposition "In a park a hippie touched a debutante" and then later hears "In a park a hippie touched a prostitute." In the mode in which partial matches are permitted, HAM would encode these two inputs into the memory structure illustrated in Figure 9.3a. That is, the second input would be encoded by simply

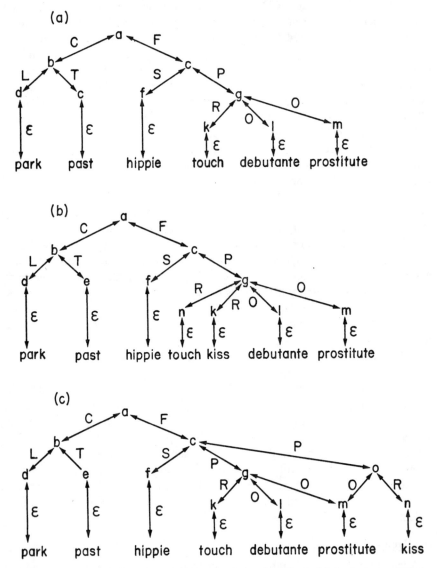

FIG. 9.3. The encoding of an additional relation branch to (a) leads to unwanted multiplication of meanings in (b). The structure in (c) illustrates a satisfactory representation that avoids multiplication of meanings.

adding an object branch to the memory structure that was constructed to encode the first proposition about the *debutante*. Incidentally, the same memory structure would be established if HAM were to encode the single proposition "In a park a hippie touched a debutante and a prostitute." Consequently, in Figure 9.3*a* HAM would be unable to determine later whether it had encoded two separate assertions or a single one. This, of course, suggests an experiment in human memory.

In any case, there is no logical problem with the memory structure set up in Figure 9.3*a*. Difficulties arise when HAM is asked to encode a third related proposition such as "In the park a hippie kissed a prostitute." The input tree for this proposition mismatches the memory structure in Figure 9.3*a* only at the relation (R) association. Therefore, at first thought, it might appear that the memory structure in Figure 9.3*b* would successfully encode the input. It differs from the old memory structure in Figure 9.3*a* only by the addition of a new relation association. But the error in Figure 9.3*b* is that HAM can now infer from it that "In a park a hippie kissed a debutante," which is a proposition it never encoded and which is probably false. The problem basically is that the two *relation* links and the two *object* links have *multiplied* together to yield four possible propositions, whereas only three of these are intended. Thus, HAM has overused the redundancy in the input or overgeneralized. Rather than the erroneous memory structure in Figure 9.3*b*, it should have produced a memory structure more like that in Figure 9.3*c*. Some of the input links and nodes, although assigned by MATCH to memory nodes, were nevertheless encoded in Figure 9.3*c* rather than replaced. The purpose of the IDENTIFY process is to identify which matched input links can be used (replaced by memory associations) and which will have to be encoded as new differentiating information.

The first step to understanding IDENTIFY is to understand the exact class of memory structures which will yield the unwanted multiplication of propositions that was illustrated in Figure 9.3*c*. In characterizing these to-be-avoided memory structures, it will be helpful to introduce the concept of a *conjunction* in a memory structure. A conjunction refers to a group of two or more identically labeled associations leading from a node. For instance, in Figure 9.3*b* there is a *relation* conjunction (node *g* is connected to the two *relation* nodes *n* and *k*) and an *object* conjunction (node *g* is also connected to the two *object* nodes, *l* and *m*). When there are two or more conjunctions in the memory structure, the propositions can "multiply" and yield undesired interpretations, as is the case for Figure 9.3*b*. However, multiple conjunctions in the memory structure do not always result in disaster, as testified by the structure in Figure 9.3*c*. In that figure there is both a *predicate* and an *object* conjunction, yet there is no unwanted multiplication.

Multiple conjunctions in the memory structure imply difficulties if there are two *distinct* sequences, $X_1, X_2, ..., X_n$ and $Y_1, Y_2, ..., Y_N$, that lead from one node in memory through two conjunctions. This condition may be illustrated by Figure 9.3*b*. From node *g*, the relation R leads into one conjunction and the relation O leads into a second conjunction. Two conjunctions need not be at the same memory node in order to have multiplication of meanings, as Figure 9.4 illustrates. Here the sequence C, L leads from the proposition node *a* to two locations, and the

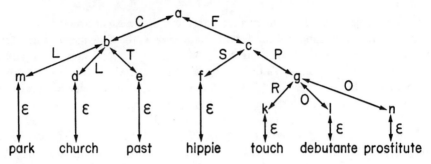

FIG. 9.4. The object and location conjunctions multiply in this memory structure.

sequence F, P, O leads to two objects. In general, according to sequence $X_1, X_2, ...,$ X_n one will have i $(i > 1)$ interpretations, and according to sequence $Y_1, Y_2, ...,$ Y_N, j $(j > 1)$ interpretations. When these two distinct paths are accessible from the root node, there are at least i-times-j possible interpretations of the propositional structure. In the encoding of inputs to partially matched structures, this multiplication of meanings is rarely if ever intended.

But now consider the situation in Figure 9.3c. This has two conjunctions, but they are both on the path P, O; consequently, interpretations do not multiply. It is necessary that the conjunctions be on two distinct paths to have multiplication of meanings.

IDENTIFY uses the list of matched memory links returned by the MATCH process to replace links in the input tree. It starts at the root node and proceeds through the input tree in a depth-first, left-to-right order, replacing paths in the input tree by memory paths. After IDENTIFY has replaced one path with a memory path that has a conjunction, it will replace no more input paths by conjoining memory paths. In this way it is guaranteed that the encoding process will never generate unwanted multiplication of conjunctions. (The exact details of the IDENTIFY process are contained in the LISP function that simulates this process. Copies are available upon request.) IDENTIFY returns to HAM the list of links it was not able to replace. These links HAM will have to store in memory as new information.

The Utility of Binary Branching

It was promised in Chapter 7 that we would have something to say about the utility of binary branching in the input tree. The time has come to make good on that promise. Clearly, some branching is needed if HAM is to connect a number of elements into a single proposition. A disadvantage of greater than binary branching is that it tends to reduce the amount of match obtained between the memory structure and the input tree. If both of these claims are accepted, it follows that binary branching is optimal in one sense. However, the second claim, that binary branching optimizes the amount of matching, is not obvious, so we will prove it. Towards that goal, it will be useful first to prove the following lemma:

Lemma. Suppose some node a in the input tree having n differently labeled downward links (i.e., labels from the set $\mathfrak{R}$) is to be matched to a memory node b which has n like-labeled associations. Then at least $n-1$ of these links must be matched if the memory structure is to be utilized in encoding the input.

Proof. Mismatching two links out of node b would simply mean that two conjunctions would have to be created from b to encode the input tree. But then two conjunctions would be accessible via different paths from memory node b. Therefore, the memory structure could not be used to encode the input because of the unwanted multiplication of meanings. This proves the lemma.

This proof depends only upon the multiplication of meanings caused by conjunctions within a proposition. It does not depend upon any special properties of our MATCH or IDENTIFY routines. Therefore, it is a general result that should be applicable to a variety of associative structures. The consequence of the lemma is that one is less likely to get useable matches between input trees and memory trees when the branching is of higher order because there is a greater likelihood of having two mismatches from a particular node.

As a further argument for HAM, its binary trees have an advantage over other binary constructions in that elements which would tend to be repeated together are close together in HAM's tree structure. For instance, *time* and *location*, which are close together in the tree structure, will often be repeated as providing the context for a number of different facts. HAM would just encode the context subtree once while storing the many facts about that context. The *proposition* node in each proposition could be associated to the same context node. In this manner, HAM can take advantage of repetitions of just pairs of elements like *time* and *location* which are close together in the input tree. However, it cannot take advantage of repetitions of just pairs of elements that are far apart in the tree, such as *time* and *object*. Intuitively, pairs of elements like *time* and *object* seem unlikely to be the only parts of an input tree that will be repeated.

However, there is a disadvantage with binary branching that somewhat cancels out this efficient utilization of known information. Lower degrees of branching tend to require more associative links to be formed to represent the proposition in memory. If there are n elements to be connected into a binary tree structure, $2(n-1)$ associative links will be required. However, if all n elements were permitted to branch directly from the root node, only n links would be required. This means that at least $n-2$ links must be matched in a binary tree if it is to require as few links as an n-ary structure. Thus, it does not seem likely that binary structures will result in substantial savings in memory requirements. The real motivation for HAM's binary representation is that it permits memory to organize itself around cooccurring elements like a particular time and location which may form the context for a large set of facts.

9.2. EXPERIMENTAL TESTS OF THE MATCH PROCESS

The proposed operation of the MATCH process suggests many psychological experiments. This section reports some of the research that we have done to test the MATCH process.

Proper Names versus Definite Descriptions

One of the more interesting features of our simulation program is the way in which it treats definite descriptions. Suppose that the parser encountered an input sentence such as "The first president of the United States was a good husband." It would take the definite description "X was the first president of the United States," match that to memory, determine that X is George Washington, and then encode in memory that "George Washington was a good husband." Thus, no record would be left in HAM's memory to the effect that the assertion had been made using a definite description rather than a proper name. HAM would only know that it was true of a particular individual node that the person referenced by the node was a good husband. It would already know that the name corresponding to that node was George Washington and that the individual was the first president of the United States; but there would be no trace left of whether the proper name or the definite description had been paired with the "good husband" predicate. Hence, we would expect HAM as well as human subjects to false alarm to "George Washington was a good husband." Our first experiment was designed to test this prediction, that there should be recognition confusions in sentence memory between proper names and definite descriptions.

This prediction is interesting for a number of reasons. First, the synonymy between definite descriptions and proper names is not a case of *conceptual synonymy*—that is, synonymy resulting from knowledge of the language. Someone may be a perfectly competent speaker of the English language, know the meanings of the words of the language, but not know that George Washington was the first president of the United States. Rather, this is a case of *referential synonymy*. It is a consequence of our general world knowledge that we know the proper name and the definite description *refer* to the same historical individual. Chapter 8 dealt with conceptual synonymy and reviewed the ample evidence that subjects make memorial confusions between sentences on this basis. No one, however, has yet researched the question of referential synonymy.

Second, the matter of definite descriptions is interesting because it is a particularly well-formulated case of the phenomena of recognition memory in HAM. That is, what HAM is really doing when it replaces the definite description by the appropriate memory node is *recognizing* that description as the individual referenced by that node. We will argue in the next section, 9.3, that all manners of recognition (e.g., recognition of faces, patterns, contexts, etc.) have the identical procedure underlying them. That is, a description is taken of the object to be recognized, the MATCH process determines the best match in memory, and this best match constitutes the basis for the recognition decision.

Now the experiment will be described in greater detail: The experimental subjects (Stanford students) studied 60 sentences that had been generated from 15 *sentence-sets.* For each sentence-set a pair of proper names was selected, such as the pair George Washington and Abraham Lincoln. Appropriate definite descriptions were selected that would uniquely reference these individuals—e.g., "The first president of the United States" and "The president who freed the slaves." Then two predicates were selected for these individuals. These predicates were chosen to be plausible, but also such that their truth value with respect to the individual was probably unknown to the subjects, e.g., "was a good husband" and "had good health." Two further predicates were created from these two by introducing slight changes in the wording that produced major reversals in the semantic import of the sentences, e.g., "was a bad husband" and "had bad health."

Fifteen such sets of two proper names, two definite descriptions, and four predicates were the ingredients that went into the construction of a recognition experiment identical in logic to the J. R. Anderson (unpublished data, 1972) and Tieman (1971) experiments reviewed in Chapter 8. From each sentence-set, four study sentences were created, one having each of the proper names and definite descriptions as subject and one having each of the four possible predicates. Thus a subject might hear the following four sentences distributed randomly throughout a study list:

George Washington had good health.
The first president of the United States was a bad husband.
The president who freed the slaves had bad health.
Abraham Lincoln was a good husband.

In this way, the subject heard each of the proper names, definite descriptions, and predicates in some sentence. His later task would be to remember which subjects went with which predicates. Semantically converse predicates were never asserted of the same individual, but rather of the other individual of a pair. For instance, we did not claim the same individual was both a good and a bad husband. In this manner 60 base sentences were constructed. Two sets of 60 sentences were created by randomly re-pairing individuals with predicates. Twenty subjects listened to each set. The sentences were presented auditorily by a tape recorder at the rate of one every 10 seconds. In the 10-second interval for each sentence, it was read twice.

After studying all 60 sentences, the subjects were tested for their recognition memory of the sentences by a four-alternative forced-choice procedure. The subject might see the following four test sentences and would be asked to indicate which was the original he had heard:

Abraham Lincoln had good health.
The president who freed the slaves had good health.
The president who freed the slaves had bad health.
Abraham Lincoln had bad health.

That is, the definite description and the proper name for a particular individual would be paired with the two semantically converse forms of one predicate in the four possible ways. Always, the subject would have heard only one of the four possible combinations. Subjects were asked to rate the sentences numerically from 1 to 4 according to their subjective likelihood of having heard each sentence, with 1 indicating the most likely sentence. Although we only analyzed data for sentences rated 1, subjects were instructed to rate all four sentences to insure that they carefully considered all four possibilities before making their choice. The subjects worked at their own pace through a recognition booklet that contained 60 four-alternative forced-choice tests, one for each of the 60 sentences heard during study. The sentences were tested in the same order that they had been studied. The total experiment, including the reading of the preliminary instructions and the filling out of a subsequent questionnaire, took about 45 minutes.

Tieman's experiment (reviewed in Chapter 8) has shown the importance of instructions on the type of results one obtains from such experiments. Therefore, the following instructions were used in the hope that they would induce the subjects to analyze the sentences in as natural a manner as possible:

> We are going to tell you a large number of facts about certain people and places you have heard of. Some of these facts you will already know, most you will not. Some of the facts you will find surprising and a few you will disagree with. Your task is to try to remember all the information that is stated. After hearing all these facts, you will be given a task that requires knowledge of them.

On a postexperimental questionnaire, about two-thirds of the subjects indicated that, upon hearing proper names and definite descriptions for the same individuals intermixed in the study sentences, they began to suspect that the purpose of the experiment was to test their memory for definite descriptions versus proper names. Undoubtedly, this affected the way they processed the sentences. Some subjects reported adopting deliberate strategies to keep the definite descriptions separate in memory from the proper names. For instance, some subjects refused to think of the definite description as referring to the appropriate individual—e.g., the first president of the United States as being George Washington. Due to the intervention of such deliberate encoding strategies, we cannot expect subjects to false alarm to the referentially synonymous sentence as often as they identify the correct sentence. However, they should false alarm to the referentially synonymous sentence much more frequently than to either of the other two alternatives. This is because these other two alternatives have predicates that are not conceptually synonymous with the original statement.

The results are summarized in Table 9.1, which classifies 2,400 observations according to whether the original sentence studied involved a definite description (D) or a proper name (N), and whether the subject selected the test alternative involving the definite description and correct predicate (+D), the proper name and correct predicate (+N); the definite description and wrong predicate (-D), or the proper name and wrong predicate (-N). Subjects selected the correct alternative much more frequently than the referentially synonymous alternative (.624 vs. .217). Importantly, however, they also false alarmed to the referentially synonymous alternative much more frequently than to one of the sentences that had the wrong predicate (.217 vs. .080). For 14 of the 15 sentence sets, the

TABLE 9.1

Classification of Subjects' Responses in Definite Description
Experiment—Proportion of Responses

Original sentence	Subjects' choice			
	+D	+N	–D	–N
D	.652	.214	.072	.063
N	.222	.596	.093	.090

referentially synonymous alternative was more frequently chosen than the conceptually distinct alternatives; hence, one can be quite confident in the result. Overall, there was a small and insignificant bias to select definite descriptions (51.9%) over the proper names (48.1%).

This experiment clearly establishes that there is considerable confusion in memory between definite descriptions and proper names, as is predicted from the use of the MATCH process by HAM's parser. This is an example of how the MATCH process can function to make difficult the recording of certain kinds of information in memory. However, this was not the intended purpose of the MATCH process. Rather, its motivation partly was to ease the recording of information by using known information to reduce the amount that needs to be stored. There are many trivial examples to demonstrate that people do use past knowledge to help reduce their storage task. For instance, American adults would presumably remember a sentence like "George Washington was the first president of the United States" much better than a sentence like "John McDonald was the first prime minister of Canada." HAM expects this trivial result because the first proposition would be matched to an existing memory structure while the second would not. Therefore, the encoding process would not need to form any new associations in the first case, but would have to form a great many in the second case. We presume that this outcome is so obvious that no experimentation is required to establish it. It clearly indicates the need for some kind of memory matching routine. However, such an outcome could be predicted by models with very different memory structures and different match routines than those embodied in HAM. The next experiment will be concerned with obtaining more discriminating evidence in favor of both the representation and the match routine employed in HAM.

Repetition of Relative Clauses

In this experiment, we will be interested in what happens when subjects study related pairs of sentences that repeat a relative clause such as Sentences (1) and (2). We will contrast these results with what happens with pairs of sentences such as (3) and (4).

The *hippie* who was *tall* touched the debutante.	(1)
The *hippie* who was *tall* kissed the prostitute.	(2)
The hippie who was *tall* touched the *debutante*.	(3)
The captain who was *tall* kissed the *debutante*.	(4)

In both sentence pairs a noun and an adjective (italicized) are repeated. Moreover, both cases are superficially very similar. However, the important difference is that the elements in the first pair—Sentences (1) and (2)—are repeated within the same proposition, whereas the repeated elements in the second case—Sentences (3) and (4)—arise out of different propositions. In fact, in the first case the entire embedded proposition "The hippie was tall" is repeated. The MATCH routine defined in HAM can take advantage of the repetition of an entire proposition in the first case, but it is unable to take advantage of the repetition of "unrelated elements" in the second case. This is because the MATCH process only works with a single proposition at one time. Therefore, it cannot detect repetition between propositions. As a consequence, after storing Sentence (1), when HAM came to Sentence (2), it could use the associative structure established for Sentence (1) to store the embedded proposition in Sentence (2) and would need only to build associations to store the embedding proposition. Therefore, HAM would require fewer associations to store the pair of Sentences (1) and (2) than the pair of Sentences (3) and (4), and so recall should be higher for the first pair than for the second pair.

In the following experiment to test this prediction, each subject studied eight successive lists of 16 sentences with recall test immediately following each study list. In each list, four of the sentences represented each of the following four conditions:

Control—Sentences were composed from new words never before encountered by the subjects in the experiment.

ASR (Across-Sentence Repetition)—The two nouns and the adjective were repeated from different sentences in the past list. Thus, the words had been studied previously, but never in that combination. This was a control for the effect of sheer repetition of the words.

APR (Across-Proposition Repetition)—This is the condition exemplified by the pair of Sentences (3) and (4). That is, the adjective and the object noun were repeated from a single sentence of the past list. The subject noun was also repeated but taken from a different sentence. So this condition differs from ASR, because in that condition the adjective and object had not appeared in the same sentences before.

WPR (Within-Proposition Repetition)—This is the condition exemplified by Sentences (1) and (2). That is, the subject and adjective had occurred in the relative clause construction of a sentence from the preceding list. The object was taken from a sentence in the past list, but had not appeared before with the subject-adjective pair.

All repetition of element pairs was between lists. Within a particular list of 16 sentences there was no repetition of any content words. So all the sentences on list 1 were equivalent because each presented a novel configuration of words. It is only on later trials that we expect differences between conditions. The words that were repeated in conditions ASR, APR, and WPR occurred once on each of the eight lists. Also, the particular pairings that were repeated in conditions APR or WPR were repeated in all eight lists. Hence, in condition WPR, by the eighth study-list the subject would have heard the phrase "The hippie who was tall . . ." eight times in the experiment. The one word that was never repeated in any of the conditions was the verb. Thus it could serve to uniquely cue the recall of a particular sentence.

A total of 35 subjects were tested in this experiment. A different set of sentences was randomly generated for each subject. The subjects studied the sentences one at a time on IBM cards at a 15-second rate. After studying the 16 sentences in a list, the subjects received a cued recall test of the sentences in the same order as they had been studied. This involved presenting on IBM cards the adjective and the verb as cues in a sentence frame such as the following:

THE WHO WAS TALL TOUCHED THE

The subject's task was to recall by filling in the missing two nouns. Subjects were given 15 seconds to make their recall for each sentence. Sentences were tested in the same order as they were studied, thereby insuring a constant lag between study and test. After completing this procedure for one list of 16 sentences, the procedure was immediately repeated for the next list, and so on through the eight successive lists. Including instructions, the experimental session lasted about 75 minutes.

Figure 9.5 displays the results of this experiment in terms of the mean number of words correctly recalled in each condition. Figure 9.5a shows the recall of the first noun in the sentence, N_1, which was the subject (i.e., *hippie*). This is the word that was constantly paired with the same adjective in condition WPR. As can be seen, recall of this subject-noun continuously improves across trials in condition WPR as it is re-paired again and again with the same adjective. In contrast, recall of N_1 for the other conditions is relatively constant, showing little in the way of reliable trends. So, we have clear evidence that subjects are able to take advantage of within-proposition repetition and hence use the memory structure established for the subject-adjective proposition in one sentence to help record it in a subsequent sentence. Overall, 66% of the N_1 words were recalled in condition WPR. This contrasts with 40% in condition APR, 41% in ASR, and 46% in the control condition. None of these latter three conditions are significantly different from one another, but all are very significantly worse than condition WPR (statistics by a Duncan's range test).

Figure 9.5b shows the results for recall of N_2, the object in the sentence (i.e., *debutante*). There seems to be little improvement across trials in any of the conditions and little difference among the conditions. Overall, 45% of the N_2 words were recalled in condition WPR, 45% in condition APR, 38% in condition ASR, and 42% in the control condition. According to a Duncan's range test, the conditions WPR and APR show significantly more recall than ASR ($p < .05$), but no other differences are significant. So, it appears that the subject derives at least some benefit in condition APR from the repetition of the adjective with N_2, despite their being in different propositions within the same sentence; this mild advantage only appears in a comparison to condition ASR in which elements were repeated from different sentences. Moreover, the improvement is not nearly so marked as the improvement in condition WPR of N_1 recall as a consequence of the repetition of

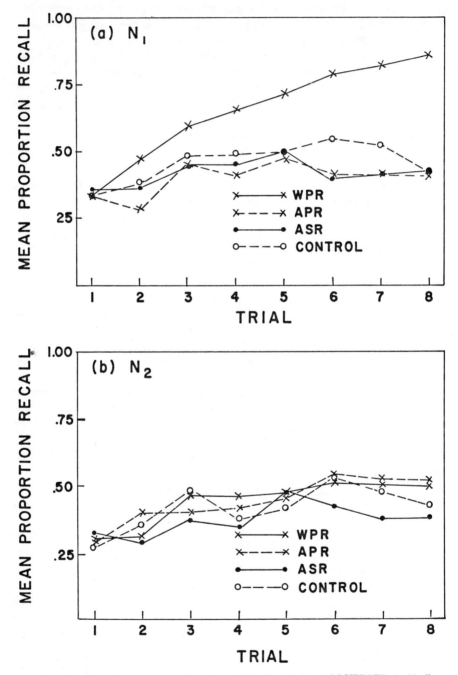

FIG. 9.5. Recall of sentences of the form: "The N_1 who was ADJ VERBED the N_2."

N_1 with the adjective within a single atomic proposition. Also, the level of N_2 recall in condition APR is no different than N_2 recall in WPR. In condition WPR the N_2 element, although repeated, had not cooccurred previously with any other element in the sentence. The improvement of N_2 recall in condition WPR may be a consequence of the fact that subjects are able to focus on the proposition in which N_2 occurs because they already have encoded from past lists the other proposition in which N_1 occurs.

Repetition of Major Clause

To summarize the results of the last experiment, repetition of elements *within* a proposition in a sentence greatly improved recall, whereas repetition of elements *between* propositions had hardly any effect. We decided to pursue this repetition phenomena in a second experiment to further establish its generality and strength. Again we were principally concerned with contrasting within- versus between-proposition repetition of elements. However, this time we tried to load the surface sentences against the within-proposition condition and more in favor of the between-proposition condition. We contrasted the within-proposition repetition exemplified by Sentences (5) and (6) with the between-proposition repetition exemplified by Sentences (7) and (8).

The *hippie* who touched the debutante was *tall.*	(5)
The *hippie* who kissed the prostitute was *tall.*	(6)
The hippie who touched the *debutante* was *tall.*	(7)
The captain who kissed the *debutante* was *tall.*	(8)

In Sentences (5) and (6), although *hippie* and *tall* are repeated from the same underlying proposition, they occur at a considerable physical distance in the surface sentence because a relative clause intervenes between the elements. In contrast, in Sentences (7) and (8), although *debutante* and *tall* are taken from different propositions, they occur in close physical proximity in the surface sentence. Thus, the between-proposition repetition is being made very salient physically, while at the same time the within-proposition repetition is made physically obscure. (In the next chapter we will report evidence that manipulating the physical contiguity of words in a sentence does slightly affect the probability of their joint recall.) It will be recalled that in the previous experiment, the cooccurring elements were at approximately equal physical distances in the two pairs of sentences.

Except for the surface structure of the sentences studied, this experiment was identical in design and procedure to the previous experiment. A total of 46 subjects were run. The results, displayed in Figure 9.6, appear quite similar to those in Figure 9.5. With respect to N_1 recall, there was the expected increase across trials in the WPR condition. The overall levels of N_1 recall were nearly identical to those of the previous experiment: 67% for condition WPR (66% in the previous experiment), 44% for condition APR (40% in the previous experiment), 40% for condition ASR (41% previously), and 51% for the control condition (46% previously). Again, recall in the WPR condition was much superior to all others. However, in this experiment recall in the control condition is significantly superior

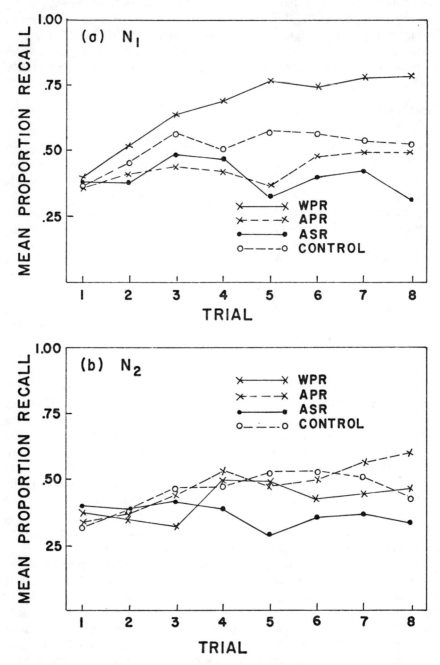

FIG. 9.6. Recall of sentences of the form: "The N_1 who VERBED the N_2 was ADJ."

to both conditions APR and ASR ($p < .05$). In the previous experiment, this difference was in the same direction but did not reach statistical significance. The difference may indicate negative transfer in conditions APR and ASR because the adjective is constantly being re-paired with a new N_1 term. There were no other significant differences with respect to N_1 recall.

Again there appears to be little effect in N_2 recall (see Figure 9.6b) either in terms of changes across trials or differences among the conditions. The overall levels of N_2 recall in this experiment were quite similar to the previous: For condition WPR, 42% in this experiment (45% in the previous), for condition APR 48% (versus 45%), for condition ASR 36% (versus 38%), and for the control condition 45% (versus 42%). However, more of the small differences between conditions achieved marginal significance (.05 level) than in the previous experiment. A Duncan's range test finds all conditions superior to the ASR condition, suggesting considerable negative transfer in this case. Condition APR is also superior to WPR, suggesting some slight benefit of the across-proposition repetition of N_2 with the adjective. However, neither condition APR or WPR is significantly different from the control condition.

So, it seems that our attempt to manipulate perceptual saliency of the repeating elements has had relatively little effect on the character of the results. The one substantial effect in the data is still the across-trials increase in N_1 recall in condition WPR. Although there was a slight improvement in the amount of N_2 recall in condition APR, it was not so much as to become a clear-cut effect statistically. Thus, we must conclude that, as predicted by the MATCH process, human memory appears to be set up in such a way that it can only easily detect and take advantage of repetition of elements within an atomic proposition.

Rosenberg's Results

We would like to relate our theory to some experiments by Sheldon Rosenberg (1968a, 1968b, 1969, 1970) that seem to establish some of the same points that we have been making in our research, but using somewhat different procedures. His 1969 experiment is rather similar in logic to our last two. He compared subjects' recall of sentences like Sentence (9) with their recall of sentences like Sentence (10).

The doctor who fired the janitor cured the patient. (9)
The doctor who fired the janitor shook the author. (10)

The important difference between these two is that in Sentence (9) the main clause "The doctor cured the patient" is likely to be already recorded in the subject's memory, probably many times over, since we all know of many different doctors having cured many different patients. In contrast, the main clause in Sentence (10), "The doctor shook the author," is likely to be a novel assertion for most subjects. Rosenberg also examined subjects' recall of sentences like Sentences (11) and (12) in which the relative clause might contain the well-known proposition.

The doctor who cured the patient fired the janitor. (11)

The doctor who shook the author fired the janitor.   (12)

The subjects in Rosenberg's experiment studied lists of 10 such sentences and then were asked to free-recall the sentences. The results he obtained are entirely consonant with our own. Recall of the well-known proposition in one sentence was higher than of the corresponding unknown proposition in another sentence. Rosenberg also examined recall of the second, novel proposition in the sentence (i.e., "The doctor fired the janitor"). Recall of this novel proposition was higher when it occurred with a well-known proposition, as in Sentence (11), than with another novel proposition, as in Sentence (12). This accords with our finding that N_2 recall was higher in the Within-Proposition Repetition condition (WPR) than in the Across-Sentence Repetition condition (ASR), although in neither condition had N_2 been repeated with an element from the sentence.

In another experiment, Rosenberg (1968b) contrasted the recall of highly interassociated sentences like Sentence (13) with sentences like Sentence (14).

The old king ruled wisely.   (13)
The poor king dined gravely.   (14)

Of course, sentences like Sentence (13) are more likely to be already partially or totally recorded in memory and hence are better recalled. The more interesting finding was that these highly interassociated sentences were recalled largely in an all-or-none manner. They did not show the same word-to-word transitional error probabilities that are found with unfamiliar sentences. The *transition error probability* denotes the probability of *not* recalling the $(n+1)$st word, given that the nth word in the sentence is recalled. In unfamiliar sentences, these transition error probabilities were high across major syntactic boundaries such as the subject-predicate boundary (see also Johnson, 1968). In contrast, higher interphrase transition error probabilities were not found with the highly interassociated sentences. Rosenberg concluded that these sentences must have been "recoded into units that transcend the phrase boundary." The unitary memory for such sentences is just what HAM would predict. Since the propositions are largely or entirely recorded in memory already, HAM only needs to tag these preexisting propositions as to-be-recalled material. In contrast, as will be shown in Chapter 10, fragmentary recall occurs in abundance when HAM must encode all the associations in a novel input sentence like Sentence (14).

On the Mnemonic Structure of SVO Propositions

The earlier experiments on the MATCH function used repetition of complete atomic propositions (e.g., "The *hippie* who is *tall* touched the debutante"). In those cases, the MATCH process was able to locate and reuse a complete propositional tree while encoding the "partially repeated" sentence. But what about repetition of subparts of a single proposition? Which subpart repetitions will HAM be able to recognize and reuse?

Consider first a pair repetition using simple SVO propositions. Let $S_1 V_1 O_1$ denote the first proposition studied. Its later mate can be either $S_1 V_1 O_2$, $S_1 V_2 O_1$, or $S_2 V_1 O_1$, where the repeated pairs have the same subscript. The MATCH and IDENTIFY processes within HAM see all these as symmetrical. In each case, HAM should recognize the cooccurring pair and reuse any old memory structure involving that pair in order to encode the new sentence. For example, in the case of a subject-object repetition, input of the second sentence $S_1 V_2 O_1$ should match up with the old memory structure $S_1 V_1 O_1$ and result in the encoding of a verb conjunction of the form $S_1 (V_1$ *and* $V_2) O_1$. Significantly, the associative path in the tree from S_1 to O_1 is strengthened just as much by a partial SO repetition with a changed verb $(S_1 V_2 O_1)$ as it would be by a complete repetition of the full proposition.

This prediction has been tested twice in our laboratory, once 6 years ago by Samuel Bobrow and again last year by Michael Fehling. The results both times were strictly in accord with the model's prediction. To describe Bobrow's earlier experiment, the subjects studied a list of 45 SVO sentences exemplifying various control and repetition conditions within the study list. For our purposes here, the conditions of relevance were: the "once-presented" control ($S_1 V_1 O_1$ once), the "twice-presented" control ($S_1 V_1 O_1$ twice), and the "changed verb" condition ($S_1 V_1 O_1$, then $S_1 V_2 O_1$).

The sentence which repeated the critical elements occurred in the input list at least 10 sentences after its initial mate. After studying all the sentences, the subjects were tested by being presented with the subject noun and were asked to recall the object noun. The average lag or number of intervening items from the last study of an item to its test trial was the same for the three conditions.

The comparison of interest is the probability of correct object recall to the subject cue. For the once-presented sentences, this probability was .33; for the twice-presented sentences (with the same verb), it was .67; for the condition with SO repetition (but different verbs), this probability was .68. So clearly, there is a pairwise repetition effect (within the repeated pair); and clearly it is about the same magnitude whether the third content element is kept the same or is changed. This is all in accord with HAM's predictions.

Consider a further prediction along these general lines. In this case, we change the object noun paired with a given subject, and we do this either keeping the same verb or changing the verb as well as the object. The case with SV (same-verb) repetition is symbolized as "$S_1 V_1 O_1$ then $S_1 V_1 O_2$," whereas with changing verb the symbols are "$S_1 V_1 O_1$ then $S_1 V_2 O_2$." Bobrow compared these conditions in a second part of his experiment. Following study of the list, the subject was given the subject-noun as a cue and was asked to recall *both* objects that had been paired with that subject. The probabilities of recall of O_1 and O_2 for the SV repetition condition were .56 and .39, respectively, with a mean of .48. For the changed-verb condition, O_1 and O_2 recall probabilities were .47 and .30, respectively, with a mean of .38. There is a "primacy" effect in these data; it is a frequent result in such within-list comparisons and is perhaps comprehensible in terms of the subject, at the time of the repetition, retrieving and rehearsing the earlier proposition (see our discussion of "negative transfer" in Chapter 15).

Disregarding that auxiliary effect, what does HAM predict for object recall in this experiment? In terms of reuseable memory structure, the condition which uses the same verb should produce a simple object conjunction (see Figure 9.7*a*), reusing the same links up to the predicate node. However, when a new verb is used, $S_1 V_2 O_2$, more new structure has to be built, because this new verb causes a predicate conjunction (see Figure 9.7*b*). The "sentence-to-predicate" link is reused in the structure in Figure 9.7*a*, but not in the structure shown in Figure 9.7*b*. For this reason, we would expect recall of either object to be somewhat higher in the same-verb condition than in the changed-verb condition. This was true, as shown by the proportions reported above.

A further, more refined prediction concerns the *correlation* between recall of O_1 and O_2 in these two cases. In the same-verb case (Figure 9.7*a*), recall of O_1 to S means that the path from S up to the predicate node is intact, so therefore further recall of O_2 requires just the two links from this predicate node to the O_2 word. On the other hand, for the changed-verb case (Figure 9.7*b*), recall of O_1 to S insures only that the path from S to the fact node is intact, so that further recall of O_2 would require three links (P, O, ϵ) to have been established and retained. For these reasons, one expects recall of O_1 and O_2 to the S cue to be more highly correlated in the same-verb case than in the changed-verb case. This is just what Bobrow found: tabulating recall and nonrecall of O_1 and O_2 in a 2 × 2 matrix (pooling across items and subjects), there was a significant positive correlation in O_1 and O_2 recall for the same-verb condition, but virtually no correlation for the

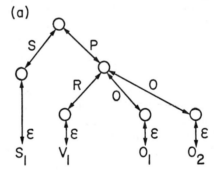

(a)

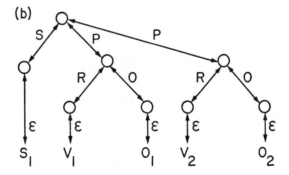

(b)

FIG. 9.7. HAM's representation of the sentence pairs from the Bobrow experiment: (*a*) Same verb conditions; and (*b*) Different verb condition.

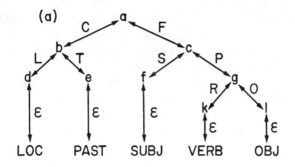

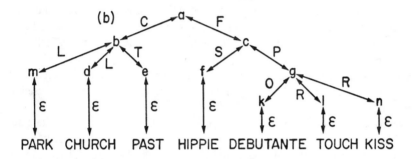

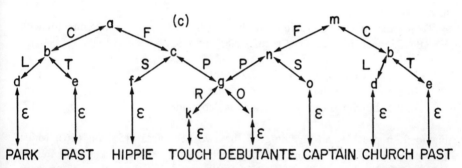

FIG. 9.8. (*a*) Standard representation for "In the LOC (during PAST) the SUBJ VERBED the OBJ." (*b*) An attempt to encode the redundancy in a SUBJ-OBJ repetition. (*c*) An attempt to encode the redundancy in a VERB-OBJ repetition.

changed-verb condition. So that detail is also in line with the sentence representations and MATCH processes used by HAM.

Repetition Effects in Four Element Propositions

We can ask more probing questions and provide more discriminating tests regarding HAM's MATCH and IDENTIFY processes by moving up to four element propositions, the SVO as previously used but with a locational element explicitly provided. Figure 9.8*a* shows the schematic diagram in terms of our deep grammar for sentences of the form "In the LOC (during PAST) the SUBJ VERBed the OBJ." The question to be researched is much as in the previous experiments: suppose we select a subset of elements from SUBJ, VERB, OBJ, which is to be repeated across successive study lists but where the other elements change in each list; which repeating subsets should the MATCH function be able to detect and reuse to ease the encoding (learning) of the successive sentences?

The MATCH function together with the IDENTIFY function deliver some firm predictions on this matter; MATCH will detect any cooccurrences of elements in memory trees, but IDENTIFY may disallow some of these so as to avoid the unwanted multiplication of meanings that would occur if the matched piece of memory were used to encode the input tree. Which cooccurring pairs allow reuse of old memory pieces formed from earlier cooccurrences? First, repetition of VERB-OBJ cooccurrences should provide useable memory structures. Both are dominated by a single node, labeled g in Figure 9.8a. This node, established during a first presentation of a VERB-OBJ pair, could be matched and used in encoding a second sentence with different LOC plus SUBJ terms but the same VERB-OBJ predicate pair. Second, repetition of the three elements SUBJ-VERB-OBJ in sentences with changing LOC should be especially well matched, detected, and learned. This is the tree dominated by the FACT node a, which would be reused in later sentences.

However, according to the current MATCH and IDENTIFY functions, there are other pairs of elements which will not lead to improved recall across repetitions. In particular, neither repetition of the SUBJ-OBJ pair nor the SUBJ-VERB can be used, because building on these repetitions would lead to multiplication of meanings.

To see that meanings would multiply with SUBJ-OBJ repetitions but not with VERB-OBJ repetitions, contrast Figures 9.8b and 9.8c.

In the park the hippie touched the debutante.	(15)
In the church the hippie kissed the debutante.	(16)
In the church the captain touched the debutante.	(17)

Figure 9.8b provides an encoding of the two Sentences (15) and (16), which exemplify SUBJ-OBJ repetition, and Figure 9.8c provides an encoding of Sentences (15) and (17), which exemplify a VERB-OBJ repetition. In both cases we have attempted to use the redundancy in one proposition to help encode the other. The result in Figure 9.8b with SUBJ-OBJ repetition has been two unintended propositions: "In the park the hippie kissed the debutante" and "In the church the hippie touched the debutante." There is no such multiplication in Figure 9.8c, where a VERB-OBJ repetition has been used. Therefore, the IDENTIFY process would permit only the second redundancy to be stored. The following experiment was performed to test this detailed prediction of HAM.

In this experiment 46 subjects studied 6 lists of 18 sentences each. All sentences were of the form location-subject-verb-object (e.g., "In the park the hippie touched the debutante"). In each list three sentences represented each of the following 6 conditions:

Control New—Sentences were composed from new words never before encountered by the subjects in the experiment.

Control Rep—The subject, verb and object were repeated from different sentences in past lists, but had never occurred together before.

SVO Rep—The subject, verb, and object of a sentence in this condition were repeated together across lists, but the locative was changed.

SV Rep—The subject and verb were repeated together across lists. The object was also repeated but never with the same subject or verb.

SO Rep—The subject and object were repeated together, and the verb was repeated separately.

VO Rep—The verb and object were repeated together and the subject separately.

As in past experiments, all repetition was between lists. The one word that was never repeated in any of the conditions was the location. Thus it could serve to uniquely cue the recall of a sentence from a list. A different set of sentences was randomly generated for each subject. The subjects studied the sentences on IBM cards at a 15-second rate. After studying the 18 sentences in a list, the subjects were given a cued recall test of the sentences in the same order. The method of *incremental cuing* was used in this experiment. First, the subject was presented with just the location and asked to recall the remainder of the sentence—that is, the subject, verb, and object. Then, the location cue was *incremented* with, randomly, the subject or the verb or the object. This two-word cue was presented immediately subsequent to the location-only cue, and the subject tried to recall the two words that remained missing. After completing his recall to the second cue, the subject went on to two more incremental cues to test his memory for the next sentence in the list. The subject had 15 seconds to write his recall to each of the cues. The sentences were tested in the same order in which they had been presented. After study and test of one list of 18 sentences, the procedure was immediately repeated for the next list. Including instructions, the experimental session lasted about 100 minutes.

We will consider separately the recall to the first location-only cue and then recall to the second, incremented cue. Figure 9.9 presents the recall to the location-only cue. In Figure 9.9a we have recall of S; in Figure 9.9b, recall of V; and in Figure 9.9c, recall of O. In these graphs, for purposes of simplicity we have collapsed two pairs of conditions from the original six conditions to yield four plotted conditions. We have plotted separately the SVO Rep and the Control New conditions. We then have collapsed the SV Rep, SO Rep, VO Rep, and Control Rep conditions into two conditions. In Figure 9.9a showing S recall, we present in the condition labeled "S conjoint" the average recall from the two conditions SV Rep and SO Rep. These are two groups in which S was repeated *conjointly* with some other element. The groups VO Rep and Control Rep contribute to the line labeled "S single." These are the two conditions in which S was repeated by itself, not in conjunction with any other element. Similarly, SV Rep and VO Rep contribute to the condition "V conjoint" in Figure 9.9b, and the conditions SO Rep and Control Rep contribute to the "V single" condition. In Figure 9.9c, the conditions SO Rep and VO Rep contribute to "O conjoint" and conditions SV Rep and Control Rep to O single.

A brief inspection of Figure 9.9 is sufficient to indicate the character of the results obtained with the location-only cue. All conditions show some improvement

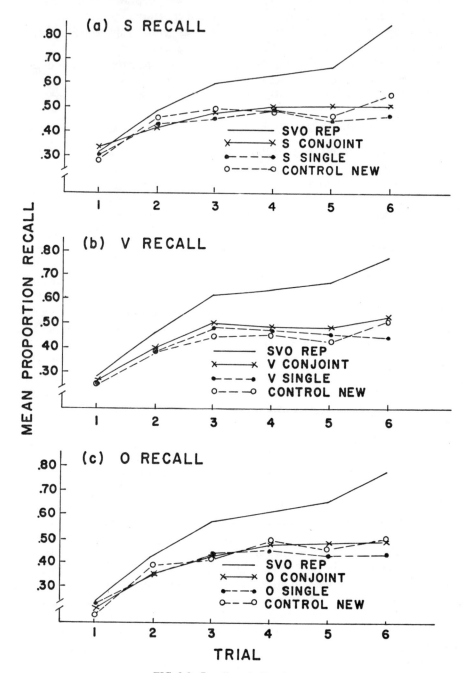

FIG. 9.9. Recall to the L-only cue.

over the first few trials, indicating something of a warm-up effect. However, the group SVO Rep is distinguished by the fact that it is improving much more rapidly, and the improvement extends to the sixth trial. The other groups are not distinguishable one from another. We had predicted the VO group would show a similar distinguished across-trial improvement. This was because our IDENTIFY process as defined will take advantage of repetition of the VO pairs, but not of other pairs. Although we have not presented data separately for the VO condition, recall in that condition is not distinguishable from the recall presented in Figure 9.9 for the various conditions (other than SVO Rep condition). Thus, it would appear that we have a clear disconfirmation of the postulated operation of the MATCH and IDENTIFY processes.

Recall to the second augmented cue might provide a more sensitive measure of whether the MATCH process is able to take advantage of VO repetition. We can cue with L plus V and observe recall of O, or cue with L plus O and observe recall of V. HAM would predict that recall in these circumstances should be greater in the VO Rep condition than any other condition except SVO Rep. We might expect to observe an effect here even though an effect did not appear to the first cue, because we are cueing with part of the repeated pair. Figure 9.10 presents the relevant data for recall to the second incremented cue. In Figure 9.10a, we have V recall to the L & S cue; in Figure 9.10b, O recall to the L & S cue; in Figure 9.10c, S recall to L & V cue; in Figure 9.10d, O recall to L & V cue; in Figure 9.10e, S recall to L & O cue; and in Figure 9.10f, V recall to L & O cue. To get acceptable frequencies of observations, we have pooled in Figure 9.10 over Trials 1 and 2, 3 and 4, and 5 and 6. We have presented the proportion recalled separately for three conditions—SVO Rep, one of the pair repetition conditions, and Control New. The other three repetition conditions were collapsed, and their recall is represented by a single line in each panel. The one pair-repetition condition represented separately in each panel is always the one where the one member of the repeated pair is part of the cue and the other member is the response. So, for instance, we have the SV Rep condition graphed separately in Figure 9.10a, because the cue for that panel contains S and the response graphed in that panel is V.

Once again the data appear to tell a consistent story. The SVO Rep condition is always best; the pairwise repetition that involves part of the cue and the response (i.e., the individually graphed condition) is second best; and there is little basis for discriminating among the other conditions. In particular, there is nothing outstanding about the VO Rep conditions as contrasted with the other pair repetitions. It is true that it is the best pair-repetition condition in Figure 9.10d and f where V and O are cue and response, but similarly the SO and SV conditions are best in their appropriate panels. So we have absolutely no evidence for the uniqueness of VO repetition as predicted by the MATCH and IDENTIFY processes.

Why is it that recall to the second incremented cue was sensitive to pair repetition, but the recall to the first, location-only cue was not? We suspect that the advantage to the second cue reflects a combination of the effects due to strategic guessing and due to memory for auxiliary observations that subjects make to themselves about pairwise repetitions. By strategic guessing we mean, for instance, that the subject may have guessed to the L & S cue the V and O elements that

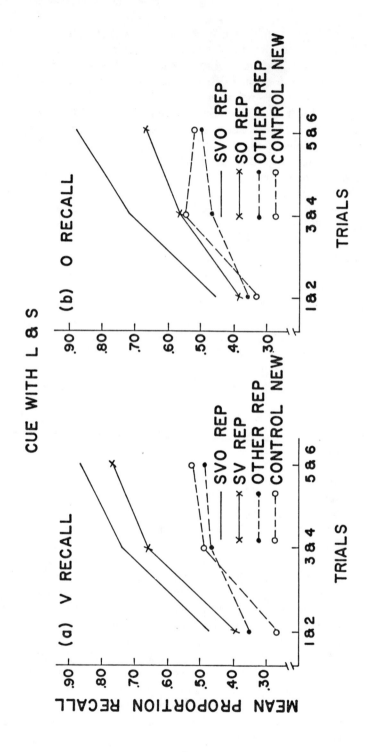

CUE WITH L & S

(a) V RECALL

(b) O RECALL

MEAN PROPORTION RECALL

TRIALS

(Continued)

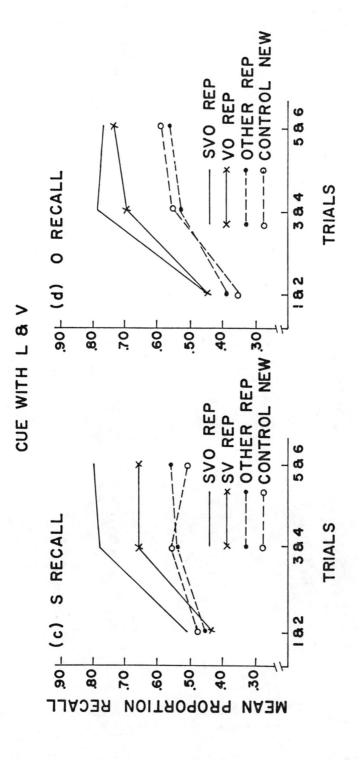

CUE WITH L & V

(c) S RECALL

(d) O RECALL

(Continued)

267

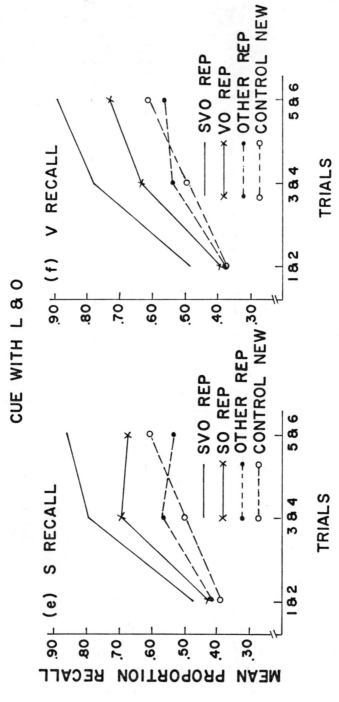

FIG. 9.10. Recall to the incremented cue.

had occurred with S in prior lists. This would lead to an increase in V recall in the SV condition, and O recall (Figure 9.10a) in the SO condition (Figure 9.10b). Similarly, we could explain the advantage of the best pair-repetition conditions to the L & V cue and to the L & O cue.

Also, subjects often report noting repetitions of pairs of elements and can recall after the experiment some of these pairwise repetitions. It is not unexpected that they should recognize such repetitions. The MATCH process would alert HAM to any repetition of a pair within a proposition. However, the IDENTIFY process inhibits use of past associative structures to encode the current proposition for pairwise repetitions (except for the VO case). The subject, noticing the repetition of S and O, could form to himself a proposition of the order: "S always cooccurs with O." Remembering that proposition, the subject would show higher recall of S when cued with O, and higher recall of O when cued with S.

Whether the subject is engaged in strategic guessing or explicitly remembering auxiliary propositions, it is the case that either of these tactics will be of avail only when he is probed with one of the members of the repeated pair. When cued with L-alone, which is never repeated, the subject will show improved recall only if he has built on a past associative structure to encode a current one and so had less work in storing the current sentence. Thus, recall to the first cue is really the most telling evidence about when a subject can use cooccurrence to reduce his encoding task. The L-only recall data seems to indicate that the SVO must be repeated in the sentences we used in this experiment.

It is difficult to isolate why we did not get a similar effect of VO repetition. In a complex model like HAM the fault may lie at many points. Perhaps our choice of representation is wrong. Maybe our definition of the IDENTIFY process is wrong. Maybe IDENTIFY will only accept a match if $n-1$ of the elements of the n-element proposition are matched, or maybe at least three elements must be matched, or maybe the fact subtree must be matched. To determine just what is wrong with our theoretical formulation will require further research.

9.3. STIMULUS RECOGNITION

Having described the MATCH process by which HAM accesses propositions stored in its memory, and having described some relevant evidence from sentence-memory experiments, it is appropriate to turn now to a somewhat more general discussion of stimulus recognition. In the following, the terms "stimulus recognition," "pattern recognition," "pattern classification," and "stimulus identification" will all be used interchangeably as equivalent terms. The issue under consideration is how the processes and structures of HAM's memory might be applied to pattern (or concept) learning and pattern identification.

In everyday parlance, we commonly distinguish between several different types of recognition performance. The first and major distinction is that between class recognition versus individual identification. In cases of class recognition, the stimulus object or event is assigned to one of several categories or classes; for instance, handwritten As, zebras, pencils, and human faces. While it is possible to talk about recognition of abstract concepts such as "male chauvinism" or "morality," we will confine our discussion to recognition of more or less perceptual concepts.

Recognition of an individual, the second major type of recognition performance, differs from concept recognition in that we do not recognize the object as a member of a class or set, but rather as an entity that shares a spatiotemporal continuity with an entity previously encountered. Namely, we conceive of the two entities as identical, independent of whether they share the same attributes or not. Thus, Joe Krud is still recognized as the same individual after he (she?) undergoes a sex change and becomes Josephine Krud. Individual identification, as a set of performances, can be subdivided into judgments of familiarity and retrieval of associated contextual facts. Examples of the first are judgments that we have or have not experienced a particular stimulus pattern before; of the second, that we can remember the context in which we last (or first) experienced this pattern. We will treat these various topics in turn.

Recognition of Perceptual Concepts

We have supposed that a complicated set of sensory analyzers connect HAM's memory with the world. Basic components of HAM's memory correspond to sensory qualities and properties. The aim of the perceptual routines is to build up a feasible and stable *description* of the current scene facing the machine. In the case of visual scene analysis, this description may be thought of as being available or elaborated at several different levels of hierarchical details. In a scene composed of boxes, bricks, and wedges stacked against one another (see Figure 8.3), the most primitive features identified are lines or contours of varying lengths and orientations, meeting so as to make angles, T-joints, arrow-joints, and so forth (see Figure 8.4). Built-in melding programs then join together several edges, identifying them as probably a pair of triad of surfaces from the same object.

After surface-clusters are tentatively identified as particular objects, the program can then decide "in-front-of" relations, where one object is partially occluding another, and other relations such as "supports," "left of," and "abuts." The output of this object-plus-relation identification program is then a relational network. To illustrate, in Winston's (1970) program (see our discussion in Section 8.1) which analyzes block scenes and develops scene descriptions, an example of an elementary object identifier would be the concept of a "wedge." Figure 9.11 illustrates a wedge and the structural description of the appearance of a wedge. The relational structure at the bottom of Figure 9.11 states that a wedge comprises (to the eye of the viewer) three surfaces, two of which are a kind of rectangle whereas the third must be a kind of triangle. The latter feature, for instance, distinguishes wedges from bricks. Thus, when shown a wedge, the lower-level program will first identify lines, edges, and surfaces, and then rectangular and triangular surfaces, gradually building up a description. When this description is matched in memory to the set of known primitive objects (concept descriptions), the best match occurs to the "wedge" concept illustrated in Figure 9.11. At the next higher level of recognition, the several objects identified and related together in a scene may satisfy a higher-order concept (e.g., a stack of wedges or a toy house); and this description

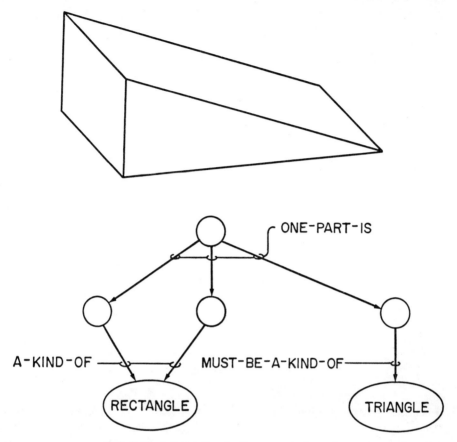

FIG. 9.11. A description for the concept of a wedge.

may in turn be passed up to a still higher level of description of the whole scene (e.g., a toy house sitting beside an arcade of arches).

Now higher-order concepts are constructed out of combinations of lower-order concepts. Figure 9.12 illustrates a few medium-level constructions which Winston's program can recognize. For example, a *tent* is two wedges that abut in a certain way, a *pedestal* is a brick lying down supported in the center by an upright brick, and so on.

An important feature of such intermediate-level concepts is that they simplify the description of a scene. For example, consider the scene composed of a tent to the left of a house, with both sitting on top of an arch (see the objects in Figure 9.12). There would be at least seven simple objects—bricks, wedges—in that overall scene, and they exhibit very many interobject relationships. *Before* the system learns these intermediate-level concepts, all of these parts and myriads of relationships would have to be entered into the description of the scene. However, *after* having learned these concepts, they can be used as units to simplify the overall description to something approximating our English proposition "A tent to the left of a house both supported by an arch." HAM would represent the scene by

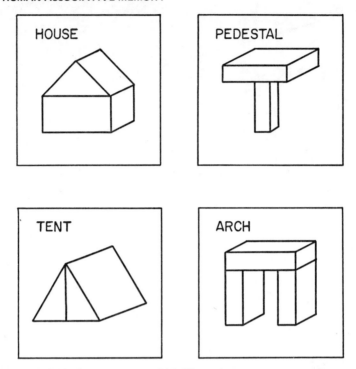

FIG. 9.12. Some structures which Winston's program can recognize.

essentially this proposition. That is because input of the structural description of a *tent* (say) will activate its idea node, and that node will enter into further predications about the scene. This is, in principle, no different from the way HAM finds and utilizes the idea nodes corresponding to definite descriptions encountered in text like "The first president of the USA" or "The fat calico cat mentioned earlier."

Feature Analysis versus Scene Description

This scene-description model of pattern recognition contrasts quite sharply with the feature-analysis model. Both models begin with the extracting of a number of elementary features by sensory analyzers, but from this point on the models are different. Rather than proceeding to build up a description, a feature-analysis model of the Pandemonium variety will simply weight each feature as giving more or less evidence for the presence of each possible concept. The total evidence for a given concept is summed across the weighted features, and that concept having the greatest degree of evidence in its favor is selected as the name of the stimulus pattern.

But there are several known deficiencies of weighted-feature Pandemoniums which cause them to be unsatisfactory models for pattern recognition. For instance, the strategy of "summing independent sources of evidence" misses the point that for many concepts, one or more critical features *must* be present and others *must not* be present in order for the concept to apply. In distinguishing a *G* from a *C*, the cross-bar is critical; a G must have one, and a C must not. No matter how great the evidence from the remaining features, it should not overwhelm this critical feature. Similarly, in distinguishing an R from a P, the oblique line (leg) of the R is critical. There are many such examples of critical features. However, in the Pandemonium model, simply weighting features and summing values does not adequately solve the problem. In Winston's (1970) program, criterial attributes are modified by the emphatic or obligatory modal, *must have* or *must not have*, appended before a property or predicate. These properties then become sufficient reasons for rejecting a particular classification for a pattern: if a *must have* property is missing in the input, the category clearly fails; if a *must not have* property is present, the input-to-category match also fails. Only after these emphatic criteria have been passed does the match function continue calculating the match score between the input tree and the given tree in memory "defining" the category.

A further inadequacy of Pandemoniums is that they lack resources for describing relations between several features or between several objects. For example, it is known (see Minsky & Papert, 1969) that a Pandemonium cannot distinguish *odd* versus *even* numbers of elements in its viewing field, nor distinguish *connected* versus *unconnected* line drawings. Pandemoniums also lack relational descriptors of the most elementary type, such as "Line A is perpendicular to Line B" or "Surface C is coplanar to Surface D." A final problem with Pandemonium systems is that they are in themselves inadequate for segmentation of a multiobject scene. An entire scene of several objects would be analyzed as a "single unit," which is ridiculous, since most scenes are novel in one respect or another, and hence would be totally unrecognizable. What clearly is needed is a device for segmenting scenes into objects, describing and recognizing these individual objects, and describing their relationships to one another in the present scene. With such capabilities, the system can perceive (describe) an infinite variety of scenes, all novel in one or another detail. These then are the various ways in which scene description programs like Winston's (and like what HAM hopes to be) are important advances over the more traditional feature-analysis models.

Recognition of Individuals

Now let us turn from recognition as classification and description to the other principle sense of recognition—recognition as individuating. In this sense, we recognize a face *as* that of our friend Tom Jones, or we recognize a dog *as* Spot, or a city *as* Paris. In this case we are identifying an individual (person, animal, or place) as a particular one known to us rather than as a member of a general class of people or dogs or structures.

But a moment's reflection reveals, however, that the individuals Tom Jones and Spot are recognized much in the same manner as conceptual categories like handwritten *A*s, *flowers*, and *arches*. The appearances of Tom Jones to us may vary dramatically from one occasion to the next, as he changes clothes, dons or removes spectacles, a beard, a wig, and gains or loses weight. But because we have reason to believe that successive "Tom Jones" appearances are caused by a single continuous entity, we say the appearances are of the identical individual, and we extract certain invariant criterial features to control our identification of the man as Tom Jones.

What obviously differs between recognition of a class and of a specific individual is the amount of detail and the number of distinguishing features in the description network for the individual. Thus, *my house* is the house with the *red tile roof* (a distinguisher). If that fails, then more distinguishers can be added to select out the referent. If some of these distinguishers are missing in a particular description and cannot be supplied by the context, then HAM would have to exit its search with a more general concept as its best matching candidate. For example, a degraded tachistoscopic flash of Tom Jones may be identified only as a man, with loss of all the individuating features.

Just as we recognize individual persons, so can we recognize individual locations, places, structures, and—in general—any particular scene. It would be assumed that we have a "perceptual model" corresponding to what the inside of our office or house looks like or what a specific street corner or a specific park looks like. These scenes are in principle characterized by some corresponding abstract description in memory, relating relevant concepts by spatial relationships along with *must have* and *may have* modals. (This abstract description need not be readily translatable into words.) Of interest, too, is our ability to recognize an old scene viewed from a novel perspective, such as a furnished room photographed from a different entrance or a familiar street corner seen from the tenth floor of a nearby building. Such performances rely on a sort of extensive match-up of parts by analogy and deduction in processes properly labeled as visual problem solving; one or a few parts are identified, then other pieces are "predicted" to be in specific relationships to the identified parts, and so only a minimal amount of evidence may be required to trigger identification. Computer programs such as those of Evans (1963) and Winston (1970) can carry out simple match-ups, identifying corresponding or analogous objects in two scenes. For instance, Winston's program can easily decide whether two scenes are symmetrical to one another by just interchanging relations in one of the descriptions (*left of* and *right of*; *in front of* and *behind*). Evans' program has the ability to describe the difference between two descriptions (scenes *A* and *B*), which difference can then be used for computing a pictorial analogy to a new picture (scene *C*). However, neither of these programs yet approximates the range of visual problem-solving skills that the human can exhibit in recognition of transformations of visual patterns.

Recognition as Context Retrieval

In the preceding examples, recognition of an individual was treated as "pattern classification" of a detailed sort, and the evidence for individual recognition was retrieval of some associated name or label (e.g., "Tom Jones" or "Spot"). However, there are many other cases in which we indicate our recognition of a stimulus pattern by recalling various facts about it other than its name. For example, a standard fact that is often recorded in propositions encoding biographical episodes (events) is the spatiotemporal context in which the event occurred. HAM "automatically" encodes this acquisition context as one of the auxiliary bits of information it appends to each focal proposition it learns. Thus, it does not simply record the proposition "Nixon is an excellent President"; rather, it will encode this as an embedded performative such as "Governor Reagan said that Nixon is an excellent President." By thus recording the source or acquisition context of a proposition, HAM tends to avoid problems arising from what would otherwise be conflicting information.

If a given pattern, scene, or event is recognized as familiar in the sense of having been experienced long before, then for most people there follows a rapid memory search for its context: "*Where* or *when* have I had this experience before?" We vaguely recognize a face in the crowd and immediately try to recall where or when we met the person and what our interactions might have been. We recognize a travel slide as of a small French restaurant along the roadside outside Rheims where we toured seven years ago, and we recall sketchily the meal we ate, the proprietor, and other parts of the tour preceding and following the restaurant snapshot. We have thus located the place and the event in a network of associations laid down in memory according to the temporal flow of causal events and coincidental happenings.

The "recognition memory" studied in learning experiments by psychologists almost exclusively concerns this "retrieval of context" aspect. The experimental subject is asked to decide whether a particular stimulus item (typically a "known" item like a word) occurred in an artificially delimited context. For each test item, the subject is asked in essentials: "Have you seen this stimulus unit before in this context?" Typically the delimiting context is temporal, stipulated as "the most recent list of items" or "those items shown to you since the beginning of this session," or the like.

This class includes so-called "item recognition" experiments of the continuous (e.g., Shepard & Teghtsoonian, 1961) or blocked variety as well as probe-recognition experiments. In such experiments using, for example, lists of words, the test question when the subject is presented with the form CAT is not whether he has ever seen that unit before in his life, nor whether he recognizes it as a word, nor as a noun, nor whether he could recognize referents of the term; the question rather is whether he has seen this word within a prescribed earlier context of this experiment. As Neisser (1967) has said, such recognition judgments comprise an "involuted association experiment," since one is testing for a temporary association between the memory node corresponding to CAT and some hypothetical context element, LIST.

This viewpoint, of recognition as retrieval of contextual associations, was fully developed in an earlier paper (Anderson & Bower, 1972), and it will be only cursorily mentioned here in passing. There it was assumed that during presentation of a list of unrelated words which the subject was to memorize, the system was at least encoding propositions of the general form "In context C_i, I thought of (was presented with) word W_i." When later asked whether word W_i had occurred in the list context, the system uses W_i as a probe to try to retrieve some link to a relevant context C_i. If that can be retrieved and properly identified, then the subject will decide *yes* and thus be scored as demonstrating "recognition memory" for W_i. In that earlier paper, we speculated regarding the composition of the context cues. We envisaged that they would include cognitive elements corresponding to the subject's thoughts at the time of presentation of a given item as well as physical characteristics of the items. Prominent though not exclusive among such contextual elements would be an implicit verbalization or count, as though the subject were in effect saying to himself "List-N" as he was presented with successive items belonging to List-N in the experiment.

Recognition without Context Retrieval

In the preceding, we have identified the memory structure that serves to describe a concept, pattern, word, or proposition as separate from the memory structure that records the context in which it was experienced or was acquired. We discussed part of the process of "recognizing" as retrieval of contextual information. But the possibility clearly exists that we can "recognize" a stimulus configuration but can retrieve no context about where or when we experienced that pattern before. The stimulus matches a stored description, but that node is not connected to an acquisition context. The search for context typically does *not* occur with category recognition or individual recognition, although it could. Frequent stimulus patterns—one's friends and relatives, his house, office, car, etc.—are tacitly recognized and reacted to according to multiple demands of the day without searching for an acquisition context. To these frequent patterns or facts, we will search for a specific context only upon a specific query, "How did you first meet your wife?" or "When did you buy this car?" or "When did you first learn that George Washington was the first President of the U.S.A.?" But for many familiar patterns, information about their acquisition context has simply been lost, and queries about this context strike us as odd. For instance, each of us can recognize many thousands of words, but we are totally unable to supply details about how, when, and where we have learned them. Similarly, most people cannot remember the context of their first learning to recognize what is a photograph, a chair, a dog, or a fire. The learning contexts are surely buried in our distant childhoods.

To return to our main point, however, it is frequently the case that we recognize a pattern or scene but cannot retrieve any further information to go along with that recognition. We simply have a "gut-level" feeling of familiarity, which in our theory means that a very good match occurs between the current situation and some memory structure; but contextual facts are no longer retrievable from that memory structure.

Learning Patterns

The preceding section dealt with retrieval of contextual information, mentioning it as the paradigm for the usual laboratory studies of recognition memory. In those terms, a given stimulus (the item *cat*) accesses a prior *collection node* in memory; the only issue is whether appropriate contextual information can be retrieved from that node. But what about the means by which this collection node in memory was formed itself: Surely *cat* and *Tom Jones* were once novel patterns; how did our memories come to contain nodes representing these patterns?

The answer to this was actually given before in our discussion of pattern learning. In brief, when a given structural description of a pattern fails to retrieve a closely matching representation from memory, then the "learning routine" gets switched in; it tries to build into memory the labeled associations between nodes comprising the input tree. It may do this by merely noting and recording how the present description differs from an already known description (e.g., "a *table* is like a pedestal except it has four legs instead of one.").

Experimental psychologists see something close to this ab initio "learning from scratch" when they have their subjects learn "nonsense" materials such as consonant letter strings or randomly generated polyhedrons. For example, in a recognition memory experiment, the subject may have to learn to identify 15 different nonsense syllables, selecting them after each study trial from a set of distractors. At this rote level, HAM has no magical strategies to deal with such situations. It would simply learn the syllables as three-letter strings (i.e., node i comprises D followed by A followed by X).

The primary complication to this type of analysis of ab initio learning of nonsense materials is that adults employ various encoding strategies to avoid rote learning. In particular, they relate the nonsense to familiar things. Nonsense syllables are thus encoded in terms of a related word plus the transformation needed to reproduce the nonsense. Thus, DAXES might be encoded as "TAXES but with an initial D," and MIB as "MOB but with a middle I." Prytulak (1971) describes a number of such transformation schemes that people use, and shows that "difficult items" are those which convert to words only by use of a low-priority transformation. In any event, rather than learning a nonsense syllable directly, the subject stores (or tags) the closest word plus a difference. This strategy is in fact also used by Winston's (1970) concept-learning program discussed earlier. It builds up new concepts by adding distinguishers and/or new relations only already known concepts. Thus, a *table* is like a *pedestal* except it has four corner legs instead of a single center leg; it is like an *arch* except it has four rather than two legs and the top must be a brick lying down. Thus, if Winston's program had to store a table scene without having a memory node corresponding to a table model, it could be described as "a sort of pedestal but with four legs."

This idea, that a novel pattern is encoded as an old pattern plus modifiers, is very ancient in psychology. Woodworth (1938) referred to it as storage of a "schema-plus-correction." It is an encoding principle that avoids some of the brute rote learning that would otherwise have to be done. What is not obvious is how and why it makes the learning easier, and under what circumstances the strategy will be used. A plausible reason for its efficiency in some instances is that the strategy reduces the total number of new associative links to be formed. An illustrative example is shown in Figure 9.13: a possible "rote" propositional structure for learning DAXES is illustrated in Figure 9.13a, and it involves 32 separate associative links. The transformed code which is illustrated in Figure 9.13b (prefix D to AXES) involves 10 links, or 22 fewer than in the rote-learning case. To proceed to the conclusion, since fewer new associations would have to be learned for the transformed code, items so treated will be learned quicker and use of the strategy will pay off in reducing errors and cognitive strain.

Expectations and Perceptual Recognition

The preceding discussion has proceeded on the assumption that pattern identification was largely a function of the amount and quality of stimulus information. However, perceptions are in many ways like hypotheses or decisions

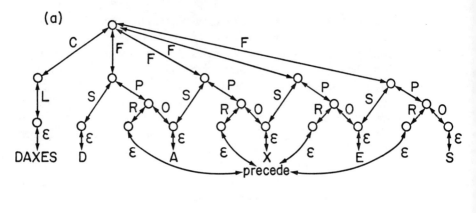

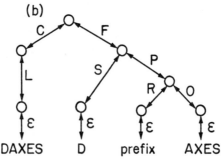

FIG. 9.13. Rote learning of DAXES (*a*) versus schema plus correction (*b*).

that the perceptual encoder makes about the stimulus situation, and these hypotheses and decisions can be shown to vary with "non-sensory" variables such as motivations, as well as with expectations established by the prevailing context (see Lindsay & Norman, 1972, pp. 131-147, for some review). When a given context establishes a particular word as the probable next stimulus, then less sensory information is required to identify that word. That is, the more probable is the stimulus pattern, the briefer and more degraded the sensory information can be and still yield accurate identification of the presented pattern.

Memory is surely involved in "computing" that a particular item is probable in a particular context. Cliches and well-worn phrases such as "How do you do" and "Mary had a little lamb" have highly predictable endings, and these endings could be smudged and blurred considerably and still be recognized. Clearly, the rest of the input sentence is treated like a retrieval cue for the blurred word. This reduces the number of plausible alternatives, and so fewer features of the blurred word are required in order to identify it. In terms used in statistical decision theory, we could say that the a posteriori odds in favor of the critical word being *lamb* are a function of the prior odds in favor of *lamb* (from the context) and the likelihood of particular features (e.g., tall letters at the ends) in a degraded stimulus presentation. Morton (1969) has offered a model whereby sensory and contextual information are combined to effect identification of a word. We accept but can add nothing important to Morton's analysis; we see no reason that his word recognition mechanisms could not be translated in toto into a word-recognition routine for HAM.

Although we have discussed pattern identification as a passive classification system, it is clear that active constructive activities are occasionally engaged; recognition becomes something akin to visual problem solving rather than passive classification. This phenomenon is subjectively prominent when we are trying to "make sense out of" a fragment of a picture or a mottled array of dark spots scattered about a paper. Figure 9.14 reproduces one such photograph. The initial impression is of just a random collection of dark blobs. However, when told that there is a familiar figure in the picture, one can almost feel himself focusing on different subareas and trying out different hypotheses. When one hits on the "dalmatian dog" hypothesis (nose forward, down, and left, near center of picture), it then becomes "transparently obvious." Moreover, upon a later presentation of the same picture, the dalmation dog is very likely to be seen and seen quickly. What is happening here? No one really knows in much detail. Every perceptual theorist agrees that the subject is searching through and testing a set of hypotheses, selecting particular pieces of the picture and filling in other gaps to fit a particular interpretation which is, almost literally, *projected onto* the amorphous and unstructured clutter that is the picture. If the misfit of internal model to reinterpreted clues in the picture exceeds a tolerance level, that interpretation is rejected and the search continues. Although this process is not difficult to describe generally, it seems to us to be very difficult to formulate it with sufficient detail for simulation purposes. Certainly, HAM is not up to such problem-solving feats.

An Overview of the Recognition Process

We have now examined the several types of recognition performance: recognition of classes, of individuals, and of familiar patterns, with or without retrieval of context. Examples would be, respectively, that I can recognize dogs, that one is Spot, and I first met Spot last week at a friend's house, or the dog is familiar but I cannot recall anything about him. In each of these cases we have supposed that the "perceptual parser" has extracted a relevant description of the critical features of the stimulus pattern and their interrelations. This description corresponds to a (possibly large) network of propositions and also constitutes the input to HAM. A "concept" or "perceptual category" corresponds, in HAM, to a stored description network. As a consequence of exposure to many variable instances, the original network has been modified, certain features have been dropped or added, some relations have been made mandatory, others optional, and so on. The concept network thus summarizes the information regarding class membership criteria abstracted from HAM's encounters with a series of instances of the class.

The description network of particular concepts is stored in memory, and the input network describing the current scene is sent to memory to find the best matching concept. The MATCH process described earlier in this chapter would be used for carrying out this memory search. The current program would report out the most specific or detailed concept giving the greatest degree of match to the input tree. Thus, given a clear perceptual description, it would say that a given

FIG. 9.14. Construction recognition processes are particularly prominent subjectively when one tries to make sense out of this fragmented picture.

pattern is "Spot" rather than saying "dog" or "hairy quadruped." Of course, the system could answer affirmatively to the question "Is the following a picture of a dog?" when shown a picture of Spot. In principle, this could be done either by identifying the individual *Spot*, then evoking the ϵ link to the concept *dog*; or the MATCH function itself, comparing the dog-template to the Spot-description, could be set to return a yes whenever a sufficient number of template features were matched, ignoring the extra features in the input that distinguish Spot from other dogs. This latter strategy is effective only when the test stimulus (Spot) is a subset of the question stimulus (dog).

As an incidental but relevant point here, it is obvious that with multiobject scenes, the question which is posed will itself direct the focus of attention. If the question is about a dog, the perceptual parser should not concentrate on encoding the mountains in the background of the picture. The question determines the way in which the picture will be processed. For the question "Is the black man tall?", a crowd scene would first be scanned to find a black man, and then check to see whether he is tall. But for the question "Is the tall man black?", the scanning would look first for a tall man, then check to see whether he is black.

To return to our comparison of recognitive types, all of these forms—class or individual recognition with or without retrieval of context—can be represented and implemented in HAM in exactly the same way. Basically, the "concept" or "event" in memory is a description network; the input is a description network; HAM's MATCH process brings them together.

The MATCH process reports out a measure of the maximal "degree of match," and we presume that this measure corresponds to the feeling of familiarity which we experience in recognition. The perceptual description may also have further information attached to its collection node—facts known about the pattern, such as its context of acquisition. This link to the context is what is accessed in the typical laboratory studies of "recognition memory" using familiar stimuli. HAM would first access the memory node corresponding to the test item CAT, and then it would check to see whether the most recent context associated to that node is a prototype of the relevant experimental context (e.g., LIST-1). This suggests that if the test stimulus itself is degraded, somewhat altered, or just poorly learned, the feeling of familiarity might be enhanced by supplying an acquisition context as an additional cue. For example, we may not fully recognize a person until he reminds us of where we had met before and of other events associated with that meeting. These extra bits of information increase the overall matching score and our sense of familiarity with the person's appearance.

A topic not specifically discussed in this last section is recognition of sentences and propositions, but our treatment of such matters is detailed in earlier sections of this chapter. It is with respect to these materials that our theory of recognition is most explicitly formulated. It is also with these materials that we have attempted careful empirical tests of this theory. In this section we have been trying to outline how the theory would generalize to the nonlinguistic domain. In summary, the associative theory embodied in HAM would seem capable in principle of dealing with all the more salient forms of recognition we have discussed. What is lacking in our efforts is an explicit development of a "perceptual parser," that wondrous machine which will sort out the relevant information from the noise in the stimulus array and deliver up to HAM a well-formed description-tree of just the critical variables and relations. Those working on scene-analysis programs know that *that* is the really tough problem. We have not worked on it at all, since our main concern has been with sentence memory. Our discussion therefore relies very heavily on the scene-analysis programs of Guzman (1968) and Winston (1970), and their logical extensions, and we have tried to show how the scene descriptions output by their programs could serve as the input to HAM's memory. Within the purview of that discussion, HAM seems to provide a reasonable hypothesis for understanding how recognition performances come about.

REFERENCES

Anderson, J. R., & Bower, G. H. Recognition and retrieval processes in free recall. *Psychological Review*, 1972, 79, 97–123.

Evans, T. G. A heuristic program to solve geometric-analogy problems. Unpublished doctoral dissertation, M.I.T., 1963.

Guzman, A. Computer recognition of three-dimensional objects in a visual scene. M.I.T. Artificial Intelligence Laboratory Project MAC-TR-59, 1968.

Johnson, N. F. Sequential verbal behavior. In T. R. Dixon & D. L. Horton (Eds.), *Verbal behavior and general behavior theory*. Englewood Cliffs, N. J.: Prentice-Hall, 1968.

Lindsay, P. H., & Norman, D. A. *Human information processing: An introduction to psychology*. New York: Academic Press, 1972.

Minsky, M., & Papert, S. *Perceptrons*. Cambridge, Mass.: M.I.T. Press, 1969.

Morton, J. The interaction of information in word recognition. *Psychological Review*, 1969, 76, 165–178.

Neisser, U. *Cognitive psychology*. New York: Appleton-Century-Crofts, 1967.

Prytulak, L. S. Natural language mediation. *Cognitive Psychology*, 1971, 2, 1–56.

Quillian, M. R. Semantic memory. In M. Minsky (Ed.), *Semantic information processing*. Cambridge, Mass.: M.I.T. Press, 1968.

Rosenberg, S. Associative facilitation in the recall and recognition of nouns embedded in connected discourse. *Journal of Experimental Psychology*, 1968, 78, 254–260. (a)

Rosenberg, S. Association and phrase structure in sentence recall. *Journal of Verbal Learning and Verbal Behavior*, 1968, 7, 1077–1081. (b)

Rosenberg, S. The recall of verbal material accompanying semantically poorly-integrated sentences. *Journal of Verbal Learning and Verbal Behavior*, 1969, 8, 732–736.

Rosenberg, S. Source of facilitation in recall of context material from high-association discourse. *Journal of Experimental Psychology*, 1970, 83, 504–505.

Shepard, R. N., & Teghtsoonian, M. Retention of information under conditions approaching a steady state. *Journal of Experimental Psychology*, 1961, 62, 302–309.

Tieman, D. G. Recognition memory for comparative sentences. Unpublished doctoral dissertation, Stanford University, 1971.

Winston, P. H. Learning structural descriptions from examples. M.I.T. Artificial Intelligence Laboratory Project AI-TR-231, 1970.

Woodworth, R. S. *Experimental psychology*. New York: Henry Holt, 1938.

10
MODEL FOR SENTENCE LEARNING

> *In thus deriving memory from association, it is never to be forgotten that every concrete memory-process is by no means a simple process, but is made up of a large number of elementary processes.*
>
> —*Wilhelm Wundt*

10.1. THE MATHEMATICAL FORMULATION

In this chapter we will develop our theory regarding the encoding of sentences into memory, provide an explicit mathematical (probabilistic) model of the process, and report several experimental tests of this explicit model. Memory for sentences has been one of the favored ways to study their mental representation. The general working premise has been that contingencies in recall of sentential elements reflect proximities of the elements in the underlying mnemonic representation of the sentence. We shall not review here the research of others using this strategy, but will refer the interested reader to reviews by Fillenbaum (1971) or Wanner (1968).

Past research efforts generally have lacked an explicit model of how a particular mnemonic representation is derived from the input, how it is stored, and how it is retrieved—all of which processes result in a particular pattern of recall probabilities of various sentential fragments. HAM provides just such a possible theory, which we will now explicate.

When HAM hears a sentence such as our standard "In a park a hippie touched a debutante," it has direct access to the word nodes in memory; it also has in working memory the parsed tree structure shown in Figure 10.1, in which lowercase letters denote newly created memory nodes which serve to group together lower elements in the labeled graph structure. The concepts or ideas are also connected to the actual words of the sentence by the relations labeled W. The concept nodes and their word associations already exist in memory. All the structure above the concept nodes in Figure 10.1 is new and is recording the novel information in the

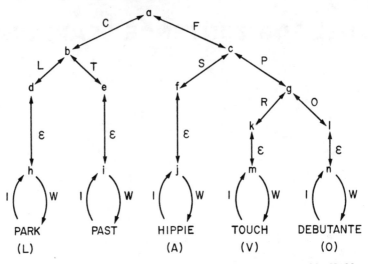

FIG. 10.1. An example of a propositional representation generated by HAM.

sentence. To encode this sentence into memory, each of the 13 links above the concept nodes must be transformed into long-term memory associations. Once a link is encoded as an association, it may be evoked in the future to retrieve information about the sentence. In later chapters (Chapters 11, 13, 14, and 15), an extensive discussion is given about matters such as guessing and deductive strategies evoked by the subject when he is asked about a proposition not explicitly recorded in memory, about implicit elaborations a subject will make when hearing the overtly stated propositions, and about interference between propositions and consequent forgetting of information. All these matters serve to enrich and complicate the study of human memory. However, in the verbatim memory tests used in the research under immediate discussion, we hope that such complicating factors have been kept to a minimum. The principal determinant of recall patterns should be the stochastic process by which links in an input tree like Figure 10.1 are converted into long-term memory associations.

We assume that the linkages between nodes in memory mechanistically determine what the subject can recall. Thus in Figure 10.1, for the subject to recall L to A there must be an intact associative path between the concept node for L and the concept node for A. If any association is missing in the path, recall will fail. In addition, for successful recall the I connection from the word A must be intact as must the W connection to the word L. For the subject to recall A to L, the same interidea associative path must be intact as well as the W connection to A and the I connection from L. By use of these W and I connections we will be able to capture the role of response availability and stimulus effectiveness in recall. The effects of the sentential representation will be reflected by the interidea associations. In this way, we hope to separate three factors that have been confounded in past research on sentence memory.

The Encoding of Associations

This conception of sentence memory may be converted into a stochastic model that delivers detailed predictions about patterns in sentence recall. All predictions will depend on the simple assumption that the probability of encoding an input link into long-term memory will depend solely on how long that link resides in working memory. In particular, this probability is assumed to be independent of how many other links are being encoded from working memory, and it is independent of how many of these links or which ones are successfully encoded.

Thus, there is no process-versus-capacity tradeoff such that the more links to be stored, the less effort devoted to the formation of any particular one link. There is only one limitation on the formation of associations, and that is the number of links that can be held in working memory. As we discussed in Section 8.2, this in turn is determined by the number of long-term memory nodes that must be recruited to support the input structure. We place only this one restriction on encoding input simply in the interest of parsimony. There is no need to assume multiple restrictions until data can be marshalled to justifiy their postulation. We shall assume a simple relationship between the time t an input link resides in memory and the probability that it is encoded into memory as an association; namely, there is an exponential distribution of times at which the encoding will succeed. The mean of the distribution will be denoted as a. Thus, letting $f(t)$ represent the probability density for forming an association, the following equation holds:

$$f(t) = \frac{1}{a} e^{-t/a} \qquad (1)$$

Letting $p(t)$ denote the probability of forming an association by time t, Equation (2) follows by integrating Equation (1):

$$p(t) = 1 - e^{-t/a} \qquad (2)$$

For reasons of parsimony, it is assumed that for a particular input tree, the parameter a is constant for all associations in that input.

Given these assumptions, some interesting facts may be derived about the encoding of an input that has n associative links. First, consider how many associations would be established if the input were studied for t seconds. The number of associations formed, k, is binomially distributed with parameters $(1 - e^{-t/a})$ and n:

$$p(k = i) = \binom{n}{i}(1 - e^{-t/a})^i (e^{-t/a})^{n-i} \qquad (3)$$

The mean number of associations formed, $E(k)$, is:

$$E(k) = n(1 - e^{-t/a}) \tag{4}$$

A related question is how long it will take to encode an input with n associations. Let T_n be the time to encode n associations. Interesting properties of the probability density of T_n depend upon three facts: (a) the time between the formation of the ith and $(i+1)$st association (out of n) will be exponentially distributed with parameter $a/(n-i)$; (b) the "interarrival" times in (a) are independent; and (c) T_n is the sum of these n interarrival times. It follows from these facts that T_n has a generalized gamma distribution (see McGill, 1963) with mean and variance as follows:

$$E(T_n) = \sum_{L=1}^{n} \frac{1}{L} \tag{5}$$

$$Var(T_n) = a^2 \sum_{L=1}^{n} \frac{1}{L^2} \tag{6}$$

The Central-Limit Theorem applies to T_n since it is a sum of independently distributed random variables. Therefore, as n becomes large, the distribution of T_n will tend to a normal distribution with the mean and variance given by Equations (5) and (6).

With this as background, let us now consider what might happen when a subject is asked to remember the sentence "In a park a hippie touched a debutante." The input structure of Figure 10.1 would be set up temporarily in working memory, and the subject would attempt to encode all 13 interidea links in the input tree. For illustration, let us suppose that he succeeds in encoding 11 of the 13 associations during the study trial and is left with the memory structure of Figure 10.2 as his record of the sentence. When we later probe his memory for the sentence with the word "hippie," the subject would recall, "I remember the hippie did something to the debutante, but I can't remember what or where."

This example illustrates the basic experimental paradigm that will concern us in this chapter. That is, after studying a sequence of unrelated sentences, a subject is presented with parts of the sentences he has studied and is asked to recall the remainder. The structural assumptions of the theory plus its encoding assumptions deliver interesting predictions about the patterns of recall that should be obtained in such experiments. For instance, consider the structure of the input in Figure 10.1. Note that V is closer in number of links to O than it is to L or A. Therefore, V should be a better cue for O simply because fewer associative links have to be established to connect the two. These are the sort of phenomena that are to be captured in the mathematical predictions derived from the model. Unfortunately, the mathematical model that will generate empirically viable predictions must be more complicated than indicated so far. Let us therefore begin to uncover these mathematical complications.

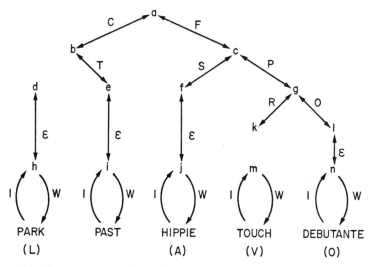

FIG. 10.2. A partial encoding of the sentence "In the park the hippie touched the debutante."

Subject and Item Differences

A first problem concerns the fact that the model, as presented so far, only describes what would happen for a single subject for a single sentence. However, the data to be predicted is average data taken from many subjects studying many different sentences. Individual subjects vary enormously in the ability they display in learning. Also, an individual subject will vary in how well he remembers different sentences. His mind will wander during the study of one sentence, whereas he may concentrate very hard while studying another sentence. The problem, then, is that while it may be reasonable to assume that the learning paramater a is constant across all associations to be formed within a sentence, it is completely implausible to assume that the parameter will be the same across sentences in a pool of observations taken from many subjects.

If we ignored this problem and fit the model to average data, assuming a constant parameter a for all sentences, what would be the consequences? Basically, the model would underpredict the frequency with which subjects recall the total sentence or recall nothing at all. The parameter a estimated from average data would be approximately the mean of the distribution of the parameter a across individual sentences and subjects in the sample. For sentences from the pool with a less than the mean we would observe more complete failures to recall than predicted, whereas for sentences with a higher than the mean we would observe much more total recall than predicted. In fact, when we tried to predict recall data with an average parameter a we consistently underpredicted the amount of all-or-none recall.

What is needed to rigorously apply the model to average data is information about the distribution of the parameter a across individual sentences in the observation pool. We will hypothesize a particular probability density of the parameter a over the sentences for the typical experiment. This hypothesis has only two things to commend it: It does not seem unreasonable a priori, and it leads to mathematically tractable results. Our hypothesis concerns the probability density of the reciprocal of a, which gives us the *speed* or *rate* at which associations are formed. We will assume that the probability density of the rate, $1/a$, is itself an exponential distribution with mean b:

$$f\left(\frac{1}{a}\right) = \frac{1}{b} e^{-1/ba} \tag{7}$$

The probability density of a can now be determined by a simple change of variable, viz.,

$$f(a) = \frac{1}{ba^2} e^{-1/ba} \tag{8}$$

One is really interested in the probability distribution of $p(t)$, the probability of forming an association in t seconds. It can be computed by another change of variable using Equations (2) and (8):

$$f[p(t)] = \frac{1}{tb} [1 - p(t)]^{-(tb-1)/tb} \tag{9}$$

This is a special case of the beta distribution which is defined as:

$$f(x) = \frac{\Gamma(\alpha + \beta)}{\Gamma(\alpha)\Gamma(\beta)} x^{\alpha-1}(1 - x)^{\beta-1} \tag{10}$$

where Γ denotes the gamma function. Our distribution has the parameter $\alpha = 1$ and $\beta = 1/tb$. The mean of this distribution, $E[p(t)]$, is

$$E[p(t)] = \frac{tb}{tb + 1} \tag{11}$$

and its variance is

$$Var[p(t)] = \frac{1}{2tb + 1}\left[\frac{tb}{tb + 1}\right]^2 \tag{12}$$

The effective parameter in this probability density is tb, which is the product of the time available for encoding, t, and the overall mean rate of encoding, b. Figure 10.3 illustrates how the probability density, $f[p(t)]$, will vary with the parameter tb. The densities are well behaved in that they shift towards 1 as tb increases. That is, the probability of forming an association will increase both with increases in the encoding time, t, and with increases in the mean encoding rate for the population of sentences, b.

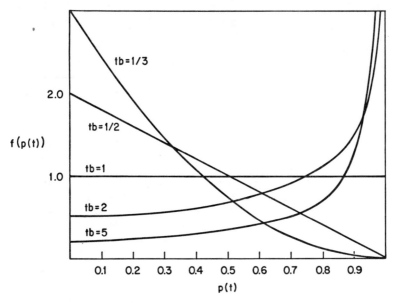

FIG. 10.3. The probability density $f[p(t)]$ for various values of tb.

To derive predictions about the average recall patterns of sentences, we need to determine the value of $Q(k, n)$, which is the probability of encoding a particular k of the n associations that are in working memory. Its value is given by the following integral:

$$Q(k, n) = \int_0^1 p(t)^k [1 - p(t)]^{n-k} f[p(t)] \, dp(t) \tag{13}$$

To explain this equation, we first are determining the probability, $p(t)^k [1 - p(t)]^{n-k}$ of forming a particular k association in the input for each value of $p(t)$, weighting this by the probability density $f[p(t)]$ at that value, and integrating this over the 0 to 1 domain of $f[p(t)]$. This integration gives the following:

$$Q(k, n) = \frac{1}{tbn + 1} \prod_{i=1}^{k} \frac{tbi}{tb(n - 1) + 1} \tag{14}$$

Again, the effective parameter is tb. To illustrate $Q(k, n)$, Table 10.1 shows it for n up to 12 when $tb = 1$. When $tb = 1, E[p(t)] = tb/(tb+1) = .5$. Note that although the mean probability of forming a single association is .5, the probability of forming n out of n associations is much higher than $.5^n$ and the probability of forming 0 out of n associations is similarly much higher than $.5^n$. The function $Q(k, n)$ thus shows a marked deviation in the direction of all-or-none encoding of

TABLE 10.1

Values of $Q(k, n)$, the Likelihood of Forming k Out of n Possible Associations.
The Parameter tb is 1.

						n						
k	1	2	3	4	5	6	7	8	9	10	11	12
0	.500	.333	.250	.200	.167	.143	.1250	.1111	.1000	.0909	.0833	.0769
1	.500	.167	.083	.050	.033	.024	.0179	.0139	.0111	.0091	.0076	.0064
2		.333	.083	.033	.017	.010	.0060	.0040	.0028	.0020	.0015	.0012
3			.250	.050	.017	.007	.0036	.0020	.0012	.0008	.0005	.0003
4				.200	.033	.010	.0036	.0016	.0008	.0004	.0003	.0002
5					.167	.024	.0060	.0020	.0008	.0004	.0002	.0001
6						.143	.0179	.0040	.0012	.0004	.0002	.0001
7							.1250	.0139	.0028	.0008	.0003	.0001
8								.1111	.0111	.0020	.0005	.0002
9									.1000	.0091	.0015	.0003
10										.0909	.0076	.0012
11											.0833	.0064
12												.0769

the associations. The function $Q(k, n)$ represents how the probabilities of individual associations covary across sentences in the data pool.

Response Availability Parameters

In fitting this model to data, a grid search will be performed over the values of tb to find a minimum chi-square estimate. However, in fitting this model to data it is necessary to estimate more parameters than just tb. The problem is that the parameter tb only governs the formation of *interidea* associations, but these associations in themselves will not permit recall of the words in the sentence. One needs to get from these ideas to the appropriate words. For instance, even if the subject perfectly encoded the input of Figure 10.1, he would not be guaranteed verbatim recall of the words "park," "hippie," "touch," and "debutante." The subject would still have to be able to get from the terminal concept nodes in the encoding of the sentence to the corresponding word nodes. The process by which one moves from a concept to a word is not well worked out in the model, but it is clear that the transition will not always be perfect. An illustration of the difficulty is the common experience of not being able to "find the words" to express an idea. A second problem involves word synonymy. That is, if more than one word expresses the same concept (e.g., postman and mailman), how does the subject remember which was the correct word he heard? We are not able to offer any enlightening solutions to these matters. We sidestep the matter by merely noting that *on the average* there will be some probability, r, of getting from the concept to the verbatim correct word and that this probability will, in general, be less than one. This probability will serve to reflect the availability of the particular word as a response to the concept.

In this research a different value of r has been estimated for each type of word in the sentence that must be recalled. There are two reasons for doing this. First, it is not unreasonable to suppose that the difficulty in getting from the concept to an appropriate word will be different for different classes of words (e.g., locations versus verbs). Second, the value of r tends to reflect biases in the encoding process. For example, the subject might focus on the first or last word in the sentence at the expense of others. One consequence of this focusing might be that the probability of getting from concept to word would be higher. Of course, it is also possible that focusing may affect the parameter a which governs the probability of forming a particular association, rather than just response availability. If focusing does have this effect, then permitting different values of r helps protect the model from disconfirmation because of that failure of assumption. A constant value of a had been assumed only for purposes of simplicity and tractability. So it would not be an interesting failure of the model in any case.

Covariation of the r_i

For each sentence, then, there is a set of parameters r_i. Presumably, the probability r_i will vary across sentences just as the probability, $p(t)$, of forming interidea associations. We previously introduced a hypothesis of how the probabilities, $p(t)$, of forming individual idea-to-idea associations within a sentence covaried across sentences. For similar reasons, the parameters r_i for different responses within a sentence may be expected to covary across sentences—that is, for some sentences in the pool these parameters will all be high, and for other sentences they will all be low. The task of producing a model of this covariance is more difficult than the previous covariance for two reasons. First, the different r_i's have different means and distributions, whereas we could assume one distribution $f[p(t)]$ for all the associative links in a sentence. Secondly, we have no clear idea of what the mechanisms are that permit the idea-to-word transitions. Therefore it is difficult to justify any probabilistic model of their effect.

Our solution to the second problem was to adopt, arbitrarily, the probability density adopted for $p(t)$. So, adapting Equation (9) we have:

$$f(r_i) = \frac{1}{\alpha_i} (1 - r_i)^{-(\alpha_i - 1)/\alpha_i} \tag{15}$$

This gives the distribution of r_i across sentences in the observation pool. There was no strong justification for this probability density of r_i except that it was well behaved and served us well in the past. In equation (15) α_i plays the same role as tb in Equation (9). We will also assume that $\alpha_i = tb_i$, where t is study time and b_i is the rate parameter. Hence, α_i should increase with study time or the mean encoding rate for word i, b_i.

Let us now turn to the difficult problem of how to express the covariance of these different distributions of r_i. With respect to the associations, it was assumed that $p(t)$ for each association within a sentence was identical. We cannot assume that different parameters r_i and r_j are identical for each sentence because r_i and r_j have different densities across sentences. Rather, we will assume that within a single sentence r_i and r_j will be associated with the same cumulative probability in the population. That is, for a particular sentence, r_i may be .7 and r_j may be .9, but the

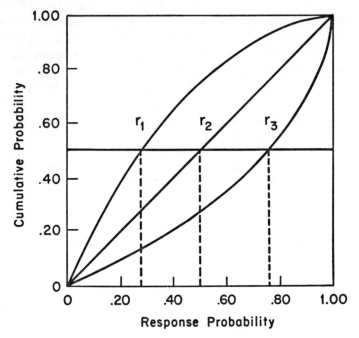

FIG. 10.4. Cumulative distributions of response probabilities.

area of the probability density to the left of r_i will be identical to the probability area to the left of r_j. That is to say, r_i and r_j for a particular sentence have the same "percentile scores" in their respective distributions.

Figure 10.4 illustrates what is being assumed. Three cumulative distributions of response probabilities are shown—for response 1 with $\alpha_1 = .5$; for response 2 with $\alpha_2 = 1.0$; and for response 3 with $\alpha_3 = 2.0$. The horizontal line intersecting the ordinate at .5 represents a sentence at the 50th percentile. The abscissa value at which it intersects the ith cumulative distribution gives the value of r_i for that sentence. In this case, we have $r_1 = .29; r_2 = .50;$ and $r_3 = .75$ for this sentence.

Probabilities of Response Availability Patterns

We want eventually to derive the probability that a specific k out of n idea-to-word associations are intact. In order to begin this computation we will need the cumulative distribution, F, for r_i, which is:

$$F(r_i) = 1 - (1 - r_i)^{1/\alpha_i} \tag{16}$$

From Equation (16) r_i can be expressed as a function of $F(r_i)$:

$$r_i = 1 - [1 - F(r_i)]^{\alpha_i} \tag{17}$$

Letting $q_i = 1 - r_i$ denote the probability that the idea-to-word connection fails, and letting $X = 1 - F(r_i)$, the following simple equation obtains from Equation

(17):

$$q_i = X^{\alpha_i} \tag{18}$$

The variable $X = 1 - F(r_i)$ is just the converse of the cumulative probability. For any i (i indexes a particular word), X has a simple density

$$f(X) = 1 \qquad 0 \leqslant X \leqslant 1 \tag{19}$$

Since all response probabilities for a single sentence have the same cumulative probability, all q_i will be functions of the same random variable, X. Therefore, to find the probability that *no* idea-to-word connections are established out of n, we need only to solve the following integral:

$$q_{12...n} = \int_0^1 \prod_i^n X^{\alpha_i} dX \tag{20}$$

On the left-hand side of Equation (20), we are using $q_{12...n}$ to denote that the idea-to-word connections are not established for words 1 through n. On the right-hand side of Equation (20), i indexes the n words. Equation (20) is derived from Equation (18), which expresses each q_i as a function of the common variable X, and from Equation (19), which gives the probability density of X. Equation (20) is weighting the value of the product Πq_i at each value of X by the probability density of X. Integrating, we find:

$$q_{12...n} = \frac{1}{\left(\sum\limits_i^n \alpha_i + 1 \right)} \tag{21}$$

Equation (21) gives the probability of having no responses available, assuming the probability of priming any response within a single sentence is identical in "percentile score" to any other response probability.

We need to be able to calculate the probability of each possible combination of availability and nonavailability of the individual responses (idea-word links). Equation (21) is sufficient for this purpose. The notation $r_{ab...c}q_{xy...z}$ will be used to denote the probability that responses a, b, ..., and c are available but responses x, y, ..., and z are not. We will illustrate its use with a simple example where we are concerned with two responses, word 1 and word 2. From Equation (20) the probability that both words are unavailable, q_{12}, is $1/(\alpha_1 + \alpha_2 + 1)$. We can also calculate from Equation (20) the marginal probability $r_1 q_2$, that response 1 is available and response 2 is not: $r_1 q_2 = q_2 - q_{12}$. Similarly, we can calculate the probability that response 2 is available, but response 1 is not: $r_2 q_1 = q_1 - q_{12}$. Finally, we can calculate the probability that both responses are available: $r_{12} = 1 - r_1 q_2 - r_2 q_1 - q_{12}$. These provide the probability of all four combinations

TABLE 10.2

Example Computation of Response Probabilities

	Available		Not available	
Response 2 Available	$r_{12} = \dfrac{\alpha_1 \alpha_2 (\alpha_1 + \alpha_2 + 2)}{(\alpha_1 + 1)(\alpha_2 + 1)(\alpha_1 + \alpha_2 + 1)}$		$r_2 q_1 = \dfrac{\alpha_2}{(\alpha_1 + \alpha_2 + 1)(\alpha_1 + 1)}$	$\dfrac{\alpha_2}{\alpha_2 + 1}$
Not available	$r_2 q_1 = \dfrac{\alpha_1}{(\alpha_1 + \alpha_2 + 1)(\alpha_2 + 1)}$		$q_{12} = \dfrac{1}{(\alpha_1 + \alpha_2 + 1)}$	$\dfrac{1}{\alpha_2 + 1}$
Total	$\dfrac{\alpha_1}{(\alpha_1 + 1)}$		$\dfrac{1}{(\alpha_1 + 1)}$	1

of availability and nonavailability of the two responses. These calculations are summarized in Table 10.2. This method can be generalized to any number of responses. That is, with Equation (21) one can calculate the probability of any combination of available and unavailable responses.

This, then, is the method by which the availability of various combinations of responses will be determined. Note that while the availability of one response covaries with that of another, these probabilities of responses, r_i, do not covary with the probability, $p(t)$, of establishing idea-to-idea associations. Different processes underlie these two mechanisms, and there is no reason to suppose that they will covary.

Stimulus-Cueing Parameters

One issue remains before turning to the experimental data. Just as it is not certain that the subject can get from a concept to a word, it is uncertain that he can get from the cue word to the concept. Words are notorious for their multiple meanings, and it is unclear how the subject manages to revive the appropriate interpretation of the word when he is cued. We have finessed this problem of how a cue word contacts a concept in the same way we finessed the problem of how a concept contacted a word. That is, we introduce a parameter, s_i, that is the probability that the cue word i makes contact with its appropriate concept. Just as with the response probabilities, a separate stimulus-cueing probability will be estimated for each word type in the sentence. These parameters tend to reflect varying stimulus effectiveness. In addition, the probabilities s_i will tend to reflect focusing and encoding biases just as had the probabilities r_i. We have not bothered to worry about possible covariances among these s_i parameters.

Summary

The mathematical complications are now at an end, and we are ready to apply our model to experimental data. We should emphasize how we have separately identified three components that have been confounded in past experimentation: The parameters r_i represent varying response availability; the parameters s_i the varying stimulus effectiveness, and the configuration of interidea associations the effects of sentential representation. Not surprisingly, to obtain separate estimates of all these factors will require an experimental design much more complicated than previous research efforts.

Our principle motivation in the experimentation will be to confirm hypotheses about the exact details of the sentential representation. One source of support for this representation will be reasonably satisfactory fits of our predictions to average data. However, as just seen, we have been forced to make a number of rather arbitrary assumptions to generate a quantitative model that yields satisfactory predictions. These assumptions were made to take account of the indisputable facts that subjects do differ a great deal in their ability, that they will favor one sentence over another in amount of processing, and that some words are more effective cues or better responses than others. Since these arbitrary assumptions play an important role in generating quantitative predictions, it would be a mistake to attach too much concern to the exact quantitative predictions of the model. Equal importance should be assigned to the qualitative predictions about ordinal trends in the data; these follow fairly directly from the sentential representation without the intercession of the mathematical model. In the analysis of the experiments, we will devote equal attention to both the qualitative and the quantitative predictions.

10.2. EXPERIMENT 1: LOCATION-AGENT-VERB-OBJECT

This experiment was the simplest of the four to be reported in this chapter. The sentences learned had the structure of location-agent-verb-object (L, A, V, O) constructions as illustrated in Figure 10.1; that is, all sentences were of the paradigmatic form "In the park the hippie touched the debutante." Each subject studied a different set of 72 sentences constructed by randomly selecting locations, agents, verbs, and objects from sets of 72 words for each function. These 72 sentences were randomly divided into three lists of 24 sentences. Each list of 24 sentences was studied twice in succession in the same order at a 10-second rate. This pair of study trials was followed by one cued recall test for that list of 24 sentences. The sentences were tested in the same order that they had been studied, and verbatim recall was requested.

Memory for the sentences in this experiment, and in the following three in this chapter, was tested by the method of incremental cueing. This involves testing each sentence with three successive cues, with each additional cue providing further information about the sentence. The first of the three cues presented just one of the four content words (L, A, V, or O), and the subject was given 30 seconds to recall (in writing) the missing three content words. The second cue followed immediately and contained the content word of the first plus an additional content word; the subject had 20 seconds to try to recall the two missing words. The third cue which then followed added another content word to the second cue, and the subject had 10 seconds to recall the one content word that was still missing from the original sentence. Thus, a subject might see the following sequence of cues:

```
IN THE         THE HIPPIE     THE
IN THE PARK THE HIPPIE         THE
IN THE PARK THE HIPPIE         THE DEBUTANTE.
```

There are 24 possible ways to create a set of three cues in this manner (4 content words to choose from for the first cue, 3 content words left to choose from for the second cue; and then 2 content words for the third cue, which is 4 x 3 x 2 = 24). Each possible sequence of cues was randomly assigned to one of the 24 sentences in each list.

After going through the first list of 24 sentences in this manner, the subjects went through the other two lists of 24 sentences in the identical manner. The study sentences and test cues were presented to the subjects on IBM cards. Before the experiment began, the exact nature of the experiment and the types of recall cues were described in considerable detail to the subjects. The total experimental session lasted about 100 minutes. A total of 41 subjects were run in the experiment.

Qualitative Results

All of the qualitative predictions for this experiment rely on the assumption that V and O are closer together in the input tree (see Figure 10.1) than either one is to either L or A. The predictions concern which words are better cues for which others, and which words tend to be recalled together. The only data that is informative on these issues comes from sentences that are partially recalled. If the sentence is perfectly recalled or not recalled at all, then there is no information about the proximity of elements in the sentence. Unfortunately, in this experiment there was a considerable portion of total recall (12%) or complete nonrecall (50%). Therefore, these predictions will be concerned with the trends in only the 38% of the data where partial sentence recall was obtained.

The first prediction is a particularly intriguing one. To illustrate it, consider this hypothetical situation: suppose the subject is cued with L and recalls V but nothing else. Then he is cued with L plus A. According to the tree structure in Figure 10.1, adding A in this case should never lead to recall of the O. If the subject were able to recall V to the first cue of the L then he must have retrieved the predicate node. In theory, the reason that he failed to recall O to the L cue must have been due to a fault in the path from the predicate node to the O response. Therefore, he should not be able to recall O to the later L-plus-A cue because O recall to this cue still demands an intact path from the predicate node to O.

The structural basis for such predictions can be made more salient by simplifying the graph structure of Figure 10.1, aggregating together nodes and links of no interest at the moment. This simplified structure is shown in Figure 10.5; the critical nodes F (fact) and P (predicate) from Figure 10.1 are preserved here, whereas all other links and nodes connecting these to the L, A, V, and O elements have been collapsed. In this diagram the prediction above is clearer: if L causes recall of V but not O, then the associative path F to P is intact, while the P-to-O path is missing; therefore, adding an A-plus-L cue cannot cause recall of O.

In contrast to the above prediction, consider this scenario: The subject is cued with L and can only recall A. Then, if he is cued with L-plus-V, it should be possible (according to Figure 10.5) for him to recall both A and O. This recall pattern could happen if the predicate link were not established from the fact node to the predicate node whereas all other links were formed. Thus, when given the L-only cue, the subject could retrieve A, but would be unable to retrieve the predicate node to recall either V or O. But when cued with V, he could reach the

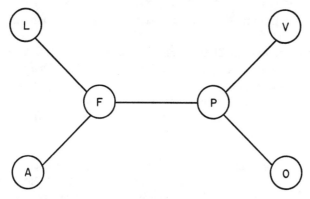

FIG. 10.5. Simplified graph of the memory structure in Figure 10.1, collapsing over nonessential nodes and links.

predicate node and so retrieve O. To summarize the significance of these two examples, when one word is recalled to a first cue, the possibility of further recall to a later cue depends upon the identity of the first word recalled.

So we eagerly went to the data to determine if this prediction would be confirmed. The results were rather disappointing. We averaged together all those situations when the model predicts the possibility of a second recall and all those when it does not. The former are called *predicted second recalls* and the latter *unpredicted second recalls.* There were 5.9% (14 of 239 opportunities) unpredicted second recalls. In the situation where recall was expected, there were only slightly more—6.5% (10 of 155 opportunities). However, there are complications in the data that make this outcome difficult to interpret. To illustrate, consider the following scenario: The subject is cued with L and recalls A. Then he is cued with L and A. Certainly, on almost any theory, he should not recall anything further. However, the data showed such further recall in 4.1% of such circumstances. Such events will be referred to as *recalls to inadequate stimuli.* It is easy to imagine conditions that might underlie these 4.1% of the cases. The subject may have been very unsure even about his recall of one word and may have inhibited his recall of another. However, upon learning that his recall of the first word was correct, he might gain the confidence to venture a second. The subject may have been in a tip-of-the-tongue state with respect to a word and only retrieved it when the second cue was presented. There are innumerable such possible explanations for these recalls to inadequate stimuli.

The point is, of course, that many of the unpredicted second recalls may be due to the same sources as the recalls to inadequate stimuli. The real test of our theory would seem to be the difference between the predicted and the unpredicted second recalls. This difference was only slightly in favor of the model—6.5% versus 5.9%. However, it should be pointed out that the model does not expect a large difference. According to the mathematical model fitted to the data and presented later, there should only be 4.8% predicted second recalls and, of course, 0% unpredicted second recalls. So, while this prediction about second recalls is intriguing in principle, it turned out to be rather indecisive in this experiment. It will prove a more informative statistic in later experiments where there was more partial recall.

We now examine two qualitative statistics that were more informative. The first statistic concerns recall of one word to the first cue *conditional* upon recall of a second word to that cue. We will illustrate these predictions again with respect to Figure 10.5. Suppose that the subject is cued with L and he recalls A. What is the probability that he will also recall O to this cue? For successful recall of A, the theory says that there must have been an intact associative path from L to the fact node F. Therefore, conditional on recall of A, the probability of O is the probability that there is an intact link from node F to the predicate node P *and* an intact path from the predicate node P to the object word O. Now, contrast this situation to a second situation in which we conditionalize upon V recall to the L-only cue. The theory infers that there is an intact path from the L to the predicate node P, and hence the conditional probability of O recall is just the probability of an intact path from the predicate node to O. Therefore, the conditional probability of O recall in this situation is higher than in the former, because only in this circumstance is it known that the predicate link between the fact node and the predicate node is intact.

So, conditional on which words are recalled, we can sometimes only know that the S has access to the fact node (e.g., recall of A to L), sometimes only that he has access to the predicate node (e.g., recall of V to O), and sometimes that he has access to both (e.g., recall of L to O). When it is known conditionally that the subject can access the predicate node, recall of V or O should be higher than when its access is uncertain. Similarly, the probability of L or A recall should be higher when it is assured that the subject has access to the fact node.

Table 10.3a presents the data relevant to these contrasts. In this table, $P(X|Y)$ denotes the probability of recall of word X in those conditional situations where the theory tells us that the subject must have access to the Y node, whereas $P(X|\bar{Y})$ denotes the comparable probability in those situations where the theory is uncertain. Observations from a number of separate cases have been pooled to give each conditional probability in Table 10.3a. We have only conditionalized on that subset of the data where there is partial recall because that is the only portion of the data which is informative. That is, we have examined recall of a third word conditional on recall of just one of the other two to-be-recalled words. For instance, contributing to $P(L|fact)$ are the probabilities of L recall, given that (*a*) O and not V has been recalled to A, (*b*) V and not O has been recalled to A, (*c*) A and not O has been recalled to V, and (*d*) A and not V has been recalled to O. (Note that symmetry of these cases in the structure of Figure 10.5.) In all these cases the model says that there has been access to the fact node. Similarly, contributing to $P(L|\overline{fact})$ are the probability of L recall, given that (*a*) O and not A has been recalled to V, and (*b*) V and not A has been recalled to O. Table 10.3a also lists the theoretical differences predicted by the mathematical model to be introduced later.

Except for L recall, the differences in Table 10.3a match the expectations of the theory. The differences in V and O recall are significant and in the predicted direction. The average difference in recall between the favored conditions and the unfavored is .083. Given that the theory only predicts a difference of .066, this

TABLE 10.3

Recall Probabilities Conditional on Node
Accessibility—Experiment 1

Conditional probability	Observed	Theoretical	n	χ^2 (1)
(a) First cue				
$P(L|\text{fact})$	.528	.535	212	.03
$P(L|\overline{\text{fact}})$	.538	.465	132	
$P(A|\text{fact})$	.459	.484	231	.61
$P(A|\overline{\text{fact}})$	.413	.393	104	
$P(V|\text{predicate})$	.458	.442	264	7.92
$P(V|\overline{\text{predicate}})$	.306	.373	121	
$P(O|\text{predicate})$	.594	.557	202	7.15
$P(O|\overline{\text{predicate}})$	.451	.524	153	
(b) Second cue				
$P(L|\text{fact})$	.583	.652	60	3.22
$P(L|\overline{\text{fact}})$	.400	.592	40	
$P(A|\text{fact})$	.553	.627	85	2.26
$P(A|\overline{\text{fact}})$	.405	.523	37	
$P(V|\overline{\text{predicate}})$	.492	.590	65	.00
$P(V|\overline{\text{predicate}})$	.500	.547	36	
$P(O|\text{predicate})$	.488	.696	43	.36
$P(O|\overline{\text{predicate}})$	.425	.667	47	

result is quite satisfactory. The chi-square values listed to the right of the probabilities provide a measure of the significance of the difference between recall in the favored and unfavored conditions.

Subjects failed to recall anything to 64.2% of the first cues. For this subset of the data, a similar analysis was performed on the recall to the second cue. For the second cue there are only two words that the subject can recall. So, we examined recall of one word conditional on the recall of the second. The important variable was whether one could infer that the subject had access to the fact or predicate nodes on the basis of his recall of the first word. Table 10.3b presents the result of this analysis. The mean difference between favored and unfavored conditions is .098; the theory expects .059. The sample sizes are not large enough to make any of the differences significant, but the results are encouraging. The theoretical values are all much larger than the observed probabilities of recall. Plausible reasons for this discrepancy will be discussed later in examining the details of the fit of the model to the data.

Model Fitting

The qualitative details of data seem consistent with the theory, though hardly overwhelming. The next question is whether we can get a reasonable quantitative fit of the model to the data. The procedure of fitting the model will be discussed in some detail now. There are 11 links in Figure 10.1 that are important to the model's predictions. The two links on the time branch are not important since the time marker was held constant (at *past*) throughout the experiment. It is necessary to compute the probabilities of all possible (2^{11}) combinations of success and failure at forming the 11 associations. These probabilities depend only upon the number of associations and not upon the particular configuration of associations (see Equation (14)).

Then we compute the probabilities p_{ij} that there was a path from the ith concept to the jth. This requires summing the probabilities of those of the 2^{11} configurations for which i and j are connected. This leads to the symmetric Theoretical Matrix given in Table 10.4b, where i indexes the rows and j the columns. The values in the Theoretical Matrix come from the best fit of the theory to these data. The value of the parameter tb, which governs the formation of associations, was estimated to be 3.9 for this best fit.

Table 10.4b is to be compared with the actual probabilities of recall of a response j to a stimulus i as the first cue. These probabilities are given in Table 10.4a, which will be called the *Data Matrix*. Letting r_{ij} represent the entries of the Data Matrix, the following relation obtains among p_{ij}, the cells of the Theoretical Matrix, r_j, the probability of a transition from the jth concept to the jth word, and

TABLE 10.4

Matrices and Parameter Estimates—Experiment 1

(a) Data Matrix — Response

		L	A	V	O
	L		.253	.225	.266
Stimulus	A	.255		.220	.264
	V	.203	.180		.221
	O	.276	.248	.243	

(b) Theoretical Matrix — Response

		L	A	V	O
	L		.557	.537	.537
	A	.557		.581	.581
	V	.537	.581		.611
	O	.537	.581	.611	

(c) Residual Matrix

		L	A	V	O
	L		.454	.418	.495
Stimulus	A	.458		.379	.454
	V	.378	.310		.362
	O	.514	.429	.398	

(d) Logarithms

		L	A	V	O
	L		-.79	-.87	-.70
	A	-.78		-.97	-.79
	V	-.97	-1.17		-1.02
	O	-.67	-.85	-.92	

(e) Parameter Estimates

$tb = 3.9$

$s_L = .833 \quad r_L = .631$
$s_A = .743 \quad r_A = .534$
$s_V = .592 \quad r_V = .503$
$s_O = .802 \quad r_O = .606$

s_i, the probability of a transition from the ith word to the ith concept:

$$r_{ij} = p_{ij} \times s_i \times r_j \qquad (22)$$

Therefore, a matrix of the values of the products $s_i \times r_j$ can be obtained by dividing the entries of the Data Matrix by the entries of the Theoretical Matrix. This yields the matrix in Table 10.4c, which will be called the *Residual Matrix*. From that matrix, estimates of $\log s_i + \log r_j$ can be obtained by taking logarithms of the entries. Table 10.4d displays these logarithms. It is a simple matter to use Table 10.4d to obtain separate estimates of $\log s_i$ and of $\log r_j$ by maximum-likelihood estimation procedures. Actually these estimates are obtained with one degree of freedom. Thus, the estimates are of the form: $\log s_i = x_i + z$ and $\log r_j = y_j - z$, where z is variable and the x_i's and y_j's are estimates obtained by the maximum-likelihood procedure. Converting from logarithms, we have $s_i = e^{x_i + z}$ and $r_j = e^{y_j - z}$. Substituting into Equation (22) yields $r_{ij} = p_{ij} e^{x_i + y_j}$.

The mechanics of the estimation procedure may be summarized as follows: We select a value of tb, compute a theoretical matrix (e.g., Table 10.4b), and from that a residual matrix (e.g., Table 10.4c). From that we estimate the four parameters s_i and the four parameters r_j by the maximum-likelihood method. These maximum-likelihood estimates have one degree of freedom, expressed by parameter z. A grid search is computed over the possible values of z, searching for the one that gives a minimum chi-square fit to the original data. Then this whole procedure is repeated with a new value of tb. This continues until a value of tb is obtained that gives the minimum chi-square. So, grid searches are conducted over the parameters tb and z, seeking minimum chi-square estimates. Given a particular value of z, the parameters s_i and r_j are determined by maximum-likelihood procedures. The estimates of these various parameters are given in Table 10.4e.

From these parameters the theoretical frequencies of various experimental events can now be estimated. Consider, for instance, the event in which the subject recalls L and A but not O to the first cue of V (which event will be abbreviated as $V \to LA\bar{O}$). There are two configurations of idea-to-idea associations for which this could happen—either all n associations are intact (prob. = .482) but response O is not available, or the object branch is missing one or both of its links (prob. = .024). The total probability of this event is the sum of the probabilities of this event when either of these two underlying configurations of associations holds; i.e.,

$$P(V \to LA\bar{O}) = .482 \cdot s_V \cdot r_{LA\bar{q}O} + .024 \cdot s_V \cdot (r_{LA\bar{q}O} + r_{LAO}) \qquad (23)$$

In Equation (23), $r_{LA\bar{q}O}$ is the probability of the responses L and A being available but not O, and r_{LAO} is the probability that all three responses are available. Remember that response probabilities covary, so that $r_{LAO} > r_L \cdot r_A \cdot r_O$. The value of $r_{LA\bar{q}O}$ is .073, and of r_{LAO} is .352. Substituting into Equation (23), it is found that $P(V \to LA\bar{O}) = .027$. Given that there were 738 observations of recall when the subject was cued with V, the expected frequency of this event is 19.77. The observed frequency was 18.

It will be informative to consider a second example of how event probabilities are predicted. What is the probability that when the subject is first cued with O, he recalls nothing, but then when cued with O plus A he recalls both L and V? This event (denoted $O \rightarrow : A \rightarrow LV$) can happen with either of two underlying configurations of associations: either all associations are intact and O was not an effective cue (it will not be effective with probability $1 - s_O$), or the object branch is missing one or both associations. These are the same two underlying configurations as in the previous example. Again, the probability of this event is just the sum of the probabilities of the event for either of these configurations; i.e.,

$$P(O \rightarrow : S \rightarrow AV) = .482 \cdot (1-s_O) \cdot s_A \cdot r_{LV} + .024 \cdot s_A \cdot r_{LV} \qquad (24)$$

Given that r_{LV} = .403, the probability in Equation (24) is .036. There are 246 circumstances in which the first cue is O and the second A. Therefore, 8.8 such events are predicted. The observed frequency was 5.

Table 10.5 provides the details of the fit of the model to the data. This is a very long table because overall there were 82 events that can be predicted. Because 9 parameters were estimated from the data and the probabilities must sum to 1, 72 degrees of freedom are associated with the chi-square measure of goodness of fit. This chi-square sum was 79.44, which is nonsignificant. Therefore, we may conclude that the model has captured most of the nonrandom variance in the data.

The event notation used in Table 10.5 requires some explanation. The first 28 events are those circumstances in which the first cue evoked some recall and the later two cues did not. The symbol to the left of the arrow provides the cue and the symbols to the right describe the recall. If the letter has a bar above it, the word was not recalled; if it has no bar, the word was recalled. So, $L \rightarrow \overline{AV}\overline{O}$ means that cue L evoked the recall of V but not A or O. The reader will note that there is a strong tendency for total recall in these data, although there is considerable partial recall as well. The model adequately predicts the relative proportions of total versus partial recall.

Events (29) and (30) summarize the circumstances in which one word was recalled to the first cue and another word to a later cue. A number of separate events have been pooled to obtain large enough expected values for these two events. In (29) are all such events where the first cue was L and the word recalled to it was A, or vice versa. The second recall in (29) involves recall of V to O or vice versa. Line (30) pools those events with V and O as the first cue and response, or vice versa. The second recall in (30) involved L and A. These are the only first-cue sequences that should permit later recall according to the theory.

Events (31) through (66) summarize those events in which the first cue evoked no recall but the second cue did. The first cue X that produced no recall is indicated by the notation $X \rightarrow :$. Events (67) through (78) summarize those circumstances in which the first two cues evoked no recall, but the third did. We have pooled over two events for each of these observations. That is, the notation XY there denotes either the case where X was the first cue and Y was added to it as the second cue, or the reverse order. In either case, the compound cue contained both X and Y, and evoked no recall. The theory predicts little difference between

TABLE 10.5

Fit of Model to Data—Experiment 1

Event	Observed	Expected	Chi-square
1) L→AVO	93	89.0	.18
2) L→AV$\bar{\text{O}}$	17	21.2	.83
3) L→A$\bar{\text{V}}$O	33	39.2	.98
4) L→A$\bar{\text{V}}\bar{\text{O}}$	41	35.1	.98
5) L→$\bar{\text{A}}$VO	33	32.6	.00
6) L→$\bar{\text{A}}$V$\bar{\text{O}}$	23	23.4	.00
7) L→$\bar{\text{A}}\bar{\text{V}}$O	37	39.4	.15
8) A→LVO	87	88.8	.04
9) A→LV$\bar{\text{O}}$	20	23.0	.40
10) A→L$\bar{\text{V}}$O	36	42.4	.97
11) A→L$\bar{\text{V}}\bar{\text{O}}$	43	39.1	.39
12) A→$\bar{\text{L}}$VO	36	26.3	3.61
13) A→$\bar{\text{L}}$V$\bar{\text{O}}$	19	22.0	.42
14) A→$\bar{\text{L}}\bar{\text{V}}$O	36	35.5	.00
15) V→LAO	78	74.2	.19
16) V→LA$\bar{\text{O}}$	18	19.8	.16
17) V→L$\bar{\text{A}}$O	30	30.3	.00
18) V→L$\bar{\text{A}}\bar{\text{O}}$	24	24.0	.00
19) V→$\bar{\text{L}}$AO	21	22.4	.09
20) V→$\bar{\text{L}}$A$\bar{\text{O}}$	16	19.2	.53
21) V→$\bar{\text{L}}\bar{\text{A}}$O	30	34.9	.68
22) O→LAV	95	87.8	.58
23) O→LA$\bar{\text{V}}$	38	39.6	.06
24) O→L$\bar{\text{A}}$V	30	32.9	.26
25) O→L$\bar{\text{A}}\bar{\text{V}}$	41	40.7	00
26) O→$\bar{\text{L}}$AV	22	24.7	.30
27) O→$\bar{\text{L}}$A$\bar{\text{V}}$	29	31.7	.23
28) O→$\bar{\text{L}}\bar{\text{A}}$V	31	37.7	1.18
29) Recall after L→A$\bar{\text{V}}\bar{\text{O}}$ or A→L$\bar{\text{V}}\bar{\text{O}}$	5	3.7	.47
30) Recall after V→$\bar{\text{L}}\bar{\text{A}}$O or O→$\bar{\text{L}}\bar{\text{A}}$V	5	3.7	.47
31) L→:A→VO	6	9.7	1.39
32) L→:A→V$\bar{\text{O}}$	6	4.9	.22
33) L→:A→$\bar{\text{V}}$O	11	7.7	1.46
34) L→:V→AO	4	8.1	2.09
35) L→:V→A$\bar{\text{O}}$	5	4.3	.13
36) L→:V→$\bar{\text{A}}$O	11	7.7	1.40
37) L→:O→AV	11	9.5	.25
38) L→:O→A$\bar{\text{V}}$	8	7.3	.06
39) L→:O→$\bar{\text{A}}$V	11	8.4	.84
40) A→:L→VO	6	11.9	2.89
41) A→:L→V$\bar{\text{O}}$	4	4.8	.13
42) A→:L→$\bar{\text{V}}$O	4	8.2	2.15
43) A→:V→LO	5	10.2	2.64
44) A→:V→L$\bar{\text{O}}$	7	4.7	1.18
45) A→:V→$\bar{\text{L}}$O	13	7.7	3.58

TABLE 10.5

Fit of Model to Data–Experiment 1 (*Continued*)

Event	Observed	Expected	Chi-square
46) A→:O→LV	9	11.8	.65
47) A→:O→L$\bar{\text{V}}$	10	8.4	.33
48) A→:O→$\bar{\text{L}}$V	13	8.4	2.52
49) V→:L→AO	12	18.6	2.36
50) V→:L→A$\bar{\text{O}}$	14	8.8	3.01
51) V→:L→$\bar{\text{A}}$O	11	10.9	.00
52) V→:A→LO	8	19.1	6.42
53) V→:A→L$\bar{\text{O}}$	13	9.9	.99
54) V→:A→$\bar{\text{L}}$O	7	10.0	.91
55) V→:O→LA	14	18.0	.89
56) V→:O→L$\bar{\text{A}}$	14	10.9	.90
57) V→:O→$\bar{\text{L}}$A	11	9.1	.41
58) O→:L→AV	13	8.7	2.19
59) O→:L→A$\bar{\text{V}}$	8	6.9	.18
60) O→:L→$\bar{\text{A}}$V	4	4.9	.16
61) O→:A→LV	5	8.8	1.63
62) O→:A→L$\bar{\text{V}}$	10	7.6	.76
63) O→:A→$\bar{\text{L}}$V	3	5.0	.79
64) O→:V→LA	8	7.4	.05
65) O→:V→L$\bar{\text{A}}$	9	4.7	3.96
66) O→:V→$\bar{\text{L}}$A	4	4.3	.02
67) LA→:V→O	7	7.0	.00
68) LA→:O→V	7	7.9	.10
69) LV→:A→O	7	8.7	.34
70) LV→:O→A	8	8.3	.01
71) LO→:A→V	11	4.6	8.78
72) LO→:V→A	5	3.9	.30
73) AV→:L→O	9	9.2	.00
74) AV→:O→L	10	9.2	.07
75) AO→:L→V	7	4.4	1.54
76) AO→:V→L	7	3.9	2.42
77) VO→:L→A	7	7.9	.11
78) VO→:A→L	11	8.4	.83
79) AVO→:	386	366.2	1.08
80) LVO→:	368	370.2	.01
81) LAO→:	358	363.8	.09
82) LAV→:	365	367.2	.01
Total	2952	2952.0	79.44

these two events. Finally, events (79) through (82) summarize those circumstances in which no cue provoked any recall. The symbol *XYZ* → : indicates that the three unsuccessful cues were words X, Y, and Z. All the six possible sequences of first, second, and third cues have been pooled because the theory predicts very little difference among them.

A few "data-smoothing" operations were performed in obtaining the observed frequencies in Table 10.5. For instance, there are those cases of recall to "inadequate stimuli" where the subject's recall to an initial cue will include X, and then when we augment a later cue with X he is able to recall a new word Y. The few events of this kind were reclassified as events where both X and Y were recalled to the first cue. There were also the unpredicted second recalls where the subject recalls X to U and then $X + Y$ to $U + Z$, but the theory predicts no second recall. These were reclassified in the same manner as the recalls to inadequate stimuli. The supposition in either case is that the subject knew Y all along, but was not recalling it. There were also some examples of what might be called *omissions*, in which the subject recalls X to one cue and then inhibits it in recall to the next cue. We count such events as if X had been recalled all along and not later inhibited. The principle in reclassifying all such aberrant data was always to give the subject the benefit of the doubt. Altogether, 2.5% of the data had to be reclassified for one of the reasons listed above. This seems a tolerable level of experimental "noise."

While the overall fit to the model is quite satisfactory, there is one point of systematic misfit which deserves comment. This involves recall to the second cue when nothing was recalled to the first cue (events 31 through 66). It is clear from inspection that the model predicts more total recall and less partial recall than was in fact occurring. That is, subjects were recalling both of the remaining two words with less than expected frequency (9 of 12 comparisons) and just one of the two with greater than expected frequency. Overall, the model expected 141.8 total recalls and 175.5 partial recalls to the second cue, but the observed frequencies were 101 total recalls and 211 partial recalls. The reason the model predicts such high total recall is because of the high covariance of response probabilities. This high covariance served us well in predicting recall to the first cue. However, it seems that, conditional on failure to recall to the first cue, the response probabilities do not covary so strongly. This suggests some covariance between the stimulus probabilities s_i and response probabilities r_j. However, it would have exceeded the powers of the estimation procedure to capture this further source of covariance. In any case, this systematic deviation from prediction on second-cue recall is the source of the discrepancies between data and theory back in Table 10.3*b* where we were examining conditional probabilities of recall to the second cue.

The outcome of the various analyses has been generally favorable to the model. It seems that the model is able to capture both the qualitative and the quantitative details of the data obtained from this cued recall experiment. The only disappointing feature was that the qualitative differences were rather marginal. The next experiment was performed in the hope of enhancing the qualitative effects predicted from the model.

10.3. EXPERIMENT 2: TWO ATOMIC PROPOSITIONS

The sentences used in the next experiment all had the form "The hippie touched the debutante who sang in the park." That is, there was a subject (S), a transitive verb (T), an object (O), an intransitive verb (I) and a location (L). Figure 10.6 indicates the structure of the input for these sentences. As can be seen, HAM's

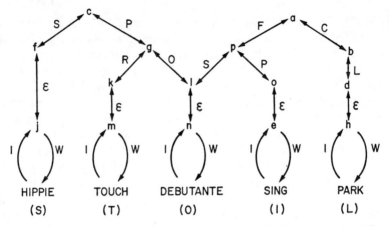

FIG. 10.6. HAM's representation of the sentences used in Experiments 2 and 3.

parser would decompose these sentences into two intersecting input trees corresponding to the two underlying atomic propositions. For simplicity, Figure 10.6 omits any representation of the *time* elements because they do not play a role in the predictions.

A total of 35 subjects were run in this experiment. Each of the subjects saw a different set of 60 sentences constructed by randomly selecting subjects, transitive verbs, objects, intransitive verbs, and locations from sets of 60 words for each function. These 60 sentences were randomly divided into three lists of 20 sentences each. Each sentence in a list was studied for 18 seconds. After the 20 sentences in a list had been studied, there followed a cued recall test for memory of the sentences. The method of incremental cueing was used as before to create three cues for each sentence. The subject had 32 seconds to recall to the first cue with four of the content words missing, 24 seconds for the second cue with three words missing, and 16 seconds for the last cue with two words missing. There are 60 possible ways to create a three-cue sequence of this sort from the set S, T, O, I, and L. Each possible cue sequence was randomly assigned to one sentence of the 60. After going through the first list of 20 sentences in this manner, subjects went through the other two lists in the identical manner. As in the Experiment 1, study sentences and test cues were presented on IBM cards. Before the experiment began, the exact nature of the experiment and the types of recall cues were described in considerable detail to the subject. The total experimental session lasted about 100 minutes.

Qualitative Results

Again, the data will first be examined for the qualitative predictions before attempting a quantitative fit of the model to the data. The first qualitative prediction concerns second recalls. These are the circumstances when the subject recalls partially to an initial cue, but with additional information in a later cue he is able to recall additional words. There are many more possibilities for a second recall in this experiment than before, because there are five target words rather than four. Therefore, this data should be more informative than in the last experiment. Three cases of second recall need to be distinguished. First is recall to an *inadequate stimulus*, where the stimulus that evoked the second recall was augmented with a word the subject had already recalled to an earlier cue. As noted earlier, such events are to be considered experimental noise. Their overall frequency in this experiment was .042 (25 of 573 opportunities).

The next class of events are the unpredicted second recalls, in which the second cue has been augmented with a word that the subject did not recall to the first cue, but the structural assumptions of the model deny the possibility of further recall. To use the example of Figure 10.6, if the first cue were "hippie" and the subject recalled "sing" or "park" or both, then he should not be able to recall "debutante" to "touch," nor "touch" to "debutante." This is because the model presumes, conditional on his success at recalling "sing" or "park" but his failure to recall "debutante" or "touch" to the first cue, that the *relation* path to "touch" or the *member* path to "debutante" cannot be intact. In 6.7% (15 out of 239 opportunities) of such cases, there was further recall to the second cue. This is more frequent than the recalls to inadequate stimuli (but not significantly so, $\chi^2_{(1)} = 1.93$). As one post hoc explanation, one might suppose that these represent cases where the subject had formed special word-to-word connections. For instance, in the above example he may have directly associated "touch" and "debutante" together in another proposition rather than connecting them through the tree structure in Figure 10.6. The subject may have accomplished this by forming spontaneously some proposition about "touch" and "debutante"—e.g., "I never touched a debutante." In these cases, "touch" could revive "debutante" even though "hippie" could not. Subjects do commonly report elaborating upon the to-be-recalled sentences with productions of their own.

The third class of second recalls are those that the structural assumptions predict. For instance, even though the subject was only able to recall "touch" and "debutante" to "hippie," he still may be able to recall "park" to "sing." He may not have been able to recall "park" to the first cue because the subject link was missing between the *member* node dominating debutante and the *fact* node dominating "sing." The path from "sing" to "park" may be intact. In 17.8% (48 out of 269) of these circumstances there was second recall. Thus, second recalls are much more frequent in this third class of situations than in the second $(\chi^2_{(1)} = 14.23)$. This clearly supports the representation generated by HAM for this class of sentences.

The other qualitative predictions concern the first cued recall of one word in a sentence conditional on a particular pattern of recall of the other words in the sentence. For instance, consider the conditional recall of the element S in the following two circumstances: (*a*) the subject has recalled T and I, but not L, to the cue of O, and (*b*) the subject has recalled I and L, but not T, to the O cue. By referring to Figure 10.6, it may be confirmed that only in case (*a*) does the model say that the subject has access to the predicate node dominating T and O. In case (*b*) we only know that the subject can access the member node dominating O. Since the predicate node is closer than the member node to S, recall of the element S is predicted to be higher in conditional case (*a*) than (*b*).

TABLE 10.6

Recall Probabilities Conditional on Node Accessibility—Experiment 2

Conditional probability	Observed	Theoretical	n	$\chi^2(1)$
(a) 2 out of 3 nontargets recalled				
$P(S\|predicate)$	.696	.650	102	9.87
$P(S\|\overline{predicate})$	.473	.626	91	
$P(T\|predicate)$	.517	.500	143	11.80
$P(T\|\overline{predicate})$	.262	.429	65	
$P(O\|object)$	.649	.676	154	—
$P(O\|\overline{object})$	—	—	0	
$P(I\|fact)$	.566	.560	145	2.64
$P(I\|\overline{fact})$	.417	.449	36	
$P(L\|fact)$	.790	.767	100	5.31
$P(L\|\overline{fact})$	.618	.688	55	
(b) 1 out of 3 nontargets recalled				
$P(S\|predicate)$	.511	.434	45	4.32
$P(S\|\overline{predicate})$	.336	.360	140	
$P(T\|predicate)$	.359	.325	78	10.09
$P(T\|\overline{predicate})$	.163	.254	123	
$P(O\|object)$	.621	.472	66	14.10
$P(O\|\overline{object})$	.336	.403	119	
$P(I\|fact)$	.457	.376	127	12.03
$P(I\|\overline{fact})$	.213	.261	75	
$P(L\|fact)$	.753	.567	73	19.78
$P(L\|\overline{fact})$	.427	.492	124	

We pooled together the cases in which it is known that the person has access to the predicate node and pooled those in which it is not known. The conditional probabilities of S recall in these two cases are given in Tables 10.6a and 10.6b. To have a fair test it was necessary to divide these cases into two subsets. Let us explain why: There are three words to be recalled besides the target word (e.g., in the preceding example, the target word was S). The conditional probability of target recall will vary with how many of these three are recalled, independent of whether the particular pattern provides any evidence for access to the target node (i.e., in the example, the predicate node). This is because the probabilities of associations and responses covary in average data. Hence, the more words out of the three that are recalled, the greater the probability of recall of the target. Therefore, the data must be examined separately for the circumstances when 3, 2, 1, and 0 words are recalled out of the three. When three words are recalled, we always know the subject has access to the target node; and when no words are recalled, we never know. Therefore, the only two interesting cases are when one or two of the three words are recalled. Table 10.6a has the analysis for the case of two words recalled, and Table 10.6b for one word recalled. These tables display the probability of recall of S, T, O, I, or L, conditional on whether the theory says that the subject has access to the target node. The notation $P(X|Y)$ gives the probability of X recall, given access to target node Y; and $P(X|\bar{Y})$ gives the probability where there is not conditional evidence of access. Depending on what the target word is, the target node is the *predicate* node, the *member* node (dominating O), or the *fact* node (dominating I).

As can be seen in Table 10.6, in all cases the observed conditional probabilities are ordered in the direction predicted by the model. The chi-square measure of the significance of these differences is given to the right of the conditional probabilities. A chi-square of 3.84 is required for significance at the .05 level. In all but one case, the differences between the favored and unfavored conditions are significant. The mean difference between the favored and unfavored conditional probabilities is .225. According to the model that will be fit to the data, the expected difference is only .077. Thus, the mathematical model underpredicts the structural effects of our representation. We shall shortly see why.

Mathematical Model

We will be somewhat more cursory in describing the fit of the model for this experiment. The technical details and procedures were described in conjunction with the previous experiment. The techniques of parameter estimation, etc., were generalized in the obvious manner to this experiment. The value of the parameter tb, which governs probability of association, was estimated to be 3.7, which is quite close to the value of 3.9 estimated in the first experiment. Using it, the Theoretical Matrix in Table 10.7b was computed. Table 10.7a shows the Data Matrix which

TABLE 10.7

Matrices and Parameter Estimates—Experiment 2

| | (a) Data Matrix | | | | | | (b) Theoretical Matrix | | | |
	S	T	O	I	L		S	T	O	I	L
S		.252	.257	.200	.267	S		.565	.565	.521	.489
T	.195		.169	.136	.183	T	.565		.596	.541	.504
O	.286	.226		.238	.338	O	.565	.596		.596	.541
I	.214	.150	.224		.267	I	.521	.541	.596		.541
L	.219	.195	.279	.283		L	.489	.504	.541	.541	

(c) Parameter Estimates

$$tb = 3.7$$

$s_S = .736$	$r_S = .666$
$s_T = .468$	$r_T = .515$
$s_O = .747$	$r_O = .627$
$s_I = .593$	$r_I = .561$
$s_L = .789$	$r_L = .796$

gives the average probabilities of recall for each response to each cue. Based on the two matrices in Table 10.7, one can compute the stimulus probabilities s_i and response probabilities r_j. The 11 parameters estimated to fit the data are given in Table 10.7c. As before, the verbs have uniformly lower parameters than the nouns.

In fitting the model to the data, it was necessary, as in the past experiment, to reclassify recall to inadequate stimuli, unpredicted second recalls, and omissions as events predicted by the model. These events were reclassified by the same system we reported for Experiment 1. Altogether, 2.4% of the data had to be reclassified. Again, this seems a tolerable level of experimental noise.

Table 10.8 summarizes the fit of the model to the data. The notation is identical to that used in Table 10.5; the letters to the right of the arrows indicate the stimuli, and to the left the responses. Overall there were 135 events to be predicted. The first 75 in Table 10.8 concern various patterns of first-cue recall to the five possible first cues. Events 76 through 95 give frequency of recall to various possible second cues, given no recall to the first cue. These second-cue events are classified by what the first unsuccessful cue was (five possible types) and by what the second cue was (four possible types). The various possible patterns of second-cue recall have been pooled to obtain acceptable event frequencies. Events 96 through 125 give frequency of recall to third cues, given the subject has failed to recall to the first two cues. Again the various possible patterns of recall have been pooled, and only the frequency with which something was recalled is presented. Similarly, the two possible sequences of the first two unsuccessful cues have been polled. Thus, ST → : can either mean the first two cues were S followed by T or vice versa. Finally, events 126 through 135 summarize the frequencies with which the full three-cue sequence led to no recall; this is pooled over all possible patterns of the three-cue sequence.

Since 11 parameters were estimated, there are 123 degrees of freedom in fitting the observed frequencies in Table 10.8. The total chi-square was 164.88. With 123 degrees of freedom, a chi-square of 150 would be significant at the .05 level. Therefore, we may conclude that the observed frequencies do deviate significantly from the model's predictions. It is easy to determine where the model is mispredicting. We have starred five events in Table 10.8—events 18, 23, 43, 58 and 63. The total chi-square associated with these events is 44.45. Had we omitted these five deviant points, the chi-square would be 126.72 with 118 degrees of freedom, which is more acceptable.

What do these five events have in common? The common aspect can be brought out by supposing that our subjects, for whatever reason, adopted a focusing strategy in which they concentrated on either just the S and T part of the structure, or just on the O, I, and L part. If so, one would expect higher cued recall within one of the groups and lower across groups than predicted by a model which assumes that effort is distributed equally over all the words. That is, one would see greater than expected recall of T when cued with S (event 8); cued with T, greater recall of S (event 23); cued with O, greater recall of I and L (event 43); cued with I, greater recall of O and L (event 58); and cued with L, greater recall of O and I (event 73). In each case the observed frequency of the event is greater than

TABLE 10.8

Fit of Model to Data—Experiment 2

	Event	Observed	Expected	Chi-square
1)	$S \to TOIL$	44	42.8	.03
2)	$S \to TOI\overline{L}$	7	4.8	.97
3)	$S \to TO\overline{I}L$	7	12.6	2.51
4)	$S \to TO\overline{I}\overline{L}$	7	5.7	.30
5)	$S \to T\overline{O}IL$	9	7.2	.45
6)	$S \to T\overline{O}I\overline{L}$	0	2.0	1.99
7)	$S \to T\overline{O}\overline{I}L$	10	6.2	2.35
8)	$S \to T\overline{O}\overline{I}\overline{L}$	22	8.7	20.61*
9)	$S \to \overline{T}OIL$	12	16.7	1.34
10)	$S \to \overline{T}OI\overline{L}$	4	4.3	.03
11)	$S \to \overline{T}O\overline{I}L$	12	12.6	.02
12)	$S \to \overline{T}O\overline{I}\overline{L}$	15	10.1	2.39
13)	$S \to \overline{T}\overline{O}IL$	6	7.9	.44
14)	$S \to \overline{T}\overline{O}\overline{I}L$	1	4.6	2.84
15)	$S \to \overline{T}\overline{O}\overline{I}\overline{L}$	13	14.3	.11
16)	$T \to SOIL$	35	32.4	.22
17)	$T \to SOI\overline{L}$	3	3.8	.19
18)	$T \to SO\overline{I}L$	9	10.8	.30
19)	$T \to SO\overline{I}\overline{L}$	5	4.9	.00
20)	$T \to S\overline{O}IL$	7	6.3	.08
21)	$T \to S\overline{O}I\overline{L}$	1	1.8	.38
22)	$T \to S\overline{O}\overline{I}L$	6	5.9	.00
23)	$T \to S\overline{O}\overline{I}\overline{L}$	16	7.9	8.22*
24)	$T \to \overline{S}OIL$	6	6.3	.02
25)	$T \to \overline{S}OI\overline{L}$	1	2.6	.99
26)	$T \to \overline{S}O\overline{I}L$	6	5.8	.01
27)	$T \to \overline{S}O\overline{I}\overline{L}$	6	6.9	.11
28)	$T \to \overline{S}\overline{O}IL$	4	3.6	.04
29)	$T \to \overline{S}\overline{O}I\overline{L}$	0	2.8	2.80
30)	$T \to \overline{S}\overline{O}\overline{I}L$	4	7.5	1.65
31)	$O \to STIL$	46	44.9	.03
32)	$O \to STI\overline{L}$	5	5.1	.00
33)	$O \to ST\overline{I}L$	18	13.7	1.36
34)	$O \to ST\overline{I}\overline{L}$	9	6.2	1.29
35)	$O \to S\overline{T}IL$	16	18.1	.25
36)	$O \to S\overline{T}I\overline{L}$	3	4.8	.66
37)	$O \to S\overline{T}\overline{I}L$	14	14.0	.00
38)	$O \to S\overline{T}\overline{I}\overline{L}$	9	11.3	.48
39)	$O \to \overline{S}TIL$	3	8.1	3.20
40)	$O \to \overline{S}TI\overline{L}$	2	3.3	.52
41)	$O \to \overline{S}T\overline{I}L$	5	6.9	.50
42)	$O \to \overline{S}T\overline{I}\overline{L}$	7	8.2	.18
43)	$O \to \overline{S}\overline{T}IL$	20	11.0	7.37*
44)	$O \to \overline{S}\overline{T}\overline{I}L$	5	9.7	2.27
45)	$O \to \overline{S}\overline{T}\overline{I}\overline{L}$	20	17.0	.54
46)	$I \to STOL$	38	38.4	.00
47)	$I \to STO\overline{L}$	8	4.5	2.74
48)	$I \to ST\overline{O}L$	8	7.1	.10

TABLE 10.8

Fit of Model to Data—Experiment 2 (*Continued*)

	Event	Observed	Expected	Chi-square
49)	$I \to ST\overline{OL}$	0	2.1	2.05
50)	$I \to ST\overline{O}L$	14	16.3	.33
51)	$I \to ST\overline{OL}$	7	4.4	1.53
52)	$I \to ST\overline{O}L$	12	8.4	1.59
53)	$I \to ST\overline{OL}$	3	5.2	.90
54)	$I \to S\overline{T}OL$	4	7.3	1.46
55)	$I \to S\overline{T}O\overline{L}$	3	3.0	.00
56)	$I \to S\overline{T}\overline{O}L$	1	4.0	2.25
57)	$I \to S\overline{TOL}$	1	3.1	1.40
58)	$I \to \overline{S}T\overline{O}L$	12	10.2	.32*
59)	$I \to \overline{S}T\overline{OL}$	8	9.0	.12
60)	$I \to \overline{S}T\overline{O}L$	23	15.5	3.61
61)	$L \to STOI$	44	43.0	.03
62)	$L \to STO\overline{I}$	7	11.5	1.77
63)	$L \to STO\overline{I}$	6	6.5	.03
64)	$L \to ST\overline{O}\overline{I}$	2	4.9	1.75
65)	$L \to ST\overline{O}I$	13	15.3	.36
66)	$L \to ST\overline{O}\overline{I}$	5	10.2	2.67
67)	$L \to ST\overline{OI}$	6	6.3	.01
68)	$L \to ST\overline{OI}$	9	10.9	.34
69)	$L \to \overline{S}TO\overline{I}$	10	6.9	1.42
70)	$L \to \overline{S}T\overline{O}\overline{I}$	3	5.1	.83
71)	$L \to \overline{S}T\overline{O}\overline{I}$	6	3.0	2.93
72)	$L \to \overline{S}T\overline{O}\overline{I}$	4	5.2	.28
73)	$L \to \overline{S}TOI$	16	8.5	6.64*
74)	$L \to \overline{S}T\overline{O}\overline{I}$	19	12.1	4.00
75)	$L \to \overline{S}T\overline{O}\overline{I}$	18	11.2	4.13
76)	$S \to : T \to$	7	8.9	.41
77)	$S \to : O \to$	16	15.9	.00
78)	$S \to : I \to$	11	9.9	.12
79)	$S \to : L \to$	12	13.3	.12
80)	$T \to : S \to$	23	21.5	.11
81)	$T \to : O \to$	25	25.0	.00
82)	$T \to : I \to$	15	19.9	1.21
83)	$T \to : L \to$	26	22.4	.59
84)	$O \to : S \to$	8	10.9	.77
85)	$O \to : T \to$	6	7.5	.31
86)	$O \to : I \to$	13	9.6	1.23
87)	$O \to : L \to$	12	10.6	.17
88)	$I \to : S \to$	15	18.3	.58
89)	$I \to : T \to$	7	12.8	2.60
90)	$I \to : O \to$	25	20.8	.86
91)	$I \to : L \to$	17	16.6	.01
92)	$L \to : S \to$	16	12.8	.78
93)	$L \to : T \to$	9	9.1	.00
94)	$L \to : O \to$	15	15.0	.00
95)	$L \to : I \to$	7	10.2	1.02

TABLE 10.8

Fit of Model to Data—Experiment 2 (*Continued*)

Event	Observed	Expected	Chi-square
96) ST→:O→	6	5.1	.17
97) ST→:I→	6	5.2	.13
98) ST→:L→	8	5.2	1.51
99) SO→:T→	1	1.2	.02
100) SO→:I→	5	2.3	3.09
101) SO→:L→	5	2.3	3.07
102) SI→:T→	2	2.8	1.69
103) SI→:O→	2	4.8	1.62
104) SI→:L→	8	3.5	5.63
105) SL→:T→	1	2.1	.60
106) SL→:T→	4	3.7	.02
107) SL→:I→	2	2.6	.16
108) TO→:S→	2	2.7	.20
109) TO→:I→	4	3.6	.05
110) TO→:L→	3	3.8	.19
111) TI→:S→	6	6.4	.02
112) TI→:O→	12	7.0	3.60
113) TI→:L→	9	6.4	1.01
114) TL→:S→	1	4.3	2.49
115) TL→:O→	7	5.4	.49
116) TL→:I→	3	3.9	.20
117) OI→:S→	5	3.3	.82
118) OI→:T→	1	2.4	.81
119) OI→:L→	1	2.7	1.05
120) OL→:S→	2	2.0	.00
121) OL→:T→	3	1.7	.91
122) OL→:I→	3	1.6	1.11
123) IL→:S→	4	4.5	.06
124) IL→:T→	5	3.2	1.06
125) IL→:O→	1	5.1	3.29
126) OIL→:	98	92.7	.30
127) TIL→:	96	98.1	.05
128) TOL→:	88	93.8	.36
129) TOI→:	95	93.5	.02
130) SIL→:	88	95.7	.62
131) SOL→:	80	91.9	1.53
132) SOI→:	86	90.9	.27
133) STL→:	98	97.4	.00
134) STI→:	95	97.1	.05
135) STO→:	99	95.8	.11
Total	2100	2100.0	164.88

the predicted. Overall the model predicts 46.3 such events, and the observed frequency is 86.

Without a doubt this is the source of the deviation between theory and prediction. Incidently, this is also the reason why the model underpredicted in Table 10.6 the structural effects of our representation. The subjects may have been forced to this focusing because the total input was too large to hold in working memory during encoding. A question that remains, however, is why subjects should fall into this manner of focusing their encoding efforts. It seems reasonable that a subject would choose to focus on the O-I-L group, since this forms one of the underlying propositions in the sentence. However, subjects did not focus on the other underlying proposition—i.e., the S-T-O group. If they had, O recall to either the S or T would have been higher than it is in Table 10.8. Rather, subjects only focused on the S-T pair from this second proposition. An explanation for this result is not apparent.

Aside from this deviation, the model fits the data very well. Even a chi-square of 164.88 with 123 degrees of freedom is a remarkably good fit with such a large number of categories and observations. The model also plays a useful role in alerting us to the fact that the S-T pair is particularly isolated from the O-I-L triple. Without a quantitative model it would be difficult to establish that this was the case in the raw data. So, except for this one perplexity of focusing, it seems that the predictions generated from HAM are uniformly supported by the data.

10.4. EXPERIMENT 3: EFFECTS OF IMAGERY INSTRUCTIONS

Subjects in these experiments frequently report use of imagery to help remember the sentences. That is, they form to themselves an image of the situation the sentence describes. They claim this is an effective means of memorization, and subjects who use this technique appear to do better than those who do not. The question obviously arises as to what the source might be of the advantage that accrues with the use of imagery. According to HAM the structure underlying memory for images should be no different from that for sentences. So what can the subject gain when he transforms his task from that of remembering a sentence to that of remembering an image? A very simple hypothesis is that the task becomes more interesting and the subject tries harder. The amount of effort displayed by the subject should be reflected by an increase in the rate parameter b in the model or, equivalently, in the parameter tb that governs $p(t)$, the probability of forming a particular association. A similar increase would be expected in the rate parameters b_i and b_j that govern the stimulus probabilities, s_i, and the response probabilities, r_j. In general, all these rate parameters would be expected to increase by some multiplicative constant a.

The purpose of this experiment was to test the viability of this simple conception of the effect of imagery instructions. Thirty-four subjects were tested in the identical paradigm as in the previous experiment, except that they received instructions strongly urging them to form vivid visual images of the sentences to be memorized. If our analysis of the effect of imagery instructions is correct, we should now see the exact same pattern of results as in the past experiment, except the overall level of recall should be higher. This prediction runs counter to one's intuitions about the difference between a sentence and an image. An image would seem to be a more wholistic construction than a sentence. Therefore, one might expect to observe more all-or-none recall of sentences learned by imagery than sentences not so learned. In contrast, our hypothesis does not expect a substantial change in this direction with imagery instructions. The increase in the rate parameters will necessarily cause more total recall of all the words, but not to any degree greater than predicted by the stochastic model. Also, one might intuitively think that an image would not have the same structural segmentation that a sentence has in memory. It is a single unit and is recorded as such in memory. If so, one would not expect to see the marked qualitative effects of sentence structure which were found in the previous experiment. Finally, one would think intuitively that imagery instructions would decrease rather than increase the parameters s_i and r_j which govern the connections between ideas and words, since an image seems abstracted away from its verbal realization. However, our hypothesis denies such intuitions about imagery.

In Section 14.5, we provide an extended discussion of why imagery instructions help improve performance in memory tasks. It is argued there that imagery instructions have their effect by encouraging the subject to spontaneously generate auxiliary propositions interconnecting the to-be-recalled material. Thus, the subject has multiple redundant paths interconnecting elements, and if one path fails he can use another. According to this more plausible explanation, it is true that imagery instructions have their effect because subjects work harder, but it is not the case that the subjects try harder at encoding the target propositions; rather, they try to encode more auxiliary propositions. The present experiment will not discriminate between these two conceptions, because the effect of spontaneously generating auxiliary propositions would be reflected in the model by an increase in the effective encoding rate. Either conception predicts increased levels of recall overall, but no change in the patterns of recall.

Qualitative Results

The first thing to note is the relative frequency of recalls to inadequate stimuli (4.4% of 568 cases), unpredicted second recalls (8.5% of 247 cases), and predicted second recalls (25% of 264 cases). The very large significant ($x^2_{(1)} = 24.68$) difference between predicted and unpredicted second recalls indicates that sentences were principally encoded according to the predicted structure.

The other qualitative result concerns the probability of recall of a particular target word to the first cue, given that a particular pattern of the remaining three words was recalled. That is, conditional on particular patterns of recall, we can know the subject has access to a node very close to the target word whose recall is of interest. Table 10.9 displays these conditional probabilities; these may be compared to those in Table 10.6 from the previous experiment. In all cases but one, the observed differences in Table 10.9 between the favored and unfavored cases were large, significant, and in the predicted direction. Again the observed effects tended to exceed those predicted by the mathematical model. The mean observed difference was .278, and the mean expected difference was .077. The reason for this discrepancy is the same as in Experiment 2.

TABLE 10.9

Recall Probabilities Conditional on Node
Accessibility—Experiment 3

Conditional probability	Observed	Theoretical	n	χ^2 (1)
(a) 2 out of 3 nontargets recalled				
$P(S|\text{predicate})$	.741	.669	85	21.31
$P(S|\overline{\text{predicate}})$	.426	.667	141	
$P(T|\text{predicate})$	.554	.508	139	27.11
$P(T|\overline{\text{predicate}})$	.221	.444	104	
$P(O|\text{object})$	.743	.735	179	—
$P(O|\overline{\text{object}})$	—	—	0	
$P(I|\text{fact})$	.672	.614	174	22.92
$P(I|\overline{\text{fact}})$	.256	.497	39	
$P(L|\text{fact})$	.879	.816	124	22.75
$P(L|\overline{\text{fact}})$	.587	.727	75	
(b) 1 out of 3 nontargets recalled				
$P(S|\text{predicate})$	.507	.443	71	6.67
$P(S|\overline{\text{predicate}})$	.317	.407	120	
$P(T|\overline{\text{predicate}})$	.380	.326	108	14.83
$P(T|\text{predicate})$	.137	.253	95	
$P(O|\text{object})$	.465	.531	71	.01
$P(O|\overline{\text{object}})$	.473	.454	131	
$P(I|\text{fact})$	.500	.436	138	24.17
$P(I|\overline{\text{fact}})$	.153	.284	72	
$P(L|\text{fact})$	.767	.619	90	29.16
$P(L|\text{fact})$	.389	.539	113	

Mathematical Model

Table 10.10 gives the Data and Theoretical Matrices for this experiment as well as the parameter estimates. A table summarizing the fit of the model to the data will not be presented, since it is 135 entries long and is largely redundant in its pattern to, say, the entries in Table 10.8 for Experiment 2. (Copies of the table of observed and predicted event frequencies may be obtained by writing to the first author.) The chi-square associated with the deviation from fit had a total value of 267.40, with 123 degrees of freedom. This constitutes a considerably poorer fit than the previous experiment. However, inspection revealed that the model misfits the data at the same points as in the previous experiment, only to a more severe degree.

The subjects apparently used the same focusing strategy as before, grouping O-I-L and S-T more closely than anticipated. This experiment constitutes the worst fit of the model to the data in the four experiments to be reported in this chapter.

However, it is important to emphasize to readers inexperienced in matters of model fitting that this is really a rather good fit. As Atkinson, Bower, and Crothers (1965) note, any model will yield significant chi-squares provided enough observations are taken. The slightest discrepancy between theory and data can be exploded into statistical significance by large numbers. In this experiment we have set ourselves a major task of attempting to predict over 2,000 observations classified into 135 separate events. Nearly half of the chi-square comes from the model's failure to capture 5% of this data where effects of the subject-imposed focusing are particularly prominent. Otherwise, the major trends in the data have been summarized by the model. For instance, the correlation between prediction and observation in this experiment, the worst of the four to be reported, is still .97. That is, the model accounts for 94% of the variance in the event frequencies, and we know that 3.8% of the remaining 6% variance is unavoidable random error. So the model is performing very well.

It seems that our hypothesis about the quantitative effect of imagery has been confirmed—i.e., that it increases the overall level of recall but leaves undisturbed all other qualitative and quantitative trends in the data. The hypothesis was that imagery instructions had their effect by increasing the rate parameters associated with the various probabilities—b, the rate parameter for probability of formation of an association, and the rate parameters b_i associated with the stimulus and response probabilities. We have already estimated the rate parameter b of association formation, but we have not directly calculated the b_i parameters for the stimuli and responses. These b_i rate parameters can be derived from the stimulus or response probabilities p_i given in Tables 10.7 and 10.10 by the following equation:

$$b_i = \frac{p_i}{18(1 - p_i)} \tag{25}$$

TABLE 10.10

Matrices and Parameter Estimates—Experiment 3

	(a) Data Matrix						(b) Theoretical Matrix				
	S	T	O	I	L		S	T	O	I	L
S		.343	.380	.304	.417	S		.661	.661	.623	.596
T	.282		.248	.235	.257	T	.661		.686	.640	.608
O	.377	.289		.321	.424	O	.661	.686		.686	.640
I	.282	.260	.343		.382	I	.623	.640	.686		.640
L	.346	.270	.431	.385		L	.596	.608	.640	.640	

(c) Parameter Estimates

$tb = 5.2$

$s_S = .804$	$r_S = .733$
$s_T = .529$	$r_T = .584$
$s_O = .744$	$r_O = .734$
$s_I = .671$	$r_I = .659$
$s_L = .843$	$r_L = .862$

Equation (25) is adapted from Equation (11). The 18 in Equation (25) represents the 18 seconds of study time. With this equation, 11 estimates of rate parameters are obtained for each experiment—the parameter b governing association formation, the five parameters governing stimulus probabilities, s_i, and the five parameters governing response probabilities, r_j. These rate parameters are given in the scatterplot of Figure 10.7. Plotted along the abscissa are the rate parameters estimated for Experiment 2 (without imagery), and along the ordinate the parameters for this experiment (with imagery). The 11 points give the rates for each parameter in the two experiments. Each point is labeled to indicate which of the 11 rate parameters it is. From inspection, it is clear that the rate parameters from the two experiments are highly correlated. The coefficient of correlation is .964. Earlier we hypothesized that the rate parameters from the two experiments would be related to each other by a multiplicative constant a, such that for each b_i from the first experiment, the corresponding $b_i = ab_i$. The best estimate of the multiplicative constant, a, is 1.40. If our hypothesis is correct, all the points in Figure 10.7 should fall on the straight line passing through the origin with slope 1.4. As can be seen, they very nearly do. Moreover, there appears no difference with respect to the multiplicative constant, a, between the parameter, b, for association formation, the

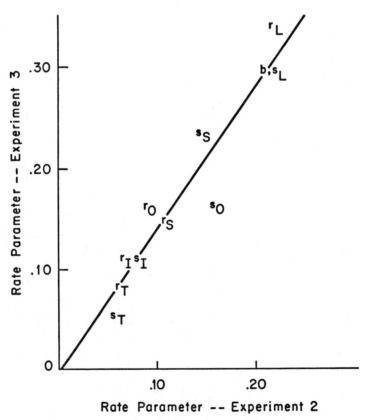

FIG. 10.7. Relation between the rate parameters in Experiments 2 and 3.

rate parameters associated with the response probabilities r_i, or those associated with the stimulus probabilities s_i. It is a rather remarkable correspondence.

10.5. EXPERIMENT 4: PHYSICAL CONTIGUITY VERSUS HAM'S DEEP STRUCTURE

There is one obvious source of confounding in the previous experiments. The elements which our representation claims should be close together in the logical

THE   HIPPIE   TOUCHED   THE   DEBUTANTE   WHO   SANG   IN   THE   PARK

FIG. 10.8. Representation of sentences in Experiments 2 and 3 according to physical contiguity.

structure were also physically close in the surface structure of the sentences studied. Therefore, if physical contiguity alone determined organization of the mnemonic representation, one would predict results identical to those predicted from our representation for those experiments. For instance, consider the sentences studied in the last two experiments, and imagine that they were stored as linear strings as illustrated by Figure 10.8. Here *tokens* of the words are ordered serially by physical contiguity. This is the representation that might be generated by HAM's perceptual parser in contrast to its linguistic parser. According to this representation, "hippie" and "touched" are close together, so are "sing" and "park," and "debutante" is midway between the two pairs. These are the same proximity relations as provided by our deep-structure representation of the sentence, which was shown in Figure 10.6.

In several experiments surface proximity of content words has been pitted against HAM's representation of the deep-structure proximity of the words. We will shortly report one of these in detail, but first we want to consider a related experiment which was performed for other purposes. In it, we had 22 subjects study 64 sentences each of the form:

> "The hippie who *kissed* the prostitute touched the debutante who *liked* the captain."

Following study, subjects were cued with the two embedded verbs that are italicized, and their task was to recall the remaining five content words in the sentence. Figure 10.9 illustrates the two alternate representations for these sentences, with Figure 10.9*a* showing HAM's representation and Figure 10.9*b* showing the physical contiguity hypothesis. The important difference between the two structures is that HAM predicts that hippie (the type *B* item) is closer than prostitute (type *A* item) to the remaining three content words to be recalled (types *C*, *D*, and *E*) in Figure 10.9. The physical contiguity hypothesis predicts just the

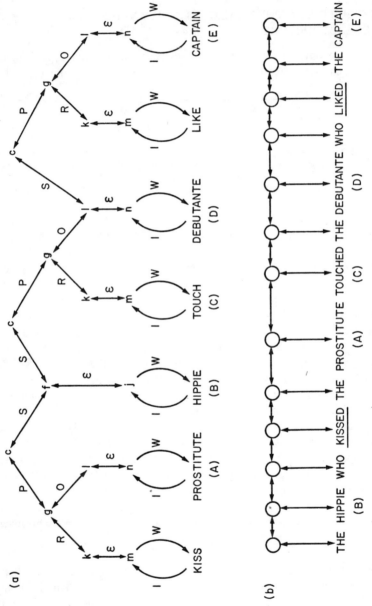

FIG. 10.9. Possible representations for the sentence "The hippie who kissed the prostitute touched the debutante who liked the captain": (*a*) according to HAM; and (*b*) according to physical contiguity.

opposite ordering. Therefore, recall of C, D, and E was contrasted on those occasions when A, and not B, was recalled (110 observations) with those occasions when B, and not A, was recalled (153 observations). The physical contiguity hypothesis predicts higher recall of the three critical items in the former case, whereas HAM predicts higher recall in the latter case.

HAM's prediction was confirmed by significant effects in the predicted direction in the cases of the recall of item C (9.1% versus 35.9% recall; $\chi^2_{(1)} = 8.72$) and D (24.5% versus 37.3%; $\chi^2_{(1)} = 4.77$). However, the outcome was nonsignificantly in the opposite direction in the case of item E (45.5% versus 39.2%; $\chi^2_{(1)} = 1.02$). It may be noted that the difference in the two conditional recall measures decreases the further away from elements A and B is the item concerned. Since item E is quite distant from A or B in either representation, it is perhaps not too surprising that its recall does not discriminate between the two representations. Overall, then, the evidence favors HAM's representation over the physical contiguity representation. This experiment confirmed HAM's prediction that elements from a *proposition*, even if separated by embedded clauses, are brought close together in memory. That is, the evidence supports HAM's *between-proposition* representation in opposition to simple physical contiguity. Other evidence for HAM's between-proposition representation over physical contiguity comes from Section 9.2, where we were examining the effects of the MATCH process. Demonstration is still required that HAM's *within-proposition* representation is more accurate than one based on physical contiguity. The next experiment was an attempt to get at that question.

Single-proposition sentences were created in which the physical order of elements conflicted strongly with the deep-structure ordering predicted by HAM. The sentences were of the following form: "In the park the debutante during the night was touched by the hippie." In such sentences the time element ("during the night") has been inserted between the logical object ("the debutante") and the verb ("was touched"). The sentence has also been rendered in the passive voice rather than in the active voice used in the prior experiments. Figure 10.10 illustrates the representation of these sentences according to HAM (in Figure 10.10a) and according to the physical contiguity hypothesis (in Figure 10.10b). Note how much the physical contiguities violate HAM's contiguities: O is physically closer to L and T than it is to R or S; T is closer to R and O than to L; and R is closer to S and T than to O. HAM predicts that T should "migrate" from its position in the physical sentence to a place in memory closest to L, thus displacing O; also, O should migrate to a place closest to R, displacing both S and T. The following experiment tests these proximity predictions.

The experiment was very similar in design to the previous two. Again, there were five content words; each sentence was tested with three incremental cues; and all 60 possible cue combinations were used. The 60 sentences were studied at a 24-second rate; test times were 32 seconds for the first cue, 24 for the second, and 16 for the third. As before, the sentences were randomly generated from sets of words for each syntactic slot and were randomly tested in three lists of 20. However, we were able to think up only 20 suitable possibilities for the time element, T. Therefore, the same 20 time elements were reused in each list of 20 sentences. If the subject

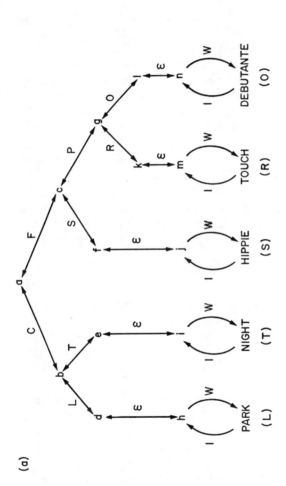

(a)

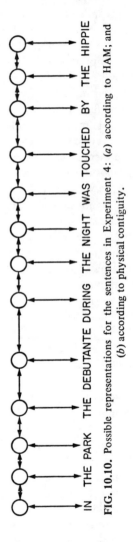

(b)

IN THE PARK THE DEBUTANTE DURING THE NIGHT WAS TOUCHED BY THE HIPPIE

FIG. 10.10. Possible representations for the sentences in Experiment 4: (a) according to HAM; and (b) according to physical contiguity.

was tested with T, his task was to recall the sentence that occurred in the most recent list. A total of 50 subjects were run in this experiment, yielding 3,000 (50 × 60) observations. In this experiment as in the previous one, subjects were given instructions that strongly urged them to form images of the situations described by the sentences.

Results

The first matter to decide is whether sentences were reordered in memory according to the representation predicted by HAM. Recall that HAM predicts a number of migrations of elements from the original physical contiguity orderings. First, T should replace O as the closest element to L. This leads to a number of predictions about recall patterns involving O versus T: First, consider recall to the first cues of R or S, where the three elements T, O, and L are all possible responses. If L is closer in memory to T than O, then L recall conditional on the recall of T should be higher than L recall conditional on recall of O. Therefore, we computed $P(L|T\bar{O})$, the probability of recall of L conditional on recall of T but not O, as well as $P(L|\bar{T}O)$, the probability of L conditional on recall of O but not T. HAM predicts $P(L|T\bar{O}) > P(L|\bar{T}O)$. This ordering was in fact the case, but the effect was exceedingly small; $P(L|T\bar{O}) = .64$ ($n = 74$) and $P(L|\bar{T}O) = .63$ ($n = 97$). On the basis of this statistic, neither HAM nor physical contiguity can be supported.

A second statistic stems from HAM's prediction that T is a better cue for L than is O, while physical contiguity predicts the opposite ordering. There is one difficulty with verifying this prediction. O may be (and indeed is) a better cue overall than T. This may simply be due to the fact that the probability of a word-to-idea transition is higher for O than T and may have nothing to do with the configuration of interidea associations. Therefore, what should be examined is the effectiveness of O as a cue for L *relative to* its effectiveness as a cue for a neutral element, R, and one should compare that effectiveness with the effectiveness of T as a cue for L relative to T's effectiveness for R. Thus, we computed the ratio, $Y_O(L|R)$, of the recall of L to O versus recall of R to O. That is, $Y_O(L|R) = P(O \rightarrow L)/P(O \rightarrow R)$. Similarly, $Y_T(L|R) = P(T \rightarrow L)/P(T \rightarrow R)$ was computed. According to HAM this second ratio, which measures the relative effectiveness of T as a cue for L, should be greater than the first ratio; that is, $Y_T(L|R) > Y_O(L|R)$. The actual result was slightly in the opposite direction: $Y_T(L|R) = 1.38$; $Y_O(L|R) = 1.42$. We took a second measure of the effectiveness of T versus O for recall of L. For this measure we used recall of S instead of R as our neutral standard. Again the outcome was slightly against HAM: $Y_T(L|S) = 1.26$, $Y_O(L|S) = 1.36$. So, these statistics offer little basis for deciding whether T or O is closer to L.

Next, we examined HAM's prediction that O should migrate to become closer than T to R. First, we computed the probability of recall of R conditional on recall of O but not T versus the probability conditional on T but not O. HAM predicts $P(R|\bar{T}O) > P(R|T\bar{O})$, while physical contiguity predicts the reverse. Physical contiguity was slightly favored: $P(R|\bar{T}O) = .40$ ($n = 127$), and $P(R|T\bar{O}) = .45$ ($n = 81$). Next we computed the effectiveness of T as a cue for R versus the effectiveness of O as a cue for R. Using S as a standard, HAM is slightly favored:

$Y_T(R|S) = .91$, and $Y_O(R|S) = .95$. However, using L as a standard, physical contiguity is slightly favored: $Y_T(R|L) = .72$, $Y_O(R|L) = .70$. Again, we seem unable to decide between contiguity and HAM's representation.

In contrast to the inability of the data to decide the last two issues, physical contiguity is clearly confirmed over HAM with respect to the relative nearness of O versus S to R. HAM had predicted that O should migrate to become closer to R. The conditional probabilities of recall strongly refute this: $P(R|O\bar{S}) = .26$ ($n = 116$), and $P(R|\bar{O}S) = .56$ ($n = 66$). Again the cueing ratios strongly favor physical contiguity: $Y_O(R|T) = .91$ versus $Y_S(R|T) = 1.17$, and $Y_O(R|L) = .70$ versus $Y_S(R|L) = .95$.

There is another possible explanation of this contingency in recall between S and R besides that of physical contiguity. It may be that the appropriate representation for these sentences is neither Figure 10.10a nor Figure 10.10b, but rather Figure 10.11. In Figure 10.11 we have introduced the passive relation "touched by" whose object is S, the subject of the corresponding active relation. Introduction of such "passive relations" is entirely reasonable, given the general approach in HAM to the representation problem. We have allowed arbitrary concepts to be represented by elementary nodes in memory, and any node can be terminal in the tree. So why not have a node for "being touched" as well as a node for "touching" and represent passives with the former relation and actives with the later relation? In Section 8.3 we have already presented reaction-time data arguing for the use of a passive relation.

If we accept Figure 10.11 as HAM's representation of such sentences, then it becomes easy to explain why physical contiguity of only R and S had an effect in this experiment—because in this case HAM's representation would correspond to the physical contiguities. In the case of the relative closeness of O versus T to R and of O versus T to L, physical contiguity and HAM's representation cancelled each other out, and the result was no overall effect. Of course, to advance this explanation is to grant to physical contiguity as well as to HAM's representation the

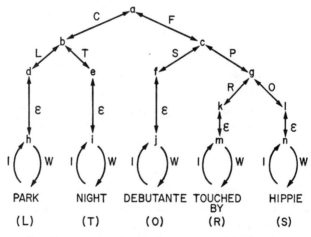

FIG. 10.11. HAM's alternate representation for sentences in Experiment 4 using passive relation.

power to connect elements in memory. It is really not unreasonable to suppose physical contiguity will have some effect on the structure of the memory representation. We have already noted evidence that subjects tend to enrich the connections among the sentential elements by spontaneously forming auxiliary propositions to interconnect subsets of the elements in the sentence. It is not unreasonable to suppose that the subjects would try to so interconnect those subsets of elements that were contiguous in the physical sentence. For example, upon reading "In the park the debutante . . ." the subject might image a debutante dancing in the park.

In further analyses of the data, the representation in Figure 10.11 will be assumed to see how much of the variance in the data it can account for. First, we examined the relative frequencies of second recalls to inadequate stimuli (7.2% of 835 opportunities), second recalls not predicted by the model (10.4% of 470), and second recalls predicted by the model (15.9% of 365). The difference between the first two frequencies of second recall is significant at the .05 confidence level

TABLE 10.11

Recall Probabilities Conditional on Node
Accessibility—Experiment 4

Conditional probability	Observed	Theoretical	n	χ^2 (1)
(a) 2 out of 3 nontargets recalled				
$P(L|\text{context})$	.688	.742	154	.63
$P(L|\overline{\text{context}})$	.736	.667	91	
$P(T|\text{context})$	.623	.558	223	1.84
$P(T|\overline{\text{context}})$	.520	.441	50	
$P(O|\text{fact})$	.680	.649	228	—
$P(O|\overline{\text{fact}})$	—	—	0	
$P(R|\text{predicate})$	.645	.540	183	18.73
$P(R|\overline{\text{predicate}})$	.370	.518	92	
$P(S|\text{predicate})$	.726	.597	157	19.43
$P(S|\overline{\text{predicate}})$	.458	.587	107	
(b) 1 out of 3 nontargets recalled				
$P(L|\text{context})$	.504	.542	127	6.72
$P(L|\overline{\text{context}})$	.349	.477	152	
$P(T|\text{context})$	.320	.382	206	4.31
$P(T|\overline{\text{context}})$	.214	.287	126	
$P(O|\text{fact})$	.411	.441	129	1.62
$P(O|\overline{\text{fact}})$	.336	.376	140	
$P(R|\text{predicate})$	.424	.353	59	23.14
$P(R|\overline{\text{predicate}})$	.137	.305	197	
$P(S|\text{predicate})$	.469	.397	98	27.57
$P(S|\overline{\text{predicate}})$	.183	.358	208	

$(\chi^2_{(1)} = 4.34)$, as is the difference between the last two $(\chi^2_{(1)} = 4.95)$. Thus, we may conclude that the revised representation in Figure 10.11 is an important determinant of the sentences' organization in memory, but that other factors are also operative.

The second analysis concerns probability of recall of particular target items conditional on whether it is known from recall of other items that the person has access to a target node dominating the target item. In this experiment the target nodes were the context node that dominates L and T, the fact node that dominates O, and the predicate node that dominates R and S (see Figure 10.11). As before, we will analyze separately the data when conditionalizing on recall of two out of the three nontarget words and when conditionalizing on recall of one out of three. The results are presented in Table 10.11, which is to be compared with Tables 10.3, 10.6, and 10.9 from previous experiments.

As in other tables, the structural assumptions of the model are strongly manifested in these conditional recall probabilities. Again the data show stronger conditional effects than the mathematical model predicts. The observed mean difference between the favored and nonfavored conditional probabilities is .168, while the expected difference is only .068. Most of this discrepancy is associated with the recall of elements R and S. It will be remembered that it was for these elements that physical contiguity coincided with HAM's contiguity in Figure 10.11. This is probably the source of the overly strong structural effects.

Mathematical Model

The model was fitted to the data using the structural representation of Figure 10.11. Table 10.12 presents the Data and Theoretical Matrices, as well as the

TABLE 10.12

Matrices and Parameter Estimates—Experiment 4

	(a) Data Matrix						(b) Theoretical Matrix				
	L	T	O	R	S		L	T	O	R	S
L		.285	.347	.242	.277	L		.774	.739	.726	.726
T	.203		.175	.147	.162	T	.774		.739	.726	.726
O	.388	.300		.273	.285	O	.739	.739		.755	.755
R	.245	.203	.227		.252	R	.726	.726	.755		.774
S	.292	.238	.253	.278		S	.726	.726	.755	.774	

(c) Parameter Estimates

$tb = 7.8$

$s_L = .714$	$r_L = .654$
$s_T = .404$	$r_T = .525$
$s_O = .734$	$r_O = .582$
$s_R = .539$	$r_R = .505$
$s_S = .630$	$r_S = .549$

parameter estimates. The table of event frequencies will not be presented here due to its length (135 entries). Interested readers may write to the first author for copies of it. The chi-square measure of goodness of fit was 204.05 with 123 df. The value of the chi-square is similar to that of the past two experiments. That is, it is clearly greater than conventional levels of statistical significance ($\chi^2_{(123)}$ = 150 for .05 level), but it is sufficiently small to indicate that the model has captured most of the variance in the data. Again, much of the chi-square is accounted for by a few discrepant events. The event where L evokes recall of just O, where O evokes just L, where R evokes just S, and the event where S evokes just R account for a total chi-square of 50.84. The theory consistently underpredicts these events. Overall, 76.9 such events are predicted, but 134 are observed. The first two events are suggestive of a greater than expected contingency between L and O, and the last two are suggestive of a greater than expected contingency between S and R. The data was ambiguous about whether to place T or O closest to L. The representation of Figure 10.11 does not underpredict the contingency between T and L, but it fits that only by underpredicting the contingency between L and O. The stronger-than-expected contingency between R and S presumably reflects the combined effects of physical contiguity and HAM's representation.

General Comments

Some interesting relations appear in comparing the parameter estimates across the four experiments. First, consider the estimates of the parameter tb: 3.9 in Experiment 1; 3.7 in Experiment 2; 5.1 in Experiment 3; and 7.8 in Experiment 4. For comparisons of the encoding rate, b, this estimate must be divided by the study times per sentence: 20 seconds in Experiment 1; 18 seconds in Experiments 2 and 3; and 24 seconds in Experiment 4. Thus, in Experiments 1 and 2, where no imagery instructions were employed, b estimates were .195 and .205, respectively. In Experiments 3 and 4, which did use imagery instructions, the b estimates are .283 and .325. So, it would appear that the encoding rate parameter is fairly constant across sentence types, but positively related to imagery instructions. The fact that the rate parameter is well behaved is encouraging with respect to the model.

It is more difficult to compare the various stimulus and response probabilities across the four experiments. Table 10.13 attempts this comparison. This lists the parameters for the locatives, the subjects, the transitive verbs, and the objects from each experiment. We have omitted the intransitive verbs used in Experiments 2 and 3 and the time elements used in Experiment 4. Subject and object refers in Experiment 4 to the grammatical subject and object which served these roles in the final representation of Figure 10.11. Since there was much sharing of the lexical items serving each function across the various experiments, one expects strong correlations between these parameters across experiments. This is indeed the case. Letting r_{ij} represent the correlation between the parameters in Experiments i and j, the coefficients of correlations are as follows: r_{12} = .69, r_{13} = .58, r_{14} = .80, r_{23} = .97, r_{24} = .84, and r_{34} = .81. All these correlations are significant by t tests. Except for Experiments 2 and 3, the sentence constructions were different. Different focusing strategies by subjects for the different sentence constructions

TABLE 10.13

Stimulus and Response Probabilities in Four Experiments

Conditional probability	Exp. 1	Exp. 2	Exp. 3	Exp. 4	Mean
(a) Stimulus probabilities					
Location	.833	.789	.843	.714	.795
Subject	.743	.736	.804	.734	.754
Verb	.592	.468	.529	.539	.532
Object	.802	.747	.744	.630	.731
Mean	.743	.685	.730	.654	.703
(b) Response probabilities					
Location	.631	.796	.862	.654	.736
Subject	.534	.666	.733	.582	.629
Verb	.503	.515	.584	.505	.527
Object	.606	.627	.734	.549	.629
Mean	.569	.651	.728	.573	.630
Mean of stimuli and responses	.656	.668	.729	.613	.667

could explain why the other correlations are not as high as that between Experiments 2 and 3.

Inspection of Table 10.12 reveals some interesting trends. First, except for the verb, the stimulus probabilities are greater than the response probabilities (a mean difference of .101). For the verb, however, the stimulus probability is just slightly higher than the response probability. The verb is also the worst item both as a stimulus and as a response in all experiments. Since verbs are generally less imageable than the nouns serving as location, subject, and object, this result seems related to findings in paired-associates learning (Paivio, 1971). Less imageable nouns make for difficult paired associates, and the detrimental effect is stronger when they serve as stimuli than as responses. Less imageable nouns also tend to be verb derivatives. It is unclear, therefore, whether the particular pattern of recall obtained with verbs and low-imagery nouns is due to imagery or syntactic class (but see Kintsch, 1972, for an attempt to separate these two factors). Some of the other trends in these parameter estimates are quite perplexing. In Experiments 2 and 3 there is little overall difference between the stimulus probabilities and the response probabilities, but the stimulus probabilities are higher than the response probabilities in Experiments 1 and 4. The bottom line in Table 10.12 reports the average of the stimulus and response probabilities for each experiment. There appears to be something of a negative relation between study time and these mean probabilities. Experiment 4, with 24 seconds per sentence, has a mean of .613; Experiment 1, with 20 seconds, .656; and Experiments 2 and 3, with 18 seconds, .668 and .729. Unfortunately, the variance in study time is not very large and in any event is confounded with sentence type. Thus, the perplexities in Table 10.12 may just reflect focusing strategies induced by the various sentential constructions.

Let us summarize the significance of the research reported in this chapter. We have taken careful and detailed measures of the patterns of sentence recall that are obtained in cued recall experiments. First, it is eminently clear that there are strong recall contingencies to be found in such data, indicating that each element does not have equal access to each other element in the memory trace. It seems that these recall contingencies are determined both by physical contiguity and by contiguities in a HAM-like deep-structure representation. We assumed that the physical factor had its influence through the auxiliary encodings that subjects report making in such experiments.

Second, there appears to be considerable validity to a stochastic model that assumes memory for a sentence depends upon the formation of a number of discrete, all-or-none connections. The model which successfully fit the data assumed that probabilities of forming these associations were independent within a sentence, but covaried across sentences in a data pool. These various findings contradict initial intuitions about a unitary, wholistic representation of the sentence. Such a wholistic representation would not predict the structural effects found nor the systematic patterns of partial recall. It is of some interest that these nonwholistic effects were maintained in the last two experiments that employed strong imagery instructions.

Finally, some comment is needed about the significance of the quantitative fit of a mathematical model to the data. The precise assumptions of the model were openly admitted to be approximate guesses. Therefore, one cannot claim a great deal for the precise predictions made. The significance of the mathematical model lies in its ability to capture and summarize most of the variance in the data. This it has done rather well, using the conventional "goodness of fit" standards of mathematical psychology. If one understands the general stochastic mechanisms and structural assumptions on which the model was based, he can be confident that he has a characterization of the principal trends determining sentence recall of the sort studied in this chapter.

REFERENCES

Atkinson, R. C., Bower, G. H., & Crothers, E. J. *An introduction to mathematical learning theory.* New York: Wiley, 1965.

Fillenbaum, S. Psycholinguistics. *Annual Review of Psychology*, 1971, **22**, 251–308.

Kintsch, W. Abstract nouns: Imagery vs. lexical complexity. *Journal of Verbal Learning and Verbal Behavior*, 1972, **11**, 59–65.

McGill, W. J. Stochastic latency mechanisms. In R. D. Luce, R. R. Bush, & E. Galanter (Eds.), *Handbook of mathematical psychology*. Vol. 1. New York: Wiley, 1963.

Paivio, A. *Imagery and verbal processes.* New York: Holt, Rinehart & Winston, 1971.

Wanner, H. E. On remembering, forgetting, and understanding sentences: A study of the deep structure hypothesis. Unpublished doctoral dissertation, Harvard University, 1968.

11
PROPERTIES OF THE
MEMORY STRUCTURE

If we believe that, in becoming associated, A and B remain two mutually neutral facts which merely happen to occur together, then some special bound, such as a particularly well conducting group of fibers, may be regarded as an adequate basis of association. In full contrast to this view, we may, however, reason as follows: When an A and B become associated, they are experienced not as two independent things but as members of an organized group unit. This may perhaps now be taken for granted.

—Wolfgang Köhler

11.1. GESTALT VERSUS MECHANISTIC INTERPRETATIONS

The preceding chapter was concerned with testing a particular mathematical model to describe the learning and retrieval of the structures allegedly underlying memory for sentences. The predictions which fit those data depended largely upon two basic assumptions: that the input tree of structural relations has a particular form, and that the associations in the input tree are formed and remembered probabilistically in an all-or-none fashion independently of one another (with due allowance for individual-difference parameters). The earlier results provided some confirmation of these general assumptions. In this chapter we seek for further confirmation of our assumptions, but this time searching for rather general *qualitative* evidence rather than the detailed quantitative fits of a model, as displayed in Chapter 10. To this end, we shall review and comment upon experiments of ours on sentence memory as well as several other critical ones appearing in the recent literature.

In this section of the chapter, HAM will be contrasted with some Gestalt-like ideas about sentence memory. Actually, the Gestalters never addressed themselves to the question of how sentential information is represented in memory. In fact, they generally avoided complex linguistic material and confined their analysis to perceptual or simple verbal materials. Therefore, it requires some extrapolation on our part to give a Gestalt interpretation for sentence memory. However, our Gestalt extrapolations do share marked similarities to Gestalt notions about memory for perceptual materials, and they also capture certain intuitions people have about sentence memory. Therefore, the empirical viability of our Gestalt interpretation is an interesting psychological question. We have been accused of beating a dead horse in this section, but that was obviously not our intent. We found our Gestalt interpretation high in initial credability and were surprised when it consistently failed. We thought these failures served to indicate a great deal about the nature of memory. Indeed the experiments we will report in this section were the ones that stimulated us to construct HAM. Our initial intention in performing them had been to show the absurdity of any associative interpretation of sentence memory. That is to say, our Gestalt interpretation antedates HAM.

Our theory provides a quite "mechanistic" interpretation of sentence learning: following parsing plus MATCH look-up processes, the independent links of the input tree are associated piecemeal, part by part. This analysis of simple sentences conflicts sharply with the layman's intuitions about the conceptual *unity* of the proposition asserted by the sentence. In contrast, Gestalt theory would give the simple sentence a unitary representation, not analyzable into independent parts. In Gestalt terms, a simple sentence like "The boy hit the girl" would constitute a single "good figure" (male chauvinism aside). It is complete in itself, its "goodness" does not gain by elaborating it with further detail. On the other hand, remove one word from the sentence, and the former unity disintegrates. For instance, the sentence fragment, "The boy hit the _____," is an unstable structure, with a gap that "begs" to be completed by an object-noun. Also, if one word in the sentence is changed (e.g., "The boy hit the booze"), the entire sentence-gestalt would appear to be changed.

The layman might describe the unitary nature of a simple sentence in terms of the mental imagery or mental pictures the sentence causes him to construct. And, to be sure, whereas "The boy hit the girl" and "The boy hit the booze" evoke quite different pictures, the fragment "The boy hit the _____" corresponds to no picture whatsoever. It is not a "good gestalt."

Fragmentary Recall?

A first elementary distinction between the two positions regards their expectation of all-or-none recall of atomic propositions. The following quotation from an earlier paper of ours tells the reasoning:

> Fragmentary recall of simple sentences (e.g., "Something about the boy and the girl") should be very rare occurrences according to the Gestalt hypothesis. This prediction follows from two principles of gestalt psychology. First, to quote Köhler (1947), "the trace of a unitary experience is itself a unitary fact" [p. 287]. That is, if an object is perceived as a unit there should be a simple all-or-none memory trace deposited. But as Köhler so cogently argues, unitary perception does not imply perfect recall of the units. The stimulus conditions at recall may not redintegrate the unitary trace, leading to complete failure of recall. However, a clear implication of the principle of a unitary trace is that, if part of a simple sentence is recalled, all must be recalled. To quote Koffka, "recall does not go from part to part, but from part to whole" [1935, p. 568]. Secondly, if for some reason, *S* did not

perceive the sentence as a unit but formed a fragmentary trace, then that fragmentary trace would have little chance for surviving until the time of recall. To quote Koffka (1935): "For if traces are exposed to forces which connect them with other traces, highly unstable trace structure will be destroyed. Chaotic patterns have neither a well-defined boundary, to keep them unified and segregated, nor interior stability. Therefore, they can have but little power of resisting outside forces. This principle seems fundamental [p. 507]."

In contrast to this Gestalt hypothesis of a unitary memory trace, the associationist hypothesis dictates that a simple sentence be represented by a configuration of several independent associations. We would expect that only some of these associations will be durably established during a single learning trial. To that extent, S should frequently give partial sentence recall. So the frequency of complete versus fragmentary recall to sentence probes will be one observation of interest [Anderson & Bower, 1971, p. 674].

It is a simple matter to check for fragmentary recall in our data, where to a probe-cue the subject recalls part but not all of a simple sentence. In many such comparisons, we have consistently found large amounts of fragmentary recall (although as this book goes to press we are currently struggling to understand a new experiment in which recall was almost completely all-or-none). For example, in Experiment 1 reported in Chapter 10, for sentences containing four content words (location, agent, verb, object), the probability of the subject recalling everything to a single cue (averaging over the four cues) was .120, and the probability of the subject recalling nothing to a single cue was .642. The remaining .238 proportion of cases represents fragmentary recall, of one or two content words being retrieved by the cue. Clearly, in this experiment, the amount of fragmentary recall even exceeds the amount of complete recall, whereas the Gestalt position expected this proportion to be nearly zero.

A Gestalter might object that four-term propositions are too complex for perceptual unification, and we must turn to simpler propositions. We have memory data for simple "subject-verb-object" declarative sentences, where the retrieval cue was the subject of each sentence, given in a test immediately after studying a list of 32 such simple sentences. Scoring protocols for recall of verb alone, object alone, or both verb and object, it was found across four experimental conditions that fragmentary recall was always at least 50% as frequent as total recall. Averaged across the four experimental conditions, the proportion of complete recalls (verb plus object to agent cue) was .263, while the average proportion of fragmentary recalls (verb or object alone) was .255. Clearly, then, the content words of the sentence are not typically recalled in all-or-none fashion.

The case is no better if one looks at free recall of sensible *two-word* phrases such as adjective-noun or noun-intransitive verb phrases. These are encoded as complete propositional trees by HAM. The all-or-none question cannot be meaningfully answered with respect to *cued* recall of two-term phrases, but it is meaningful for free recall. In free recall, the subject is asked to recall in any order all the words he saw in a study list of two-word phrases, including in his recall any single words he can remember without their neighbor. HAM expects the amount of fragmentary recall to be generally much less here than for the more complex structures, since there are fewer component associations to establish. In general, all-or-none recall exceeds fragmentary recall in these cases, but there is significant partial recall. As expected, the level of fragmentary recall varies with the same factors that make for difficulty or ease of associating items in sentences—e.g., semantic anomaly of the phrases, normative associative frequency, concreteness of the terms, whether the subject is asked to "image" the concept described, etc. (cf. Horowitz & Manelis, 1972).

The classification of recall employed in the above discussion was simply whether or not each content word was recalled correctly. What happens when the subject fails to recall a given term? Overwhelmingly in our experiments, the subject simply draws a "blank," and says something like "I can remember only that the boy hit someone or something." One can raise the level of intrusion errors by instructions or other motivational devices that encourage guessing. In these cases, the subjects typically guess words of the appropriate case function that appeared in other sentences of the study list. It has been proposed to us (R. C. Anderson, personal communication) that the errors in the protocols which create partial recall might mainly be intrusions that are semantically close to the correct word (e.g., prostitute versus whore) and that perhaps if we scored for "gist" recall, the pattern would appear more all-or-none. In our data, this is clearly not the case. Subjects generally do not make many intrusions that have meaning similar to the correct word, so that counting them in as "correct" does not much affect the overall conclusion. For instance, in Experiment 4 of Chapter 10, there were 32% words correctly recalled and just 1% semantic intrusions. Of course, semantic intrusions should be higher in sentences that are "semantically well integrated" in Rosenberg's (1968) sense—e.g., "The grocer sold the goods." With such sentences, intelligent subjects can plausibly guess at missing elements, given part of the sentence, and thus possibly record a "correct gist" response while recalling nothing specific about the correct object noun. For these reasons, we have tended in most of our work to use sentences which are not semantically well integrated, although they are perfectly sensible propositions such as "The major telephoned the librarian" or "The farmer bought a package."

The Verb-Repetition Experiment

The verb-repetition experiment concerned sentence recall accuracy when a given verb occurs in several different sentences. In our experiment (Anderson & Bower, 1971), the same verb was used in either one, two, four, or eight different sentences distributed among a set of 32 which the subject studied. Consider how an associative theory might reconstruct the situation when the subject has studied two sentences with the same verb, such as the pair of sentences, "The boy hit the dog" and "The girl hit the ball." Figure 11.1 shows how HAM would represent this pair of sentences.

The question of interest in this research was how the patterns of recall to various cues would be related to the variable of number of propositions in which the verb occurred (1, 2, 4, or 8). Consider first cueing with the subject noun

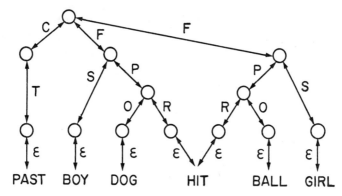

FIG. 11.1. Memory representation for a pair of sentences using the same verb.

(BOY) only, and we ask about recall of the object noun (DOG). In this case, object recall depends on having formed five links in the direct chain from the concept node of the cue, BOY, to the concept node of the object, DOG. The verb is in no way involved at this point. Therefore, a first expectation of the structure in Figure 11.1 in this experiment is that the probability of object recall to a subject cue should be independent of the number of different propositions in which a given verb occurred within the study list. This "null result" was confirmed in our experiment. Object recall proportions to the subject cue were .31, .30, .32, and .29 for sentences using verbs occurring in 1, 2, 4, and 8 sentences, respectively. These proportions obviously do not differ from one another. This replicates a finding reported by Rowher and Lynch (1967). While it is true that this result is predicted by our theory, it is also true that it is predicted by Gestalt theory. That is, according to the Gestalt theory, each sentence is a different patterned whole, whether or not the verb is repeated. Thus repetition of an element, the verb, should have no effect on probability of object recall.

However, the two theories differ with respect to a more refined prediction. Suppose that to the cue of the subject BOY, the S is unable to recall either remaining item in the sentence. The question is what the model implies about the S's ability to recall the object if he is now cued with the "subject plus verb" compound. From Figure 11.1 and the S's failure to recall anything to BOY, we may infer that his memory structure for that sentence does not contain an intact associative path from the concept node for BOY to the concept node for the verb HIT. At least one of the five associative links in that chain must have failed to be established. Similarly, due to the S's failure to recall the object, we know that there cannot be an intact path from BOY to DOG. Therefore, when cued with the subject plus verb, the S should be unable to recall the object via an associative path from the subject. (If there had been an intact path from subject to object, the S would have already recalled the object to the subject-only cue.) The only possibility for recall in this set of circumstances is if an associative path exists from the verb concept to the correct object.

However, it is precisely at this point that the multiple contexts of a verb's occurrence lead to its ambiguity as a recall cue. If the verb has occurred in several sentences, the concept node of the verb will lead to many instances connected in turn possibly to their respective objects. Since there is no association from the subject to the verb, the S will probably not be able to select with certainty the correct path from the verb type to the appropriate object. The S in this predicament would have to guess among several equally likely paths from the verb concept. Hence, conditional upon nonrecall of both verb and object to the subject-only cue, the associative model predicts confusion in object recall to the cue of subject-plus-verb if that verb occurred in several study sentences. Moreover, this confusion or competition among objects at recall should increase and correct recall should decrease as a given verb occurs in progressively more sentences. Gestalt theory makes the same prediction in this conditional circumstance as it had in the first, namely, it predicts no effect anywhere of verb repetition.

The experimental results are shown in Table 11.1, and they are completely in accord with predictions of the associative model. Line 2 is critical in differentiating the two hypotheses; as verb-repetition increases, there is a decrease in correct object recall to subject + verb, conditional upon nonrecall to the subject alone. This was as predicted by the associative model.

A further prediction of the associative hypothesis is that there should be increased *intrusions* of other objects with which the verb was paired. Such intrusions should occur everytime the S decides to guess among the competing verb-to-object paths (he may sometimes simply inhibit overt recall altogether), and selects the wrong path and hence the wrong object as an intrusion error.

To test this last prediction we will require the notion of an intragroup intrusion. A *group* refers here to the eight experimental sentences in the set of 32 that contributed to one of the four verb-repetition conditions. An intragroup intrusion is the intrusion (recall) of an object from one of the other sentences in the same group as the test sentence. The number of such intrusions in the condition where the verb occurs in only one sentence provides a baseline measure of how frequently such intrusions should occur when there is no specific confusion of objects due to verb repetition. Such baseline intrusions are due to unidentified factors which

TABLE 11.1

Mean Probability of Recall

Cueing condition	Item recalled	Number of sentences in which verb occurred			
		1	2	4	8
1. Agent	Object	.307	.300	.316	.285
2. Agent + verb given nonrecall to agent	Object	.186	.078	.094	.051
3. Agent + verb	Intragroup object intrusion	.112	.156	.170	.211

Note.—Adopted from Anderson & Bower (1971).

presumably are constant across the levels of the verb repetition factor. But if intrusions arise due to verb repetition, then the number of intragroup intrusions to the cue of agent plus verb should increase with verb repetition in some monotonic manner from this baseline.

Line 3 of Table 11.1 reports the mean proportions of such intragroup intrusions to the cue of subject-plus-verb. These show the predicted increase in intrusions with higher verb repetition, and the linear trend was very significant statistically.

So, in this second, refined prediction for the verb-repetition experiment, the associative theory is confirmed, whereas the Gestalt hypothesis is disconfirmed. As expected, verb repetition does not harm recall except in those special circumstances where the person must rely upon the verb alone, and then he shows "response competition" among various objects to recall, intrusion errors, and reduced correct recall. Several other effects were present in these data (e.g., correct verb recall increased with verb repetition); they do not contradict the basic ideas of the associative model. The original Anderson and Bower (1971) paper may be consulted for these ancillary details.

The Cross-over Experiments

Another experiment in this series (Anderson & Bower, 1972a) tests a different facet of the contrast between the Gestalt and associative theories. The associative account stresses the functional independence of the various associations in a structure. The Gestalt principle of emergence (see Section 3.2) contrasts sharply with that independence; it is alleged that a structure "is not just the sum of its parts," but rather has new emergent properties that are dependent upon the configuration of parts. For example, a single slanting line on paper suggests nothing regarding depth; but put two slanting lines close together and converging, then the attribute of depth "emerges" from that linear perspective. When applied to sentences, the principle of emergence implies that the information conveyed by a sentence is not just a combination of the information conveyed by its separate parts. New properties should emerge from the sentence because of the configuration of its parts.

The associative theory denies these emergent, configural properties of a proposition. The representation of a sentence in the theory is as a set of concepts linked into a particular structure by labeled associations; it is this mechanical compounding of the parts to form a representation of the sentence which leads associative theory to the counterintuitive predictions that are tested in the Cross-Over experiments.

Consider the associative structure that should develop after studying a pair of sentences like (1) and (2), which have the same direct object of the verb:

The child hit the landlord.   (1)
The minister praised the landlord.   (2)

The associative structure for these two sentences is illustrated in Figure 11.2. The crucial question of interest is how would a cue (prompt) such as Frame (3) compare with a cue such as Frame (4) in terms of eliciting recall of the common object noun.

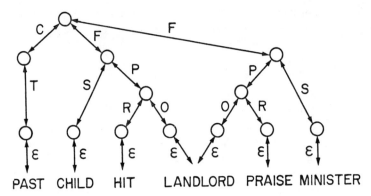

FIG. 11.2. Memory representation for a pair of sentences using the same object.

The child hit the _____.   (3)

The child praised the _____.   (4)

In Frame (3), the subject-noun and verb are reproduced from the same study sentence, whereas in Frame (4) they were selected from different sentences or are crossed-over. Since in both cases the subject and the verb have been associated with the same object-noun (i.e., landlord), there should be no ambiguity about what to recall in either case. The Gestalt hypothesis would predict that recall to Frame (3) should exceed that to Frame (4) because the acquired pattern of parts is maintained in Frame (3) but destroyed in Frame (4). Consequently, the "emergent" information should be maintained in Frame (3) but not in Frame (4). This prediction of the Gestalt hypothesis has been judged to correspond with intuition by most of our colleagues.

However, associative models like HAM lead to just the opposite prediction. An examination of Figure 11.2 will give the reason. We will explain HAM's predictions by assigning probabilities to various pieces of the graph structure in Figure 11.2. Let a be the probability that the path from the subject noun (e.g., "child") to the predicate node is intact. Let b be the corresponding probability that the path is intact from the verb (e.g., "hit") to the predicate node. Finally, let c be the probability that the path is intact from the predicate node to the object. To expedite explanation we will assume the various probabilities are independent. The model set forth in Chapter 10 concerned itself with the covariance of these probabilities, but such covariance is irrelevant to the qualitative predictions that will concern us here. In the following, we shall be concerned with the probability that S recalls the object-noun when cued with various other parts of a sentence. We shall write these recall probabilities like conditional probabilities. Thus, $P(O|S)$, $P(O|V)$, $P(O|S_1 V_1)$, and $P(O|S_1 V_2)$ will denote the probability of object-noun recall, given a recall test-cue of, respectively, a subject, a verb, a subject and verb from a studied sentence, and a subject plus verb from different sentences of pairs like Sentences (1) and (2). An $S_1 V_1$ test frame like Sentence (3), with S and V from the same sentence, will be called a *Same* cue; the $S_1 V_2$ test frame like Sentence (4) will be called a *Crossed-over* cue.

By inspection of Figure 11.2, the following equations are found to describe the recall probability for Same versus Crossed-over test frames:

$$P(O|S_1 V_1) = ac + (1-a)bc \tag{5}$$
$$P(O|S_1 V_2) = ac + (1-ac)bc \tag{6}$$

Subtracting Equation (5) from Equation (6), we have

$$P(O|S_1 V_2) - P(O|S_1 V_1) = abc(1-c) \tag{7}$$

In words, recall to the Crossed-over cue is predicted to exceed recall to the Same cue. Now the difference in Equation (7) in favor of the Crossed-over cue may not be very large. For instance, if the probability for each association were .67, the difference would be only .033. However, even the prediction that these two test frames should elicit about equal recall is counterintuitive.

Recall of the object to the Crossed-over cue will succeed if either of two separate associative paths are intact, the one from the subject in the first sentence to the object, or the one from the verb in the second sentence to the object. In contrast, for the Same cue the two associative paths, from the verb and from the subject, share two links in common, specifically the two from the predicate to the object concept. It is this difference which gives the Crossed-over cue the slight advantage in the associationist theory.

A second interesting prediction can be derived from Figure 11.2. It concerns the probability of successful object recall to a cue like Frame (8) which only contains a subject-noun, and a cue like Frame (9) which only contains a verb:

The child _____ the _____.   (8)
The _____ praised the _____.   (9)

The probabilities of recall for Frame (8), $P(O|S)$, and for Frame (9), $P(O|V)$, are:

$$P(O|S) = ac \tag{10}$$
$$P(O|V) = bc \tag{11}$$

The interesting observation is their relation to the probability of object recall to the Crossed-over cue, which is given in Equation (12):

$$1 - P(O|S_1 V_2) = (1 - P(O|S))(1 - P(O|V)) \tag{12}$$
$$\text{or } P(O|S_1 V_2) = 1 - (1 - P(O|S))(1 - P(O|V)) \tag{12a}$$

That is, the associative model predicts that the probability of nonrecall to the Crossed-over cue should equal the product of the probabilities of nonrecall to the subject-only cue and the verb-only cue. This follows because the Crossed-over cue is viewed as just as independent combination of subject and verb cues. This prediction can be shown to hold for almost any associative structure, not just the particular structure shown in Figure 11.2. In fact, in our original paper we explicated it with respect to the ELINOR (see Section 4.4) representation. Combining Equation (7) with Equation (12a) leads to the predicted inequality:

$$P(O|S_1 V_1) \leqslant 1 - (1 - P(O|S))(1 - P(O|V)). \tag{13}$$

Equation (7) and the inequality in Equation (13) rest on the assumption of any associative model, that there is no further information in the Same cue than that

TABLE 11.2

Proportion Object Recall—Experiment 1

1. $P(O|S)$	.470
2. $P(O|V)$	.292
3. $P(O|S_1 V_1)$	.579
4. $P(O|S_1 V_2)$	.611
5. $1 - (1 - P(O|S))(1 - P(O|V))$ (computed from Lines 1 and 2)	.624
6. $1 - (1 - P(O|S))(1 - P(O|V))$ (computed for each S and then averaged)	.604

Note.—736 observations contribute to each of Lines 1 to 4.

contained in its parts, the subject and the verb. In contrast, if the Gestalt hypothesis is correct in its claim of emergent information, then both the inequality in Equation (13) should be reversed and the Same cue should also be superior to the Crossed-over cue.

The experiments testing these predictions are reported in detail in Anderson and Bower (1972a); however, the principle results will be briefly reviewed here. The results of the main experiments are shown in Table 11.2, which reports the proportions of object-noun recall to the several cues. As is usually the case, the subject-noun is a more effective cue than the verb; also the $S_1 V_1$ cue shows an advantage over either cue singly. The really interesting result is that recall to the Crossed-over cue (Line 4 of Table 11.2) exceeds recall to the Same cue (Line 3 of Table 11.2). The difference is not large, but as we noted with respect to Equation (7), it was not expected to be a large difference. Given the strength of one's intuitive expectation of the opposite ordering, even the slight superiority of the Crossed-over cue is surprising.

Lines 5 and 6 in Table 11.2 are testing the ability of the model to predict object recall to the Crossed-over cue (Line 4) from recall to the subject-alone and verb-alone cues. Two slight variants are shown, one computed from group averages and the other computed for each subject before taking the group average. These predictions differ little, and they bracket the observed recall of .611 to the Crossed-over cue. Thus, this experiment gives strong support to the class of "independent associations" models such as HAM. Not only was recall to the Crossed-over cue slightly above recall to the Same cue, but the former was quantitatively predictable from alternate measures of object recall to the subject-only and verb-only cues.

The associative model predicts that during testing, the subject will often be able to recognize or label the Crossed-over cues for exactly what they are. In theory, S_1 could retrieve all or part of proposition 1, and/or verb V_2 could retrieve all or part of proposition 2 in such manner as to warrant the claim that $S_1 V_2$ was a Crossed-over cue. A later, unpublished experiment of ours has shown that, as expected, the subjects can identify with reasonable accuracy (circa 80%) which were Same and which were Crossed-over subject-verb cues. Furthermore, as predicted by the theory, object recall was higher when the cue type was correctly identified than when it was incorrectly identified.

In conclusion, the facts reviewed above—on fragmentary recall of sentences, on selective interference in the verb-repetition experiment, and on the retrieval efficacy of Crossed-over versus Same cues—convince us to reject the Gestalt interpretation we have given of sentence memory. Like many of the other Gestalt-like notions that have appeared in psychology, it had intuitive appeal, but it just failed to live up to the empirical facts of the matter.

11.2. ON CUEING EFFECTIVENESS

As a further illustration of the predictions of HAM, we shall review predictions and results concerning the relative power of certain retrieval cues, given a particular sentence structure. The first experiment to be reviewed is by Wanner (1968). Wanner was concerned with finding a deep-structure parameter which would predict the relative effectiveness of various items in the sentence as prompts for recall of the complete sentence. He proposed that the efficacy of a prompt word should vary directly with the number of times a lexical item is entered in the deep-structure derived from the surface sentence. This corresponds to the number of atomic propositions in which the word appears. For instance, in standard transformational grammar, the surface sentence "The lazy student was spanked by the cruel principal" can be "de-transformed" into the elementary (or atomic) propositions: "The student is lazy," "The principal spanked the student," and "The principal is cruel." Several different surface strings can be derived from these three logical propositions, depending on the sequence of transformations followed to generate a surface form from the deep-structure (e.g., "The principal who spanked the lazy student was cruel"). In any event, Wanner's hypothesis would examine such surface strings, note their deep-structure propositions, then index each item according to the number of propositions in which it occurs. Prompt effectiveness of a word would then be expected to vary directly with this index number.

In Wanner's experiment, he used slightly more complex sentences in order to obtain results discriminating between his own hypothesis and an alternate hypothesis (which is of no interest here). Examples of Wanner's sentences are the following:

The governor asked the detective to cease drinking.   (14)
The governor asked the detective to prevent drinking.   (15)

The graph structures assigned to these two types of sentences by HAM are shown in Figure 11.3. In the "cease" sentence, "detective" occurs in three propositions, whereas in the "prevent" sentence, with an understood "some people drink," "detective" appears in only two propositions.

To test his predictions, Wanner had subjects (college students) study a list of sentences and then try to free-recall as many sentences as they could. The free-recall measure was to check whether there was any intrinsic difference in difficulty or memorability of the class of "cease" compared to "prevent" sentences. There was no significant difference between the two types of sentences. The critical data came when Wanner then cued recall of each sentence by giving either the surface subject, "governor," or the embedded subject, "detective."

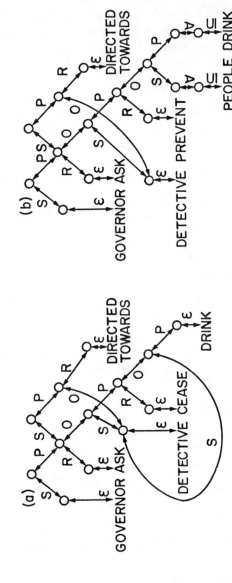

FIG. 11.3. HAM's representation of the sentences in the Wanner (1968) experiment: (*a*) "cease" sentences, and (*b*) "prevent" sentences.

A first fact was that the prompting effectiveness of the surface subject, "governor," was equally good (or poor) in the *cease* and the *prevent* types of sentences. Second, and most important, prompt effectiveness did increase directly (almost linearly) with the number of deep-structure propositions in which the cue word appeared. Thus, the best prompt was "detective" in *cease* sentences, next best was "detective" in *prevent* sentences, and poorest was "governor" in either sentence; these occur, of course, in three, two, and one atomic propositions, respectively.

We mention Wanner's result because we find it one of the more appealing and intuitively satisfying findings to come out of the deep-structure approach to sentence memory. Furthermore, the result is precisely what is expected by the learning and retrieval mechanisms embodied in HAM. As a particular item appears in more propositional subtrees of the total sentence, the more central it becomes. That is to say, the mean distance (in number of associations) from "detective" to the to-be-retrieved items is less in Figure 11.3*a* than in Figure 11.3*b*. Since the probability of recalling an item varies inversely with number of links from the cue to the item, Wanner's results are just as HAM predicts.

A second experiment that strikes near the same point is one by Lesgold (1972) regarding the role of pronominal reference in "unifying" two successive predications. Lesgold compared subjects' memory for the following two classes of sentences:

The postman opened the gate and George was exhausted.   (16)
The baker drove the van and he was happy.   (17)

The sentences are similar in almost all respects: they have two clauses in the surface, two propositions in a Chomskian deep-structure, written in almost the same way, containing the same number and kinds of content words, etc. They differ only in whether "George" or "he" is in the second clause. In HAM, however, the two sentences are parsed and represented as quite different memory structures. These structures are shown in Figure 11.4, the *George* sentence in Panel *a* and the *he* sentence in Panel *b*. The differences derive from the fact that the pronoun "he" refers back to "baker," whereas "George" does not refer back to "postman."

In Lesgold's experiment, the subject studied eight sentences, four *pronoun* sentences and four *proper noun* sentences. Two of each set were presented with the clauses in the order shown in Sentences (16) and (17), with the verb-phrase first and adjective-phrase second; the other two had the clauses in the reverse order (but with the pronoun always in the second phrase). Following study of each set of eight sentences, the subjects were cued for complete "recall of the gist" of each sentence by prompting with the first noun ("postman"), the verb ("opened"), the object-noun ("gate"), or the adjective ("exhausted").

Comparing the two associative structures in Figure 11.4, the pronoun structure in Panel (*b*) is simpler and has fewer links than the proper noun structure, because both predicates in Panel (*b*) are connected to the one subject "baker." Thus, recall of pronoun sentences should be higher because fewer associations need to be formed to record the sentences.

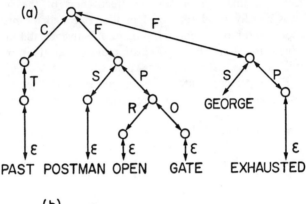

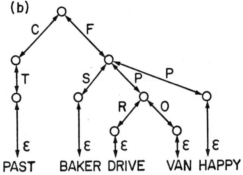

FIG. 11.4. HAM's representation of the sentences in Lesgold's (1972) experiment: (*a*) proper noun sentences, and (*b*) pronoun sentences.

Lesgold's results came out as predicted by our model. Recall was generally much higher for the *pronoun* sentences than for the *proper noun* sentences, for any cue. Lesgold found that cues from *pronoun* sentences elicited 70% recall of the other lexical items, with 58% of the full sentences being completely recalled; for the *proper noun* sentences, recall of lexical items averaged 55%, and full recall of the complete sentence compound averaged 40%. So the *pronoun* sentences, which predicate two things of the same concept, are more easily learned and recalled than the sentences having two independent clauses.

A further prediction for Lesgold's data can be derived from the associative structures in Figure 11.4, and it concerns the fact that the *pronoun* serves to unify or integrate the second clause more closely to the first clause than is the case for the *proper noun*. For instance, given "baker" as a cue in a *pronoun* sentence (Figure 11.4*b*), according to a node-distance measure it is just as close to the second clause ("was happy") as it is to the first clause. So in this *pronoun* case, one would expect words from the two clauses to be recalled about equally well whether the retrieval cue comes from the same clause or from the different clause. For the *proper noun* sentences (Figure 11.4*a*), however, the two clauses are structurally more independent, and only connected at the highest-level proposition node.

In this *proper noun* case the node distance from a cue word to the other words in its clause is shorter than to the words in the other clause. We would therefore expect, for *proper noun* sentences, that the lexical items recalled would come disproportionately from the same clause as the cue word.

Lesgold's data completely confirmed these predictions. Considering those cases in which some but not all of the lexical items were recalled to the prompting cue (i.e., the "all-or-none" cases are not discriminatory), he counted the number of items recalled from the same clause as the cue and from the other clause in the sentence. Due to the nature of the cues and the differing clause lengths, if subjects had been recalling lexical items uniformly from the two clauses, then 56% of them would be expected to come from the same clause as the cue. For the *pronoun* sentences, the observed proportion was 61%, showing fairly close to the expected probability of accessing the two propositions from the cue. On the other hand, the *proper noun* sentences yielded 72% of lexical recalls from the same clause as the cue. This proportion is significantly higher than that for the *pronoun* sentences and is significantly higher than the chance baseline. Hence, in sentences containing two independent clauses, the retrieval cue is most likely to gain access to the other elements of its clause before it retrieves elements in the other proposition. The results therefore are in line with expectations.

11.3. ABSTRACTION AND DISTORTION OF LINGUISTIC MATERIAL

The first section of this chapter demonstrated that the ideas of Gestalt psychology did not predict certain features of sentence memory. However, the other rationalist counternotion to associaton theory, the Reconstruction Hypothesis (see our review in Section 3.3) does appear to fare much better with sentential material. Indeed, much of the support for this hypothesis comes from research with sentences and larger units of discourse. Such research has shown that memory for such material is often very abstract and distorted. It sometimes appears that new linguistic information becomes rapidly assimilated into the subject's total structure of knowledge and beliefs and that very little, if anything, is left as a record of what was actually said. These features of memory are just what would be expected if, as Reconstruction theory claims, memory recorded only very fragmentary traces of the actual experiences and constructed overt recall by fleshing out these traces with general schemas and impressions. The question to which we will be addressing ourselves in this section is whether HAM is embarrassed by the data showing abstraction and distortion of connected discourse.

The classic research in this tradition was performed by Bartlett in 1932. He had subjects attempt to memorize a passage, "The war of the ghosts," which tells a tale from North American Indian culture. Bartlett found many errors besides simple omissions of details. Subjects tended to change, distort, and even import new material into their reproductions. For instance, in the original story, as the Indian died, "Something black came out his mouth." Subjects had difficulty remembering this accurately. One subject recalled instead that he "foamed at the mouth." These distortions had the effect of making the passage more "rational" or "conventional"—that is, from the ethnocentric point of view of his World War I English subjects. Bartlett argued that the recall was distorted because the passage had been assimilated into their knowledge and belief structure.

While there is no denying that extraexperimental knowledge was affecting Bartlett's results, there is ample room for disputing his theoretical interpretation. Consider the apparent distortion of "Something black came out of his mouth" to "he foamed at the mouth." There are a number of ways HAM could have produced this error, without assuming the actual recording of the story was distorted. HAM might only have partially stored the information as "Something about the Indian's mouth." We have seen that sentences are frequently only partially remembered. However, "Something about the Indian's mouth" would not be a very acceptable report to make under the task demands of Bartlett's experiment. Therefore, the subject might call on his past experiences to guess what that something about the mouth might be.

Thus, much of what Bartlett identified as distortion of memory might be deliberate confabulation on the subject's part in an attempt to "smooth out" the telling of the story. This suggests that careful instructions by Bartlett not to confabulate may have largely eliminated the distortions. This is just what Gould and Stephenson (1967) found in a replication of Bartlett that examined the instructional variable. They also found that subjects were fairly accurate, when asked, at identifying the portions of their reproductions which were confabulation.

Bartlett used the method of multiple reproduction in which subjects would reproduce the passage a number of times, each reproduction separated from the others by periods varying from days to years. Bartlett found the greatest distortions at long temporal delays when there had been a number of intervening reproductions. This could just reflect the fact that the subject forgot more and consequently introduced more confabulations to make the story cohere. It is also possible that confabulations would begin to compound one upon another, since the subject would find it hard to discriminate between his earlier confabulations and the original passage.

A related problem in Bartlett's experiment is that subjects may fail to discriminate between what they actually read and their implicit thoughts at the time of reading. Then they might recall their implicit elaborations. For instance, a subject upon reading "Something black came from his mouth," might think "I wonder if that means he was foaming at the mouth." Later he might recall the implicit thought "he was foaming at the mouth," fail to recognize it as such, and give it in overt recall. In HAM there are mechanisms which would permit discrimination between the actual passage and covert elaborations, earlier confabulations, or other deliberate additions by the subject. HAM can store with each fact its source (HAM or the experimenter) and can use this information to effect the discrimination. But the mechanism with fail if HAM fails to form the requisite associations to encode the source information or if it looses (forgets) these associatons.

For these various reasons we do not find the research of Bartlett and others in this tradition (e.g., Dawes, 1966; Frederiksen, 1972) embarrassing for HAM. At best they argue that HAM's strategy-free memory component is less interesting than the generative processes that smooth out the story. But questions of what is interesting, like questions of fashion, always reduce to matters of personal taste.

Bransford and Franks: Abstraction of Linguistic Ideas

We will now examine a recent study by Bransford and Franks (1971) which is commonly interpreted as providing strong support for reconstructionlike notions. Again we want to argue that HAM expects similar results but for reasons distinct from those of the reconstruction hypothesis. Again it will be necessary to emphasize the methodological problems in such research.

Bransford and Franks (1971) presented subjects with a series of simple sentences which used one, two, or three atomic propositions of a four-proposition construction. This can only be illustrated with an example. Example Sentence (18) can be seen to be composed of the four atomic propositions given in Sentences (19) to (22):

The rock which rolled down the mountain crushed the tiny hut beside   (18)
the woods.

The rock rolled down the mountain.	(19)
The rock crushed the hut.	(20)
The hut was tiny.	(21)
The hut was beside the woods.	(22)

It is possible to combine two or three of these atomic propositions in Sentences (19) to (22) in order to make up new compounds. For instance, a two-atom compound of Sentences (21) and (22) would be "The tiny hut was beside the woods," and a three-atom compound of Sentences (20), (21), and (22) would be "The rock crushed the tiny hut beside the woods." There is in fact a set of 12 such combinations of the four atoms: Four singlets, four doublets, three triplets, and the one quartet sentence as shown in Sentence (18) above. Let us call each such set of sentences an *idea cluster*.

Bransford and Franks had their subjects study sentences which contained one, two, or three atoms of an idea cluster, interleaving across trials sentences from several different idea clusters. About half the possible sentences within an idea cluster were presented. After these sentences had been studied, the subjects were then shown all the sentences of all idea clusters as well as several distractors that were produced by interchanging terms of atomic propositions *across* two idea clusters; the subjects were asked to rate how certain they were that a particular sentence had or had not been presented in the study list.

Three main results were obtained. First, the subjects were able to reject sentences that violated the sense of the atomic propositions or was not mentioned in them. Second, subjects were more confident that a sentence from an idea cluster had been presented the greater was the number of atomic propositions embedded in the tested sentence. Third, considering only the proper sentences within a given idea cluster, the subjects were largely unable to discriminate between sentences they had seen and sentences they had not seen. As expected from the two preceding remarks, subjects gave their highest recognition rating to the full sentences like Sentence (18) which embedded all the atomic propositions, although at no time during the study period had *any* of the full sentences like Sentence (18) been presented. So subjects were most sure about remembering something which they had not in fact experienced; however, that full sentence did epitomize the accumulation or integration of all the parts and pieces of the idea cluster.

The Bransford and Franks result is quite startling and also quite robust. It suggests that subjects are discarding surface information and integrating individual sentences into complex ideas—something equivalent to an image, scenario, or schema of the overall situation being described in piecemeal fashion—and then rating test sentences according to how many details of that situation they reinstate.

However, HAM expects some of these results and can at least give a plausible (albeit posthoc) explanation of the remaining results. Let us go through the results one at a time. First, of course, if HAM stores the study propositions, it will have no problem rejecting the noncases, i.e., novel propositions composed by crossing elements from different idea clusters. Thus, having stored atoms like "The rock crushed the hut" and "The wind blew the trailer," HAM will reject "The rock crushed the trailer" as a study sentence because intersections from the cues in the test sentence will not be found; rather, the original two atomic propositions may be retrieved, thus insuring to HAM's satisfaction that the test sentence is a distractor to be rejected.

Consider the second result of Bransford and Franks, viz., no discrimination within an idea cluster regarding which combinations had or had not been presented as input sentences. HAM predicts a result *close* to this because of the nature of its MATCH and IDENTIFY processes in looking up and storing new statements, and the fact that specific contexts of occurrence may be interfered with and forgotten. After a few sentences of an idea cluster have been heard and stored, HAM will have stored, in essentials, the four atomic propositions contained in that cluster. Therefore, any combination of propositions, whether old or new, will achieve a complete match to memory.

HAM does have the means at its disposal to identify which combination of propositions it has heard. That is, HAM will not (nor will a human subject) when it studies a sentence like "The rock crushed the tiny hut," store just an encoding of the stated sentence. If it did, HAM would leave the experiment believing a rock actually crushed a tiny hut. Think of what brainwashing possibilities would exist in the simple sentence memory experiment! Rather, what HAM must store is something of the order "In context C_1 I studied that the rock crushed a tiny hut." Figure 11.5 shows how HAM would represent the elaborated proposition. Presumably, in all sentence experiments, the propositions are tagged in this manner with information about their context of acquisition. At most points in this book, such contextual taggings have been ignored as inessential to the points being made, but they are crucial to understanding the Bransford and Franks research just as they were in our previous discussion of Bartlett's results.

HAM is thus able to tag each proposition with the contexts in which it was heard. We give Figure 11.6 as a highly schematic diagram of what HAM's memory representation would be after it had encountered six sentences from a particular idea set. Each of the four propositions (the P_i) have occurred three times. Since we assumed the various contexts of occurrences are slightly different one from

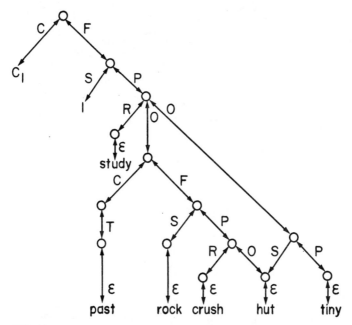

FIG. 11.5. HAM's representation of a sentence in Bransford and Franks'
(1971) experiment.

another, we have the propositions attached to different contexts (the C_i). Figure
11.6 encodes the hypothetical case where the subject has encountered P_1, P_2,
$P_1 + P_4$, $P_3 + P_4$, $P_1 + P_2 + P_3$, $P_2 + P_3 + P_4$. Supposing that the structure in
Figure 11.6 is HAM's memory representation of the six sentences above, how is
HAM to decide exactly which combinations of nodes has it experienced or which
has it not?

One assumption that predicts the Bransford and Franks recognition results
supposes that the subject responds to a test sentence according to the number of
contextual markers that are retrievable when the GET routines are activated
starting at the root nodes of the atomic propositions in the test question. The
number of retrieved contexts will increase, on average, with the number of atomic
propositions in the test string. The average number of contexts evoked will be
about the same for old, presented compounds as for new, nonpresented compounds
of the idea cluster. In our hypothetical case of Figure 11.6, each atomic proposition
has occurred in three sentences and hence has three context tags associated to it.
Therefore, each old or new compound with n propositions will have retrievable
from it $3n$ contextual tags. Therefore, if the recognition rating is done on the basis
of the number of context markers retrievable from the test propositions, then the
subjects would be unable to discriminate between old and new legitimate
combinations, which is, of course, the Bransford and Franks result. Moreover,
recognition ratings should increase with number of propositions in either old or
new combinations. Again, this is just what Bransford and Franks found.

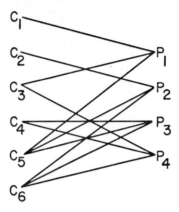

FIG. 11.6. Schematic representation of HAM's memory structure after studying six sentences in the Bransford and Franks' (1971) paradigm.

There is one disconcerting aspect to this explanation. A careful inspection of Figure 11.6 actually reveals a means by which HAM could discriminate OLDs from NEWs. For example, there is evidence that $P_1 + P_4$ has occurred and $P_1 + P_2$ has not. That is, the two propositions in the first case have a context marker that leads to them and no others, i.e., C_3. Now it is true that P_1 and P_2 both lead to C_5, but C_5 is also connected to P_3. The problem with this mechanism for separating the OLDs from the NEWs is that it is a difficult computational feat for the human subject to accomplish. He must examine all the contextual linkages of all the propositions in the target sentence, determine if there are any intersections, check whether these intersecting contexts lead to all the target propositions, and finally make sure that no nontarget propositions are connected to any candidate contexts. Moreover, all these operations would have to be done with contextual tags that are virtually indiscriminable one from another. Exactly what description will be attached to a contextual tag is uncertain (see, however, Anderson & Bower, 1972b), but it would probably be little more than the fact that context was a particular moment in the experimental session. Moreover, because of the limitations of study time, it is highly improbable that all the requisite contextual associations will have been formed.

So, it should not be surprising that subjects would balk at attempting to discriminate OLDs from NEWs by this context-searching procedure and would resort to the context-counting strategy we elaborated earlier. Also, Bransford and Franks used a yes-no recognition procedure which (see our discussion in Chapter 8) would not be as sensitive as a forced-choice procedure in which the S was explicitly confronted with an old sentence like $P_1 + P_4$ and a new one like $P_1 + P_2$, was told he had only encountered one, and was forced to choose. Actually, Bransford and Franks did find marginal ability to discriminate among OLDs and NEWs when they contained only one proposition. With one-proposition sentences, the context-searching strategy we outlined is quite tractable; whereas it becomes mind boggling for multiproposition sentences, particularly when all the intersections among three or four propositions must be considered.

A Follow-up to Bransford and Franks

We ran a modification of the Bransford and Franks experiment to check our interpretation. This experiment, run with 12 Yale students, used a forced-choice recognition procedure. That is, rather than the Bransford and Franks procedure of presenting one sentence at a time for recognition judgment, we presented all 12 sentences from an idea cluster and requested the subject to identify the six study sentences. We have argued at many points in this book that a forced-choice procedure should be more sensitive than a yes-no procedure because it forces the subject to attend to subtle differences in sentence memory.

Our subjects studied lists of four idea clusters. For each idea cluster there were 6 study sentences and 12 test sentences. So in all, there were 24 study sentences and 48 test sentences. Each subject studied and was tested with two such lists. Results on the first and second lists did not differ, so we will present pooled results. Exactly half the test sentences of each propositional length were presented for study. That is to say, in a study list of 24 sentences there were 2 FOURs, 6 THREEs, 8 TWOs, and 8 ONEs. The idea clusters used were the same as in the Bransford and Franks experiment.

In Table 11.3 we have the pooled results, from this experiment, classified according to whether the test sentence was OLD or NEW, and according to the number of atomic propositions in the sentence; chance discrimination would be a 50-50 split in choices between OLDs and NEWs.

There are a number of notable differences between these results and those reported by Bransford and Franks. Overall, there is a clear ability to discriminate between OLDs and NEWs (.59 versus .37). If we look at this result as a function of number of propositions, we see a steady decline in the ability to make the discrimination. That is, discrimination is high for ONEs, still quite significant for TWOs, marginal for THREEs, and nonexistant for FOURs. For FOURs, there is even a slight difference in favor of the NEWs, reflecting the small number of observations for each probability ($n = 48$). The other feature of this data which does not accord with Bransford and Franks is that there is no bias to select sentences with more propositions. This is as HAM would predict if the subjects

TABLE 11.3

Probability of Choice for Various Alternatives
in the Forced-Choice Design

	FOUR	THREE	TWO	ONE	Mean
OLD	.42	.58	.56	.71	.59
NEW	.46	.53	.37	.22	.37
Mean	.44	.56	.46	.46	.48

were not using number of contexts to make their recognition decision, but rather were attempting to determine if all the propositions in a test sentence intersected at a unique context.

So, a forced-choice procedure does get subjects to process the sentences in a more discriminative manner. Subjects are able to discriminate between old and new information for ONEs and TWOs where the information load in making that discrimination is not excessive. Thus it is clearly wrong to claim that subjects do not record which individual propositions occur together. However, when multiple-overlapping sentences are presented, this co-occurrence information becomes hard to retrieve and to utilize.

Thus, HAM's mechanisms appear capable of dealing with all the salient results in sentence memory experiments. Certainly, it can address itself to a much broader range of phenomena than can any other theory. What is still lacking in our theoretical efforts is a detailed analysis of the inferential and problem-solving procedures that utilize this information. Undoubtedly, such processes have an important role to play in experimental paradigms such as Bartlett's or Bransford and Franks' as well as in many naturalistic memory phenomena. In Chapter 13, we will sketch an outline of the role of the inferential and problem-solving processes in question answering. But before we get into that, we must explore the more mundane problem of fact retrieval—how information gets retreived from a large data-base like human memory. This is the topic for the next chapter.

REFERENCES

Anderson, J. R., & Bower, G. H. On an associative trace for sentence memory. *Journal of Verbal Learning and Verbal Behavior*, 1971, **10**, 673–680.

Anderson, J. R., & Bower, G. H. Configural properties in sentence memory. *Journal of Verbal Learning and Verbal Behavior*, 1972, **11**, 594–605. (a)

Anderson, J. R., & Bower, G. H. Recognition and retrieval processes in free recall. *Psychological Review*, 1972, 79, 97–123. (b)

Bartlett, F. C. *Remembering: A study in experimental and social psychology*. Cambridge: The University Press, 1932.

Bransford, J. D., & Franks, J. J. The abstraction of linguistic ideas. *Cognitive Psychology*, 1971, **2**, 331–350.

Dawes, R. M. Memory and distortion of meaningful written material. *British Journal of Psychology*, 1966, **57**, 77–86.

Frederiksen, C. H. Effects of task induced cognitive operations on comprehension and memory processes. In R. Freedle & J. B. Carroll (Eds.), *Language comprehension and the acquisition of knowledge*. Washington, D.C.: Winston, 1972.

Gould, A., & Stephenson, G. M. Some experiments relating to Bartlett's theory of remembering. *British Journal of Psychology*, 1967, 58, 39–50.

Horowitz, L. M., & Manelis, L. Toward theory of redingrative memory: Adjective-noun phrases. In G. H. Bower (Ed.), *The psychology of learning and motivation*. Vol. 6. New York: Academic Press, 1972.

Koffka, K. *Principles of Gestalt psychology*. New York: Harcourt, Brace & World, 1935.

Köhler, W. *Gestalt Psychology: An introduction to new concepts in modern psychology*. New York: Liveright, 1947.

Lesgold, A. M. Pronominalization: A device for unifying sentences in memory. *Journal of Verbal Learning and Verbal Behavior*, 1972, **11**, 316–323.

Rosenberg, S. Association and phrase structure in sentence recall. *Journal of Verbal Learning and Verbal Behavior*, 1968, 7, 1077–1081.

Rohwer, W. D., Jr., & Lynch, S. Form class and intralist similarity in paired-associate learning. *Journal of Verbal Learning and Verbal Behavior,* 1967, 6, 551–554.

Wanner, H. E. On remembering, forgetting, and understanding sentences: A study of the deep structure hypothesis. Unpublished doctoral dissertation, Harvard University, 1968.

12
FACT RETRIEVAL

It is better to confine it (memory) to ideal revival, so far as ideal revival is merely reproductive, and does not involve transformation of what is revived in accordance with present conditions.

—G. F. Stout

12.1. FACT RETRIEVAL

An elementary distinction that can be made in the artificial intelligence literature is between "fact-retrieval" systems and "question-answering" systems. In fact-retrieval systems, the user wishes to store vast quantities of data (e.g., indexing key words of abstracts of papers on organic chemistry) and then retrieve relevant parts of the information by sending a few key words into the system. In such systems, there is almost no inference to be done, no deduction, no subtle semantic interpretation of the question itself. The user is usually restricted to a small vocabulary of specified key words, and the syntax of his retrieval requests is usually restricted to only a few standard syntactic frames, with no possibility of complex embeddings or the like. The issue in such systems is efficiency of a given coding (keying) and organization of the information files, so that the user obtains rapid and maximum return of documents or facts relevant to his request, with a minimum of irrelevant information that must be scanned for significance. These are "fact-retrieval" or "document-retrieval" systems.

Question-answering (QA) systems have as one of their principal aims the generation of as many "correct" answers to questions as is logically possible, given a particularly *economic and efficient* organization of the data files, and given a particular set of *inference heuristics* that permit deduction or indirect calculation of an answer from the facts known. QA systems emphasize the information which is *implicit* in the data base, which is not directly stated but which is deducible from what is known. Although some questions can be answered by direct look-up (e.g., 9 times 3 equals ?), the QA system builders have been much more interested in those cases where direct look-up fails, and answer-search and inference heuristics must be invoked. It is at this point that QA research makes contact with problem-solving and theorem-proving programs; an answer to be deduced from the known facts is viewed much like a theorem in mathematics which is to be proved by applying admissible rules of inference to the axioms; and formal methods for theorem proving, using so-called "resolution techniques," are quite advanced now in the artificial intelligence field (see Nilsson, 1971). However, the relevance of these theorem-proving techniques to elucidating how people actually answer inferential questions is problematic.

Experimental psychologists working on memory have almost always investigated fact retrieval (e.g., what syllable occurred beside JIR?). Our model HAM has been developed specifically for this task. Our ideas about question answering are much more programmatic, but are reviewed nonetheless in the next chapter. In the current chapter, we will discuss the mechanisms of fact retrieval in HAM. Since our conception of fact retrieval is much the more articulated, we will be able to bring experimental data to bear in much more detail on our hypotheses.

In describing HAM's mechanisms for fact retrieval, we will be restating several points made earlier in Chapter 9, which discussed how the MATCH process was employed in stimulus recognition. The same MATCH process will be employed here to describe how HAM searches memory for an answer appropriate to a particular probe or query. To review, there are two types of probes that HAM deals with. First, yes-no questions which query whether a particular proposition is true (e.g., "Did the hippie touch the debutante in the park?"). The probe tree for such a query is a complete encoding of the proposition. HAM attempts to match the probe tree to memory, returns as output the best match, and determines whether there are any negations attached to the proposition (e.g., "It is false that the hippie touched the debutante in the park" would yield a perfect match to the probe, but an outer negation is attached). From this yield HAM must intelligently compute an answer to the question. The second class of questions are the wh-questions that interrogate specific elements within a proposition (e.g., "Who touched the debutante?"). Their probe trees are identical to the yes-no probes, except that "dummy" elements exist at each of the terminals which have been queried. Identical mechanisms search the memory as in the yes-no case. This section reviews the mechanisms that intervene between the stating of the question and HAM's output of the answer. First is the linguistic analysis of the question.

The Question Grammar of HAM

The surface grammar accepted by HAM was described in Chapter 8 in conjunction with the parsing system (see Table 8.1). There is a subset of seven rules (Rules 3a to 3f) for writing questions, permitting expression of most of the significant ways of querying particular elements in a complex question. To show this, consider as an example the sentence "Yesterday, in the zoo a topless dancer fed the lions." Rule 3a is used to query the context: "Where and when did the dancer feed the lions?"; Rule 3b queries the agent: "Who fed the lions yesterday in the zoo?"; Rule 3c queries the action: "What did the dancer do to the lions?"; Rule

3d queries the object: "What was fed by the dancer?"; Rule 3e asks a yes-no question: "Did the topless dancer feed the lions yesterday in the zoo?"; Rule 3f queries an adverb of manner: "How did the dancer feed the lions?" Only the last question, querying an adverb of manner (or the instrument by which the action will be done), has no answer stipulated by the example sentence. Relevant information, for example, would be that "she fed them *hurriedly*" or "*with a ten-foot pole*," answering the foregoing questions by giving an action modifier or an instrument for the act.

As indicated in Chapter 8, HAM's parser accepts English sentences and rewrites them in terms of a "deep grammar," as a binary tree of associations. When analyzing questions, the parser produces as output an incomplete tree with a "dummy element" at the specific information slot which is being queried and into which the answer is to be inserted, when (and if) it is found. Figure 12.1a and b shows question trees querying the subject and the predicate nodes of the sentence "The dancer fed the lions at the zoo." The question mark in the diagrams indicates the dummy node which is to be filled by the answer. The answer is defined only in terms of what constants can fill these variables (slots) so as to make the filled-in sentence true or at least consistent with the beliefs of the question-answerer. Obviously, there will be several dummy nodes if several parts of a proposition are being queried.

In the idiom of the human-memory literature, a question is a "retrieval cue," or rather, a compound of retrieval cues. Almost all psychological theories of memory

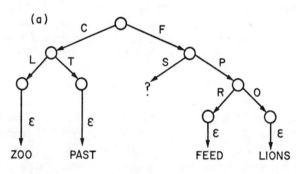

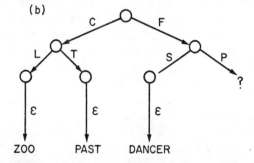

FIG. 12.1. Examples of probe trees: (*a*) "Who fed the lions in the zoo?" and (*b*) "What did the dancer do in the zoo?"

suppose that access of a retrieval cue to a stored memory trace occurs on some basis of "similarity" or "resonance" between the two information structures. This principle is true for HAM, too, except that the "similarity" between the initial study string and the later test string is not determinable from the surface features of the two strings. Rather, similarity will depend upon the deep-grammar propositions extracted from the two strings by HAM. If propositions were encoded and remembered perfectly, then the overlap of deep-structure propositional concepts and of the relations among them would be an accurate metric of similarity for HAM's retrieval mechanisms.

The MATCH Process

Once the probe tree has been set up by the parser, the MATCH process is evoked to interface the probe with memory. To briefly recapitulate how the MATCH process works, HAM always matches the terminal nodes of the input tree to nodes in memory (dummy nodes in wh-questions are not matched initially to anything). This match to the nodes of the input tree can always be done, since it is assumed that HAM can access the nodes directly from the words in the sentence (the assumption of content-addressability). If an unfamiliar word is input to HAM, it will be accepted as such, but a new node will be created to begin collecting information about that unit, such as how it is spelled and what predicates have been associated to it in input trees.

Once the terminal nodes in memory have been accessed, HAM then tries to find paths through the memory structure which connect terminal nodes of the input tree and which correspond to paths in the input tree. An associative path in the memory structure corresponds to a path in the input tree if and only if the following two conditions are satisfied: (a) they connect the identical terminal nodes, and (b) the labels or relations on the path segments occur in an identical sequence for the two paths. To illustrate, predicating that someone "hit Bill," we would have stored in memory the links labeled ϵ^{-1}, R^{-1}, O in that order from *hit* to *Bill.* Then a later "*X* hit Bill" would match memory as would "*X* struck William." But "Bill hit *X*" would not match the prior "hit Bill" memory structure because the paths from *hit* to *Bill* would be different in the two cases.

By these graph-searching techniques the MATCH process attempts to obtain the maximum MATCH between the current input pattern and the patterns stored in memory. Of all HAM's theoretical mechanisms, this MATCH process is the one that has figured most centrally in our experimental predictions. And it is clear that something like the MATCH process is central to human intelligence, since it brings past knowledge to bear in interpreting current experience.

Reducing Search Time

When a probe sentence is given (e.g., "A dog bit Bill"), what is to guide the search for its matching structure in a vast memory network that contains many thousands of facts? Even confining the search to tokens of *dog, Bill,* and *bite* may not restrict the search sufficiently, since the system might know many facts about dogs, many facts about Bill (or many Bills), and also be able to access many episodes involving biting. How can the search process be curtailed?

In HAM there are two devices which shorten the search. First, it uses the labeled relations of the input tree (the probe) to search selectively from the memory nodes accessed by the input words. Thus, if the node dominating *dog* in the input tree is labeled with the ϵ relation, then HAM will consider only ϵ^{-1} links leading out of the *dog* node, and thus not search from the node any links labeled with $\forall^{-1}$ (which tell universal facts about all *dogs*) or with $\subseteq$ (which list supersets of *dog*) or $\subseteq^{-1}$ (which list kinds of *dogs*). This is one way that relational information attached to links is used to guide the search through memory.

There will probably be a large number of ϵ^{-1} associations from *dog*, corresponding roughly to some facts one can remember about particular instances of dogs. That is, the list of memory nodes returned by the function GET (dog, ϵ^{-1}) could be very long. In Chapter 9 it was assumed that the entries on a given "GET-list" were being constantly updated according to their recency of being experienced. This mechanism of recency updating of a GET-list was used in Chapter 8 as a heuristic solution to the problem of determining anaphoric reference. Problems of anaphoric reference arise whenever pronouns, definite articles ("The dog---"), and definite descriptions ("The brown dog who likes ice cream---") are used to refer to specific concepts introduced earlier in the text or dialogue. HAM selects as the referent the most recent node on a concept's GET-list for the ϵ^{-1} relation. This heuristic usually works because an anaphoric referent is almost always the most recently mentioned instance of a given concept in a particular dialogue.

To return to our description of the MATCH process for "A dog bit Bill," the GET-list for ϵ^{-1} of *dog* may be quite long; moreover, the particular dog who bit Bill may not even be on this list. To forestall possibly fruitless and lengthy searches, HAM will search a GET-list to only a probabilistically determined depth (the exact rules are given in Chapter 15). As a consequence, very old associations that have not been recently revived will tend to be low in the GET-list, and so are unlikely to be searched. This is the main mechanism in HAM for "forgetting" of information that was once encoded into long-term memory.

On Incomplete Matches

The discussion so far has focused on the simple case where the test probe finds a perfect match in memory, leading to a fully confident yes or confident filling in of the dummy elements in the probe tree. Alas, life is not always so simple. Much of the time the probe tree will not be matched perfectly, either because the question is probing for slightly different information than the system knows or because some original information was never encoded or has been forgotten. We will deal here with the issue of matching fragmentary material; the other issue, answering slightly modified questions, will be discussed in the next chapter.

HAM will retrieve the best-matching tree it can find which does not contradict information in the probe question. To a recall probe, HAM will recall those parts of a full proposition it can retrieve, but will remain vaguely neutral about the forgotten remainder. For example, if we input the proposition and then later ask "Did a hippie touch a debutante in the park?" but HAM had forgotten the context, it would answer something like "I know a hippie touched a debutante, but I don't know where or when." The system admits its ignorance about appropriate elements. If it had forgotten the verb then to the recall cue "What did the hippie do?", HAM would output "The hippie did something involving the debutante in the park, but I forget exactly what it was."

In principle, there could be a conflict between which of two partial structures provide the better or more important match to the probe. However, HAM gives equal importance to all elements of the probe. For example, consider a query stipulating a SUBJECT, RELATION, OBJECT, and LOCATION. Suppose memory structure M_1 matches the probe on the SUBJECT, RELATION, and LOCATION (and has no contradictory elements for the remaining elements), whereas memory structure M_2 matches the SUBJECT, RELATION, OBJECT. Then these two matches are equally valid, and HAM would arbitrarily select the first one it encountered in its memory search. In fact, in conducting its search, HAM keeps track of the most successful matching M_i found so far. Unless a new partial match M_j exceeds M_i in the number of content elements matched, M_i just maintains its preferred position as the best match found so far. Since the M_i will be accessed in the order of their relative recency of predications involving the elements of the probe, this arbitrary heuristic gives preference to more recent rather than distant fragmentary matches.

Response or Decision Rules

In the abstract, the retrieval probe specifies k propositional elements explicitly; wh-queries stipulate some d further dummy cases to be filled in by memory. In wh-questions, HAM will select the best-matching memory structure to the k elements of the probe, and use whatever this memory structure contains to fill in whatever it can of the d dummy elements being queried. For those elements it cannot fill in, it admits its ignorance. In case only a partial match can be found for the k retrieval cues of the probe, say j (when $j < k$), then depending on how an adjustable "recall threshold" is set, HAM will either (a) output nothing in case j is below the recall threshold, or (b) in case j exceeds the criterion, output what it is able to of the d queried dummies, with the qualification that it is not sure of the unmatched elements of the question probe. If one follows through what this strategy means, it seems to accord intuitively with the patterns of vagaries and confidences that characterize human memories of complex propositions.

If the probe is a yes-no question, akin to a recognition memory test, with k cues specified, then the system may match j ($j \leq k$) elements, mismatch on none or some, and it must decide whether the test sentence is true. Here, decision criteria enter very heavily; how the subject should respond to this matching-mismatching evidence will be strongly influenced by strategies, general knowledge about the test conditions, and payoff contingencies for correct and incorrect True and False responses. The factors influencing this criterion for saying "Yes" or "True" are summarized in statistical decision theory. Given the maximal match of j elements in memory to a k-element probe with no contradictions, and given that some i elements of the memory structure were not stipulated in the probe, how confident should HAM (or the human) be that the test query is true? Such questions have been addressed in the multicomponent theory of the memory trace (see Bower, 1967). In general, if one supposes that the number of matches (j) is probabilistically distributed (say, binomial) for both True and False probes, but with a lower average number of matches for False sentences, then the theory will predict the proper kind of memory operating characteristic (or "MOC curve") that has been observed in recognition memory experiments (see Wickelgren & Norman, 1966). We will not pursue this discussion of decision criteria further here, because it is really ancillary to the theory of memory structures under test. We turn now to some empirical evidence for the search heuristics of HAM, where the scan is over a data base which one can be reasonably confident that it knows.

12.2. EVIDENCE FOR HAM'S SEARCH STRATEGIES

This section reports the results of several experiments performed at Stanford to test HAM's search strategies for propositional materials. Under consideration is the sequential manner in which associations on various GET-lists are searched. This process leads to strong predictions about how reaction times (abbreviated RTs) should increase as the associative branching in a memory structure is varied.

The experiments below first teach the subject a set of artificial facts such as "A hippie is in the park," or "The miner helped the judge," and so forth. Following learning of these facts, the person receives a series of true-false questions about these facts, and we measure his reaction time. We then try to relate these RTs to the structural interrelations of the fact base and to our hypotheses regarding search over that data base. We are sometimes asked why we use artificial facts rather than making use of the common stock of facts which most college students (our subjects) would know. The difficulty with using commonly known facts (e.g., "Chicago is in Illinois") is that one does not know exactly how they are stored and interrelated in the person's memory, nor does one know the recency of the subject's having thought about the various facts. With artificial facts, we know not only the exact interrelations among the facts but also the subject's methods of learning and rehearsal, and his relative recency of having experienced the various facts. In the model, all of these factors are expected to be potent determinants of RTs. So these factors must be controlled in experimental tests of the model. Later, in Section 12.4, we will review the research done on "natural" facts, and the problems inherent in such research.

Thorndyke's Experiment

An experiment by Perry Thorndyke, a colleague at Stanford University, provides the first test of HAM's strategies. He was interested in simple subject-verb-object propositions like "The boy saw the girl." Figure 12.2 shows HAM's representation for such sentences. The contextual element specifying the time (past) has been omitted as it is not a factor in the experiment. Subjects studied lists of nine sentences (see Table 12.1), three sentences of which contributed to each of three experimental conditions: (a) the "1-1" propositions, which used a single subject and verb with three different objects; (b) the "3-3" propositions, which used a unique subject, verb, and object in each proposition; and (c) the "3-1" propositions, which used three distinct subject-object pairs all linked by the same verb. The numbers identifying the condition refer to the number of distinct subjects and verbs in each condition. Table 12.1 illustrates a sample list from

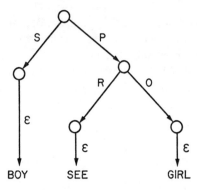

FIG. 12.2. HAM's representation for the sentences used in the Thorndyke experiment.

Thorndyke's experiment. That table also lists the false sentences created by recombining subject, verb, and object from the nine true sentences.

After the subject had memorized the nine target sentences (as judged by two successful free recalls), his memory was tested by presenting the nine Trues and nine Falses and requesting truth judgments. Presentation was done with a tachistoscope, and the subjects indicated their decision by pressing a button. The mean verification time for the true sentences in the 1-1 condition was 1,488 msec.,

TABLE 12.1

Sample List

Condition	Mnemonics	Sentence
1-1	$S_1 - V_1 \begin{cases} O_1 \\ O_2 \\ O_3 \end{cases}$	The queen rescued the professor. The queen rescued the grocer. The queen rescued the hunter.
3-3	$S_2 - V_2 - O_4$ $S_3 - V_3 - O_5$ $S_4 - V_4 - O_6$	The thief tackled the singer. The miner helped the judge. The addict scolded the infant.
3-1	$\begin{cases} S_5 \\ S_6 \\ S_7 \end{cases} V_5 \begin{cases} O_7 \\ O_8 \\ O_9 \end{cases}$	The gentleman watched the poet. The priest watched the officer. The father watched the miser.

The nine "true" sentences comprise the study list. The test list is composed of the nine true sentences plus the following "false" sentences:

F1	$S_1 - V_2 - O_5$	The queen tackled the judge.
F2	$S_2 - V_3 - O_6$	The thief helped the infant.
F3	$S_7 - V_1 - O_6$	The father rescued the infant.
F4	$S_1 - V_2 - O_4$	The queen tackled the singer.
F5	$S_4 - V_4 - O_1$	The addict scolded the professor.
F6	$S_1 - V_1 - O_7$	The queen rescued the poet.
F7	$S_5 - V_5 - O_2$	The gentleman watched the grocer.
F8	$S_1 - V_5 - O_4$	The queen watched the officer.
F9	$S_3 - V_5 - O_4$	The miner watched the singer.

in the 3-3 condition 1,386 msec., and in the 3-1 condition 1,488 msec. So in the two conditions where elements were repeated in multiple propositions, longer reaction times occurred. This is as expected by HAM, since the repetition of an element results in multiple propositions leading from that element's node in memory. Figure 12.3 illustrates the memory structures that are set up in each of the experimental conditions. In the 1-1 condition, associative fanning (multiple paths with the same label) occurs at the object branches leading out of the predicate node; in the 3-1 condition, the fanning occurs with respect to the member branches leading from the verb concept. At each point of fanning the subject would often have to search multiple branches before he found the appropriate one resulting in verification of the proposition. This is the main cause of the longer RTs in these cases.

(a) 1-1

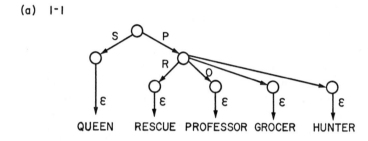

(b) 3-3

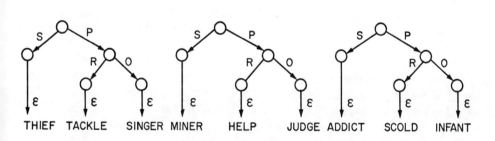

(c) 3-1

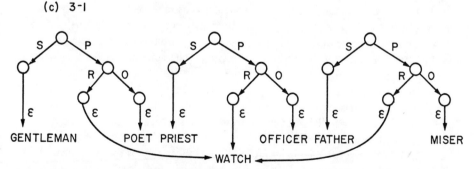

FIG. 12.3. The memory structures HAM would set up in the three conditions of the Thorndyke experiment: (a) 1-1 condition; (b) 3-3 condition; (c) 3-1 condition.

A Model for Verification Times

An interesting question is whether we can predict the result obtained of near-identical verification times in the 1-1 and 3-1 conditions. To answer this question and to make predictions for later experiments in this chapter, an explicit model for predicting verification times will be required. One hypothesis would be that there is linear relation between computation time for the MATCH function to run in the computer program and the corresponding reaction times in a verification task. However, this would be to attribute unjustifiable significance to many of the programming details in HAM. Rather, we propose a simple but plausible hypothesis: Reaction time should be proportional to the number of associative links that must be examined to obtain a MATCH.

To illustrate, let us consider verifying one of the 3-3 examples in Figure 12.3b. To obtain a complete match of the whole tree starting from the subject node, seven associative links must be examined. Thus the mean reaction time for path-tracing, starting from the subject node, should be $7a$, where a represents the time per link. However, a critical and significant part of our search hypothesis must now be added; we assume that a parallel search process occurs, with the MATCH process being *simultaneously* evoked from all the content words of probe. In Thorndyke's experiment, that means that three independent search processes are initiated simultaneously from the subject, verb, and object of the probe. The verification time will be determined by whichever process first succeeds in obtaining a complete match. Thus, in this case there will be a race between three processes, each with mean time $7a$.

To determine the mean verification time for the *fastest* of three searches, one needs to first characterize the distributions of verification times from each entry point considered in isolation. For purposes solely of mathematical tractability, we will assume that this distribution of completion times is exponential with mean na, where n is the number of links searched before completion. Equivalently, we may assume that the rate parameter of the distribution is the reciprocal, $1/na$. The advantage of the exponential distribution is that the distribution of the fastest of k exponentials, with rate parameters $r_1, r_2, ..., r_k$ is easily characterized. The fastest has another exponential distribution, with a rate parameter equal to $r_1 + r_2 + ... + r_k$ and a mean which is the reciprocal of this summated rate.

Initially we considered it more reasonable to assume that the time to examine *each* link would be exponentially distributed with mean a. If so, then the time to examine n associative links would have a gamma distribution with parameters n and a. But this is intractable since there is no simple characterization for the fastest of several gamma-distributed random variables.

With these assumptions, the expected verification times for the 3-3 condition may now be derived. For verifying any single S-V-O proposition in this condition, there will be three parallel MATCH processes, each proceeding simultaneously with rate $1/(7a)$. Therefore, the rate parameter for the distribution of the fastest of the three is $1/(7a) + 1/(7a) + 1/(7a) = 3/(7a)$, and its mean time is the reciprocal, $2.33a$. This gives us the mean time for the memory match. But time is also required for analysis of the sentence, for word look-up, for response generation, and so on.

Since these processes do not involve the MATCH process, their times are assumed to be identical for all true conditions (i.e., 1-1, 3-3, and 3-1) and to be independent of the time for the MATCH process. These non-MATCH times will be assigned a mean value K_T (subscript T for True). Hence, the predicted mean verification time for true sentences in the 3-3 condition is $K_T + 2.33a$.

Consider now the prediction for the 1-1 condition in Figure 12.3a. Here the scanning rate starting from the object of the probe will still be $1/(7a)$ because only seven links must be examined to match the memory structure from the object. The situation is more complicated for MATCH processes that begin from the subject and the verb. When a MATCH process starting from subject or verb attempts to access the object association from the predicate node, it will retrieve via the GET function an ordered list of three object associates which it will have to search *serially*. We will assume that the search will terminate when the association to the desired object (of the test probe) is obtained. That is, the search of a GET-list is self-terminating (see Sternberg, 1969). If the desired association is the first on the GET-list, the subject will have to search seven links; if it is second, he will have searched nine links; if third, eleven links. We can assume each possibility is equally likely (since all three propositions in the 1-1 case were tested). For the present illustration, then, with probability 1/3, the search rates from subject and verb will each be $1/(7a)$; with probability 1/3, these search rates will be $1/(9a)$; and with probability 1/3, $1/(11a)$. Therefore, the following distribution of rate parameters is predicted for the fastest of the three MATCH processes:

$$\text{rate} = 1/(7a) \ + 1/(7a) \ + 1/(7a) = .429/a \qquad \text{with probability } 1/3$$
$$\text{rate} = 1/(9a) \ + 1/(9a) \ + 1/(7a) = .365/a \qquad \text{with probability } 1/3$$
$$\text{rate} = 1/(11a) + 1/(11a) + 1/(7a) = .325/a \qquad \text{with probability } 1/3$$

The average MATCH time may be obtained by weighting the mean times (reciprocals of the above rates) in each of these cases by their one-third probability: mean MATCH time = $1/3 \, (a/.429) + 1/3 \, (a/.365) + 1/3 \, (a/.325) = 2.716a$. So, adding the constant for encoding and true responses, the predicted verification time for the 1-1 condition is $K_T + 2.716a$.

Finally, predictions for the 3-1 condition will be derived. Referring to Figure 12.3c, it may be verified that seven links must be searched to obtain a MATCH from either the subject or the object. The complications are produced by the verb from which three ϵ^{-1} associations lead. These links will be returned as a list when the function GET (verb, ϵ^{-1}) is evoked at the beginning of the search. The number of links to be searched depends on where the desired association (tree) is on this verb-instance list. If it is the first verb-instance, then only seven links will have to be considered. However if it is second, the MATCH process will then have to examine 14 associations: 7 involving the first incorrect proposition (to which the first ϵ^{-1} association led), and 7 more for the correct proposition. Finally, if the association leading to the correct response is the last on the GET (verb, ϵ^{-1}) list, then 21 associations will have to be searched. Thus, the distribution of rates for the fastest of the three MATCH processes is:

$$\text{rate} = 1/(7a) + 1/(7a) + 1/(7a) \quad = .429/a \qquad \text{with probability } 1/3$$
$$\text{rate} = 1/(7a) + 1/(7a) + 1/(14a) = .354/a \qquad \text{with probability } 1/3$$
$$\text{rate} = 1/(7a) + 1/(7a) + 1/(21a) = .331/a \qquad \text{with probability } 1/3$$

From these, the mean MATCH time for the fastest of the three is found:

$$\text{Mean MATCH time} = 1/3 \, (a/.429) + 1/3 \, (a/.354) + 1/3 \, (a/.331) = 2.693a$$

Therefore, the expected verification time in the 3-1 condition is $K_T + 2.693a$.

To summarize, the theory predicts the verification time in the 1-1 condition $(K_T + 2.716a)$ to be very close to that in the 3-1 condition $(K_T + 2.693a)$, but both would be longer than in the 3-3 condition $(K_T + 2.333a)$. This is precisely what Thorndyke observed, with the reaction times of 1,488.2 in the 1-1 condition, 1,487.6 in the 3-1 condition, and 1,386.3 in the 3-3 condition. It is worth emphasizing why the 1-1 and 3-1 conditions are so similar. The MATCH process can become slowed down in searching multiple object paths starting both from the subject and from the verb in the 1-1 condition, while it encounters multiple paths only from the verb in the 3-1 condition. However, this tends to be balanced by the fact that the MATCH process requires much longer to explore the rejected propositions in the 3-1 case.

From Thorndyke's data we may compute an estimate of the parameters a and K_T, which will be useful for comparisons with other experiments. The estimate of a is 273 msec. and of K_T is 748 msec.

The Person-Location Experiment

The next experiment was performed to obtain data more discriminative regarding two matters: (a) the parallel (or simultaneous) application of the MATCH process to each memory node in the probe; and (b) the serial scanning of associations leading from the memory nodes. All of the facts taught to the subjects were of the type "A PERSON is in the LOCATION." Examples are "A hippie is in the park" and "A policeman is in the store." What was varied was the number of locations a particular person could be in (1, 2, or 3) and the number of people who could be in a particular location (1, 2, or 3). Thus, "hippie" might occur in two propositions: the one above, and "A hippie is in the church." The item "park" might occur in three propositions: the one above, "A policeman is in the park," and "A sailor is in the park." If so, the sentence "A hippie is in the park" would represent what we shall call a "2-3" proposition, since the person of the probe occurred in two locations and the location of the probe contains three people. These two factors were varied orthogonally over the fact base, yielding $3 \times 3 = 9$ conditions. All these conditions were exemplified in a list of 26 sentences which the subject studied until he could recall all of them perfectly. Recall was tested by asking him to enumerate to the questions "*Where* are the hippies?" and "*Who* are the people in the park?" For some subjects, recall was accessed equally often from the person and from the location; for others, just from the person (i.e., "Where are the hippies?"); and for still others, just from the location. No reliable differences appeared as a function of the questions used in the recall test. Therefore, only the pooled data will be presented.

Once the facts could be perfectly recited, the verification RT phase of the experiment began. The subject was shown a declarative sentence, "A PERSON is in the LOCATION" and had to judge it as True or False, pressing one of two buttons. The sentences were back-projected on a screen before the subject by a Carousel slide projector with an electronic shutter. Reaction times were measured from the opening of the shutter (projecting the sentence) to depression of the correct response button. The tests may be conceived as six replications of a basic block of 50 tests, or 300 trials in all. First, nine basic sentences were selected as critical targets, one exemplifying each of the 3 x 3 experimental conditions. (The exact sentences exemplifying particular conditions were completely counterbalanced over subjects.) In each block of 50 tests, these nine basic sentences were tested as True twice each. Also, a set of 18 False sentences were composed by mispairing these nine basic sentences; these 18 false sentences occurred once in each block of 50. Just as the Trues, the Falses represented the nine experimental conditions depending on how many places the person of the false probe was in (1, 2, or 3) and how many people were in the location. The remaining 14 tests in each block were "filler tests" constructed from the other $26 - 9 = 17$ sentences of the training list. About half of these tests were Trues and half were Falses. Although data from these filler items were not analyzed, the tests were included to keep active in the subject's memory the "nonbasic" propositions in the training list. If this had not been done, the target propositions might have risen to the top positions in the "GET-lists" of ϵ associations leading from each of the terminal nodes in the probe tree. We needed to keep all relevant predications "active" rather than letting only the nine basic propositions work their way into the top-priority ("most recent") positions in the GET-lists. If that were to happen, then the predictions below would have to be altered. The predictions presuppose that the elements of the test sentence are located at some random position in the GET-lists corresponding to the person and location conditions of the test elements. Eighteen subjects were selected from a pool of subjects in the introductory psychology course at Stanford. The total experimental session, including the learning of the 26 sentences and the 300 RT trials, lasted about 2 hours.

Figure 12.4 illustrates four possible representations that HAM might generate for the 2-3 example of "A hippie is in the park." In Figure 12.4a, HAM has taken advantage of the fact that "hippie" occurs with two locations and has thus produced multiple object branches from the predicate node to these locations. In contrast, in Figure 12.4b HAM has taken advantage of the fact that "park" occurs with three people by building multiple subject branches from the fact node. Now, such subject and object conjunctions cannot be combined within a single proposition, since that will produce unwanted multiplication of meanings as discussed earlier in Section 9.1 In Figure 12.4a the subject may have to search up to 9 associations from "hippie" to obtain a match, and up to 21 associations from "park." In contrast, in Figure 12.4b there is a maximum of 14 associations from hippie and only 11 from park. So in Figure 12.4a search is faster from "hippie," but in Figure 12.4b it is faster from "park." It is also possible for HAM to partially

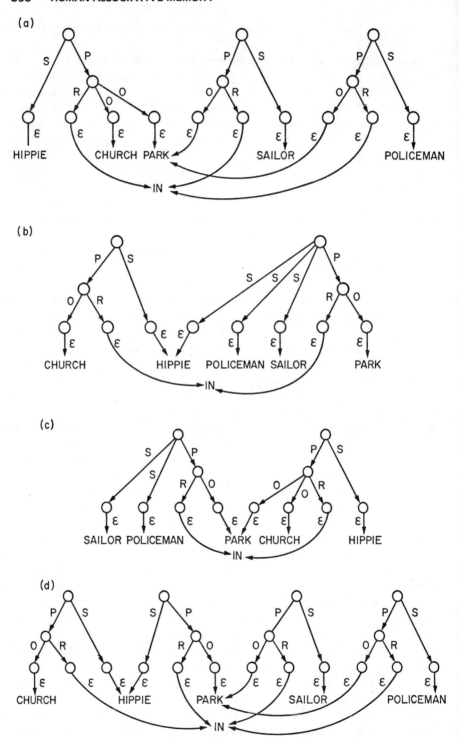

FIG. 12.4. Possible memory structures that might be set up in HAM for the 2-3 condition.

use the object branching and partially the subject branching, as Figure 12.4c illustrates. We will be unable to obtain precise reaction-time predictions if we must worry about all these and other possible overlappings of redundant trees. Therefore, in our work here, we shall adopt the representation shown in Figure 12.4d, in which each proposition is encoded separately and there is no attempt to take advantage of redundancy among the 26 propositions input to HAM. As discussed in Section 9.1, the current simulation of HAM has the option of either attempting to take advantage of partial overlap, as in Figure 12.4a to c, or not so doing, as in Figure 12.4d.

In Figure 12.4d, then, the maximum number of associations to be searched from the person and location will vary from 7 to 14 to 21 as the items appear in 1, 2, or 3 propositions. The maximum number of links that must be searched from the relational element "in" is $26 \times 7 = 182$. We will ignore the contribution of successful searches from "in" to the overall reaction time as it is relatively negligible. The reaction times will be usually determined by the MATCH processes starting from the person or location. So we shall be considering a simple race between these two MATCH processes in deriving the predictions.

In this experiment both the False and the True reaction times will be predicted. (In Thorndyke's experiment, insufficient observations were collected for false-item types to obtain reliable data.) To falsify a particular probe, HAM must examine either all the stored propositions accessible from the person or all from the location given in the probe. Since all seven associations in each proposition will be examined by HAM, to falsify a probe HAM must exhaustively search $7n$ associations from the person and from the location, where n is the number of propositions in which the person or location is involved. The subject can respond "False" as soon as the fastest one of these searches is exhausted without verifying the probe question. Hence, the following is the expected value for $F_{i,j}$ the time to respond "False" to a false proposition in which the stated person is involved in i true propositions stored in memory and the location in j propositions:

$$F_{i,j} = K_F + a/(1/7i + 1/7j) = K_F + 7aij/(i+j) \qquad (1)$$

In this equation, K_F is the constant associated with encoding and response execution for False sentences. This function $F_{i,j}$ increases continuously with i or j, and it is symmetric with respect to i and j. Figure 12.5 illustrates this function for various values of i and j. A distinctive feature of the function $F_{i,j}$ is that if j is held constant and i varied (or vice versa), the increments in $F_{i,j}$ decrease with equal increments in i. Thus, the curves in Figure 12.5 are negatively accelerated. This is because the value of $F_{i,j}$ is always bounded above by $K_F + 7a$, which is the mean time for successful verification from a single entry node with n propositions. That is, the value of $7ja$ would be the MATCH time if there were no race. The expected value for the winner of the race cannot be slower than this bound, but will approximate it as i becomes large.

To falsify a proposition, the MATCH process must exhaustively search all the propositions retrieved by the GET process at a particular entry node. To verify a proposition, however, it is only necessary for HAM to search until it finds the

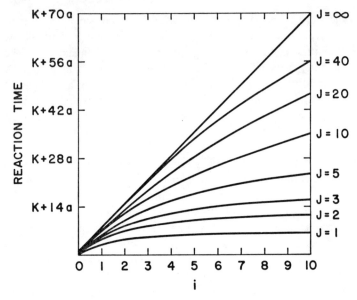

FIG. 12.5. Possible values of the function $F_{i,j}$—the time to respond "False" to a probe in which the person is in i propositions and the location is in j propositions.

proposition to match the probe, at which time it may terminate the search. This option has been denoted a "self-terminating" search by Sternberg (1969). The expected time of a self-terminating search is determined by the location of the target proposition on the GET-list of associations that leads from the entry node. As before, it is assumed that all positions on the GET-list are equally likely to hold the sought-after item. Thus, if the person is involved in ℓ propositions and the location is involved in m propositions, there are $\ell \times m$ equally likely configurations of the target proposition on the two GET-lists. If the target proposition is at the ith position on the person GET-list and at the jth position on the location GET-list, the MATCH time should be the same as that to falsify an i, j proposition, namely, the fastest of two exponentials which proceed at rates a/i and a/j. Letting K_T denote the constant time associated with the non-MATCH processes for true propositions, the following equation for $T_{\ell,m}$ describes the time to verify an ℓ, m proposition:

$$T_{\ell,m} = K_T + 1/(\ell \times m) \sum_i^\ell \sum_j^m 7aij/(i+j) \qquad (2)$$

With the theory explicated, we are now prepared to deal with the data from this experiment; this is presented in Table 12.2 for correct responses only (errors were less than 4%) for Trues in the left half and for Falses in the right half of the table. About 200 observations contribute to each entry. Progressing across any row or down any column, HAM expects a monotonic increase in RTs as the person or location appears in more propositions. For the True data this is nearly always the case:

TABLE 12.2

Verification Times for the Person-Location Experiment

		Trues No. props. person in						Falses No. props. person in			
		1	2	3	Mean			1	2	3	Mean
No. props. location in	1	1.022	1.068	1.076	1.055	No. props. location in	1	1.110	1.112	1.149	1.124
	2	1.040	1.068	1.159	1.089		2	1.128	1.298	1.170	1.199
	3	1.075	1.116	1.271	1.154		3	1.139	1.379	1.441	1.320
Mean		1.046	1.084	1.169	1.100	Mean		1.126	1.263	1.253	1.214

the only discrepancy is a tie between the 2,1 and 2,2 cells. For the False data there is one reversal: that between the 2,2 and 3,2 cells. Altogether there are 36 pairwise comparisons along rows and columns. Of these only 2 (or 6%) fail to conform to the monotonicity predictions. So at the level of ordinal predictions, HAM's search mechanisms are clearly supported. The orderliness of the RT functions reduces the credibility of those models (e.g., Quillian's, 1968, intersection search—see Sections 4.3 and 12.4) which suppose that search proceeds in parallel along all possible paths leading out from an entry word, and that speed of search is not affected by the number of paths. However, the data are consistent with a "parallel" model whose search rate is slower in proportion to the number of paths that must be searched (see Townsend, 1971).

Model Fitting

The search model will be fit separately to the True data and then to the False data. The reason for this separate treatment will soon be apparent. The model's predictions for the True data, assuming a self-terminating search, are given in the "self-terminating" column of Table 12.3. An independent fit of the model to the False data is given under the column labeled "exhaustive." For the True data the additive constant, K_T, was estimated to be 712 msec., and the rate per association, a, was estimated to be 81 msec. For the False data, K_F was estimated at 900 msec. and a at 49 msec. The discrepancy between the two estimates of a suggests that the search for the True propositions may have been exhaustive rather than self-terminating. That is, the MATCH process may have continued searching past the target proposition and proceeded to the end of the GET-list. A model with such an exhaustive search would result in a lower estimate of a. Fitting an exhaustive search model to the True data (in the column labeled "exhaustive search" under Trues), the estimate of K_T is 902 msec. and of a is 31 msec. Thus, when we assume a pure exhaustive search, the estimate of a is now less than the estimate based on the False data. The self-terminating model's predictions have an average discrepancy of 21 msec., whereas the exhaustive model has an average discrepancy of 22 msec. So, there is little basis to choose between the two search strategies for the True data. In fact, it would seem that the truth lies somewhere

TABLE 12.3

Fit of Model to Data

Condition	Observed	Self-terminating	Exhaustive	Single-access
		Trues		
1-1	1.022	.996	1.011	1.089
2.1	1.068	1.043	1.047	1.045
3-1	1.076	1.074	1.065	1.100
1-2	1.040	1.043	1.047	1.045
2-2	1.068	1.114	1.119	1.100
3-2	1.159	1.164	1.162	1.156
1-3	1.075	1.074	1.065	1.100
2-3	1.116	1.164	1.162	1.156
3-3	1.271	1.231	1.228	1.211
		Falses		
1-1	1.110		1.072	1.053
2-1	1.112		1.129	1.134
3-1	1.149		1.157	1.214
1-2	1.128		1.129	1.134
2-2	1.298		1.243	1.214
3-2	1.170		1.312	1.295
1-3	1.139		1.157	1.214
2-3	1.379		1.312	1.295
3-3	1.441		1.415	1.375

between a pure exhaustive search and pure self-terminating search. That is, subjects would appear to self-terminate only some of the time.

Parallel or Single Access?

One assumption makes our model difficult to simulate, namely, that the MATCH process proceeds simultaneously in parallel from every entry node in the probe. Is this assumption really necessary? Would it not be simpler to assume that the subject randomly accessed one of the nodes, in this case either the person or the location, each with 50% probability, and then searched for the full tree from only that one entry node? We call this the "single-access" model, and it differs from the parallel model in the curves predicted for Figure 12.5. The single-access model predicts the following relation between verification time for Falses and the variables i and j:

$$F_{i,j} = K_F + 7a(i+j)/2 \qquad (3)$$

That is, for each value of j, reaction time should increase linearly as a function of i with a slope of $7a/2$. Similar linear functions are predicted for the True data. Thus, the increment in verification time as i varies from 1 to 3 should be independent of j. Since $F_{i,j}$ is symmetric in i and j, the single-access model similarly predicts that the effect of increasing j should be independent of i. In contrast, the parallel-access model predicts that the effect of manipulating one variable will be more pronounced for larger values of the other variable. The data in Table 12.2 clearly support the parallel model. The mean effect associated with varying i or j from 1 to 3, when the other variable has value·1, is 44 msec.; when the other has value 2, it is 119 msec.; and when the other has value 3, it is 246 msec.

The last column in Table 12.3 gives for the Trues and Falses the best fit of the linear, single-access model (estimating different slopes for True and False data). The single-access model is off by a mean of 27 msec. for the True data, compared to 21 and 22 msec. for the two versions of the parallel model. It is off a mean of 65 msec. for the False data, compared to 41 msec. for the parallel model.

Comparison with Thorndyke's Experiment

It is interesting to compare the present parameter estimates with those obtained in Thorndyke's experiment. Using the estimates obtained with the self-terminating parallel model applied in the True data, which was the model fit to Thorndyke's data, the estimate of a is 81 msec. and of K_T is 712 msec. The estimates for Thorndyke's experiment were 273 msec. and 748 msec. Several reasons may be cited for the large discrepancy in a between the two experiments. First, a tends to decrease as the subject becomes more practiced. In the first 150 trials in the person-location experiment, a was estimated to be 100 msec.; in the second 150 trials, a was 62 msec. Since Thorndyke tested his subjects for only 18 trials on a particular propositional base (they learned nine such bases), his data should yield much higher estimates than in the agent-location experiment which involved 300 trials of continuous testing. Another reason for the lower estimate of a is that in our representation of the person-location experiment, we have supposed that there was no redundancy of encoding as there was in the 1-1 conditions of Thorndyke's experiment. As a consequence, in fitting HAM to the person-location experiment, each additional proposition to be searched was presumed to require an additional seven links. In contrast, in Thorndyke's 1-1 condition each additional proposition merely added an object branch (or two more links). The net effect of this difference is that the same reaction-time differences would result in a higher estimate of a in Thorndyke's experiment.

12.3. MEMORY SCANNING EXPERIMENTS

The reader may have noticed the similarity between the previous RT experiments and the general class of "memory-scanning" experiments begun by Sternberg (see Sternberg, 1969, for a review). In such experiments, the subject commits a short list of items to memory, then receives a probe item, and has to respond yes or no to the question of whether the probe item is in the most recent list learned. The standard result is that RT for both Yes and No responses increases linearly with the number of items on the memorized list (called "memory-set size"), with a slope of between 30 and 50 msec. per item in the memory set. This result, supposedly showing a sequential scan over items in short-term memory, has been seminal in inspiring many investigations of memory scanning.

Without going into great detail here, we shall indicate briefly how HAM's search mechanisms are consistent with at least the salient results from the Sternberg paradigm. When HAM is told that the memory list for one or more tests will be the digits 7, 9, 4, HAM will construct the compound proposition "List-K has-as-parts 7, 9, 4," for which the memory structure will be as shown in Figure 12.6. The term "List-K" simply is the internal indexing by which the system keeps track of the most recent list in the experimental series. The representation in Figure 12.6 is identical to that for the 1-1 case in Thorndyke's experiment. The only difference is that in the typical Sternberg procedure the memory set is altered every trial, so this structure would reside in working memory only temporarily rather than in long-term memory. There may be relatively little of permanence deposited in HAM's associative network about the transient digit string. Moreover, any digit series deposited there would suffer interference from other digit series encountered during the experiment.

We will assume basically the same search processes for the Sternberg task as for Thorndyke's experiment. That is, when HAM is probed with "8," this is equivalent to constructing and inputting the probe "List-K has-as-parts 8?", and HAM will attempt to match that probe to memory. The MATCH process will begin the search simultaneously from the three entry nodes for "List-K," "has-as-parts" and "8." HAM will be able to identify that it is a false proposition by failing to get a successful match from any one of the three entry words. Since this is a negative case, the MATCH processes that begin from "List-K" or "has-as-parts" will have to exhaustively search the object conjunction leading from the predicate node.

The element 8, while not in the current list, is likely to have been in earlier lists (say LIST K-*i*). The search from 8 might find this old list name, permitting fast falsification of the "LIST-K has 8" query. Conceivably, the temporal discriminability between the two internal list tags (for LIST K versus LIST K-*i*) could slow the rejection process due to list-differentiation problems. Even in case the negative probe has not been previously used in this experiment, instances of it will still have been hooked into other preexperimental propositions (e.g., "The movie starts at 8"). Retrieval of the subject of the most recent preexperimental proposition involving the negative probe would permit direct falsification of the probe question. These remarks are to deny the thought that the negative probe can "retrieve nothing" so will therefore lead to an indefinitely long search.

One may ask why this fast backpath (from "8") doesn't always win out in the race against the MATCH processes which begin from "LIST-K" and from

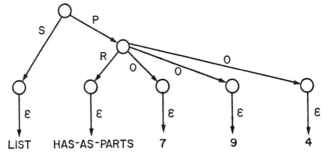

FIG. 12.6. HAM's encoding of a memory set in the Sternberg experiment.

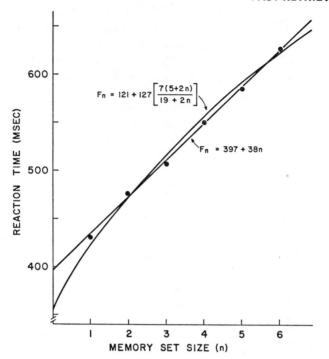

$$F_n = 121 + 127\left[\frac{7(5+2n)}{19 + 2n}\right]$$

$$F_n = 397 + 38n$$

FIG. 12.7. HAM's predictions for the Sternberg data.

"has-as-parts." This should especially happen for large memory sets, since these latter searches are slowed down by the multiple object paths (see Figure 12.6) which they will encounter in their search. However, in the Sternberg task one usually finds linear increases in reaction times as memory sets increase in size from 1 to 6.

But it turns out that the effect predicted by HAM is nearly linear over the shorter range of set sizes that are typically explored in the Sternberg task. From either LIST-K or "has-as-parts," there are $5 + 2n$ associates which must be searched (where n is the size of the memory set). From the probe digit, seven links must be examined. Putting together the three components, then, the rate parameter for the fastest of the three-way race is the sum $1/[(5 + 2n)a] + 1/[(5 + 2n)a] + 1/[7a]$, all of which simplifies to $(19 + 2n)/[7(5 + 2n)a]$. Thus, the function relating the time to falsify a probe given a memory set of size n is given in Equation (4):

$$F_n = K_F + a[7(5 + 2n)/(19 + 2n)]. \tag{4}$$

Figure 12.7 illustrates the predictions of this model, Sternberg's straight-line function, and the data (given by the dots) from an illustrative experiment reported in Sternberg (1969). In this fit K_F was estimated to be 121 msec. and a to be 129 msec. As can be seen, the linear prediction and the prediction from HAM are virtually indistinguishable over this range. The function predicted by HAM is negatively accelerated and asymptotes at $K_F + 7a = 1024$ msec., but over the range of set size explored in the typical short-term memory experiment, the negative acceleration is not sufficient to be detected empirically.

Sternberg has found no difference between the slope obtained for saying yes that a probe is in memory set, or for saying no that a probe is not in the set. He interpreted this as evidence for an exhaustive search of the memory set. It will be recalled that with respect to long-term memory searches (the person-location study), our results were ambiguous between exhaustive or self-terminating search. If HAM is to predict identical effects of memory-set size for Yes and No responses in the short-term task, we must assume the subject exhaustively scans the memory structure in working memory. This contrasts with the assumption we favor for long-term memory, but is clearly forced upon us by the data.

List-Scanning in Long-term Memory

Atkinson and Juola (1972) have extended the Sternberg paradigm by using memory sets of sizes up to 48 words. These memory sets are well learned as serial lists by the subject before the experiment begins. Therefore, much as in the experiments in Section 12.2, it may be assumed that the information is stored in long-term memory. We will assume a memory representation that is identical to Figure 12.6, which was suggested for the Sternberg task. However, unlike the application to Sternberg's data, it will be assumed that the search is self-terminating; that is, the subject is presumed to stop his search of a GET-list as soon as he arrives at the positive item. This assumption of self-termination is consistent with the models favored in Section 12.2 for search of long-term memory; with respect to our analysis of the Atkinson and Juola data, little of an empirical issue hinges on the assumption of self-termination.

Using the representations and derivations from the above analysis of the Sternberg task, Equation (4) above gives HAM's predictions for the No times. Assuming a self-terminating search, Equation (5) describes the Yes times for tests of items that were in fact on the memory list:

$$T_n = K_T + a/n \sum_i^n 7(5 + 2i)/(19 + 2i). \tag{5}$$

This model will be applied to an experiment reported by Atkinson and Juola in which they had subjects commit to memory lists of length 16, 24, and 32. Following learning of his list on one day, the subject returned for reaction-time tests the next day. On this day, single words were presented as probes, and the subject decided as quickly as possible whether or not the probe was in the memorized list. Half the test probes were on the memory list (called targets) and half were not (called distractors). Over the course of an hour's testing, some of the targets (requiring a Yes answer) occurred up to four times; also, some of the distractor words (requiring a No answer) occurred up to four times. Atkinson and Juola found rather different results, depending on whether the subject was dealing with the list targets and distractors for the first time or for a later time. We will consider the data obtained for targets and distractors that had already been presented at least once. The RTs did not change much over presentations 2, 3, and 4 of the distractors or targets. The data from these repeated presentations is shown in Figure 12.8 as a function of the memory-set size. As can be seen, both the time to identify targets (positives) and to identify distractors (negatives) increases with list length. The curved lines represent the best predictions of HAM, with an a estimate of 46 msec., a K_F estimate of 559 msec., and a K_T estimate of 520 msec. The straight lines represent the predictions from the theory presented by Atkinson and Juola. The two theories are closely comparable in their predictions. The Atkinson and Juola model which assumes linear functions has a mean discrepancy from the data of about 4 msec., whereas ours is off by about 5 msec.

One interesting feature requires comment in connection with the theoretical fits that HAM displays in Figure 12.8. There is virtually no difference between positive and negative predictions with respect to the increase in verification time as a function of list length. This virtual equality occurs despite the fact that a self-terminating search is assumed in the case of the positive probes. It has been frequently remarked (e.g., Sternberg, 1969) that a self-terminating search expects a 2 to 1 ratio in the slopes of the positives and negatives. But this assumes that the verification times increase linearly with the list length. If the increase is negatively accelerated (as we assume), then ratio of the negative-to-positive slopes will range from almost 2 to 1 for the low values of list length, to 1 to 1 in the range Atkinson and Juola explore, to a ratio *less* than 1 at still larger values of list length. This shifting ratio results because both positive and negative RT functions approach the same asymptote, but the negative function approaches it more rapidly than the positive function under the assumption of a self-terminating search.

Atkinson and Juola assume essentially a serial scan of lists, just as Sternberg proposed for the short-term memory case. However, they assume that this serial search is only invoked occasionally when the subject is uncertain as to whether the

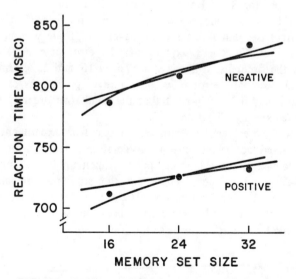

FIG. 12.8. HAM's predictions for the Atkinson and Juola data.

word is actually in the list. Usually, the subject makes his decision as to list membership by the relative "strength" of the items. We find the strength arguments generally unconvincing (see Anderson & Bower, 1972) but will not enter into a detailed critique of those models here.

Before leaving this area, brief mention will be made of another confirmatory experiment on long-term memory search done at Stanford by Keith Wescourt (personal communication, 1972). His subjects first learned on Day 1 three lists of 12 words, the three lists printed on green, yellow, or red cards and denoted the Green List, the Yellow List, and the Red List. Each list comprised three subsets of four words: one subset of four words was unique to that list, appearing only in it; the other two subsets of four words were shared between this list and one or the other of the two other lists. For instance, the Green List consisted of four words unique to the Green List, four words that were on the Green List and the Yellow List, and four words that were on the Green and the Red Lists. The same overlapping structure characterized the Yellow and Red Lists. Over the next two sessions the subject received a series of memory-search tests. A probe word would be shown on a card of a specific background color (green, yellow, or red); the implicit probe question was "Did WORD appear in the LIST of this COLOR?" Alternatively, HAM would translate the probe as "COLORLIST contains WORD?" since this will match its representational format "GREENLIST contains WORD 1, WORD 2, ..., WORD 12" (see Figure 12.6).

The queries may be considered to be of four types: first, they query either a unique word belonging to one list or an overlapping word that had two instances in different color lists; second, the query is either True or False. HAM expects the queries involving unique words to be answered faster than those involving overlapping words. Wescourt's results came out as expected. The mean reaction times for correct responses, averaged over eight subjects with 42 tests of each type, were 1,848 msec. for True Unique queries, 2,298 msec. for True Overlapping queries, 2,281 for False Unique queries, and 2,656 for False Overlapping queries. Each main effect is about 400 msec. in magnitude. There was an unfortunately large error rate in Wescourt's experiment; the error percentages for the four conditions in the order listed above were 7, 21, 15, and 23%, respectively. With such high and systematic error rates, quantitative applications of the model are uncertain. However, it is of interest that the qualitative ordering of the queries came out in the expected direction.

Having now some evidence for our search model from experimental studies with especially contrived fact bases, we turn consideration to reaction-time studies which utilize the data base presumably stored preexperimentally in the long-term memory of our well-educated subjects. These are the studies of so-called "semantic memory" which use verification times to try to infer something about the organization of the knowledge store as well as the search processes which sift through this data looking for answers to specific questions.

12.4. SEMANTIC MEMORY

Partly in response to Quillian's memory model (see Section 4.3) and partly for autonomous reasons, there has been a recent spate of research studying the search processes that operate on natural memories rather than on some artificial memory structure created for experimental purposes. That is, subjects are interrogated about facts which are presumably part of their everyday world knowledge, and interest centers on how fast various types of questions can be answered. Such research is fraught with experimental dangers due to the confounding of experimental manipulations with inherent characteristics of the materials. The experimenter is not totally free to choose his experimental materials. He must select from what has been provided by the whims and quirks of natural language and culture. When the experimenter assigns material to conditions on the basis of some semantic criterion, he is also probably producing differences between conditions on the basis of word frequency, conjoint propositional frequency and recency, concreteness, or some other dimension. It thus becomes very difficult to assess the significance of a difference in RT between the conditions. Is it due to the specified change in the semantic variable, or is it some unspecified variable that happens to correlate with the semantic variable? For an extensive discussion of these methodological problems, the reader is directed to a paper by Landauer and Meyer (1972). Despite these inherent problems, many researchers have moved to natural materials. The principal motivation is the suspicion that the search processes that operate on the highly overlearned natural knowledge structures may be different from those that operate on memories acquired only briefly and imperfectly for the purposes of a psychological experiment.

Much excitement was created by a seminal paper by Collins and Quillian (1969) which proposed that the organization of semantic memory could be revealed by the time subjects needed to answer queries which required some inferences. Specifically, Quillian (1968) had postulated that concepts were hierarchically organized into logically nested subset-superset chains, and that particular predicates or properties would be attached directly only to that node designating the most general class to which that property applied. Thus, the superset of *pekinese* was presumed not to be *animal*, but rather was first *dog*, which has superset *mammal*, which then has superset *animal*. Thus, to verify that a *pekinese* is an *animal* would require three deductive steps, whereas to verify that a pekinese is a dog would require but one deductive step, and so less time to respond. The further assumption, that properties are attached to the most general concept to which they could possibly apply, leads to similar predictions regarding reaction time to verify subject-property conjectures. Thus, if *sings* is a property stored directly with the concept *canary*, whereas *has skin* or *breathes* are properties stored only at the superordinate category *animal*, then it will take less time to verify that "A canary can sing" than "A canary has skin." Presumably, to verify that "A canary has skin" the subject must search through superset chains to get from *canary* to *animal*, and thence to the fact that all animals *have skin*.

The Collins and Quillian proposal was really concerned with how a certain type of deduction would be made in memory. That is, if we know A is a subset of B, and B a subset of C, then we may properly conclude that A is a subset of C. Similarly, if we know A is a subset of B and that B has property P, we may correctly deduce that A have property P. What is novel and intriguing about the Collins and Quillian proposal is their claim that these deductions can be largely effected by simple search routines defined on a hierarchical memory structure. The important predictor of reaction time is the number of superset chains that must be searched to accomplish the inference. For this reason this research has been included in this chapter on fact retrieval rather than the chapter on question answering which follows. Collins and Quillian interpret their data not as evidence about the character of human deduction, but rather as evidence about how memory is structured and searched.

Their basic claim is that reaction time should increase with the number of nodes to be traversed; this claim is perfectly compatible with the inference processes in HAM. Where we differ with Collins and Quillian (see our earlier discussion in Section 4.3) is in regard to the degree to which memory is hierarchically organized and the degree to which properties are only stored with supersets. We think that when we assent to the fact "Canaries can fly" it is probably because the "can-fly" predicate is stored directly with *canary* rather than inferred from *bird*. It is only for rare subject-predicate combinations (e.g., "Spinoza had an elbow") that inferences are likely to occur and that the Collins and Quillian predictions should hold. In fact, Collins and Quillian chose their experimental items so that the subject-predicate combinations used were rare and likely to require inference making (e.g., "A birch has seeds").

The initial data reported by Collins and Quillian on these issues confirmed their hypotheses both for subset questions ("A canary is an animal?") and for property questions ("A canary can breathe?"). Statements requiring longer pathways to be traced out to connect them in the alleged hierarchy were also found to take longer to verify. However, given the selection of stimulus materials, it remained unclear whether all property information was stored in the hierarchical, nonredundant manner proposed by Quillian. Later research concerned itself more directly with this question.

Effects of Associative Strength

A first complication in the results was shown by Wilkins (1971), who found that reaction times to verify subset relations such as, "An A is a B," depend strikingly upon the preestablished "associative strength" between instance A and category B. Wilkins measured the subject's time to decide whether a particular word belonged to a given category. Sample sentences would be "Is the following an instance of a *bird*: . . . *robin*? . . . *flamingoo*? . . *ostrich*? . . . ." The RT to verify that "A *robin* is a *bird*" was correlated with the relative frequency with which a normative group of English speakers gave *robin* as a categorical associate to the concept *bird*. This associative strength is presumed to index the frequency with which the two terms occur conjointly in discourse.

This result is easily accounted for with the ordered GET-list of bird instances that would be delivered when HAM-evoked GET (bird, $\subseteq^{-1}$). The position of a particular bird subset on this GET-list is determined by the recency of its experience. In the absence of specific recency information, a good predictor of an item's position in the GET-list is its frequency of occurrence in contexts in which the category is under discussion; this amounts to saying that category-instance cooccurrence frequency is the critical variable. These simple mechanisms, of recency and frequency effects on an item's location on a GET-list, would thus account for Wilkin's verification latencies. Rips, Shoben, and Smith (in press) have observed similar effects of "associative strength" on verification latencies for instance-category questions.

It is also plausible that a similar ordering influenced by recency and conjoint frequency of supersets on a GET-supersets list would account for much of the so-called "distance" effect on verification latencies with superset statements. If one asks for superordinates of *sparrow, bird* is the most frequent, and *animal* is less frequent; *aves*, which is technically near *bird*, does not occur (Loftus & Scheff, 1971). Similarly, to *collie* as a cue, the listing of categorical associates supersets come out in the order *dog*, then *animal*, with *mammal* (which is logically intermediate) following far behind in the listing. In HAM this would clearly be simulated by the order of categories on the list returned by GET (*pekinese, superset*); this order would be determined primarily by conjoint frequency. The farther down in the ranking a given superset is, the longer HAM must search to find it. Since supersets that are semantically far removed from the subject-word tend to have low rankings, they would tend to take a longer time to verify. This simple notion would seem to account for the "superset distance" results in the literature without necessitating the assumption of a hierarchy of nested sets. The above discussion assumes that single links to the various supersets of a given concept are stored directly at a given node. This is, of course, a procedure that is wasteful of "storage space," since the system could infer (from subset relations) much of what it thus stores redundantly. Quillian (1968) in particular offers this spacesaving as an argument for eliminating all redundant facts stored in semantic memory. Quillian's position in the extreme claims that if the system learns that all dogs have fleas, it should *erase* the prior information it had stored about Fido having fleas, because that old fact would now be derivable from the new fact plus the fact that Fido is a dog.

We disagree fundamentally with this space-saving assumption and with the erasure idea to which it leads. There is no compelling reason to believe that human memory cannot retain many redundant facts; there is no strong need for erasure or "garbage collection" of redundant facts just to "clean up" the memory system. We handle forgetting in HAM by essentially making a certain fact very difficult to retrieve from particular concepts, by its gradually settling far down in the GET-lists associated with these concepts through its disuse but multiple uses of the concepts with other interpolated, interfering facts. Quillian's hypothesis, that predicates are erased from specific instances and attached as a generalization about the class of instances, is simply implausible.

Let us enumerate a few of the problems with the Quillian model: First, subjects do not have stored in logical order the various supersets to which each concept belongs. As Collins and Quillian (1969) point out themselves, *mammal* is technically between *dog* and *animal*, so therefore *mammal* should be closer to *dog* in a semantic hierarchy than *animal* is to *dog*. However, animal is a more frequent associate of dog than is mammal. The reaction time to verify "A dog is a mammal" is found to be much longer than for "A dog is an animal" (see Rips, et al. in press). This is true even for adult subjects who know the logical nesting relations among these three concepts. Therefore, when we pit associative frequency against logical nesting, it is the former variable that is the effective predictor of categorization times.

Second, Conrad (1972) has shown that RTs to verify property statements like "A canary has skin" are predicted more accurately by association norms than by one's intuitions about the highest level in the hierarchy at which a given property generalization would be attached. For example, Quillian has proposed that a predicate like "has wings" would be attached directly to the *bird* concept since it applies generically to all birds, while "has skin" would be attached to the *animal* node. Conrad (1972) collected property-association norms to each concept (noun) in a typical hierarchy used by Collins and Quillian; that is, subjects would be asked to describe a *canary*, or a *bird*, or an *animal*, and so forth. These norms showed clearly that high associates of *canary* tended to be those properties presumed by Collins and Quillian to be stored directly with *canary*, whereas the properties used by Collins and Quillian for testing more distant subject-predicate constructions tended to be of much lower associative frequency. This confound, of alleged hierarchical distance with associative frequency, is not necessarily damning to the hierarchical viewpoint, since distance in the logical concept hierarchy may itself be determining the association data.

To assess such confounds, Conrad ran several experiments to factor out the effects on verification latencies of associative frequency versus alleged hierarchical distance. In each case, the associative probability of a property to the subject of a True statement (or to a superordinate of the subject) strongly determined reaction times (with more probable properties being verified faster), whereas logical distance in the hierarchy between the subject and predicate gave inconsistent effects overall. For example, in her Experiment II, Conrad used high- versus low-frequency predicates of the highest-level concepts like *animal*, and used subjects (nouns) which were logically either zero, one, or two hierarchical levels removed from the predicate (e.g., *animal, bird,* or *canary*). She found that predicate frequency (to *animal*) had a large effect on RT (approximately 250 msec. difference), whereas hierarchical distance did not contribute significantly to the variation in RTs.

One would not wish to give up entirely on the Collins and Quillian idea of superset chaining, but the various negative results suggest caution in exactly how the process is to be formulated and when it is to be activated. In HAM, we envision essentially two mechanisms for verifying property statements—either a direct associative link or, if that fails, a chaining through supersets. Conjoint frequency of experiencing a particular concept-predicate pair would determine the probability that the association can be directly retrieved. This means, of course, that a given predicate may be duplicated redundantly and many times all over the network. This violates Quillian's assumption of cognitive economy. As Conrad (1972) says:

> Thus, there seems to be little evidence to support the hypothesis that all properties are stored only once in memory and must be retrieved through a series of inferences for all words except those that they most directly define [p. 153].

> ...it was shown that the Collins and Quillian data which supported this hypothesis could be attributed to a failure to control for the frequency with

which a property is stored with its assumed superordinate in memory. In addition, a somewhat stronger test of the hypothesis [Experiment II reviewed above] failed to provide supportive data. This suggests that properties are stored in memory with every word which they define and can be retrieved directly rather than through a process of inference [p. 154].

Some recent research at Stanford by S. M. Kosslyn and K. E. Nelson (personal communication, 1972) adds a final blow to the Collins and Quillian proposal. They used individual subject's ratings of the "saliency" and conjoint frequency of the subject-predicate combination. These various ratings were highly intercorrelated; more importantly, they were much better predictors of verification reaction times for subject-predicate test probes than was the logical node distance in a Quillian hierarchy. As we have assumed for HAM, Kosslyn and Nelson interpret their results in terms of a serial self-terminating search of a property list associated with the subject noun. More "salient" properties are simply ones that are higher on these lists.

To place some perspective on the issue, however, it is clear that something like superset chaining must be used to answer the thousands of queries a person encounters which require some inference. Let us call these the queries with an "almost-zero" conjoint frequency between the subject and predicate. Some examples would be: "Did Leibnitz have a four-chambered heart?", "Did Martha Washington have a mouth?", or "Is the climate of Yucatan hot?" No one has probably heard precisely those predications, yet they are inferred directly (in two-steps) by moving up to a superset (*is a person* or *is in Mexico*) and finding the property. This sort of inference would take more time than the direct association. However, it is not clear that there is much need for very lengthy chains of deductions. Each of the above bizarre examples used exactly one "superset" link. We doubt that people frequently carry through inferential chains of much greater length.

Effects of Category Size

We have argued that propositions like "A canary is an animal" are stored directly, even though they could be inferred from pairs of propositions like "A canary is a bird" and "A bird is an animal." Also more remote superset relations will lead to longer verification times insofar as the more remote superset is less accessible on the GET-list. For the above example it would be claimed that the GET (*canary, superset*) list would tend to be ordered "bird, animal, living thing, physical object, etc." However, another factor would predict the same result. The proposition "An A is a B" can be verified in two ways: either B is found on the superset list of A, or A can be found on the subset list of B. As in the previous discussions, one may conceive of a race between these two search processes, with the fastest determining the verification time. If B is logically a second-order superset of A (as *animal* is of *canary*), its subset list will be much longer than if it is a first-order superset (as *bird* is of *canary*). Consequently, it will probably take longer to find A among the many B subsets. Therefore, first-order superset statements may be faster to verify simply because more often an A is found on the

GET (*B, subset*) list, thus "beating out" the search process operating on the GET (*A, superset*) list.

In fact, Wilkins (1971) found that the time to verify categorical statements of the form "An *A* is a *B*" was slightly faster for smaller *B* categories. Unlike other researchers (e.g., Landauer & Freedman, 1968), Wilkins' smaller *B* categories were not nested within larger *B* categories (e.g., as *bird* is in *animal*). Therefore, his category-size effect is not confounded with node distance. A second example comes from an experiment by Meyer and Ellis (1970) who found that the time to determine that a nonword was not a member of a specified category (e.g., "A Mafer is a bird") increased with category size. Since nonwords cannot enter into semantic hierarchies, Meyer and Ellis argue that their effect cannot reflect node distance. Rather, they argue for a sequential search of the category which can sometimes exhaust small categories before the determination is made that the item is a nonword. This is approximately what happens when HAM evokes its GET (*bird, subset*) function while simultaneously searching for associations to Mafer.

Freedman and Loftus (1971) reported an experiment which is sometimes interpreted as evidence that category size does not affect verification time. They had subjects generate instances of categories that satisfied a certain criterion—for instance, an animal whose name begins with the letter *Z* or a season that was hot. Response latencies were only slightly and negatively related to the rated size of category. However, there is no reason to expect an effect of category size in such a task. If it is assumed that a subject scans a serial list of category instances, what should determine his response time is how far down the list is an instance that satisfies the criterion, rather than how long the list is. There is no reason to suppose the required instance will be further down a longer list. Assuming that the position of the instance is related to its frequency in the language or the frequency with which it is given as an instance to the category (see Battig & Montague, 1969), then reaction time should display a strong negative relation to such frequency measures. In fact, this is just what Freedman and Loftus (1971) found.

A recent experiment by Loftus (in press) is very encouraging with respect to HAM's race model for categorization judgments. Loftus had her subjects judge whether an instance belonged to a category. Either the instance was presented one second before the category or the order of presentation was reversed. By presenting instance or category first, Loftus was giving a "head start" to the search process proceeding from that member of the pair. That is, HAM could access that word and ready it for a search that would begin immediately with the presentation of the other member of the pair. Therefore, the effective predictor of RT should be how quickly the search process from the initially presented member would find the target association. This is just what Loftus found. When the instance preceded the category, the effective predictor of RT was how dominant the category was as an associate to the instance. When the category preceded, the effective predictor was how dominant the instance was as an associate to the category.

Thus, most of the evidence seems consistent with the claim of HAM's search model: namely, that search processes in long-term memory will be slowed down in proportion to the number of competing associations that must be examined to retrieve the desired information, but that several such search processes (beginning from the separate elements of a compound probe) race against one another in the attempt to verify a test proposition. On the other hand, the assumption of Quillian's search model was that activation (the search) spreads out in parallel from a node, down all paths, and that the speed of this radiation was independent of the number of associative paths leading from the node. This assumption should be laid to rest, for it appears to be incorrect.

The denial of Quillian's memory-search assumptions has serious consequences. These may be illustrated by propopositions of the form "*A* has relation *R* to *B*." The time to verify this proposition should vary with the number of propositions stored individually about *A*, *R*, and B, and should be very long when the number of propositions is very large for all three elements. Does this claim coincide with the everyday facts of memory? Is it not the case that we can quickly verify propositions involving much-used concepts and individuals? For instance, consider the proposition "Nixon is the president of the U.S.A." We immediately recognize it as true (in 1973), but how many facts do we know about "Nixon," about the relation "is-president-of," and about the "U.S.A."? Many hundreds, so how can we verify this one quickly? HAM's answer to this query rests upon the saliency of the test proposition. While these items are indeed involved in a great many propositions, it seems likely that this particular proposition would be near the top of any GET-list leading from "Nixon," "is-president-of," or "U.S.A."

But let us consider a less salient proposition about Richard Nixon, such as "Richard Nixon consults with Billy Graham." Many of us can quickly affirm the truth of this, but for most of us it is not a very salient feature of Richard Nixon. HAM's mechanisms nonetheless predict relatively rapid verification in this case because the proposition is a relatively salient fact about Billy Graham. Recall that for rapid verification, it suffices if just one of the racing MATCH processes obtains a quick result.

Finally, consider a proposition that is not only nonsalient with respect to Nixon, but also with respect to the other elements of the proposition. Understandably, it is difficult to come up with such propositions, but consider this one: "In 1964 Richard Nixon supported Barry Goldwater." Presumably, for most of us, the proposition is not a very salient fact about 1964, Nixon, "supports," or Barry Goldwater. Yet it was well reported in the news media at the time and presumably was deposited firmly in our long-term memory. Most people cannot even recall whether this particular fact is true. A typical response is "Well, I know Nixon was a loyal Republican, and loyal Republicans supported Goldwater in 1964, so I suppose that Nixon did too." HAM interprets this failure of memory by supposing that the proposition had become "buried" far down on all GET-lists so that it was practically unavailable. Chapter 15 gives a thorough discussion of such interference effects; but basically it is assumed that there is a "cutoff" time after which a MATCH process ceases to search memory anymore. If the desired proposition is not found by that time, the system gives up and believes that it does not know (or has forgotten) the proposition.

So, perhaps, what at first seems an unpalatable assumption may be viable after all. In the absence of countervailing evidence, we will continue with the claim that the time to verify a proposition should vary with the saliency of the proposition for its various elements. Moreover, the principal determinant of verification time will be the highest saliency it has for some element. The lower saliencies it has for other elements will be less important. This certainly suggests a systematic research program on semantic memory.

The Mysterious Case of Negatives

Some data on "False" judgments appear to upset the consistent picture developed so far. Schaeffer and Wallace (1970) examined the time required to verify that two instances came from the same category. The possible categories were *tree, flower, mammal,* and *bird.* The striking result concerned the time to decide that the two instances were not from the same one of these categories. This "different" judgment was over 100 msec. longer when the two instances were similar (i.e., both were plants, one being a tree and the other a flower) than when they were dissimilar (i.e., one was a tree and the other a bird). A simple prediction from Quillian's hierarchical model would have been that reaction time would be less for similar "differents" because the node distance between the two items is less (i.e., *tree* and *flower* intersect at *plant,* but *tree* and *bird* only at *living thing*). Therefore, it would take longer for dissimilar "differents" to find the path that justified a different response. Meyer (1970) and Collins and Quillian (1972) report similar findings in terms of subjects' speed of rejecting subset statements like "All *A* and *B*." When the sets overlap (e.g., "All mothers are writers"), it takes approximately 100 msec. longer to reject these statements than when the sets are disjoint (e.g., "All typhoons are wheat").

The way HAM should handle these distance effects with false statements is not obvious. Consider falsifying statements like "All women are writers." A first pass by HAM would not find "writers" among the supersets of "women." A second pass might evoke GET (ϵ^{-1}, woman), yielding a list of known individual women. These exemplars may then be checked for being writers. The first failure found would disconfirm the universal test probe. The more overlapping are the two concepts (e.g., "All women are students"), the longer would be this expected scan over exemplars before a disconfirming instance would be found, causing a judgment of False. This hypothesis, which Meyer (1970) called "exemplar searching," would explain part of the semantic-distance effect. For even more distant, almost bizarre, probes like "All typhoons are wheat," these superset and exemplar checking procedures seem counterintuitive; rather it would seem that people note the incompatibility of one or more of the inalienable properties of the two concepts, and so exit "False" without further ado. Such restricted search strategies *could be* programmed into HAM, of course, if we felt there were sufficient rationale for doing so.

Both Schaeffer and Wallace (1970) and Meyer (1970) propose two-stage models to explain their results. Schaeffer and Wallace propose that in the first stage the meaning of the two words are compared. If the two words have little in common semantically, the threshold is lowered for making a different response in the second stage. Meyer argues that the first stage determines if the concepts have any overlap. If not, the subject can give a fast No response. If they do overlap, the subject must move to a second stage in which information is retrieved to determine if S is a B-subset.

Several comments are in order regarding these developments. A first complaint is that these results typically are based upon very restricted sampling of different item types, despite the fact that there are usually large item-specific effects. If different items had been included as a variable factor contributing to the variance among RTs, then it is doubtful whether the observed mean differences would have been statistically significant. This is to argue that use of just a few exemplars of given material conditions limits one's ability to generalize from the observed results to the entire population of such exemplars. H. Clark (personal communication, 1972) has forcefully advanced this argument of "inadequate design" against many of the experiments on "semantic memory," including those by Meyer (1970) and by Schaeffer and Wallace (1970).

A second problem with the two-stage models, particularly that of Meyer (1970), is that they assume that true "Some A are B" statements are always verified faster than corresponding true "All A are B" statements. But we now have evidence, to be reviewed in the next chapter, that this generalization is incorrect. Under many circumstances, true "All" statements can be faster than true "Some" statements—a fact which leaves the evidential status of the two-stage models somewhat in limbo.

A further problem with the search models of Meyer and of Schaeffer and Wallace is that they appear usable only for deciding whether subset conjectures are true or false, and they do not extend in any obvious way to searching fact bases for more complex predications (e.g., a four-case proposition), nor for filling in the missing parts of a complex retrieval query. In brief, their search models are rather "task-specific," and reflect more on the decision components of a verification task than upon retrieval from long-term memory.

Despite these detracting comments, we feel that the phenomenon is important; if there is a reliable semantic-distance effect with false subset statements, then it is not obviously explained by the current memory structures and search processes now present in HAM. The next chapter, which deals with inference and deduction in question answering, will find us making similar comments frequently.

REFERENCES

Anderson, J. R., & Bower, G. H. Recognition and retrieval processes in free recall. *Psychological Review*, 1972, 79, 97–123.

Atkinson, R. C., & Juola, J. R. Factors influencing speed and accuracy in word recognition. In G. Kornblum (Ed.), *Attention and performance*. Vol. 4. New York: Academic Press, 1972.

Battig, W. F., & Montague, W. E. Category norms for verbal items in 56 categories: A replication and extension of the Connecticut category norms. *Journal of Experimental Psychology Monograph*, June, 1969.

Bower, G. H. A multicomponent theory of the memory trace. In K. W. Spence & J. T. Spence (Eds.), *Psychology of learning and motivation*. Vol. 1. New York: Academic Press, 1967. Pp. 229–325.

Collins, A. M., & Quillian, M. R. Retrieval time from semantic memory. *Journal of Verbal Learning and Verbal Behavior*, 1969, 8, 240–247.

Collins, A. M., & Quillian, M. R. Experiments on semantic memory and language comprehension. In L. Gregg (Ed.), *Cognition and learning.* New York: Wiley, 1972.

Conrad, C. Cognitive economy in semantic memory. *Journal of Experimental Psychology,* 1972, 92, 149–154.

Freedman, J. L., & Loftus, E. F. Retrieval of words from long-term memory. *Journal of Verbal Learning and Verbal Behavior,* 1971, 10, 107–115.

Landauer, T. K., & Freedman, J. L. Information retrieval from long-term memory: Category size and recognition time. *Journal of Verbal Learning and Verbal Behavior,* 1968, 7, 291–295.

Landauer, T. K., & Meyer, D. E. Category size and semantic-memory retrieval. *Journal of Verbal Learning and Verbal Behavior,* 1972, 11, 539–549.

Loftus, E. F. Category dominance, instance dominance, and categorization time. *Journal of Experimental Psychology,* 1973, in press.

Loftus, E. F., & Scheff, R. W. Categorization norms for fifty representative instances. *Journal of Experimental Psychology Monograph,* 1971, 91, 355–364.

Meyer, D. E. On the representation and retrieval of stored semantic information. *Cognitive Psychology,* 1970, 1, 242–300.

Meyer, D. E., & Ellis, G. B. Parallel processes in word recognition. Paper presented at the meeting of the Psychonomic Society, San Antonio, November 1970.

Nilsson, N. J. *Problem-Solving Methods in Artifical Intelligence.* New York: McGraw-Hill, 1971.

Quillian, M. R. Semantic memory. In M. Minsky (Ed.), *Semantic information processing.* Cambridge, Mass.: M.I.T. Press, 1968.

Rips, L. J., Shoben, E. J., & Smith, E. E. Semantic distance and the verification of semantic relations. *Journal of Verbal Learning and Verbal Behavior,* 1973, 12, 1–20.

Schaeffer, B., & Wallace, R. The comparison of word meanings. *Journal of Experimental Psychology,* 1970, 86, 144–152.

Sternberg, S. Memory-scanning: Mental processes revealed by reaction-time experiments. *Acta Psychologica,* 1969, 30, 276–315.

Townsend, J. T. A note on the identifiability of parallel and serial processes. *Perception and Psychophysics,* 1971, 10, 161–163.

Wickelgren, W. A., & Norman, D. A. Strength models and serial position in short-term recognition memory. *Journal of Mathematical Psychology,* 1966, 3, 316–347.

Wilkins, A. T. Conjoint frequency, category size, and categorization time. *Journal of Verbal Learning and Verbal Behavior,* 1971, 10, 382–385.

13
QUESTION ANSWERING

How do people answer questions? At first, the process appears reasonably simple. A person is asked a question, he retrieves the relevant information from his memory, and then he responds with the appropriate answer. According to this notion, the traditional psychological studies of memory should tell us something about the way that knowledge is used to answer questions. This is not so; there is much more to understanding questions than simple retrieving from memory.

—D. A. Norman

13.1. INTRODUCTION

To put it crudely, the difference between retrieving a fact and answering a question is that the latter requires us to think. Almost all the questions that we encounter in our daily trials and tribulations require that inferences be drawn from stored information. Presumably, the executive first checks to see whether the answer to the query is known directly; it may then analyze the question to see whether it is probable that the answer can be inferred; if so, it then sets up a procedure for calculating the answer. For instance, if a middle-aged man were asked "How many automobiles have you owned in your lifetime?", he probably would not have that number stored directly. But he would know that he probably can retrieve some or all of the separate bits of propositions that are needed to give a good estimate. Once determined to do the computation, he would execute some calls to memory with a list of known context cues (times-plus-places of his life) compounded with other retrieval cues ("my car"), and set up a scheme for counting positive instances.

Baseball

This is what was done in an early question-answering system developed by Green, Wolf, Chomsky, and Laughery (1963). The data base employed was the month, day, place, teams, and scores for each baseball game in the American League for 1 year. The aim of the program was to answer complex questions phrased in ordinary English regarding this data base. The individual game

TABLE 13.1

A Portion of the Data Structure for
BASEBALL

---

1 month = July
  Place = Boston
    Day = 7
      Game Serial No. = 96
        Team = Red Sox, Score = 5
        Team = Yankees, Score = 3
  Place = Chicago
    Day = ...

---

information is stored within a list structure as in Table 13.1, with the time and place being the primary indexes in memory, and with the other information being a list of attribute-value pairs. The complete baseball season is stored in this tabular form.

When a question is read into the program, a linguistic parser creates a *specification list* for the question. The specification list is the input to the question-answering program; it lists a set of attribute-value pairs, some of which are to be filled in. The specification list for the question "Who did the Red Sox play on July 7?" is as shown in Table 13.2a. The retrieval cues in panel a directly access the appropriate information molecule in memory (in Table 13.1), so that the queried element can be filled in by the answer "Yankees."

But consider the more complex question in Table 13.2b; this modified specification list corresponds to the question "What teams won 10 games in July?" This leads to an initial interpretation in terms of a program for counting the number of games won in July by each team. The program tabulates the number of games won by each team during July by comparing the two scores and adding a +1 to the "games won" counter for the team having the larger score. When this is finished for all games in July, the program exits with a list of games won in July by each team. The next part of the query is then attacked, namely, to list the names of the teams that won exactly 10 games in July. This would be interpreted as another program, wherein the "games won in July" list would be scanned for entries equal to 10. The executive would note which teams gave a match to the criterion figure of 10 wins. Following its scan, the program might then print-out, e.g., "Yankees and Tigers" as the only teams to win exactly 10 games during July.

We see in this illustration several cycles of question interpretation. "What teams. . ." calls for a list of team names having criterial attributes to be specified; the predicate ". . .won 10 games in July" stipulates the criterial properties. But this is not in a form that will match the game molecule. So "winning 10 games in July" is interpreted to "time = July; number of games score X exceeds score Y," which leads to the counting program. At the very "bottom" is a routine that is comparing the scores of the two teams in each July game and entering a count in one or another counter.

Frequency judgments of this sort are just one illustration of inferences from a memory base. There are many other illustrations that depend upon the semantics of relational predicates, the interpretation of questions, superset chaining, autonymous relations, and assessment of the truth of queries regarding complex propositions by combining the known truth values of elementary propositions. Question-answering programs to handle such queries constitute an extensive area of investigation in artificial intelligence (see Minsky, 1968, and Simmons, 1970, for reviews). However, the concern of all such programs is computational power and efficiency, rather than simulation of how people in fact answer such questions. These priorities clearly underlie the presently popular view in artificial intelligence that question answering is a "theorem-proving" problem.

One of the more powerful question-answering systems, QA3 (see Green & Raphael, 1968), proceeds by converting all its input to statements in first-order logic, so that answering a question corresponds to deriving it as a logical consequence of the known facts, which are considered as axioms of the system. The logical derivations use Robinson's "resolution method," (see Robinson, 1965) which converts all propositions into prenex conjunctive normal form and then forms resolvents of resulting conjoined clauses. Although this procedure makes for inferential power, it also places the program beyond the pale of plausibility as a psychological simulation. In certain respects, the program is much more powerful than humans, deriving implications with flawless logic which humans could rarely do without benefit of paper and pencil. But in other respects, the program is inefficient insofar as it considers all varieties of deductions which are clearly irrelevant to the question at hand.

A further problem in considering the logic-oriented question-answerers as simulations is that the program cannot abide contradictions in their data base. Since the data base is considered as an axiom-set for deriving answers to queries, an internal contradiction in the axioms is disastrous, since logically any theorem can be proved from a set of contradictory premises. On the other hand, people seem to function reasonably well while all the time harboring various degrees of direct and indirect contradictions in their belief systems. The conflict between two beliefs may be implicit and go unnoticed for years until the relation is explicitly drawn out, say, in an argument with an adversary.

TABLE 13.2

Specification Lists for Two Questions
to BASEBALL

(a) Opponent = ?
     Team = Red Sox
     Month = July
     Day = 7

(b) $Team_{(winning)}$ = ?
     $Game_{(number of)}$ = 10
     Month = July

Rather than reviewing and criticizing the various question-answering programs available in the artificial intelligence field, we will instead discuss the inference mechanisms available to and projected for HAM. HAM's capacities are rather minimal at the moment; HAM as programmed is *not* a powerful inference machine. However, the projected capabilities do have psychological plausibility. The evidence on how people perform complex inferences from memory, is, in fact, quite weak and fragmentary, so that it places few constraints on the nature of the theoretical assumptions regarding inference making. But more on this anon after we have discussed HAM's rudimentary capabilities.

Word Synonymity and Definite Descriptions

A first rudimentary ability that HAM has is recognition of synonymous words or phrases. This is because synonymous words are attached to the same "idea node," and it is the latter node that enters into factual propositions about that concept. Thus, if it has stored the sentence "The young lad was bitten by a dog," it will be able to match this structure to answer the query "Was a boy bitten by a canine?"

A similar one-step inference is available in HAM for definite descriptions which are known to refer to a particular individual. In HAM, the concept of a given individual would be represented as a single node about which numerous predications could be made. Thus, a given node, say #3158, might be linked into a series of propositions such as "George Washington is the name of individual 3158," "Individual 3158 was the first president of the United States," "Individual 3158 was married to individual 4275," and so on. Because such definite descriptions point to the same concept node, they can be used interchangeably in retrieving facts which HAM has been taught. For example, if it is told that "George Washington lived at Mt. Vernon," it can retrieve this fact from the query "Where did Martha Washington's husband live?"; it can do this because the definite description accesses the same idea node as does the name George Washington. In experiments on sentence memory, we have shown too that subjects easily confuse in recall a person's name with a familiar definite description of him (e.g., "Richard Nixon" and "The current president of the U.S."—see the experiment in Section 9.2). Schematically, if the subject studies two sentences like "Name has property P_1" and "Definite description has property P_2," he will later be confused about the pairings, having difficulty remembering which property was paired with the name and which property with the definite description.

Referential Distinguishers in Context

There is a second kind of elementary contextual inference which HAM can do because of its manner of dealing with anaphoric reference and with conjoining of predications to the same idea node. Suppose HAM is confronted with a scene of two objects characterized by the proposition "Scene is composed of a red triangle on the left and a blue triangle on the right." We then input the sentence "The triangle on the left belongs to Harry." In looking up the phrase "triangle on the left," HAM's recency mechanism identifies this with the earlier concept node representing the "red triangle on the left," and it attaches the predication "belongs to Harry" to this node. Later we can ask "Who does the *red* triangle belong to?", and HAM can answer "Harry," since the "red triangle" of the query retrieves the same concept node to which the phrase "belongs to Harry" was attached. This is an example of how two partial descriptions (red or left triangle) can access the same concept node, so that information inserted under one description is retrievable from the other partial description.

The example also illustrates contextual determination of reference. The uniqueness of reference of an expression depends critically on the context in which the utterance occurs. Thus, "the blue object" has no unique referent if there are several blue objects under discussion. Olson (1970) has argued that selection of a referring utterance depends critically on the features distinguishing among the set of objects under consideration. Such matters can be handled adequately in HAM by supposing, for instance, that a visual scene is encoded by a perceptual parser in terms of a set of descriptive propositions, such as a list of objects with certain properties, in particular relations to one another. A given expression would then retrieve (select) a unique concept node or not in this scene-description, depending on whether the expression uses a distinguishing retrieval cue.

These are the sorts of simple inferences that HAM regularly makes (almost flawlessly) in our current program. The reader may be somewhat perplexed by our reference to these as "inferences." Really they are just "gifts" of our representation and our recognition routines. That is, HAM can "infer" "George Washington was a good husband" from "The first president of the United States was a good husband" simply because the two statements receive identical representation in memory with the same individual node being used for "George Washington" or "The first president of the United States." In fact, HAM at no point goes through an explicit step of inferring "George Washington is the first president of the United States." We regard this proper name–definite description example as an excellent demonstration of the importance of the choice of good representation.

It would be clearly desirable if this sort of inference through representation could be extended to handle other of the inference demands in question answering. But our representation and all others we have examined seem clearly limited in this respect. It seems that if a program is going to correctly solve most questions, at some points it will have to explicitly step through stages of an inference. Our purpose in subsequent sections will be to examine in some detail what inferential procedures HAM would have to employ to obtain appropriate inferences from its memory. Always our selection of inferential processes is constrained by the representational assumptions that we tied ourselves to in earlier chapters. Thus, to the extent we can succeed in providing an account of inference making, we will have provided further empirical support for our representational assumptions.

13.2. NEGATION

So far we have talked as though information were stored primarily in positive assertions. But clearly a good deal of our knowledge is in the form of explicit or implicit negations. Linguists believe that an explicit denial like "Harry didn't kill the cat" has at least two components: a presupposition and an assertion. The presupposition of the utterance is that the speaker thinks that the listener believes that Harry killed the cat; the assertion is that the speaker thinks that that proposition is false. In terms of the logical deep-structure, then, the denial is equivalent to "False (suppose (Harry killed the cat))."

In HAM, denials or explicit negatives are parsed and encoded as a subject-predicate construction, of the simple form *"Proposition* is false." Thus "Harry didn't lie" would be equivalent to *"That Harry lied* is false." This form of encoding can then be easily accessed to answer questions. Specifically, whenever the MATCH process signals a match on a proposition, the question-answering routine checks for a "is false" predicate attached to the matched proposition. To a question like "Did Harry lie?", HAM would find a perfect match to the embedded proposition in memory, but would then notice that False is predicated of this proposition. Thus, it will retrieve the statement *"That Harry lied* is false" and report out a False (or No) answer to the question. If the question probe were negative, "Is it true that Harry didn't lie?", then the probe will exactly match the memory structure, and HAM will report out a True answer.

The procedure of comparing embedded propositions for a match before examining sentence predicates is the principle advocated by Clark (1972) and Chase and Clark (1972) for verifying a sentence against a picture. We will describe the Chase and Clark experiment in some detail, because their model for the task is isomorphic to that of HAM. The basic procedure is to show the subject a simple statement and then a picture (or vice versa); the subject is instructed to decide as fast as he can whether the statement is true of the picture. For example, the picture may show a small star located above a small plus sign. The sentence might be something like "The star isn't below the plus," and the subject is to decide as rapidly as possible whether the sentence is true or false of the picture. The sentence can take one of eight forms: the preposition can be "above" or "below," the subject of the sentence can be "star" or "plus," and the statement can be *positive* or *negative* ("is" or "isn't"). The picture can also be one of two forms (star above plus, or plus above star). Crossed with the eight sentence types, the two pictures yield 16 trial types. The typical experiment would test practiced subjects for hundreds of trials with repeated cycles of the 16 trial types in random order.

The theory which fits the reaction-time data hypothesizes four phases: (*a*) a sentence-encoding phase, where, in particular, negative statements such as *"A* isn't above *B"* are converted internally into propositional predicates of the form "False (*A* above *B*)"; it is assumed that negative sentences take slightly longer to encode than do positive sentences, and we let *b* denote this excess setup time for negations; (*b*) a stage for encoding the picture into a proposition, but with the same preposition ("above" or "below") as used in the sentence; (*c*) a comparison stage in which the executive compares the sentence proposition to the picture proposition to see whether they match; and (*d*) a response stage during which a Yes or No response is generated.

It is assumed that when the picture comes after the sentence, subjects will encode the picture using the same preposition as used in the sentence. This facilitates the comparison stage and also reduces the number of distinct cases to be handled theoretically to four. These four paradigmatic cases are shown in Table 13.3 (from Clark, 1972) for use of the "above" preposition. The procedures within

TABLE 13.3

Latency Components for the Sentence-Picture Verification Task

Sentence type	Stage 1: Sentence representation	Stage 2: Picture representation	Latency components
True Positive	(*A* above *B*)	(*A* above *B*)	t_o
False Positive	(*B* above *A*)	(*A* above *B*)	$t_o + c$
True Negative	(false (*B* above *A*))	(*A* above *B*)	$t_o + c + (b+d)$
False Negative	(false (*A* above *B*))	(*A* above *B*)	$t_o + (b+d)$

the critical comparison process are shown in Table 13.4. The representation of the picture is compared to that of the sentence (in memory) in a series of steps, to decide whether the sentence is true or false. For this purpose, the execution is said to keep track of a *truth index*. This index starts out with the value *true* in it; the value might then be switched by operations 1*a* or 2*a* (see Table 13.4) during the comparison stage. The final value of the index at the end of the comparison stage determines whether the response is True or False.

The various cases will be enumerated to illustrate the quantitative predictions of the model (see Tables 13.3 and 13.4). The True Positive sentence is most quickly verified, in t_o milliseconds, because it occasions no mismatches. The False Positive statement causes a mismatch at Step 1, so branch 1*a* is taken and the truth index is flipped. It is supposed that this branch requires an additional time of *c* milliseconds. The negative statements in lines 3 and 4 of Table 13.3 require a time of *b* milliseconds longer to encode (initially set up) than the positive sentences. The False Negative statement (line 4 in Table 13.3) produces a match at Step 1, the comparison of the two inner strings, but it causes a mismatch at Step 2, when the two outer predicates, False ( ) and ( ), are compared. This causes the executive to branch to Step 2*a* and flip the truth index to False. This extra operation is assumed to take *d* milliseconds. Thus, the total excess time for the False Negative statement is *b+d*. The True Negative sentence (line 3) is the most complex: first, it requires an extra *b* milliseconds of setup time because it is negative; second, in Step 1, the inner strings mismatch, so the 1*a* flip is executed, requiring *c* extra milliseconds; third, in Step 2, the outer predicates mismatch, so the 2*a* branch flips the index back to True, but requires an extra *d* msec.

TABLE 13.4

The Comparison Process (Stage 3) of the Model

1. Compare the embedded (inner) strings of sentence and picture.
   A. If they match, go to 2.
   B. If they do not match, go to 1*a*.
1*a*. Change value of truth index into its opposite; then go to 2.
   2. Compare the *embedding* (outer) strings of sentence and picture.
   A. If they match, stop.
   B. If they do not match, go to 2*a*.
2*a*. Change value of truth index into its opposite; then stop.

This model fits the reaction-time data extremely well. It predicts quantitatively that the RT increment (of $b+d$) between True Positives and False Negatives should be the same as the increment between False Positive and True Negatives. These predictions are always confirmed. A typical estimate of c, for Step $1a$, is 187 msec.; while for $b+d$, for negation setup plus Step $2a$ times, a typical estimate is 685 msec. These estimates fall consistently in this range across several experiments of this type (see Chase & Clark, 1972). Chase and Clark also report several variations on this basic experiment—for example, giving the picture before the sentence and using "above" or "below" equally often in the sentence. In these cases, it is assumed that the picture is naturally encoded in terms of "above" relations. A sentence like (B below A) would then be verified in three comparisons: first, the subjects of the inner propositions are compared, with the truth index changed if the subjects mismatch; then, the prepositions of the inner strings are compared, with the truth index changed if they mismatch; finally, the outer predicates of the two strings are compared, with a mismatch causing a final flip of the truth index. Thus, for a picture encoded as (A above B), the subsequent sentence (false (B above A)), or "B isn't above A," takes the longest time to verify. Chase and Clark also report experiments in which they alter the encoding of the picture by instructing their subjects to concentrate on the bottom figure, so that the picture becomes encoded in terms of "below," as (B below A). This has the expected effects on RT to verify the various sentences using "above" and "below."

A further experiment by Young and Chase (cited in Clark, 1972) instructed subjects to convert all negative statements into positive ones before beginning the comparison to the picture. Conversion was done by simply interchanging mentally the subject and object of negative sentences; thus "A isn't above B" converts to "B above A." It will be appreciated that, although this conversion takes time, it totally eliminates final sentence representations of the form (false (A above B)). And it was such sentence predicates that necessitated the former Operation 2 in Table 13.4 which checked for a match of the outer predicates. If k is the conversion time, then the expected RT for the four cases (successive lines) in Table 13.3 should be t_o, $t_o + c$, $t_o + k$, and $t_o + k + c$, respectively. That is, given the conversion-encoding strategy, the True Negative sentence should now be verified faster by c milliseconds than the False Negative sentence. This model gave a very good fit to the RT data collected by Young and Chase from subjects instructed and practiced on using the conversion strategy. The results illustrate how a conscious strategy can cause different representations to be set up from the same information and how this representation influences later performances which utilize this information.

We mention these results and the model of Chase and Clark because HAM uses precisely the same encoding of explicit negations and the same comparison operations for deciding whether a statement is true. The notion of a "truth index" that flips around is not essential to the model. All that really is needed is some way of keeping track of the number of mismatches—0, 1, or 2—in the comparison process, and a device that responds True, False, or True, respectively, for 0, 1, or 2 mismatches. The "truth index" or "number of mismatches" notions work when one is dealing with two-valued pictures and oppositional predicates, where negation of predicate 1 is equivalent to predicate 2 (not above = below). However, the computation rules would have to be modified to deal with nonopposites. For instance, if the picture was equally often a plus either above, below, to the left of, or to the right of the star, then "isn't above" would not be equivalent to "is below," etc. Thus, in this respect the Chase and Clark analysis is very task-specific. Another comment about the Chase and Clark comparison model is that there is no reason to require the comparison to begin with the inner strings; the same number of mismatches and total RT would be obtained regardless of whether the comparison began at the inner string or at the outer predicate.

Implicit Negations and Inferences

The preceding section has illustrated how HAM deals with full sentence negation and uses such predicates for answering questions and verifying statements. However, use of the explicit negative particle (no, not, none, never, etc.) is but one of the modes of negation in English. Another whole class deals with *implicit* negations (see Klima, 1964; Clark, 1972) in which a particular word carried negative implications or connotations. Examples occur in abundance in the so-called "oppositional contrasts" such as *in-out, open-closed, remember-forget, same-different, present-absent*, and many others. These pairs are contradictories, in the sense that each term is equivalent to the negation of the other member of the pair. For many contradictories, English provides a negative prefex to mark one of the terms, as in *happy-unhappy, possible-impossible, economic-uneconomic, profit-nonprofit*, and so on. In contrast to contradictories, there are contrary pairs which designate predicates that cannot both be true of an object but which are not mutually contradictory. Examples of contrary pairs are *above-below, smart-dumb, beautiful-ugly, tall-short, heavy-light, top-bottom, near-far*, and so on. Although these words designate end-anchors on a dimension, the negation of one is not equivalent to the assertion of the other term, because many possible values (predicates) are commonly recognized along the dimension. Someone who is not beautiful is not necessarily ugly; someone who is not at the top of his class is not necessarily at the bottom.

A current question within linguistics and psycholinguistics concerns how one should analyze and understand such implicit negations. An appealing hypothesis promoted by Clark (1972) is that in each polar pair, one element is the simple form (the "unmarked" form), and the other term is derived by the negation of the simple form. Clark assumes that the cognitive representation of the marked form is always in terms of the negation of the positive, unmarked form. Thus, he supposes that *closed* is interpreted directly as *false* (*open*), and *forget* is interpreted as *false* (*remember*). Although we agree with the basic distinctions about marked and unmarked forms, we are not yet convinced that predications using marked forms are always represented directly in terms of the negation of the unmarked term.

Although nothing of this nature is currently programmed, we think we can see how we would represent implicit negation in HAM, and how this would be used in inference and in question answering. The basic idea is to introduce an oppositional predicate of the form "x is the opposite of y," which we will abbreviate here as "x OPP y." For purposes of deductive inference, we need also to store some properties of the OPP relation; a first property is that it is a *symmetric* predicate, so that (x

OPP y) implies (y OPP x); a second property states that oppositional predicates cannot both be true of the same subject (S), so that ((x OPP y) and (S has property x)) imply (false (S has property y)).

It will be noticed that our class of oppositional pairs includes both contradictories and contraries. These subsets would differ in that, for contradictories, a second proposition would state explicitly that *closed* is defined as *false* (*open*) or the like. The reason for grouping contraries and contradictories together into our oppositional class is that they have a certain inference potential in common. That is, if HAM has stored the fact that "John is fat," it can answer no to the query "Is John thin?" because it retrieves "John is fat" from memory; and in comparing *fat* and the *thin* of the query, HAM would quickly discover the proposition "Fat OPP thin." By similar means, looking up the predicates of the subject and checking for an OPP relation to the predicate of the query, HAM would answer False to all questions asserting antonymic relations to predications it knows (and takes as truths). Thus, it would answer no to such queries as "Is Alaska hot?", "Is Wilt Chamberlain short?", and "Is San Francisco north of Seattle?"

In his research, Clark has compared the contradictory pair *present-absent*, involving an implicit negation, with the pair *present-not present*, involving an explicit negation. In understanding Clark's analysis of these predicates, it is important to separate their *reference* from their *suppositions*. With respect to their referential meaning, Clark argues that they are identical and that sentences like "The plus is absent" are rewritten referentially as (false (plus present)), which is the same representation as is given to "The plus isn't present." The difference between the two occurs with respect to their suppositions. "The plus is absent" affirms the supposition that the plus is not present, whereas "The plus is not present" denies the supposition that the plus is present. Thus, if we expand our notation to include these suppositions, Clark would represent "The plus isn't present" as (false (suppose (plus present))), whereas "The plus is absent" is represented (true (suppose (false (plus present))))). Clark's research strategy is to find data to indicate that "absent" and "isn't present" have identical referential representations. Any differences between the two he will attribute to their suppositional differences. Let us examine how successful his attempt is:

To simplify matters, we will only consider the case where the picture is a plus and receives an encoding of (present plus). Against this, the representation of the sentence will be compared. In Table 13.5 we have the analysis assigned by Clark and by HAM to the various sentences. Section A of the table presents the analysis for the "isn't present" sentences where Clark and HAM concur. This portion of the table is very similar to Table 13.3 for the "star above plus" case that we examined earlier in this section. The assumption is that the comparison operation begins at the innermost string, and works outwards. The constant c is added for a mismatch of the innermost element; $b+d$ is added for True Negatives as the time to initially setup the False representation (b) and the time added when the outer predicate mismatches the picture code (d). Section A of Table 13.5 may be compared to Section B, which gives the predictions for the *present-absent* data. Here the sentence was either "The star (or plus) is present" or "The star (or plus) is absent." Comparing these to the picture code of (plus present) yields the latency

TABLE 13.5

Analysis of Clark and Young's Experiment

A. Isn't present data

Type	Analysis (Clark or HAM)	Latency component (Clark or HAM)
True Positive	(plus present)	t_o
False Positive	(star present)	$t_o + c$
True Negative	(false (star present))	$t_o + c + (b+d)$
False Negative	(false (plus present))	$t_o + (b+d)$

B. Absent data

Type	Clark's analysis	HAM's analysis	Latency (Clark)	Latency (HAM)	Observed
True Present	(plus present)	(plus present)	t_o	t_o	1463 msec.
False Present	(star present)	(star present)	$t_o + c$	$t_o + c$	1722 msec.
True Absent	false (star present)	(star absent)	$t_o + c + (b+d)$	$t_o + c + x$	2028 msec.
False Absent	false (plus present)	(plus absent)	$t_o + (b+d)$	$t_o + x$	1796 msec.

components listed. Clark's hypothesis is that *absent* rewrites as (false (present)), as shown in Lines 3 and 4 for the column labeled "Clark's analysis." The data, shown in the far right column (from Clark, 1971) support this analysis, with best-fitting parameters t_o = 1490 msec., c = 232 msec., $(b+d)$ = 306 msec.

Although these data are consistent with Clark's analysis, they do not discriminate against our hypothesis that *absent* is stored and used directly as a predicate (see column marked "HAM's analysis" in Section B of Table 13.5). This hypothesis supposes that a mismatch of the subject (star vs. plus) adds c msec. to the RT, whereas a mismatch on the predicate (*absent* versus *present*) adds x msec. to the RT. This time x represents the time to evoke the "absent OPP present" proposition and use it to make the necessary inference. Clearly, x plays the same role in HAM's search and match routines as does $(b+d)$ in Clark's theory. So the data do not prove that *absent* is treated directly as *not present*. The only evidence in favor of our view, vis-à-vis Clark's, is that the constant x (or $b+d$) was only 306 msec. in the *absent* experiment, whereas it was estimated to be considerably higher (640 msec.) for the explicit negative, *not present*, as HAM's analysis might expect. Clark related the difference in the two estimates of $(b+d)$ to the difference in the suppositions of "absent" and "isn't present."

A similar interpretation can be provided for the verification RT data on *same-different* and on *agree-conflict* that were offered by Clark (1971) as evidence for the hypothesis that the marked form is represented as the negation of the unmarked form. For example, in answering whether a color name and a color patch conflict (differ), the person is assumed to be filling in color codes for the word X and the color patch Y in the proposition (conflict (X, Y)). The comparison process looks first for a match of X and Y; then looks for whether conflict is the outer predicate, in order to alter the truth index in case it is. These simple assumptions will handle the verification RT data just as well as does Clark's implicit negation thesis (see Clark, 1972). To conclude, there is no evidence that requires HAM to decompose implicit negatives as Clark advocates.

The Presuppositions of Negations

In the preceding discussion, it was pointed out that denials involve certain presuppositions as well as particular assertions. It happens that this distinction is almost captured exactly in HAM according to what is expected to be true of memory and what elements within a larger propositional structure are being negated. Suppose we say to HAM something like "It wasn't in the park that the hippie touched the debutante." The way this input gets encoded by HAM's parser (see Figure 13.1) is as "At some place the hippie touched the debutante, and it's false that that place was the park." The first part may be called the presupposition of the denial; it presupposes that the episode happened. The second part of HAM's input tree asserts that it wasn't in the park that the episode occurred.

Other elements can be negated with the consequent presupposition of the rest of the complex proposition. As an illustration, when we say "It wasn't the debutante whom the hippie touched in the park," we thereby presuppose that the hippie touched someone in the park, and we assert that that someone was not the debutante. All such statements can be properly represented and partitioned into

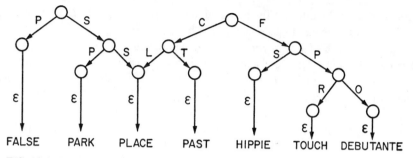

FIG. 13.1. Representation of the proposition "It wasn't in the park that the hippie touched the debutante."

significant parts by HAM's parser. The presuppositional part will be sent to memory by HAM's encoding function, looking for a match to decide whether the presupposition is true. Unless a satisfactory match is obtained, HAM will not encode the assertion.

While we are on the topic of presupposition, we might note that HAM's parsing routines also provide a satisfying analysis of the presuppositions that occur in definite descriptions. For instance, consider the sentence "The fat man who married Julia owns a farm." In currently popular linguistic analyses, this statement is said to *presuppose* that (*a*) A man married Julia, and (*b*) The man is fat; but the statement is said to *assert* that the man owns a farm. Evidence of this distinction is the fact that if either of the presuppositions are false, the sentence fails to have a truth value, and communication totally breaks down, a listener is likely to mutter "Who are you talking about?" In contrast, if the assertion is false, the total statement is considered false. A listener is likely either to accuse the speaker of lying or to correct him.

HAM captures just this difference in the way it analyzes such a sentence. The definite description sends a probe into memory to retrieve the node corresponding to the man who fits the descriptions. If HAM can find an individual satisfying the definite description, all is well and fine. Being a gullible program, HAM just passively encodes the assertion. The definite description need not be encoded, as it is already in memory. However, if HAM cannot find an individual satisfying one or more of the presuppositions, it protests and announces that it cannot find a suitable referent and that it therefore cannot encode the assertion.

On Disjoint Sets

The discussion above indicates how HAM would answer questions using explicit as well as implicit negation, by checking for sentence predicates (e.g., "*p* is false") and for OPP relations. It is not so easy, however, to implement the procedures by which we reject false conjectures involving disjoint sets. For example, how do people reject the conjecture "Chicago is in Florida"? Presumably, they retrieve the fact that Chicago is located in the state of Illinois, which is not Florida. But how are we to represent that latter jump, that "in Illinois" implies "not in Florida"? We need some notions of mutually exclusive or *disjoint* sets, the idea being that a given element cannot simultaneously be a member of both sets. Fido cannot be both a collie and a chihuahua; if he's one, he can't be the other.

We do not really know how to represent economically in HAM these elementary facts of disjunction. It is surely implausible to store with every possible noun pair whether or not they constitute disjoint sets; there are simply too many millions of things that Fido isn't or places where Chicago isn't located. The most plausible proposal is to store with each list of distinguishers of a general category a proposition stating whether or not the subsets listed are to be interpreted as disjoint. Thus, a *professions* list would not have the "disjoint" marker (since one can be, say, a lawyer and a professor); however, with a list of *colors* or *dog species*, the auxiliary information would be supplied that the subsets are mutually exclusive. This auxiliary rule would then enable HAM or any question-answerer to reply False to "Chicago is in Florida," "A robin is a canary," or "Fido is a chihuahua." Such class rules would also enable rejection of even more distant and bizarre conjectures such as "All grains are typhoons" or "All rugs are minds." These statements are rejected obviously because the nouns fail on the *organic-inorganic* exclusion and the *concrete-abstract* exclusion, respectively.

13.3. QUANTIFICATION AND LOGICAL CONNECTIVES

We noted in Chapter 7 that HAM had the expressive power equivalent to second-order predicate calculus, but that is a very weak statement indeed. That abstract fact doesn't do HAM a lot of good. We need to define inferential procedures that will enable HAM to squeeze out of its representational formalisms the inferential potentials that exist therein. As we noted in the introduction, the theorem-proving techniques of artificial intelligence provide a set of very powerful and uniform procedures for deriving inferences. Unfortunately, any reasonable soul would have to balk at their psychological plausibility. What we would like to do in this section is provide some further information about how we can get the necessary inferences from HAM in psychologically viable ways. In the last section (13.2) we examined the matter of negation extensively; in the next section (13.4) we want to expand further on the implicational connections between various relations and predicates. Our focus in this section will be on the quantificational aspects of HAM's representation as well as conjunction ("and") and disjunction ("or").

The Subset, Generic, and Set-Membership Relations

The subset relationship ($\subseteq$) serves to encode many of the important implications that are contained in the universal quantification of the predicate calculus. The association $<A \subseteq B>$, stating that the A is a subset of B, would be translated into the predicate calculus as $(\forall x) (A(x) \rightarrow B(x))$. Suppose we substitute "dog" for A and "pet" for B. Now we can infer from "Fido is a dog" that "Fido is a pet." This is a simple case of universal instantiation accomplished by substituting "Fido" for x in the predicate calculus formula. The other important means by which universal quantification is encoded into HAM's representation is through the generic relation ($\forall$). Thus, we can encode such things as "All pets are bothersome" (see Figure

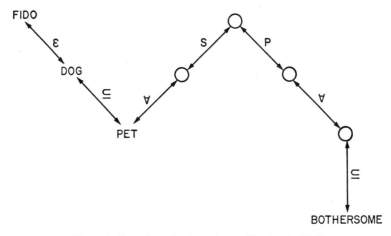

FIG. 13.2. Encoding of universal quantification in HAM.

13.2). The structure in Figure 13.2 would be translated into predicate calculus as $(\forall x)$ $(\text{pet}(x) \rightarrow \text{bothersome}(x))$. With these predicate calculus formulae, we can infer that "Fido is bothersome" through operations known in logic as universal instantiation and modus ponens.

If HAM is to match the above exercise in predicate calculus, it must be programmed on when and how to use the three important quantifiers in Figure 13.2—subset ($\subseteq$), set membership (ϵ), and generic ($\forall$). It seems quite obvious how to program HAM to perform the proper inferential steps in response to a question like "Is Fido bothersome?" (Figure 13.3a). HAM would not find the overtly stated probe in memory nor anything that would even yield a partial match to that probe. However, it could loop back through memory a second time asking "What kind of things are bothersome?" This probe is illustrated in Figure 13.3b. Note that we have a dummy terminal node to which the generic quantifier leads. In matching this probe to memory, the dummy node will be matched to the list of classes of things that are bothersome. On that list will be "pet." HAM has, in two cycles through its memory, isolated the fact that is relevant to verifying the proposition. Now, to verify that "Fido is bothersome," it becomes only necessary to prove that "Fido is a pet," which involves chaining along the ϵ and $\subseteq$ links.

In this example we verified a proposition by finding a more general proposition that implied it. Another task would be to verify an existential proposition by instantiating it with a particular proposition. For instance, consider how HAM would verify "Does John hit girls?" if it had learned "John hit Mary." The question will obtain its best match to the "John hit Mary" proposition, but HAM will note that the objects of the probe and the memory trace differ. So, before answering no, a subproblem would be set up, equivalent to the query "Is Mary a girl?" This subproblem query can be sent into memory as a probe, which will evoke the ϵ^{-1} links out of the individual-*Mary* node. If *person* is on this list, then the subquery exists with a yes, and control would transfer back out to the top-level question-answering program. Having found two Trues, for "John hit Mary" and "Mary hit a person," the inference rule for set membership enables the inference

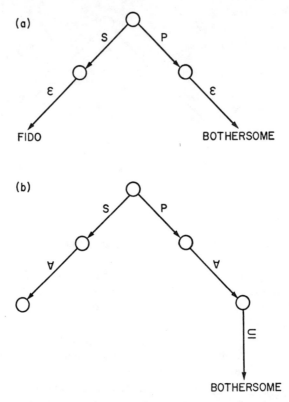

FIG. 13.3. (*a*) Encoding of probe for "Is Fido bothersome?" (*b*) Encoding of "What kind of things are bothersome?"

"John hit a person," which was the query. So the top-level program exits with true as an answer.

An important point to glean from these two examples is how HAM's memory-matching routines can be evoked to direct the program to the relevant parts of memory. One of the classic problems in theorem proving is directing the theorem-prover to the proper subset of the data base so that it doesn't waste time with propositions irrelevant to the question at hand. This is what HAM's recognition mechanisms do very well. Of course, what our system lacks is any comprehensive scheme for inference making. What we are doing in this section is just describing procedures that would enable HAM to answer particular classes of questions.

Existential Instantiation

Suppose that HAM knows a generic fact about a general class such as "All dogs have a nose." The question is how this universal generalization is used to verify an existential statement "*Some* dogs have a nose." The issue concerns how *some* questions are verified against *all* facts. The issue arises too with subset relations: If all dogs are animals, then are *some* dogs animals? One representation of the known universal statement and the *some* query are shown in Figure 13.4. The query in Figure 13.4*b* will achieve a partial match to the predicate structure of the known universal in Figure 13.4*a*. Thus, the only mismatch is on the links out of *dog* to the "subject" node in the two structures. Here a simple inference rule must be invoked, to the effect that *all* includes *some*. Thus, HAM would treat the two links $<\subseteq,\forall>$ in that order as implied by $\forall$; every predication true about *all* dogs is also true about *some* dogs. Quite explicitly, this rule does not work in the reverse direction; *some* doesn't imply *all* (e.g., it is true that some birds are yellow, but false that all are). So the inference rule must be carefully applied in only one direction, from *all* to *some*.

This representation of *all* versus *some* statements leads to the prediction that when the person knows a universal generalization, then it will be matched and responded to more quickly by a true universal (*all*) query than by a true particular (*some*) query. This is expected by HAM's current representation because the *some* query mismatches the *all* premise and so requires invocation of an inference rule, which adds the excess time. This accords with our informal observations with questions posed to "nonsophisticated" subjects. If asked whether "Some tuna are fish" or similar questions, they will boggle, balk, and frequently say "No; not some, but *all* tuna are fish." Meyer (1970) found *some* questions to be verified somewhat faster than *all* questions, but this comparison was possible only across different experiments he did, one involving only *all* universal queries and the other involving only *some* queries. Clearly, subjects could have evoked some experiment-specific strategy that bypassed the inference from *all* to *some*. The issue needs resolving with a controlled experiment directly comparing the two types of questions and avoiding such experiment-specific strategies.

As this book goes to press, we can report that such an experiment has just been performed by a colleague of ours, A. Glass (personal communication, 1973). His experiment mingled a rich variety of *all* and *some* statements. Confirming our expectations, he found *all* statements were verified more rapidly (1091 msec.) than were *some* statements (1158 msec.). It is a very gratifying experience to go out on a limb as we had in the preceeding paragraph and then to be vindicated.

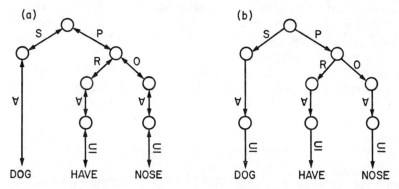

FIG. 13.4. The universally quantified memory structure in (*a*) about dogs is used to verify the existentially quantified probe in (*b*).

Compound Questions and Truth-Tables

We have considered heretofore true-false answers to simple queries. It is, of course, possible to introduce compound queries which require combining assessments of the truth of many atomic queries. For instance, we may ask tag questions such as "Mary was driven home by John or Keith, wasn't she?"; the answer is to be yes if the system gets a match either to the atom "John drove Mary home" or "Keith drove Mary home." In this case, the *or* of the query should call a "truth-evaluation" function which supplies a procedure for evaluating inclusive disjunctions. The procedure for this case would be to test the first atomic proposition; if it is true, then exit True; if it is false, then test the next atomic proposition of the query in a recursive loop; if all atoms are false, then exit False for the compound query. In similar fashion, a conjunctive query like "Both John and Keith voted for Nixon" would call a truth-evaluation procedure which would return True only in case both atomic propositions were found to be true or known in memory. This truth-table approach is equivalent to that advocated by Trabasso, Rollins, and Shaughnessy (1971) to account for the RTs of their subjects verifying compound propositions against pictures.

13.4. EXPANSION OF RELATIONS AND PREDICATES

One of the standard procedures for answering questions, when the answer is not directly stored, is to semantically interpret or expand relational and predicate components of the query. Thus, the command to "List the siblings of Bill" may fail initially because the facts are stored in terms of *brother* and *sister* relations. Thus, a first move would be to semantically expand the *sibling* relation of the command into the transformed probe "List the *brothers* and *sisters* of Bill."

The inference potential that exists with the predicate and relational elements represents one of the most important features of language. Roger Schank (1972) employs an approach to capturing this inference potential that is growing in popularity. His parser derives all the salient inferences from a relation and represents the relation and its inference in terms of a primitive set of atomic concepts. Thus, "John kicked Bill" would be encoded in memory as something like "John moved his foot forcefully against Bill causing Bill to feel pain." Thus, when later queried, a subject can reply affirmatively to "Did John move his foot?", "Was Bill hurt?", "Did a foot touch Bill?", etc., because all this information was explicitly stored in memory upon receipt of "John kicked Bill."

As discussed in Chapter 8, we are reluctant to accept Schank's point of view. Rather, we prefer to think that the subject *can* store just the overtly stated proposition and make inferences from it at the time of test. The reader should understand, though, that we are not claiming that people cannot derive inferences like "John moved his foot" and store these directly. Undoubtedly, people often do, and they can even make overt reports of the fact. We are claiming, rather, that it is not necessary to decompose a relation into atomic elements and store all inferences. The relation can be stored directly in an unelaborated form. And when a person does analyze a relation into its inferences and more elementary terms, he need not always pursue this de-composition to the most atomic level.

If, as we claim, the immediate inferences of a proposition are not always stored upon the input of a proposition, we are led to a powerful prediction about verification latencies. This means if we assert P_1 (e.g., "John kicked Bill") to HAM and later interrogate it about P_2 (e.g., "John hurt Bill"), and P_1 implies P_2, HAM should take longer to verify P_2 than if it had heard P_2 originally. In contrast, Schank would claim there should be no difference because we would have derived P_2 and stored it when P_1 was input. The data that does exist seems to support HAM over Schank's analysis. The negation data we reported from Clark clearly indicates that the immediate representation of a sentence does not include all its inferences. For instance, unless given explicit conversion instructions, subjects do not derive the positive equivalent of a negative statement (e.g., infer "The star is above the plus" from "The plus is not above the star"). Indeed, much of the research Clark (1972) reviews in his "Semantics and Comprehension" paper brings home the same theme: Many of the obvious inferences about P_1 are only made when subjects are required to verify P_2. However, all of Clark's work is concerned with the immediate representation of P_1. Given the results on recognition confusions in sentence memory (see our reviews in Sections 8.3 and 11.3), we might suspect that the long-term representation of a sentence is often enriched with many of its allowable inferences. We will consider one recent experiment in which there was no discrimination at all between what was said and what could be inferred.

Inferences about Spatial Dimensions

The experiment by Barclay (1973) used pairs of relations like "is to the left of" and "is to the right of." Subjects were told 10 facts about five objects that produced a linear ordering of the objects with respect to the relations. For instance, subjects might be told "The giraffe is to the right of the tiger" and "The tiger is to the left of the cow," etc. Barclay found subjects were quite good at deriving from these 10 pairwise orderings what was the linear ordering of the five objects (viz., "monkey, tiger, giraffe, cow, and donkey" from left to right). Most people experience visual imagery in doing this task; the several objects are visualized arrayed in a row, and their respective positions are juggled so as to accommodate the most recent pair relation learned. By successive jugglings of the array, the correct final order is arrived at from the pairwise relations. One might say that the person has *integrated* the separate bits of information into a full description of the complete situation under consideration.

This sort of construction would never occur with a passive learning-machine which simply records the pairwise relations as independent facts. Rather, it appears as though the input sentences themselves are being *recoded* and stored in relation to a developing description of the full situation. We think we could have HAM produce such representations, but only if it were actively processing and transforming incoming information. For example, this recoding might involve translating all inputs into the same predicate; thus, "B right of A" would be recoded and stored as "A left of B," if "left of" were the initializing relation.

Again, a person upon learning "*A* left of *B*" and "*B* left of *C*" might infer "*A* left of *C*" and store that also. Figure 13.5 illustrates a complete representation of the array.

Probably, the first-order spatial relations (i.e., "*A* left of *B*" and "*B* left of *C*," rather than "*A* left of *C*") would be held primary and stored high on the object GET-lists leading from the predicate nodes in Figure 13.5. This is because these first-order relations are the essential ones to encoding the linear order. Although the first-order relations are the only essential ones, there are two aspects of the task that would strongly orient the subject to form encodings of the higher-order relations. First, the instructions orient him to focus on the linear ordering of the elements rather than the exact propositions encountered. The subject is not even told that there will a memory test. Thus, the subject was motivated to make the higher-order inferences and encode them. Second, the propositions are not presented in a neat orderly fashion. The subject may be first told "*A* left of *C*," then "*B* left of *C*," and only then "*A* left of *B*." Thus, he was given the second-order A-C pair before he was told the two first-order pairs from which it could be inferred. Since he had no way of knowing at input of "*A* left of *C*" that it was a second-order pair, he would naturally have to encode it in case it turned out to be a first-order pair.

Barclay found that subjects who were set to construct the full linear ordering of the objects from the pairwise relations were unable to discriminate, on a later memory test, which pairwise propositions they had actually heard during the training session versus those true propositions which they had inferred from what

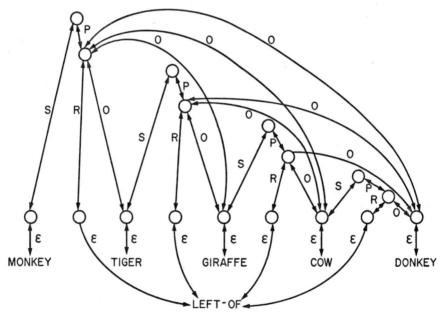

FIG. 13.5. A possible representation in HAM of the information possessed by subjects in Barclay's experiment.

they had heard. Subjects were very good at deciding whether a given statement was true or false of the situation (e.g., "Was the piano to the left of the chair?"); but they were practically at the chance level in deciding whether a true test sentence had been given explicitly during training.

Such failure of memory for specific details is likely to be a function of procedural details of the experiment. Important factors include the fact that a particular noun (for example, C) is being used repeatedly, sometimes as the object of "left of" and sometimes as the subject of the same predicate or its opposite; Barclay's procedure thus has "double-functioning" of most terms, which is likely to produce associative interferences operating against verbatim recall. Another factor is that the learner's strategy very likely results in the input sentence being recoded in terms of one predicate (left of) and that, as Figure 13.5 illustrates, the subject probably supplements the overtly stated relations with any he can infer.

At present, we see no convincing arguments against our proposal that linear orderings, such as those in Barclay's experiment, should be represented as the propositional structure shown in Figure 13.5. This is the way we would program HAM to encode the information. A possible prediction from this structure is that reaction time to verify the true statement "X is left of Y" will increase with the ordinal distance between X and Y in the linear ordering. Potts (1972) tried to test this prediction but encountered several complications that prevented a usable test. His subjects received only a low degree of learning on the basic ordering, so they made appreciably more errors on ordering a pair the closer were the two members. Second, he found second-order artifacts due to end-anchor effects. In the ordering of objects A, B, C, D in their "goodness," one can form the auxiliary propositions that "A is best" and "D is worst," and these enable rapid response to any test pair containing these elements. With such end-anchor artifacts, it is impossible to test the distance versus RT conjecture with four elements, which is what Potts used. The issue awaits some experimental resolution.

On Storing Inferences

A point in the prior discussion should be emphasized; HAM can store (learn, encode) inferred propositions just as though they were input trees to be memorized. We can ask you now, "Did Leibnitz have a four-chambered heart?", and you will answer yes more readily now than you did before you answered this bizarre question in the previous chapter. We assume that if the answer to a question is not directly stored but required some inference, then HAM will try to store directly the answer it has found by inference. (If an answer is retrieved directly, then it is not re-stored but its components may have their recencies updated on the relevant GET-lists).

It appears plausible that a human memory not only would store final inferred answers to questions, but also would try to store intermediate results in a derivation or inference chain. This would be like a mathematician remembering the small lemmas he proves along the way in carrying out a larger proof sequence. Certainly, Winograd's (1972) program stored intermediate action sequences that its robot hand performs while moving around blocks in a scene to achieve a specified goal configuration. These intermediate stages correspond to solutions of subproblems, namely, how to achieve particular subgoals within the context of the larger problem. Given an initial configuration of colored blocks, wedges, and boxes in a scene, and given a command to construct a given goal scene (e.g., "Make it so that a blue pyramid is on top of a green cube, and both are inside the big box"), Winograd's program "thinks out" the sequence of movements, then executes a series of *move, grasp,* and *ungrasp* motor commands to its artificial hand, and it stores a record of significant subgoals of this movement sequence. This record is accessed whenever the program is asked *how* or *why* questions, such as how it achieved a particular subgoal or why it performed a particular action. For example, to the query "Why did you pick up the red cone?", Winograd's program might answer "To clear off the top of the green cube." To a recursive series of *why* questions it might answer successively "To grasp the green square," "To put the green cube in the big box," "So I could place a blue pyramid on top of it," and finally "Because you told me to" when it is backed up to the original command.

These intermediate results in Winograd's program (as in the mathematician's lemmas) are nonetheless carried out overtly in the world (or on paper) rather than existing in "mere thought." It is still somewhat moot how much a person will recall of an intermediate result serving only as a momentary thought supporting a derivation within a larger context. The issue is currently being researched by Jim Levin (personal communication, 1972) at the University of California at San Diego. For instance, consider kinship relations as a testing situation. The subject learns a number of separate facts such as "John is Mary's brother," "Jane is Mary's mother," and "Harry is Jane's brother." When given the problem "Is John Harry's nephew?", the program must proceed through a series of steps trying to link John to Harry. One pair of the links corresponds to the lemma "Jane is John's mother," established as an intermediate result. The question is whether this intermediate result, established in the John-Harry search, is then primed so that the experimental subject can now react more quickly than a control subject to the question "Is Jane John's mother?" We suspect the answer is affirmative.

Notice that the "Jane is John's mother" lemma arises when the derivation begins at John and "moves out towards" Uncle Harry. But suppose the derivation were biased by the form of the query to start at Harry (e.g., "Is Harry John's uncle?"); then the intermediate lemma would be "Harry is Mary's uncle," and the "Jane is John's mother" intermediate result would never materialize. Such an activation pattern might then yield different orderings of the verification latencies to the John-Jane and the Harry-Mary questions, depending on the surface form of the original query about John-Harry.

Of course, a strong possibility is that these separate facts become integrated into one symbolic structure equivalent to a visual diagram of a family tree, which is the introspection of many people (Lindsay's, 1963 "Sad Sam" program does just this). This representation is *not* equivalent to the derivation and storage of all possible pairwise relations among the persons in the set, as the basic facts are learned. According to either theory, subjects would probably be unable to discriminate later whether they had learned a given relation directly or had inferred it, much as in the Barclay (1973) and Bransford, Barclay, and Franks (1972) studies mentioned earlier. However, the two representations differ in their predictions regarding the time taken to verify conjectures relating two persons as a function of their node distance in the family tree. The "visual diagram" representation would imply that path tracing and RT would vary with the node distance in the diagram; the "derive and store all relations" theory would imply that RT would not vary as a function of either structural distance or directness of experience (versus inference) of the relation. These possibilities await experimental test.

13.5. THE COMPLEXITIES OF QUESTION ANSWERING

So far we have proceeded through the topic of question answering as if the only difficulty were to construct psychologically plausible procedures for performing low-level inferences. This part of the question-answering topic seems to us to be fairly tractable experimentally and theoretically. However, what we have discussed so far is only a small component of what would have to go into a system that would successfully simulate the question-answering capacities of a human. When we consider the system in its totality, it is truly mind boggling. The purpose of this section is to boggle the reader's mind a bit so as to provide him with a proper perspective of the task at hand.

There is a real sense in which the semantic interpretation of the question, and calling of procedures for searching a data base, is just like problem-solving activity. A number of psychologists have viewed memory searching in terms of the construction of problem-solving strategies. Lindsay and Norman (1972) illustrate the matter with the query, "What were you doing on Monday afternoon on the third week of September two years ago?" They then say the following about this example:

The type of response people typically produce when asked this kind of question goes something like this:

1. Come on. How should I know? (Experimenter: Just try it anyhow.)
2. O.K. Let's see: Two years ago. . . .
3. I would be in high school in Pittsburgh. . . .
4. That would be my senior year.
5. Third week in September—that's just after summer—that would be the fall term. . . .
6. Let me see. I think I had chemistry lab on Mondays.
7. I don't know. I was probably in the chemistry lab. . . .
8. Wait a minute—that would be the second week of school. I remember he started off with the atomic table—a big, fancy chart. I thought he was crazy, trying to make us memorize that thing.
9. You know, I think I can remember sitting. . . .

Although this particular protocol is fabricated, it does catch the flavor of how the memory system works on this kind of retrieval problem. First, the question of whether or not to attempt the retrieval: The preliminary analysis suggests it is going to be difficult, if not impossible, to recover the requested information and the subject balks at starting at all (line 1). When he does begin the search, he does not attempt to recall the information directly. He breaks the overall question down into subquestions. He decides first to establish what he was doing two years ago (line 2). Once he has succeeded in answering this question (line 3), he uses the retrieved information to construct and answer a more specific question (line 4). After going as far as he can with the first clue, he returns to picking up more information in the initial query, "September, third week." He then continues with still more specific memories (lines 5 and 6). Most of what happened between lines 7 and 8 is missing from the protocol. He seems to have come to a dead end at line 7, but must have continued to search around for other retrieval strategies. Learning the periodic table seems to have been an important event in his life. The retrieval of this information seems to open up new access routes. By line 8, he once again appears to be on his way to piecing together a picture of what he was doing on a Monday afternoon two years ago.

Here memory appears as a looping, questioning activity. The search is active, constructive. When it cannot go directly from one point to another, the problem is broken up into a series of subproblems, or subgoals. For each subproblem, the questions are: Can it be solved; will the solution move me closer to the main goal? When one subproblem gets solved, new ones are defined and the search continues. If successful, the system eventually produces a response, but the response is hardly a simple recall. It is a mixture of logical reconstruction of what must have been experienced with fragmentary recollections of what was in fact experienced (Lindsay & Norman, 1972, pp. 379–380).

This lengthy quotation does illustrate many of the complexities of answering involuted questions; the protocol is much like that a problem-solving subject gives while "thinking aloud." The question is approached in successive indirect passes, supplying oneself with progressively finer contextual retrieval cues, using the information retrieved at subgoals as new access cues for helping formulate and answer more refined or detailed questions. Subjectively, the experience involves putting oneself back into the approximate context (place and time) of the requested events. But plausible or logical information ("third week of September" implies "school classes were in their second week") intervenes at practically every step in the self-cueing scheme.

Although such problem-solving sequences are clearly beyond the pale of current models of question answering, it should not prove too difficult to teach people a few general strategies to follow in reconstructing answers to such complicated questions. In brief, the prescription would supply the subject with a set of rather general queries or retrieval cues to which he was to associate in a depth-first manner, with the further prescription that he was to combine information retrieved from one area to aid cueing of memories about another area. The list of probe queries would refer to all aspects of contextual information surrounding the main event in question. For example, to retrieve the names of the guests at one's tenth birthday party, one can list a number of direct and indirect cues such as: Where did I live then? Who were my neighbors? My friends and relatives? What school class was I in then? Who was my teacher? What other children were in my class? Can I remember anything from around that time about *any* of my birthday parties or that of any of my friends? This sort of self-probing activity could be extended indefinitely. However, it constitutes only a first pass at the original question. The second and subsequent passes are to pick over and use the more relevant pieces of information retrieved in the initial pass. It is our belief that this is a lawful, reasonable process of constructing a series of retrieval probes to answer subgoal queries; it is not unlike theorem proving or general reasoning in problem solving (see Newell & Simon, 1972). However, we harbor no illusion that HAM has advanced us very far along the path to the distant goal. Moreover, we are very dubious that a program will be developed in the foreseeable future that will be able to simulate the human question-answerer when he is put to such complex tasks.

Norman's "Problems"

Recently Donald Norman (1972) at San Diego has written a curious document that serves to lay out some of the enormous complexities of question answering. He has isolated a number of major problems and has dubbed each with a catchy title. We will conclude this chapter with a review of Norman's "problems." If the reader still harbors any illusions about the tractability of question answering, this review should serve to correct his perspective.

The Telephone Number Problem   What is Charles Dickens' phone number? If we asked this question of HAM or of any other currently programmed question-answerer, it would search its data base to see if it had the information stored, determine that it did not have a phone number stored with Charles Dickens, and reply, "I don't know." A human would reply, "That's a stupid question." Norman is pointing out that before (or besides) invoking fact retrieval or inference routines, we do certain plausibility checks on the question.

The Floor Plan Problem   Marc Eisenstadt and Yaakov Kovarsky at San Diego had graduate students there draw floor plans of their apartments. Despite the fact these people had often lived in this apartment for years, they made a number of systematic errors. They incorporated structural features which were normative for apartment architecture, but which were not in fact the case for their particular apartments. As Norman concludes, our recall of a particular fact is seldom a simple readout from memory. Rather, we are forever calling on our general knowledge, knowledge of what is normative or prototypical, to fill in gaps of our particular memories. This normative knowledge can be so potent that we even fail to perceive or remember the true relations in an apartment where we spend much of our lives.

The Three Drugstores Problem   Norman takes this example from Abelson and Reich (1969). Consider how HAM would respond to the assertion "I went to three drugstores." It would passively consume this phrase and build up the appropriate tree-structure encoding it in memory. However, an intelligent system should be processing this information, should note the peculiar fact, and should respond appropriately with a question like "Did the first two drugstores not have what you were looking for?" That is, a successful question-answering program should check each assertion input to it, should try to integrate it with past knowledge, and should seek further information if the current statement is lacking in some respect.

A more complex example of the same point is to be found in the many interactions we psychologists find ourselves in, one with another. When we start to tell our colleague about a study or theory, we expect to be constantly interrupted with questions. If he is asking us about how many subjects in particular conditions, significance levels, etc., we have good grounds for believing he is bored and just being polite. However, we know we've caught his interest when he begins to ask the pointed questions, get red in the face, challenge our derivations, etc. We have stepped on a sensitive point in his theory, and he is attempting to defend himself. Our response to a piece of information goes beyond the effort to make sense of it (as in the "three drugstores" example). Often we have other purposes—to be polite, to defend a theory, etc. In general, a question-answering program that adequately simulated the human, would have to be able to respond to an information source variably and adaptively according to its current needs and purposes.

The Empire State Building Problem   Consider what would be a reasonable answer to the question "Where is the Empire State Building?" As Norman (1972) notes:

> If I were asked this question in Russia, I might well respond "In the United States." If I were asked by an adult in Europe, I would probably respond "In New York City." In the United States—especially in New York City, I would respond "On 34th Street." Finally, if asked in the New York subway system I would not answer with a location but rather with instructions on how to get there [pp. 25-26].

As this example points out, in order to appropriately answer a question, it is necessary not only to be able to know and retrieve the answer; one must also know his interrogator and understand which, of a number of acceptable answers, is the one desired. Thus, any adequate question-answerer must be building up a model of the interrogator's world view as the conversation proceeds. Thus, every sentence our question-answerer received must be processed, not just as a source of information about the world, but also as information about the interrogator.

Conclusions from Norman's Problems   In these examples Norman is illustrating the extreme complexity and open-endedness that characterizes human question answering. The examples serve to reinforce the conclusion we came to in Chapter 6, about the futility of a general all-purpose question-answerer. When we observe psychologists struggling with the full complexities of question answering, we cannot help but be struck by the analogy to a physicist walking through a forest and trying to explain all the physical events that are occurring about him. No doubt he might be able to provide an enlightening qualitative description of the principle forces that govern the descent of a leaf to the ground, but surely he would never set himself the task of simulating in the laboratory the descent of that leaf and surely would not consider simulating the entire forest. Similarly, we find it mistaken to attempt to mimic the question-answering behavior of the human. Rather, like the physicist, we have, and will continue to try to abstract from the real world, significant components of the phenomena at hand. In the artificial confines of the laboratory, we will study and theorize about these components, using all the currently available experimental methodology to disentangle each component from the many interactions it normally has with the rest of the human mind.

REFERENCES

Abelson, R. P., & Reich, C. Implicational molecules: A method for extracting meaning from input sentences. *Proceeding of the International Joint Conference on Artificial Intelligence*, Washington, D.C., 1969, 641-647.

Barclay, J. R. The role of comprehension in remembering sentences. *Cognitive Psychology*, 1973, 4, in press.

Bransford, J. D., Barclay, J. R., & Franks, J. J. Sentence memory: A constructive versus interpretive approach. *Cognitive Psychology*, 1972, 3, 193-209.

Chase, W. G., & Clark, H. H. Mental operations in the comparison of sentences and pictures. In L. Gregg (Ed.), *Cognition in learning and memory*. New York: Wiley, 1972.

Clark, H. H. The chronometric study of meaning components. Paper presented at the CRNS Colloque International sur les Problèmes Actuels de Psycholinguistique, Paris, December 13-18, 1971.

Clark, H. H. Semantics and comprehension. In T. A. Sebeok (Ed.), *Current trends in linguistics*. Vol. 12. The Hague: Mouton, 1972.

Green, B. F., Wolf, A. K., Chomsky, C., & Laughery, K. Baseball: An automatic question answerer. In E. Feigenbaum & J. Feldman (Eds.), *Computers and thought*. New York: McGraw-Hill, 1963.

Green, C., & Raphael, B. Research on intelligent question answering systems. *Proceedings of the 23rd Association for Computing Machinery National Conference*. Princeton: Brandon Systems Press, 1968. Pp. 169-181.

Klima, E. G. Negation in English. In J. A. Fodor & J. J. Katz (Eds.), *The structure of language*. Englewood Cliffs, N.J.: Prentice-Hall, 1964.

Lindsay, P. H., & Norman, D. A. *Human information processing: An introduction to psychology*. New York: Academic Press, 1972.

Lindsay, R. K. Inferential memory as a basis of machines which understand natural language. In E. Feigenbaum & J. Feldman (Eds.), *Computers and thought*. New York: McGraw-Hill, 1963.

Meyer, D. On the representation and retrieval of stored semantic information. *Cognitive Psychology*, 1970, 1, 242-300.

Minsky, M. (Ed.), *Semantic information processing*. Cambridge, Mass.: M.I.T. Press, 1968.

Newell, A., & Simon, H. A. *Human problem solving*. New York: Prentice-Hall, 1972.

Norman, D. A. Memory, knowledge, and the answering of questions. Paper presented at the Loyola Symposium on Cognitive Psychology, Chicago, 1972.

Olson, D. R. Language and thought: Aspects of a cognitive theory of semantics. *Psychological Review*, 1970, 77, 257-273.

Potts, G. R. Information processing strategies used in encoding of linear orderings. *Journal of Verbal Learning and Verbal Behavior*, 1972, 11, 727-740.

Robinson, J. A. A machine-oriented logic based on the resolution principle. *Journal of the ACM*, 1965, 12, 23-41.

Schank, R. C. Conceptual dependency: A theory of natural-language understanding. *Cognitive Psychology*, 1972, 3, 552-631.

Simmons, R. F. Natural language question-answering systems: 1969. *Communications of the Association for Computing Machinery*, 1970, 13, 15-30.

Trabasso, T., Rollins, H., & Shaughnessy, E. Storage and verification stages in processing concepts. *Cognitive Psychology*, 1971, 2, 239-289.

Winograd, T. Understanding natural language. *Cognitive Psychology*, 1972, 3, 1-191.

14
VERBAL LEARNING

The domain of psychological research known today under the title of verbal learning has suffered through a long and dull history.
—*Tulving and Madigan*

14.1. A PROPOSITIONAL ANALYSIS OF VERBAL LEARNING

In this chapter we wish to interpret some of the more salient procedures and results of verbal learning research in terms of our theory. Although HAM is really a theory about learning and retrieval of propositions rather than lists of single items, we nonetheless think it advisable to try to link up the theory with the verbal learning research. This is because most of the laboratory studies of human memory have been done in the verbal learning tradition, and it is from these that we have our most reliable findings. It is clear too that if HAM is to initiate very many experimental tests of its claims, they will come largely from the members who comprise this "human-memory" group rather than from the linguists or computer scientists. Although this chapter attempts to interpret or "translate" some of the verbal learning results in terms of the theoretical mechanisms of HAM, we should emphasize that HAM was not specifically designed for this interpretive task, we have not invested as much time as we should have liked in these thoughts, nor should the model stand or fall on the strength of these interpretations.

This chapter is organized into five sections. The first section will introduce HAM's propositional interpretation of verbal learning—an interpretation which is both novel and, we think, quite important. The next three sections will apply HAM's propositional representations to interpret the three principle verbal learning paradigms—paired associates, serial learning, and free recall. The last section will argue for HAM's propositional system as the representation of information during mental imagery. This analysis of imagery is even more radical than our propositional interpretation of verbal learning. A discussion of mental imagery is included in the verbal learning chapter because much of the research on imagery has used verbal learning paradigms.

Most research in verbal learning has not taken the proposition as the basic unit of analysis, as we have done for HAM. Rather, the traditional units in verbal learning studies have been the single nonsense syllable or the single word. Behind the bias for the nonsense syllable was the desire to study learning in the raw, beginning from scratch, with unorganized materials to which no prior knowledge or meaningful associations were relevant. The nonsense syllable was supposed to catch the learner at ground zero and enable the psychologist to study the learning process as the subject slowly memorized the material by the sheer heave of the will. Although this assumption of "rote learning" of nonsense materials is sometimes justified, it is just as frequent that subjects learn nonsense by use of linguistic coding strategies which convert a nonsense unit into a meaningful word or phrase (e.g., Prytulak, 1971). The use of such encoding strategies varies considerably across subjects and items, making the results somewhat variable and erratic—in fact, defeating the original purpose for which nonsense syllables were designed, viz., to homogenize the process of learning across subjects and materials.

The use of single words as learning materials was partially motivated by the belief that propositional thoughts or sentences were decomposable into word-to-word associations. This *associative chain hypothesis* is refuted by many lines of data (e.g., the sentence recognition data reviewed in Chapter 8) and is clearly inept for explaining any interesting linguistic performance. The associative chain hypothesis is denied by HAM. In HAM, words are not directly associated together. They become connected one to another only in that the ideas which they reference can be terminal nodes in the tree structures that encode a sequence of propositions.

However, for many theoretical analyses of verbal learning paradigms, the important fact is that two words are or are not connected together. It is irrelevant whether the connecting bond is a single unanalyzable link, a propositional structure as in HAM, or the emergent relation as proposed by the Gestalters. Indeed, in many of our subsequent analyses, we will proceed as if words were connected by single labeled associations rather than propositional tree structures. However, the reader should always keep in mind that this is just a "shorthand" to facilitate explication, and we remain firmly committed to the tree structures that were used in the representation of memory in earlier chapters.

Since HAM only learns complete propositions, it is clear that in order to learn single words or a list of single letters (a nonsense trigram), HAM must "propositionalize" the single-term information to be learned. It is a relatively easy matter to convert most single-term learning tasks into tasks requiring encoding of a corresponding proposition. Plausible propositions would be: "In the list, I was presented with word X," or ". . . I thought of word X, then thought of word Y," or ". . . idea X occurred before idea Y." These essentially encode autobiographic events—what Tulving (1972) has called "episodic" memories. If such propositions are learned, then presentation of appropriate cues would cause retrieval of the propositional memory structures. In other words, when presented with the context query "What items were presented in the list?", this probe would access propositions like "In the list, I thought of ideas $X, Y, \ldots$" Similarly, the query "What item followed or was paired with item X?" could access a proposition enabling paired-associate recall.

A basic problem with this approach is that there is an abundance of propositions that could be formulated surrounding presentation of a single unit in a learning list—depending on how the person encodes that item in relation to other items and other things he knows. The theory embedded in HAM does not provide any magical truths about the encoding strategies used by subjects on isolated verbal units presented for memorization. In this regard, we confront the same issues as do other verbal learning theories concerning the encoding variability injected into the acquisition process by virtue of different strategies used by subjects. Therefore, in what follows we identify one or another propositional encoding of material as "probable" in a given situation, doing this to get on with our analysis of paired associates or serial learning or free-recall learning. But these propositional encodings are to be viewed as suggestive rather than as ironclad premises of the analysis.

On Encoding Nonsense

Nowhere is this propositional variability more apparent than with nonsense syllables like CHP. At a primitive level, HAM has "idea nodes" corresponding to the individual letters, $C, H,$ and P. One proposition exemplifying learning of the trigram is illustrated in Figure 14.1a (compare with Figure 9.12): "Within a CHP, a C precedes an H which precedes a P." Note that, although the context node has been denoted "CHP" in Figure 14.1a, it is an unanalyzable idea node in memory. We have labeled that node CHP only for expository purposes, to indicate what concept it represents; we cannot "explode" that node itself into the letters $C, H,$ and P. Such orthographic information is only retrievable from the fact subtrees to which this context had been attached. For shorthand purposes, we will have occasion to rewrite the structure in Figure 14.1a as that in Figure 14.1b. The dominating node in Figure 14.1b represents the concept of the nonsense syllable.

The compound proposition in Figure 14.1a involves a goodly number of associative links. The number of links would, of course, increase as we increased the length of the nonsense syllable. It is easy to imagine that in a brief study period, HAM would only encode enough of the associative structure to retrieve part of the nonsense syllable. This partial learning would lead to later partial recall of fragments, and to confusions with similar trigrams during retrieval. For instance, if HAM had only learned C-P, then much like EPAM (see Section 4.2) it would yield the same match and ensuing behavioral result whether CQP or CHP were the test stimulus.

The coding above might be classed as "rote memorizing" of the trigram since each letter of the trigram corresponds to a distinct memory-node, and the relations were only ones characterizing spatial or temporal contiguity of elements. But there are alternate ways to proceed. One coding possibility recognizes that two-letter pairs (digrams) may already exist as units, that is, as regular or familiar spelling patterns. Thus, ZAT could be coded as "Z followed by AT-node" and BEQ as "BE-node followed by Q." In this case, the memory already contains the digram as

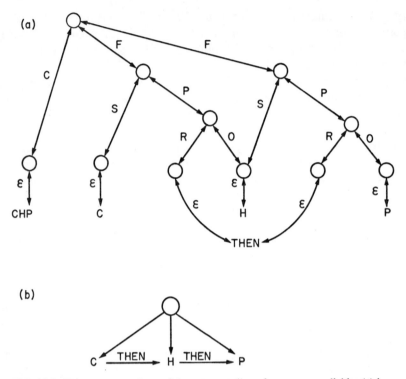

FIG. 14.1. Two representations of the rote encoding of a nonsense syllable: (*a*) longhand, and (*b*) shorthand.

a familiar spelling pattern or word, so a *token* of that digram is referenced in the tree encoding ZAT, BEQ, or similar syllables. An implication of this encoding style is that trigrams containing digram spelling patterns should be easier to learn than trigrams which do not. One rough index of whether a digram forms a spelling pattern is the relative frequency of the digram in words randomly sampled from text. This was the measure used by Underwood and Schultz (1960) in scoring a set of digrams. These digrams were then used as response terms in a paired-associate learning task. As expected, the more frequent digrams were easier to learn, even though none of them were actual words.

A third alternative encoding of a nonsense trigram is in terms of a word or phrase that it suggests. This tends to be done when the presentation rate is slow enough. In the literature, these transformed codes are called "natural language mediators" (NLMs), and we shall use that term in our discussions. A quite extensive analysis of NLM selection and use was given by Prytulak (1971), and we have little to add to his analysis. He enumerates many of the transformations which adults can and do use to convert a nonsense syllable into a word or phrase. What happens in encoding a particular trigram depends on what it is as well as on which of an ordered set of transformation rules first succeeds in converting it into a word. From various sources, Prytulak hypothesized a modal rank ordering of the most frequent transformations he observed, called the transformation-stack (or T-stack). For instance, the first "transformation" of the trigram was "identity," which just checks memory to see whether the trigram is a known word. If not, then the next transformation to be tried is to "add a suffix." For instance, this converts LOV to LOVE, and GOL to GOLF or GOLLY or GOLD, etc. If a high-frequency word can not be found in this manner (e.g., ROF would fail), then the next transformation on the T-stack would be tried. This might be something like inserting an additional letter at a particular place (e.g., ROF to ROOF, HIN to SHIN) or replacing a letter by a substitute (e.g., ROF to ROT, HIN to HIT or SIN or HEN).

HAM's MATCH process would identify potential transformations out of partial matches it obtained with memory. For instance, ROOF would be encoded in memory (see Figure 14.2a) or "R-THEN-O-THEN-O-THEN-F." The encoding of ROF would be "R-THEN-O-THEN-F" (see Figure 14.2b). The MATCH process would discover the substantial overlap between the two structures. HAM could then encode this new stimulus as "ROOF without an O" (see Figure 14.2c). This is the scheme-plus-correction notation that we introduced in Section 9.3. Prytulak's "transformations" are just various classes of "corrections" that can be applied to the schema. Prytulak's ordering of transformations in the T-stack would essentially correspond to a priority ordering on the acceptability of (a) different partial matches recovered by HAM's MATCH process, and (b) the corrections applied to these partial matches. For instance, the "add suffix" transformation corresponds to finding a memory tree (e.g., for GOLLY) which matches the stimulus (e.g., GOL) exactly except it has more elements to the right. The second transformation mentioned above, insertion of a new letter in the middle (ROF → ROOF), would find as the best match (according to the priority rules) the word which adds a middle element. Replacing a letter, signaled by a positive mismatch between the input and the best-matching memory tree, would be of even less priority because a lesser match would be obtained to memory. Even less acceptable transformations in Prytulak's scheme were those involving two or more alterations of the trigram to get a word. For example, PYM might go to PAYMENT, having a middle-letter insertion plus a heavy suffix added.

The importance of Prytulak's T-stack theory is that it provides an explanation for why trigrams of low meaningfulness are harder to learn than trigrams of high meaningfulness. The idea is that the harder it is to convert a trigram into a word—the further one has to search the T-stack for a successful transformation of the trigram—the less study time there will be left to actually encode the trigram after the transformation is uncovered. Moreover, if the transformation is a very low priority one, it might not be uncovered in the available study time (being at a lower T-stack depth). Even if a successful transformation is found, it will probably contain two or more elementary operations. Each detail of a transformation rule (e.g., "PAYMENT except delete A and delete the suffix") adds further associations to be learned by HAM, creating greater likelihood of a recall failure.

14.2. PAIRED-ASSOCIATE LEARNING

Paired-associate learning (PAL) appears to fit the "stimulus-response association" paradigm of behaviorism almost exactly. The learner acquires a list of

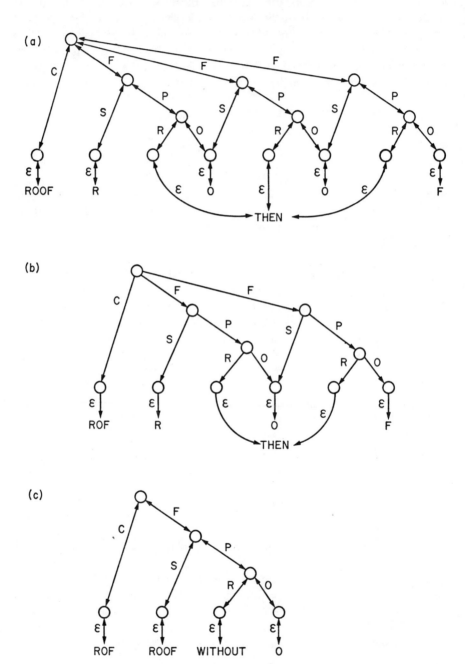

FIG. 14.2. (*a*) The representation of ROOF in memory; (*b*) the immediate representation of ROF; and (*c*) the schema-plus-correction encoding of ROF with respect to ROOF.

artificial pairs of items; the first or left-hand member of the pair is the nominal "stimulus" term used as a retrieval cue for the pair; the second or right-hand member is the "response" term which is to be recalled to the appropriate stimulus cue. The stimulus and response terms can be any type of material—words, digits, syllables, pictures, sounds—and they are typically paired together arbitrarily, and the subject learns concurrently a list of, say, 10 to 20 of such pairs.

From the time of McGuire's classic paper (1961), it has been widely recognized that paired-associate learning is conceptually analyzable into three components: stimulus discrimination, response learning, and stimulus-response association. To illustrate, in order to learn a pairing such as BEQ-713, the subject must discriminate the stimulus BEQ from similar trigrams in the list, learn the three-digit response 713 as a unit, and learn that 713 goes with BEQ. The heart of our propositional analysis of PAL concerns the association phase. Our claim is that stimulus and response will become associated if and only if a proposition is formed to link them. So given a pair like "cow-lawyer," the subject might form and learn the proposition "*Cow* is next to *lawyer*" or the mnemonic elaboration "The cow kicked the lawyer." But before we develop the propositional connecting further, it is necessary to consider the logically prior stimulus and response learning.

Stimulus and Response Learning

If the stimuli and responses are common words, then HAM does not have to bother learning them since they are already represented by word nodes in memory. However, when they are nonsense syllables, a major portion of HAM's learning task will be to construct representations of the stimulus and response terms. In the past section we outlined various means for representing nonsense syllables in memory. Using the rote encoding option and the shorthand introduced in Figure 14.1, the paired associate "BEQ-713" has been encoded in Figure 14.3. Given this information structure, the query "What is paired with BEQ?" will match and retrieve the stimulus subtree in the usual fashion, and the response subtree will be output.

The major difference between response and stimulus learning is that the response has to be entirely encoded so the subject can generate it, but the stimulus need be only sufficiently encoded to discriminate it from the other stimulus members. Thus, if BEQ were the only stimulus beginning with *B*, it would be sufficient for HAM to encode "B is paired with 713." The general reasoning here is the same as in EPAM or in E. J. Gibson's (1940) original analysis of PAL in terms of stimulus differentiation. Such analyses predict that PAL becomes harder as the stimuli are more similar and that more of a stimulus structure must be encoded to permit discrimination from other stimuli. Such similarity effects with nonsense syllables are well documented, and HAM predicts them for the same reasons the other analyses do.

However, unlike the earlier analyses, HAM also explains why semantic similarity interferes with learning when words are used as stimuli. To understand HAM's explanation, consider how HAM would deal with lists that contained semantically similar words such as *dog, mutt, hound,* and *canine.* When one of these words is used in PAL, an idea node connected to that word is selected by HAM for use in a

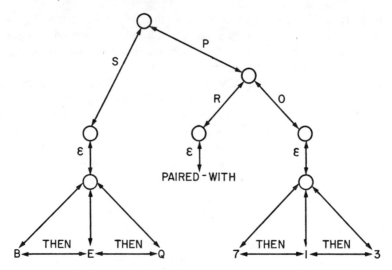

FIG. 14.3. A rote encoding of the paired-associate pair "BEQ-713."

proposition conjoining the "stimulus word" to the "response word" of the pair. A given word is usually associated to several different idea nodes, representing the differing "meanings" to which that word is associated (see Figure 8.2). These idea nodes correspond intuitively to the different nuances of meaning people have for one word. For example, comparing *dog* and *hound*, in a primary meaning *hound* is a subset of *dog* (poodles are dogs but not hounds); in particular, hounds are hunting dogs. But *dog* as a word also references other meanings, such as metaphorical extensions (e.g., to refer to a homely woman, or a low-quality performance, or persistent following). *Hound* also has metaphorical extensions, being using frequently as a verb (e.g., "He was hounded by the tax man").

In the abstract, then, we may conceive of a set of idea nodes in HAM accessed by a given word; the sets corresponding to two words may overlap with shared concepts. For instance, *hound*, just as *dog*, can refer to the general species of canines. The greater the degree of overlap of the two sets of idea nodes, the greater the "semantic similarity" of the two words. A few word pairs like *mailman* and *postman* are almost complete synonyms in the sense that they seem to be connected to the same set of idea nodes. The word nodes themselves might have different predications attached to them—for instance, "The word *postman* is used more frequently in England but *mailman* more frequently in America."

From the above characterization of the similarity of meaningful words within HAM, it should be apparent how we explain the effect of semantic similarity on paired-associate learning. Two pairs like *boy*-R_1 and *lad*-R_2 will be confused with one another in case the idea node primed for use in the *boy*-R_1 association is the same as the one used by the *lad*-R_2 association. These confusion errors will continue until a distinct idea node is referenced by at least one word of the confusing pair. Thus, although both *boy* and *lad* reference the idea node "young male human," in a particular person's lexicon *boy* might also reference "big bully boy," whereas *lad* does not. This "big bully boy" concept node thus provides a distinct, potentially useful idea node for reducing confusions during the learning of the *boy* and *lad* pairs. The more semantically similar are the stimulus members of the list of pairs, the more overlap there will be in idea nodes referenced by the different words, and the more difficult will be the subject's task of selecting a distinct, discriminating idea node to represent each word in the list to be learned. Much as in "hypothesis-testing" models of discrimination learning, HAM would try out one idea node after another for a given stimulus word on the list, searching for a successful discriminator. The current idea node being used for a given word would be the top item (most recent one) returned by the GET (word, IDEA) function called from the stimulus word. Thus, once a distinct idea node was found, it would thereafter be immediately accessible from the word, at least until that word were used in different, interfering contexts. In those rare cases where two words are complete synonyms, so that no distinct idea nodes exist for the two words, HAM would have to resort to learning a rote proposition about the words qua words rather than ideas. HAM would learn something like "The input to word node X occurred next to the input to word node Y."

Stimulus-Response Association Learning

The crux of the paired-associate task, of course, is associating the cue term appropriately to the response term. We suppose that this is always done by propositionalizing the relationship—either finding a preexisting relationship between the two concepts corresponding to the stimulus and response terms, or confabulating an "artificial" relationship (such as "is paired with") to deal with the exigencies of the learning task itself.

This analysis of PAL leads to an interest in preexperimental association norms that characterize the availability of associations issuing from a particular stimulus word. We do not interpret free-association norms as indicating direct connections between ideas. While some associations reflect phonetic or orthographic relationships, those of a "semantic" variety are to be interpreted as indicating some propositional connection between the two words. Thus, the pair "cow-milk" may reflect the underlying proposition "Cows give milk"; "cat-dog" the proposition "Cats are chased by dogs"; and "oak-tree" the proposition "An oak is a tree."

If a proposition already exists in memory connecting stimulus and response, HAM is saved the need to form a new one. If idea S has *any* association to idea R, then that (or an equivalent) connection would probably be located in the PDS on Trial 1 (of the S-R pairing) and tagged as usable for later trials. This means, in effect, that the connection from S to R has, after a single trial, been primed into dominance when S is presented as a recall cue. A clear implication is that rate of "association learning" of an S-R pair will not be dependent on where the response occurs in the rank-ordering of the associate in the norms for the S-term; rather, learning rate will depend on whether or not any preexperimental association is available from the S-concept to the R-concept. This implication seems to accord with the facts of the case. Postman (1962) found that there was little or no difference between high and low associates; but Postman, Frazer, and Burns (1968) did find a difference between associates and completely unrelated pairs.

The Propositional Structure

We have supposed that in learning an arbitrary word pair, the subject locates in memory or constructs a new relation between the two concepts and tries to learn a proposition using this relation. If it is a pair of nouns, then probably a verb or preposition would be found to relate them; if a pair of adjectives, then probably a noun having both properties would be found; if a noun-adjective pair, then the adjective may be predicated of the noun, or if that fails, the adjective may be applied to a new noun dredged up to form an association to the initial noun. To illustrate this last case: to learn an arbitrary pair like *horse-icy*, the adjective is difficult to predicate directly of horse, but we could apply it to, say, the horse's drinking trough or the horse's hair or his breath, etc.

Figure 14.4 illustrates the kind of proposition HAM might find to relate the noun pair *cow-lawyer*. The basic relation which HAM might find to connect these concepts is the transitive verb *kick*, so the proposition would be "A cow kicked a lawyer." Further information is also predicated about various parts of this structure. For instance, HAM learns that *cow* is the first word of the pair and *lawyer* is the second. It also learns that the "cow-kick-lawyer" proposition is something it thought of in the context of the experiment. Of course, these auxiliary propositions are attached to each of the pairs being learned in the list. Because they are used repeatedly, these auxiliaries are easily attached to each new propositionalized pair.

There are good reasons for encoding these auxiliary propositions around each pair. First, they enable the subject to discriminate between list words versus nonlist

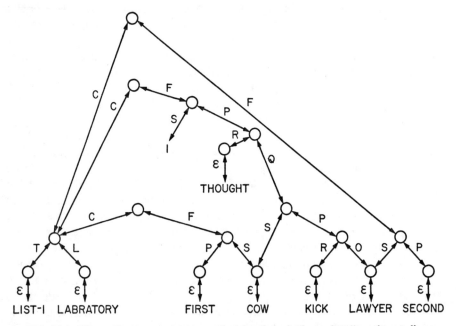

FIG. 14.4. The total memory structure underlying the paired associate "cow-lawyer."

additives (like *kick*). Second, they enable him to discriminate first words or "stimuli" from second words or "responses" in the list of pairs. This prevents the subject from using stimulus words as possible guesses for response terms. Such intrusions are known to be quite rare in such experiments.

The "second word" node in Figure 14.4 also provides the list of responses from which guesses can be made in case the stimulus word *cow* fails to access its response term directly. HAM could implement various sophisticated guessing strategies, provided time is available on the retention test. A particularly good strategy uses backward associations when the forward association fails, trying thus to weed out unlikely guesses. The prescription of the strategy is to scan through the "second word" response list looking for one having a backward association to the current test stimulus; if one is found, to give that as the response to the test stimulus; if the backpath for a response leads to a stimulus word differing from the test cue, then to eliminate that response as a possible guess; and when all list responses have been so scanned, to guess from the set not eliminated by the above backpath-scanning strategy. This is the kind of guessing strategy which permits success at a greater than chance level even before the forward associations from S to R are fully formed and accessible. Execution of that guessing strategy takes a lot of time, however, so the subject could not complete it in a fast-paced retention test.

The context tag in Figure 14.4, "In the experiment I thought of . . .," is necessary because we do not want the subject to leave the experiment with various mistaken beliefs. He knows that the event, of a cow kicking a lawyer, did not really happen. He only thought of it for purposes of the experiment. Thus, the context is a sort of tag marking the embedded proposition as a hypothetical.

A few psychologists to whom we have shown propositional structures such as Figure 14.4 have exclaimed at the number and complexity of associations required by our theory. Why not, they urge, simple associate *cow* to *lawyer* directly with one link? The answer, of course, is that *cow-lawyer* is not a proposition, and we believe that human memory only stores propositions. The simple associative link conception also does not begin to deal with all the auxiliary knowledge which we can demonstrate that the subject has about the pair (e.g., recalling the list of stimuli separately or the responses). Also as mentioned before, the auxiliary predications are used so frequently throughout a list that they are overlearned subtrees which are easily attached to a new pair-proposition with relatively little cognitive strain. Such considerations therefore make our propositional theory of PA learning not so unwieldly in comparison to the "direct link" hypothesis.

Backward Associations

Our theory supposes that associations are always formed in a bidirectional manner. Thus, the associative path in Figure 14.4 leading from *cow* to *lawyer* can also be traversed backwards from *lawyer* to *cow*. This forms the basis for "backward recall" of the stimulus word when cued with the response word. A strong qualification on all this, however, is that the accessibility of the forward path may be greater than that of the backwards path. Specifically, from the node representing the lawyer-instance in Figure 14.4, there is a single "is a member of" link to the concept *lawyer*. However, if the MATCH process begins at the concept node *lawyer* (as it does in a backwards-recall test) and evokes GET (lawyer, ϵ^{-1}), the particular instance-node in question may not be the first element on the GET-list. The general principle is that for the triple $<A\ R\ B>$, B may be on the top of the GET(A,R) list, whereas A need not be on the top of the GET (B, R^{-1}) list. The principle applies to our present case where R is the relation ϵ, A is the instance-node for a particular individual, and B is the concept-node *lawyer*. The upshot of these considerations is that backwards recall could fail despite the ability to do forward recall.

These backward associations reveal themselves indirectly in causing slow learning of "double function" lists. In double-function lists, a given item appears as a stimulus of one pair and a response of another pair. An example would be the list *A-B, B-C, C-D, D-A*. In such lists, when the person is cued with item *C* he is supposed to give only the forward association, *C-D*. However, the backward association from *C* to *B* (from the *B-C* pair) intrudes and interferes with recall of *D* to *C*. HAM would have exactly the same difficulties as do people, as is illustrated by Figure 14.5. This shows two propositions, one linking the pair *cow-lawyer*, the other linking the pair *lawyer-butcher*. The auxiliary propositions in Figure 14.5 are deleted to reduced clutter and in any case are of no use here, since *lawyer* (as well as *cow* and *butcher*) is a first word in one pair and a second word in another, and there is no simple, direct way to encode in which pair it is first and in which pair it is second. This is the cause of the confusion and interference when *lawyer* is the test cue. How does the person (or HAM) know whether to recall "The *lawyer* was kicked by the *cow*" or "The *lawyer* sued the *butcher*"? He might use a fact such as that the stimulus and response of a given pair generally fill the subject and object positions in the propositional constructions, but that is not a perfectly reliable cue. The alternative is to encode a rote proposition regarding cooccurrence of the words. That is, the subject would learn propositions similar to "Word *A* was to the left of Word *B*," "Word *B* was to the left of Word *C*," and so forth. This would solve the confusions, but it also considerably slows down the learning because predications about words qua objects are always more difficult to learn than meaningful predications involving the ideas and concepts associated to the words.

Rote versus Meaningful Learning

That "rote" learning should be harder than "meaningful" learning is one of those transparent facts which everyone readily accepts, but which turns out to be

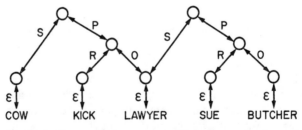

FIG. 14.5. The word *lawyer* encoded both as stimulus and response in a double-function list.

very difficult to explain with any cogency. After all, "Word *cow* next to word *lawyer*" is a perfectly decent proposition. Yet subjects who encode all pairs in terms of relationships between items qua physical words will in general learn much more slowly than subjects who concoct "meaningful" relationships among the conceptual ideas. But why? We suspect that the outcome depends on the fact that predications about ideas can be expanded and elaborated into a large set of related propositions, whereas predications relating words as objects cannot be expanded into anything other than what they already are. The proposition "The cow kicked the lawyer" can lead to some mental imagery or propositions regarding what parts of the cow and lawyer got contacted, what this caused the lawyer to do, and so on and on, to a rather full-blown description of the scenario, its setting and sequel. These subsidiary propositions provide multiple connecting pathways between the two concepts which are to be associated together for the paired-associate task. Consequently, there are just many more opportunities for at least one pathway to be learned and retrieved at the time of the later recall test. On the other hand, in the "rote" proposition, a spatially static (nonaction) predicate (x to the left of y, x beside y, etc.) provides for no elaborate unpacking of its underlying semantics. Also, the objects "Word A" and "Word B" can support no particular elaborations in their own right. Therefore, the rote proposition "Word A beside Word B" is likely to be encoded alone, without elaboration and embellishment.

According to this view, then, pairs leading to meaningful propositions are learned more rapidly than pairs leading to "rote" propositions because of redundant, multiple pathways elaborated in the former but not in the latter case. This characterizes the meaningful-rote difference as a quantitative difference. What differs in the two cases is the way that our semantic memories are primed to elaborate and process the two classes of propositions.

Type of Connectives in PA Learning

A set of experiments in paired-associate learning, with noun-noun pairs, has investigated learning rate when a connective of some kind is placed between the two nouns. Rohwer (1966) reported, for example, that when the connective between two nouns is a verb ("*cow* kicked *lawyer*"), PA learning is facilitated relative to a condition in which the connective is a simple conjunction ("*cow* and *lawyer*"). Prepositions like *in, outside, beside, near* (as in "*cow* near *lawyer*") produce variable results, sometimes yielding recall as high as verb-connectives, and in other experiments producing recall comparable to that of conjunctions.

HAM can explain the basic differences observed by Rohwer. Verb-connectives produce better subject-object learning than do conjunctions (and, or) because an "S-V-O" combination constitutes a complete proposition whereas "S and O" is not a proposition at all; nothing is yet predicated of the S and O conjunction. HAM stores only complete propositions, so the subject must find or supply some predicate in the noun conjunction case. Since subjects may not do the necessary search for a predicate, or the search may fail, pairs linked by the conjunction will be acquired more slowly than pairs presented with a verb, yielding a complete proposition.

As the foregoing indicates, a subject may attend in only a cursory manner to a paired associate without trying to find and tag a meaningful linkage from the stimulus term to the response term. Perhaps no linking proposition is formed at all, or perhaps only the "rote" proposition referring to coocurrence of the two physical symbols is encoded. In any event, learning or long-term remembering is unlikely to result from such cognitive processing of the pair. Different individuals will vary in their strategies for the paired-associate task; there will be those who predominantly search for meaningful relationships to learn the pairs, and those who try to learn primarily by rote. These individual differences in strategies create corresponding differences in learning rate; subjects who search for meaningful relational mnemonics learn faster than those who do not (see Bean, 1971). But instructing the poorer subjects to always search for and remember meaningful relations for the pairs enhances their learning appreciably, so that individual differences in learning are reduced, though not eliminated. We suspect that this result is the general rule: subjects who learn and remember a lot do so because they use more efficient and powerful encoding strategies. If mnemonic strategies are equated by instruction and tutoring, the individual differences are expected to be reduced, if not eliminated.

14.3. SERIAL LEARNING

The serial learning experiment is characterized by the primary requirement that the subject recall the items in a specific serial order. Typically the serial lists are arbitrary items (words, digits, letters), presented in an arbitrary serial order with little, if any, organization to the presentation order. The recall-testing procedure either can be full unaided recall of the complete list or can be prompted recall of one probed item at a time. Instructions for recall to the probe element would be either to recall its serial location (e.g., "fifth item in list") or to recall the next item following the probe. The traditional "serial anticipation method" presents the probes and the next successors in a constant serial order from the beginning to the end of the list, recycling through the list in this manner for many trials. Experiments can be further differentiated according to whether the same list is presented for only one trial or for many trials. The one-trial experiments (e.g., digit-span tests) typically use complete serial recall.

There is a vast range of facts now known about serial learning in laboratory settings. In this section we will indicate how HAM's mechanisms can handle some of the more salient of these findings. But first we must address ourselves to the question of how we would represent a serial list of items such as *ABCD*. One possibility, illustrated in Figure 14.6, is to borrow directly from our representation for nonsense syllables (e.g., refer to Figure 14.1) and encode the list in terms of left-to-right successor relationships.

However, it is well known in the literature that serial-order information could also be carried by serial-*position* information. To be specific, the string in Figure 14.6 could have been encoded as in Figure 14.7 by the propositions "First element is *A*, second element is *B*, third element is *C*, and fourth element is *D*." One need not tie the representation to the *numbers* "first, second, ..." All that is required are some cognitive elements that are distinguished by being linearly ordered along a dimension. These linearly ordered elements then serve like "implicit stimuli" to which the items in the series become attached like paired-associate

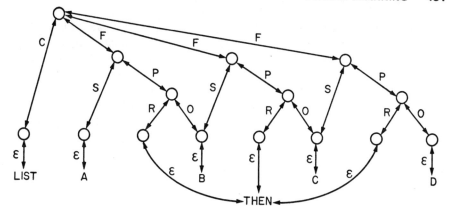

FIG. 14.6. An encoding of the serial string *ABCD* according to successor relationships.

responses. Ebenholtz (1972) has recently summarized the evidence for this positional view of serial-order learning as contrasted to the sequential learning hypothesis.

These two hypotheses—sequential versus positional learning—are alternative types of descriptions which HAM's *perceptual parser* could output. It goes without saying that no assumption we have made requires the output descriptions to be in one form rather than another. Presumably the encoding format is a strategic matter that varies with materials, procedures, and subjects. We know of situations (e.g., serial learning of a cyclic list with a different, random starting point each trial) which clearly induce sequential encoding based on temporal precedence. Other situations (e.g., constant spatial locations for the items presented in a changing temporal series) tend strongly to induce serial-position encoding. On the question of how much of each encoding is involved in particular tasks, we have no better guesses than what are currently available in the field. That is, HAM does not automatically solve for us the problem of the "functional stimulus" in serial learning. We are not certain the problem is "solvable" in the sense people once hoped it would be.

Interference among Serial Strings

According to the No Forgetting Postulate of Section 7.4, once a propositional structure has been stored in long-term memory it will never be lost. However, it is possible to lose accessibility to that structure. For example, in a digit-span

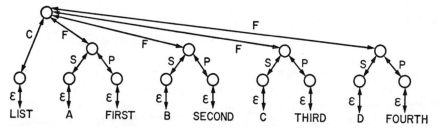

FIG. 14.7. An encoding of the serial string *ABCD* by positional information.

experiment, a particular string 7319 may be encoded in LTM. Yet because these same digits are reused repeatedly in other strings and other contexts, the 7-instance (as well as the other digit instances) involved in the 7319 structure will descend to inaccessible depths on the GET $(7, e^{-1})$ list. Consequently, the tree structure encoding 7319 in LTM is eventually unlikely to be matched to an input of 7319, and will not be recognized as a familiar sequence. This is why it is difficult for HAM to "retain" a random number or letter series for very long in a multitrial digit-span or letter-span experiment which composes new series by permuting a small vocabulary of elements.

This analysis accords with an observation by Melton (1967), who studied the improvement in immediate recall of a nine-letter series which recurred on Trials 3, 6, 9, 12, 15, and 18 of an 18-trial block of immediate-recall tests. On the interpolated trials 1, 2, 4, 5, 7, 8, . . ., new different letter-strings were presented for immediate recall. These used either the same nine letters as in the recurring string (except permuted in a different order) or used an entirely different set of nine letters from those in the recurring string. As HAM would expect, Melton found much greater trial-to-trial improvement in recall of the recurring string in the case where the nonrecurring items were composed of different letters. There was only slight improvement in recall of the recurring string when the interstitial strings were just permutations of the same elements. The interfering effect of these strings would prevent HAM's MATCH process from making contact with the string's trace, and so the encoding process could not take advantage of the associations already in memory in trying to store the string. In another experiment reported in the same paper, Melton varied the number of interpolated letter series between presentations of the recurrent series. As HAM expects, he found less trial-to-trial improvement in recall of the recurrent series the greater the number of interpolated series. In fact, with four interpolated strings, there was no improvement at all in recall of the recurrent series.

Given such results, one might question how it is that people (or HAM) ever remember numerical sequences for a long time, as we surely can with historical dates, population figures, street addresses, and phone numbers. Often these are stored as objects in propositions whose subject provides a distinct entry point; thus, when HAM evokes the GET-list for the probe "John's street address is . . .," the string "7319 Elm Street" can be retrieved directly. In contrast, in Melton's experiment, retrieval of the digit string had to occur from the digit elements of the string. Consequently, the multiple occurrences of the digits had severe interfering effects.

On Perceptual Groupings of a Series

A series of elements such as letters or digits is rarely encoded as a monotonous series; rather a preferred strategy of the learner is to segregate the stream of items into groups or chunks, and then to deal with these chunks as units in learning. HAM offers an obvious explanation for this chunking. Long strings cannot be totally held in working memory, and so HAM would need to break the string into workable chunks. It would then hold each chunk in working memory for a short while, restricting for that while its MATCH processes and encoding processes to that chunk.

The segmentation and assignment of successive items of a series to groups is a function carried out, presumably, by HAM's *perceptual parser*. Since the writings of Max Wertheimer (1923), there have been several well-known principles of perceptual grouping, i.e., specification of variables determining which elements of an input get grouped together in a perceptual description. The first variable is *proximity*: elements that are close together on the relevant dimension will tend to be aggregated in favor of elements that are farther apart. This proximity can be temporal or spatial in character. An example of a spatial discontinuity is the letter series PZN LKB WFT, where blank space separates the three triplets of letters (a dash or asterisk or parenthesis or any other boundary marker would serve as well as a blank). Such spaces are needed in reading, since wo-rdsw-itho-utsp-ace-sar-edi-ffic-ult-tore-ad. The same "blank spaces" can be located in a temporal series, where they are called pauses, defined as relatively long interelement times. Such pauses (as well as intonation contours) are part of the so-called "prosodic" features of speech, enabling the parser to identify major clause boundaries, questions, and the like. These prosodic analyzers are apparently recruited for the use of segmenting and learning most series of arbitrary elements.

Somewhat more generally, the space between letters in the series PZN LKB WFR may itself be thought of as just a null character which the parser is to treat as a group boundary but is otherwise to "ignore" in constructing a description of the groups in the string. If this were true, then similar subjective groupings should be produced by use of a homogeneous "spacer character" which the subject is told to ignore in his encoding. Thus, if the subject is told to ignore the symbol $\emptyset$ in the input string, then he will encode and later recall the string $\emptyset$PZN$\emptyset$LKB$\emptyset$WFR$\emptyset$ in substantially the same way as before when blank spaces or pauses replaced the $\emptyset$ spacer. Winzenz (1972) found precisely this result in an immediate serial recall paradigm.

Proximity is one of the most potent variables determining perceptual grouping of elements in a series. Another determining variable is the similarity of the elements as physical stimuli; similar elements are more likely to be grouped together. This similarity of adjacent elements can be on the basis of shape (e.g., AAbbAAbb), or color (e.g., ○○●●○○●●), or size (e.g., OOooOOoo), or any other such attribute. Bower (1972b) has shown that these similarity variables affect the grouping and encoding of visually presented letter-strings as inferred from their recall patterns. Thus, in a letter series defined by spatial adjacency, adjacent letters were more likely to be grouped together if they were similar in size, shape, or color. These are elementary "grouping principles" which we would want our perceptual parser to utilize.

Hierarchical Representation of a Series

If the elements of a series are being chunked by the perceptual parser into a set of groups, then the full description of a series is similar to that of a *hierarchy* with various levels. Figure 14.8 shows as an illustration a possible three-level hierarchy encoded in HAM for the sample letter-string PZN LKB WFR. Here we are again using the shorthand introduced in Figure 14.1. In Figure 14.8 the string is encoded in terms of three groups, G1, G2,

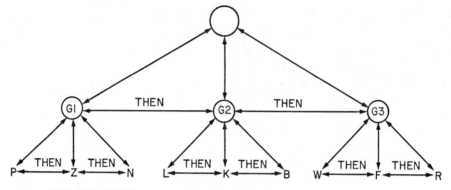

FIG. 14.8. HAM's representation of a serial string broken into three chunks.

G3, with each group in turn encoded as having certain elements in a particular order.

This representation of the memory structure implies a number of results for the learning of grouped series. A first elementary prediction is that elements within a group should tend to be recalled in relatively "all-or-none" fashion,–either all elements of a group recalled together, or none at all. An elementary index of this all-or-none recall is the transition error probability (TEP) in position n, defined as the conditional probability of an error in recall of the element in position n, given a correct recall of the element in position $(n$-1). If elements n-1 and n tend to be recalled together, then the TEP will be small; if these elements are recalled independently, then the TEP will be large, approaching the unconditional error probability at position n.

Figure 14.9 shows a graph of empirical TEP data from Bower and Winzenz (1969) illustrating this point regarding differential recall within a chunk versus between a chunk. This graph is for immediate recall of 12-digit strings presented auditorily and segmented by temporal pauses into successive groups of sizes 2, 3, 2, 3, 2, respectively. The point plotted above position n in the graph is the TEP, the conditional probability of an error in recalling the nth element, given that the $(n$-1)st element was recalled in its correct location in the series. At position 1 we have plotted just the unconditional probability of an error in recalling the first element of the series. The important point to be gleaned from Figure 14.9 is the saw-toothed pattern, with high TEPs at the transition beginning a group and lower TEPs for within-group transitions.

Such TEP patterns confirm a hierarchical structure for representing the series. For a series like PZN LKB WFR (see Figure 14.8), it is just a much shorter distance in the associative graph structure between Z and N than it is between N and L. Moreover, conditional upon recall of Z, N can be recalled if either of two links have been formed (Z to N or G1 to N). But conditional upon recall of N, L can be recalled only if at least two links have been formed (G2 to L, and either G1 to G2 or the root node to G2).

Another fact that should be apparent from the graph structure in Figure 14.8 is that, given recall of the nth element, the time before locating and producing the $(n$+1)st element should be greater for between-group than for within-group

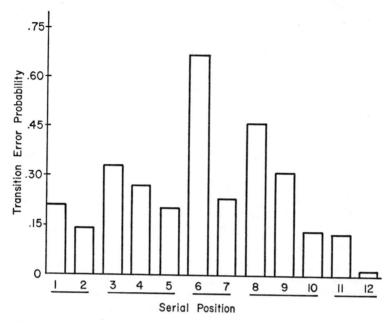

FIG. 14.9. Representative TEP data: Conditional probability of an error in Digit $n + 1$ given correct for Digit n for items in a serial string. (From Bower & Winzenz, 1969.)

transitions. This predication of larger reaction times for between-group transitions has been confirmed for interresponse times during full serial recall by McLean and Gregg (1967), and for probed recall by Wilkes and Kennedy (1970). In the Wilkes and Kennedy study, for example, after thoroughly learning a chunked-letter series, the subject received reaction-time trials on which he would be probed with a random letter of the series and then have to recall the next successor to the probe. The expectation from the graph structure in Figure 14.8 is that within-chunk successor latencies will require traversing just one link and should be less than between-chunk successor latencies which require at least three steps in the graph from N to get G1, from G1 to get G2, and from G2 to get L. The Wilkes and Kennedy experiment confirmed these expected differences.

Part Learning and Serial Groupings

We have supposed that perceptual variables partly determine the groupings of elements which are identified by the perceptual parser. Recall that when an input tree is entered into HAM's working memory to be encoded, initially there is a call of the MATCH process to see how much of an input can be identified as familiar material.

Experiments by Bower and Springston (1970) and by Bower (1972b) bring out these points clearly for serial recall of letter strings utilizing familiar sub-sequences. Their subjects studied, then immediately recalled, strings of 12 letters, segmented by pauses into successive groups of sizes 4, 3, 3, 2 or into successive groups of sizes 2, 3, 3, 4 across the 12-letter series. Unknown to the subjects, the series were in fact composed by stringing together familiar acronyms—abbreviations for companies (IBM, TWA), governmental agencies (FBI, DOD), familiar personalities (JFK, FDR), university initials (UCLA, CAL, USC), and other assorted miscellany familiar to most American college students (TV, UFO, USSR, etc.). The 12-letter strings were composed of a digram, then two trigrams, then a quadragram, in that order or in the reverse order of chunks. The strings beginning with a digram will be referred to as D-strings; those beginning with a quadragram will be referred to as Q-strings. Half of each kind of string were presented with pauses so as to be segmented perceptually into groupings of 2-3-3-4; the other half of the strings were presented so as to be perceptually grouped into a 4-3-3-2 structure.

The empirical hypothesis under test was that immediate recall would be best when the perceptual groups coincided with the familiar acronyms. For example, the 2-3-3-4 perceptual grouping would be optimal for a D-string like TV IBM TWA USSR but nonoptimal for a Q-string like IC BMF BIU SCBO. But the 4-3-3-2 perceptual grouping would reverse this recall order of D-strings and Q-strings. Exactly this result was obtained: when the perceptual and acronym groupings coincided, recall was best, averaging 9.6 letters; when the groupings were out of phase, recall averaged 6.7 letters. This effect, of about 3 letters or 42% over the baseline, is very large, given the usual stability and low variance of memory-span measures."

The correspondence hypothesis confirmed above fits perfectly with the encoding functions in HAM. The perceptual parser delivers a particular description of the input to working memory. This description, as we have said, is a hierarchy of groups (actually, propositions about the precedence relations noted by the parser). These groups are determined largely by perceptual variables. Once in working memory, the MATCH process checks to see whether the group is familiar. A graph of the process used by Bower (1972b) is reproduced in Figure 14.10. Here, MRL denotes "Most Recent List" and the Gi reference the successive groups. To the letter group I, B, M in that order, HAM would call its MATCH function and find immediately that IBM was a known unit, with a corresponding node in long-term memory. The encoding routine then would use that old memory node to replace the entire subtree corresponding to the parser's lengthy description of the group I, B, M. Thus, what was formerly, say, G2 in the tree structure of Figure 14.10 gets replaced by a token of the IBM node. When the entire string is composed of appropriately grouped acronyms, then the memory structure consists essentially of a record of their tokens in particular precedence relations.

This sort of match-up of incoming letters to familiar memory nodes will not occur when the parser breaks the acronym in its middle and groups it with other elements. Thus, IBM LA is not recognized in the groupings IB MLA. The MATCH function checks for full groups, and does not rearrange or repartition the groups; that is, failing on IB, HAM will not resegment and pull in the M from the second group in order to get a match on IBM. Not having a match for IB or MLA, HAM would have to encode all the links in the input tree. Because it has many more links to learn, HAM will fail to recall IB MLA much more frequently than it fails on IBM LA.

These perceptual grouping variables can be quite powerful, and they can be "undone" or reversed cognitively only with special effort. In an experiment by

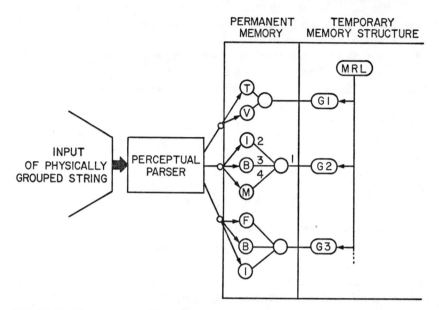

FIG. 14.10. The operation of the perceptual parser in representing a serial string chunked into familiar acronyms.

Winzenz and Bower (1970), subjects were trained to group auditory digit series into triplets regardless of the group structure in the physical acoustic stream. This was a difficult task; subjects could perform successfully only when the input rate was slowed considerably (to one digit per second, whereas prior experiments have used rates of two to four per second), and then only by conscious focusing on and articulation of the new groupings in a vocal rehearsal loop. Their recall TEPs showed evidence of a conflict between the physical groupings (say, 4-3-3-2) and the subjectively attempted groupings (of 3-3-3-3), and they clearly recalled a lot more when the physical groupings coincided with the triplet format into which they were forcing each input.

Recognition Memory

The foregoing illustrated how a series of familiar acronyms will not be recognized as such when it is segmented into unfamiliar letter groups. A similar phenomenon occurs in recognition memory experiments using arbitrary strings of letters or digits. Experiments by Bower and Winzenz (1969) had subjects making Old-New recognition memory judgments for a long series of five-digit items. The items were presented auditorily, grouped by pauses and numerical naming into structures such as 2-3, or 2-1-2, or 1-2-2, etc. The task used the continuous recognition paradigm introduced by Shepard and Teghtsoonian (1961), in which the subject gives recognition responses to a long series of items, half of which are repeats of earlier ones. The variable studied was the similarity in group structure of the first versus second presentation of a given five digit string. The subject was to respond "Old" if he thought the underlying string of test digits matched a string presented earlier, irrespective of whether the digits were grouped differently from before. Half of the strings at random were repeated with identical group structures, while half were repeated with a change in group structure.

The primary result was that recognition memory was very much worse when the string repetition occurred with changed groupings than with unaltered groupings. Thus, a string like 83-5-96 was unlikely to be recognized later when tested as 8-359-6. The difference in correct "Old" responses between the two conditions was about 20%, and it held up across lags of from 1 to 24 intervening items. The main result, of poorer recognition with changed groupings, is expected by HAM's representation of a series as a hierarchy of groups. When the groupings are changed, the input does not match the old memory structure set up by the earlier presentation of the same digit series. Thus, recognition should be seriously impaired, as it clearly was in the experiment.

Accumulative Learning from Repeated Series

Other experiments by Bower and Winzenz (1969) examined serial learning of a repeated digit string, in which the group structure of the string was either constant across repeated trials or variable across repetitions. This manipulation was done in the context of a Hebb-like experimental paradigm (Hebb, 1961), in which a particular digit string (the "target") periodically recurs among a set of constantly changing "noise" items; the subject listened to each string, then attempted immediate recall of it. The target string recurred at lags of 2 or 3; for half of the trial-blocks, the target string was always grouped the same on each of its presentations; for the other trial-blocks, the target string was grouped differently upon each of its presentations, although it contained the same serial order of digits. To be specific, the recurrent string might appear on Trials 3, 6, 9, 12 of a 12-trial block. If it were to have changing groupings, then it might be chunked as (17) (683) (945) (2) on its first presentation, but on its next three presentations on Trials 6, 9, 12 as (176) (8) (394) (52), then as (1) (768) (39) (452), and then as (1768) (3) (94) (5) (2).

The result quite simply was that recurrent strings that were grouped identically upon each repetition showed considerable increase in their recall across repetitions. However, when the group structure of the recurrent string was changed at each of its presentations, there was no accumulative learning whatsoever for the recurrent string. That is, the normal improvement in recall with repetition was practically annihilated by changing the group structure at each repetition. It thus appears that perceptual chunking determines similarity of the memory structures established by two presentations of the same digit series. If two series are identical in constituents and in group structure, then it is possible for the second input to make contact with the memory trace of the first input; this contact of new input with old trace evidences itself in recognition of familiarity and also in accumulative learning effects—that is, the subject's immediate recall following the second presentation of the series is higher than it was following the initial presentation. On the other hand, if perceptual groupings are changed, the repeated string is not recognized and there is no accumulative learning. Note how similar these accumulative learning results are to the pattern we obtained with across-trial repetition of parts of sentences (see Section 9.2).

The theoretical explanation in terms of the MATCH process is similar for the two cases.

This discussion of hierarchical group structures and their memory representations concludes our discussion of serial learning. We have not touched on many interesting phenomena of this topic, but rather have focused on those for which HAM could provide explanations that were not post hoc. We have thought about how HAM would handle many other phenomena, but these explanations rested on unmotivated, post hoc assumptions about how HAM would represent the serial lists. We have decided not to annoy the reader with such post hoc explanations and have largely confined our analysis to those experiments where HAM's representation was obvious. We also want to emphasize that the MATCH process, which carried much of the burden of explanation in the foregoing discussions, was not originally designed to explain serial learning. We now move on to discussion of a final procedure in verbal learning research, namely, free recall.

14.4. FRAN: A SIMULATION MODEL OF FREE RECALL

The basic free-recall experiment involved the presentation to a subject of a list of words, one word at a time. After seeing all the words in the list, the subject is asked to recall them in any order he chooses. The experimental paradigm derives its name from the fact that the subject is not constrained to a particular order by recall. The free-recall paradigm has attracted much research interest because of evidence indicating the strong influence of various types of conceptual organization upon the subject's recall.

We have already worked out in detail how an associative model might be applied with some success to free recall (Anderson, 1972; Anderson & Bower, 1972). This model of free recall is embodied in a simulation program dubbed FRAN, an acronym for Free Recall in an Associative Net. FRAN begins the experiment with a preexperimental associative network of interconnected words or concepts. FRAN's various study and recall processes are defined in terms of this network of interword associations. HAM does not permit such direct associations between words. Words become interconnected only as they participate in particular propositions. So part of our task in describing FRAN will be to convey how it is to be reconceptualized in the broader framework provided by HAM.

It is easy to map FRAN's initial structure into an initial structure for HAM. As we noted in earlier sections of this chapter, interword associations become elaborated in HAM into propositional tree structures that serve to link two elements. So where FRAN might have had the bare association "dog-cat," HAM will have a proposition of the order "Dogs chase cats." Note that this proposition produces more than a binary linkage. Beside connecting *cat* and *dog*, it links both to *chase*. Thus, FRAN's initial network of associations becomes in HAM an initial network of propositions. Of course, because each proposition in HAM is composed of a set of associations, in HAM too we would have at a more microscopic level a network of associations. However, the proposition will be the important unit of analysis in translating FRAN into HAM. FRAN's routines are divided into STUDY processes and RECALL processes, and each will be described briefly.

STUDY Routines in FRAN

When word i is being studied during input of a free-recall list, it is as though a set of activities is going on around node i in the semantic network. During study of word i, FRAN attempts to do two things: (a) to mark node i with an association to LIST, which information is used later for recognition that word i appeared in the LIST context; and (b) to follow out one or more associative pathways stemming from node i, searching for other list-words (i.e., nodes with association to LIST). If such pathways to other list-words are found, then those pathways are associated to (marked with) a LIST tag. The effect of such marking of pathways is to tell the executive during retrieval to use these marked pathways to move from recall of word i to recall of other list words.

Word tagging in the old FRAN model involved the formation of a single association between the word and LIST. In HAM this association would become translated as a contextual proposition of the order "Word i occurred in the context of LIST" where LIST now references the concept of the list in which the word occurred. Path tagging in the old FRAN involved the formation of an association between each association in the path and the node LIST. This formation of associations between associations and nodes was a particularly ad hoc assumption in the old model with which we never did feel entirely comfortable. There are all sorts of vagaries in such a system that are avoided in HAM, where only nodes can be connected. For instance, it is hard to specify how retrieval mechanisms should treat an association between a node and another association (represented in FRAN as $<A \ R_1 \ <B \ R_2 \ C>>$). For instance, when one traverses along R_1 from A, exactly what does he retrieve? And, whatever it is that he does retrieve, how does he continue the search from there? Again, is it possible to go in the reverse direction from the association $<B \ R_2 \ C>$ to the node A along R_1^{-1}? To travel from a node X to Y along R, it is necessary that the processor be in possession of X and evoke GET (X, R). What are the corresponding necessary conditions to travel from an association like $<B \ R_2 \ C>$? These and other perplexing questions did not arise in implementing FRAN because in the program we needed only to articulate the functional consequences of the representation for a particular free-recall strategy.

One of the advantages of HAM is that it is no longer necessary to introduce associations between associations and other elements. FRAN's unarticulated association has been replaced by a proposition. One can tag a proposition simply by tagging its root node. For example, let us consider the differing manners in which FRAN or HAM would tag the connection between *cat* and *dog*. The two alternatives are illustrated in Figure 14.11. In Figure 14.11a, FRAN has bound the association $<$cat dog$>$ into a new association with LIST. In Figure 14.11b, HAM has taken the proposition "Dogs chase cats" and embedded it in an autobiographical proposition: "In the context of LIST, I thought of the fact that dogs chase cats." Note that in Figure 14.11b HAM would also have to tag the words *cat* and *dog* to recognize that they and not the other elements were the list words.

There are three other components to be described regarding the study processes. One of these is a rudimentary short-term store (STS) which holds on the order of the last two to four items besides the current one it is working on (in the "memory

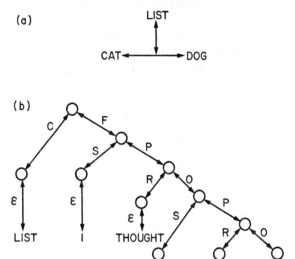

FIG. 14.11. Tagging a connection between *cat* and *dog*: (*a*) in FRAN, and (*b*) in HAM.

drum window"), plus any associates it has uncovered. Of course, FRAN's STS corresponds to HAM's working memory. As in HAM, structural modifications are made to only those parts of FRAN's memory currently residing in STS. It is recall from this short-term memory that gives the recency effect in free recall, and which accounts for above average associative strength for items occurring close together in the input list (cf. Glanzer, 1972).

A second component to be described is construction of a special set of "starters," which are list-words with associations *from* LIST. Along with items in STS, these items are used by the person to begin his recall chains during output. In the program, these starter associates to LIST correspond to a small list we call ENTRYSET (in the current program, it is constrained to be three items or less). The algorithm for placing elements on the ENTRYSET is as follows: at the initial trial, place the first three items on ENTRYSET (this assumption, by the way, produces a "primacy effect" in the serial-position recall curve on Trial 1); if any item in the list is found which leads to more list items in its associative neighborhood than does an item currently on ENTRYSET, then the latter is replaced by the former item; if one item on ENTRYSET is found to lead associatively to recall of a second item on ENTRYSET, then the second one is replaced by some other word from the list under study. The reader should recognize that these are relatively crude heuristics for converging on those items that are most central in the list, that lead to recall of the largest number of associates. With repeated practice on a list, more and more pathways among list items become tagged, so that the whole list becomes a single interconnected cluster of marked nodes and pathways.

Of course, the ENTRYSET associations from LIST are just the converses of the associations to LIST involved in word tagging. In HAM, the identical proposition (with its symmetric associative structure) would be involved in word tagging and construction of ENTRYSET. Thus, HAM would form to itself a proposition of the order "In the context of LIST, I studied cat, house, potato. . . ." This is illustrated in Figure 14.12. While it is easy in such a propositional structure to go from a particular word to LIST (i.e., to determine if the word has a list tag), it is very much more difficult to go from LIST to the words in the list. This is because of the excessive branching on the object relation from the predicate node. When HAM would evoke GET (X, OBJECT) it would be faced with a very long list of associates which it would only search to a probabilistically determined depth. This limitation on the search of the GET-list is why ENTRYSET in FRAN is constrained to a certain size. FRAN's heuristics for determining the constitution of ENTRYSET become in HAM heuristics for selecting which associates to keep at the top of the GET-list.

The third learning process that should be mentioned is the learning that is assumed to go on during output (recall test) trials. Recall of a given word is assumed to provide the subject with another "study" opportunity during which he searches out associative pathways radiating from the recalled node, seeking to find and mark pathways leading to other words of the list. In this way, the subject may learn quite a bit on test trials in the sense of later recalling previously unavailable words, and increasing the probability of stereotypy in recall order across trials.

To summarize, the learning processes which go on in FRAN during study are: tagging of list-words, searching for associative pathways between list-words, marking the successful pathways so found, replacing items on the ENTRYSET by items that are associatively more central, and the learning of retrieval pathways during recall itself.

RECALL Routine

In recall, FRAN first dumps out the five more or less recent words in her STS (unless these have been erased by interpolated activity of some kind). These STS items plus the three on ENTRYSET are then sampled, one at a time, and used to commence associative chains for recall. In recalling from word i, the executive

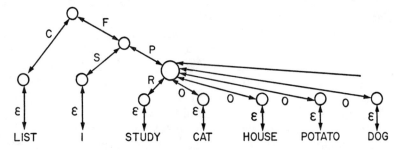

FIG. 14.12. HAM connects the list words to LIST.

examines the several associative branches radiating out from node i to check whether any of them has been marked (with a LIST tag) as a retrieval route to another list word. If such a marked link is found, it is followed to its terminus, which node may be tagged with a LIST tag, in which case the corresponding word is recalled. Whether tagged or not, FRAN will search any tagged paths accessible from this node in the same manner it searches from i. When the search of these tagged paths is exhausted, FRAN returns to node i to check for any other tagged paths from it. In this manner a depth-first search is effected of all the tagged paths leading from each of the entry words taken from STS and ENTRYSET. When it has exhausted her eight entrywords, FRAN's recall protocol comes to a halt, and the output trial has ended.

Some Properties of FRAN's Behavior

We have run a number of simulations of FRAN's behavior under various experimental conditions. FRAN's behavior is quite variable from one simulation run to the next because the tagging operations are probabilistic, as are important parts of the search process by which FRAN scans the neighborhood of the word it is studying, looking for other list-words. We will give a few averaged results to illustrate the explanatory powers of such a model before turning to enumerating its deficiencies.

First, in simple multitrial free-recall experiments, FRAN shows the typical exponentially increasing learning curve for recall (cf. Figure 14.13). More importantly, measures of stereotypy or subjective organization match those of human subjects (cf. Figure 14.14). The data in these figures were collected from 18 Stanford students doing free recall of two 32-item lists of unrelated nouns; 36 individual simulations of FRAN were run, and their averages are indicated in the figures. In Figure 14.14, the measure of stereotypy is the proportion of adjacent pairs recalled in Trial n which are recalled, also adjacently, on Trial $n + 1$. Without any special effort at parameter estimation or curve fitting, FRAN is seen to fit the data fairly well.

FRAN also shows, on Trial 1 especially, a tendency towards recalling, adjacently, items which were close together in the input list (cf. Glanzer, 1972; Kintsch, 1970). This is produced by the short-term memory assumptions: Suppose there is an associative link from word n to word n-k; word n-k might not have been tagged, but it is more likely to be in STS at the same time as word n the smaller k is; therefore, it is more likely that word n-k will be recognized, and the path from word n to word n-k will be tagged the smaller k is.

FRAN also shows a proper serial-position curve in recall probability on every trial. The recency effect due to STS is present on every trial. The primacy effect (due to priority of initial items on ENTRYSET) is predicted on Trial 1 only; with random reshuffling of the list items on each trial, the primacy effect disappears on later trials on the list. These predictions fit the results reported by Shuell and Keppel (1968).

FRAN also displays the appropriate relation between words recalled and list length and study time (or number of presentations) per item. Figure 14.15 shows the fit of FRAN to some of Waugh's (1967) data in which free recall was studied as a function of number of distinct word types (list length) and study time per word type. Study time per word type was varied either by presenting a word once for *n* seconds or presenting it *n* times for 1 second, each of its presentations distributed among presentations of other items. In FRAN, increases in list length increase total words recalled (although proportion recalled decreases), because with more words it becomes somewhat more probable that an associative search from any list-word will come across other list-words. The effect of study time is simple, direct, and two fold: increasing the study time on a word: (*a*) increases the number of pathways that can be searched out from that node, and (*b*) increases the probability that the node itself will be tagged (associated to LIST-N), as well as the probability of tagging pathways between words stemming from the study word. These assumptions suffice to account for the standard effects of list length, study time, and number of repetitions.

The model can also simulate the results of Tulving (1967) on multiple test trials interspersed between study trials. There is a definite "learning effect" from test trials. Moreover, FRAN shows considerable variability in its output on consecutive recall trials without an intervening study trial; as in Tulving's study, many words recalled on one test may be missing in the next consecutive recall test, and vice versa.

Another fact of free recall which FRAN will obviously handle is one reported by Deese (1959), relating recall of a list to the average degree of interitem associations preexisting among the list-words. We have not expended the computer costs to

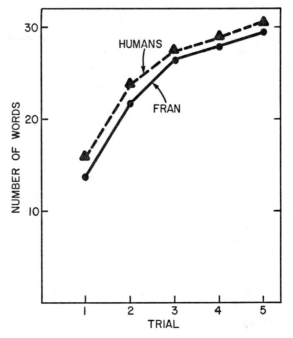

FIG. 14.13. FRAN and human *S*s compared with respect to mean numbers of words recalled as a function of trial.

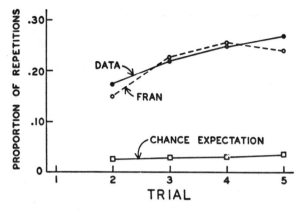

FIG. 14.14. FRAN and humans compared with respect to
stereotypy of output order.

simulate Deese's exact results, but it is obvious that associative retrieval pathways
among multiple list-words will be more easily found in a word list having many
close associations at the beginning of the experiment. Similarly, the clustering in
recall of highly associated word pairs, reported by Jenkins and Russell (1952), is
just the kind of result FRAN is designed to explain.

Recognition and Free Recall

Another implication of FRAN is that is fits the more obvious facts regarding
recognition memory in relation to free recall (see Anderson & Bower, 1972, for a
detailed analysis.) Kintsch (1970), in particular, has argued that recognition is
independent of associative retrieval processes, and has shown this in several
experiments. FRAN "recognizes" a test word as having been on LIST-N if an
association exists between the corresponding node and the cognitive element
"LIST-N." Even assuming the association from word to LIST-N is all-or-none,
Bernbach (1967) has still shown how reasonably continuous recognition ratings
could be derived from such two-state memory structures. For the moment, what
needs to be pointed out is that recognition in FRAN is almost independent of recall
in the way Kintsch (1970) hypothesized, with "recognition monitoring" of items
before they are recalled. If recognition fails on an item, then recall will most
probably fail; if recall succeeds, then recognition will most probably succeed.
FRAN can also recognize many items it cannot free-recall. Recognition of a word
depends on marking its corresponding node; however, recall of that same word
usually (except for STS) depends on the marking of associative pathways into it
from other words in the to-be-recalled list.

As a consequence of these assumptions, FRAN also fits the results on free-recall
versus recognition measures following intentional versus incidental learning of a set
of words (e.g., Eagle & Leiter, 1964). In the model, we suppose that
incidental-learning subjects spend their time tagging word nodes but not searching
out or tagging iteritem relationships or "retrieval routes," since they are not
expecting a memory test. On the other hand, intentional learners not only tag word

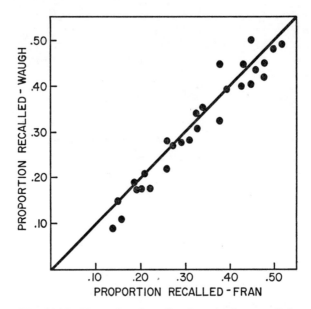

FIG. 14.15. Observed and predicted proportions recalled
from lists of length 24 to 120 words, with each unit presented
for 1, 2, 4, 5, or 6 seconds.

nodes (leading to good recognition performance) but also search out and tag associative pathways between list words. This results in their having significantly higher free recall, despite no difference in recognition between the intentional and incidental subjects.

These various "successes" of FRAN could also be reproduced by HAM if we translated FRAN into HAM. They provide support for associative models of memory like FRAN or HAM. Perhaps more enlightening than these successes of FRAN are the points where she misfits the data, but where HAM offers the possibility of explaining FRAN's failures. These points serve to help justify the translation from FRAN into the more complex model.

Repairing FRAN's Deficiencies

FRAN has no "encoding" process, so it encounters no recognition difficulties due to encoding variability. A word has one corresponding concept node in FRAN's network, and presentation of that word to FRAN always activates that one node. However, a word typically has several alternative senses or conceptual encodings, and which of these is activated depends on the context in which the item is experienced. So in humans, recognition memory will fail if the item is tested in a context differing from that prevailing when it was studied (Light & Carter-Sobell, 1970; Tulving & Thomson, 1971). Such results can be interpreted in HAM where we have the idea-word distinction. Corresponding to each word in memory will be several distinct idea nodes corresponding to the varying senses of the word. One of these idea nodes would be activated and tagged during the study trial, but, with changed context, a different node may be activated and interrogated for a list tag during the test trial.

Another deficiency of FRAN is that she is not a language comprehender; she does not "understand" sentences in any different sense than she understands random strings of words. If the successive words in the list were those of a sensible sentence, FRAN would not treat them any differently than she would a randomized list of the same words, and her recall would be about the same in the two cases. People, of course, recall the linguistically structured lists much better, and the more so the closer the word order approximates grammatical English (Miller & Selfridge, 1950). Of course, this is just the sort of result that HAM was designed to handle. Word strings that it can make sense of are translated directly into propositions and encoded. When faced with random word combinations, HAM must create new interlinking propositions or search its memory and tag old propositions that already interlink the elements. HAM's currently programmed parser would have difficulties with some of the approximations to English that Miller and Selfridge employed, but presumably a more realistic and powerful parser could be constructed that would detect partial propositions in these approximations.

Category Blocking

While HAM provides the solution to these failings of FRAN, there are other shortcomings in FRAN that HAM cannot ameliorate. A first difficulty is that FRAN does not show enough recall nor nearly enough category clustering when she is learning categorized word lists. She particularly lags behind human subjects in these respects when the list items are presented blocked by categories. FRAN does recall and cluster categorized lists more than unrelated-word lists, and she clusters a bit more on blocked than on randomized lists. But the effects in the simulation are far too small to fit the human data when the categorized lists are blocked (see Anderson, 1972).

What is wrong here? What is wrong is that FRAN uses the instance-to-instance associative strategy, and despite frequent conjectures to the contrary, that strategy simply does not provide the amount of category clustering which adults exhibit in their recall. What is needed is to allow FRAN to use a nonlist word (specifically, the name of the category) as a central entryword into the instances of a category. That would implement the "superordinate" retrieval route which was proposed in Bousfield's (1953) earliest papers on the topic.

This failing of FRAN is not that serious with respect to her associative mechanisms nor the mechanisms of her translation in HAM. It is simply a case of too narrowly formulating the processes by which she studies and recalls the list. If we permitted her more flexible and adaptable behavior in free recall, she could bring her associative mechanisms to bear in a way that would generate the typical categorical effects. However, the next misfit of FRAN seems more fundamental in that it is not just a case of our having programmed an inappropriate mnemonic strategy. It seems to suggest something fundamentally wrong with the basic associative mechanisms that we have postulated.

Slamecka's Results

FRAN fails badly in its attempt to simulate the results of experiments by Slamecka (1968, 1969). Following one or more input trials, some subjects were given half the list on a sheet and told to recall only the remaining half of the list. Their recall of this remaining half was no better (in fact, was frequently worse) than that of control subjects who were trying to recall the entire list. Later experiments by Allen (1969) and Anderson (1972), have shown that with various methodological refinements, the half-list "cued" subjects may recall 7 to 15% more than the noncued control subjects. But the fact remains that these effects are very small considering the measures taken to produce positive cueing effects.

FRAN was run on a 40-item simulation of Slamecka's procedure. A study-then-test cycle was done, followed by a second study trial, followed by a cued or noncued recall test. The cued condition was simulated by composing FRAN's entry words of the 20 cue (list) words, as well as the usual five from its STS, and the three from ENTRYSET. This takes the hard line that the optimal strategy is for the experimental subject to try to cue recall from the presented half-list. In the control simulation, FRAN recalled all of the 40 words she could, then was allowed to study those words recalled for an extra time, trying to stumble across another list word or two to recall. This extra time proved almost completely ineffectual for FRAN, as it is, too, for humans. FRAN recalled 14.8 words out of 40 on Trial 1 (7.4 out of each half-list). On Trial 2, on the to-be-recalled half-list of 20, FRAN recalled 14.6 when cued, but only 10.6 in the noncued, control condition. So with half-list cueing, FRAN recalled 42% of the words she could not recall without cues. The size of the predicted effect is to be compared to the 0 to 15% improvement observed by half-list cueing under more or less optimal conditions.

The conclusion, much as Slamecka indicated, is that either subjects do not use the half-list cues in the way they should (or there is something inhibiting about its use), or else we are seriously in error, theoretically, in assuming that subjects are using interitem associations as their primary retrieval routes. The conclusion from Slamecka's result, as from FRAN's attempted simulation, is essentially negative: A simple prediction of an associative model is not confirmed. So far as we are aware, there is no compelling theoretical analysis of Slamecka's findings. It is clear that we could make ad hoc assumptions about how FRAN deals with the half-list cueing procedure, so that we would predict the lack of a cueing effect. But ad hoc assumptions specifically designed to fit one piece of data are not very satisfying.

Despite its various misfits, we do regard FRAN as the most viable theory of free recall available in terms of its range of applicability. In comparison with current mathematical models of free recall (e.g., Shiffrin, 1970; Norman & Rumelhart, 1970), FRAN is to be favored because it fits some of the elementary "organizational" facts about free-recall protocols (e.g., increasing subjective organization over trials of unrelated words). Such facts are typically not addressed by those models, for the very good reason that those models typically assume that individual list items are stored and retrieved independently of one another. The item-independence assumption is extremely useful for simplifying mathematical derivations. One of the advantages associated with the move to a simulation program is that we were no longer theoretically constrained by considerations of mathematical tractability. In comparison to other nonmathematical formulations of free recall, FRAN is to be favored because she is a going, operative program that, in fact, fits some data. FRAN's manifest superiority, plus the admitted existence of her empirical imperfections, should provide ample incentive for some nonassociative theorists to formulate an equally explicit model that can compete with FRAN in the empirical domain. Models like FRAN or HAM are in desperate need of some well-formulated countertheory, for then we would all have a clearer conception of what the significant questions are for future research.

14.5. IMAGERY

In recent years, there has been a renewed interest in nonverbal imagery and the role it plays in verbal learning. The research surrounding this issue has been amply summarized in Allen Paivio's book *Imagery and Verbal Processes* (1971), and we will not attempt a competing summary here. Suffice it to say that visual imagery seems subjectively to be a principal representation of the meaning of words and propositions. It is particularly relevant to the referential function of language. It is also our principal way of thinking about or processing spatially organized information.

An example task used by Paivio (1971, p. 34) to illustrate imaginal processes is to have the person visually image a large block letter (e.g., an E) and, beginning at an arbitrary place and proceeding in any specified direction, to have him begin counting the interior angles or corners of the figure. Most people can do this comfortably with any figure, starting anywhere and proceeding in either a clockwise or counterclockwise direction. The example illustrates several significant points. First, the internal symbolic structure which describes the block letter is not "directionally specific"; we can "focus" our information processor (attention?) on any part of the structure, and proceed in any direction. Second, the task of counting angles is a verbal process, performed sequentially under the control of a sequential "internal scan" of the corners of the figure. Third, we proceed systematically in one direction around the corners of the imagined figure, not because we must scan in that order but because it simplifies keeping track of where on the figure we began our count. We could have our internal scan "leap" erratically from one corner to any other, but we would soon lose track of which corners had or had not been counted.

Given the sensationalist basis of HAM's concepts, and given our acceptance of something like Winston's (1970) program as an adequate beginning for describing scenes, we have at least the rudiments for representing such performances. The block-letter E would be described by the perceptual parser in terms of the connectivity relations between lines, angles, etc. A "counting" program called by the executive could then scan systematically through the elements of this description tree counting angles, much as a person would proceed if he had the block letter before him. Such programs are not at all beyond implementation. For example, Baylor (1971) has developed a detailed information-processing model to characterize how people might solve visual puzzles in imagery. His program works on "cube-dicing" problems such as the following: "Take a 3-inch white solid cube, paint all six sides red, then dice it into 1-inch cubes by making six slices (two slices in each of three dimensions); now, how many cubes have three red faces, how many two, how many one, and how many have zero red faces?" This performance too can be represented in terms of problem-solving maneuvers operating over a symbolic graph structure.

The *subjective* counterpart of processing these symbolic descriptions of spatial information is that we are "seeing images" of successive parts of the puzzle, much as we would see an actual cube that we were dicing. There is no denying the validity of such subjective reports. What is to be cautioned against is the common view that the subjective imagery *explains* the performance in any acceptable sense. Pylyshyn (in press) has argued, correctly we think, that even granting the subjective validity of having images, one still needs an information-processing analysis of (*a*) what is the symbol structure that represents spatially distributed information, and (*b*) what executive processes can operate on that information. The preceding discussion shows our bias to have HAM represent spatial information as in Winston's (1970) program, as a description-tree of elementary perceptual properties, objects, and spatial relations connecting them.

It is clear that man's perceptual and linguistic systems are very closely linked together; for instance, we can describe our perceptual experiences to someone else, and he can in turn "understand" and be somewhat in contact with our experience. But in order to describe perceptual scenes, we must first interpret them; and this interpretation is itself strongly controlled by a preceding context, established particularly by language as well as by pragmatic considerations regarding the actors, objects, and actions in a given episode. The effect of a prior sentence on the interpretation of a perceptual event has been extensively documented in a paper by Clark, Carpenter, and Just (1972). The effect is most obvious with ambiguous figures, such as the duck-rabbit figure, or the wife–mother-in-law picture (see Figure 14.16), etc. If, before showing the subject the picture, he is asked to "Find the duck," he will practically never see the opposite interpretation. In this instance, he would store his "duck description," noting, for example, which way it was oriented, etc. But he would suppose there to be little or no information left over in this instance for HAM to later reimage that picture in memory and reinterpret it as a rabbit. The perceptual descriptions stored are inferential conclusions; the raw texture of appearance which initially supported those conclusions are rarely stored in any detail.

Verbal Learning and Imagery

In recent years considerable research has investigated the role of mental imagery in verbal learning. As the mnemonic experts have been saying since ancient times, the explicit use of mental images or pictures to represent verbal materials enhances people's memory for the material. What is currently a controversial issue is the exact interpretation of that fact. There are three main lines of evidence to indicate that mental imagery aids verbal learning. First, words which have concrete referents and which elicit vivid imagery are learned faster in almost all situations than are

FIG. 14.16. Famous ambiguous figures: (*a*) the duck-rabbit figure; and (*b*) the wife–mother-in-law picture.

words which are abstract and which arouse little imagery; second, subjects report spontaneous use of mental pictures to learn particular paired-associate word pairs, and these tend to be the pairs that they learn the quickest; and third, instructing subjects to form mental pictures of imaginal interactions among the referents of the words of a pair greatly enhances paired-associate learning of nouns. A fourth fact that is frequently cited in such discussions is that actual pictures of objects are easier to remember than are the names of the objects. Logically, however, that fact is not strictly relevant to whether *verbal* materials are aided by evocation of imagery.

There have been essentially three theoretical postures taken in interpreting such results. We will call them the "radical imagery" hypothesis, the "conceptual-propositional" hypothesis and the "dual-coding" hypothesis. The radical imagery hypothesis (e.g., Bugelski, 1970) supposes that subjects convert the verbal materials to mental pictures, store these pictures away in memory, then revive and describe these pictures at the time of the retention test for learning. At the other extreme is the conceptual-propositional hypothesis of HAM which supposes that knowledge—even knowledge that is derived from pictures or that is used in generating images—is always represented in the form of abstract propositions about properties of objects and relations between objects. According to this view, concrete words are more easily learned than abstract words because of the lexical complexity of the items themselves and because concrete concepts are more easily related by way of the exceptionally rich set of *spatial* predicates that exist for binding together concepts.

Finally, there is the "dual-coding" hypothesis that was advocated vigorously by Paivio (1969, 1971) and was subscribed to earlier by the second author (Bower, 1972a). In rough outline, the hypothesis supposes that there are two distinct representational and storage systems—the verbal and the imaginal. They are richly interconnected and often operate in conjunction in encoding and recording experiences. The two systems are presumed to be specialized for handling somewhat different tasks and have somewhat different capabilities. For example, Paivio (1971) mentions that the verbal system is specialized for representing and processing sequentially presented information, whereas the imaginal system is specialized for representing simultaneous arrays of information, the parts of which may be processed in parallel. The dual-coding hypothesis supposes that when a person tries to memorize concrete verbal materials using mental imagery, he establishes two distinct memory traces, one in the verbal-associative store, and a second, redundant one in the imagery store. The redundancy of the traces makes for better memory of concrete materials, since the learning event can presumably be reconstructed later on the basis of either memory trace. Abstract materials suffer because they are naturally encoded primarily in just the verbal-associative store, establishing but one trace. Therefore, memory for abstract materials is more vulnerable to disruption, more likely to be forgotten, than for concrete materials.

It is proven difficult to achieve any clear-cut differentiation and testing among these several points of view. Part of the problem of distinguishing the hypotheses is that the denotations of the "verbal" and "imagery" systems change in the theoretician's hands according to the explanatory demands of the situation.

Imagery refers not only to our detailed memory of pictures and melodies, but also to vague, schematic memory for such stimuli, as well as to memory for the *meaning* of a sentence. On the other hand, the verbal medium is taken variously not only to denote words as acoustical stimuli, but also to denote semantic interpretations and rich, meaningful relationships among concepts. The terminology in this nether world has just become exceedingly imprecise. Paivio (1971) offers a similar opinion on the distinction between verbal and imaginal systems:

> Our goal of differentiating these two symbolic processes is an extraordinarily difficult empirical problem at best, but is especially so when the theoretical goal is the explanation of verbal behavior, for here it is difficult to rule out verbal mediation as the most parsimonious interpretation and at the same time isolate whatever contribution may have been made by imagery [p. 9].

The problem, as we see it, involves confusions regarding theoretical representations of knowledge. And until those representations are made sufficiently explicit in theoretical detail, we can do little but thrash about with the vagaries of the layman's terms.

We have said that HAM comes down on the side of the conceptual propositional hypothesis regarding the role of imagery in verbal learning. Our principal point of disagreement with both the radical imagery and the dual-coding hypotheses is that they are too "peripheral" in their conception of the memory trace. The radical imagery hypothesis only permits raw sensory information; the dual-coding hypothesis augments this with memory for exact lexical items. We insist that the principal representation in memory is neutral with respect to the question of modality and that information is represented in abstracted, conceptual, propositional structures. Therefore, our arguments for the conceptual hypothesis will largely take the form of an attack on peripheral encoding as a viable memory system.

Against the Mental-Picture Metaphor

Our first arguments are simply that it is not scientifically viable to suppose that memories, or other sorts of knowledge, are carried about in a form like an internal photograph, videotape, or tape recording, which we can reactivate and replay in remembering an image. This is not to deny the subjective experience of imagery; we mean to distinguish, however, between that subjective experience and a scientific account of the symbolic structures and information-processing components which underlie our competence in carrying out imaging tasks.

We would argue that people store perceptual interpretations of scenes rather than "raw, unanalyzed, textured details" of such scenes. (The one exception known to us is an incredible eidetiker of Stromyer, 1970.) The visual scene is filtered, abstracted, summarized—in something like the propositional descriptions we would hope to have as output from HAM's perceptual parser. The abstract character of images shows up in the typical vagueness and sketchiness of memory images; they are frequently very schematic, categorical, and focused on only salient features. If one thinks on the matter for a moment, storage of textured details in all their minutiae would require gigantically large storage and retrieval capabilities.

Furthermore, it would be ultimately useless to store full pictures of scenes, because they could never support any usable performance. It is well known that pattern recognition cannot be explained by comparing an external scene to an internal picture (or template). Some intelligent device would still be needed to decide which are the relevant features and which are irrelevant for a particular classification or purpose. Also, if thinking is to be conceptualized as a kaleidoscope of mental pictures like a videotape, what is the homunculus that sits inside our head and "reads" and interprets these internal pictures? Doesn't he have to do the perceptual interpretations? If so, then why not do them neat, an input, rather than storing a passive videotape, which is then interpreted only upon later reruns?

It is perfectly clear, too, that in recognition memory for pictures, subjects are in fact recollecting their earlier interpretations of the pictures rather than comparing a raw, textured template of the initial study patterns and later test patterns. This is shown most clearly, perhaps, in an experiment by Wiseman and Neisser (1971) on recognition memory using the Mooney pictures, which are relatively unstructured blobs and snatches of ink scattered about (actually obtained by deletion of contours from a naturalistic scene). An example was shown in Figure 9.13, of the hound dog pointed to the left. The concealed figures were difficult to find, and many of the subjects of Wiseman and Neisser failed to "construct" an interpretation of a given Mooney picture. The picture series was shown a second time, with some old (previously shown) pictures and some new (distractor) pictures. For each test pattern, the subject was to (a) try to "see" some object in the jumbled ink patches and say what he saw, and (b) judge whether or not he had seen this exact stimulus pattern before in the training series.

Wiseman and Neisser found that complex visual patterns will be stored and recognized only if (a) they yield a familiar interpretation—the subject "sees" something in the picture—and (b) upon re-presentation, he "sees" the same interpretation of the test pattern, in which case he recognizes it as one seen before. If the visual pattern remains uninterpreted (e.g., not "seen" as a dog) either at study or at the test trial, then the raw, uninterpreted textured visual stimulus will hardly be recognized at all from memory. Such results argue that what is stored in memory from an encounter with a visual scene is dependent upon the interpretation "projected" onto that scene by the perceptual parser.

A related argument that fits in here is that people can comprehend and remember conceptual distinctions that would appear very difficult to represent, at least in naive imagery. We argued this point earlier, in Chapter 8, with respect to confusions in recognition memory for sentences. Some examples which appear difficult to distinguish in imagery involve judgments of mental traits ("He speaks *dishonestly*" or "He *forged* a name to the check"), negations of all varieties ("John isn't present" or "Only a few babies are unloved"), causality versus temporal precedence ("John's arrival made Mary cry" versus "Soon after John arrived, Mary began to cry") different temporal locations ("John thought" versus "John will think"), and different anchor reference points for measuring an event ("The glass is half empty" or "half full"; "Stephen's hair is long because he let it grow" or "because he didn't cut it"), and so on. One can multiply such examples ad infinitum in which there is a perfectly clear conceptual distinction between two

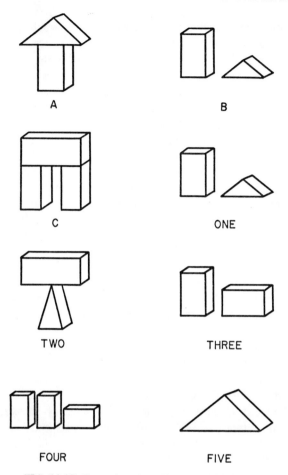

FIG. 14.17. Examples of visual analogy problems.

propositions, but no compelling distinction between the *static* images aroused in the two cases. And although such pairs of propositions will be confused somewhat in a recognition memory experiment, the significant point is that the particular proposition studied is remembered and discriminated quite well from its "imaginally similar" alternative.

Representing visual scenes as unanalyzed pictures in all their textured detail is also useless for doing any kind of visual search or visual problem solving. A simple illustration is solution of visual analogy problems, such as those shown in Figure 14.17. The analogy question is: "Figure *A* is to Figure *B* as Figure *C* is to which: one, two, three, four, or five?" Representation and storage of these line drawings as just pictures is of no help at all. We need interpretations and descriptions of objects, parts, and relations within a figure as well as the ability to describe the difference between Figures *A* and *B*, and the ability to apply that difference description to Figure *C* to generate a plausible answer figure. The computer programs of Evans (1968) and Winston (1970) perform these feats but only by first interpreting each figure and representing it as a relational graph structure.

A further note here regarding the "mental-picture" metaphor is that it will not suffice really to deal with the referential interaction between language and the external world. We have already seen earlier how a prior linguistic context biases how we interpret and encode a visual scene, e.g., the duck-rabbit ambiguous figure. But to even verify propositions about a scene, such as "The wedge is above the block," it is necessary that the scene be converted into something like a proposition. Chase and Clark (1972), in their many studies of subjects' reaction times to verify sentences against pictures (see our discussion in Chapter 13), have repeatedly shown the necessity for assuming that the sentence and picture are coded into a common format for comparison, and that this format must be propositional in character rather than imagistic. For example, negated sentences or negated predicates are readily verified against a picture, yet they lead to no particular images (i.e., no particular image encodes "The ball isn't present").

On Imagery Effects in Verbal Learning

We would suppose that the so-called "imagery effects" found in memory for verbal materials are not primarily due to the subjective experience of mental pictures (or because such images are "remembered better"—which explains nothing), but rather are due to a combination of factors, some due to the mnemonic coding strategies engendered in subjects given imagery instructions, and some due to the encoding of propositions using spatial relationships, which can be very efficient for storage.

It was mentioned earlier that learning of word-word paired associates can be greatly enhanced by instructing the subject to concoct mental images of the two referents (of the word pair) interacting in some vivid way. It is clear, however, that at the least this induces subjects to search out and activate sensible conceptual-semantic relationships between the two concepts. Practically the same benefits can be produced in PA recall of noun pairs by simply instructing subjects during the study trial to find and report sensible sentences connecting the concepts of a pair (see Bobrow & Bower, 1969; Bower & Winzenz, 1970). Typically the sentence-generation subjects will learn just as well as the imagery subjects, and both will far exceed control subjects instructed to learn by overt rote repetition of the word pairs.

Moreover, in an experiment by Bower, Munoz, and Arnold (1972), it was shown that subjects instructed at the time of study to learn some pairs (designated at random) by imagery and some other pairs by sentence generation could not remember very well later which mnemonic method they had used for a given pair, even though they could recall the pair itself. Although they correctly identified the mnemonic used 70% of the time (chance was 50%), in a control condition where they used the same mnemonic for all pairs but where half were presented on the left and half on the right edge of the study card, they remembered the location of presentation (which was the cue for the other subjects to image or not) at the same 70% level. In short, subjects could not remember for each pair whether they had been told to generate a sentence or an image to learn it, any better than they could remember whether it was presented on the left or right. If subjects were following instructions, to image or generate sentences, then one must conclude that not much distinguishable residue of the two activities was left behind. Such negative results are inconclusive, however, since subjects might not have been following instructions.

Somewhat more convincing evidence that imaging and propositional relating share common features arises when we constrain via presented materials or instructions the kinds of relations between items that the person tries to learn. If the subject uses a verb or locative preposition to make up a phrase relating two nouns, then he associates the two items together better than if he uses a simple conjunction (and, or). Similarly, one can show pictures of two objects interacting in some action photograph or show the two objects as static, standing singly side by side without interaction. In such cases, the interactive picture promotes better associative learning of the object pairs than does the noninteractive picture. As a third point in this comparison, consider a paired-associate experiment by Bower (1970) in which subjects were told to learn the pairs either by use of interaction imagery or separation imagery. In the former case, subjects were to image the referents of the to-be-learned word pairs and to image some interaction between them. In the latter case, subjects given separation-imagery instructions were told to imagine the two objects of a pair as two separate noninteracting pictures, as though they were two still pictures hanging on opposite walls of a room, with the contents of one "picture" not being influenced in any way by the contents of the other. This kind of separation imagery resulted in very poor *associative* recall compared to the interactive imagery condition. That is, when cued with one word of the pair, the separation-imagery subjects could not recall the other word of the paired associate nearly so well as the interaction-imagery subjects; in fact, subjects doing separation imagery recalled at the same level as control subjects instructed to learn by rote repetition of the word pairs.

If one examines the verbalizations or descriptions of the images generated by these subjects, the interaction-imagery subjects invariably use verbs or locatives, as in agent-action-object constructions (e.g., "Cow *kicked* lawyer") or agent-preposition-object constructions ("lawyer *on top of* cow"). On the other hand, separation-imagery subjects invariably use simple *conjunctions* to describe the two objects: "A picture of a *cow* over here and a picture of a *lawyer* over there." There might be many adjectival embellishments of each object singly, but the primary connective between the two objects was the simple conjunction *and*.

We believe that all these results are showing the same thing. Sentences, pictures, or images which lead to propositions relating the two terms produce greater associative learning than do stimuli that lead merely to coordinate conjunctions or simple static predicates of the kind "*X* beside *Y*." Coordinate conjunctions by themselves do not provide any propositional structure at all, and the static predicates are not much better. Such static relations as *next to* place virtually no semantic constraints whatsoever on *X* and *Y*. Therefore, if a subject is cued with *X* and retrieves the predicate *next to*, he has done little to narrow down the possible alternatives for the object. Thus, if the object association to *Y* is not intact, there will be little avail in guessing strategies of various sophistication. For instance, consider the contrast between "Cowboy beside steer" and "Cowboy ropes steer." Given "Cowboy beside ...," it is unlikely that steer will be provided as a guess to complete the phrase, whereas such a guess is very likely to "Cowboy ropes . . . ." Moreover, the static relation permits little elaboration, whereas other relations permit elaboration into new propositions interconnecting X and Y. Thus, "Cowboy ropes steer" suggests such additional facts as "Cowboy chases steer," "Cowboy bulldogs steer," "Cowboy brands steer." Moreover, each of these episodes can be expanded into its microstructure, providing further interconnections. For instance, "Cowboy ropes steer" expands into the cowboy taking aim, letting go of the rope, the rope encircling the steer, the rope becoming taut, the steer tripping, the cowboy's look of accomplishment, etc. This sort of expansion is much less readily accomplished with a predicate like "Cowboy beside steer."

Concreteness-Abstractness of Verbal Materials

It was mentioned earlier that learning is usually faster with concrete words than with abstract words. How might the conceptual-propositional hypothesis explain that abstract-concrete difference? At least part of the usual effects result from other attributes of the words that are typically confounded with concreteness-abstractness. One of these confounded attributes is the complexity of the lexical item as an English word, which determines the complexity of its entry in our internal lexicon. Frequently, abstract nouns are derived morphemically by adding prefixes or suffixes to verbs or adjectives, whereas concrete nouns tend to be lexically simple and not derived. This is how we get the abstract nouns *explanation, interpretation,* and *liberation* from the transitive verbs *explain, interpret,* and *liberate*, or how we derive *ability* and *difficulty* from the adjectives *able* and *difficult*. In fact, Kintsch (1972) has shown that lexically complex words are learned more slowly in a paired-associate task than are lexically simple words, even when the words were equated on imagery value.

A second overlooked contaminant in the comparison of abstract versus concrete words is the number of different semantic senses or dictionary meanings which a word has. In a paired-associate task, Schnorr and Atkinson (1970) found that words with many dictionary meanings were learned more slowly than words with fewer meanings, perhaps due to greater variability in encoding of the former items. This effect held for words equated on their imagery value. Furthermore, there is known to be a positive correlation between the average abstractness of a word and its number of dictionary entries—which may be why it is so difficult for people to communicate their exact meanings in abstract discussions.

There may be other confounding "linguistic" attributes correlated with the concreteness-abstractness ratings of words. The reason for mentioning these confounding factors is to illustrate that one should exercise extreme caution in basing major conclusions on the correlation between word abstractness and verbal learning rates. The correlation might be substantially reduced when various possible confounding word attributes are controlled.

Modality-Specific Interference?

There was a short-lived hope that the imaginal versus semantic representation of the memory trace could be distinguished by so-called "modality-specific interference" effects, an idea adapted from earlier work by Lee Brooks (1968). The basic notion is that if visual imagery involves some specifically visual process, then it must engage some of the same brain mechanisms as are engaged in visual perception. If this is true and if these visual mechanisms have a limited processing capacity, the visualization should suffer if the subject tries to visualize learning materials at the same time as he is required to do a visual perception task. On the other hand, according to this hypothesis, the subject's visualization should not be reduced nearly so much by having visualized learning material while he is doing a nonvisual distraction task. In brief, according to this hypothesis, it should be hard to do two visual things at once, even when one of the things is only visually imagining; the outer eye should compete with the inner eye.

This idea, based on Brooks' (1968) performance results, was tried out in the context of a memory experiment by Atwood (1971) with apparently positive results. He found that a *visual* distractor task (given during study of a paired-associate list) reduced later recall of concrete, imageable material more than it reduced recall of abstract material. On the other hand, a comparable *auditory* distractor task had the reverse effect, reducing recall of abstract verbal material more than recall of concrete material. This was the "modality-specific interference" effect that was being sought.

The interpretive problem is that the Atwood results have not stood up under systematic replication (Bower, Munoz, & Arnold, 1972; Lee Brooks, personal communication, 1972). Thus it appears best not to rely too heavily on that result for drawing theoretical conclusions. Moreover, later experiments by Brian Byrnne (reported in Brooks, 1970) have cast an entirely new light on the interpretation of Brooks' original results. In brief, Byrnne showed that in order to scan in memory over a spatially distributed array of information (e.g., an image of words in a 3 x 3 matrix), the person must be permitted to move his eyes in a homologous sequence. If his reporting task requires him to carry out completely conflicting eye movements (e.g., to report the serial order of the words in the matrix by finding them in a scrambled list), then his memory scan suffers. If the report task requires eye movements in a serial order that is spatially compatible with the spatial array of memory information the subject is scanning, then there is no conflict between visual perception and remembering in visual imagery. So, the conflict is not between imaging and visual perception, as originally supposed, but rather is between the motor (eye movement) scanning of sensory arrays and the scanning of mnemonic information structures encoding spatial information (e.g., about the location of words in a 3 x 3 matrix).

The upshot of these various considerations is that we cannot rely on the "modality-specific interference" effect to dictate our memory representation in favor of imagery versus a propositional base. Quite the contrary, the present results appear particularly insufficient to support a firm conclusion on such a major matter.

HAM's View of Imagery

In concluding, we would like to emphasize that we are not downgrading the importance of imagery. Rather, we are disputing one interpretation frequently given to the effects of imagery in memory. We have been arguing that the representation of an image should be in terms of the abstract propositional system of HAM and neither in terms of internal "pictures" nor in terms of verbal associations. In fact, as we argued in Chapter 7, we think such a propositional system initially evolved to deal effectively with perceptual material, and that language attached itself parasitically onto this propositional base. As a consequence, most of the primitives in HAM's base set of simple ideas correspond to elementary sensations.

The only difference between the internal representation for a linguistic input and a memory image is detail of information. A moment's reflection will reveal that most of what we say is very abstract and quite removed from a complete description of the causal microstructure of the concrete happenings. The listener either can be content to comprehend at this abstract level what we are saying, or he may choose to form an image of what we are asserting. If he chooses the latter, he will *unpack* each of our concepts into its more primitive terms.

Our words spoken to a listener are like the cryptic directions a playwright provides for a play director, from which a competent director is expected to construct an entire setting, an expressive mood, or an action episode in a drama. To illustrate, in the course of reading a story, you might read the sentence "James Bond ran to his car and drove to the casino." As you read, you can concretize that sentence by bringing to bear all sorts of facts and sensory images about running, about getting into cars, about driving, and so forth. These "fill-ins" would be called upon, for example, if you were to be asked simple questions like "Did James Bond sit in a car? Did he start its motor? Did he move the steering wheel?" Such trivial implications seem immediately available from the referential semantics of the verb phrase "drive a car." What the sentence does is merely mention a couple of signposts (source, instrument, goal) along the way in the description of an event sequence; the listener interpolates or fills in all the interstitial events between the mentioned signposts. Of course, at a later time, the listener is hardly able to say exactly what he heard as compared to what he filled in; if he is asked to tell the story "in his own words," he will probably select slightly different descriptions or signposts to mention in reconstructing the salient episodes.

All this can be represented in the structures of HAM, although we make no pretense to having programmed all the processes necessary to effect the unpacking of concepts. Note also that, in this view, the difference between abstract comprehension and imagery is one of degree. That is, the unpacking need not go all the way to the visual primitives, but can stop at some intermediate level. To the extent that the level of unpacking remains removed from the primitives, to that extent the image will be described as schematic and incomplete. We would suppose that such expansion goes progressively deeper the more time a person is allowed to think about or image the meaning of the sentence.

Summing-up

We have presented a very strong version of the conceptual-propositional hypothesis, arguing that HAM's representation is sufficient to handle all information processing associated with visual imagery. We are aware that this is probably too strongly stated, that there are imaginal processes that seem to require a representation of a mental object that is isomorphic to the structure of the physical object, rather than a propositional representation. Particularly striking evidence for the former representation comes from Shepard and Metzler (1971), who showed that the time to recognize that two perspective line drawings portray objects of the same three-dimensional shape is a linear increasing function of the angular difference in the orientation of the objects. Thus, figures which were 180° apart took the longest to identify. In contrast, network models like Winston's find 180° equivalences quite easy to identify. Such recognitions only require a switching of right and left relations in one description and a test whether the transformed description matches the other. Network models would find harder the recognition of equivalences between objects at less than 180° rotation. The introspections of Shepard and Metzler's subjects is that, unlike Winston's program, they mentally rotate one object into the other. In general, it would seem difficult for network systems like Winston's or like HAM to deal with continuously varying visual attributes such as degree of rotation, size, shape, and color. Presumably, the mind processes such information in analog fashion while the information is in a rather raw, textured form.

However, there are important limitations on the usefulness of such an information representation. As Posner (1969) has demonstrated, it appears to be very fragile and does not last well in the absence of the physical stimulus. Certainly, it is completely useless in reasoning tasks such as reported by Clark, Carpenter, and Just (1972). Finally and most important, whatever its value as an immediate representation for visual information, our preceding arguments still hold in implying that it cannot serve as a basis of representation in long-term memory.

We have now covered the main points we wished to make regarding imagery, the conceptual-proposition hypothesis, the relation between them, and their relation to verbal learning studies. We have devoted considerable space to the topic because it concerns a fundamental issue in current-day cognitive psychology, namely, how to represent theoretically our knowledge of the world. Also, mental imagery is currently a very fashionable topic for psychologists to study, and any newly proposed theory dealing with a representation of cognitions must confront and come to grips with the expanding experimental literature on imagery and cognition. Although there are many further details we have skipped concerning our views on imagery, the main points have been stated, and it is time to conclude our general review of verbal learning. The next chapter will be devoted to a detailed analysis of the topic of interference and forgetting, which has received extensive investigation in the verbal learning literature.

REFERENCES

Allen, M. M. Cueing and retrieval in free recall. *Journal of Experimental Psychology,* 1969, **81,** 29–35.

Anderson, J. R. FRAN: A simulation model of free recall. In G. H. Bower (Ed.), *The psychology of learning and motivation.* Vol. 5. New York: Academic Press, 1972.

Anderson, J. R., & Bower, G. H. Recognition and retrieval processes in free recall. *Psychological Review,* 1972, 79, 97–123.

Atwood, G. An experimental study of visual imagination and memory. *Cognitive Psychology,* 1971, **2,** 290–299.

Baylor, G. W. A treatise on the mind's eye. Technical report, Institute of Psychology, University of Montreal, July 1971.

Bean, J. The effects of subject-generated strings on noun pair learning in children: Population differences. Unpublished doctoral dissertation, University of California, Berkeley, 1971.

Bernbach, H. A. Decision processes in memory. *Psychological Review,* 1967, **74**, 462–480.

Bobrow, G., & Bower, G. H. Comprehension and recall of sentences. *Journal of Experimental Psychology,* 1969, **80**, 455–461.

Bousfield, W. A. The occurrence of clustering in recall of randomly arranged associates. *Journal of General Psychology,* 1953, **49**, 229–273.

Bower, G. H. Imagery as a relational organizer in associative learning. *Journal of Verbal Learning and Verbal Behavior,* 1970, **9**, 529–533.

Bower, G. H. Mental imagery and associative learning. In L. Gregg (Ed.), *Cognition in learning and memory.* New York: Wiley, 1972. (a)

Bower, G. H. Perceptual groups as coding units in immediate memory. *Psychonomic Science,* 1972, **27**, 217–219. (b)

Bower, G. H., Munoz, R., & Arnold, P. G. On distinguishing semantic and imaginal mnemonics. Unpublished manuscript, 1972.

Bower, G. H., & Springston, F. Pauses as recoding points in letter series. *Journal of Experimental Psychology,* 1970, **83**, 421–430.

Bower, G. H., & Winzenz, D. Group structure, coding, and memory for digit series. *Journal of Experimental Psychology Monograph,* 1969, **80**, 1–17.

Bower, G. H., & Winzenz, D. Comparison of associative learning strategies. *Psychonomic Science,* 1970, **20**, 119–120.

Brooks, L. R. Spatial and verbal components of the act of recall. *Canadian Journal of Psychology,* 1968, **22**, 349–368.

Brooks, L. R. Visual and verbal processes in internal representation. Paper presented in a colloquium series sponsored by the Salk Institute, La Jolla, California, July 1970.

Bugelski, B. R. Words and things and images. *American Psychologist,* 1970, **25**, 1002–1012.

Chase, W. G., & Clark, H. H. Mental operations in the comparison of sentences and pictures. In L. Gregg (Ed.), *Cognition in learning and memory.* New York: Wiley, 1972.

Clark, H. H., Carpenter, P. A., & Just, M. A. On the meeting of semantics and perception. Paper presented at the Eighth Carnegie Symposium on Cognition, Carnegie-Mellon University, Pittsburgh, Pennsylvania, 1972. (W. G. Chase (Ed.), *Visual information processing.* New York: Academic Press, in press.)

Deese, J. Influence of inter-item associative strength upon immediate free recall. *Psychological Reports,* 1959, **5**, 305–312.

Eagle, M., & Leiter, E. Recall and recognition in intentional and incidental learning. *Journal of Experimental Psychology,* 1964, **68**, 105–111.

Ebenholtz, S. N. Serial learning and dimensional organization. In G. H. Bower (Ed.), *The psychology of learning and motivation: Advances in research and theory.* Vol. 5. New York: Academic Press, 1972.

Evans, T. G. A program for the solution of geometric-analogy intelligence test questions. In M. Minsky (Ed.), *Semantic information processing.* Cambridge, Mass.: M.I.T. Press, 1968. Pp. 271–353.

Gibson, E. J. A systematic application of the concepts of generalization and differentiation to verbal learning. *Psychological Review,* 1940, **47**, 196–229.

Glanzer, M. Storage mechanisms in recall. In G. H. Bower (Ed.), *Psychology of learning and motivation: Advances in research and theory.* Vol. 5. New York: Academic Press, 1972.

Hebb, D. O. Distinctive features of learning in the higher animal. In J. F. Delafresnoye (Ed.), *Brain mechanisms in learning.* Oxford: Blackwell, 1961.

Jenkins, J. J., & Russell, W. A. Associative clustering during recall. *Journal of Abnormal and Social Psychology,* 1952, **47**, 818–821.

Kintsch, W. Models for free recall and recognition. In D. A. Norman (Ed.), *Models of human memory.* New York: Academic Press, 1970. Pp. 307–373.

Kintsch, W. Abstract nouns: Imagery vs. lexical complexity. *Journal of Verbal Learning and Verbal Behavior,* 1972, **11**, 59–65.

Light, L. L., & Carter-Sobell, L. Effects of changed semantic context on recognition memory. *Journal of Verbal Learning and Verbal Behavior*, 1970, 9, 1-11.

McGuire, W. J. A multi-process model for paired-associate learning. *Journal of Experimental Psychology*, 1961, 62, 335-347.

McLean, R., & Gregg, L. Effects of induced chunking on temporal aspects of serial recitation. *Journal of Experimental Psychology*, 1967, 74, 455-459.

Melton, A. W. Relations between short-term memory, long-term memory, and learning. In D. P. Kimble (Ed.), *The organization of recall.* New York: New York Academy of Sciences, 1967.

Miller, G., & Selfridge, J. Verbal context and the recall of meaningful material. *American Journal of Psychology*, 1950, 63, 176-185.

Norman, D. A., & Rumelhart, D. E. A system for perception and memory. In D. A. Norman (Ed.), *Models of human memory.* New York: Academic Press, 1970. Pp. 65-102.

Paivio, A. Mental imagery in associative learning and memory. *Psychological Review*, 1969, 76, 241-263.

Paivio, A. *Imagery and verbal processes.* New York: Holt, Rinehart & Winston, 1971.

Posner, M. J. Abstraction and the process of recognition. In G. H. Bower (Ed.), *The psychology of learning and motivation.* Vol. 3. New York: Academic Press, 1969.

Postman, L. The effects of language habits on the acquisition and retention of verbal associations. *Journal of Experimental Psychology*, 1962, 64, 7-19.

Postman, L., Fraser, J., & Burns, G. Unit-sequence facilitation in recall. *Journal of Verbal Learning and Verbal Behavior*, 1968, 7, 217-224.

Prytulak, L. S. Natural language mediation. *Cognitive Psychology*, 1971, 2, 1-56.

Pylyshyn, A. W. The problem of cognitive representation. *Cognitive Psychology*, in press.

Rohwer, W. D., Jr. Constraint, syntax and meaning in paired associate learning. *Journal of Verbal Learning and Verbal Behavior*, 1966, 5, 541-547.

Schnorr, J. A., & Atkinson, R. C. Study position and item differences in the short- and long-run retention of paired associates learned by imagery. *Journal of Verbal Learning and Verbal Behavior*, 1970, 9, 614-622.

Shepard, R. N., & Metzler, J. Mental rotation of three-dimensional objects. *Science*, 1971, 171, 701-703.

Shepard, R. N., & Teghtsoonian, M. Retention of information under conditions approaching a steady state. *Journal of Experimental Psychology*, 1961, 62, 302-309.

Shiffrin, R. Memory search. In D. Norman (Ed.), *Models of human memory.* New York: Academic Press, 1970.

Shuell, T. J., & Keppel, G. Item priority in free recall. *Journal of Verbal Learning and Verbal Behavior*, 1968, 7, 969-971.

Slamecka, N. J. An examination of trace storage in free recall. *Journal of Experimental Psychology*, 1968, 76, 504-513.

Slamecka, N. J. Testing for associative storage in multi trial free recall. *Journal of Experimental Psychology*, 1969, 81, 557-560.

Stromeyer, C. F. Eidetikers. *Psychology Today*, 1970, 4, (November) 76-81.

Tulving, E. The effects of presentation and recall of material in free recall learning. *Journal of Verbal Learning and Verbal Behavior*, 1967, 6, 175-184.

Tulving, E. Episodic and Semantic Memory. In E. Tulving & W. Donaldson (Eds.), *Organization of memory.* New York: Academic Press, 1972.

Tulving, E., & Thomson, D. N. Retrieval processes in recognition memory: Effects of associative context. *Journal of Experimental Psychology*, 1971, 6, 175-184.

Underwood, B. J., & Schultz, R. W. *Meaningfulness and verbal learning.* Philadelphia: Lippincott, 1960.

Waugh, N. C. Presentation time and free recall. *Journal of Experimental Psychology*, 1967, 73, 39-44.

Wertheimer, M. Untersuchungen zur Lehre von der Gestalt, II. *Psychologische Forschung*, 1923, 4, 301-350.

Wilkes, A. L., & Kennedy, R. A. The relative accessibility of list items within different pause defined groups. *Journal of Verbal Learning and Verbal Behavior*, 1970, 9, 197-201.

Winston, P. H. Learning structural descriptions from examples. M.I.T. Artificial Intelligence Laboratory Project AI TR-231, 1970.

Winzenz, D. Group structure and coding in serial learning. *Journal of Experimental Psychology,* 1972, *92,* 8–19.

Winzenz, D., & Bower, G. H. Subject-imposed coding and memory for digit series. *Journal of Experimental Psychology,* 1970, *83,* 52–56.

Wiseman, G., & Neisser, U. Perceptual organization as a determinant of visual recognition memory. Paper presented at meeting of the Eastern Psychological Association, Spring 1971.

15

INTERFERENCE AND FORGETTING

Interference theory occupies an unchallenged position as the major significant analysis of the process of forgetting.

—Leo Postman

15.1. FORGETTING IN HAM

A fault found in most of the current stock of computer simulations of human memory is that they have forgotten that people forget. In the few programs that do forget (e.g., Reitman, 1965), information loss is viewed as simple decay of the strength of past memories. The research on EPAM and SAL (Feigenbaum, 1963, 1970; Hintzman, 1968; Simon & Feigenbaum, 1964; see our discussion in Section 4.2) has been the only attempt to produce simulation models that make contact with the basic facts of forgetting from long-term memory. However, as we noted in Chapter 4, these conceptions of memory are not adequate for the task of expressing the propositional character of memory.

In contrast, experimental psychologists have developed an impressive body of data and theory surrounding the process of forgetting. This, the work of the interference theorists, has been the major substantive accomplishment of American associationism. However, these efforts suffer from difficulties similar to those of EPAM and SAL. That is, the interference research has been conducted within the framework of an inadequate conception of the character of human memory. The basic unit of knowledge has pretty much still been taken to be the S-R habit, undifferentiated according to the relations among the terms; human knowledge is equated with just a list of habits. Recent papers by Underwood (1969) and Wickens (1970) recognize several different "attributes" of memories but do not go beyond cataloging some of the evidence that people can remember all sorts of things about past events. What is lacking in these efforts is an attempt to characterize the associative organization of long-term memory and how the "mind" brings that to bear in recording new facts and events, while forgetting others. Another aspect that has been conspicuously lacking is the study of interference and forgetting of sentences and textual materials. Interference theorists are probably uncomfortable analyzing the learning and forgetting of propositional materials because they have not developed any viable ideas regarding the structure of sentences (they are obviously not serial lists of words), nor any specific ideas regarding how the person brings his cognitive equipment to bear upon comprehending, storing, retrieving, and using propositional information.

In past chapters we have outlined the beginnings of a more adequate conception of human memory. In this chapter we will try to indicate how forgetting would occur in such a memory. This section discusses the basic mechanism that produces forgetting in HAM. We will illustrate how it accounts for some of the salient facts of forgetting. In Section 15.2 this theoretical conception is compared with others, and we will note how HAM can account for data previously thought to be solely favorable to other theories. However, in reviewing the recent evidence for "response-set suppression," we will find ourselves forced to make some kind of concession to the notion of a generalized loss of response availability. Section 15.3 will examine the evidence for interference and forgetting with sentences and larger linguistic units. Finally, in Section 15.4 we will present the results of efforts to obtain "relation-specific" interference.

The basic facts of forgetting that demand explanation are now fairly well documented. The learning of laboratory materials tends to interfere with memory for other laboratory material that precedes or follows it. In serial learning, this interference increases with the similarity of the two lists of items. In paired-associate learning, increasing similarity of the stimuli in the successive lists of materials increases the interfering effect, but increasing the similarity of the responses has inconsistent effects and may actually facilitate memory. Retroactive interference (RI) refers to the effect of later learned material on retention of earlier material; proactive interference (PI) refers to the effect of learning earlier material upon retention of later learned material. In this section we will focus on how HAM would handle RI. The next section considers, among other things, the problem of how HAM could be extended to deal with PI and the related matter of negative transfer.

Stimulus-Specific Interference in HAM

The mechanism for stimulus-specific interference lies in HAM's search of the GET-lists when the MATCH process is evoked to search memory for information which will match an input or probe tree. When HAM searches from a node a for associations having relation Y to a, it must serially search the list (the GET-list) of all nodes b such that $<a\ Y\ b>$ is an associative link. This list may contain many members, and HAM will search only a probabilistically determined portion of the list for an association to match the input probe. HAM always searches the GET-list from the beginning and moves down the list examining member after member, to a randomly determined depth. This serial search process was used in explaining the search-time data of Chapter 12. Since the GET-list of a given relation out of a given node is constantly updated to reflect the most recently used associations, this search routine guarantees that the most recent associations are the most likely to be examined. Consequently, the acquisition of new associations will tend to "bury" old associations and make them inaccessible when the GET-list is searched. That is, the probabilistic retrieval mechanism may not search far enough down the GET-list to find the desired association. In barest terms, this is the mechanism for retroactive inhibition in HAM.

An important feature of this search process is that it was originally motivated solely to provide for an efficient search of memory, not to fit the interference data. Since the GET-lists that must be searched can become inordinately long, it is necessary to have some mechanism to inhibit long and fruitless searches that would result in excessive verification times.

The Stop Rule

Let us consider a simple model of how the search from a memory node is terminated. The model is tentative, and little in this chapter rests on this specific formulation. However, we prefer to have something explicit to reference in later discussions of interference. Basically, it is assumed that the MATCH process will terminate after T seconds of search. Thus, the mechanisms developed in Chapter 12 may be used to give a precise characterization of the amount of memory that will be searched from a particular entry node. In that chapter we assumed that there was an exponential distribution of search times for completely examining N memory associations from a terminal node in a probe tree. This distribution had mean aN:

$$f(t) = \frac{e^{-t/aN}}{aN} \tag{1}$$

Using Equation (1) we can derive the probability that N associations will be searched by time T:

$$\text{Prob(Completing } N \text{ associations in time } T) = 1 - e^{-T/aN} \tag{2}$$

This model may be applied to particular examples to compute the probability that a particular fact will be retrieved. As an example, consider the case of a sentence in the "3-3 true" condition in the agent-location experiment described in Section 12.2. To refresh the reader's memory, that experiment varied the number of places a particular class of people (e.g., hippies) were and the number of people in a particular location (e.g., park). Thus, if "A hippie is in the park" is a "3-3 true" sentence, then hippies were in two other locations, and the park had two other people in it.

Thus, from the "hippie" node in memory, three ϵ^{-1} associations would lead to three separate propositions; similarly, three ϵ^{-1} associations would fan out from "park." Retrieval of the "hippie in park" proposition would be particularly difficult when it is the last proposition leading out of both the "hippie" node and the "park" node (as in Section 12.2, we will just ignore the contribution of search from the "in" node). Suppose, then, that when the subject calls the function GET (hippie, ϵ^{-1}), the ϵ^{-1} association leading to the proposition "A hippie is in the park" happens to be the last on the GET-list. Suppose that similar misfortunes arise when the system evokes the function GET(park, ϵ^{-1}). In this set of disastrous circumstances, HAM would have to search 21 associations from either entry node in order to verify the test assertion. We wish to calculate the probability that the subject will fail to retrieve this proposition if we fix time for retrieval, T, at, say, 2 seconds. Having estimated a to be 81 msec. for that experiment, we can determine the probability that a MATCH process will not succeed in examining 21 necessary associations in 2 seconds from Equation (2); it is Prob(failure) = $e^{-2,000/(81 \times 21)}$ = .31. Since the two MATCH processes from the two entry nodes are independent, the probability of failure of search from both is the product of the two identical values above, or .095.

Now, compare this unfortunate case with the favorable case where the "hippie in park" proposition is on the top of the two GET-lists leading from "hippie" and "park." Again, we compute the probability that the MATCH process fails from both nodes in 2 seconds, but this time the MATCH process need only consider seven associations from each node. Again, using Equation (2) we find for either node, Prob(failure) = $e^{-2000/(81 \times 7)}$ = .029. The joint probability of the failure of both MATCH processes is the product, which is .001. Comparing these two cases, the probability of successfully retrieving a proposition depends markedly upon how far down it is on the appropriate GET-lists of associations.

Assuming the "stop rule" above means that the distribution of MATCH times will be truncated at time T. Consequently, the model fit to the RT data in Chapter 12 was only approximate because it assumed that the exponential distribution of MATCH times had positive probability for values beyond any cutoff point T.

An intuitively satisfying feature of this interference mechanism is that it offers a partial explanation of the fluctuating availability of information in long-term memory. It is a common experience to try to retrieve a particular fact but to fail, only to have it later "come to mind." According to HAM, the interpretation is that a later activation of the MATCH process has scanned through long-term memory at a more rapid rate and has come to the criterion information before the cutoff time T.

This fluctuating availability not only holds over days, but also occurs from moment to moment. Upon hearing "The president hurt the dog," we might initially fail to match this to memory. That is, in searching GET-lists from "president," "hurt," and "dog," we might initially retrieve nothing appropriate. However, the probe could be reentered again and again into memory, rematched and rematched, and eventually the GET(president, ϵ^{-1}) list would be searched to the instance "Lyndon Johnson," and the GET(Johnson, S^{-1}) list would be searched to the proposition referring to that occasion when Johnson tugged on the ears of a beagle for the national news media (see Figure 15.1). In this eventuality, the proposition would be recognized. Most experimenters have observed subjects that "strain" at a memory for a while and then recall it successfully. How often a subject will reenter memory with the same probe, trying to find a match, is presumably affected by such factors as motivation, expected reward for recall, and how sure the subject is

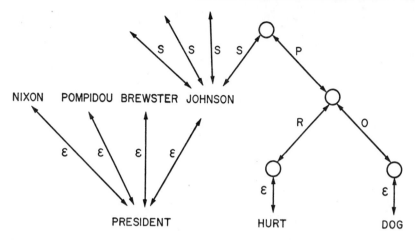

FIG. 15.1. An example of how multiple-branching associations make it difficult to verify the proposition "The president hurt the dog."

that he knows the answer. Shiff in (1970), p. 434) has reported evidence that requiring subjects to "search memory" again after an initial failure to recall may dredge up some more information.

Comparison with the Data of Retroactive Interference

The mechanism proposed above accounts for the gross fact of interference, i.e., that new information will tend to interfere with recall of old learning. What needs to be examined is the extent to which this mechanism can explain some further details of retroactive interference (abbreviated as RI). This discussion will be confined principally to the literature on the paired-associate learning (PA) of words, since most of the careful research on the topic of interference has been done in this context. We will use the same mechanisms for paired-associate learning as were developed in Section 14.2. That is, HAM will learn by embedding the two members of a paired associate into some proposition. The tree structure encoding this proposition will contain a pathway interlinking the stimulus and response of the paired-associate pair.

Stimulus Similarity

First, we examine the effects on RI of stimulus similarity. HAM clearly predicts maximal interference when the stimuli of the two lists are identical, i.e., in the so-called *A-B, A-C* paradigm. A detailed examination of how HAM produces RI in this paradigm will be informative. HAM initially established an associative path from word *A* to word *B*. During the course of second-list learning the path from *A* to *C* will have to branch off from the former *A*-to-*B* path. The *A-B* and the *A-C* paths could branch immediately at the word *A*. In this case, the *A-C* path may involve a different word-to-idea link than the *A-B* path, a circumstance illustrated in Figure 15.2*a*. In this case, word *A* is being used in two different semantic senses in the two PA pairings. Figure 15.2*a* illustrates two senses of the word "crab." As another alternative, if both propositions used the same word-to-idea link, then the

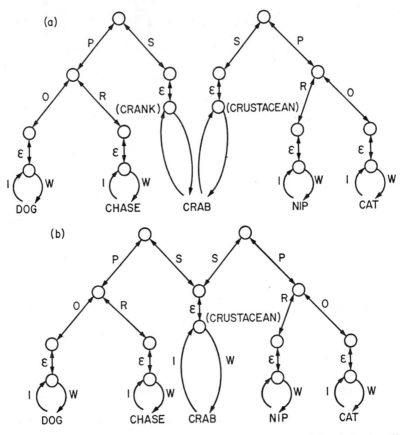

FIG. 15.2. Two alternate memory structures that encode the *A-B* pair "crab-cat" and the *A-C* pair "crab-dog."

point of branching would occur at one of the idea-to-idea associations. The illustration in Figure 15.2*b* has the branch point at the S^{-1} (subject) associations leading from the crab-instance node; other illustrations would have the branch points at somewhat different places in the tree depending on the nature of the *A-B* and *A-C* propositions the subject composes. But the important point is that the two paths from word *A* *must* branch at some point before they arrive at the words *B* and *C*.

The *A-C* path will interfere with the *A-B* path at the point of branching if that branching introduces a *conjunction* in the memory structure. To review Section 9.2, a conjunction occurs when two identically labeled associations are attached to one node. The *A-B* and *A-C* paths may branch in this identically labeled manner, or they may branch by the *A-B* path leaving the branch node *a* via one label ℓ_1 and by the *A-C* via a different label ℓ_2. These two distinct cases are illustrated in Figure 15.3*a* and *b*. In Figure 15.3*a*, an S^{-1} conjunction occurs since both associations leaving the hippie-instance have an S^{-1} label; on the other hand, in Figure 15.3*b*, one association leaves the hippie-instance node via an S^{-1} association and the other via an O^{-1} association. The theory expects RI to occur only in the former case where there is a conjunction. In the conjunctive case both the B associate and the C associate will be on the list returned when GET(a, ℓ_1) is evoked, and the C associate will be the first on the list. If HAM searches this GET-list to only a depth of 1 (which event will happen with some probability), then HAM will not be able to recall in A-B retest. We would have thus observed RI in this case. Note that it is by no means "complete" or a "massive" forgetting effect.

Let us now consider the A-B, A'-C paradigm, where the stimuli in the two lists are semantically similar (e.g., "boy-lad") and the responses different. HAM predicts RI in this circumstance, although not as much as in the A-B, A-C paradigm; and this is found. HAM predicts this finding because, with semantically similar stimuli, the A-B and the A'-C paths are likely to converge at some point. That is, the two paths which start at different word nodes A and A' are likely to contain idea nodes in common. If they do converge, then they must branch at a later point in order to accommodate the new A-C proposition. For those A-B and A'-C paths that do converge, the same mechanism will produce interference as in the A-B, A-C case. That the A-B and A-C paths will often converge is easily argued for pairs of stimuli such as "boy" and "lad." Although both words are likely to lead to the same idea node, the two paths may diverge by selection of a different instance (ϵ) for the two paired associates. Figure 15.4 illustrates how the two paired associates "boy-dog" and "lad-chair" might be encoded. Note the divergence from the idea node for boy. This is the point in this memory structure where interference would occur during retrieval.

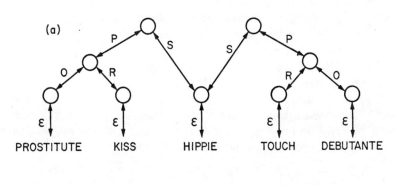

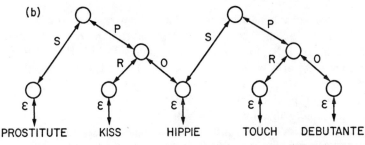

FIG. 15.3. Two alternate memory structures that encode the A-B pair "hippie-prostitute" and the A-C pair "hippie-debutante." HAM only expects RI in panel (a), where there is competition of identically labeled relations.

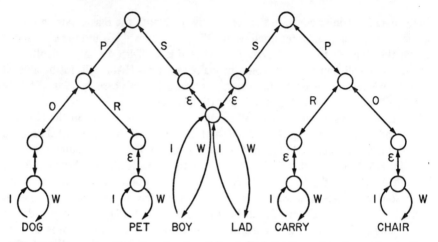

FIG. 15.4. Example of how learning the *A'-C* pair "lad-chair" may interfere with retention of the *A-B* pair "boy-dog."

Now consider the question of how HAM performs in an *A-B, C-D* paradigm—that is, when the stimuli for the two lists are dissimilar. While there is less interference in this paradigm than with similar or identical stimuli, it is known that *A-B, C-D* conditions produce reliably more interference than rest-control conditions where some unrelated activity like solving jigsaw puzzles is substituted for learning of the interpolated *C-D* list. Since the *A* and *C* stimuli are not related, there seems little possibility for a convergence of the *C-D* path with the *A-B*, as there was in the *A-B, A'-C* condition. It seems rather that forgetting in this situation results from a general loss of the availability of the *B* responses as a consequence of the interpolated *C-D* learning. This is an example of interference that is not stimulus-specific; it is difficult to produce from the mechanisms of HAM. The research regarding this general loss of response availability will be reviewed in Section 15.2 and evaluated alongside the mechanism of response-set suppression advanced by prominent interference theorists. At that point we will also consider how such data might be accommodated within HAM.

Number of Trials

Let us continue applying HAM to the basic findings in RI. The basic effects on forgetting of the number of trials of original and interpolated learning (see Slamecka & Ceraso, 1960, for a review) can be handled within HAM. We will briefly indicate how these effects would be predicted. First, it is known that RI for the *A-B* list increases with the number of interpolated trials on *A-C*. Two mechanisms would combine to produce this effect in HAM. First, with more *A-C* trials, there is a greater probability that the subject will successfully construct an *A-C* path to compete with the *A-B* path. Furthermore, as noted in Section 14.2, subjects in paired-associates experiments tend to form multiple redundant paths to interlink stimulus and response terms. With more *A-C* trials, then, more *A-C* paths should be formed that would compete with the original *A-B* path. Wherever this competition resulted in conjunctions, the *A-B* path would fall to less and less accessible regions of a GET-list.

It seems reasonable that, on the later trials of an *A-C* list, the subject is more likely to rehearse old connections than to form new ones. Consequently, later *A-C* trials should produce lesser increments in RI. It is generally observed that amount of RI does asymptote with large numbers of *A-C* trials. It has also been shown a number of times (e.g., Underwood, 1945; Postman, 1965) that it is more effective to have a number of distinct interpolated lists (i.e., *A-C*, *A-D*, etc.) than just one list, even though the same total number of IL (interpolated learning) trials are administered. That is, *m* trials on each of *n* IL lists causes more forgetting of *A-B* than *m* x *n* trials on one interpolated list. This is as it should be. With each new list HAM must learn, it will be forced to add new associative paths to compete with the originally learned paths. If those trials learning more interpolated lists had been spent overlearning the first interpolated list, then HAM might just rehearse the same *A-C* associative paths rather than construct new ones.

Consider further details of RI as the number of interpolated-learning trials on *A-C* is increased. As IL increases, the amount of RI (as measured by recall errors of *A-B*) increases monotonically, whereas the number of intrusions of *A-C* first increases, reaches a maximum at intermediate degrees of IL, then decreases with further learning of the *A-C* list. These details can be produced within HAM by using the "list discrimination tags" that are part of our representation for paired-associate learning (see especially Figure 14.4). As *A-C* training commences, a branch point in the *A-B* structure will have to be found to fit in the required *A-C* association. The increasing success in doing this accounts for the general rise in RI. However, with increasing trials on *A-C*, it becomes increasingly likely that response *C* will be tagged with an association to a "List 2" marker. If, in attempting recall of the first list associate (*A-B*), the executive monitor checks for the list membership of the retrieved association, then the "*C*-List 2" association would prevent intrusions of *C*. Thus, *C* intrusions in *A-B* recall would rise, then decline as *A-C* trials are extended, despite the fact that total RI increased. This is the standard explanation of this result (e.g., Thune & Underwood, 1943); our discussion demonstrates that the standard explanation in terms of list discrimination has a natural formulation in the mechanisms of HAM.

Another well-documented fact is that resistance to interference increases with the number of trials on the original *A-B* list. With extra *A-B* trials, HAM could form multiple paths interlinking *A* and *B*. The example in Figure 15.5 will serve to illustrate that this multiple pathing would produce in HAM greater resistance to interference. Here, "hippie" and "debutante" have been linked during *A-B* learning by two propositions: "The hippie touched the debutante" and "The debutante slapped the hippie." In *A-C* learning, "hippie" is paired with "sailor," and the subject encodes the proposition "The hippie kicked the sailor." This new proposition interferes with the "hippie touch debutante" proposition leading from the hippie-instance; but not with the "debutante slap hippie" proposition. The second proposition is not interfered with because it is a subject (S) branch that leaves the hippie-instance in the *A-C* proposition, and this branch will interfere only with earlier propositions in which that hippie-instance was the subject. In this case,

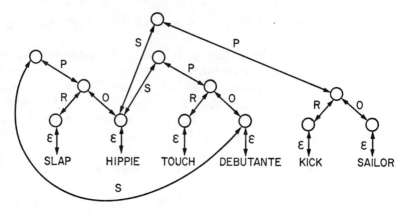

FIG. 15.5. An example of how forming two associations to encode the *A-B* pair "hippie-debutante" protects from interference by the *A-C* pair "hippie-sailor."

by encoding two original *A-B* propositions, HAM has protected itself from interference in *A-C* learning. However, the reduction in RI depends upon having at least one of the *A-B* propositions relate *A* and *B* by a different *sequence* of syntactic links than occurs for the *A-C* proposition. Of course, on later trials of original learning the subject may rehearse old *A-B* paths rather than form redundant new ones. Hence, the effect of number of original-learning trials in reducing RI should asymptote. This is clearly the case (e.g., Briggs, 1957).

In HAM, the *A-B* path is not destroyed by *A-C* learning; rather the *A-C* path (or paths) competes with it for availability. Even though HAM can no longer recall *A-B*, the path remains between *A* and *B*. Therefore, it is not surprising that the interfering effect of *A-C* quickly dissipates with one or two relearning trials on *A-B* (e.g., Osgood, 1948; Underwood, 1945). The interpretation within HAM is that these relearning trials update the "recency" of the *A-B* path, making it once again available by raising its position on the GET-list at which the branch with *A-C* paths had occurred.

One point of interest in this analysis of retroactive inhibition is that it identifies the theoretical communality between the mechanisms contributing to the increases in times to search memory in fact retrieval (reviewed in Chapter 12) and the interference mechanism. That is, the reaction times reflect the time to search particular connections on the GET-list, while the phenomenon of interference in recall occurs when the GET-list becomes longer than can be searched before a preset cutoff time. An experiment by Postman and Kaplan (1947) is particularly interesting in relating these measures. They examined the latencies with which subjects could retrieve their correct responses in the *A-B* retest. Subjects in the *A-B*, *A-C* paradigm showed consistently longer latencies than in the control condition. Moreover, although the difference in recall scores between the control and experimental subjects quickly dissipated after a few relearning trials, the latency difference was maintained. These findings suggest that even when the *A-B* path remained or became accessible on the GET-list, the interfering *A-C* connection still made its presence felt in terms of the time to search the GET-list and retrieve the *A-B* association.

Recall that in the person-location RT experiment of Section 12.2, we found that subjects had relatively little difficulty in searching through three propositions. Given this result, we have been asked why it is we postulate considerable interference between just a pair of elements, A-B and A-C. A number of technical points need to be made in response to this question. First, because of the possibility that the subject encodes multiple propositions in learning A-C, more than two propositions may have to be searched to arrive at the A-B proposition. Second, in the person-location experiment, subjects had two points from which they searched memory, whereas in the paired-associate experiment there is only one entry point, the stimulus A. If the subject has a probability p of not retrieving the proposition when one entry point is available, the probability is reduced to p^2 with two entry points. Finally, we should point out a third fact for which HAM has no compelling explanation: As propositions are more practiced, they are searched more rapidly. For instance, in our person-location experiment, the search rate parameter a was 100 msec. for the first 150 trials and only 62 msec. for the second 150 trials. Moreover, subjects in our person-location experiment already had a half hour's practice with the material before the experiment began. Thus, it would be expected that their memory structures are being searched more rapidly than in the typical paired-associates experiment where the material is only imperfectly learned. Consequently, in the person-location experiment the memory structures could be searched to a greater depth. So for these three reasons, we may expect moderate interference in the typical A-B, A-C paired-associates paradigm.

15.2. COMPARISON TO OTHER INTERFERENCE THEORIES

To use the terms of the interference literature, the mechanism that produces RI in HAM is a hybrid combination of *response competition* and *unlearning*. Like McGeoch's (1936) original notion of response competition, it is assumed that the A-B connection fails because it is overcome by one or more competing A-C connections. It is often assumed in the response-competition hypothesis that the subject must either overtly or covertly recall the competing C responses during the A-B retest. These recalled C responses compete with and hinder the subject's recall of the appropriate B responses. There are a number of well-known empirical embarrassments to this version of the response-competition hypothesis. It has been shown that most of the forgetting in A-B retest does not manifest itself as intrusions of the competing C responses, but rather as total failures to recall (e.g., Melton & Irwin, 1940; Thune & Underwood, 1943). Moreover, at high levels of IL where RI is maximal, the number of overt intrusions is very negligible. If the C responses were competing with and displacing the B responses, we would expect to see an increase in overt intrusions. Earlier, we indicated how such results can be explained by "list-discrimination" factors in HAM.

The modified–modified free recall (MMFR) experiment reported by Barnes and Underwood (1959) is another classic demonstration of the deficiencies of a simple response-competition hypothesis. Barnes and Underwood asked their subjects to recall both the B and the C responses to the A stimulus, during the retention test following A-B, A-C learning. They found that as their subjects had more A-C trials, their ability to recall the B terms decreased. It was argued that the loss of the first-list responses in this case could not be due to response competition because the subject was free to recall both responses, and in fact was even instructed to do so.

While such data embarrass the traditional response-competition mechanism, they are as expected from the interference mechanism in HAM. In HAM, even though A-C paths compete with and make A-B paths unavailable, it is not the case that C responses will be intruded in the A-B retest. Through the list-discrimination mechanism discussed earlier, HAM can inhibit C responses to A stimuli when first-list recall is requested. As noted earlier, HAM expects fewer C intrusions in A-B retest with greater IL training, which is what Melton and Irwin (1940) found.

Of course, when list discrimination fails, HAM will incorrectly recall the C response (although B was available) because C is more accessible than B. Such cases exemplify overt competition of responses, with C dominating B, which was the original response-competition thesis regarding forgetting. However, in HAM associative paths also compete for availability on the GET-lists. This means that even if HAM is urged to recall both responses as in the Barnes and Underwood MMFR experiment, it still may fail to "get at" the B response.

In this way the mechanism of interference in HAM is like the unlearning mechanism that has been traditionally advanced to account for findings such as those of Melton and Irwin or Barnes and Underwood. The unlearning postulate claims that A-C learning produces unlearning of the prior A-B associations. Underwood (1948a, 1948b) suggested that this unlearning may be similar to the phenomenon of "experimental extinction" seen in classical and instrumental conditioning; i.e., B responses are extinguished because they are evoked but not reinforced during A-C learning. (A curious paradox is that prominent contemporary accounts of experimental extinction in the animal conditioning area—e.g., Amsel, 1967; Logan, 1960; Spence, 1960—attribute extinction to response-competition-like factors such as avoidance of frustrative nonreward.) Underwood found evidence that RI decreases over the retention interval. This was attributed to "spontaneous recovery" over time of the unlearned A-B associations. Spontaneous recovery of an extinguished response is usually found in classical and instrumental conditioning paradigms. Much research has investigated the "spontaneous recovery" of verbal responses in interference paradigms. Absolute recovery of A-B is sometimes found, sometimes not, depending on a variety of circumstances such as the degree of original learning of A-B, the retention interval, and so on. Recent reviews are contained in papers by Postman, Stark, and Fraser (1968) and by Postman, Stark, and Henschel (1969).

The unlearning and the response-competition hypotheses are generally considered complementary (e.g., Keppel, 1968). Proactive interference (PI) was thought to reflect only response competition, whereas retroactive interference was assumed to reflect a combination of both factors. Unlearning was presumed to be absent in PI because the interfered-with material is learned last, so it cannot suffer from unlearning due to a subsequent interpolated task. An embarrassment for this analysis is evidence that PI is not solely a result of response competition. For instance, in an MMFR retention test the subject is asked to recall both responses to the stimulus, one from each list (i.e., both B and C). This should eliminate any interfering effects of response competition since the subject is free to give both responses. However, PI has been found in MMFR tests (e.g., Koppenaal, 1963; Koppenaal, Krull; Katz, 1965), contrary to the early prediction. But how can previous learning cause later-learned material to be unlearned? We shall return later to this issue of PI.

At this point it will be instructive to note the differences between our interference mechanism and the unlearning mechanism. The major difference is that there is no committment in our theory to notions of reinforcement and extinctive inhibition. Unlearning is often conceived of as caused by the unreinforced evocation of the B responses during A-C learning. As Melton (1961) noted, this implies that "there is some correlation between the specific responses that are unavailable in specific subjects and the specific nonreinforced intrusions of these same responses during IL [p. 184]." But there is no evidence for such a correlation. In fact, in an experiment that manipulated IL intrusion rate by guessing instructions, Keppel and Rauch (1966), found no relation between RI and intrusion rate. HAM does not require this dependence of RI on the overt elicitation of the B response. The A-B path will tend to be buried by the A-C path purely as a function of acquiring A-C. One way to keep the A-B path from sinking too far below the A-C paths on GET-lists is to require the subject to explicitly recall both the B and C responses throughout interpolated learning of A-C. Postman and Parker (1970) found, in fact, that simple instructions to maintain B responses during IL did reduce (although not eliminate) RI.

Spontaneous Recovery

One of the more persuasive pieces of evidence for the inhibitory conception of unlearning has been the demonstration of spontaneous recovery from RI. Sometimes, the number of A-B items that can be recalled actually increases over a short interval between A-C learning and retest. This is referred to as *absolute spontaneous recovery*. Sometimes, however, there is only *relative spontaneous recovery*, in which loss of A-B items is less rapid relative to their loss rate in a control condition. For instance, immediately after IL, recall of A-B items may be 70% for subjects who have had A-C interpolation but 90% for subjects without any interpolation. However, at a 24-hour delay these recall percentages may become, respectively, 60% and 70%. Thus, subjects in the A-C group have lost only 10% of the items over the 24-hour retention interval, relative to the 20% loss for the control group.

It might seem that HAM would not produce spontaneous recovery, particularly of the absolute variety. Once the A-B had been buried by the A-C path, how could it ever become available again? A possible solution to this dilemma lies in the observation that while the A-B path may not be any longer available, the B-A path may be. Recall that the branch that causes interference occurs along the path from A to B. In contrast, there is no such branching on the path from B to A. With respect to the backpath, the A-B, A-C paradigm is actually a retroactive facilitation paradigm (i.e., B-A, C-A). Therefore, should HAM in its random mental wanderings, ever generate the B responses during the interval between A-C learning and retest, it is likely to revive its memory of the B-A backpath. As a consequence of reactivating that connection, the forward A-B path would rise to the top of the GET-list at that point where the branch occurred with the A-C paths. Hence, B would become once again available as a response to A. Of course, the probability that the subject will think about the B response and its backpath to A, and thus revive the forepath, will increase with the interval between A-C learning and the retention test. Hence we would have the phenomena of spontaneous recovery.

There are two lines of evidence which suggest this "backpath" analysis of so-called spontaneous recovery. First, no spontaneous recovery can be found with "associative matching" tests under comparable conditions which produce recovery in the case of PA recall (L. Postman, personal communication, 1972). In associative matching tests, the stimuli and responses of the A-B list are given in scrambled sets, and the subject must pair them according to the A-B pairings learned. This is a kind of "pair-recognition" test. HAM can perform pair recognition on the basis of either the A to B path or the B to A path (see also Wolford, 1971); so A-C learning should not seriously degrade pair recognition. But more importantly, since pair-recognition tests already tap both A-B and B-A, there can be no evidence of "spontaneous recovery" over time due to the B-A path inadvertently making the A-B path more available than the A-C path.

A second bit of positive evidence has been provided by Merryman and Merryman (1972). They considered the increase in A-B recall (following A-C interpolation) which accompanies repeated nonreinforced test trials with the subject trying to recall A-B. HAM expects some improvement in A-B recall over repeated test trials for two reasons: first, successive retrievals at the branching point out of the A stimulus are independent, and a low A-B associate which is not retrieved on initial trials may be retrieved at later opportunities, recognized as the first-list response, and so updated to the top position in the GET-list. The second reason for improved test performance is the backpath argument given above: repeated tests provide more opportunities for the subject to scan the list of B responses retrievable from the context cues (i.e., "LIST 1 contains responses B_1, B_2, ..., B_m"), and to recognize the backpath from a B to its appropriate A stimulus. This then reinstates that A-B forepath to have priority over the A-C forepath, thus appearing to be "spontaneous recovery" of the unlearned A-B pair.

Merryman and Merryman (1972) tried to eliminate this second source of recovery. To do this, they arranged the interpolated learning so that both forward and backward associations were "unlearned." Following A-B learning, the interpolated list contained D-B pairs as well as A-C pairs—the former to lower the availability of the B-A path, and the latter to lower the availability of the A-B path. The series of 10 nonreinforced tests for A-B retention which followed showed considerably less "recovery" in this condition of double unlearning than in the condition of just A-C forward unlearning only. The result is relevant to HAM's interpretation of "spontaneous recovery" of A-B over time if it is supposed that the multiple test trials in the Merrymans' experiment are simply measuring explicitly what is implicitly occurring over an "unfilled rest interval" when the A-B associations recover.

This analysis also suggests why subjects display progressively increasing proactive inhibition with the interval between A-C learning and retest. The subject is ruminating over old *A-B* connections and reviving them so that they have a degree of availability greater than *A-C*. Of course, on the traditional two-factor theory, the reason for increasing PI was the recovery of the *A-B* associations. What is novel in our account is the belief that the subject's conscious ruminations are an important causal factor. Houston (1969) has performed an interesting experiment relevant to this issue. He supposed that PI was particularly marked in the normal laboratory experiment because subjects were expecting to be retested. Therefore, in the retention interval they would rehearse *A-B* pairs, making the *A-C* pairs less available. Houston's experiment tested this possibility by using four groups of subjects, two learning only a single *A-C* list, and two learning *A-B* and then *A-C* lists. Within each condition, one group was told that it should return to the lab in 7 days for a retention test for what had been learned, whereas the other group was told (falsely) that the experiment was completely finished. Six days later, the experimenter unexpectedly telephoned each subject and administered the MMFR retention test over the telephone. The recall results were entirely consistent with the implicit-rehearsal hypothesis; that is, (*a*) subjects expecting to receive a retention test showed significant PI, comparing recall by the double-list group to that by the single-list group, whereas (*b*) subjects not expecting to be tested did not show significant PI on the MMFR test, the double-list group recalling the *A-C* pairs just as well as did the single-list controls. In addition, those subjects expecting to be tested reported that they had consciously rehearsed the test lists several times throughout the retention interval. Such results (which have been replicated— Houston, 1971) provide a plausible interpretation of PI in the usual MMFR tests—a result that could not be accommodated by the two-factor theory that attributed PI to response competition.

The Differentiation Hypothesis

Another dimension of complexity was added to interference theory by Underwood (1945) when he proposed the *differentiation* hypothesis. The basic idea is that in *A-B, A-C* learning the subject requires some means to distinguish when to respond with *B* and when with *C*. Underwood supposed that subjects use various temporal and contextual cues to differentiate between Lists 1 and 2 but that the discriminative power of these cues would deteriorate as the retention interval increased. Birnbaum (1965) has shown that in an MMFR test, the subject's ability to identify the list membership of a response does deteriorate from about 99% immediately, down to about 78% at one week's delay. So clearly, list discrimination may be another factor promoting both PI and RI in non–MMFR recall tests.

HAM contains a reasonably satisfactory analysis of list discrimination and the causes of its deterioration over time. This mechanism was developed more fully elsewhere (Anderson & Bower, 1972), and only its basic characteristics will be indicated here. List discrimination occurs by means of retrieval of contextual information stored with the elements of the list (the stimuli and/or responses). This contextual information constitutes basically a description of the situation in which the responses occurred. On the basis of the contextual information, the subject makes a decision about whether the word appeared in List 1 or 2. With the passage of time, the word will occur in additional contexts, and new context descriptions will be stored with it. These will tend to interfere with and make less available the old contextual descriptions. The mechanism of interference among contextual descriptions is the same as our mechanism for interference among responses to the same stimuli in PA, namely, loss of availability of associative paths. So, HAM's basic interference mechanism is responsible for the loss of list discrimination over time and for the consequent misidentification of B and C responses in a paired-associates paradigm.

Response Set Suppression

The basic notion of list differentiation and its role in retention is an important addition to interference theory. We use the idea in HAM, and try to suggest the bases for list identification. We are somewhat less sympathetic to the use of list-differentiation principles to bolster the theory of response-set suppression (see Postman, Stark, & Fraser, 1968), an approach that has become somewhat popular in the recent literature of interference theory.

The hypothesis is that during A-C learning following A-B learning, the subject soon comes to confine his response selections to the C response set and to avoid or "suppress" the B response set (which produces intrusions). The response-suppression mechanism is assumed to show "inertia," so that once it is set to select from the C responses, this setting persists willy-nilly for a while, causing difficulty in recalling the B responses on an MMFR retention test. Such assumptions predict RI, especially on tests that require the B responses to be recalled (rather than recognizing A-B pairs presented for test); the assumptions also imply that RI will appear strongly in the A-B, C-D paradigm despite the absence in this design of stimulus-specific interference. It is further hypothesized that the set to select C responses and suppress B responses "spontaneously dissipates" over the retention interval, so that eventually neither response set will be dominant. This hypothesis of the dissipation of response-set suppression predicts, correctly, the A-B recall will recover from RI in the A-B, A-C paradigm; it also predicts, correctly again, that just as much recovery of A-B occurs in the A-B, C-D paradigm as in the A-B, A-C paradigm (see Postman, Stark, and Henschel, 1969).

We personally find this notion of *response-set suppression* unattractive. The mechanism is unexplained, it seems disturbingly ad hoc, and its theoretical properties are not yet fully developed. To postulate that the subject is a helpless victim of a perseverating tendency to suppress B responses runs counter to the increasing acceptance of the importance of cognitive control and the speed with which people can switch their "cognitive set" or search strategies. But our theoretical biases are not at issue here. Let us examine the empirical evidence for response-set suppression. It is useful to discriminate and examine separately three empirical claims that have been made by its promoters: (*a*) there is a generalized competition between B and C responses for availability; (*b*) the mechanism underlying this competition is the conscious or unconscious *suppression* of one entire set of responses; and (*c*) all RI observed in the A-B, A-C paradigm is a consequence of this generalized response loss—there is no stimulus-specific interference as postulated in HAM. The available evidence forces acceptance of claim (*a*), is rather weak with respect to claim (*b*), but clearly refutes claim (*c*). We now review this evidence.

Generalized Response Loss

It seems clear that as interpolated learning progresses, the subject's ability to access the original responses deteriorates, while the interpolated responses become ever more available. After IL, the originally learned responses gradually recover in strength at the expense of the availability of the IL responses. The facts in this case evoke metaphorical imagery of an army of OL responses and an army of IL responses battling for control of the high ground of response availability. Using the *A-B, A-C* paradigm Ceraso and Henderson (1965, 1966) have shown that the *B* responses become more available over a 24-hour interval after *A-C* learning, but that *C* responses become less available as measured in either MMFR or free recall.

Postman and Warren (1972) have examined the effect of the temporal point of the interpolated learning in the interval between original learning and its relearning. They found that the point of maximal interference was just before relearning, and this was true for both *A-B, A-C* and *A-B, C-D* designs. Newton and Wickens (1956) had reported similar results. The interpretation is that the *B* responses recover their availability in the interval between *A-C* learning and before retest. Lehr, Frank, and Mattison (1972) have shown that interpolation of free-recall learning can also have an interfering effect on *A-B* retention, although the interference is not as strong as that caused by new paired-associate learning. Thus, simply requiring the subject to learn and make available a new set of responses interferes with *A-B* recall. Moreover, the spontaneous recovery of the *A-B* list over the retention interval was about the same for either source of interference. This suggests that spontaneous recovery may be largely a matter of recovery of response availability.

There is also some evidence that requiring the subjects to free-recall the *B* responses after interpolated *A-C* learning will reduce the interfering effect. Postman, Burns, and Hasher (1970) found that reexposure to the *B* responses had a beneficial effect for the weak *A-B* pairs (i.e., those correctly anticipated only a few times in acquisition), but there was no effect of free recall on the strong *A-B* pairs. Cofer, Faile, and Horton (1971) report extensive research on the effect of interpolated study and free recall of *B* responses. Free-recall tests on the *B* responses were given either during or after learning of the interpolated list. Either procedure reduced *A-B* forgetting in the *A-B, A-C* paradigm. However, none of their various manipulations were able to completely eliminate RI in the *A-B, A-C* paradigm, nor to eliminate the greater RI in this paradigm than in the *A-B, C-D* paradigm, Thus, while response availability is clearly one factor in RI, there appears to also be a role left for stimulus-specific interference.

Evidence for the Suppression Mechanism

The research reviewed shows that general loss of response availability is one factor contributing to forgetting. But what is the evidence for a response-set suppression mechanism? Need we believe that a selector mechanism, "suffering from inertia," is withholding the *B* responses? The evidence for such a mechanism is presently not very compelling.

Some of the existing evidence derives from the assumption that the subject will show more inertia in repressing B responses the more difficulty these B responses produce in retarding A-C acquisition. Postman, Keppel, and Stark (1965), Friedman and Reynold (1967), Birnbaum (1968), and Shulman and Martin (1970) have examined the effect of manipulating the similarity between the B and C sets of responses. The consistent finding is that there is more RI when the B and C responses come from the same class (e.g., words of the same conceptual category in the Shulman and Martin study). It is argued that since the response classes are similar to one another, the responses would tend to compete more during A-C learning, the selector mechanism would have to become even more discriminating to keep out B responses during A-C learning, and would consequently show more inertia in the A-B retest. The logic of this argument is not unassailable.

Postman, Stark, and Fraser (1968) have shown that, when the subject is presented with A and its second-list response C and asked to recall its first-list response B, RI is greater than when the subject is asked either to recall just B or to recall both B and C to the stimulus of A alone. They suggest that this greater interference is because presentation of the C response maintains the bias of the selector mechanism in favor of the C response over the B response.

Unfortunately, manipulations designed to bias the selector mechanism do not always have their intended effect. Postman and Stark (1965) reexposed subjects at the end of IL to the B responses by means of an incidental task. The hope was to increase the dominance of the B responses. The tactic succeeded in that the B responses were more likely to be given first before the C responses in MMFR. However, the amount of RI was unchanged. That is, the B response was no more likely to be recalled, despite the fact it was more likely to be emitted first when it was recalled. So, a manipulation that should have reduced the RI due to the inappropriate suppression failed.

To summarize, then, the evidence reviewed does not provide a conclusive case for the concept of response-set suppression.

Evidence for Stimulus-Specific Interference

A question asked in the recent interference literature is whether there is any evidence for the loss of specific A-B associations in the A-B, A-C paradigm, as opposed to the hypothesis that all RI is a matter of general loss of response availability. If one tries to explain all forgetting in terms of generalized response loss, it becomes problematical why there is more RI in the A-B, A-C paradigm, where there is opportunity for stimulus-specific interference, than in the A-B, C-D paradigm, where this opportunity does not exist. It has been suggested (e.g., Postman & Stark, 1969) that the response-set suppression may be more severe and more persistent with A-C interpolation because the occurrence of explicit B intrusions early during A-C learning calls forth greater efforts to suppress B terms, or efforts to find more bases for distinguishing B and C responses and thus to edit out and suppress the B terms.

Postman and Stark attempted to test this notion with a multiple-choice PA retention test that would negate the effects of response-set suppression. That is, instead of having to recall the B responses to the A stimuli, the subject was given a set of possible responses and asked to select the correct one. They argued that in this circumstance, since the subject was given the correct B response along with the irrelevant distractors (incorrect B responses), there was no way to suppress the set of B responses. Consequently, they predicted and found no RI with such tests in the A-B, A-C paradigm relative to a rest control. There was also no RI in the A-B, C-D paradigm with the multiple-choice recognition procedure. Thus, it would appear that in an associative matching test that eliminates the factor of response availability, there is no RI for either paradigm.

Several objections can be advanced regarding the conclusions from the Postman and Stark experiment. First, other researchers (Delprato, 1971; Garskof, 1968; Garskof & Sandak, 1964) have found some RI in a response-matching task. Second, a model like HAM does not predict much RI in the A-B, A-C paradigm when retest involves response matching. As noted before, if HAM were given the B response as one choice in a set of alternatives, it could determine that B was the correct one either by (a) finding a path from A to B, or by (b) finding a path from B to A. The possibility of using this second path, or backpath, is what is distinctive about the multiple-choice task, and it is the reason HAM predicts little or no RI (see Wolford, 1971). The only standard PA paradigm which HAM expects to produce large RI in a multiple-choice test is the A-B, A-Br paradigm—that is, when the responses and stimuli are kept in the interpolated list but are just re-paired in new ways. There should be considerable RI in this circumstance because there will be branching on both forward and backward paths of the old A-B structure. In fact, Postman and Stark did find quite large RI in this circumstance, even in a multiple-choice test, just as HAM would predict.

Several recent experiments support this analysis of the Postman and Stark experiment. Anderson and Watts (1971) tested first-list retention using one of three types of unpaced multiple-choice tests. When each multiple-choice test for A-B included the specific competing response, C, from the second list, there was a substantial amount of RI, whereas no RI appeared when the multiple-choice tests contained only first-list responses or noncompeting second-list responses. Recent experiments by Merryman (1971) and by Greenberg and Wickens (1972) are particularly enlightening on this issue. They guaranteed that backward associations were unlearned by having the subjects learn both A-D and B-E during interpolated learning after originally learning A-B. They found significant RI in a multiple-choice test when the backward associations were selectively interfered with. Postman and Stark (1972) have criticized the design of these experiments, but have replicated this result, although their effect was not statistically significant.

Another line of evidence commonly given against stimulus-specific interference comes from the apparent independence of A-B and A-C recall in MMFR tests (see Greeno, 1969; Martin, 1971). That is, the probability of retrieving the B response to the A stimulus in MMFR appears to be independent of whether or not the C response is retrieved—i.e., $P(B) = P(B|C)$. This would appear to provide a substantial embarrassment to a model like HAM, since it predicts that the availability of the B response decreases as a consequence of competing A-C paths. Hence, one might expect that, conditional on recall of C, the number of A-C paths displacing the original A-B paths would be greater, so that recall of B would be less likely.

However, a serious problem in interpreting the data indicating independence of associations is that it is average data pooled over many subjects and items (i.e., *A* terms). As Hintzman (1972) has recently observed:

> Thus, quite apart from any theoretical prediction, one should expect to find a positive relation between recall of *B* and *C*. Good subjects will tend to recall both *B* and *C* while poor subjects will recall neither, and easily encoded stimuli will tend to elicit both responses while hard to encode stimuli will not [p. 261].

Thus, Hintzman's argument is that the positive relation due to subject and item differences may be cancelling out the negative relation due to item-specific interference. Martin and Greeno (1972) countered Hintzman's criticisms by presenting data that showed that independence held for good and poor subjects, for easy and difficult items, and for any combination of these two factors. Basically, the variance in subject ability or item differences was not sufficiently large to introduce a substantial positive relation between the average recall of *B* and *C* items. Nonetheless, Hintzman's argument might hold if there were strong subject-by-item interactions in that some stimuli are easily encoded for some subjects and other stimuli for other subjects. This variance in the effectiveness of particular stimuli for particular subjects could be very large and hide a negative relation due to the stimulus-specific interference. Unfortunately, it is difficult to estimate empirically the magnitude of subject-by-item interactions. But because of this point, the empirical phenomena of independence of associations is at best inconclusive evidence against stimulus-specific interference. There are several plausible sources of strong positive covariance in *B* and *C* availability which makes the failure to find a negative covariance uninterpretable.

The most clearly devastating evidence against the hypothesis that all RI is due to general response competition comes from demonstrations of interference with mixed-list designs. That is, some of the items in the interpolated list are *A-C* pairs with respect to certain first-list *A-B* pairs, whereas other second-list pairs are functionally *C-D* pairs. If RI is greater for those *A-B* pairs whose stimuli are paired with new responses in IL, such evidence would indicate that particular *A-C* associations interfere with particular *A-B* associations. Birnbaum (1970) has reported weak and nonsignificant effects in this direction. Ceraso (1964) found evidence for specific interference in a mixed-list design but only when OL items were well learned. Merryman (1971), Weaver, Duncan, and Bird (1972), and Wichawut and Martin (1971) have also reported evidence for stimulus-specific interference of varying magnitudes. Very impressive evidence for stimulus-specific interference in a mixed-list design comes from our research reported in the fourth section of this chapter. Deliberate and concerted efforts were made to produce massive stimulus-specific interference; *A-B* retention when followed by *C-D* items was 84%, whereas only about 50% retention was obtained with *A-C* interpolation. In light of these many results, there can be no doubt that there is stimulus-specific interference in the *A-B*, *A-C* paradigm.

In conclusion, most of the forgetting in the *A-B*, *C-D* paradigm appears to be a matter of loss of general response availability, but stimulus-specific interference also plays an important role in the *A-B, A-C* paradigm. This explains why manipulations reinstating *B* responses improve recall in both paradigms, but do not eliminate the difference between the two paradigms (e.g., Cofer, Faile, & Horton, 1971). It also explains why there is little difference between *A-C* and *C-D* interpolation in terms of reducing free recall of the old *B* responses, while there is a considerable difference in terms of cued recall of old *A-B* associates (e.g., Delprato & Garskof, 1969; Keppel, Henschel, & Zavortink, 1969).

A Mechanism for Generalized Response Competition

We clearly have to admit generalized response competition as a fact of life. The theoretical question is how to conceive of it. One approach would be to assign strengths or availability measures to each response, and to make the probability of recall in a paired-associates paradigm a function of both the response strength and the intactness of an associative path. In Chapter 10 we were forced to assume a similar response-availability factor to account for the detailed characteristics of the recall data from sentence-memory experiments. We could assume that these response availabilities behave in an appropriate manner, increasing with repeated exposure to the response, but decreasing with exposure to other responses. Thus, the response strength of any particular item is both a function of the total time spent studying it and the time devoted to making other responses available. This viewpoint is similar to Slamecka's (1969) hypothesis which supposes that the probability of recall of an item is a function of both the absolute time spent studying it and the relative amount of the total study time devoted to that item as opposed to others. Slamecka shows that this hypothesis predicts the basic interference effects associated with temporal manipulations. The problem with the hypothesis, of course, is that it is not really a mechanism at all, but rather only a compact description of the results. We will attempt an alternative formulation that is compatible with the mechanisms of HAM.

The formulation we shall propose is very similar to McGovern's (1964) analysis of the role of contextual stimuli in paired-associate learning. We shall identify the concept of "response availability" with the association of a response to the contextual stimuli of the experimental situation. In FRAN (see Section 14.4) there is an explicit model of how the responses in a list can become connected to the contextual stimuli. It will be remembered that FRAN succeeded in free-recalling responses by building and tagging associative paths that permit access to the responses from the list-marker, which was FRAN's concept of the list context. In the following discussion, *X* will denote the list-marker or contextual cues. Thus, in learning the first list of *A-B* pairs, the subject is conceived to be simultaneously learning the *X-A* and *X-B* pairs. That is, associative paths would develop to connect the items *A* and *B* to *X*. In learning an interpolated *C-D* list, *X-C* and *X-D* paths would be learned, thus to compete with and to make less available the old *X-A*, and *X-B* paths. Moreover, by the same mechanism as outlined above for spontaneous recovery of the *A-B* connection, the *X-A* and *X-B* paths should recover over the retention interval. These statements correspond substantially to the assumptions regarding the buildup and dissipation of suppression of List 1 responses during List 2 learning.

Although this proposed contextual unlearning notion appears plausible, some further thought is required to show its relevance for RI. The question, in brief, is why should loss of the *X-B* connection seriously affect recall of the *A-B* connection? This issue has not received a detailed analysis in the interference literature. In the following we therefore construct a plausible explanation for how *X-B* unlearning could affect *A-B* recall.

Basically, the idea is that recall of response *B* to stimulus *A* can occur either if there is an intact *forward* association leading from *A* to *B*, or if there is an intact *backward* association from *B* to *A* and the subject can generate the *B* response (and possible others in List 1) from an intact *X-B* association (see Wolford, 1971). We may conceive of performance within an *A-B* recall trial to proceed as follows:

1. Check for a forward path from cue *A*: if one exists, give the response to which it leads; if none exists, go to step 2.

2. Retrieve List 1 responses at random from the list of *X-B* connections; for each response generated, check if it has a backward path to the current stimulus.

3. If so, give that as the overt response.

4. If the candidate response has a backward path to a different stimulus than the current test cue, then eliminate that response from the current "guessing pool" to that test cue.

5. If the candidate response has no backward association, then put it into the guessing pool.

6. Return to *X* and try to generate a new List 1 response (i.e., go back to step 2).

If the correct response has not been found by either a forward or a backward association by the end of a certain time, then the person either omits giving any answer, or he guesses randomly from the reduced set of alternatives in his guessing pool. These are plausible guesses, since they are known to be on List 1 but are not known to belong to other stimuli.

The foregoing outlines a very rational guessing strategy for a subject to use if he has forgotten (or not yet learned) the forward connection from *A* to *B*. In conjunction with the notion of loss of availability of specific connections (backward or forward), this analysis has a number of implications regarding different interference paradigms. For example, the *A-B, C-D* paradigm will exhibit RI to the extent that *X-B* associations are unlearned during *C-D* and consequently the *B* response is not available to be considered as a guess or examined for a backpath to cue *A*. This assumes that there will be some base-level forgetting of forward associations in the rest-control group (for a variety of reasons). Roughly speaking, the probability (*P*) of *B* recall to the *A* cue will be:

$$P = f + (1 - f)bc \tag{3}$$

where *f* is the probability of retrieving the correct forward path, *c* is the probability that response *B* is retrieved from the *X-B* connection, and *b* is the likelihood that it has a backward path to *A*. Compared to the *A-B* rest controls, subjects learning in the *A-B, C-D* paradigm will have a lower value of *c* in Equation (3) due to unlearning of *X-B*. But the magnitude of variation in *P* with *c* depends on $(1 - f)$—that is, some substantial loss of forward but not backward associations is required to cause an appreciable difference.

It seems reasonable to suppose that the parameter *c*, giving the probability that the *B* response is retrieved from *X*, should increase with the time the subject has to respond. That is, if the subject is given more time to respond, he has longer to search for and access the appropriate *B* response from *X*. This implies that the effects of manipulating response availability should be stronger with unpaced retention tests when the subject has unlimited time to make his recall. There is some evidence that this is the case. For instance, Cofer, Faile, and Horton (1971) found that reinstatement of first-list responses by free recall reduced RI in an unpaced recall test, but not in a paced test. In fact, most of the experiments cited as evidence for the importance of response availability used unpaced retention tests.

Let us summarize HAM's analysis of interference in a paired-associate task. Four sets of associative paths must be considered: the *A-B* paths that are particularly prominent in forward recall, the *B-A* paths that become very important in backward recall and in recognition tests, the *B-X* paths that permit list discrimination, and the *X-B* paths that determine response availability (and, partly, free-recall performance). Forgetting is both a matter of new paths being encoded and displacing old paths, and of old paths being revived and displacing new paths. It seems that this analysis of the associative connections underlying paired-associate learning and this displacement mechanism will handle many of the facts of retroactive and proactive inhibition.

Negative Transfer

A remaining problem is to provide some analysis of the phenomena of negative transfer. That is, after learning *A-B*, it is frequently found that it is harder to learn *A-C* than to learn a new pair *C-D*. In part, this can be viewed as an instance of proactive interference. That is, in *A-C* learning each pair must be retained over the interval from when it was acquired on trial *n*−1 until the time it is tested on trial *n*. This is a retention interval over which the mechanisms of PI may operate to reduce the probability of successful reproduction of *C* to *A* on trial *n*. However, PI over such short intervals is typically weak, whereas the amount of negative transfer relative to the *C-D* group can be considerable. Therefore, it seems unlikely that one can successfully account for negative transfer by identifying it as solely proactive interference. Moreover, we have conjectured that PI is a consequence of the subject's conscious ruminations about old *A-B* associations. But during the retention interval defined by one trial to the next of *A-C* learning, the subject is unlikely to have much time for leisurely thinking over his old associations.

Subjects' introspections in such an experiment suggest a slightly different mechanism that might be important for producing negative transfer. They frequently say that when seeing the pair *A-C*, they will call to mind the old *A-B* pair. Thus, time and effort are expended wastefully reminiscing over the old *A-B* memories, time that is more profitably spent learning the new pairs in the *C-D* case. This conception of negative transfer is testable. Subjects could be asked to introspect out loud during second-list acquisition. It should be found that probability of recall of a second-list pair is a positive function of the amount of time spent considering it rather than other matters. It should be the same function of rehearsal time for A-C as for C-D pairs. However, the amount of time given to rehearsing the C-D pairs should be greater than for the A-C pairs. We would expect to observe A-B reminiscences creeping into the introspections and taking time away from A-C rehearsal.

Possibly as important as its effect on A-C study time is the fact that "stolen" A-B rehearsals would alter the relative availability of A-B and A-C paths. In such cases, A-B paths may come to temporarily dominate the A-C paths on the relevant GET-lists. So, in this way, this suggested mechanism of negative transfer is like that for proactive interference. The only difference is that revival of A-B paths is not the result of a random free association occurring sometime in a rather long interval; rather, it occurs in response to the stimulus of A-C presentations.

15.3. INTERFERENCE WITH LINGUISTIC MATERIALS

This review of interference has so far been confined to examining interference effects in learning and retention of arbitrary paired associates. The question naturally arises as to whether HAM's mechanism will generalize to provide an adequate account of forgetting as it occurs with linguistic materials. It has often been claimed (e.g., Ausubel, 1963; Ausubel & Blake, 1958; Ausubel, Robbins, & Blake, 1959; Miller, 1951) that the concepts of interference theory would not generalize from nonsense syllables and single words to meaningful linguistic material. If this were the case, it would be disastrous for our theoretical enterprise, since we have argued that interference in paired-associate learning depends crucially upon interference among meaningful propositions that the subject has constructed to learn the pairs. Therefore, it is crucial that HAM's predictions hold for propositional materials. The evidence reviewed in this section establishes that natural-language materials show interference effects in conformity to HAM's expectations.

Several early attempts to produce interference with prose passages (Ausubel, Robbins, & Blake, 1959; Deese & Hardman, 1954) turned up negative results. For instance, Ausubel et al. found that a passage about Christianity did not interfere (proactively or retroactively) with retention of a passage about Buddhism (comparing such subjects to rest controls). Slamecka (1960a, 1960b) noted that the experimental methodology used with such materials was rather different from that typically used in serial-learning experiments. Rather than the serial anticipation method of presenting the words one at a time and asking for recall of the next word, the whole passage had been presented, and the subject received a recognition test for the substance or gist of the text. Slamecka demonstrated that if the sentence material is presented by the serial anticipation method, with verbatim recall required, the typical interference results are obtained. Basically, this just demonstrates that the subject can treat connected discourse as a random list of words, and if he does, the typical interfering effects are obtained. However, Slamecka's research leaves unchallenged the claim that when connected discourse is normally comprehended and remembered, the laws of interference do not apply.

More recent research (Anderson & Myrow, 1971; Crouse, 1971; Myrow & Anderson, 1972) has challenged this negative conclusion and produced clear evidence for interference with naturally acquired connected discourse. The basic problem with the earlier research on the topic is that it failed to distinguish between the conditions when retroactive facilitation should obtain and when retroactive interference should obtain. When two similar passages are memorized, one must pay careful attention to details of which aspects can be expected to show interference and which not to. If the same proposition from the first passage is repeated in the second passage, then one obviously expects memory for that proposition to improve. When completely different propositions occur in the two passages, no effect can be expected. The only time that interference is to be predicted is when propositions are partially repeated and partially changed. But even in this condition, interference is expected only if the right method of testing is used. That is, one must probe with the repeated portion of the proposition and ask for recall of the portion that is not repeated. In terms of the concepts derived from paired associates, the text must exemplify an *A-B, A-C* paradigm, and testing must probe for recall with *A*. The early experiments did not selectively examine changed propositions with the appropriate test.

The experiment by Crouse (1971) is a good example of research that met the necessary conditions for interference. Subjects first learned a biographical passage such as the following:

JOHN PAYTON

Payton was born in Liverpool at the end of October, 1810. When he was only five years of age, his father, who was a servant, was killed by a robber. Before Payton was thirteen, his mother died of appendicitis leaving him the eldest of six orphans. After the death of his parents he was left in the hands of his paternal uncle. Meanwhile, he was attending a small school at Greenmount. After four years of apprenticeship (1826-30), Payton entered Gate's hospital, Brentford, as a medical student, remained there for almost two years, and received a certificate allowing him to practice. However, his ambitions had now turned to writing poetry, and in the spring of 1832 he went to Rydal Lake and began his long poem *Ode to Jupiter*, which he finished the following autumn. By the time he was trying seriously to write poetry, his brother Matthew left England and emigrated to America, and in the same year (1834) his brother Franklin died of pneumonia. Yet, from the autumn of 1835 through the summer of 1836 Payton composed his best poetry. Soon after this, however, he began to suffer hemorrhages in the lungs, and after much misery, he died in Geneva on April 12, 1859.

After studying and recalling such a paragraph, two related passages were interpolated such as the following:

SAMUEL HUGHES

Hughes was born in Paddington at the end of October, 1805. When he was only nine years of age, his father, who was a weaver, was killed in a swimming accident. Before Hughes was fourteen, his mother died of diphtheria leaving him the eldest of three orphans. After the death of his parents he was left in the hands of his grandfather. Meanwhile, he was attending a small school at Woolwich. After four years of apprenticeship (1821-25), Hughes entered Royal hospital, Camberwell, as a medical student, remained there for almost four years, and received a certificate allowing him to practice. However, his ambitions had now turned to writing poetry, and in the spring of 1829 he went to Eaton Square and began his long poem *Dreams on End*, which he finished the following autumn. By the time he was trying seriously to write poetry, his brother Richard left England and emigrated to America, and in the same year (1831) his brother Arthur died of pneumonia. Yet, from the autumn of 1832 through the summer of 1833, Hughes composed his best poetry. Soon after this, however, he began to suffer hemorrhages in the lungs, and after much misery, he died in Paris on March 18, 1846.

This similar paragraph is much like the original one except that many particulars regarding names, places, ages, dates, causes of death, etc., have been changed. Following study of two such interpolated passages, retention of the original passage was tested; performance in this condition was contrasted with retention observed after interpolation of two unrelated passages (about a hypothetical island and a hypothetical library). Retention was tested by questions which selectively probed for propositions that had been changed in the interpolated passage (e.g., Payton was born in what city?). On the retention test for the original passage, subjects receiving interpolation of unrelated passages were able to recall as many facts as were recalled by rest controls who had no interpolated material. However, subjects with the related passages interpolated correctly recalled only 54% as much as the controls. Clearly, massive retroactive interference can be obtained if the experiment is done properly.

An Experiment: Extension of Crouse's Result

We have performed an experiment that elaborates upon these results of Crouse. An interesting point about the passages that Crouse employed is that while a great many specific details were changed across related passages, the general structure or general nature of the predications is repeated across passages, as are many other specific facts. For instance, consider the first three sentences of the two paragraphs from Crouse's experiment:

> Payton was born in *some* city at the end of October in *some* year. When he was only *some* years of age, his father, who was *some* occupation, was killed by *some* means. Before Payton was *some* age, his mother died of *some* illness leaving him the eldest of *some* number of orphans.

The various *somes* indicate the changed specific details. It was memory for these specifics that Crouse tested. However, many other specifics are not changed; and of course, all general facts remain unchanged (e.g., that Payton was born in some month and that he was born in some year both will be called "general facts"; that Payton was born at the end of October will be called a "repeated specific fact").

Therefore, we thought we should be able to show, in a free-recall experiment, facilitation in memory for the repeated specifics and for the repeated general facts. That is, all general facts should be better recalled after interpolation of a related passage than after interpolation of an unrelated passage. However, the subjects should be better able to recall the specifics of the general facts only when these specifics have not been changed in the interpolated material. We also attempted a replication of Crouse's experiment by further cueing recall of the changed specific facts.

In all, 26 subjects participated in this experiment. Thirteen studied two related passages interpolated before retention testing, and thirteen studied two unrelated passages. The passages were those used by Crouse, slightly modified for this experiment. A set of 20 questions were constructed for cued recall, most of which were identical to Crouse's. (We wish to express our appreciation to Dr. Crouse for supplying us with copies of his experimental materials.) The twenty questions for the original passage queried all but two of the changed specifics in the passage. The paragraphs were presented to the subjects one sentence at a time by means of an overhead projector at the rate of one sentence per 5 seconds. After presentation of the paragraph, subjects read projected numbers for 20 seconds to reduce recall from short-term memory. Then the subjects received a second study trial with the same paragraph. Following the second study trial and 20 seconds of number reading, 6 minutes were given for the subject to write his free recall of the paragraph on a sheet which was provided to him. The experimenter then handed out a sheet containing 20 questions, interrogating specific facts from the passages. The subjects were instructed to write their answers and then to turn over their recall sheets. This cued test usually required 2 to 3 minutes. The identical study and testing procedures were used for the original passage and for the two interpolated passages. Following the third paragraph, retention of the original paragraph was retested by another sequence of a 6-minute free-recall test followed by cued recall of the 20 specifics. The total experiment required about 55 minutes.

Cued Recall

In the cued test, control subjects receiving interpolation of unrelated stories correctly recalled a mean of 11.85 of the specific facts about John Payton in the first test, and a mean of 11.62 in the delayed test. Individual control subjects did not gain or lose more than a single item. However, subjects receiving interpolation of related passages recalled a mean of 10.77 items immediately, but only 8.00 items at the delayed-retention test. Thus the (control) subjects had a mean loss of .23 items, whereas the experimental subjects had a loss of 2.77 items. The difference between the loss scores for the two groups of subjects is highly significant ($t_{24} = 3.41$). Therefore, the main result of Crouse's experiment was replicated; retroactive interference occurs in cued recall of specific, factual details.

Free Recall

The data from the free-recall tests are presented in Table 15.1. Altogether there were 63 atomic facts in the story. For 22 facts, the specific detail (e.g., a date) was changed in the related interpolated passages, whereas for the remaining 41 facts the

TABLE 15.1

Mean Number of Atomic Facts Free-Recalled from Original Paragraph

		Changed		Unchanged	
		Specific	General	Specific	General
Related	Original	10.46	13.54	24.08	27.07
	Delayed	7.54	16.69	31.23	32.84
Unrelated	Original	11.69	14.69	27.92	29.54
	Delayed	11.20	15.54	30.15	31.46
	Total possible	22	22	41	41

specifics were maintained throughout the interpolated material. The data in Table 15.1 are separated according to these two types of facts—changed or unchanged. Each free-recall protocol was separately scored for whether the general fact was recalled, and if it was recalled, whether the specific detail was recalled correctly. For example, recalling that John Payton had an occupation would count as correct recall of a general fact, but recalling that John Payton was a poet counted as correct recall of a specific detail. Needless to say, recall of a correct specific fact implies recall of a correct general fact, but the converse implication does not hold. In Table 15.1, specific and general recall are reported separately for both changed and unchanged facts. For example, if one story said Payton was a poet and the other story said Payton was a doctor, that Payton had an occupation would count as a general fact associated with changed specifics. These recall scores are presented in Table 15.1 for both the original and delayed free recall for the experimental subjects with related interpolation and for the control subjects with unrelated interpolation.

Although none of the general facts were repeated in the unrelated interpolated material, there was a slight improvement ("reminiscence") in their recall by these control subjects at the delay test. Combining both the changed and unchanged generals, an additional 2.77 general facts were recalled in the delayed condition. This improvement is of marginal statistical significance ($t_{12} = 1.82; p < .05$). More importantly and as predicted, subjects receiving related interpolation showed an increase in recall of general facts whether the specifics were changed or not. The most striking contrast in the free-recall data is the memory for changed versus unchanged specifics for those subjects receiving interpolation of related stories. A mean of 7.15 *more* unchanged specifics is recalled but a mean of 2.92 *less* changed specifics is recalled by the experimental subjects. Both the gain in unchanged specifics and the loss in changed specifics are highly significant statistically. None of the 13 subjects with related interpolation showed a gain in changed specifics whereas every subject showed a gain in unchanged specifics.

It seems that our expectations about retroactive interference and facilitation have been confirmed in this experiment, that predictions of a model like HAM can be applied to a connected thematic paragraph as to a paired-associate pair. However, the unit of analysis with which HAM is comfortable is neither the paired-associate nor the paragraph but the single sentence. With the paired-associate there are always uncontrolled generative processes that convert the pair into a proposition. With paragraph material, the subject may interconnect the stated propositions with many unstated, but plausible, inferences. Thus, memory for the paragraph is only partially determined by what is overly stated and partially by what the subject decides to fill in. At present HAM has little to offer in an analysis of this elaboration process (see Crothers, 1972; Frederiksen, 1972). We feel more comfortable using simple sentences as learning units, since we are somewhat more sure about the propositional representation given to the material to be recalled. Let us therefore consider studies of interference in memory for sentences.

Interference in Sentence Memory

There are few reported experiments on interference effects with single sentences. An experiment by Anderson and Carter (1972) is one that fits our preconditions for a test. Subjects in their experiment learned an original list of sentences and then learned an interpolated list. Three of their conditions are particularly interesting. In the control condition, the two lists of sentences were unrelated. In the verbatim condition, the sentences in the second list were identical to sentences from the first list except for the subject-noun. Finally, in the paraphrase condition, the sentences of the second list were paraphrases of first-list sentences except again for the subject-noun. In all three conditions the subject-nouns in the two lists were completely unrelated. The experimental task was to recall the subject-noun to a sentence frame in which the subject was missing. Thus, Anderson and Carter have an *A-B, A-C* paradigm in the verbatim condition in which the stimulus was the sentence predicate and the response the subject-noun. The control condition is an *A-B, C-D* design, and the paraphrase condition is a *A-B, A'-C* design. The *A-B* retention test yielded 2% forgetting in the control condition, 12% in the verbatim condition, and 19% in the paraphrase condition. The ordering of the verbatim and paraphrase conditions is unexpected and probably a chance result, but their relation to the control condition is much as expected.

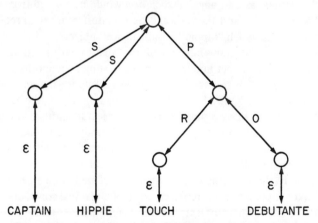

FIG. 15.6. HAM's representation of the two interfering sentences in the Anderson and Carter experiment.

An attractive feature of the Anderson and Carter paradigm is its control over the representation of the material and the point of interference in that representation. For instance, Figure 15.6 illustrates HAM's representation of the two interfering sentences in the Anderson and Carter design. In this representation, the point of interference should be at the subject branches fanning out from the fact node. In the next section we will use this control over point of interference to test some predictions made by HAM about relation-specific interference.

15.4. RELATION-SPECIFIC INTERFERENCE?

In HAM , interference is assumed to be relation-specific. That is, associative links leading from node a only interfere with one another if they involve the same relation X. It is only then that more recent links will tend to bury older ones on the GET-list from node a. This is because there is a different GET-list for each relation. Consequently, when HAM searches for a node b having relation X to a, it does not search the GET-lists for relations other than X. Therefore, if in one list a subject learns a proposition that requires him to form an X_1 relation from node a, there should be no interference if the subject has to learn an interpolated proposition requiring him to encode a different X_2 association leading from a.

To illustrate, suppose the sentence in original learning was either "The hippie touched the debutante" or "The debutante was touched by the hippie." Assuming that the person naturally converts the passive into the active form in parsing, we expect for either sentence the memory structure illustrated in the right-hand portion of the graph structure in Figure 15.7a. Suppose that the person in interpolated learning hears either the sentence "The hippie kicked the prostitute" or the sentence "The prostitute was kicked by the hippie." In either case, a second subject association would be formed out of the "hippie" node (see Figure 15.7a), and we would expect interference. On the other hand, suppose that "hippie" was the logical object in the interpolated study sentence. That is, the person might encounter interpolated propositions like "The prostitute kicked the hippie" or "The hippie was kicked by the prostitute." In either case, an object association would be created from the "hippie" node (see Figure 15.7b), and there should be no interference with retention of the original proposition in which "hippie" was the logical subject.

One problem with using items like "the hippie" to create the relational branching is that even if it is used as object in one sentence and subject in another, one could still obtain interference just in case the representation set up for the sentences in Figure 15.7b might instead be Figure 15.7c. That is, instead of making the same instance of "hippie" the subject in one proposition and the object in another, there would be a different hippie-instance for each proposition. This leads to a fanning at the member (ϵ) association leading from "hippie," and consequently forgetting would be predicted in this altered-relation case also, as in the same-relation case.

Our solution to this dilemma was to use names of well-known people rather than class names like "hippie." In our representation of individual constants, then, there is no possibility to create different instances for different sentences since we can specify the same individual. Therefore, the subjects in this experiment studied interrelated sentences like "Nixon touched the debutante" and then "The prostitute kicked

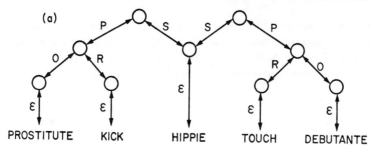

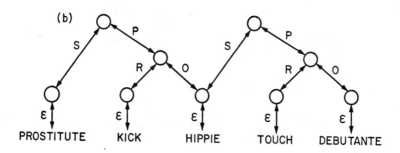

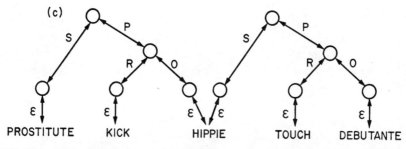

FIG. 15.7. Different memory structures involving "hippie." Interference is expected in panels *a* and *c*, where there is conjunction of identically labeled associations.

Nixon." The last names of 32 familiar and current American political figures were chosen for this experiment. There were 20 separate conditions in the experiment. The original sentences were either active or passive and had the critical political figure either as grammatical subject or object. Thus, in the original list (OL) there were sentences of the following four kinds:

Nixon kissed the baby.
The baby kissed Nixon.
Nixon was kissed by the baby.
The baby was kissed by Nixon.

These OL sentences could have any one of five relationships to the IL sentences.

1. Control: The particular political figure was not reused in the IL sentences. Instead, some statement was substituted about a political figure not used in OL. This corresponds to the *A-B, C-D* condition in the typical paired-associates paradigm. The other four conditions will all correspond to various forms of *A-B, A-C*.

2. *+L, +G*: The political figure was used in a new proposition but in the same *logical* (*L*) and *grammatical* (*G*) role as before. So if *Nixon* had appeared in OL as object in a passive sentence, he was used in that role in IL.

3. *+L, −G*: The political figure was used in the same logical role but a new grammatical role. This required a switch in the voice of a sentence. So, in this condition, *Nixon* might occur as surface object in a passive OL sentence but as surface subject in an active IL sentence. Thus, *Nixon* would remain logical subject in the underlying proposition, but would switch surface roles.

4. *−L, +G*: In this condition, the surface role of the name was maintained while its logical role was changed. Again a change in voice of proposition was required. *Nixon* might appear as subject of an active sentence in OL but subject of a passive sentence in IL.

5. *−L, −G*: In this condition both surface and logical roles were changed. In this condition, no change of voice was required. Thus, *Nixon* might appear as object of an active sentence in OL but subject of an active sentence in IL.

Examining our theoretical expectations for this paradigm, HAM clearly predicts interference relative to the control condition in the *+L, +G* condition. Whether there should be interference in the *+L, −G* or *−L, +G* conditions really depends upon whether subjects are converting sentences in parsing to their logical active forms or not. In some past experiments we have found evidence for this, in other experiments we have not. If the subject does convert to active form, there should be fanning of the same relationship (either object or subject) in the *+L, −G* condition and hence interference. If the subject does not convert passive but rather uses passive relations directly in his representation, there should be interference in the *−L, +G* condition. In either case, there should be no interference in the *−L, −G* condition.

The 20 separate conditions in the experiment are created by combining orthogonally the four possible types of OL sentences with their five possible relations to IL sentences. These 20 conditions were each represented by one of the sentences each subject had to study, making for a within-list interference paradigm. As reviewed in Section 15.2, this is the circumstance that should not produce interference if all interference were due to response-set suppression. We tried to design the experiment to provide maximal RI in the experimental conditions relative to the *A-B, C-D* control. From previous pilot research we had determined that five OL trials were sufficient to bring most subjects to near-perfect performance in cued recall on the OL list. The amount of RI possible, of course, is limited by the final level achieved in OL. Therefore, we selected five OL trials as a value that would give asymptotic acquisition with a minimum of overlearning; such overlearning is to be avoided since it produces resistance to RI. Following OL, subjects had two trials each on three separate IL lists. As reviewed in Section 15.1, this should produce considerably more interference than six trials on one IL list.

Thus, the experiment required four lists of 20 sentences each. Since the political figures were repeated in experimental conditions across lists, only 32 names were required. However, 80 distinct verbs were required and 80 distinct class names of people (e.g., hippie) to fill the other person role in the sequence. The verbs were chosen so that their logical subject would be assigned to the agentive role in a Fillmore case grammar and their logical object to an objective role. Each sentence in the OL list represented one of the 20 possible conditions. Corresponding to each sentence in OL was one sentence in each of the three IL lists. The relation between the OL sentence and its corresponding IL sentence was constant for all IL lists. Within the various design constraints, the OL and IL sentences were randomly generated for each subject by computer from the master set of words.

The sentences were printed on computer cards, and each subject studied his own deck of cards. The order of the sentences within a trial was randomized, but sentences were tested in the same order that they had been studied on any particular trial. Within a trial the 20 sentences were first studied at the rate of 12 seconds per sentence, and then were tested at the same rate. Thus, sentences were tested at a constant lag.

Subjects wrote their recall on the cards. Always, the subjects were presented with the political figure's name in a sentence frame, and they were to recall the missing person and verb. The subject might see:

THE   WAS   BY NIXON.

This kind of probe provides information regarding the "relation link" from Nixon that is being queried. After the five OL trials and six IL trials, subjects received one retention test for the 20 OL sentences. The manner of testing was identical to that used in OL and IL. Altogether the experimental session lasted about 100 minutes. Thirty-seven subjects participated in this experiment. We adopted the policy of rejecting any subject who had not achieved a criterion of at least 75% recall of the nouns by the fifth OL trial. By this criterion two of the subjects were rejected from the data analysis.

Results

With respect to the five OL trials, the only meaningful variable was sentence structure. The input sentence was active or passive, and the probe (the political figure) served as either grammatical subject or object. Figure 15.8 presents the across-trial recall for the noun (panel *a*) and the verb (panel *b*) for these four conditions. We have pooled here the results obtained from the 35 subjects from 31 subjects in a second unreported experiment. With respect to the five OL trials, the two experiments were identical, and they were run concurrently using subjects from the same population. Pooling the data from the 66 subjects, we have 330 observations contributing to each data point. As can be seen, there is little difference among the conditions with respect either to noun recall or to verb recall. As we have found in other experiments (see Chapter 10), verb recall tends to be somewhat lower than noun recall. Over the five trials, the mean level of verb recall was .658, compared to .691 for noun recall.

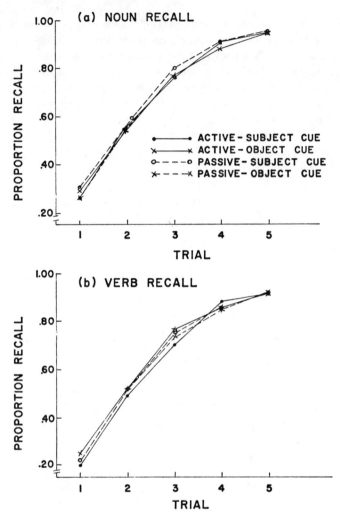

FIG. 15.8. Proportion recalled as a function of number of OL trials for various sentence types.

Transfer Data

Figure 15.9 presents recall on each of the two trials for the three interpolated lists. Panel *a* illustrates the noun recall and panel *b* the verb recall. For Lists 3 and 4 (the second and third interpolated lists), all experimental conditions are clearly inferior to the control condition but show little difference among themselves. The List 3 experimental sentences are in a negative-transfer relation with respect to the List 2 sentences as well as to the List 1 sentences. List 4 experimental sentences are in a negative-transfer relation with respect to all three preceding lists. Control sentences are not in a negative-transfer relation with respect to any list. The negative-transfer List 3 receives from List 2, and that which List 4 receives from Lists 2 and 3 is of the same character for all experimental conditions, since the cue word was kept in the same logical and grammatical role across the three IL lists. Using our earlier notation, the negative-transfer relation among IL lists was always of the form +*L*, +*G*.

Therefore, the most interesting transfer data is that obtained from List 2, since different List 2 experimental sentences displayed different relationships to the corresponding List 1 sentences. For the same reasons that HAM predicts relation-specific interference, it also predicts relation-specific negative transfer in List 2. Table 15.2 displays the appropriate transfer data. Here we have pooled recall of nouns and verbs for both trials on List 2 and present mean proportion recalled for each condition. The values from the experimental conditions in Table 15.2 are to be compared with the mean proportion of .557 recalled in the control condition. It would appear that our various predictions from HAM have been confirmed for negative transfer. An analysis of variance for a within-subjects design was performed

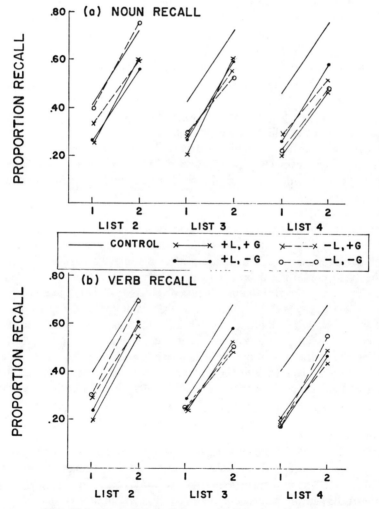

FIG. 15.9. Proportion recalled on each of the three IL lists.

TABLE 15.2

Mean Proportion of Nouns and Verbs
Recalled in List 2

Control: .557

Experimental:

	+L	−L	Mean
+G	.398	.450	.424
−G	.416	.532	.474
Mean	.407	.491	.449

to test the significance of the various results. The differences among the conditions is quite significant $(F_{4,136} = 5.25;\ p < .001)$. We divided the four degrees of freedom associated with the between-conditions sum of squares into four orthogonal comparisons to test specific questions. First, recall in the experimental conditions was significantly worse than in the control condition $(F_{1,136} = 9.84;\ p < .005)$. Second, negative transfer was significantly less in those experimental conditions where the *logical* relation of the cue was changed between lists (i.e., comparing −L to +L conditions; $F_{1,136} = 7.43;\ p < .01$). The difference between those conditions in which the cue word maintained its grammatical function across Lists 1 and 2 as contrasted with those where it did not (i.e., +G versus −G) was only marginally significant $(F_{1,136} = 2.64;\ p < .2)$. There was no interaction in Table 15.2 between whether the logical role of the cue was maintained or changed and whether the grammatical role of the cue was maintained or changed $(F_{1,136} = 1.08)$.

Thus, it appears that we have obtained relation-specific negative transfer. The marginally significant effect of grammatical role may be due to the fact that subjects sometimes encoded passive sentences using the passive relation directly, rather than converting it into the active form. It is particularly encouraging that there is no significant difference between the control condition and the (−L, −G) condition $(F_{1,136} = .33)$. Thus, just as HAM would predict, negative transfer was obtained only when the cue word was in the same logical relation in the two sentences. Overall, this outcome is very encouraging as it is clear evidence that a matter like logical role of a word is important in learning. To our knowledge, it is the only such data extant. Unfortunately, this negative-transfer result was not paralleled in the retroactive-interference results obtained with respect to List 1 retention.

Retention

We now consider the data from the List 1 retention test which is given in Table 15.3. Again the proportion recalled has been pooled over noun and verb recall. The recall proportions in these experimental conditions are to be compared to the mean recall of .839 in the control condition. Again, a within-subjects analysis of variance was performed, and the differences among the conditions were statistically significant ($F_{4,136}$ = 11.34; p < .001). However, all the variance is accounted for by the difference between the experimental condition and control conditions ($F_{1,136}$ = 43.46). Although the difference among the experimental conditions tends to be in the predicted direction, the variance among the conditions is not significant ($F_{3,136}$ = .71). That is to say, all four experimental conditions exhibit retroactive interference, but the amount of RI does not differ significantly among the four conditions.

The control condition yielded 30% higher recall than the experimental conditions. Thus, we have obtained very strong RI in a mixed-list design. It will be recalled from Section 15.2 that the pure response-suppression position does not expect such stimulus-specific RI in the mixed-list design. Therefore, this is a result of considerable theoretical importance.

It is not clear why HAM's prediction of relation-specific interference was confirmed with respect to the transfer data, but not the retention data. We cannot claim the experiment was insensitive, because we did obtain very strong RI. It is just that the amount of RI was not related to the logical or grammatical role of the cue word. Thus, it might seem that we can no longer maintain that associations are searched in relation-specific manner. We find it difficult to give up this assumption, as it has been our constant companion throughout the book. Perhaps, this failure can be attributed to the relation-specific negative transfer obtained in IL. As HAM had expected, there was much more negative transfer when the logical relation was maintained in IL. This meant that there was less learning of IL material to compete with OL in the +L conditions. Consequently learning IL material in the +L conditions might have been more interfering, but this +L detrimental effect may have been cancelled by the lower IL learning rate.

The argument is that the failure to find relation-specific RI may be related to our use of a fixed number of IL trials. If we rather had brought all conditions to a fixed performance criterion in IL, then it is quite likely that we would have obtained relation-specific RI. (Bob Crowder pointed this possibility out to us.) Of course, this tack will not explain why we did obtain such strong RI in the −L conditions of the current experiment. Perhaps this was due to interference at the level of word-to-idea associations. That is, subjects might have been encoding *Nixon* in different senses in the IL lists. For instance, *Nixon* can be encoded from the

TABLE 15.3

Mean Proportion of Nouns and Verbs
Recalled in List 1 Retest

Control: .839

Experimental:

	+L	−L	Mean
+F	.532	.507	.520
−F	.521	.582	.552
Mean	.527	.547	.536

point of view of a liberal, a conservative, a libertarian, a black, or a North Vietnamese. Each of these points of view provides us with a quite distinct sense of *Nixon*. The senses of *Nixon* used in IL could interfere with the OL sense, producing RI. In any case, it is clear that a further experiment is required using a fixed performance criterion.

Further Evidence for Stimulus-Specific Interference

An interesting claim of our theory is that the probability of recall of *A-B* should covary with number of correct recalls of *A-C* in the interpolated learning. This prediction derives from the fact that more correct recalls of *A-C* should reflect the existence of more *A-C* paths to interfere with *A-B* retention. Runquist (1957) failed to find the predicted relationship. However, he did not control for degree of *A-B* acquisition. It is to be expected that degree of *A-B* and *A-C* acquisition will covary because of differences in subject abilities and stimulus effectiveness. Since retention does increase with degree of *A-B* acquisition, we may have the effect of degree of *A-C* cancelled out by the covarying *A-B* effect. Therefore, in the data to be presented we will examine the effect of degree of *A-C* learning for each level of *A-B* acquisition.

We measured *A-B* acquisition for an item-subject combination in terms of the number of correct recalls of noun plus number of correct recalls of verb. Degree of *A-C* acquisition was similarly measured. Thus the maximum score for *A-B* was 10 (5 trials × 2 responses) and for the three pooled *A-C* lists the maximum was 12 (6 trials × 2 responses). These data are summarized in Table 15.4. We have represented each of the 11 possible values of degree of OL but have aggregated degree of IL into two values. The proportion retention is entered in each cell along with the sample size, *n*, on which these proportions are based. It can be seen that retention improves with degree of OL, but there was no overall effect of degree of IL. However, for 9

TABLE 15.4

Probability of Recall of an OL Response as a
Function of Degree of IL

Number of correct OL recalls	Number of correct IL recalls		
	0 – 4	5 – 12	Overall
0	.079 (*n* = 38)	.000 (*n* = 2)	.075
1*	.000 (*n* = 10)	1.000 (*n* = 2)	.167
2	.250 (*n* = 48)	.125 (*n* = 8)	.232
3	.357 (*n* = 28)	.250 (*n* = 8)	.333
4*	.500 (*n* = 66)	.625 (*n* = 16)	.524
5	.656 (*n* = 32)	.500 (*n* = 28)	.583
6	.477 (*n* = 86)	.446 (*n* = 74)	.463
7	.625 (*n* = 72)	.488 (*n* = 82)	.552
8	.635 (*n* = 74)	.582 (*n* = 134)	.595
9	.875 (*n* = 48)	.587 (*n* = 92)	.686
10	.774 (*n* = 62)	.581 (*n* = 110)	.651
Overall	.535 (*n* = 564)	.536 (*n* = 556)	.535

of the 11 separate values of degree of OL, degree of IL influenced retention in the anticipated direction. The two deviant observations are starred, and in neither case is the sample size very large. Nine out of 11 observations in the predicted direction is significant at the .05 level by a sign test. In summary, then there is a clear trend in the predicted direction when we control for degree of OL.

It will be remembered that we argued in Section 15.2 that the failure to find a negative relation between availability of B and C in MMFR is because of subject-by-item interactions, in that some stimuli are more easily encoded for some subjects. This leads to a positive relation between the availability of B and C in MMFR, cancelling out the negative one that we would expect because of stimulus-specific interference. The data of Table 15.4 clearly indicate that such item-by-subject interactions can hide a negative relation due to stimulus-specific interference. It is an interesting question whether a similar item analysis would turn up a negative relation in the MMFR data of Martin and Greeno (1972).

As things now stand, we can be fairly confident in HAM's prediction that there should be stimulus-specific interference. There is some evidence for relation-specific interference in the negative-transfer data of this experiment, but the matter is left uncertain by the null result obtained with respect to OL retention. We clearly need a better conceptualization of the interrelations among the memory representation, negative transfer, and retroactive interference. There are now sufficient uncertainties as well as obvious candidate hypotheses to make this general topic a gold mine for future research. In pointing out this uncertainty, and calling for more insightful research on the topic, we close out this chapter.

REFERENCES

Amsel, A. Partial reinforcement effects on vigor and persistence. In K. W. Spence & J. T. Spence (Eds.), *The psychology of learning and motivation: Advances in research and theory.* Vol. 1. New York: Academic Press, 1967.

Anderson, J. R., & Bower, G. H. Recognition and retrieval processes in free recall. *Psychological Review*, 1972, 79, 97–123.

Anderson, R. C., & Carter, J. F. Retroactive inhibition of meaningfully-learned sentences. *American Educational Research Journal*, 1972, 9, 443–448.

Anderson, R. C., & Myrow, D. L. Retroactive inhibition of meaningful discourse. *Journal of Educational Psychology*, 1971, 62, 81–94.

Anderson, R. C., & Watts, G. H. Response competition in the forgetting of paired-associates. *Journal of Verbal Learning and Verbal Behavior*, 1971, 10, 29–34.

Ausubel, D. P. *The Psychology of Meaningful Verbal Learning.* New York: Grune & Stratton, 1963.

Ausubel, D. P., & Blake, E. Proactive inhibition in the forgetting of meaningful school material. *Journal of Educational Research*, 1958, 52, 145–149.

Ausubel, D. P., Robbins, L. G., & Blake, E. Retroactive inhibition and facilitation in the learning of school materials. *Journal of Educational Psychology*, 1959, 48, 334–343.

Barnes, J. M., & Underwood, B. J. "Fate" of first-list associations in transfer theory. *Journal of Experimental Psychology*, 1959, 58, 97–105.

Birnbaum, I. M. Long-term retention of first-list associations in the A-B, A-C paradigm. *Journal of Verbal Learning and Verbal Behavior*, 1965, 4, 515–520.

Birnbaum, I. M. Response-class similarity and first-list recall with mixed and unmixed transfer designs. *Journal of Experimental Psychology*, 1968, 77, 542–546.

Birnbaum, I. M. Response selection in retroactive inhibition. *Journal of Experimental Psychology*, 1970, **85**, 406–410.

Briggs, G. E. Retroactive inhibition as a function of degree of original and interpolated learning. *Journal of Experimental Psychology*, 1957, **53**, 60–67.

Ceraso, J. Specific interference in retroactive inhibition. *Journal of Psychology*, 1964, **58**, 65–77.

Ceraso, J., & Henderson, A. Unavailability and associative loss in RI and PI. *Journal of Experimental Psychology*, 1965, **70**, 300–305.

Ceraso, J., & Henderson, A. Unavailability and associative loss in RI and PI: Second try. *Journal of Experimental Psychology*, 1966, **72**, 314–316.

Cofer, C. N., Faile, N. F., & Horton, D. L. Retroactive inhibition following reinstatement or maintenance of first-list responses by means of free recall. *Journal of Experimental Psychology*, 1971, **90**, 197–205.

Crothers, E. J. Memory structure and the recall of discourse. In R. O. Freedle & J. B. Carroll (Eds.), *Language comprehension and the acquisition of knowledge*. Washington, D.C.: Winston, 1972.

Crouse, J. H. Retroactive interference in reading prose materials. *Journal of Educational Psychology*, 1971, **62**, 39–44.

Deese, J., & Hardman, G. W. An analysis of errors in retroactive inhibition of rote verbal learning. *American Journal of Psychology*, 1954, **67**, 299–307.

Delprato, D. J. Specific-pair interference on recall and associative matching tests. *American Journal of Psychology*, 1971, **84**, 185–193.

Delprato, D. J., & Garskof, B. E. Free and modified free recall measures of response recall and unlearning. *Journal of Experimental Psychology*, 1969, **81**, 408–410.

Feigenbaum, E. A. Simulation of verbal learning behavior. In E. A. Feigenbaum and J. Feldman (Eds.), *Computers and thought*. New York: McGraw-Hill, 1963.

Feigenbaum, E. A. Information processing and memory. In D. A. Norman (Ed.), *Models of human memory*. New York: Academic Press, 1970.

Frederiksen, C. H. Effects of task-induced cognitive operations on comprehension and memory processes. In R. O. Freedle & J. B. Carroll (Eds.), *Language comprehension and the acquisition of knowledge*. Washington, D.C.: Winston, 1972.

Friedman, M. J., & Reynold, J. H. Retroactive inhibition as a function of response-class similarity. *Journal of Experimental Psychology*, 1967, **74**, 351–355.

Garskof, B. E. Unlearning as a function of degree of interpolated learning and method of testing in the A-B, A-C and A-B, C-D paradigms. *Journal of Experimental Psychology*, 1968, **76**, 579–583.

Garskof, B. E., & Sandak, J. M. Unlearning in recognition memory. *Psychonomic Science*, 1964, **1**, 197–198.

Greenberg, G., & Wickens, D. D. Is matching performance an adequate test of "extinction" effects on individual association? *Psychonomic Science*, 1972, **27**, 227–229.

Greeno, J. G. A cognitive interpretation of negative transfer and forgetting in paired-associates. (Human Performance Center Memorandum Rep. No. 9) Ann Arbor: University of Michigan, 1969.

Hintzman, D. L. Explorations with a discrimination net model for paired-associate learning. *Journal of Mathematical Psychology*, 1968, **5**, 123–162.

Hintzman, D. L. On testing the independence of associations. *Psychological Review*, 1972, **79**, 261–264.

Houston, J. P. Proactive inhibition and undetected retention interval rehearsal. *Journal of Experimental Psychology*, 1969, **82**, 511–514.

Houston, J. P. Proactive inhibition and undetected rehearsal: A replication. *Journal of Experimental Psychology*, 1971, **90**, 156–157.

Keppel, G. Retroactive and proactive inhibition. In T. R. Dixon & D. L. Horton (Eds.), *Verbal behavior and general behavior theory*. Englewood Cliffs, N.J.: Prentice-Hall, 1968.

Keppel, G., Henschel, D. M., & Zavortink, F. Influence of nonspecific interference on response recall. *Journal of Experimental Psychology*, 1969, **81**, 246–255.

Keppel, G., & Rauch, D. S. Unlearning as a function of second-list error instructions. *Journal of Verbal Learning and Verbal Behavior*, 1966, **5**, 50–58.

Koppenaal, R. J. Time changes in the strengths of A-B, A-C lists: Spontaneous recovery? *Journal of Verbal Learning and Verbal Behavior*, 1963, **2**, 310–319.

Koppenaal, R. J., Krull, A., & Katz, H. Age, interference, and forgetting. *Journal of Experimental Child Psychology*, 1965, **1**, 360–375.

Lehr, D. J., Frank, R. C., & Mattison, D. W. Retroactive inhibition, spontaneous recovery, and type of interpolated learning. *Journal of Experimental Psychology*, 1972, **92**, 232–236.

Logan, F. A. *Incentive*. New Haven: Yale University Press, 1960.

McGeoch, J. A. Studies in retroactive inhibition: VII. Retroactive inhibition as a function of the length and frequency of presentation of the interpolated lists. *Journal of Experimental Psychology*, 1936, **19**, 674–693.

McGovern, J. B. Extinction of associations in four transfer paradigms. *Psychological Monographs*, 1964, **78** (Whole No. 593).

Martin, E. Verbal learning theory and independent retrieval phenomena. *Psychological Review*, 1971, **78**, 314–332.

Martin, E., & Greeno, J. G. Independence of associations tested: A reply to D. L. Hintzman. *Psychological Review*, 1972, **79**, 265–267.

Melton, A. W. Comments on Professor Postman's Paper. In C. N. Cofer (Ed.), *Verbal learning and verbal behavior*. New York: McGraw-Hill, 1961.

Melton, A. W., & Irwin, J. M. The influence of degree of interpolated learning on retroactive inhibition and the overt transfer of specific responses. *American Journal of Psychology*, 1940, **53**, 173–203.

Merryman, C. T. Retroactive inhibition in the A-B, A-D paradigm as measured by a multiple-choice test. *Journal of Experimental Psychology*, 1971, **91**, 212–214.

Merryman, C. T., & Merryman, S. S. Improvement during nonreinforced trials: Confounded with backward associations? Paper presented at the meeting of the Psychonomic Society, St. Louis, November, 1972.

Miller, G. A. *Language and communication*. New York: McGraw-Hill, 1951.

Myrow, D. L., & Anderson, R. C. Retroactive inhibition of prose as a function of type of test. *Journal of Educational Psychology*, 1972, **68**, 303–308.

Newton, J. M., & Wickens, D. D. Retroactive inhibition as a function of the temporal position of the interpolated learning. *Journal of Experimental Psychology*, 1956, **51**, 149–154.

Osgood, C. E. An investigation into the causes of retroactive interference. *Journal of Experimental Psychology*, 1948, **38**, 132–154.

Postman, L. Unlearning under conditions of successive interpolation. *Journal of Experimental Psychology*, 1965, **70**, 237–245.

Postman, L., Burns, G., & Hasher, L. Response availability and associative recall. *Journal of Experimental Psychology*, 1970, **84**, 404–411.

Postman, L., & Kaplan, H. L. Reaction time as a measure of retroactive inhibition. *Journal of Experimental Psychology*, 1947, **37**, 136–145.

Postman, L., Keppel, G., & Stark, K. Unlearning as a function of the relationship between successive response classes. *Journal of Experimental Psychology*, 1965, **69**, 111–118.

Postman, L., & Parker, J. F. Maintenance of first-list associations during transfer. *American Journal of Psychology*, 1970, **83**, 171–188.

Postman, L., & Stark, K. The role of response set in tests of unlearning. *Journal of Verbal Learning and Verbal Behavior*, 1965, **4**, 315–322.

Postman, L., & Stark, K. The role of response availability in transfer and interference. *Journal of Experimental Psychology*, 1969, **79**, 168–177.

Postman, L., & Stark, K. On the measurement of retroactive inhibition in the A-B, A-D paradigm by the multiple-choice method: Reply to Merryman. *Journal of Verbal Learning and Verbal Behavior*, 1972, **11**, 465–473.

Postman, L., Stark, K., & Fraser, J. Temporal changes in interference. *Journal of Verbal Learning and Verbal Behavior*, 1968, **7**, 672–694.

Postman, L., Stark, K., & Henschel, D. M. Conditions of recovery after unlearning. *Journal of Experimental Psychology*, 1969, **82**, 1–24.

Postman, L., & Warren, L. Temporal changes in interference under different paradigms of transfer. *Journal of Verbal Learning and Verbal Behavior*, 1972, **11**, 120–128.

Reitman,W. *Cognition and thought.* New York: Wiley, 1965.

Runquist, W. N. Retention of verbal associates as a function of strength. *Journal of Experimental Psychology*, 1957, **54**, 369–375.

Shiffrin, R. Memory search. In D. A. Norman (Ed.), *Models of human memory.* New York: Academic Press, 1970.

Shulman, H. C., & Martin, E. Effects of response-set similarity on unlearning and spontaneous recovery. *Journal of Experimental Psychology*, 1970, **86**, 230–235.

Simon, H. A., & Feigenbaum, E. A. An information processing theory of some effects of similarity, familiarity, and meaningfulness in verbal learning. *Journal of Verbal Learning and Verbal Behavior*, 1964, **3**, 385–396.

Slamecka, N. J. Retroactive inhibition of connected discourse as a function of practice level. *Journal of Experimental Psychology*, 1960, **59**, 104–108. (a)

Slamecka, N. J. Retroactive inhibition of connected discourse as a function of similarity of topic. *Journal of Experimental Psychology*, 1960, **60**, 245–249. (b)

Slamecka N. J. A temporal interpretation of some recall phenomena. *Psychological Review*, 1969, **76**, 492–503.

Slamecka, N. J., & Ceraso, J. Retroactive and proactive inhibition of verbal learning. *Psychological Bulletin*, 1960, **57**, 449–475.

Spence, K. W. *Behavior theory and learning: Selected papers.* Englewood Cliffs, N.J.: Prentice-Hall, 1960.

Thune, L. E., & Underwood, B. J. Retroactive inhibition as a function of degree of interpolated learning. *Journal of Experimental Psychology*, 1943, **32**, 185–200.

Underwood, B. J. The effect of successive interpolations on retroactive and proactive inhibition. *Psychological Monographs*, 1945, **59** (Whole No. 273).

Underwood, B. J. Retroactive and proactive inhibition after 5 and 48 hours. *Journal of Experimental Psychology*, 1948, **38**, 29–38. (a)

Underwood, B. J. "Spontaneous recovery" of verbal associations. *Journal of Experimental Psychology*, 1948, **38**, 429–439. (b)

Underwood, B. J. Attributes of memory. *Psychological Review*, 1969, **76**, 559–573.

Weaver, G. E., Duncan, E. M., & Bird, C. P. Cue specific retroactive inhibition. *Journal of Verbal Learning and Verbal Behavior*, 1972, **11**, 362–366.

Wichawut, C., & Martin, E. Independence of A-B and A-C associations in retroaction. *Journal of Verbal Learning and Verbal Behavior*, 1971, **10**, 316–321.

Wickens, D. D. Encoding categories of words: An empirical approach to meaning. *Psychological Review*, 1970, **77**, 1–15.

Wolford, G. Function of distinct associations for paired-associate performance. *Psychological Review*, 1971, **78**, 303–313.

16
AN EPITAPH

Of making many books there is no end and much study is a weariness of the flesh.

—Solomon

The previous chapter was the last concerned with review, research, and theory about human memory. The time has come to close out the book, and in so doing we would like to try our hand at writing a critique of it; in short, we want to write our own epitaph. We will do this in two parts: first, we will state the various criticisms that we anticipate; second, we will state what we believe to be the significance of the work.

THE CRITICISMS

The introduction (Chapter 1) listed four fundamental questions about the theoretical biases that went into the construction of HAM. To review, they were:

1. HAM has been too strongly determined by what is easy to simulate on a computer rather than by considerations of psychological plausibility.
2. HAM's strategy-free memory component was too passive, too much of a tabula rasa.
3. The price HAM paid for item 2 was an excessively complicated set of interfacing mechanisms to link it to the external world.
4. HAM's propositional base was too logical and abstract; perhaps a diffuse sensory base would have been more appropriate.

We hope these initial criticisms have been largely answered by the chapters that followed, demonstrating HAM's success in addressing a wide range of mnemonic phenomena. Success is the only way to respond to such fundamental criticisms.

We solicited from a number of colleagues further criticisms about this book. They responded with a rather mixed bag of negative statements. We would like to acknowledge all these and thank our critics for their efforts. The following is a list of the criticisms to which we have decided *not* to respond. This lack of response does not always indicate that we think the criticisms are inappropriate, just that there is nothing to say.

1. The book is too (philosophical, mathematical, experimental, conversational, wordy, terse, long, broad, or narrow).

2. The book doesn't deal with the really interesting phenomena of memory.

3. HAM really isn't an associationalist theory; really it is a (Gestalt or Reconstruction) theory.

4. You haven't developed a (Gestalt or Reconstruction) alternative with the same care, detail, and explicitness that you used in developing an associationist theory.

5. The simulation program doesn't do anything interesting.

6. The formalisms in Chapter 7 don't prove anything.

7. HAM's network representations are too rigid and geometrical.

8. You use the word "we" too often.

9. The word "HAM" has confused reference. Sometimes it refers to the simulation program, sometimes to the theory, sometimes to a theoretical (simulation) subject, and at other times to a seemingly omniscient scientist who explains and predicts data, and seemingly is never embarrassed.

Finally, there are four criticisms which we feel are very serious and which require special acknowledgment:

1. No attempt has been made to carefully work out the semantics of HAM's representation. A set of rules or procedures has not been defined that will permit HAM to deduce the obvious implications from a set of propositions stored in memory. As an example of the inferences HAM should be able to make, it should deduce from "John is taller than Bill" and "Bill is not as short as Pete" that "John is taller than Pete." As another example, HAM should be able to infer from "Red-headed chickens are good layers" that "Some chickens are good layers." Again, from "John kicked Mary" HAM should be able to infer that "John moved his foot." These are elementary deductions that intelligent adults can make, so HAM should be able to make them also. Without some concrete demonstration of how the implications of a set of facts may be obtained, the claims in Chapter 7 about the expressive sufficiency of the representation lack convincing force. So, clearly a high-priority goal in the future development of HAM will be to program such a deductive or inferential system.

2. There is not a formally defined procedure for assigning propositional representations to English sentences. Largely, in our exposition we have called upon intuition as to what was the appropriate representation for a sentence. A parser *is* programmed that will assign HAM-like representations to a well-defined subset of English sentences. However, a program listing is not a systematic or very satisfactory representation of the translation procedure being sought. Moreover, our

parser fails to deal with a number of critical linguistic phenomena such as quantification and various complex forms of conjunction. The translation problem is a very difficult one, and its seems unlikely that anyone is going to rapidly hit upon a solution. For instance, despite the many bright people who have concerned themselves with the matter, there is no formal translation procedure between English sentences and the predicate calculus of formal logic.

3. Despite our hopes that one could avoid such problems with sentential materials, our research still seems plagued by subjects' use of variable coding strategies. Certain matters such as the representation of active versus passive sentences seemed to be affected by changes in task demands. Furthermore, subjects' introspections indicate that they are engaged in various unscheduled activities in order to improve their recall performance—guessing strategies, deliberate encoding of surface information, mnemonic elaboration, imaging, and so forth. It seems very difficult to use a particular memory phenomena to obtain firm inferences about a strategy-free component of memory. It is often plausible to attribute any feature of that phenomena to a mnemonic strategy of one sort or another. We occasionally worry that the Reconstruction theorists may have been right at least in their claim that it is impossible to separate memory from the operation of other cognitive processes.

4. While evidence was collected supporting many assumptions of the theory, we have failed to produce decisive evidence with respect to HAM's within-proposition representation. The experiments in Chapter 9 provided clear support for the postulated between-proposition effects of the MATCH process, but the one critical experiment that involved within-proposition assumptions failed. Again in Chapters 10 and 11, much evidence was accumulated for the independent formation of associations and for HAM's between-proposition representation, but the results were ambiguous with respect to the within-proposition question of whether the verb is closer to the object than to the subject. Similarly, while strong interference effects were obtained in Chapter 15, there was little to indicate that these effects were specific to associative relations like OBJECT and SUBJECT.

SIGNIFICANCE

While these four criticisms temper any strong conclusions one can make, we still believe that several matters of significance were accomplished in the preceding chapters. The theory advanced in this book constitutes a significant advance in sophistication over past theories of memory. HAM provides such major elaborations and extensions of the general associative approach that it is unclear to what extent the title "associationist" is appropriate to HAM. Although we began with the belief that HAM would be fairly faithful to the associationist tradition (Anderson, 1971), we were gradually forced to abandon this position as untenable. Rather, HAM has been labeled "Neo-Associationist" to acknowledge that it represents a mixture of methodological rationalism and empiricism. However, the book is more than an ambitious enterprise; it contains what we believe to be significant contributions of empirical, theoretical, and metatheoretical varieties. Among these contributions we would list the following points:

1. An attempt has been made to identify the defining features of associationism and the dimensions of its contrast with Gestalt theory and the Reconstruction Hypothesis. Fundamentally, these differences center around contrasting methodologies for theory construction. Metafeatures were identified that typified associative theories generated by methodological empiricism, and contrasting metafeatures were proposed for methodological rationalism.

2. Chapter 7 provided an exposition of the representation problem and motivated a well-defined solution.

3. Chapter 7 also characterized the structure of memory and its dependence on experience. Significant theorems were proven regarding what initial primitives were necessary and what kinds of memory structures were possible. A distinction was made between universal and particular ideas.

4. Chapter 9 introduced the MATCH process and indicated its implication in all varieties of recognition phenomena. Relevant experimentation provided clear support for its predictions.

5. Chapters 10 and 11 proposed a mechanism for association formation, and considerable evidence was advanced to support the salient features of the formulation.

6. Chapter 12 provided a general and successful model of fact retrieval from memory.

7. Chapter 14 provided a propositional reinterpretation of the major findings from verbal learning.

8. Also in Chapter 14, a conceptual-propositional interpretation of imagery was offered as an alternative to either the radical imagery or dual-coding hypotheses.

9. In Chapter 15 a new interpretation was offered for interference effects. This interpretation seems at least as successful as the existing ones. Also, new experiments studying interference with sentential materials were reported.

10. A significant feature of points 2 through 9 is that they were accomplished within a single theoretical framework. Therefore, HAM provides a major integration of empirical research on human memory.

11. HAM is the first of the network theories (compare to Quillian, 1969; Rumelhart, Lindsay, & Norman, 1972) in which the *psychological meaning* of the networks has been carefully developed. It is not enough merely to construct an intuitively satisfying graph and assert that it represents certain information in memory. Such graphs acquire psychological meaning only after one has addressed himself to the necessary task of defining the functional properties of the networks—the mechanisms by which they are constructed, stored, searched, recognized, forgotten, used in reasoning, etc. HAM is distinguished from other models by the explictness and detail with which these functional properties and their corresponding mechanisms have been developed and tested.

Despite these laudatory and self-serving remarks, it is abundantly clear to us that much remains to be done. Almost every question considered in this book was left in a state requiring further theory and experimentation. With respect to experimentation, we have been frequently asked by colleagues to state what are the *crucial* assumptions of our model, what an experimentalist would have to do to *disprove* the theory. However, there are no such crucial assumptions. HAM consists of a collection of specific theoretical claims, none of which are particularly crucial in their own right. If anything is at stake, it is the overall plan or structure that is imposed upon these particular claims. This structure is more or less a direct consequence of the Neo-Associationist methodology that we have followed in theory construction. No simple experimental test can disconfirm a theoretical methodology. The ultimate test concerns the generality, power, parsimony, and empirical accuracy of the theory that it generates.

In conclusion, we would emphasize that this book is very much a progress report, that a lot of relevant theorizing and experimentation within this framework is going on and will continue for quite some time. Although unable to provide final answers, we hope we have achieved the goal set for ourselves in Chapter 1—to help all of us to better understand the nature of human memory and its myriad complexities.

REFERENCES

Anderson, J. R. Human associative memory: A dissertation proposal. Unpublished manuscript, 1971.

Quillian, M. R. The teachable language comprehender. *Communications of the ACM,* 1969, **12,** 459–476.

Rumelhart, D. E., Lindsay, P. H., & Norman, D. A. A process model for long-term memory. In E. Tulving & W. Donaldson (Eds.), *Organization of Memory.* New York: Academic Press, 1972.

AUTHOR INDEX

Numbers in italics refer to the pages on which the complete references are listed.

A

Abelson, R. P., 413, *415*
Abrahams, P. W., 67, *99*
Allen, M. M., 448, *461*
Amarel, S., 151, *197*
Amsel, A., 476, *503*
Anderson, J. M., 114, *132*
Anderson, J. R., 25, *38*, 140, *149*, 216, 224,
 228, 229, 230, 231, *234*, 275, *282*, 333,
 334, 336, 337, 340, 350, *352*, 378, *387*,
 439, 445, 447, 448, *461*, 479, *503*, 509,
 511
Anderson, R. C., 483, 489, 493, *503*, *505*
Arnold, P. G., 53, *64*, 456, 459, *462*
Asch, G. E., 52, 53, *64*, *65*
Asch, S. E., 155, *197*
Atkinson, R. C., 216, *234*, 317, *329*, 376,
 387, 458, *463*
Atwood, G., 459, *461*
Ausubel, D. P., 488, *503*

B

Bain, A., 18, *38*
Bandura, A., 106, 107, *132*
Barclay, J. R., 407, 410, *415*
Barlow, H. B., 48, *64*
Barnes, J. M., 475, *503*

Bartlett, F. C., 58, 59, *64*, 93, *98*, 345, *352*
Battig, W. F., 384, *387*
Baylor, G. W., 449, *462*
Bean, J., 430, *462*
Beare, J. I., 17, *38*
Begg, J., 232, *234*
Bergman, G., 31, *38*
Bernbach, H. A., 445, *462*
Bever, T. G., 12, 13, *39*, 108, *132*, 154,
 197, 205, *234*
Bird, C. P., 484, *506*
Birnbaum, I. M., 479, 482, 484, *503*
Blake, E., 488, *503*
Bloomfield, L., 109, *132*
Bobrow, D. G., 68, *99*, 121, *132*
Bobrow, G., 456, *462*
Bolinger, D., 79, *98*
Boring, E. G., 18, 26, *39*, 58, *64*
Bousfield, W. A., 447, *462*
Bower, G. H., 45, 52, 53, 54, 57, *64*, *65*,
 275, *282*, 317, *329*, 333, 334, 336, 337,
 340, 350, *352*, 360, 378, *387*, 433, 434,
 435, 436, 437, 438, 439, 445, 452, 456,
 457, 459, *461*, *462*, *464*, 479, *503*
Bransford, J. D., 233, *235*, 347, 350, *352*,
 410, *415*
Bratley, P., 121, *133*
Bregman, A. S., 154, *198*, 224, *234*
Briggs, G. E., 474, *504*
Brooks, L. R., 458, 459, *462*

513

SUBJECT INDEX

A

Aristotle's theory of memory, 9, 12, 16–18, 186
Associationism, 3, 9–39
    American, 16, 26–38
    British, 12, 16, 17–26
    German, 26
    See also Aristotle's theory of memory, Associations, Behaviorism, Functionalism, Ideas, Methodological empiricism
Associations, 22, 28, 181–190
    free association, 425
    HAM, 181–190
    successive vs. synchronous, 22
    See also Contiguity, Similarity

B

Behaviorism, 28–37, 136
    habit memory, 33–37
    intervening variables, 31–33
    theory of language, 103–109
Binary branching, 246–247
    See also Ideas (duplex)
Bloomfieldian linguistics, 108–109

C

Center-embedding, 216, 221–222
Chomskian transformational linguistics, 108–114, 157–158
Competence-performance distinction, 101–102, 153
Complex ideas (*See* Ideas)
Computational linguistics, 120–131
    augmented transition networks (Woods), 121–124
    conceptual dependency analysis (Schank), 128–131, 196–197, 209–210
    procedural systems (Winograd), 125–128
    See also Parsers (HAM)
Computer simulation, 67–98
    effects on theory construction, 6, 67–69, 448–449
    models of memory, 5
    See also Computational linguistics, ELINOR, EPAM, FRAN, HAM, TLC, Parser (HAM)
Connectionism, 10, 12, 68, 81, 96, 186
Conjunction, 245–247, 470–471
Contiguity, 17, 22–23, 251–257, 319–327, 433